SPOILS *of* WAR

SPOILS
of WAR

The Fate of Enemy Fleets after the
Two World Wars

AIDAN DODSON

SERENA CANT

Seaforth
PUBLISHING

Title page: *U126* at Plymouth in November 1918. *(NHHC NH 43791)*

Copyright © Aidan Dodson and Serena Cant 2020
First published in Great Britain in 2020 by
Seaforth Publishing,
A division of Pen & Sword Books Ltd,
47 Church Street,
Barnsley S70 2AS
www.seaforthpublishing.com

British Library Cataloguing in Publication Data
A catalogue record for this book is available from the British Library
ISBN 978 1 5267 4198 1 (HARDBACK)
ISBN 978 1 5267 4199 8 (EPUB)
ISBN 978 1 5267 4200 1 (KINDLE)

Pen & Sword Books Limited incorporates the imprints of Atlas, Archaeology, Aviation, Discovery, Family History, Fiction, History, Maritime, Military, Military Classics, Politics, Select, Transport, True Crime, Air World, Frontline Publishing, Leo Cooper, Remember When, Seaforth Publishing, The Praetorian Press, Wharncliffe Local History, Wharncliffe Transport, Wharncliffe True Crime and White Owl

Typeset and designed by Stephen Dent

Printed and bound in India by Replika Press Pvt Ltd

Contents

Preface

The genesis of this book came during the research for Aidan Dodson's earlier book, *The Kaiser's Battlefleet* (2016), when it became apparent that, when checked against contemporary archival data, many of the published details of the post-1918 fates of German capital ships were incomplete, garbled or simply wrong. When extended to other categories of vessel, this proved to be even more the case, in particular as regards submarines of the era, where a significant number of entries in Erich Gröner's *Deutschen Kriegsschiffe*, long the baseline source for German warships, proved completely fictitious. In particular, six boats among a dozen stated to have 'run aground' or 'sunk' 'on the East Coast of Great Britain while en route to being broken up, 1921' were actually scuttled in the English Channel, south of the Isle of Wight, by the Royal Navy in the summer of that year. Another boat similarly listed had been sunk in the Solent as a target the previous year. Others allegedly scrapped or expended in France had actually foundered or been wrecked in the English Channel en route, while a set of submarines allegedly 'blown ashore in a storm' had actually been dumped on a beach after being mangled in explosives trials. Further confusion has been caused by misprints or misunderstandings of *U-* versus *UB-* numbers in contemporary and later sources, leading to vessels' fates being mixed up or even conflated, exacerbated by using the incorrect fate listings in Gröner, and the many 'standard sources' (including on the internet) that largely copy him.

However, contemporary press reports, archival sources, in particular the Admiralty Sales register for 1919–39 (which includes the disposal of ex-German vessels ceded to the UK during 1919/20) and the records of the Naval Inter-Allied Control Commission, together with the positive identification of a number of wrecks by divers – demonstrating the importance of archaeology to the writing of even modern history – have allowed most of the picture to be cleared up.

The focus of this book concerns the warships, submarines and major auxiliaries of ex-enemy navies as disposed of by the victorious powers, but is not extended to cover prizes taken in wartime (e.g. *U505*), minor auxiliaries requisitioned for naval use (e.g. trawlers as minesweepers) or national commercial assets such as ocean liners. These, too, were subject to disposal and allocation agreements, retrocessions and recommissioning by the victorious powers, but this history is secondary to the primary aims of the present work. The presentation of what we believe to be a near-definitive list of the fates of the significant German (and other Central Powers') warships extant at the end of the First World War has thus been a major objective in writing this book, as well as highlighting the key outstanding queries in the hope that this may contribute to their final resolution.

Problems also exist regarding the situation after the Second World War, exacerbated by the wide distribution of a much larger number of ex-enemy ships, some of which had long service lives under their new owners. For a long time, the careers of vessels ceded to the Soviet Union remained obscure, although from the 1980s onwards significant amounts of new data began to become available, allowing the ultimate fates of the most important vessels to be understood. On the other hand, data from different sources are on occasion contradictory, and thus the final fates of certain vessels remain provisional.

As well as providing this kind of data, a further objective has been to tell the story of the weeks leading up to the ends of hostilities with the various enemy navies during the two World Wars, and the decisions made by their opponents as to the fates of their fleets following armistice or surrender. These followed prolonged negotiations between the victorious powers, some of which became distinctly acrimonious, and exposed underlying tensions between certain countries, especially France and Italy.

While the headlines are fairly well known, much of the detail of these discussions, their outcome and their implementation has often been obscured or confused in published treatments. Thus, for example, we read of the submarine *U119* being 'surrendered to France on 24 November 1918' (Gröner); in fact, the boat was surrendered on that date at

Harwich in the UK to the Allies in general, moved to a French port to relieve pressure on the facilities at Harwich in the spring of 1919, and only formally ceded to France in January 1920, with the promulgation of the results of the inter-Allied negotiations. Indeed, some of the boats moved to French waters in 1919 were ultimately allocated to the UK, although in the end only the value of their scrap was actually returned to Great Britain.

Similarly, after the Second World War, an ex-German vessel may be found cited as having been taken as a 'French prize'. However, only the UK, USA and USSR actually received formal allocations of ex-German tonnage: with a handful of anomalous exceptions, all such vessels that came into French hands were actually ceded to her by the UK from the latter's share, supplemented by a few from the US portion.

A further area where confusion has arisen is over the use of ex-German ships to dispose of chemical munitions. A considerable number of vessels were scuttled in the North Sea following the end of the war, some of which were cer-tainly sunk with such ammunition aboard as part of a formal programme. However, there seems to have been a wide later assumption (e.g. in Gröner) that this was the case with *all* scuttlings, whereas in reality most sinkings were carried out to dispose of unallocated, often damaged, tonnage to meet a deadline agreed between the Allies, with nothing on board. Accordingly, in carrying out our key objective, there has been a underlying secondary one of 'myth-busting' such misunderstandings.

In writing this book, we are of course in the debt of a number of friends and colleagues for all their help, in particular LaVerle Berry, Ian Buxton, David Chessum, Innes McCartney, Ramón J Miró, Martin Woodward and Jenny Wraight. Responsibility for all errors, misinterpretations and other infelicities remain, of course, solely ours.

Aidan Dodson **Serena Cant**
University of Bristol Historic England

4 October 2019

Introduction

While a large number of books have dealt with the navies and war at sea of the World Wars, the immediate aftermaths have generally been dealt with in passing only, as a coda to the main narrative. However, the political machinations and technical discussions that surrounded the determination of the fates of the surviving navies of the defeated powers are of considerable interest from a number of perspectives. These include the relative priorities of the victorious nations, acquisition and testing of ex-enemy materiel and the intended future capabilities of those ex-enemy navies that were to be allowed to continue to exist.

Accordingly, this book is intended to trace the histories of navies and ships of the defeated powers from the months leading up to the relevant armistices or surrenders, through to the final execution of the appropriate post-war settlements, and the uses made by the victors of ex-enemy vessels

Spoil of an earlier war: the Japanese battleship *Iwami*, formerly the Russian *Orel*, captured after the Battle of Tusushima in 1905. She is shown here after reconstruction by her new owners. *(NHHC NH 45832)*

ceded to them. In doing so, it also narrates and discusses the way in which the victorious powers reached their final demands, how these were implemented, and to what effect. In doing this, much of the material has been drawn from archival sources, some of which seem never previously to have been used to inform published work on the topic.

The narrative is accompanied by tabulated lists of all major navy-built (and certain significant ex-mercantile) enemy ships in commission at the relevant date of armistice/surrender, or whose hulks were specifically listed for attention in post-Second World War inter-Allied agreements. This includes the key dates in their careers and, most crucially, their ultimate fates, insofar as these are available, correcting as far as possible the many errors that have crept into 'standard' published reference and secondary works.

Separate parts deal with each of the two World Wars, each with a similar structure. This begins with a look at the last months of the naval war for each of the defeated protagonists, and then the discussions between the victorious powers over the terms of the prospective settlement(s). They then move on to the events following the various armistices/surrenders, including treaty negotiations, the decisions taken as to the disposition of the ex-enemy fleets, and the implementation of those decisions. Finally, there is a survey of the uses to which the victorious powers put the vessels surrendered to them – ranging from short-term trials and/or destruction as targets, to long-term service, during which extensive alterations sometimes took place.

Conventions and Abbreviations

ACC	Allied Control Commission	MMS	Motor Mine Sweeper
AD	Aidan Dodson (in image credits)	MoD	Ministry of Defence, UK
ANAC	Allied Naval Armistice Commission	MRVC	Minenräumverbandes Cuxhaven
BA	Bundesarchiv (in image credits)	MSA	Maritime Safety Agency (Japan, 1948)
BU	Broken Up (in tables)	MSDF	Maritime Self Defence Force (Japan, 1952)
CID	International Danube Commission	MTB	Marine Transportation Bureau
(D)	Disarmed (in tables)	MTB	Motor Torpedo Boat
DMRVBC	Deutscher Minenräumverband Cuxhaven (Jan 48 to Jun 51)	NACDEV	Naval Allied Commission for the Disposal of Enemy Vessels
FAA	Fleet Air Arm (Royal Navy)	NHHC	Naval History and Heritage Command, US (in image credits)
FO	Flag Officer	n/l	never launched
FPB	Fast Patrol Boat	NMM	National Maritime Museum, London (in image credits)
FR M/S	Minesweeping under French control (in tables)	OD	Sunk in Operation 'Deadlight' (in tables)
GM/SA	German Mine Sweeping Administration (Deutschen Minenräumdienst)	OMGUS	Office of Military Government, United States (in Germany, 1 January 1946–5 December 1949)
HA	high altitude	ORP	Okręt Rzeczypospolitej Polskiej (Polish navy ship prefix) (in tables)
HC	Horizontal Compound (in tables)	(P)	'propaganda' ship (in tables)
HE	Historic England (in image credits)	R-boat	Minenräumboot (German coastal motor minesweeper)
HE	high-explosive	SF	Submarine Flotilla
HSE	Horizontal Single Expansion (in tables)	SG	Scouting Group
HTP	high-test peroxide	shp	shaft horsepower (in tables)
ihp	indicated horsepower (in tables)	TB	Torpedo Boat
IWM	Imperial War Museum, London (in image credits)	TE	Turbo-Electric (number of shafts, in tables)
KFK	Kriegsfischkutter (German small navy-built trawler)	TNA	The National Archives, UK (in references)
KUJ	Kriegs-Unterseebootjäger (German large navy-built trawler)	TT	Torpedo Tubes (in tables)
LCS	Light Cruiser Squadron	Tu	Turbines (number of shafts, in tables)
LCU	Landing Craft (Utility) (in tables)	UE	Uniform Expansion (in tables)
LSU(B)	Labor Service Unit (B) (in Germany, February 1951–57)	UKHO	United Kingdom Hydrographic Office
M-boat	Minensuchboot (German fleet minesweeper)	US NA	US National Archives (in image credits)
MDG RN	Marinedienstgruppe Royal Navy, Cuxhaven	VC	Vertical Compound (in tables)
ML	Motor Launch	VQE	Vertical Quadruple Expansion (in tables)
MLR	Muzzle Loading Rifle (in tables)	VTE	Vertical Triple Expansion (in tables)

Country codes (in tables)

AL	Albania	FRV	Vichy France	PE	Peru
AH	Austria-Hungary	GE	Germany	PL	Poland
AR	Argentina	GED	German Democratic Republic	PT	Portugal
AT	Austria	GEF	Federal Republic of German	RO	Romania
AU	Australia	GR	Greece	RSI	Italy – Social Republic
BE	Belgium	HR	Croatia	RU	Russia
BG	Bulgaria	ID	Indonesia	SA	South Africa
BR	Brazil	IN	India	SG	Singapore
CN	China	IR	Iran/Persia	SU	Union of Soviet Socialist Republics
CNP	People's Republic of China	LT	Lithuania	SY	Syria
CO	Columbia	LV	Latvia	UA	Ukraine
DK	Denmark	ME	Montenegro	UK	United Kingdom
FI	Finland	NL	Netherlands	US	United States
FR	France	NO	Norway	YU	Yugoslavia[1]

Full texts of all treaties and agreements mentioned or cited in the text are available in C. Bevans (ed.), *Treaties and Other International Agreements of the United States of America, 1776–1949*, 13vv (Washington, DC: US Government Printing Office, 1968–76), and *US Treaties and Other International Agreements*, 35vv (Washington, DC: US Department of State, 1950–84).

In the context of the First World War and its subsequent treaties and agreements, the term 'Allied powers' or 'Allies' is used to cover all the nations fighting against the Central Powers, although legally speaking, the USA and Brazil were 'Associated Powers'.

[1] Although anachronistic before 1929, when the Kingdom of Serbs, Croats and Slovenes, established on 1 December 1918, was renamed that of Yugoslavia – and even more so during October/November 1918 when the State of Slovenes, Croats and Serbs existed as a provisional entity embracing only those parts of the eventual Yugoslavia that had lain within the Austro-Hungarian Empire (i.e. not the Kingdoms of Serbia and Montenegro) – the term 'Yugoslav(ia)' will be used throughout this book for reasons of simplicity.

1

Endgame 1918

GERMANY

By the summer of 1918, Germany's war-position was on a knife-edge. On land, the spring's Ludendorff Offensive had ground to a halt, while the Allies were building up towards their August counter-offensive. At sea, the conflict for Germany was now a matter for light forces – torpedo boats, submarines and minesweepers – the big ships of the High Seas Fleet having largely remained in harbour since the Battle of Jutland in 1916.[1]

Following the introduction of the Allied convoy system in May 1917, the German submarine force had suffered both a drop in its levels of success, and a rise in its own loss-rate. In the late spring of 1918, it had been decided to take the submarine campaign right up to the US coast, using the big *U139*- and *U151*-class cruiser-submarines, beginning with *U151* during April/July, which sank twenty-three ships totalling 61,000 tons, and laid mines that sank another four. However, the subsequent deployment of *U140*, *U151*, *U156* and the large minelayer *U117* proved less successful, *U156* being mined on the way home in September, although having actually fired on the US coast at Orleans, MA, in July. *U139*, *U152* and *U155* were en route to American waters when the war ended.

German submarine operations were further constrained by the increasing use of aircraft in anti-submarine roles, and also by creation of the North Sea Mine Barrage, which has been credited with sinking six submarines. By November, sinkings of Allied shipping had been declining month-on-month, while no fewer than sixty-nine submarines had been sunk since the beginning of the year.

Mutiny

August 1918 marked the turning point in the war in the West. On the 8th, at Amiens, a massive tank-supported offensive by British, French, Australian and Canadian forces broke through the German lines. Two days later, the German retreat back towards their Hindenburg Line defences began. Allied consolidation was followed by a fresh offensive on 21 August, the German front line being hopelessly broken by the end of the month. The Grand Offensive, launched on 26 September, broke the Hindenburg Line on 8 October, the rest of the month witnessing a German retreat back towards their own borders. The Flanders coast was evacuated by the German navy from the end of September.

Emperor Wilhelm II was informed of the hopelessness of the situation on 29 September, and on 5 October, the German government, headed since the 3rd by Prince Max of Baden, put out feelers to President Woodrow Wilson of the USA towards agreeing an armistice: the latter's response required German withdrawal from occupied territory; the ending of the submarine campaign against trade; and the abdication of the emperor as preconditions to any agreement.

The end of the submarine campaign against merchant shipping was implemented on 24 October 1918. However, with the new availability of submarines for fleet support – and with a wider notion of maintaining the 'honour' of the navy and possibly influencing the peace settlement – the German Admiralty (without reference to the government) revived an operational plan originally drawn up in 1916, with the aim of provoking a final battle with the Grand Fleet.

By this point the Grand Fleet of the Royal Navy outnumbered the High Seas Fleet of the Imperial German navy by 35:18 in battleships (including five US vessels),[2] 9:5 in battle-cruisers, 36:14 in light cruisers and 146:60 in destroyers/torpedo boats (not counting the Harwich Force and other detached commands in the North Sea, with eight light cruisers and ninety-nine destroyers). However, the view of the German command was that the ends –

---

1. The only substantive role played by some of its ships had been during Operation 'Albion', the Baltic landings in the spring of 1918. For an overview of the German navy from Jutland to the end of the war, see D Woodward, *The Collapse of Power: Mutiny in the High Seas Fleet* (London: Arthur Barker, 1973).

2. On the US contribution to the Grand Fleet, see J W Jones, *U.S. Battleship Operations in World War I* (Annapolis, MD: Naval Institute Press, 1998).

influencing peace negotiations and salvaging the reputation of the German navy – justified the means and likely tactical outcome.

The order for the operation was thus issued on 24 October, with sailing scheduled for the 30th. The ships began assembling in Schillig Roads, off Wilhelmshaven, on the 29th, but while passing through the Wilhelmshaven locks, the battlecruisers *Derfflinger* and *Von der Tann* temporarily lost between 200 and 300 men by desertion. There was also unrest aboard the battleships *Markgraf, König, Kronprinz Wilhelm* and *Thüringen*. In light of this, it became clear that it would be impossible to sail the III. Sqn, and it was accordingly decided, around 22:00 that evening, to scale back the operation to just the cruiser raids, ostensibly because of bad weather. To support these, the I. Sqn would cover minesweepers in home waters. However, the next morning, the crew of *Thüringen* refused to weigh anchor, making it apparent that the I. Sqn was also not able to play a part, even in the reduced operation.

Suggestions that the fleet should be forced to sea under the threat that any ship refusing would be sunk were wisely rejected, and instead it was planned that while the IV. Sqn would remain at Wilhelmshaven, the I. SG should go to Cuxhaven and the III. Sqn to the nearby Altenbruch Roads, to try and minimise the risk of mutinous 'infection'. However, it was then decided to send the III. Sqn to its home port of Kiel, in the hope that the presence of family would ease the men's mood. On the other hand, Kiel was already in a state of unrest, and its port-admiral was concerned at the likely impact of the squadron's arrival – quite rightly, as it turned out.

Meanwhile, the capital ships sailed from Schillig Roads, leaving the mutinous *Thüringen*, and *Helgoland*, which was also now suffering from major unrest. The intent was that marines would take back control of *Thüringen* on the 31st, covered by the 15cm-armed submarine *U135* and the IV. TB Half-Flotilla destroyers *B97, B109, B110, B111* and *B112*, standing ready to torpedo the rebel battleship if necessary.

German submarines at Kiel hoist the red flag in November 1918; the vessel in the background is the disarmed cruiser *Veneta*, employed as an accommodation ship for submarine crews. *(AD collection)*

Thüringen, with *B109* and *B112* close by, and *U135* on the left, during the Wilhelmshaven mutiny. *(Dirk Nottelmann collection)*

Helgoland was also now in the hands of mutineers, and trained her own 15cm guns on the two vessels carrying the marines – and on *U135*. In the meantime, loyalists aboard *Thüringen* had seized her aft turret, which they trained on *Helgoland* until ordered to return to midships by *U135*.

B97 approached *Thüringen* at 14:00, warning that she was about to open fire, before the order was countermanded at the last moment, *Thüringen's* crew having been prevailed upon to surrender. Those in *Helgoland* also gave up, and the mutineers were imprisoned ashore, along with mutinous members of the crews of *Markgraf*, *König*, *Oldenburg* and *Friedrich der Große*.

The III. Sqn arrived at Kiel, having passed through the Kiel Canal, on 1 November. The effect was exactly as the port-admiral had feared, and the presence of rebellious sailors from the battleships soon further stoked a situation already enflamed by rumours of what had been happening in Wilhelmshaven. Light cruisers of IV. SG (*Bremse*, *Brummer*, *Regensburg*, *Straßburg*), plus *Dresden*, arrived at Kiel on the 3rd, and on the following day there was a stand-off between *Dresden* and *Markgraf*, the latter training a turret on the cruiser, in an attempt to stop her sailing for Eckernförde, to become a repeating ship in view of communications difficulties arising from current circumstances. She eventually sailed, as did the IV. SG, which made its way to Glücksburg.

Although the III. Sqn had been successfully sent to Travemünde on the 4th (except for *König*, now in dry dock), some of their crews remained in Kiel, taking part in an expanding uproar, which was a key catalyst of the revolution that was now spreading across Germany, with sailors in the vanguard. The news from Kiel led to upheavals in the I. Sqn, now at Brunsbüttel, on 5 November, while the III. Sqn at Travemünde continued in revolutionary mode.

The IV. SG, excluding *Straßburg*, together with *Dresden*, moved to Swinemünde as the revolt spread, arriving on the 7th, where rumours of an attack by rebel ships from Kiel led to the ships being placed out of commission, and left with their magazines (and, inadvertently, other compartments as well in *Dresden*) flooded and confidential books destroyed.

On the 9th, the cadet training ship *Schlesien* arrived from Sweden, where she had briefly taken refuge, by which time work had begun to pump-out and dry the ammunition of the four cruisers. The latter were ultimately recommissioned on the 18th.

Armistice and Internment

Progress towards an armistice was slowed by opposition from within the German army, disagreements among the Allies over the shape of any post-war settlement, and now the fallout from the revolution. However, final negotiations were authorised on 5 November, and began on the 8th. The following day, the emperor abdicated,[3] a republic was proclaimed, and Prince Max replaced as chancellor by the Social Democrat Friedrich Ebert. The terms were harsh, but there was little scope for German manoeuvre (apart from correcting factual errors), and the Armistice of Compiègne was thus signed on the morning of 11 November, to come into effect at 11.00 Paris time that day. Due to expire on 13 December, it was then prolonged until 16 January 1919, then to 16 February 1919, and finally to the point when the peace treaty (which would be signed on 23 June) came into effect on 10 January 1920.

Surface Vessels

Article XXIII of the Armistice stated:

> German surface warships which shall be designated by the Allies and the United States shall be immediately disarmed and thereafter interned in neutral ports or in default of them in allied ports to be designated by the Allies and the United States. They will there remain under the supervision of the Allies and of the United States, only caretakers being left on board. The following warships are designated by the Allies: Six battle cruisers, ten battleships, eight light cruisers (including two mine layers), fifty destroyers of the most modern types.

The light cruiser *Königsberg* brought delegates to Rosyth to arrange the transfer of the ships to be interned on 15 November, escorted into harbour by the 6th LCS (*Cardiff* flag) and ten destroyers, Rear Admiral Hugo Meurer being taken by the destroyer *Oak* to confer with Admiral Beatty on board *Queen Elizabeth*.[4]

The capital ships to be interned were essentially the newest of each category (the III. and IV. Sqns, and I. SG of

3. Between then and the end of November all other German monarchs would also vacate their thrones, the last being Wilhelm II of Württemburg on the 30th.
4. TNA ADM 137/2483.

HMS *Cardiff* leads the vanguard of the High Seas Fleet to internment on 21 November 1918. Immediately behind her are *Seydlitz*, *Von der Tann* and *Hindenburg*. *(US NA 165-WW-330B-002)*

the High Seas Fleet), but excluding the fleet flagship *Baden*. However, poor intelligence on the part of the Allies meant that the far-from-complete battlecruiser *Mackensen*, and also the incomplete light cruiser *Wiesbaden* were included on the original internment list. Although the Allies initially demanded that the battlecruiser be towed if unable to proceed under her own steam – she actually had not yet had her engines installed – it was eventually decided by the Allies (under German protest) that *Baden* should be substituted for the battlecruiser, while the light cruiser *Dresden* stood in for *Wiesbaden*.

Norway and Spain having declined to host the interned fleet, it had been directed that they should be laid up at Scapa Flow, guarded by the Grand Fleet. Led by the light cruiser *Cardiff*, and met by the whole Grand Fleet (including the American 6th BS), the German vessels sailed in line-ahead to the Firth of Forth on the 21st, with the battlecruiser *Seydlitz* in the van, followed by the battle-cruisers *Moltke*, *Hindenburg*, *Derfflinger*, *Von der Tann*, and then the battleships *Friedrich der Große* (flag), *König Albert*, *Kaiser*, *Kaiserin*, *Prinzregent Luitpold*, *Bayern*, *Kronprinz Wilhelm*, *Markgraf* and *Großer Kurfürst*. Then came HMS *Phoebe*, leading the light cruisers *Karlsruhe*, *Frankfurt*, *Emden*, *Nürnberg*, *Brummer*, *Cöln* and *Bremse*; forty-nine torpedo boats followed (a fiftieth, *V30*, had been mined and sunk en route). Having anchored temporarily in the Forth

estuary, the German ships subsequently sailed in batches to Scapa Flow.

Twenty destroyers moved to the Flow on 22/23 November, twenty more on the 23rd/24th, the battlecruisers and the remaining destroyers on the 24th/25th; *Friedrich der Große*, *König Albert*, *Kaiserin*, *Prinzregent Luitpold*, *Kaiser*, *Karlsruhe*, *Nürnberg* and *Emden* were transferred on the 25th/26th, and *Bayern*, *Großer Kurfürst*, *Kronprinz Wilhelm*, *Markgraf*, *Frankfurt*, *Cöln*, *Bremse* and *Brummer* on the 26th/27th. The transports *Sierra Ventana* and *Graf Waldersee* arrived on 3 December to begin the repatriation

German destroyers at Scapa Flow. In the foreground is *V45*, with *S131* beyond; one of the two pairs of boats in the distance comprised *S49* and *S50*. *(AD collection)*

Scapa Flow, with *Kaiser* in the foreground, *Moltke* and destroyers directly behind, the foreparts of *Seydlitz* and *Nürnberg* on the left, and the stern of *Hindenburg* on the right. In the far background in the British depot ship (ex-battleship) *Victorious*. *(AD collection)*

of those not required to form the ships' caretaker crews: 4,000 left on the 3rd, 6,000 on the 6th and 5,000 on the 12th, leaving 4,815; subsequently, some 100 were repatriated each month. On the 4th, *König*, which had been unable to sail with the main body owing to being in dock at Kiel, the light cruiser *Dresden* and the destroyer *V129* (vice *V30*) also dropped anchor in the Flow.

The final arrival was the fleet flagship *Baden* (vice *Mackensen*) on 9 January 1919, which had left Wilhelmshaven on the 7th, escorted by the light cruiser *Regensburg*, which then repatriated her crew; on arrival, the battleship was inspected by a team from HMS *King George V*. In early December 1918, *Regensburg* had been used to escort the battleship *Hercules*, carrying members of the Allied Control Commission to Wilhelmshaven. She was

subsequently used to escort the passage of submarine support vessels from Germany to the UK during April/June (see p 19, below).

As regards the remainder of the surface fleet, the final part of Article XXIII had stated:

> All other surface warships (including river craft) are to be concentrated in German naval bases to be designated by the Allies and the United States and are to be completely disarmed and classed under the supervision of the Allies and the United States.

Under these terms, the *Nassau*s, *Helgoland*s and remaining seagoing older ships had their guns disabled, and were laid up at their home ports to await events. A handful of ships were permitted to remain operational, including a number of light cruisers, although of these only two – *Regensburg* and *Graudenz* – were permitted to have both guns and a crew aboard; all ships had to have their torpedo tubes removed and the gap in their bulwarks plated over. *Königsberg*, although fully crewed, thus had to have her guns removed. The Germans made a point of immediately destroying the new 60cm torpedoes and tubes fitted in the newest cruisers, to avoid any danger of them falling into Allied hands.

In addition, *Straßburg* was employed as flagship of the Baltic Minesweepers, with a single 15cm gun on the forecastle for the destruction of mines: minesweeping was a naval activity permitted by the Allies. As a result, four disarmed pre-dreadnought battleships, *Wittelsbach*, *Schwaben*, *Lothringen* and *Preußen* were fitted as carriers for motor minesweepers, although the latter proved unsuitable and was replaced by the old cruiser *Arcona* as parent ship for the minesweepers based at Wilhelmshaven.

The battleship *Preußen* as carrier of F-boats (motor mine sweepers). *(AD collection)*

The cruiser *Arcona*, which replaced *Preußen* as the F-boat support ship at Wilhelmshaven. *(AD collection)*

Members of Germany's active destroyer force of the immediate post-war era, the so-called Eisernen Flotille, on 24 February 1919. Second from the left is *V79*, the remaining ships being *S133*, *S134*, *S135* and *S136*; note the absence of torpedo tubes, removed from all vessels to meet Armistice requirements. All still fly the old Imperial ensign, the new Reichsmarine ensign not being introduced until 1921. *(AD collection)*

Some destroyers were also permitted, the big *V116*, and *V26*, *V28*, *V79*, *S63*, *S133–S135*, *S139* and *H146* serving in the Eisernen Flottille ('Iron Flotilla'), a 'voluntary' formation under the auspices of the new Provisional Reichsmarine, the embryonic new German navy, which played a security role during the political and social upheavals of the spring of 1919. Like the cruisers, all the destroyers had their torpedo tubes removed, and were limited as to gunpower.

Also impacting surface vessels was Article XXIX:

All Black Sea ports are to be evacuated by Germany; all Russian war vessels of all descriptions seized by Germany in the Black Sea are to be handed over to the Allies and the United States of America; all neutral merchant vessels seized are to be released; all warlike and other materials of all kinds seized in those ports are to be returned and German materials as specified in Clause Twenty-eight are to be abandoned.

The most significant vessels involved were the battleship *Volya* (ex-*Imperator Aleksandr III*), and the destroyers *Schastliviy*, *Bystriy*, *Gnevniy*, *Kapitan Saken*, *Zorkiy*, *Zvonkiy*, *Zutkiy*, *Zivoy* and *Zavidniy*, all of which had been considered for commissioning, or had actually been commissioned, into German service. Having been taken over by Allied forces at Sevastopol on 24 November 1918, the formal position taken was that the ships were henceforth 'in trust', pending the establishment of a stable government in Russia. In practice, they were handed over to the White forces of General Denikin, with the result that most ended up being evacuated to Bizerte, Tunisia, in 1920, and broken up during the 1930s. The exceptions were *Schastliviy*, sunk in a storm in 1919, *Bystriy*, which became the Soviet *Frunze* in 1925, and *Zutkiy* and *Zavidniy*, which were broken up by the Soviet authorities in the early 1920s.

Submarines

Under Article XXII of the Armistice, Germany was to:

Surrender to the Allies and United States of all submarines (including submarine cruisers and all mine-laying submarines) now existing, with their complete armament and equipment, in ports which shall be specified by the Allies and United States. Those which cannot take the sea shall be disarmed of the personnel and material and shall remain under the supervision of the Allies and the United States. The submarines which are ready for the sea shall be prepared to leave the German ports as soon as orders shall be received by wireless for their voyage to the port designated for their delivery, and the remainder at the earliest possible moment. The conditions of this article shall be carried into effect within the period of fourteen days after the signing of the armistice.

It should be noted that while surface vessels that passed into Allied custody under Article XXII of the Armistice would be *interned* until a peace treaty had been agreed, submarines were to be *surrendered* from the outset. This stringency relating to submarines was largely motivated by worldwide concern at the capability of the submarine as a war machine. Germany's two iterations of unrestricted submarine warfare (in 1915, and from 1917 onwards)

had played a key role in bringing the USA into the war. During the war 5,798 British, Allied and neutral ships had been sunk directly by submarine (torpedo or shellfire), a tonnage of over 11,000,000 tons, while a further 774 ships of over 1,000,000 tons had been sunk by mine during the period 1915–18, attributable in large part to the *UC*-minelaying submarines that had come into operation from 1915: mines were, of course, no respecters of neutrality.[5] These statistics included small wooden fishing vessel fleets that were targeted on multiple occasions around the British coastline, particularly from 1916 onwards. The deep naval and mercantile concern over the capabilities of the submarine found its echo in a public, press and political milieu that were actively hostile to the memory of what was routinely termed 'submarine piracy'. There would thus have never been public acceptance of any retention of submarines by Germany.

5. Lloyd's of London, *Lloyd's War Losses: The First World War: Casualties to Shipping through Enemy Causes 1914–18* (London: Lloyd's of London Press Ltd., facsimile edition, 1990).

Three German submarines arriving at Harwich on 21 November 1918. *(NHHC NH 111172)*

Crews disembarking from their surrendered submarines at Harwich on 5 December 1918. *(Western Newspaper Union)*

A *U151*-class cruiser-submarine and two smaller boats laid up at Harwich. *(AD)*

A German preparatory commission having been conveyed to Harwich by the battleship *Helgoland*, the first vessels arrived at Harwich on 20 November, a steady stream then crossing the North Sea until 1 December.[6] Under the agreed protocol, each group of approximately twenty submarines[7] was to be accompanied by a transport to repatriate their crews, and be escorted from the rendezvous point (52° 05′ N, 2° 05′ E) by British light cruisers and destroyers, columns of five boats each being led by a destroyer. Each submarine was supposed to have fully charged batteries, a full set of torpedoes, all ballast tanks empty, and free of booby-traps. For the second batch, of nineteen boats from the II. Flotille and arriving on 21 November, *Helgoland* acted as the transport. Not all boats made it, with *U97* and *U99* of the third batch sinking en route. *U35*, which had been at Barcelona, reached Harwich to surrender on 26 November 1918. By 1 December 1918, when the sixth batch arrived, 122 boats had been surrendered at Harwich which were moored in the River Stour, forming what came to be known as 'U-Boat Avenue' (see further pp 94–96). Four vessels, *UB14* (which had previously had a spell as the Austro-Hungarian *U26*), *UB42*, *UC23* (AH *U63*) and *UC37* (AH *U77*), had been taken over by the Allies at Sevastopol on 25 November 1918. *UB14* was scuttled off the port early in 1919, but the other three were taken to Malta (*UB42* and *UC37*) or Bizerte (*UC23*) for formal surrender, and sold for scrap locally (*UB14*, *UB42*, *UC 23* and *UC37*). According to information held by the Allies, this left sixty-four still to be delivered.[8]

There was then a hiatus until 16 January 1919, when thirteen further vessels (the seventh batch, ten of the boats having recently returned from the Mediterranean) arrived. On 25 January, the Germans were advised that forty-nine[9] complete boats still needed to be surrendered (*UC71* [at Wilhelmshaven], *U148*, *U150*, *UB144*, *UB145*, *UB150* [building at Vulcan, Bremen], *U165–U169* [building at Vulcan, Vegesack], *U181*, *UC40* [which had, however, foundered in the North Sea on the 21st], *UC106–U114* [building at Blohm & Voss, Hamburg], *U121*, *U145*, *UB154*, *UB155* [building at Vulcan, Hamburg], *U16*, *U21*, *U25*, *U38*,

U71, *U118*, *U136*, *U140*, *UB76*, *UC28*, *UC60*, *UC91* [Kiel], *U127*, *U142*, *U143*, *U144*, *U173*, *UB133*, *UB136*, *UB137* [building at Germania, Kiel]), and work began on breaking up incomplete vessels, before the forthcoming renewal of the Armistice on 17 February.[10]

The Germans responded on 30 January/1 February with a proposal to surrender twenty-four, of which twenty-one would be delivered to an Allied port, the remaining three having been already so far dismantled that they could no longer be towed, and would be broken up in Germany. Twenty of the newest boats would also be placed at the disposal of the Allied Naval Armistice Commission (ANAC) – but not brought over by the Germans. All remaining boats would be 'disabled' and the submarine salvage vessels and pressure docks placed at the disposal of the ANAC.

On 3 February, three boats (the last to return from the Mediterranean) arrived at Harwich. The same day, the Allies responded to the German offer by insisting that they required the remaining balance to be delivered, which was now calculated at forty-five boats. Any boats that had been, in the Allied view, 'wilfully rendered unfit for sea' should be 're-assemble[d]' and towed over.

On the 6th, however, the Germans essentially repeated their original offer, listing twenty-one boats for immediate delivery from German ports: *U1*, *U2*, *U16*, *U21*, *U25*, *U38*, *U71*, *U118*, *U136*, *U140*, *UB2*, *UB5*, *UB9*, *UB11*, *UB76*, *UB89*, *UC28*, *UC40*, *UC60*, *UC71* and *UC91*. Seven currently interned boats (*U39*, *U157*, *UB6*, *UB23*, *UC48*, *UC56* and *UC74*) would be delivered on release. Seventeen boats in building yards would be 'placed at the disposal of' the Allies. However, the Allies responded by noting that the original number of sixty-four boats (on which the current demand for forty-five was based) had *not* included boats currently interned, *nor* obsolete vessels such as *U1*, *U2*, *UB2*, *UB5*, *UB9* and *UB11*, and that they had specified the boats required in their list of 25 January. On 8 February, *U157*, which had been interned in Norway, arrived at Harwich in tow, but the same day *U16* sank in the Elbe. *UB76* and *UC28* arrived at Harwich from Germany on the 12th, but had, however, originally been accompanied by *UC91*, which had foundered in the North Sea on the 10th.

On 16 February, the terms of the renewal of the Armistice were adjusted to confirm the requirement that forty-five further boats be surrendered, explicitly excluding those still interned in neutral countries, and also the obsolete *U1*, *U2*, *UB2*, *UB5*, *UB9* and *UB11*, which could be broken up in Germany. Of them, *U1* was sold to her builder in early 1919 to become an exhibit in the Deutsches Museum at Munich;

6. TNA ADM 116/1826.

7. In practice, twenty came on the 20th, twenty on the 21st, nineteen on the 22nd, twenty-eight on the 24th, twenty-seven on the 27th and eight on 1 December.

8. TNA ADM 116/1975, dated 11 February 1919.

9. Starting with the previous sixty-four, less the thirteen surrendered on the 16th and one at Hamburg, but plus an extra boat now judged to be towable at Kiel, and less '3 small submarines seized by the Germans from Russia, and stated to be at Germania, Kiel'. Their identity is unclear: the only Russian submarines to fall into German hands had done so in the Black Sea (*Burevestnik* = *US1*, *Orlan* = *US2*, *Utka* = *US3*, *Gargara* = *US4*, plus others not taken under the German flag), and had in any case come into White Russian hands in November 1918.

10. TNA 116/1975.

UC122, *UC123* and *UC124* being broken up incomplete at Hamburg-Moorburg, near the Blohm & Voss yard where they had been launched shortly before the Armistice; their minelaying tubes are exposed. *(AD collection)*

sectioned for display, her retention was formally endorsed by the Naval Inter-Allied Control Commission (NIACC – see Appendix 3.1). *U2*, *U4*, *U17*, *UB2*, *UB5*, *UB9* and *UB11* were broken up during 1919/20.[11]

For boats listed for handing over, but unfit for towing, engines and motors could be substituted (either belonging to the boats themselves or, if already mutilated, equivalent items from other sources); likewise, should boats sink on passage, they were to be replaced by engines and motors of the appropriate type. Accordingly, the previously commissioned *U21*, *U25*, *U38*, *U71*, *U118*, *U136*, *U140*, *UB76*, *UC28*, *UC40*, *UC60*, *UC71*, *UC89* (in lieu of the sunken *UC91*) and the brand-new *U121*, *U165* (which, however, proved to have foundered at her builder's yard soon after the Armistice), *U166*, *U167*, *UB133*, *UB136*, *UB 144*, *UB145*, *UB150*, *UB154*, *UB155*, *UC106*, *UC107*, *UC108*, *UC109*, *UC110*, *UC111*, *UC112*, *UC113* and *UC114* would be physically surrendered, as would the engines and motors of *U127*, *U142*, *U143*, *U144*, *U145*, *U148*, *U150*, *U168*, *U169*, *U173*, *UB137* and *UC181*.

The first of this new series of deliveries arrived at Harwich on 23 February, with smaller numbers being received during March and April. Although the earlier arrivals had come straight from operations and had sailed under their own power, those from February onwards nearly all had to be

towed, some lacking engines, some electric motors as well. Thus, when *U21*, *U25*, *U38*, *U71*, *U118*, *U136*, *U140*, *UC40* and *UC60* left Germany on 20 February, all but *U118* were in tow of the light cruiser *Graudenz*. The poor condition of some of the 'later' boats is indicated by the fact that while only two of the November 1918 sailings (*U97* and *U165*) had been lost on passage, no fewer than five of the 1919 boats (*U16*, *U21*, *UC40*, *UC71* and *UC91*) foundered before reaching Harwich. Many others broke tow on passage, and were retrieved only with difficulty.

The hulk of *UB89*, which had been sunk in collision with the cruiser *Frankfurt* three weeks before the Armistice and salvaged a week later, had been added to the surrender list in lieu of the lost *UC91*; she was in tow to Harwich in a storm off the Dutch coast on 7 March 1919 when the boat (along with *UB133* and *UB154*) broke tow off course and had to be brought into IJmuiden. She remained in the Netherlands, being sold for breaking up at Dordrecht. Even once at Harwich, leaky boats were not yet safe: *UB117* foundered at her moorings, the wreck being fouled by the recently docked *UB105*, which then capsized on the falling tide.

Five boats had been interned in Spanish ports during 1918 (*U39*, *UB23*, *UC48*, *UC56* and *UC74*), and significant negotiation was required to secure their release, to allow them to be surrendered at French ports. *UC48* had been interned at Ferrol on 23 March 1918 as a result of action damage. On 15 March 1919, she sailed from Ferrol, nominally to surrender, but was in fact scuttled about 5km offshore. As a violation of Armistice conditions, this act would contribute (along with the much more notorious scuttlings at Scapa Flow three months later) to a demand for additional reparations from the Allies. However, the other boats reached France intact, *U39* arriving at Toulon on 24 March, *UB23* Brest on the 25th, *UC56* Rochefort on the 27th and, finally, *UC74* Toulon on 6 April.

In addition to actual boats, dismounted machinery began to arrive in March. As initially batched, SS *Portia* brought the engines intended for *UC106*, *UC108*, *UC109*, *UC110*, *UC114* and *UC116*, plus the motors for *UC106*, *UC107* and *UC113* (one only), received on 17 March, while *Adeline Hugo Stinnes* shipped the auxiliary diesel (for battery charging) of *U145*, the engines of *U165*, *U168*, *U169*, *UC107*, *UC111* and *UC113*, and motors of '*U21*',[12] *U145*, *U149*, *U150*, *U165*, *U168*, *U169*, *UB166*, *UC40* and *UC71*, received on the 25th. The latter cargo vessel had large hatches particularly suitable to carrying such material, and thus on 4 April she delivered the auxiliary diesels of *U142*, *U143*, *U144* and

---

11. A report on the disposal of German naval assets, dated 31 July 1921 (our Appendix 3.1), includes the note:

U.B.3. An old small coastal boat was found at Neugebauer Works. G[erman].N[aval].P[eace].C[omission]. made repeated efforts to obtain permission to use the vessel for various purposes, but the demolition was insisted on by N.I.A.C.C. and carried out.

The identity of this boat is obscure, as the actual *UB3* disappeared in the Aegean in May 1915, while *U3* was surrendered and *UC-3* mined in 1916. One assumes that this is a misprint for the other boats left in Germany, perhaps *U2*, for which no sale details are recorded by Gröner (all the others are listed as sold in 1919 or 1920).

12. Clearly wrong: this boat had been lost en route to Harwich in February, and in any case engines and motors were from vessels under construction.

The submarine salvage ship *Vulcan*, which foundered in a storm en route to Harwich on 26 April 1919. *(AD collection)*

The first of the 'pressure' or 'tubular' docks to be built by the German navy (Brückenbau Flender 21) to pressure-test submarine hulls. Unlike a second example, which never reached the UK, this one was acquired by the shipbreakers Cox & Danks and, after the removal of the pressure-cylinder, reconfigured as a salvage-platform. *(AD collection)*

U173, the engines of *U127*, *U142*, *U143*, *U144*, *U173* and *UB157*, and the motors of *U127*, *U137*, *U142*, *U143*, *U144* and *U173*. Another large shipment arrived at Barrow for storage on 26 May, other batches having already been deposited on the Tyne and at Greenock.

The surrender was also required of the submarine salvage dock ships *Cyclop* and *Vulcan*, together with two special floating docks, each of which carried a cylinder for the pressure-testing of submarine hulls, as well as the capability to dock a submarine alongside the cylinder. On 4 April 1919, *Cyclop* and *Vulcan* sailed from Brunsbüttel in the tow, respectively, of the tugs *Wendemuth* and *Loewer*, and *Retter* and *Schelde*, escorted by the light cruiser *Regensburg*. However, they ran into a storm in the North Sea, *Vulcan* foundering in 40 metres of water on the morning of the 6th;[13] *Cyclop* nevertheless reached Harwich on 9 April, her crew being repatriated by *Regensburg*.

The first of the 'pressure docks' to be handed over (Brückenbau Flender, Lübeck, builder's number 25, apparently not fully complete) was towed out of Wilhelmshaven on 8 May, again escorted by *Regensburg*, but the tow broke on the 10th, the dock being later recovered and towed to IJmuiden by the Dutch trawlers *Gorredijk* and *Liesbeth Betty*.[14] The dock was then sold by Germany directly to the Dutch government for the sum of 750,000 Marks – before the signing of the peace treaty. The sale was not traced by the Allies until December 1919: the Dutch authorities were then keen to assure the British naval authorities that '[t]his sum, however, did not reach Berlin … Different people took a

piece of the pie.'[15] The dock's subsequent history is not recorded, but it is likely that, like *UB89*, which had also inadvertently ended up at IJmuiden on 6 March, it was sold for scrap locally. The second dock (Brückenbau Flender 21), was towed out of Wilhelmshaven on 23 May, also accompanied by *Regensburg*, arriving safely at Harwich on the 30th (for its subsequent history, see pp 53–54, below).[16]

Given their surrendered status, the submarines' fates were entirely in Allied hands. Within weeks a number were put to use in an ambitious programme of visits to ports around the UK and Ireland over December 1918 to January 1919. These port visits served both to satisfy public interest in the fearsome submarines about which they had heard so much, and to raise money for naval and mercantile charities. The original programme was rapidly extended in a remarkable feat of organisation, with more ports and boats being added. Occasionally there was great disappointment from potential venues that would have liked to host such a visit but missed out, while others hosted more than one submarine concurrently or consecutively. A motor launch was sent for display in York to test the viability of getting a submarine through inland waterways to the city, but even the launch met with difficulties, so the idea of even attempting to navigate a submarine to the city was abandoned as impractical.[17]

The U- and UB- prefixes were often used interchangeably, in error, by Allied media (as had indeed been the case during the war), leaving scope for confusion, but the programme can largely be reconstructed as follows: *U54* went on show at Dover; *U62* called at Dundee; *U67* made her way to Southampton, where she was joined by *UB122*; *U70* and *UB92* went to the Firth of Forth, the latter continuing to

13. The wreck was demolished by destroyer depth charges later that month in Operation 'D.V.' (presumably for 'Destroy/Demolish Vulcan'), to prevent potential salvage by Germany (orders issued 27 April 1919: see TNA ADM 116/1975).

14. The arrival of the dock in the Netherlands was covered by the local press (e.g. *Algemeen Handelsblad*, 29,509 [13 May 1919], p 2; *Delftsche courant*, 111 [13 May 1919]).

15. Letter from S C L Reygersberg, Vice-Consul at IJmuiden, 20 December 1919, in TNA ADM 116/1974.

16. Curiously, some British authorities were under the impression that *both* pressure docks *had* 'been delivered to British custody by Germany', expressly stating that there was no confusion with a salvage dock (ADM 116/1974, dated 15 August 1919, from Admiralty M Branch.)

17. *Yorkshire Evening Post*, 8,815 (13 December 1918), p 7.

Montrose, Aberdeen and Peterhead; *U86* and *UC92* visited Bristol; *U94* made two visits to Newcastle and one to Hartlepool, while *U98* made a call at Whitby; *U100* was displayed at Blyth; *U101* called at Penzance; *U107* made a tour of Portland, Weymouth and Poole, before returning to Portland; *U111* called first at Liverpool, where she was exhibited at Wallasey Dock simultaneously with *U162* at Canning Dock, thence to Manchester's Pomona Docks; *U123* and *U141* visited Portsmouth; *U126* and *U161* were sent to Devonport; *U152*, *U153* and *U155* all went to the Thames on 2 December, the first two to Greenwich, and *U155* to St Katherine's Dock, next to Tower Bridge; *UB21* was exhibited at Ramsgate; *UB28* went to Great Yarmouth; *UB64* was moored by the House of Commons in the Thames; *UB91* went on display at Cork Wharf, Cardiff; *UB93* visited Kingstown (now Dún Laoghaire); *UB111* was exhibited at Liverpool and Manchester; *UB120* visited Dufferin Dock, Belfast; *UC59* went on a tour of Humber ports, visiting Hull,

Immingham, Grimsby and Goole; and, lastly, *UC95* went on display at Westminster Pier.

The demand to view the submarines was high, with crowds regularly being reported, and occasionally the newspapers deprecated the tendency of the public to abstract souvenirs from their visit. More positively, the nominated charities did well out of the proceeds.[18] A common thread was a supporting cast of the British 'Mystery Ships' or 'Q-ships', which were at the same time gaining publicity for their wartime exploits against German submarines. Groupings of Q-ships and U-boats were to be seen at Aberdeen (HMS *Fresh Hope* and *UB92*),[19] Liverpool (*Hyderabad*, *U111* and *U162*), and St Katherine's Dock, London (*Suffolk Coast* and *U155/Deutschland*).

18. *The Cornishman*, 8 January 1919.
19. Takings for *UB92* at Aberdeen on 14 Jan 1919 during its Scottish tour of Dec 1918-Jan 1919, amounted to £14 3s, representing 568 visitors at 6d each. (*Aberdeen Press and Journal*, 19,981 [15 January 1919], p 2.)

U155 arriving in London's St Katherine's Dock to moor alongside the Q-ship Suffolk Coast *on 2 December 1918. (US NA 165-WW-330C-012)*

U86 and *UC92* moored in the River Frome at Bristol during their November/December 1918 tour. *(Reece Winstone collection)*

U155 being demilitarised at the yard of Clover, Clayton, & Co at Birkenhead-Woodside, prior to her tour under her previous name *Deutschland*, under the auspices of Horatio Bottomley's *John Bull* magazine. *(AD collection)*

Of these boats, *U155* was a vessel not only of impressive size, but also a 'celebrity', having been built as the mercantile *Deutschland*, which had made two Atlantic crossings as a cargo-carrier in 1916. Thus, in early 1919, an offer of purchase was made by Horatio Bottomley, MP (1860–1933), with a view to displaying the vessel around British ports, the profits from which would go to the King George V Fund For Sailors.[20] The offer was accepted, subject to the submarine being fully disarmed; she was formally sold to James Dredging Co on 3 March for £3,500, with refitting carried out by Clover, Clayton, & Co at Birkenhead-Woodside. James Dredging then towed her to London, where she began her tour in May 1919 under the auspices of Bottomley's John Bull Victory Bond Club. She then went for an 'overhaul' at the Tyne Dock Engineering Company, South Shields, in August 1919, where she was made available for an invitation-only tour of inspection.

Under her original name of *Deutschland*, the boat then commenced her tour proper, being towed from South Shields for display at Great Yarmouth in September 1919, thence to London, where she arrived at the Victoria Embankment on 7 October 1919. Later that month a full crew was recruited for the submarine, under a national scheme for the resettlement of disabled ex-servicemen at a weekly salary of £4 10s each.

Deutschland then remained in London until April 1920, before visiting Ramsgate in May and Brighton in June, where special coaches were laid on to see the 'super-submarine'. She then visited Southport and Douglas, Isle of Man, in September 1920. By October 1920 she was back in Birkenhead, where a school party visited her as an essay prize. These visits reveal that the public interest in former

enemy submarines remained unabated. Over the course of the tour, she received some 150,000 visitors, but allegedly made a £15,000 loss – part of a broader fraud that led to Bottomley being convicted and imprisoned in June 1922. *Deutschland/U155* was taken into dock in June 1921 to be stripped; five men were killed in September 1921 by an explosion in the engine room. The hulk was sold for scrap in June 1922, with Clover Clayton still owed £3,356 by Bottomley for labour, materials and docking fees, of which only £200 could be recovered by the sale.

At the end of their government-sponsored tours, some of the boats concentrated at Rosyth, before returning to lay-up, while others remained in ports closer to the ends of their tours. An ulterior motive on the part of the Admiralty in commissioning the tours may have been to enable the boats to be viewed by prospective scrap-purchasers. In any case, once all the submarines had completed their tours, the Admiralty turned its attention to disposing of them (and other ex-German boats) for sale by tender. Advertisements in carefully targeted publications were placed to that effect from early February 1919 onwards, for the sale of 'a number of German submarines as they lie in England, Scotland and Ireland at Harwich, Rosyth, Buncrana, and other Naval Ports', for 'breaking up only, under bond and inspection'.[21]

The day that saw the initial sale of *U155*, 3 March 1919, also witnessed that of fifty-three other boats by the British Admiralty, to be scrapped on behalf of the Allies in general, with proceeds to be distributed proportionately once those proportions had been agreed (see pp 39–40). These initial transactions sold the engines separately from the hulls,

20 D R Messimer, *The Baltimore Sabotage Cell: German Agents, American Traitors, and the U-boat* Deutschland *during World War I* (Annapolis, MD: Naval Institute Press, 2015), pp 201–5; this contains a number of errors, some apparently owing to mis-transcriptions from <www.old-merseytimes.co.uk/ Deutschland.html> (which itself also contains errors of transcription).

21 For example, *Sheffield Daily Telegraph*, 19,835 (5 February 1919), p 1: contemporary shipbreakers, such as George Cohen, Sons & Co. and T W Ward, had offices in Sheffield and yards in many different locations.

mainly to the primary purchaser, but some to separate firms, in particular with the vessels sold to Cohen's (see pp 92–94).

The buyers accordingly made arrangements over the coming weeks for the removal of the vessels. Cohen's representative was initially optimistic that the first ten submarines would 'be brought, within the next fortnight or three weeks, to our River Lea wharf at Canning Town', although in practice it would be May or June before the majority of vessels were removed.[22]

The famous *U9*, which had sunk four cruisers in 1914, was sold on 3 March 1919 at Harwich, having lain there since 26 November 1918. She met with mishap on her first voyage to the breakers, foundering at Dover on 13 March, but was salved on 2 April, returning to Harwich within the next few weeks. As a British submarine depot, Harwich

22 *Hampshire Telegraph*, 7,197 (7 March 1919), p 10; ADM 116/1975.

Above: *U118* ashore at Hastings, having broken tow on 15 April 1919, while in tow for Brest. She was sold for scrap six weeks later and broken up on the beach. *(AD collection)*
Below: In company with *U118* en route to France, *UB121* also broke tow, and came to rest at Birling Gap a little further along the English coast, alongside *Oushla*, wrecked there in November 1916. *(AD collection)*

Above: *U151* moored at Cherbourg in 1920. Behind her are the stricken French reciprocating-engined boats *Thermidor* and *Fructidor*. The German submarine would be sunk as a target by the cruiser *Gueydon* the following year. *(NHHC NH 43778)*

would have been well placed to effect running repairs sufficient to withstand another attempt at the long journey to the breakers. *U9* accordingly left Harwich for good on 19 May, successfully arriving at Morecambe on 30 May. Not all the vessels sold on 3 March made it to the scrapyard: *U60* and *UB60*, both sold to Cohen's, sank while under tow from Chatham to South Wales (pp 96–97) and *U3* was lost before delivery from Harwich to Preston. Later sales would also see a number of losses in transit (see below). After these fifty-four boats had been sold, a hiatus in destructions was agreed among the Allies pending an overall decision on the fate of the enemy fleets.

Alongside the surrendered boats, the UK also had in her hands *UB110*, which had been sunk by the destroyer *Garry* in July 1918 off the Tyne, and salved in October and patched up by the Swan Hunter yard. In May 1919 she was lying at Jarrow, and was sold to George Clarkson, at Whitby. However, her equipment was excluded from the sale, her four torpedo tubes being removed for examination, three going to Portsmouth Dockyard and one to Armstrong Whitworth. The oscillator from her Fessenden echo-ranging device was also sent to Portsmouth. On arrival from the Tyne for demolition, she struck the pier at Whitby.[23]

In parallel with the sale of these boats, on 20 March France agreed to take up to twenty-seven vessels to relieve congestion in British ports, pending final allocations. Four boats, *U108*, *U113*, *U139* and *UC103*, had previously been transferred at Brest from the UK, arriving on 1 January 1919 to the strains of 'La Marseillaise' as they manoeuvred between two lines of French submarines.[24] Twenty-six boats were initially listed to be towed from Harwich to French ports; some were intact, but others lacked various fittings: *U25* (no engines), *U38* (no engines or electric motors), *U71* (no engines or motors; stripped), *U91*, *U118* (engines and motors in poor condition), *U121*, *U136* (no engines), *U153*, *U157*, *U160*, *U166* (parts of engines missing), *UB6*, *UB84*, *UB100*, *UB114*, *UB130*, *UB142*, *UB154*, *UB155*, *UC22* (one engine in bad condition), *UC27* (likewise), *UC28* (no engines or motors), *UC100*, *UC107* (no engines or motors), and *UA*. In the event, some on the initial list were swapped with other boats, *U153* being replaced by her sister *U151*, and *UB97* and *UB121* by *UB99* and *UB100*; *U90* was later reallocated to Belgium (p 31, below). Fifteen further vessels from Harwich were subsequently added, but in the end six failed to make it to France, breaking tow and drifting ashore (*U118*, *UB121*, *UB130*; the wrecks were sold by the Admiralty) or foundering (*U114*, *UA*) en route. *UB84* later

foundered in tow between Cherbourg and Brest. In addition, as noted above, France later became custodian of German submarines released from Spanish internment, and six Austro-Hungarian ones (*U4*, *U22*, *U31*, *U41*, *U43*, *U47*), all lying at Cattaro.

AUSTRIA-HUNGARY

By the middle of 1918, Austria-Hungary had been both in military difficulties and suffering from the progressive disintegration of its multi-ethnic state. In addition, food supplies were increasingly problematic, with hunger stalking even the major cities. Defeat at the Second Battle of the Piave River (15–23 June 1918) marked the beginning of the end, both militarily and for the monarchy. The Battle of Vittorio Veneto, which began on 24 October, marked the death blow, coinciding with declarations of independence by various elements of the empire. Already, on 14 October, an approach had been made to the Allies with a view to an armistice, and on 4 November hostilities were ended by the Armistice of Villa Giusti, signed the day before.

The Austro-Hungarian navy's role in the war had generally been marginal, other than submarine operations and the convoying of supplies down the Adriatic.[25] The appointment of Miklós Horthy (later Regent of Hungary) as CinC in February 1918, in the wake of the Cattaro Mutiny, had led to a range of reforms, including the paying off of many the older big ships, concentrating the fleet around the four *Tegetthoff* and the three *Radetzky*-class modern battleships, with the older three *Erzherzog* class as heavy support to light forces. A major operation against the enemy units guarding the barrage across the Strait of Otranto was planned for both strategic and morale reasons, but ended in disaster when the battleship *Szent István* was sunk by an Italian FPB on 10 June.

The final action by the Austro-Hungarian navy was on 2 October, when Durazzo was attacked by an Allied force comprising three Italian armoured cruisers, five British light cruisers, sixteen destroyers, plus smaller craft. All Austro-Hungarian vessels present, including the destroyers *Dinara* and *Scharfshütze*, the torpedo boat *87F* and the submarines *U29* and *U31*, survived, the latter torpedoing the light cruiser HMS *Weymouth*. But on 30 October, Emperor Karl agreed to the transfer of all Austro-Hungarian warships (except the Danube Flotilla) to the South Slav National Council (the incipient Yugoslavia: see

23 *Leeds Mercury*, 24,834 (19 May 1919), p 4.

24 Press Association War Special release, widely reproduced in the British press, for example in the *Western Daily Press*, 18,892 (2 January 1919), p 6.

25 For a history of the Austro-Hungarian navy during the First World War and it dissolution, see L Sondhaus, *The Naval Policy of Austria-Hungary 1867–1918: Navalism, Industrial Development and the Politics of Dualism* (West Lafayette, IN: Purdue University Press, 1994), pp 256–361; E Cernuschi and V P O'Hara, 'The Naval War in the Adriatic', *Warship* XXXVII (2015), pp 161–73, [XXXVIII] (2016), pp 62–75.

p 9 n.1), with the formal transfer of the ships at Pola taking place the following morning, the ships at Cattaro being handed over on 1 November. Over the previous five days, the Germans had scuttled, mainly at Pola, ten submarines (*U47*, *U65*, *U72* [Cattaro], *U73*, *UB48*, *UB129* [Fiume], *UC25*, *UC34*, *UC53*, *UC54* [Trieste]) that they had operated out of the Adriatic; fourteen more boats sailed for Germany (see above, p 17).

However, that very morning, an Italian human torpedo had attacked the new Yugoslav flagship, the battleship *Viribus Unitis*, in Pola harbour.[26] Debate continues as to whether the sinking was an error, the operators not being privy to intelligence certainly available to senior Italian officers, or whether it was allowed to continue to reflect the Italian view that the handover was illegitimate, intended to deny Italy what she saw as her spoils of war.[27] This view was certainly implicit in the Armistice documents.

Under the emperor's order of 30 October, the monitors and patrol boats on the Danube were to pass to the Kingdom of Hungary. Except for *Bodrog*, which had run aground

following an action with Serbian artillery on the 30th, the flotilla concentrated at Novy Sad (Újvidék) on 2 November, before sailing for Budapest, where they arrived on the 6th.[28]

The Naval section of the main armistice protocol included the following provisions:

2. Surrender to the Allies and to the United States of America of 15 Austro-Hungarian submarines, completed between the years 1910 and 1918, and of all German submarines which are in or may hereafter enter Austro-Hungarian territorial waters. All other Austro-Hungarian submarines to be paid off and completely disarmed, and to remain under the supervision of the Allies and United States of America.

3. Surrender to the Allies and to the United States of America, with their complete armament and equipment, of 3 battleships, 3 light cruisers, 9 destroyers, 12 torpedo boats, 1 mine layer, 6 Danube monitors, to be designated by the Allies and the United States of America. All other surface warships (including river craft) are to be concentrated in Austro-Hungarian naval bases to be designated

---

26 Although often alleged to have been renamed *Jugoslavija*, there seems no evidence for a formal renaming during the few hours that separated the ship's cession and her sinking.

27 Cf. E Cernuschi, in 'A's & A's', *Warship* [XL] (2018), pp 203–4.

28 On the Austro-Hungarian Danube monitors, see F Prasky, *Donaumonitoren Östreich-Ungarins – von 1872 bis zur Gegenwart* (Vienna: Neuer Wissenschaftlicher Verlag, 2004).

Pola harbour early in 1919. From the left are: the French cruiser *Waldeck Rousseau*; *Tegetthoff* and *Prinz Eugen*, with the old battleship *Mars* (ex-*Tegetthoff*) between them; *Erzherzog Franz Ferdinand*; and the Italian cruiser *San Marco*; in the right foreground is the minelayer *Chamaeleon*. (*NHHC NH 95007*)

by the Allies and the United States of America, and are to be paid off and completely disarmed and placed under the supervision of the Allies and the United States of America.

Supplementary Naval clauses included:

2. The units referred to in Articles II and III, to be surrendered to the associated powers, must return to Venice between 8 a. m. and 3 p. m. on November 6; they will take a pilot on board 14 miles from the coast. An exception is made as regards the Danube monitors, which will be required to proceed to a port indicated by the commander in chief of the forces of the associated powers on the Balkan front, under such conditions as he may determine.

3. The following ships will proceed to Venice:

Teghetthoff   *Saida*
Prinz Eugen   *Novara*
Ferdinand Max   *Helgoland*

Nine destroyers of the *Tatra* (at least 800 tons) of the most recent construction.

Twelve torpedo boat (200-ton type)

Mine layer *Chamaleon*

Fifteen submarines built between 1910 and 1918, and all German sub-marines which are, or may eventually be, in Austro-Hungarian waters.

Premeditated damage, or damage occurring on board the ships to be surrendered will be regarded by the Allied Governments as a grave infringement of the present armistice terms.

However, neither the Armistice not the supplementary terms had been seen, let alone agreed, by the other Allies, and the supplement was formally annulled at the end of November.[29]

The requirement that the ships proceed to Venice had also not been agreed with the other Allies, and was not implemented, although some vessels eventually went there (see p 28, below). Rather, the joint Allied intent was that the vessels should go to Corfu. But in the event, all remained in their Adriatic ports, where all of the fleet, not just those listed in the Armistice, were interned under Allied control, to await the outcome of the peace conference.

On 16 November 1918, a meeting took place at Venice between Italian, UK, French and US naval representatives to establish a Naval Commission for the Adriatic, with initial sessions held in Rome from 26 November. This divided the Adriatic coastline into three occupation zones: Italy was to

Erzherzog Friedrich and *Novara* at Cattaro in 1919. *(US NA 165-WW-329D-001)*

control the north (Istria, Gorizia/Gradisca and Trieste), the USA in the middle (mainly Dalmatia) and France the south (mainly Albania); each zone would come to contain a group of former Austro-Hungarian warships, respectively at Pola and Sebenico, at Spalato, and at Cattaro.

Six Danube monitors had been specified for surrender under the terms of the Armistice, although initially only *Sava*, *Temes*, *Körös*, *Bosna* and *Enns* were delivered to Belgrade by British crews in November 1918, with the patrol boats *Wels* and *Barsch* accepted in lieu of the sixth monitor. However, monitor numbers were made up by the addition of *Bodrog*, salvaged after having been run aground near Belgrade. All were provisionally taken over by Yugoslavia in December, *Bodrog* being renamed *Sava*, *Bosna* as *Vardar*, *Enns* as *Drava*, *Körös* as *Morava*, *Sava* as *Soca* and *Temes* as *Drina*. However, not all would remain Yugoslav under the final Allied division of prizes (see p 46, 74).

Of the rest of the Danube Flotilla's monitors, the old *Leitha*, *Szamos* and *Maros* and modern *Inn* remained at Budapest, under Hungarian control, but laid up. The Hungarian Communist regime that came to power on 21 March 1919 remilitarised the vessels in contravention of the Armistice terms, *Inn* being renamed *Újvidék*, and then *Marx*. However, *Leitha* and *Maros*, together with four patrol boats, surrendered to British forces at Baja on 26 June 1919, following an attempted counter-revolution. This British squadron, comprising the river gunboat *Aphis* and *Ladybird* (both relieved by *Glowworm* in 1920) plus motor launches, had deployed on the Danube in December 1918, where *Glowworm* would remain until 1925. Prize crews were placed aboard and the ex-Hungarian vessels sailed for Bucharest on 1 July. With the fall of the Hungarian Communist regime in August 1919, the remaining monitors *Szamos* and ex-*Inn* were laid up unmanned at Budapest under British surveillance, alongside the patrol boats *Compó* and *Viza*, while *Leitha* and *Maros* were taken under Yugoslav

29 A C Davidonis, *American Naval Mission in the Adriatic, 1918–1921* (Washington, DC: Navy Department, 1943) <www.history.navy.mil/research/library/online-reading-room/title-list-alphabetically/a/american-naval-mission-adriatic-1918-1921.html>.

Radetsky and *Zrinyi* at Spalato with USS *Birmingham* around the beginning of 1919. *(US NA 165-WW-329D-002)*

guard at Novi Sad, along with the patrol boats *Fogas*, *Csuka*, *Pozsony* (ex-*Stör*) and *Komarom* (ex-*Lachs*).

The fundamental Italian view as to the fate of the ex-Austro-Hungarian fleet was that, as the new Yugoslav state did not yet formally exist, it was thus not capable of acquiring the fleet – and that, in any case such a fleet would present a threat to Italian security. Accordingly, its opinion was that the fleet's ships should pass to Italy or be destroyed. Although there was some sympathy for the Yugoslav position among the other Allies, it was politically impossible for any of them to accept the validity of the emperor's gift, and on 10 November the Yugoslavs began to give up the ships. Italian forces had occupied Trieste, Pola and Fiume on 4 November, Sebenico being taken the following day. *Radetzky*, *Zrinyi* and the torpedo boats *12* and *52T* had nevertheless sailed with Yugoslav crews from Pola on the 7th, as did the admiralty

yacht *Lacroma*, carrying the new Yugoslav CinC, with the aim of making a port not yet under Italian control. *Prinz Eugen* attempted to sail with them, but was turned back; by the 9th all ships still at Pola were flying the Italian flag. The *Radetzky* group ended up near Spalato on the 14th, within the US zone of occupation, from whence they radioed a request to surrender to US forces: the ships were handed over to skeleton crews from a group of US navy submarine chasers on the 21st.[30] The battleships and torpedo boats hoisted the US flag on 22 November, the Yugoslav crews departing by the end of the year; the ships were then used as store hulks for the US occupation forces. The vessels remained in formal US custody until November 1920; the two torpedo boats went

30 E E Hazlett, 'The Austro-American Navy', *US Naval Institute Proceedings* 66 (1940), pp 1757–68.

Radetzky and USS *Pittsburgh*, with an Eagle-boat alongside, later that year. *(NHHC NH 60156)*

Erzherzog Franz Ferdinand and *Tegetthoff* arriving at Venice on
22 March 1919. *(NHHC NH 87219)*

Helgoland, Novara and *Sankt Georg* at Tivat (Cattaro Bay) on 10 January
1919, flying the provisional Yugoslav quadricolour (red-white-blue-red) flag.
(AD collection)

aground in a storm in December and were still there when
the USA evacuated the port in 1921 (see p 46, below).

In February 1919, the armoured cruiser *Kaiser Karl VI*
moved from Sebenico to join the main group of ships at
Pola. On 23 March, a number of vessels were finally transferred to Venice from Pola, *Tegetthoff, Erzherzog Franz
Ferdinand*, the light cruiser *Admiral Spaun*, two destroyers
(*Balaton* and *Tátra*), five torpedo boats (including *80T, 86F*
and *92F*) and four submarines (including *U29* and *U40*)
taking part in the Italian victory review on the 25th.

At Cattaro, under French control, were some forty ex-
Austro-Hungarian vessels. Of them, *Kaiser Franz Joseph I*
was temporarily manned by a French crew, and anchored in
Zanijsa Bay as an ammunition and store hulk. As such, she
foundered in a storm in October, coming to rest on the
bottom on her port side, in some 40 metres of water.
Although subject to salvage work in 1922 and 1967 (when a
15cm gun was recovered), the wreck remains largely intact.
On 4 December 1919, a meeting of the Supreme Council
considered the ships remaining at Cattaro, addressing
concerns by the French officer in overall charge that their
position was 'precarious'.[31] Accordingly, it was agreed that all
could be transferred to Bizerte, although in the event only
the battleship *Erzherzog Karl*, the light cruiser *Helgoland*,
the destroyer *Reka* and the gunboat *Satellit* were actually
towed there.

BULGARIA

In contrast to the other Central Powers, Bulgaria had a tiny
navy that played little part in the war at sea, although the
torpedo boat *Shumni* (1908) was mined and sunk in

September 1916. In 1918, the occupation of Sevastopol by the
Germans was used as an opportunity by the Bulgarians to get
the decrepit torpedo gunboat *Nadezhda* overhauled in the
dockyard there.[32] However, she did not arrive until mid-
September, and was being dismantled prior to refit when the
Armistice of Salonica, bringing an end to Bulgaria's participa-
tion in the war, came into effect on 30 September. The ship's
skeleton crew came under the influence of Russian revolu-
tionaries and mutinied in December, the ship subsequently
being abandoned at Sevastopol when the city was taken by
the Red Army in April 1919. Taken over by the Soviet authorities, she was added to the Soviet navy list on 2 December
1920, and formally placed in storage at Sevastopol in June
1921. Ordered to be scrapped in June 1923, the hulk was
handed over in September 1924 for breaking up, which was
undertaken over the following year.[33]

The rest of the Bulgarian navy (including the submarine
Podvodnik No. 18 [ex-German *UB8*]), was seized by the
French, the torpedo boat *Letyashchi* being wrecked while in
their hands on 28 November. Their ultimate fate awaited the
agreement of a peace treaty (see p 39).

TURKEY

During the latter part of 1918, although experiencing
success in the Caucasus, Ottoman forces started to lose
ground to the British in Syria, and in September the collapse
of Bulgaria meant that there was no prospect of victory on
the Macedonian front. An armistice was sought in the
middle of October, negotiations (between the British and the
Ottomans only) beginning aboard the battleship HMS
Agamemnon, moored at Mudros, on the 27th.

The naval section of the Armistice of Mudros, signed on

31 E L Woodward and R Butler (eds), *Documents of British Foreign Policy
1919–1939*, First Series, II: 1919 (London: His Majesty's Stationery Office, 1948),
pp 483–4.

32 R Greger, 'The Bulgarian Nadezda', *Warship International* X/2 (1973),
pp 183–85.

33 I Todorov, 'Fifty Years of the Bulgarian Navy', *Warship International* XXXIII/1
(1996), pp 16–17 n.2; Greger (previous note) states, however, that the remains of
her hull were still at Sevastopol in 1941.

Yavuz Sultan Selim and a British S-class and 24-class sloop at İzmit during 1920/21. *(AD collection)*

the 30th, and coming into force at midday the following day, ran as follows:

VI. Surrender of all war vessels in Turkish waters or in waters occupied by Turkey; these ships to be interned at such Turkish port or ports as may be directed, except such small vessels as are required for police or similar purposes in Turkish territorial waters.

On 3 November, all warships at the principal naval anchorage at the Golden Horn were placed out of service, and all vessels disarmed over the following weeks under Allied supervision, Anglo-French forces having occupied Constantinople on 12/13 November, joined by Italians on 7 February 1919.

2

Dividing the Spoils – 1

SUBMARINES FOR DISPLAY AND EXPERIMENT

As already noted, four of the already-surrendered German submarines had been transferred to French waters at the end of 1918, while the UK had placed a number of boats on public display in the weeks following the end of the war. Ten boats (*U54*, *U95*, *U102*, *U114*, *U120*, *U163*, *UB80*, *UC93*, *UC94* and *UC98*) were transferred to Italian control at this time, Italian sailors arriving in the UK at the turn of the year to take them over, some arriving aboard the cruiser *Libia*. *UC94* and *UC98* sailed for Palermo with the tugs *Frisky* and *Saucy* on 18 February 1919, they and the other eight boats joining the eighteen Austro-Hungarian submarines in Italian hands.

In addition to these changes of custodianship, it was agreed that a number of boats should be allocated for 'propaganda' purposes (public display and testing), pending definitive allocations (for which, see pp 40–41, below). The UK was to have twenty-two (*U112*, *U123*, *U152*, *U161*, *UB21*, *UB76*, *UB93*, *UB98*, *UB99*, *UB106*, *UB112*, *UB118*, *UB122*, *UB128*, *UB131*, *UB133*, *UB136*, *UB144*, *UB145*, *UB150*, *UC101* and *UC110*), the USA six, Japan eight and Belgium two.

The boats originally earmarked for the USA were *U53*, *U124*, *U140*, *U164*, *UB149* and *UC105*, but *U53* foundered and, although salvaged, was no longer in a fit state to sail. In addition, *U124*, *U164*, *UB149* and *UC105* had already been placed on the UK's sale list,[1] and although it proved possible

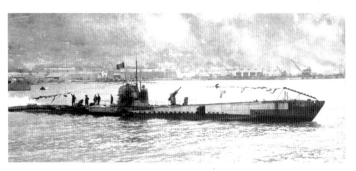

UC93 arriving at La Spezia in early 1919. She was broken up later that year. *(AD collection)*

U46 (to be *O2*), *UB143* (*O7*) and *UC90* (*O4*) at Portsmouth in early 1919, preparing to sail for Japan. In the background are some of the eight destroyers that would escort them, together with the cruiser *Nisshin* (see p 67). *(IWM SP 1052)*

to withdraw *U164*, other boats had to be substituted for the rest, giving an allocation of *U117*, *U140*, *U161*, *UB88*, *UB148* and *UC97* (the last two being boats originally allocated to the UK).[2] However, when ferry crews had arrived at Harwich in March 1919 to commission the boats and take them across the Atlantic, *U161* proved to have been so heavily stripped to provide spares for boats already taken over by the French, Italians and Japanese that *U111* was substituted. Nevertheless, she, and *U117*, *UB88*, *UB148* and *UC97*, having lain unmaintained for some months, all required work to make them seaworthy. *U140*, which had been towed to Harwich in February, lacked engines completely, but as an example of one of the purpose-built U-cruisers,[3] she was felt worth towing across the Atlantic (France and the UK having the other two complete examples, *U139* and *U141*, respectively).

U117, *UB88*, *UB148* and *UC97* left for the USA, via the Azores and Bermuda, on 3 April, all under their own power,

---

1. *U124* later sank in the scrapyard at Swansea (reported as '*U134*' in the *Western Mail*, 16,027 (7 October 1920), p 8).

2. TNA ADM 1/8558/132.

3. As compared with the ex-mercantile *U151* class.

except for *UC97*, which was initially towed by the submarine tender *Bushnell*, owing to engine defects, which were subsequently repaired sufficiently for *UC97* to arrive in New York under power. As a late substitute, *U111* was not ready to go with them, departing on the 7th, her captain deciding to sail direct, with the aim of getting to New York before the inauguration of the Bond drive on the 21st. In spite of bad weather, she made it on 19 April, well ahead of the other four, *U117* and *UB88* arriving on the 26th, *Bushnell*, *U148* and *UC97* a little behind. *U140* arrived at Brooklyn in May, in tow of a collier.

U43, *U46*, *U122*, *UB125*, *UB143*, *UC90* and *UC99* were originally set aside for Japan, but *U43* was apparently rejected, and *U125* substituted for the defective *U122*; thus, seven boats were formally taken over by personnel from the cruiser *Izumo*. Eight destroyers and the cruiser *Nisshin* then

escorted the submarines, renamed *O1–O7*, to Japan, sailing at the end of March via Malta, arriving on 18 June 1919.

Belgium was assigned two boats, *U90* (at one time earmarked to go to France) and *UC92*,[4] and preparations began in Belgium to gather crews.[5] However, both were listed in October 1919 as having '[b]atteries run down, and needing considerable refit to bring to seagoing condition', and while it was noted on 28 November that 'Belgium has been loaned one for a few weeks', it was reported the very next day that the boat in question had 'been sunk on the way to Belgium'.[6] That this was *U90* is clear from *UC92*'s survival to eventually be expended in British explosive trials (pp 51–53, 98–99, below), while the location of *U90*'s wreck, just south of the Isle of Wight, is consistent with her being on passage from her lay-up location of Pembroke to Belgium.[7] There is no evidence that any attempt was taken to tow

4. TNA ADM 1/8576/337, dated 15 October 1919; curiously, the boats in question are named as *U91* and *U112* in R H Gibson and M Prendergast, *The German Submarine War 1914–1918* (London: Constable, 1931), p 377, perhaps reflecting an earlier proposal. Such changes would be not-inconsistent with the shuffling of boats within other countries' allocations (cf. p 30).

5. F Philips, *14–18 op zee. Belgische Schepen en zeelui tijdens de Grote oorlog* (Tielt: Lannoo, 2013), pp 84–5.

6. TNA ADM 1/8576/337.

7. On *U90* and her wreck, see Maritime Archaeology Trust, *Forgotten Wrecks of the First World War: SM U-90 Site Report* (April 2018) <https://forgottenwrecks. maritimearchaeologytrust.org/uploads/images/Articles/Site%20Reports/ FW_Site%20report_U-90_FINAL.pdf>; see also p 98, below.

U117, UC97, UB88 and *UB148* at Brooklyn Navy Yard at the end of April 1919. *(AD collection)*

UC92 across, and in any case it seems that the Belgians decided that the costs of refit and a lack of suitable personnel contributed to their rejection of any idea of becoming submarine operators.

In addition to the allocation of boats to foreign nations, there was also a thought that one might be preserved in the UK as a museum piece: 'Their Lordships have under consideration the allocation of another submarine, whose number will be considered later, to the Imperial War Museum.'[8]

THE RITES OF PARIS

The conference to agree treaties to end the First World War assembled in Paris on 19 January 1919, and ended a year later.[9] Twenty-seven nations were represented, but the main work was done by a core of the UK, the USA, France, Italy and Japan, with the first four dominating proceedings. Five treaties were prepared: that of Versailles (signed on 28 June 1919 with Germany); Saint-Germain (10 September 1919: Austria); Neuilly (27 November 1919: Bulgaria); Trianon (4 June 1920: Hungary); and Sèvres (10 August 1920: Ottoman Empire). The defeated powers were given no opportunity for any meaningful negotiation of terms.

GERMANY

The Treaty of Versailles

The drafting of the German treaty was completed in early June. Its principal naval clauses ran as follows:

Article 181

After the expiration of a period of two months from the coming into force of the present Treaty the German naval forces in commission must not exceed:

    6 battleships of the Deutschland or Lothringen type;
    6 light cruisers;
    12 destroyers;
    12 torpedo boats;

or an equal number of ships constructed to replace them as provided in Article 190.

No submarines are to be included.

All other warships, except where there is provision to the contrary in the present Treaty, must be placed in reserve or devoted to commercial purposes.

8. TNA ADM 1/8576/337, dated 15 October 1919.
9. For a sketch of the proceedings, see M MacMillan, *Peacemakers: The Paris Peace Conference of 1919 and its Attempt to End War* (London: John Murray, 2001).

Article 182

Until the completion of the minesweeping prescribed by Article 193 Germany will keep in commission such number of minesweeping vessels as may be fixed by the Governments of the Principal Allied and Associated Powers.

Article 183

After the expiration of a period of two months from the coming into force of the present Treaty, the total personnel of the German Navy, including the manning of the fleet, coast defences, signal stations, administration and other land services, must not exceed fifteen thousand, including officers and men of all grades and corps.

The total strength of officers and warrant officers must not exceed fifteen hundred.

Within two months from the coming into force of the present Treaty the personnel in excess of the above strength shall be demobilised.
No naval or military corps or reserve force in connection with the Navy may be organised in Germany without being included in the above strength.

Article 184

From the date of the coming into force of the present Treaty all the German surface warships which are not in German ports cease to belong to Germany, who renounces all rights over them.

Vessels which, in compliance with the Armistice of 11 November 1918, are now interned in the ports of the Allied and Associated Powers are declared to be finally surrendered.

Vessels which are now interned in neutral ports will be there surrendered to the Governments of the Principal Allied and Associated Powers. The German Government must address a notification to that effect to the neutral Powers on the coming into force of the present Treaty.

Article 185

Within a period of two months from the coming into force of the present Treaty the German surface warships enumerated below will be surrendered to the Governments of the Principal Allied and Associated Powers in such Allied ports as the said Powers may direct.

These warships will have been disarmed as provided in

Article XXIII of the Armistice of 11 November 1918. Nevertheless they must have all their guns on board.

BATTLESHIPS:
  Oldenburg
  Thuringen
  Ostfriesland
  Helgoland
  Posen
  Westfalen
  Rheinland
  Nassau

LIGHT CRUISERS:
  Stettin
  Danzig
  München
  Lübeck
  Stralsund
  Augsburg
  Kolberg
  Stuttgart

and, in addition, forty-two modern destroyers and fifty modern torpedo boats, as chosen by the Governments of the Principal Allied and Associated Powers.

Article 186
On the coming into force of the present Treaty the German Government must undertake, under the supervision of the Governments of the Principal Allied and Associated Powers, the breaking up of all the German surface warships now under construction.

Article 188
On the expiration of one month from the coming into force of the present Treaty all German submarines, submarine salvage vessels and docks for submarines, including the tubular[10] dock, must have been handed over to the Governments of the Principal Allied and Associated Powers.

Such of these submarines, vessels and docks as are considered by the said Governments to be fit to proceed under their own power or to be towed shall be taken by the German Government into such Allied ports as have been indicated.

The remainder, and also those in course of construction, shall be broken up entirely by the German Government under the supervision of the said Governments. The breaking-up must be completed within three months at the most after the coming into force of the present Treaty.

Article 189
Articles, machinery and material arising from the breaking-up of German warships of all kinds, whether surface vessels or submarines, may not be used except for purely industrial or commercial purposes.

They may not be sold or disposed of to foreign countries.

Article 190
Germany is forbidden to construct or acquire any warships other than those intended to replace the units in commission provided for in Article 181 of the present Treaty.

The warships intended for replacement purposes as above shall not exceed the following displacement:

  Armoured ships 10,000 tons
  Light cruisers 6,000 tons
  Destroyers 800 tons
  Torpedo boats 200 tons

Except where a ship has been lost, units of the different classes shall only be replaced at the end of a period of twenty years in the case of battleships and cruisers, and fifteen years in the case of destroyers and torpedo boats, counting from the launching of the ship.

Article 191
The construction or acquisition of any submarine, even for commercial purposes, shall be forbidden in Germany.

Signature was initially planned for 21 June, which subsequently slipped to the 23rd.

June
The Scapa ships had remained in their remote anchorage while deliberations proceeded in Paris. It was becoming clear that the ships would all fall to the Allies under the prospective treaty, and thus, contrary to Article XXXI of the Armistice's stipulation that 'No destruction of ships or of materials to be permitted before evacuation, surrender, or restoration', 'unofficial' plans were being hatched to scuttle the ships rather than hand them over. Cut off from direct communication with home, the German flag officer, Ludwig

10. Submarine pressure-test (see p 19, above).

Bayern (top) and *Derfflinger* (bottom) sinking. *(C W Burrows via TNA; NHHC NH 49920)*

Frankfurt and *Baden* beached in Smoogro Bay, Scapa Flow. *(Burrows,* Scapa with a Camera, *p 121)*

Destroyers sunk in shallow water off Fara island, Scapa Flow; on the left: *S51*; behind her: *S137* and *G89*; right: *V80, S65, V82* and *S54. (NHHC NH 426)*

von Reuter, was unaware of the delay of signature of the treaty, and thus on the morning of the 21st, when almost all British ships were absent on a training sortie, he gave the order to scuttle all ships.

With British presence initially restricted to the destroyers *Walpole* and *Westcott* and service vessels – although the main British fleet returned while some ships were still afloat and immediately joined in the efforts – it was difficult for the Royal Navy to hinder the process, especially as valves and other openings had often been sabotaged after opening, making them impossible to close. On the other hand, nearly half the destroyers were beached or got into the shallows before sinking, and one – *S132* – was prevented from sinking entirely. Of the light cruisers, *Emden* was beached after a boarding party managed to close valves, and *Nürnberg* drifted ashore after her cables parted, while *Frankfurt* was towed into the shallows before she sank; *Bremse* was also towed, but capsized and sank just as her bow touched ground, her stern in 23 metres of water, but with her bow protruding from the water, supported on a rock. The remaining four light cruisers, *Dresden, Karlsruhe, Brummer* and *Cöln* all sank at their moorings, as did all the capital ships apart from the battleship *Baden*, whose scuttling had been delayed, and was brought into shallow water before she foundered forty-eight hours after the beginning of the scuttle, and the battlecruiser *Hindenburg*, which had nearly been brought inshore before foundering. All but these two capital ships capsized, *Seydlitz* coming to rest on her side, the remainder fully inverted.

Of the vessels left above the surface, all were the subject of salvage work by the Royal Navy. *Emden* was pumped out using her own generators and was afloat by 28 June, while *Nürnberg* was afloat on 3 July, *Baden* on the 11th, and *Frankfurt* on the 12th. Most of the destroyers were afloat by the middle of July, although the salvage of *G92* was not complete until 15 August, and *G89* and *V83* were abandoned as total losses. *Baden* had been towed to Invergordon for docking by early August, but the rest of the ex-German ships remained at Scapa with small maintenance crews until 1920. Then, they were towed south, most to ultimately be broken up in the UK (with *S54* and *V81* lost en route), although the cruisers and some of the destroyers would be distributed among the Allied nations as part of the broader sharing-out of ex-enemy vessels (see pp 43–44, below).

After Scapa

As the bulk of the High Seas Fleet thus settled into the mud on the floor of Scapa Flow, the Allied delegations in Paris were already discussing the impact of the scuttling on the terms of the settlement with Germany. While no changes were made to the terms of the actual treaty, signed two days after the scuttling, it was soon decided that further

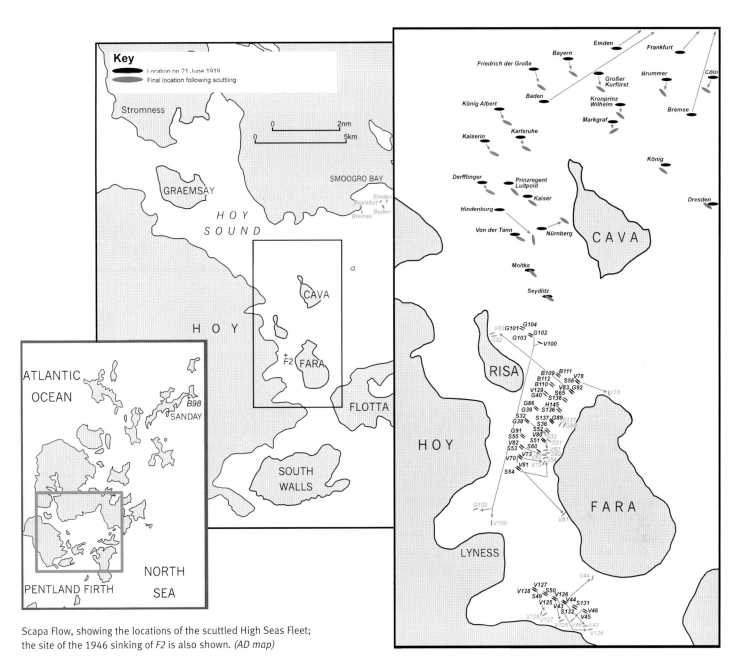

Scapa Flow, showing the locations of the scuttled High Seas Fleet;
the site of the 1946 sinking of *F2* is also shown. *(AD map)*

surrenders would be required to make up for the ships sunk
at Scapa. Listed in a note dated 2 September, the demands
were formalised in part of a draft protocol annexed to a note
to the German government dated 1 November 1919. This
covered various areas in which Germany was failing to
comply with the Versailles Treaty – including the obligation
to maintain and not to destroy ships covered by Clauses
XXXI and XXXIII of the Armistice. It thus stated that:[11]

> [T]he Allied and Associated Powers cannot overlook,
> without sanction, the other infractions committed against
> the Armistice Conventions, and violations as serious as

11. Woodward and Butler (eds), *Documents*, II, pp 143–6.

the destruction of the German Fleet at Scapa Flow, the
destruction of the submarine U.C.48 off Ferrol, and the
destruction in the North Sea of certain submarines proceeding to England for delivery.

Consequently, Germany agrees:

1st. (A) to deliver as reparation for the destruction of
the German Fleet at Scapa Flow:

(a) Within a period of sixty days from the signing of the
present protocol and under the conditions provided for by
paragraph 2 of Article 185 of the Treaty of Peace, the following five light cruisers: *Königsberg, Pillau, Graudenz,
Regensburg, Strassburg.*

(b) Within a period of ninety days from the signing of

Regensburg, one of the handful of German cruisers left active after the Armistice: she would act as escort to *Baden* en route to Scapa and to (inter alia) the 'tubular dock' en route to Harwich. *(AD collection)*

the present protocol, and in all respects in good condition and ready to function, such a number of floating docks, floating cranes, tugs and dredgers, equivalent to a total displacement of 400,000 tons, as the Principal Allied and Associated Powers may demand.

As regards the docks, the lifting power will be considered as displacement. In the number of docks above provided for, there should be about seventy-five per cent of docks of over 10,000 tons. The totality of this material must be delivered in situ.

(B) To be delivered within a period of ten days from the signing of the present protocol:

A complete list of all the floating docks, floating cranes, tugs and dredgers which are German property. This list, which will be delivered to the Inter-Allied Naval Control Commission, provided for by Article 209 of the Peace Treaty, will include the material which, on the 11th of November, 1918, belonged to the German Government, or in which the German Government had an important interest at that date.

(C) The officers and men who formed the crews of the battleships sunk at Scapa Flow, and who are actually detained by the Principal Allied and Associated Powers, with the exception of those whose surrender is provided for by Article 228 of the Peace Treaty, will be repatriated at the latest when Germany will have complied with the above paragraphs A and B.

(D) The destroyer B 98 will be considered as one of the 42 destroyers, the delivery of which is provided for by Article 185 of the Peace Treaty.

2nd. To deliver within a period of ten days from the signing of the present protocol: the machinery and engines of the submarines U-137, U-138[12] and U-150, to

offset the destruction of the submarine U.C.48, as well as the three engines of the submarine U-146, which is still to be delivered, to offset the destruction of sub-marines in the North Sea.

3rd. To pay to the Allied and Associated Governments: the value of the ex-ported aerial material, according to the decision and the estimation which will be made and notified by the Aerial Control Commission, provided for by Article 210 of the Peace Treaty, and before the 31st of January, 1920.

In case Germany should not fulfil these obligations within the time above specified, the Allied and Associated Powers reserve the right to have recourse to any coercive measures, military or other, which they may deem appropriate.

B98 had been used to carry post between Germany and the interned fleet and had been seized by the British when she arrived at Scapa the day after the scuttling. However, while in tow to Rosyth she broke her cable and grounded on the beach at Lopness, Sanday (Orkney), on 17 February 1920 and, as her loss was through no fault of the Germans, she was offset against the Versailles 'debt'. Her wreck was sold for scrap on 25 June, although parts of the wreck, including turbine casings, remain visible to this day and one of her guns is a museum piece on Orkney.[13]

In an attempt to save the five modern cruisers as the core of their new fleet, Germany proposed in December 1919 that she should instead be allowed to complete and hand over five of the cruisers under construction at the Armistice. France counter-proposed that if this were to be done, the five existing ships should be handed over 'on account' and returned as the new ships were delivered. This was prompted by the realisation that if Germany were stripped of her modern cruisers, she would be entitled to replace the ancient (1899–1903) ships that would thus be left to her with new construction straight away, rather than being left with a set of increasingly obsolescent ships into the mid-1930s, when the first of the 'five' (the 1913-launched *Graudenz*) would finally fall ready to be replaced under the treaty.

However, on 7 January 1920 it was officially determined that such an arrangement would be contrary to Article 181 of the Treaty of Versailles, which required 'the breaking up of all the German surface warships now under construction'. Accordingly, when the protocol was finally signed by the Germans on 10 January 1920, the five cruisers were indeed to be delivered.

---

12. These two boats' engines arrived at Rosyth on 5 August 1920, aboard one of the ships of the convoy of surrendered warships (see p 45, below).

13. <http://canmore.org.uk/site/102230/sms-b98-west-langamay-bay-of-lopnesssanday-orkney-north-sea>.

The baseline numbers of floating docks in existence had been the subject of considerable dispute between Germany and the Allies, in particular over the existence of an 80,000 ton dock at Hamburg (actually two smaller ones), a 4,500-tonner at the Howaldtswerke at Kiel, and large docks at Danzig (all non-existent). In addition, Germany had, soon after the issue of the draft Allied demands, sold a number of docks to Dutch, Norwegian and Danish owners (which resulted in a warning from the British Foreign Office that such transfers would not be recognised by the Allies). Then, on 17 December 1919, Germany made a counter-offer of 192,000 tons of docks and harbour equipment (rather than the demanded 400,000 tons).[14] In response, the Allies offered a reduction from 400,000 tons to around 300,000 tons (to make up for incorrect initial assessments), with a potential further reduction of 25,000 tons, to take into account German economic arguments for the retention of privately owned docks. However, this offer was subject to the immediate delivery of the German-proposed 192,000 tons, with additional tonnage to be delivered within two years. This formed the basis of the final agreement.[15]

Of the docks and equipment handed over, the 40,000-ton lift *Kiel VIII* was retained by the British Admiralty, and lengthened to become the 65,000-ton lift *AFD.VIII*, which would serve at Malta from 1925 to its sinking by bombing in June 1940.[16] *Kiel VII* (40,000t) was considered for use at Singapore, but in the event was sold for scrap at Portsmouth on 1 September 1926 for £23,220, being cut up at Rosyth and Charlestown during 1926/28. *Wilhelmshaven XXIII* was also sold, in 1925, but in its case for further service, being used for salvage work on the High Seas Fleet at Scapa (see p 53–54, below).

Even after signing the protocol, Germany attempted to avoid being left with only antiques as a cruiser force. A letter of 27 January argued that Articles 181 and 190 (which allowed the replacement of ships over twenty years old), when read together, gave Germany the right to have a force of six under-age ships. To achieve this, she proposed that the two 2,060-tonne 15cm-armed big destroyers *S113* and *V116* should be reclassified as cruisers and be retained by Germany, which should also be allowed to keep and complete *Wiesbaden*, the most advanced of the nine incomplete light cruisers. This proposal was rapidly rejected by the Allies, pointing out that *S113* and *V116* had been listed as torpedo craft in the protocol; the Germans were also reminded of the requirements of Article 186.

Thus, the final list of ships to be surrendered comprised eight battleships, eight Article 185 cruisers, five 'protocol' cruisers, forty-one destroyers and fifty torpedo boats. The latter groups were stricken from the German navy list on 3 November 1919, with the battleships and cruisers on the 5th, the exception being the 'protocol' cruisers, stricken on 10 March 1920, except for *Königsberg*, which went on 31 May. All battleships and cruisers were 'renamed' with letters, in preparation for handover.

All surviving destroyers of the *V25* and later classes were to be handed over, as were all Type A-II (*A26*) and A-III (*A56*) coastal torpedo boats. In addition to these modern vessels, a number of older destroyers were on the surrendered-list, particularly those which had hitherto been used for minesweeping duties.[17] As already seen, the submarine force had been surrendered at the time of the Armistice, but Article 188 of the treaty swept up such assets as remained in German hands, which thus finalised the terms of the Armistice as far as the submarines themselves were concerned, but also now provided for the surrender of their surviving infrastructure.

AUSTRIA AND HUNGARY

With the end of the war, the Austro-Hungarian empire was dissolved. Its navy was dealt with under the Treaties of Saint-Germain (StG) and Trianon (T) as follows:

Article StG136/T120
From the date of the coming into force of the present Treaty all Austro-Hungarian warships, submarines included, are declared to be finally surrendered to the Principal Allied and Associated Powers.

All the monitors, torpedo boats and armed vessels of the Danube Flotilla will be surrendered to the Principal Allied and Associated Powers.

[Austria/Hungary] will, however, have the right to maintain on the Danube for the use of the river police three patrol boats to be selected by the Commission referred to in Article 154 of the present Treaty.

Article StG137/T121
The Austro-Hungarian auxiliary cruisers and fleet auxiliaries …will be disarmed and treated as merchant ships …

Article StG138/T122
All warships, including submarines, now under construction in [Austrian/Hungarian] ports, or in ports which

14. TNA ADM 116/1974.

15. Woodward and Butler (eds), *Documents*, II, pp 684, 697.

16. I Buxton, 'Admiralty Floating Docks', *Warship* XXXII (2010), pp 30, 38.

17. *T159–T160, T165, 166, 169, T174, T181–T184, T192, T195, T197* and *V106.*

previously belonged to the Austro-Hungarian Monarchy, shall be broken up.

The work of breaking up these vessels will be commenced as soon as possible after the coming into force of the present Treaty.

Article StG139/T123

Articles, machinery and material arising from the breaking up of Austro-Hungarian warships of all kinds, whether surface vessels or submarines, may not be used except for purely industrial or commercial purposes.

They may not be sold or disposed of to foreign countries.

Article StG140/T124

The construction or acquisition of any submarine, even for commercial purposes, shall be forbidden in [Austria/Hungary].

Article StG141/T125

All arms, ammunition and other naval war material, including mines and torpedoes, which belonged to Austria-Hungary at the date of the signature of the Armistice of 3 November 1918, are declared to be finally surrendered to the Principal Allied and Associated Powers.

TURKEY

The Treaty of Sèvres was signed between the Allies and the Ottoman government on 10 August 1920. The naval clauses reduced the fleet to a rump:

Article 181

From the coming into force of the present Treaty all warships interned in Turkish ports in accordance with the Armistice of October 30, 1918, are declared to be finally surrendered to the Principal Allied Powers.

Turkey will, however, retain the right to maintain along her coasts for police and fishery duties a number of vessels which shall not exceed:

7 sloops,
6 torpedo boats.

These vessels will constitute the Turkish Marine, and will be chosen by the Naval Inter-Allied Commission of Control referred to in Article 201 from amongst the following vessels:

SLOOPS:
Aidan Reis.
Burack Reis.
Sakiz.
Prevesah.
Hizir Reis.
Kemal Reis.
Issa Reis.

TORPEDO-BOATS:
Sivri Hissar.
Sultan Hissar.
Drach.
Moussoul.
Ack Hissar.
Younnous.

The authority established for the control of customs will be entitled to appeal to [France, Great Britain and Italy] in order to obtain a more considerable force, if such an increase is considered indispensable for the satisfactory working of the services concerned.

Sloops may carry a light armament of two guns inferior to 77 m/m and two machine guns. Torpedo-boats (or patrol launches) may carry a light armament of one inferior to 77 m/m. All torpedoes and torpedo tubes on board will be removed.

Article 182

Turkey is forbidden to construct or acquire any warships other than those intended to replace the units referred to in Article 181. Torpedo-boats shall be replaced by patrol boats.

The vessels intended for replacement purposes shall not exceed:

600 tons in the case of sloops;
100 tons in the case of patrol launches.

Except where a ship has been lost, sloops and torpedo-boats shall only be replaced after a period of twenty years, counting from the launching of the ship.

Of the vessels over and above those allowed under Article 181, all were to be handed over to the Allies. Curiously, however, the extant distribution lists omit the torpedo cruisers *Peyk-i Şevket* and *Berk-i Satvet*. Also inconsistent was the fact that while listed in the treaty for retention, the distribution lists give the named torpedo boats to the UK. In the event, such issues remained academic as, by the middle of 1919, the Turkish War of Independence had begun between the Turkish National Movement and foreign intervention and occupation forces – and implicitly the now-moribund Ottoman regime of Sultan Mehmed VI. The victory of the National Movement, under the leadership of Mustafa Kemal (Atatürk) was followed by the overthrow of the monarchy in November 1922, and a fresh peace conference at Lausanne. The resulting treaty, signed on 24 July 1923, replaced that of Sèvres – and contained no naval clauses whatsoever.

BULGARIA

The Treaty of Neuilly-sur-Seine was signed on 27 November 1919, and was principally concerned with the territorial changes imposed on Bulgaria, including losing her outlet to the Aegean. Its naval terms mirrored those of the treaties of Versailles and Sèvres, reducing the size of the permitted maritime forces (Article 83), ordering ships under construction to be broken up (Article 84) and prohibiting submarines (Article 86).

Article 83 provided that:

> Bulgaria will, however, have the right to maintain on the Danube and along her coasts for police and fishery duties not more than four torpedo boats and six motor boats, all without torpedoes and torpedo apparatus, to be selected by the [Naval Inter-Allied Commission of Control].

> The personnel of the above vessels shall be organised on a purely civilian basis.

> The vessels allowed to Bulgaria must only be replaced by lightly-armed patrol craft not exceeding 100 tons displacement and of non-military character.

The ships allowed to Bulgaria essentially comprised the navy's vessels still afloat and in Bulgarian waters in 1919. The exception was, of course, the submarine *Podvodnik No 18* (ex-German *UB8*), which was sold by the UK Admiralty to a Constantinople-based British businessman in March 1921. However, she seems never to have moved from Bulgarian waters, her wreck being identified off Varna in 2010.[18]

THE ALLOCATIONS

Having determined what each ex-enemy navy should give up to the Allies, there was the small matter of deciding who got what – and what they could do with the vessels received. During the treaty-drafting phase, this had been left open, and no decision had been made by the Allied Supreme Council, although discussions on 24/25 June had included the possibility that, given that France's naval programme had been effectively given up during the war, she might benefit from special considerations. In addition, the UK had expressed her willingness to take her own eventual share in the form of ships sunk at Scapa Flow.[19]

It was in mid-November 1919 that naval representatives of the Allied powers met to work through the options.[20] The first issue discussed was the ultimate fate of surrendered vessels: if all were to be destroyed, detailed allocation seemed pointless. Second, if ships were to be distributed, what would the basis be? Although there was general agreement that this should be in proportion to war losses by the receiving power, the French and Italians raised issues of quality as well as quantity. Finally, there was the question whether, assuming a distribution took place, any such vessels might be allowed to enter service with the receiving power, rather than be simply broken up or sunk.

The formal national positions in October, at the outset of the discussions, had been:

UK: all vessels to be broken up, with proceeds distributed in proportion to war losses, with the exception that, owing to the limited construction carried out by France and Italy during the war, they should be allowed to embody their shares into their fleets.

Italy: in agreement with the UK, but military value should be incorporated into the sharing formula.

France: freedom to dispose of allocated vessels as the recipient wished; distribution on the basis of numbers of each category of ships equalling losses in that category; quality as well as quantity to be considered; additional vessels to be allocated, over and above loss-compensation, to take into account suspension of much of the French naval programme.

USA: first preference for all vessels to be sunk; second that they be broken up. If a distribution were to occur, the USA would wish it to be on the basis of total national war effort, with free disposal of the allocated vessels.

Japan: in agreement with UK, but would insist on equal

18. '[I]n July 2011 Viceadmiral Manushev, Commander of the Bulgarian Navy, announced that the submarine, discovered in 2010 at the sea bottom near the town of Varna, is UB-8. Divers discovered manufacturer numbers and according to them the identity is confirmed' <https://en.wikipedia.org/wiki/SM_UB-8>, accessed 21 July 2018. Her periscopes are now on display in the Bulgarian naval museum at Varna.

19. Woodward and Butler (eds), *Documents of British Foreign Policy 1919–1939*, First Series, I: 1919 (London: His Majesty's Stationery Office, 1947), pp 249–52.

20. Woodward and Butler (eds), *Documents*, II, pp 343–5.

rights if principle of free disposal were to be adopted.

On 14 November, the British put forward a suggestion that, as a general principle, and with certain exceptions, all surrendered vessels be broken up and proceeds distributed in proportion to war losses (UK: 70 per cent; FR: 10 per cent; Italy: 10 per cent; Japan: 8 per cent; US: 2 per cent; Greece: 1 x destroyer; Romania: 1 x torpedo boat; Portugal: 1 x gunboat). The UK would take the Scapa Flow scuttlings as part of her share, while 'protocol' equipment ceded by Germany in compensation (pp 35–37) would be allocated in the same proportions as ships for scrap. France and Italy would each receive five cruisers and ten destroyers that could be incorporated into their fleets, and each of UK, France, Italy, USA and Japan would be loaned one battleship, one cruiser and three destroyers for one year, which could be used for any purpose, save longer-term incorporation into national fleets.

Although the USA now abandoned their idea that 'effort' should be the determining factor for allocations, they felt that the 2 per cent being proposed for them undervalued the American contribution to victory (although actual losses were well below even a level reflecting a 2 per cent share). They also raised the issue of how far nations should be compensated for losses other than in action – which drew a riposte from Italy that their losses of big ships in harbour (the battleships *Leonardo da Vinci* and *Bendetto Brin*, destroyed by internal explosions) 'had clearly been destroyed by enemy action' as was 'susceptible of proof by documents' in Italian possession.[21]

There remained also the question of the fate of surrendered vessels destined for destruction, and how far material derived from their breaking up might be reused for warlike purposes. However, it was agreed on 29 November that, subject to US confirmation of their position on percentage allocations, the British proposal on surface warships be accepted.[22]

Apropos submarines, France put forward a proposal that they should be allocated in proportion to national losses in that category: UK 70 per cent (on the basis of the loss of fifty-five boats); France 18 per cent (fourteen); Italy 10 per cent (eight); US 2 per cent (one). All should be disposed of, except for ten to be allowed to France as compensation for

not having constructed submarines during the war.[23] An Italian variation on the theme required that boats that 'have taken part in the war on commerce and which have committed acts contrary to the laws of humanity' should be broken up and the proceeds distributed in proportion to submarine losses in wartime, while those 'whose entry into service took place at a time that they could not participate in such acts' should be distributed proportionately, but each recipient should be permitted full freedom to deal with them as they wished. This formula gave 106 'used' boats, and seventy 'not used' examples, based on vessels that had run trials within three months of the Armistice.

There was general sympathy for the French position, and it was agreed, resulting in a British formal proposal, in part based on the impracticability of asking for boats previously distributed to be returned to Great Britain:[24]

(a) That each Power should keep the enemy submarines now in its ports, those surrendered by Austria being allotted to Italy.

(b) That France and Italy, being the two nations which, owing to their pre-occupation with the war on land, were unable to continue warship production during the war, should be free to embody their share of the enemy submarines in their fleets should they desire to do so, pending a decision by the League of Nations as to a continuance of submarine warfare in general.

(c) That the other Allied and Associated Powers should undertake to break-up or sink their share of enemy submarines by 31 March 1920.

(d) That no enemy submarines should be allocated to the smaller Allies or neutral powers.

Of the 190 ex-enemy submarines then extant, 103 were in UK waters (forty-nine intact, plus fifty-four already sold for scrapping), forty-six in French, twenty-eight (ten ex-German + eighteen ex-Austro-Hungarian) in Italian, six in American and seven in Japanese. Of these, it was agreed on 9 December 1919 that forty-three could be counted as 'propaganda' boats, to be retained for a limited period, for public display or experimental purposes, at the end of which they should be destroyed or sunk, by the latest 1 July 1920.[25] The UK could so employ five, France fifteen, Italy ten, the

---

21. Woodward and Butler (eds), *Documents*, II, p 416; on the question of the cause, cf. the British understanding that the explosion in *da Vinci* was the result of a petrol fire caused by a leaking tin, exacerbated by the slow flooding of her magazines once the fire had taken hold ('Storage and Handling of Explosives in Warships', *Technical History and Index*, 2/24 [CB 1515 (24)] (October, 1919), §98 (text available at <www.gwpda.org/naval/thist24.htm>).

22. Woodward and Butler (eds), *Documents*, II, p 420.

23. Some of the French 1914 submarine programme had not been completed

until after the war, all of the 1915 programme had been cancelled, and none of the 1917 programme was launched until 1921. Six boats being built for foreign customers had been requisitioned, but only three were in commission before the end of the war.

24. TNA ADM 1/8576/337, dated 9 October 1919.

25 In view of the congestion of scrapyards, this was subsequently amended so that boats should be 'incapable of further service' within twelve months, and 'completely destroyed' in a further twelve months; this would later be further extended (p 54).

Submarines laid up at Cherbourg during 1920. The three ex-German boats in the centre, *U105*, *UB94* and *U79* later became, respectively, the French *Jean Autric*, *Schillemans* and *Victor Reveille* (see pp 60–61). In the foreground is the French *Cornélie*, with *Joessel*, *Clorinde* and *Nivose* behind the ex-German boats. (*NHHC NH 43779*)

USA six and Japan seven. The boats in excess of these numbers (held by the UK, France and Italy) would be broken up by their current guardians, with the exception of the ten that France was now allowed to commission for long-term service, to make up for the aforementioned disruptions caused by the war.[26] Italy had initially pressed for a similar (but lower) concession, but this was rejected once the size of her own wartime submarine-building programme was seen to be very different from that of France.[27]

It was not only complete boats that were to be distributed: there were sixty surrendered submarine diesel engines and sixty-one electric motors, currently stored at Barrow, Wallsend, Greenock and other UK locations (pp 18–19, above), with six/nine more due.[28] A discussion of September 1919 proposed that they be distributed according to aggregate horsepower in the same proportion as complete submarines, the result being that the UK would get thirty-four diesels, France ten, Italy twelve, the USA four and Japan one. As far as surplus submarine diesels were concerned in general, it had been decided that motors of 1,200bhp and above could not be regarded as commercial machines, and thus should be destroyed. Smaller ones could, however, be allocated for commercial use (see Appendix 3.2).

It was also agreed that Belgium should be allowed to keep the small ex-German warships that were in her ports (removing an earlier reservation that she could do so only if they were solely for police work). These comprised three Type A-I small torpedo boats (*A4*, *A12* and *A14*) that had been found at Antwerp following the German evacuation, plus another six A-Is (*A5*, *A8*, *A9*, *A11*, *A16* and *A20*) and five Type A-IIs (*A30*, *A40*, *A42*, *A43* and *A47*) that had taken refuge at Hellevoetsluis in the Netherlands on 16 November. These were handed over by the Netherlands on 25 June 1919, in accordance with Article 184 of the Versailles Treaty. It was also agreed that other smaller states should receive allocations of torpedo boats:[29] for Greece, Romania and Portugal, this would be in addition to the destroyer, torpedo boat and gunboat that had already been proposed for them.

On the basis of these discussions, and subject solely to a continuing US reservation over the calculation of their

26. TNA ADM 116/1992, dated 17 January 1920.
27. TNA ADM 1/8576/337, dated 29 November 1919; twenty-nine boats were launched by Italy in wartime, with fifteen acquired from the UK and one captured.
28. TNA FO 608/248/29.
29. Woodward and Butler (eds), *Documents*, II, p 516.

share, the following final agreement covered the distribution of surface warships:[30]

In accordance with the preamble to the naval, military and air clauses of the Treaty of Peace with Germany, with the general spirit of that Treaty and of those concluded with the other enemy powers, all surface warships surrendered by enemy powers shall, with the exception of the few noted in paragraphs 2 (b) 5 and 6 below, also paragraph (5) (II) and (5) (III) of Draft orders to I.N.C. be broken up or sunk under the superintendence of an Interallied Naval Commission.

2. (*a*) Enemy Tonnage of Surface Warships shall be divided up between the Allied and Associated Powers in accordance with the following computation of losses of surface warships sustained by these powers during the war:–

Great Britain	70%
France	10%
Italy	10%
Japan	8%
U.S.A.	2%

(*b*) Other Allied Powers which lost surface warships during the war shall have these losses replaced by an enemy ship of a type similar to that lost. These ships may be used for any purpose to which these powers may desire to put them. The distribution under this head shall be as follows:

Greece	1 T.B.D.
Roumania	1 T.B.
Portugal	1 Gunboat

3. (a) Enemy tonnage above proportions is to be allocated to each country for breaking up or sinking, under the superintendence of the Inter-Allied Naval Commission. Should any country be unable to break up its share, it may place it in another country for breaking up, subject to conditions detailed below, preference being given to Allied countries.

(b) The ships are to be sunk or rendered incapable of any further service as Naval War vessels, in the judgment of the Inter-Allied Naval Commission, within a period of 18 months and to be completely broken up within 5 years from the date when they arrive in a port of the power to whom they are allocated.

4. As regards the sinking of the German ships at Scapa Flow Great Britain has stated her willingness to bear the

loss arising from that incident; but now that it is probable that compensation will be forthcoming from Germany in material which is not naval construction, Great Britain agrees that such compensation should be divided in a similar proportion to that adopted for the enemy surface warships (Para. 2 (a) above).

5. In view of France and Italy being unable to build surface warships during the war, owing to their preoccupation with the war on land, it is proposed that they should be granted the following compensation in warships surrendered from the enemy fleets for use in their fleets or for any other purpose they may desire.

France	5 light cruisers & 10 T.B.D.
Italy	" " " " "

6. It is further proposed that the Naval Inter-Allied Commission shall loan to each of the Five Principal Allied and Associated Powers:—.

1 Battleship
1 light cruiser
3 T.B.D.

This loan will be for one year and during this time these ships may be used for any purpose whatsoever provided that they are not incorporated into the navies of these Powers. At the end of a year after these ships have arrived in a port to the power to which they have been allotted they shall be broken up under the supervision of the I.N.C. or sunk in deep water, under conditions identical to those which were set forth in paragraph 3 (b) above.

The material from the breaking up of these ships will belong to the Powers to which they were allotted.

In addition, draft orders for implementing this agreement were agreed:

1. (a) The Inter-Allied Naval Commission for superintending the disposal of enemy warships will be referred to as the I.N.C. and will consist of a British Flag Officer as President and a flag officer or captain from the U.S., France, Italy and Japan.

(b) Technical Advisers will be attached to the Commission as each member may desire.

(c) The I.N.C. may delegate such of its duties as it may consider desirable to the Naval Attache in any of the countries concerned.

(d) Any of the Principal Allied and Associated Powers which may not have ratified the Treaty of Peace with

30. Woodward and Butler (eds), *Documents*, II, p 526–9.

Germany when the I.N.C. first meet, may, pending ratification of the Treaty of such power, have a representative at the meetings, who may take part in the discussions, but will not be empowered to vote on decisions.

2. The I.N.C. is to assemble in London at as early a date as practicable without necessarily waiting for the Treaties of Peace to come into force.

3. The pay of the officers as allowed by their Governments, also then-actual and necessary expenses, will be paid by each Government concerned. The general expenses of the I.N.C. will be shared by the various Governments concerned in the same proportion as the percentages decided on for the division of the enemy surface warships.

4. *Surrendered Enemy Warships*

(*a*) The Inter-Allied Naval Commission of Control (A.N.A.C.) will supervise the transfer of ships from German to Allied Ports, where they will be held in trust for the I.N.C. by the Powers in whose ports they are until they are definitely allocated to the Powers concerned.

(*b*) The I.N.C. will make agreements with the Naval Authorities of the countries concerned to have the ships sunk or rendered incapable of any further service as Naval War vessels, in the judgment of the I.N.C., within a period of 18 months, and to be completely broken up within 5 years from the date they are handed over to the said authorities in their ports.

(*c*) The I.N.C. will arrange with the interested Naval Authorities as to their visiting the yards where the breaking up of the enemy vessels is in progress.

(*d*) The I.N.C. are to render half-yearly reports to the Allied and Associated Powers as to the progress of demolition of the Enemy warships.

5. *Ex-Enemy Warships and submarines which need not be broken up.*

Ex-enemy ships are allotted to the following Powers and are exempted from being broken up or sunk:—

(i) Vessels to be employed as the Government to which they are allotted may desire:—

France:	5 light cruisers, 10 destroyers, 10 submarines
Italy:	5 light cruisers, 10 destroyers
Greece:	1 destroyer, 6 T.B.
Portugal:	1 Gunboat, 6 T.B.
Roumania:	1 Torpedo Boat, 6 T.B.
Brazil:	6 T.B.

(ii) To be disarmed with the exception of one gun to be used for police duties:

| Poland: | 6 torpedo boats. |
| Serb-Croat-Slovene: | 12 torpedo boats (These vessels will not be employed until the maritime frontier[s] of the Serb-Croat-Slovene State are defined.) |

(iii) The following States to have the option of receiving similar vessels if they desire them: Greece 6 T.B., Portugal 6 T.B., Roumania 6 T.B., Brazil 6 T.B.

6. *Surrendered German ships*

(*a*) With a view to facilitating the selection of the ships for the French and Italian Navies, vide paragraph 5, the 13 light cruisers and also 20 destroyers to be surrendered by Germany will proceed to a French port in the first instance, the French Government being responsible for these ships until the final allocation concerning them has been made.

(*b*) With regard to the remaining German ships, those allotted to the United States and Japan will proceed in the first instance to a British port and those for France and Italy to a French port. The United States, Italy and Japan should take over their responsibilities regarding the ships allotted to them, as soon as such ships arrive in a British or French port.

7. The following ex-enemy ships are to be loaned to the Principal Allied and Associated Powers for the purpose of propaganda and experiments.

Capital Ships:

Great Britain	Baden.
United States	Oldenburg Class one vessel or Hindenburg if U.S. desires to salve her.
France	Baden, Goeben, or Oldenburg Class one vessel.
Japan	Oldenburg Class one vessel.
Italy	Tegetthoff.

Light Cruisers:

Great Britain	Nürnberg.
United States	Frankfurt or one of the latest type L.C.s which may be available after the 10 L.C.s referred to in par. 5 (i) have been allocated.
France	Emden.
Italy	Sankt Georg.
Japan	Strassburg or one of the latest type L.C.s which may be available after the 10 L.C.s referred to in par. 5 (i) have been allocated.

T.B.D.s. The U.S.A., Great Britain and Japan are entitled to choose 3 T.B.D.s each from those saved at Scapa Flow.

The allocation of the remaining T.B.D.s is deferred until the T.B.D.s referred to in par. 5 (i) have been selected.

In connection with the above the following vessels are provisionally selected:—

Great Britain V.46, G.102, S.137.

United States V.100 (1 1,300 ton 1916–17 class), 1 1,000 ton 1916–17 class, 1 750 ton 1916–17 class.

France

Italy

Japan   (1 1,300 ton 1916–17 class), 1 1,000 ton 1916–17 class, 1 750 ton 1916–17 class.

In the middle of January 1920, the various decisions on the allocations of ex-enemy warships were consolidated into a final list, issued on the 17th. As a result the following surface vessels were formally transferred as 'propaganda' ships:

	Battleship	Cruiser	Destroyers
UK	*Baden*	*Nürnberg*	*V44; V82; V125*[31]
France	*Thüringen*	*Emden*	*V46; V100; V126*
Italy	*Tegetthoff*	–[32]	3 *Huszár* class
Japan	*Oldenburg*	*Augsburg*[33]	*S60; V80; V127*
USA	*Ostfriesland*	*Frankfurt*	*V43; G102; S132*

Apart from *Augsburg*, all the cruisers and ex-German destroyers had been beached in shallow water at Scapa during the scuttling, and thus had inoperable machinery.

As far as the selection of the cruisers and destroyers for the Franco-Italian division of ships for commissioning was concerned, the final arrangements were that '[a]t least six [German cruisers] from those vessels that are in the best condition are to proceed to a French port, and if after their selection there are any more in a serviceable condition they should also go to France'; all four of the modern Austro-Hungarian cruisers were to be considered. Fifteen (if possible twenty) German destroyers would accompany them. Then '[r]epresentatives of France and Italy should inspect the German and Austro-Hungarian light cruisers and destroyers and draw up priority lists of their fitness, the

Tegetthoff at Venice in 1920. *(NHHC NH 87220)*

two Ministries of Marine subsequently deciding between themselves … which vessels they will incorporate in their respective fleets.' All leftover vessels from this process would go to the UK for scrapping, to join others to be delivered for that purpose to Rosyth.

In December 1919, Poland requested an increase in their allocation of torpedo boats, and that the requirement that they be disarmed waived; the same month Cuba asked to be added to the recipients of ex-German vessels. Brazil followed this in January with a request that full-size destroyers be substituted for the torpedo boats allocated, as these were regarded as too small for operation in Brazilian waters, with Belgium at the same time asking for light cruisers, destroyers and submarines. Finally, later the same month, the Yugoslavs reiterated their demand for a large proportion of the former Austro-Hungarian fleet. All these bids were rejected.

Making it happen
Ex-German ships

The Versailles Article 185 ships were all stricken from the German Navy list on 5 November 1919 (but with the out-of-commission *Pillau* replacing *Stralsund* at this point), with *Graudenz*, *Regensburg*, *Straßburg* and *Stralsund* following on 10 March 1920, and finally *Königsberg* on 31 May; all battleships and cruisers were then 'renamed' with letters, in preparation for their handover. The first cruiser to arrive at Cherbourg (the 'French port'), on 5 April 1920, was the former *Kolberg*, from Rosyth, together with six destroyers (and also the battleship *Thüringen*: see p 56) from Germany. The steamer *Ceuta* (a German merchantman under the aegis of the British Shipping Controller) accompanied the destroyers to repatriate the German crews.[34] The former *Graudenz*, *Regensburg*, *Stuttgart*, *Straßburg*, *Pillau*, *Königsberg* and *Stralsund* would

---

31. The original UK allocation was *S60*, *V44* and *V125*, with Japan to receive *S51*, *V80* and *V127*, but *S51* was in poor condition, and had to be beached at Rosyth to stop her from foundering; Japan was thus given *S60* instead, and *V82* allocated to the UK.

32. The previously earmarked *Sankt Georg* ended up in the UK main allocation; presumably, having received two of the modern Austro-Hungarian cruisers for further service, Italy had no interest in the obsolete *Sankt Georg*.

33. Cf. n.36, below.

34. *Le Gaulois*, 45,544 (27 April 1920), p 4; this incorrectly gives the number of destroyers as seven.

join them over the next four months, making a total of seven cruisers, as would fourteen more destroyers, making a total of twenty-one.

Discussions over the allocations between France and Italy took place over the late summer of 1920, with an initial agreement assigning *Regensburg* and *S113* to France, and their sisters *Graudenz* and *V116* to Italy. The final allocation was placed before the Conference of Ambassadors and agreed in late September 1920, with a simultaneous announcement of their new French names.[35] Thus, France also took the former *Stralsund*, *Königsberg* and *Kolberg*,[36] with the Austro-Hungarian *Novara*, at Bizerte, comprising their fifth cruiser. Italy additional cruisers were the former, *Straßburg* and *Pillau*, plus the Austro-Hungarian *Helgoland* and *Saida*. Twenty additional German destroyers (mainly ex-'Eisernen Flotille') were delivered to Cherbourg during May/July 1920. As already noted, France took the big *S113*, plus eight smaller boats (*V79*, *V130*, *S133*, *S134*, *S135*, *S139*, *H146* and *H147*), with Italy adding *B97* and *S63* to her already-agreed *V116*. Both nations' balance of destroyers was made up with Austro-Hungarian tonnage (see overleaf).

35. *Le Figaro*, Ser 3, 66/261 (18 September 1920), p 2; 267 (24 September 1920), p 4; 273, (30 September 1920) p 2.
36. It had been assumed for planning purposes that *Kolberg*, as one of the oldest cruisers delivered to Cherbourg, would probably be rejected and fall to the UK for disposal. However, she was taken by France and it was the much newer Austro-Hungarian *Admiral Spaun* that ended up surplus. It may also be noted that rather than taking 'one of the latest type L.C.s' for her propaganda cruiser, Japan received *Kolberg's* sister *Augsburg*.

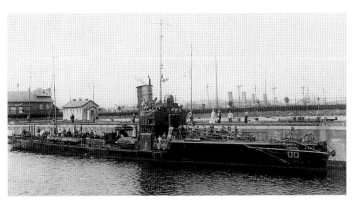

The German torpedo boat *A68*, later the Polish *Kujawiak*. *(AD collection)*

All other ships due to be surrendered by Germany were delivered to Rosyth for further distribution or disposal. The transfers of ships from Germany may be summarised as in the table below: Total surrenders of German ships, including the ill-fated *B98*, but excluding the unseaworthy *Rhineland*, laid up at Kiel after damage suffered when stranded in April 1918, numbered seven battleships, thirteen cruisers, forty-one destroyers and fifty torpedo boats.

As noted above, Brazil and Poland had each been allocated six torpedo boats, and while Poland had the option to take Austro-Hungarian vessels, both nations' shares were taken in their entirety from the fifty German torpedo boats delivered to Rosyth. Brazil did not take over her ships (*A65* [substituted for *A81* after the latter was damaged by grounding], *A74*, *A78*, *A93*, *V105* and *V106*), instructing the British Admiralty to sell them for scrap on her behalf.

TRANSFERS OF GERMAN WARSHIPS TO ALLIED PORTS, 1920

Ships	Echelon	Sailed	Arrived	Place
Nassau; *Ostfriesland*	I	1 Apr	5 Apr	Rosyth
Kolberg; *S24*; *T189*; *T192*; *T193*; *T195*; *T197*	II	21 Apr	25 Apr	Cherbourg
Thüringen	III	24 Apr	25 Apr	Cherbourg
Oldenburg; *Posen*; *V71*	IV	8 May	12 May	Rosyth
V28; *S63*; *B97*; *S113*; *V116*; *H146*	V	20 May	23 May	Cherbourg
Graudenz	VI	28 May	1 Jun	Cherbourg
Regensburg	VII	1 Jun	5 Jun	Cherbourg
V26; *V79*; *S134*	VIII	10 Jun	14 Jun	Cherbourg
München	IX	1 Jul	5 Jul	Rosyth
Königsberg; *Straßburg*; *Pillau*; *Stuttgart*; *S133*; *S135*; *S139*; *H147*	X	14 Jul	19/20 Jul	Cherbourg
Stralsund; *V130*	XI	28 Jul	3 Aug	Cherbourg
Helgoland; *Westfalen*; *G95*; *T164*; *T166*; *T169*; *T178*; *T179*; *T180*; *T182*; *T183*; *T184*; *T186*; *V108*	XII	31 Jul	5 Aug	Rosyth
A27; *A28*; *A29*; *A31*; *A35*; *A36*; *A39*; *A41*; *T159*; *T160*; *T174*; *T181*; *V105*; *V106*	XIII	14 Aug	19 Aug	Rosyth
Augsburg; *Lübeck*; *A45*; *A46*; *A48*; *A65*; *A68*; *A69*; *A74*; *A78*; *T161*; *T163*; *T173*	XIV	28 Aug	2 Sep	Rosyth
Danzig; *Stettin*; *A33*; *A34*; *A37*; *A38*; *A44*; *A49*; *A53*; *A61*; *A62*; *A87*; *A92*; *T165*; *T176*	XV	9/11 Sep	17 Sep	Rosyth
A52; *A54*; *A55*; *A59*; *A63*; *A64*; *A66*; *A70*; *A75*; *A76*; *A80*; *A81*; *A86*; *A88*; *A89*; *A90*; *A91*; *A93*; *A94*; *A95*	XVI	25 Sep	30 Sep	Rosyth

Königsberg (inboard) and *Graudenz* berthed at Wilhelmshaven on 31 March 1920; *Königsberg* was still on the German navy list, but her companion had been stricken some two weeks previously, although still flying her jack. *(AD collection)*

Z (ex-*Stralsund*) following her arrival at Cherbourg on 3 August 1920 for the Franco-Italian selection of cruisers and destroyers for further service; she became the French *Mulhouse*. *(Jean Moulin collection)*

However, before being handed over to the breakers, *V105* was swapped with the Poles for *A69*, which had been allocated to them but proved to be in very poor condition. The latter thus went for scrap along with the remaining unwanted Brazilian vessels.

Ex-Austro-Hungarian ships

As noted above, of the Austro-Hungarian cruisers, *Helgoland*, still at Bizerte, and *Saida*, were incorporated into the Italian navy on 19 September as *Brindisi* and *Venezia*, respectively, the former being transferred to La Spezia during 22–26 October Their French-allocated sister *Novara* became, after some mis-adventures (see p 57, below), *Thionville*. Italy took over at Adriatic ports for further service the destroyers *Balaton, Csepel, Lika, Orjen, Tátra, Triglav* and *Uszok*, France taking their sister *Dukla*.

Of the former Austro-Hungarian Danube Flotilla (of which Hungary had fought hard to be allowed to retain the whole),[37] the initial allocation gave ex-*Bodrog*, ex-*Bosna* and ex-*Enns* to Yugoslavia, and ex-*Sava*, ex-*Temes* and ex-*Inn* to

Romania. The other four monitors were to be handed over to the International Commission of the Danube for potential use as pontoons. In the event, of the latter, the Yugoslavs were allowed to keep ex-*Körös* as well. *Moros* was soon scrapped by the Commission, but *Leitha* and *Szamos* would embark on long careers as dredgers, *Leitha* surviving to be restored as a museum in the twenty-first century.

The remaining ex-Austro-Hungarian ships were due for scrap or destruction. *Radetzky* and *Zrnyi*, together with the two now-stranded torpedo boats at Spalato, had originally been allocated to France, and *Prinz Eugen* to Italy, but soon afterwards discussions resulted in a swapping of vessels, to give both powers an Austro-Hungarian dreadnought. Accordingly, the Italians approached the Americans, who were acting as guardians of *Radetzky* and *Zrnyi* (pp 28–29), for an early release of the vessels.[38] However, the USA was not willing to do so until the St Germain Treaty had been ratified, and thus it was not until 7 November 1920 that the US cruiser *Olympia* and two destroyers towed the two battleships to Sebenico to be handed over to the Italians. The battleships carried fittings removed from the wrecked torpedo boats, whose hulls were finally broken up in 1922.

Throughout the Allies' discussion on the distribution of ex-enemy vessels, the Yugoslavs had continued to lobby for a generous share, in April 1919 requesting the four ex-Austro-Hungarian light cruisers, seventeen destroyers, twenty-seven torpedo boats, twenty submarines (plus a further seventeen under construction), six river monitors and a repair ship – i.e. essentially all the modern non-capital ships of the Austro-Hungarian navy.[39] This was rejected out of hand, and in May 1920 a revised bid was submitted,

37. TNA ADM 1/8565/231.

38. Davidonis, *American Naval Mission,* pp 92–5.

39. See M Vego, 'The Yugoslav Navy 1918–41', *Warship International* XIX/4 (1982), pp 344–5; R Greger, 'Yugoslav Naval Guns and the Birth of the Yugoslav Navy 1918–1941', *Warship International* XXIV/4 (1987), pp 344–5.

Erzherzog Franz Ferdinand and *86F* at Venice in 1919; the latter became the Portuguese *Ave* in 1921. *(NHHC NH 87688)*

boats (see p 43, above), plus an old battleship, four minesweepers (ex-torpedo boats), four river monitors, a depot ship, and various subsidiary and harbour service vessels. Even then, their handover was delayed until after the signing of the Treaty of Rapallo the following month, which agreed the mutual boundaries of Yugoslavia and Italy, and was further held up by the ongoing French occupation of Cattaro, which finally ended only in March 1921.

Turkish ships

While German and Austro-Hungarian ships were all handed over and distributed as planned, this was not the case with Turkish vessels. The January 1920 list gave almost all the fleet to the UK for scrap, the exceptions being the battleship *Turgut Reis*, allocated to Japan for scrap, and a gunboat (apparently never precisely identified) that Portugal was to be allowed to place in service. However, the replacement of the Sèvres Treaty by that of Lausanne meant that in the event no ships were ever handed over, many remaining in Turkish service for decades.

reduced to two old cruisers, six destroyers, twelve large and twelve small torpedo boats, and four submarines. In the end, following the signing of the Treaty of St Germain in October 1920, Yugoslavia was granted a core fleet of a dozen torpedo

Appendix 2.1: SUMMARY ALLOCATION OF EX-GERMAN AND AUSTRO-HUNGARIAN NAVAL VESSELS

Category	UK		FR		IT		US	JP	BR	PT	GR	YU	PL	RO
GE Battleships	1P 4		1P		–		1P	1P 1	–	–	–	–	–	–
AH Battleships		6		3	1P 3		–	–	–	–	–	–	–	–
GE Cruisers	1P 6		1P 4*		3*		1P	1P	–	–	–	–	–	–
AH Cruisers		8		1*		2*	–	–	–	–	–	–	–	–
GE Destroyers & torpedo boats	3P 74		3P 9*		3*		3P	3P 1	6*	–	–	–	6*	
AH Destroyers & torpedo boats		25		1* 6		3P 7* 21	–	–	–	6*	7*	12*	–	7*
GE Submarines	105		10* 27		10		6	7	–	–	–	–	–	–
AH Submarines	–		6		–	12	–	–	–	–	–	–	–	–
GE+AH submarine entitlement	[124]		[34]		[19]		[0]	[0]	–	–	–	–	–	–
AH minelayers	2		2		–		–	–	–	–	–	–	–	–
AH gunboat	–		1		–		–	–	–	–	–	–	–	–
AH river monitors	– –		– –		–		–	–	–	–	–	4*	–	3*
TOTALS	194	41	55	20	16	49								
	235		75		65		**11**	**14**	**6**	**6**	**7**	**16**	**6**	**10**
GE sunk at Scapa	58													
UK GRAND TOTAL	**293**													

P = Propaganda vessels
* To be taken into service
All others for scrap/sinking

NOTE: the fourteen torpedo boats taken over by Belgium were not part of the formal allocation process.

3

Under New Management – 1

UK

With the coming into effect of the Versailles Treaty on 10 January 1920, the UK had formal possession of three distinct groups of vessels. First were the vessels she was scrapping under her own auspices or on behalf of the Allies. These included both those of the submarines sold in early 1919 that had not yet been fully dismantled, and a whole swathe of vessels now to be sold. Second were the UK's set of 'propaganda' ships – and third the hulks of the scuttled vessels on the bottom of Scapa Flow.

For disposal

Of the first group, some were already in UK waters, in particular the balance of submarines. As described in the previous chapter, most of the German surface vessels due for disposal were delivered to Rosyth during the late summer of 1920 to await disposal, although the Franco-Italian rejects, *Stuttgart*, *S24*, *V26*, *V28*, *T189*, *T192–T193*, *T195* and *T197*, remained at Cherbourg. The latter were all sold in October 1920, *Stuttgart*, *S24* and *T189* to a Teignmouth-based breaker. Although the cruiser arrived safely, the two destroyers were caught in a gale on 12 December 1920 near Torquay, *S24* running onto Preston Beach at Paignton, and *T189* onto rocks near Roundham Head. *S24* was towed off the next day, but *T189* broke her back (see p 98, below).

The UK's share of Austro-Hungarian vessels, none of which were removed from ex-Austro-Hungarian Adriatic ports by the British, had all been sold to Italian firms during August 1920, with the exception of the Franco-Italian reject *Admiral Spaun*, which was sold at Venice in November. Breaking up of these vessels was slow to get under way, and would become an issue the following year.

Of the remaining Article 185 vessels, one was still overseas – *Rheinland*. Insufficiently seaworthy to be towed to the UK (following grounding in April 1918), she was sold to Dutch breakers in June 1920 while still at Kiel. Of the other three battleships allocated to the UK, which had arrived at Rosyth

D (ex-*Westfalen*) being stripped at Birkenhead in 1921; in May 1922 she sailed under her own steam to Barrow for breaking-up. *(AD collection)*

in April/May, *Westfalen* and *Helgoland* were not sold for a year, with *Posen* being sold only in July 1921. However, this sale was cancelled and the ship re-sold to Dutch breakers in August 1921, finally leaving Rosyth in early October (cf. p 55). Three of the cruisers, *Lübeck*, *Stettin* and *Danzig*, were sold in February/March 1921, while *München* was expended in torpedo trials in October 1921. The destroyers and torpedo boats (*T159*, *T160–T161*, *T163–T166*, *T169*, *T173–T174*, *T176*, *T178*, *T179*, *T180*, *T182–T184*, *T186*, *A27–A29*, *A31*, *A33–A39*, *A41*, *A44–A46*, *A48–A49*, *A52–A55*, *A61–A63*, *A66*, *A70*, *A75–A76*, *A81*, *A86*, and *A87–A95*) were sold during February/March 1921.

Two submarines under UK control at Malta, *UB42* and *UC37*, had been sold during December 1919/January 1920, but disposals of those in UK waters did not begin again until June/July 1920, when eighteen (*U67*, *U101*, *U167*, *UB64*, *UB133*, *UB136*, *UB144*, *UB145*, *UB150*, *UC60*, *UC95*, *UC106*, *UC108*, *UC109*, *UC111*, *UC112*, *UC113* and *UC114*) were sold. Sales resumed in September, when *UB76*, *UB93*, *UB98* and *U112* were sold (see p 101, below), but no more passed to breakers until the following year (see below, pp 53–55).

The monitor *Terror*, employed as firing ship for most of the 1921 trials against ex-German vessels. *(AD collection)*

Trials and Targets

Ten vessels had been explicitly allocated to the UK for 'propaganda' or trials purposes: the battleship *Baden*, the light cruiser *Nürnberg*, three destroyers (*V44*, *S82* and *V125*) and five submarines (*U126*, *U141*, *UB21*, *UC102* and one other). The British intent was that all should be expended in ordnance trials, in particular to determine the effect of the latest British shells[1] on a wide variety of targets.

These were carried out off Portsmouth during late 1920 and the early months of 1921, the principal firing ship being the monitor *Terror*, her twin 15in (381mm) main turret and 4in (102mm) secondary battery being supplemented for the purposes of the trials by a 7.5in (190.5mm) weapon on a special proof mounting loaned by the Shoeburyness range, plus a 6in (152mm) and a 4.7in (120mm) pieces.[2]

First up was the destroyer *V82*, subjected to 4.7in fire on 13 October 1920. The trials were carried out at short range (300m) to ensure hits, but with reduced charges and the ship heeled by 12 degrees to simulate long-range plunging shellfire; a similar protocol was employed for all firings during the overall trials programme. Damage after three hits was such that trials had to be suspended to allow *V82* to be patched up, before resuming on the 15th, five more hits being scored. Divers managed to further patch the destroyer sufficiently for her to be towed back into Portsmouth harbour, but she had to be beached near Whale Island.

V44 was taken under fire on 8 December, taking four 6in, two 4.7in and eight 4in hits, with further strikes from bursts of 2pdr pom-poms. Dragged back into Portsmouth, she was beached alongside *V82*. Both were sold to T W Ward on 30 March 1921, but remained in place, the hulks being re-sold to the local shipbreakers H Pounds in 1927; although

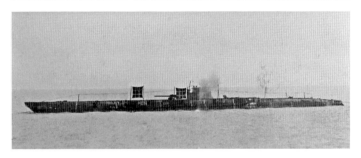

Baden, *V82* and *U141*, shown while being employed as targets off Portsmouth in 1921. *(Gunnery Manual 1921, figs 52, 34 & 41)*

stripped *in situ*, parts of their hulks remain visible at low tide in 2020 (see p 101, below). *V125* was not employed in the trials and was sold to John Cashmore in July 1921, and towed away on 2 September.

Three submarines had been earmarked for the ongoing trial programme: *U126*, *U141* and *UB21*, to assess the effects of hits on the conning tower, the superstructure and the pressure hull; the same protocol of reduced charges and ranges, and inclination of the target vessel were employed. *UB21* was brought forward on 30 September 1920, and took 4.7in, 4in and 12pdr hits, totalling eighteen, from *Terror*. Damage was such that the small boat sank as a result;[3] her wreck was dispersed between 1970 and 1998, but remains were still extant in 2013. *U141* took no fewer than twenty-five hits from guns of the same spread of calibres on 7 October but, doubtless helped by being over seven times the size of *UB21*, was nursed back to Portsmouth and beached, later being laid up with *U126*, not finally employed in the trials.

Nürnberg was brought onto the range for the first time on 5 November 1920, 400m away from *Terror* and heeled at

---

1. I McCallum, 'The Riddle of the Shells', *Warship* XXV (2002–3), pp 3–25; XXVI (2004), pp 9–20; XXVII (2005), pp 9–24.

2. See I Buxton, *Big Gun Monitors: Design, Construction and Operations 1914–1945*, 2nd edition, Seaforth Publishing (Barnsley, 2008), pp 157–58; *Progress in Gunnery Manual 1921* (C B 1594).

3. *UB21* has on occasion been confused with *UB121*, wrecked at Birling Gap en route to France (p 22, above).

NOT JUST THE SUBMARINES: *CYCLOP* ON TRIAL

From the outset of her U-boat building programme, Germany had realised the possibility that such vessels could be lost, and the attendant necessity of a new type of ship – the submarine salvage vessel. The salvage vessel *Vulcan* was accordingly commissioned in 1908, hard on the heels of *U1*, commissioned in December 1906. She was built on catamaran principles with a twin hull joined by an upper deck and superstructure, and saw service with three recoveries.[1]

Her 'half-sister' *Cyclop* was more than twice the size, with a displacement of 4,010 tons, and unlike *Vulcan*, survived the journey to surrender in April 1919, although it is noteworthy that both vessels required two tugs to negotiate the North Sea for delivery to the UK. She belonged to a small group of vessels, with nothing like it in the Royal Navy, although in 1912 the French had built the *Kangourou*, a twin-hulled submarine transport vessel for commercial delivery of overseas orders, which was requisitioned for war service in 1914 and torpedoed in 1916. Closest to the German vessels was the Russian *Volkov*, midway in size between *Vulcan* and *Cyclop*, and launched by the Putilov yard at St Petersburg in 1913. As of 2019 she remains in service in the Black Sea as the submarine rescue ship *Kommuna* (as she was renamed in 1922), after over a hundred years in commission.

Cyclop's appearance was even more striking than *Vulcan*'s, gigantic and skeletal. After arrival at Harwich she seems to have remained inactive until moved to the Nore in the Thames Estuary in August 1920, where her 'peculiar profile' aroused interest.[2] On that voyage she passed her namesake and British repair ship HMS *Cyclops* at Sheerness,[3] The coincidence was more than just the name: *Cyclops*, purchased by the Admiralty on the stocks in 1905, had served as a repair ship during the war and was at that time in the process of being converted into a submarine depot ship.

This coincidence would lead to the ex-German vessel being renamed *Cyklop* when formally commissioned as a Royal Fleet Auxiliary (RFA) some time before December 1920: her new name both nodded to her German origins,[4] and allowed her to be distinguished from HMS *Cyclops*, particularly while both were in commission in very similar roles.

There was some public enthusiasm for seeing how *Cyklop* would perform under trial, but the Admiralty was rather less keen. According to one observer in Portsmouth who saw her arrive there under her own steam in November 1920, she afforded 'a striking example of how very much ahead of us were the Germans in devices for submarine salvage' but he also noted that '[o]ur service was slow to believe that there was any virtue in such contraptions as those above described.'[5]

Thus, how better to employ her than in test trials of vessels with which she was initially designed to work, six former German submarines? She was, in fact, relatively untried, having only raised one boat, *UB89* in

The submarine salvage ship RFA *Cyklop* (ex-SMS *Cyclop*) at Falmouth for the 1920/21 submarine explosive tests. *(C B 1622)*

October 1918 at the Holtenau Lock end of the Kiel Canal. During the trials at Falmouth (described in detail on pp 52–53), *Cyklop* was used to suspend and retrieve the submarines, as an examination platform to inspect the damage sustained, and in assisting in beaching the submarines. During this work, she shuttled regularly between Falmouth and Devonport to bunker coal. In some ways, this was a double trial of both the submarines, which were tested to destruction, and of the salvage vessel. The trials, begun on 20 November 1920 with *UB112*, were completed on 7 March 1921 with the experiments on *UC92*.

Despite these regular voyages to Devonport as part of the trial programme, her arrival there on 22 January 1921 gave rise to rumours that she would be deployed in raising the steam-powered fleet submarine *K5*, which had gone down with all hands on 20 January southwest of the Isles of Scilly. This was swiftly denied as 'there was no chance of raising that vessel in the deep water in which it is believed she lies'; and in any case, *Cyklop* was still involved in the highly important experiments on the former German submarines. It was noted that her unusual design made her cumbersome even in fair weather, with a top speed of 6 knots, but at this stage her potential future in the British service was still being explored. There were hopes that she would be able to rescue vessels from relatively shallow depths and thus prevent the recurrence of pre-war tragedies such as those of *A7* and *A8*.[6] Shallow depths posed hazards of their own, but, as the Falmouth trials demonstrated, *Cyklop* was able to manoeuvre in a shallow, rocky environment without herself coming to grief.

10 degrees by shifting coal. A range of 7.5in and 6in shell-types were used, with specific parts of the ship once again targeted, in this case the conning tower, light structures, belt and upper deck. During this first series, flooding was caused by one hit, reducing the ship's heel to 7.5 degrees. For the second series, on 8 November, the heel was increased to 20 degrees by also flooding the bunkers. Although battered, the cruiser remained afloat, and was returned to Portsmouth, from which she was towed the following year,

on 7 July 1922, well in advance of her 'ineffective' date of 30 September 1922, to be sunk by gunfire from the battle-cruiser *Repulse*, coming to rest on her port side in 62 metres of water halfway between Poole and Cherbourg.[4]

The final set of trials employed *Baden*, which, once pumped out at Scapa, had been towed to Invergordon for docking in floating dock *AFD.V*. While in dock there, an

4. See <www.wrecksite.eu/wreck.aspx?30575>.

It appears that it had originally been hoped that *Cyklop* could be used for towing the submarines to Falmouth but, in the end, the tug-trawler *Strathcoe* was used instead. In any case, *Cyklop*'s departure in March 1921 for Portsmouth following the end of the trials was postponed on account of 'rough weather', apparently substantiating concerns over her manoeuvrability and stability. By April 1921 it was becoming public knowledge that, while she had been 'satisfactory enough' on trial, she was now 'discredited' and being offered for sale by the Admiralty. Press opinion suggested that it was 'soothing' to domestic prestige given that '[s]o much has been said regarding the backwardness of our own naval methods, and the wonderful superiority of the Germans in various directions ...'[7]

Cyklop was therefore paid off in June 1921, with advertisements for sale stressing her five 'very strong transverse girders'. The conditions of sale were explicit: '[p]ermission to transfer the vessel abroad cannot be given.'[8] Despite this it seems that there were no potential purchasers in the UK prepared to give the vessel another use either in whole or in part – for example, her girders could have been cannibalised for use in other contexts – or for scrapping. Thus, the vessel was in the end sold to Alfred Kubatz, Schiffs- und Abwrackwerft, Berlin, in May 1922, for breaking, either at Rönnebeck, Bremen, or at their new yards in Wilhelmshaven, which were under expansion due to the volume of shipping being broken up at that time.[9]

It is clear that the journey from Harwich to Portsmouth under her own steam in 1920 was regarded as something of a feat for *Cyklop* and that poor weather generally put paid to even relatively short journeys. As such she was effectively a white elephant, and there was little benefit in restricting her sale back to Germany in 1922, since, by that time, there were no German submarines left for her to raise. With no military context in which to operate, and little possibility of conversion for civilian use, there was no further option but to send her to the breakers.

1 *U3* in 1911; *U30* in 1915 and *UC45* in 1917.

2 *Pall Mall Gazette*, 17,230 (13 August 1920), p 3.

3 Ibid.

4 It was also an up-to-date linguistic move, with the contemporary spelling reform in Germany that led, among other things, to the treatment of foreign names on German lines and the substitution of 'k' where 'c' had previously been used, as in *Cöln = Köln*.

5 *Hampshire Telegraph*, 3,775 (12 November 1920), p 7.

6 *Western Morning News*, 18,997 (24 January 1921), p 7.

7 *Western Morning News*, 19,065 (14 April 1921), p 7.

8 *The Times* 42,825 (14 September 1921), p 2.

9 Alfred Kubatz, proprietor of the Schiffs- und Abwrackwerft, Berlin, *Jahrbuch der Schiffbautechnischen Gesellschaft*, 27th edn, 1926; auf dem Garten 2012 pp 86–8; Stadtarchiv Stadt Wilhelmshaven 4630/74.

explosion occurred deep in the ship on 5 August 1919, killing one workman. Pronounced as 'cleared of free water and rubbish and ... watertight' and 'fit to be towed' on 8 October, she was then taken to Portsmouth, where she was prepared for her trials.[5]

First, the ship also had charges ignited within the superimposed turrets to test flash-tightness. The live-firing tests

UB131 ashore at Hastings, 9 January 1921. *(AD collection)*

then began on 2 February 1921, using an updated version of the latest British 15in (381mm) shell, and with the usual range/charge/heeling protocol. These confirmed the enhanced effectiveness of the new shells, one penetrating the upper belt, armour deck and inner bunker bulkhead and bursting in the forward boiler room. Leaking badly, the ship foundered the following day in bad weather, albeit in shallow water, with a 10-degree list to starboard. Three months later, *Baden* was refloated and patched up for the next trial on 10 August 1921, with *Terror*'s sister *Erebus* as firing ship. As well as more 15in shellfire (fourteen hits), six aerial bombs were placed aboard and detonated. On 16 August 1921 *Baden* was scuttled midway between Weymouth and Jersey, coming to rest on her side in 180 metres of water, her turrets having apparently fallen out during her descent. Trials were by no means restricted to vessels formally designated as 'propaganda' ships: as already noted, *München* was expended as a torpedo target in September 1921.

During the autumn of 1919, a number of ex-German submarines were used for engine and diving trials: *U86* (based at Portsmouth), *U126* (ditto), *U135* (Blyth), *U141* (Portsmouth) and *U162* (Campbeltown).[6] Others, 'which have not been maintained', were earmarked for 'experiments' (*U112* [at Pembroke], *U122* [Harwich], *U152* [Chatham], *UB21* [Portsmouth], *UB93* [Pembroke], *UB98* [Queenstown], *UB99*, *UB106*, *UB112* [all Harwich], *UB118*, *UB128* [both Chatham], *UB131*, *UB133* [both Harwich], *UB144*, *UB145*, *UB150* [all Chatham] and *UC101* [Harwich]) or the removal of fittings (*U161* [Devonport], *U123* and *UB122* [both Portsmouth]). Three boats 'not complete when delivered' were also on the 'experiments' list (*UB76*, *UB136* and *UC110* [all Harwich]).

Six boats (*UB86*, *UB97*, *UB106*, *UB112*, *UB128* and

5. W Schleihauf, 'The *Baden* Trials', *Warship* XXIX (2007), pp 81–90.

6. TNA ADM 1/8576/337, dated 10 October 1919.

UC92), supported by the ex-German submarine salvage ship *Cyklop* (see text-box on preceding pages), the British submarine depot ship *Maidstone*, and the trawler *Strathcoe*, acting as a tug, were the subject of experiments at Falmouth, the first boats arriving during November 1920.[7] In addition, *UB118*, which broke tow halfway between Devonport and Falmouth and had to be sunk by gunfire on the 21st,[8] and *UB131*, wrecked in tow at Hastings in January 1921, and sold for scrap in May, may have also been intended for use.

The trials were intended to explore the effects of underwater explosions on submerged submarines. Accordingly, *Cyklop* was used to suspend the boats at specific depths – 150ft when using 300lb charges, and 100ft when using smaller ones. Negative buoyancy was achieved through the use of the boats' ballast tanks, and the admission of water into the pressure hull itself where necessary to make up for

equipment and stores stripped out. Booms fitted to the side of *Cyklop* were used to lower charges into position at the appropriate distance from the submarine.

UB112 was the first boat to be employed, suffering leaks (attributed to poor workmanship) sufficient to have sunk her in the first firing, on 20 November 1920. On 1 December she was used again, this time suffering penetration of the pressure hull, and again 'sunk', although of course hauled back to the surface by *Cyklop* for full examination. She was recorded as beached in the inter-tidal zone by mid-December 1920.[9] Next to be used was *UB106*, which ended the trial with superficial damage on her first trial (13 January 1921), but which suffered fatal penetration of the pressure hull on the second (17 January). *UB128* only lasted one trial, being 'sunk' on 1 February. Likewise, *UB86* suffered fatal damage on the 14th, although *UB97* (which had been towed from Devonport for Falmouth on 17 February) suffered two charge failures on 25th, before 'sinking' on the 28th. The last Falmouth trial was on 7 March, when *UC92* suffered non-threatening damage in 7 March.

7. *Report on Explosive Trials, Carried out against ex-German Submarines, 1920 and 1921*, C B 1622 (London: Admiralty, 1922) = TNA ADM 186/360; see also <http://atlanticscuba.co.uk/the-falmouth-u-boats-the-factual-story/>.
8. On her wreck, see p 98.

9. *West Briton and Cornwall Advertiser*, 2,716 (16 December 1920), p 3.

UB112 slung and listing below *Cyklop* after a trial. *(C B 1622)*

UB86 and *UB112* beached at Falmouth in early 1921 after being damaged in the explosive trials. *(C B 1622)*

UB106 and *UB112* were both sold locally on 30 March, the other four to the same firm on 19 April. Salvage work seems to have begun in June, when the tug *Alice* is reported as foundering at her moorings while employed in the work. Although partly broken up, with the remains allegedly 'flattened' in 1966/67, vestigial remains of five boats still seem to survive *in situ* (see pp 98–99). Local tales later had it that the six boats had actually been blown ashore in a gale while awaiting target use in February 1921, with three more having been sunk as targets.

A final trial in the same series took place at Spithead on 23 March, when *UB100* also received non-fatal damage. Two further trials were, however, carried out at Spithead, when howitzer shells were exploded abeam the surfaced *UC101* (7.5in calibre, on 26 March) and *UC102* (11in, on 30 March). The former boat suffered serious, but not fatal, damage, but *UC102* was left in a sinking condition.

The hulk of the destroyer *G98* at Stromness, Scapa Flow. She was one of the first ex-German wrecks sold, to a local firm for £500 in 1920. Finally raised at the end of 1922, she was taken to Stromness, where demolition was begun, and then abandoned. Re-sold to Cox & Danks, who were by then systematically salvaging the wrecks in the Flow in August 1928, she was taken to Lyness, where she was finally demolished over the next few years. *(AD collection)*

Scapa Flow

Of the ships on the bottom of the Flow, it was initially anticipated that most would be left on the seabed. However, it was soon realised that a number were hazards to navigation and, from 1920, the wrecks began to be sold for salvage and scrap.[10] First, the two remaining beached destroyers, *V83* and *G89*, were sold that year.[11] The first sunken examples were sold in April 1923, when *V45*, *S49*, *S50* and *S131* were purchased by Scapa Flow Salvage & Shipbreaking; they were subsequently refloated and sold for scrap.

The following January, the shipbreakers Cox & Danks acquired further vessels – not just the relatively easy-to-salvage destroyers (buying *S53*, *S55*, *V70* and *G91*), but also the only partly submerged battlecruiser *Hindenburg*. At the same time, they obtained options on further wrecks, again a mixture of destroyers (twenty-one: *S32*, *G38*, *G39*, *G40*, *G86*, *S36*, *S52*, *S56*, *S65*, *V78*, *G101*, *G103*, *G104*, *B109*, *B110*, *B111*, *B112*, *V129*, *S136*, *S138* and *H145*) and an apparently easy battlecruiser, *Seydlitz*.

For salvaging the destroyers, Cox & Danks acquired from the Admiralty, for £8,500, the pressure-testing dock that had arrived at Harwich in May 1919. Its pressure cylinder was removed for scrap at Queenborough, additional equipment installed, and the dock towed to Scapa. Once there, one sidewall was cut away, and the dock cut in two, allowing it to be deployed on both sides of a sunken vessel; further salvage equipment was also installed. A further, larger, floating dock was acquired by Cox & Danks on 3 June 1925, for £29,255; this was also ex-German, *Wilhelmshaven XXIII* (1914), surrendered after the Scapa scuttlings, comprising six separable sections, and with a total designed lift of 40,000 tonnes.

Four sections appear to have been broken up at Queenborough, but one (including the machinery) arrived at Scapa on 27 August, with the intent that destroyers would be lifted off the seabed by the ex-pressure test dock halves, which would then be towed with their burden into the sunken larger dock; this would then raise the combination to the surface. The pressure dock halves having been disconnected and floated off, the dock section was used to make the destroyers seaworthy for towing to shipbreakers. A second section was also used at Scapa, both remaining

10. On the salvage of the Scapa ships and their subsequent disposal, see S C George, *Jutland to Junkyard: The Raising of the Scuttled German High Seas Fleet from Scapa Flow – the Greatest Salvage Operation of All Time* (Cambridge: Patrick Stevens Ltd, 1973); I Buxton, *Metal Industries: Shipbreaking at Rosyth and Charlestown* (Kendal: World Ship Society, 1992); T Booth, *Cox's Navy: Salvaging the German High Seas Fleet at Scapa Flow, 1924–1931* (Barnsley: Pen & Sword, 2005); I McCartney, *Scapa 1919: The Archaeology of a Scuttled Fleet* (Oxford: Osprey, 2019).

11. Both boats were later sold-on, the wreck of *V83* being later abandoned, with the remains still *in situ*; *G89* was finally broken up from 1928.

The hulk of *Bayern* being towed into Rosyth on 30 April 1935. *(AD collection)*

1927, and from then until 1939 a steady procession of wrecks were raised by Cox & Danks and, from 1933, by Metal Industries, most being scrapped in dry dock at Rosyth. The last ship to be raised was the battlecruiser *Derfflinger*, on 25 July 1939, but because of the outbreak of the Second World War the Rosyth docks were no longer available, and it was not until 1946 that she was actually broken up.[13]

Of the remaining wrecks, those of the battleships *König*, *Markgraf* and *Kronprinz Wilhelm*, had been sold to Metal Industries along with *Derfflinger* in April 1936, as was the light cruiser *Karlsruhe* in 1955, but they were left on the bottom, being sold on, from the mid-1950s, to a series of salvagers who removed armour and other valuable material using explosives, but made no attempt to actually raise the wrecks. Salvage rights for the light cruisers *Brummer*, *Dresden* and *Cöln* were also sold during the late 1950s and early 1960s, with similar salvage work carried out.[14] These latter rights having expired on 17 September 1985, the three cruiser wrecks were then sold to the Orkney Islands Council by the Ministry of Defence for the nominal sum of £1; in recognition of the ships' historic importance, all wrecks were scheduled in 2001.[15] However, the formal ownership of *König*, *Markgraf*, *Kronprinz Wilhelm* and *Karlsruhe* was auctioned online via eBay in June 2019, a century on from their sinking; the battleships were sold in July to Middle Eastern interests for £25,000 each, and *Karlsruhe* to a UK private individual for £8,500.

Leftovers

As the deadline of 1 July 1921 for most submarines being 'rendered incapable' approached, eleven still lay at Portsmouth and Devonport, unsold. Accordingly, plans were laid to sink *U86*, *U135*, *U122*, *U123*, *U152*, *U153*, *U161*, *UB100*, *UB122 UC101*, and *UC110* in deep water by 30 June. Nine were thus towed out into the English Channel on 28 June (*U123*, from Portsmouth), 30 June (*U86* [Portsmouth], *U135* [Devonport], *U152*, *U153* [Portsmouth], *U161* [Devonport] and *UB122* [Portsmouth]), and 1 July (*U122* [Chatham], *UC110* [Portsmouth]). *U135* and *U161* were towed out together to be sunk by gunfire from British submarines *L21* and *L52* of the 2nd Submarine Flotilla some 60 miles south of the Eddystone.[16] However, *UB100* and

parts of *Wilhelmshaven XXIII* being cut down to act as pontoons/work platforms for the salvage of larger ships from 1926 onwards.[12]

Although twenty-six destroyers were successfully refloated between August 1924 and April 1926, the two big ships, *Seydlitz* and *Hindenburg*, actually proved to be problematic, in spite of being partly above water at all tide conditions, as did the cruiser *Bremse*, purchased in October 1925. However, the fully submerged battlecruiser *Moltke*, bought in August 1926, was successfully raised using compressed air in June

---

12. There was a hiatus in salvage work between 1931 and 1934, owing to a depressed scrap market (*Von der Tann* and *Prinzregent Luitpold* being laid up inverted between 1931 and 1933, when they were actually sold), operations then being taken over from Cox & Danks by Metal Industries. The latter scrapped the ex-pressure-dock sections at Rosyth in June 1934 (Buxton, *Metal Industries*, p 71[29A]: our thanks go to Professor Buxton for the information that this disposal concerned these, rather than a part of *Wilhelmshaven XXIII* as stated there, and other information on ex-German docks). The two ex-*Wilhelmshaven XXIII* sections were broken up in July/August 1937 (Buxton, *Metal Industries*, p 80[25C]).

13. A Dodson, '*Derfflinger*: An Inverted Life', *Warship* [XXXVIII] (2016), pp 175–8.

14. For their history since 1919, see McCartney, *Scapa 1919*, pp 147–276.

15. Historic Scotland, scheduling document dated 23 March 2001.

16. *Western Morning News*, 19,131 (1 July 1921), p 3. Neither vessel has been definitively identified, with a submarine discovered in 2005 and variously attributed to *U135*, *U123* and a U-boat of Second World War vintage; the identification of *U161* as now charted (at the time of writing) is tentative and does not tally with the position as reported in 1921.

UC101 were at the last minute (29 June) sold for scrapping in the Netherlands, on the condition that they be mutilated beyond use by 1 August; the 'propaganda' *U126*, *U141* and *UC102* remained at Portsmouth, although the latter was sold in August, again to go to the Netherlands for scrap, and be mutilated by 18 October.

As shown by placing such contractual terms on purchasers, mere sale to shipbreakers was not sufficient to fulfil a nation's commitment to dispose of ex-enemy vessels. But, as had been foreseen by some parties during the inter-Allied negotiations, the practicalities of the shipbreaking process meant that such rigid timescales could be problematic, and by the middle of 1922 it was clear that a considerable number of vessels that were the responsibility of the UK were overdue, or soon would be.[17] This was a particular concern to the Admiralty, as the French and Italians were apparently meeting their deadlines – albeit with a far smaller throughput of vessels. Not only did the UK have many more ex-enemy ships to deal with, but she had an extensive programme of disposals of her own surplus vessels, some of which had timelines mandated by the Washington Naval Treaty, signed in February 1922.

As already noted, non-'propaganda' submarines had been 'due' on 1 July 1921, but in May 1922, *U19*, *U30*, *U35*, *U70*, *U94*, *U101*, *U112*, *U126*, *U141*, *UB50*, *UB51*, *UB62*, *UB79*, *UB92*, *UB98*, *UB105*, *UB111*, *UB117*, *UB120*, *UB121*, *UB128*, *UB132*, *UB136*, *UB144*, *UB145*, *UB149*, *UB150*, *UC76*, *UC92*, *UC95*, *UC105* and *UC113* had not yet met the appropriate standard of dismantling. Most had been sold back in 1919 or 1920 and, in most cases, it is likely that the sheer numbers of vessels being scrapped at the same time caused the backlog. Others had gone ashore while in tow (*UB121* and *UB128*) and had not yet been broken up, as had the destroyer *B98* ('due' on 29 October 1921), making their scrapping part of a broader salvage issue. The now-overdue 'propaganda' *U126* and *U141* still languished in Portsmouth Dockyard.

Other 'overdue' vessels in British waters were *Helgoland* and *Westfalen* ('due' 5 February 1922), *T160* (17 February), *T192*, *T193* and *T195* (25 February), *Stuttgart*, *S51*, *T164*, *V26*, *V28*, *V73*, *V128* (15 March; *V26* and *V28* not yet sold), *Danzig* (16 March), *A70* (29 March) and *A81* (4 May – not yet removed from Limekilns, where she had been sold in March 1921). While it was relatively simple to 'encourage' local breakers, other vessels for which the UK was responsible had been sold abroad. Thus, *Posen* (13 November 1921), *Rheinland* (20 January 1922), *T166*, *T169*, *T178* and *T182* (15 March) were in the Netherlands, and *Stettin* (16 March) at Copenhagen.

17. TNA ADM1/8641/119.

The cruiser *R* (ex-*Danzig*), soon after her arrival at Whitby to be broken up. *(AD collection)*

Even more remote were various ex-Austro-Hungarian vessels, *Arpád*, *Babenberg*, *Hapsburg* and *Kaiser Karl VI* (12 February 1922), *Budapest* (28 February) and *Admiral Spaun* (7 May). In the cases of the big ships, the UK Director of Contracts had visited them at Pola shortly before, and reported that none showed any sign of being broken up, apart from rendering the guns useless, and in one case having had her foreturret removed.

At the end of June it was suggested that if Italian shipbreakers had not fulfilled their contracts, their performance bonds could be forfeited, and the ships broken up in Malta as an unemployment relief measure. This had been suggested by Luigi Camilleri (1892–1989), a pioneer member of the newly established Malta Legislative Assembly, as it would certainly be unaffordable to bring ships from the Adriatic to the UK for scrapping. On the other hand, it was noted that in at least the case of *Admiral Spaun* at Venice, delays had been caused by strikes by metal workers that had halved the projected work carried out to date, and by the middle of July considerable progress had been made with her. Pressure appears to have been applied more widely, and on 21 August it was reported that the other ships were now unseaworthy, with the more valuable parts and metals removed.

Posen was a particular problem, as she had not been sold by the UK until the summer of 1921, by which time her November 1921 'due' date was wholly impossible for a ship of her size. For her, a prospective concession from the other Allies had been required, as without one no shipbreaker would have been prepared to take her. It was presumably for this reason that *Posen*'s initial sale to Ward's had been cancelled, with her resale in the Netherlands being for only half the sum previously agreed with the British shipbreaker. As a result of having to seek this concession, the UK had no

The British submarine-cruiser *X1*, whose battery-chargers were powered by two 1,200bhp MAN diesels removed from *U126*. *(AD collection)*

Emden and *Nürnberg* after being refloated at Scapa Flow in the summer of 1919. *(Burrows,* Scapa with a Camera, *p 129)*

option but to agree to a similar request from Italy to delay the 'incapable' date for *Tegetthoff* from 1 January 1923 to 1 July of that year (cf. p 61).[18]

The last disposals of ex-enemy vessels took place with the sale of *U126* and *U141* in February 1923: when *U126* left Portsmouth under tow on 19 March, the final ex-German submarine afloat in UK waters had gone. However, her main diesels remained at sea in a submarine, being installed for battery-charging purposes in the new British submarine-cruiser *X1*, launched in November of that year – where they caused considerable trouble, mainly owing to defects caused by their age.[19]

That all ex-German submarines, except for the French 'ten', had been destroyed was underlined by the fact that in 1927 none were available for use (and ultimately destruction) in the film *Q-Ships* (New Era, 1928), an Anglo-American co-production that depicted the historic action between the British decoy-ship *Stock Force* and *UB80* on 30 July 1918. Thus, '*U98*' (at that time erroneously believed to be the German protagonist) was 'played' by the surplus British submarine *H52* (1919), one of a number of boats of her class sold out of service during 1926–28. Her sinking by gunfire in January 1928 during the filming[20] was surely an unintended consequence of the disposals programme.

FRANCE

The 'propaganda' allocation to France comprised the battle-ship *Thüringen*, the light cruiser *Emden*, the destroyers *V46*, *V100* and *V126*, and fifteen submarines. *Thüringen* was to be handed over at Brest, and on 24 April 1920 she set out from Germany with a German mercantile crew. However, on the

25th she was diverted to Cherbourg (arriving at the same time as *Kolberg* and six destroyers: see p 45, above), with twelve boilers (out of fifteen) being non-operative and allegedly only 12 tons of coal left, with an apparent attempt to scuttle the ship having been made: significant amounts of water were found in her hull. The ship finally arrived at Brest under tow in February 1921, where she was stripped of her armament, and in June she was taken to Gâvres, near Lorient, and beached for use in trials (in particular regarding the spread of fire following shell hits), which lasted through the summer. The hulk soon afterwards broke in two and in February 1923 was sold for scrap. Although partially broken up *in situ*, with stripping of the wreck continuing in 1925, the hulk continued to be used on occasion as a target. However, by 1933 the abandoned remains were considered a hazard to navigation: a 100m section of the hull still lies in the shallows, some 200m off shore, with tops of the engines visible at low tide.[21] Of the smaller 'propaganda' vessels, despite her use for explosive trials, *Emden* survived to be scrapped at Caen in 1926. *V100* was scrapped in 1921, with the other two lasting as trials vessels until 1924 (*V46*) and 1925 (*V125*), when they were also broken up.[22]

Three battleships had fallen to France's basic share of surrendered tonnage, all of Austro-Hungarian origin, and of which *Erzherzog Friedrich*, and *Erzherzog Karl* were of little technical interest. The latter had been one of the ships transferred to Bizerte (p 28 above), and stranded and capsized off that port in a storm in 1920, being subsequently broken up *in situ*. More interesting was *Prinz Eugen*, which was exam-

18. TNA FO 893/20.

19. R Branfill-Cook, *X.1: The Royal Navy's Mystery Submarine* (Barnsley: Seaforth), p 80.

20. In spite of the fact that both *U98* and *UB80* survived the war. The wreck of *H52* lies at 50° 11.55′ N, 04° 17.27′ W, UKHO No.17584 (see I McCartney, *Lost Patrols: Submarine Wrecks of the English Channel* [Penzance: Periscope Publishing, 2003], pp 45–56; S Cant, *England's Shipwreck Heritage* [Swindon: English Heritage, 2013], pp 100–1).

21. *L'Ouest-Éclair*, 7,709 (12 November 1922), p 7; 13,265 (2 March 1933), p 6; *L'homme libre*, 3,228 (26 May 1925), p 3; UKHO No.26150, first charted 1933; now charted in position 47° 41.20′ N 003° 18.476′ W.

22. The boilers from *V100* and *V126* were used respectively to reboiler the destroyers *Aventurier* and *Intrépide* during 1924/27.

Prinz Eugen at Toulon in 1920, after the removal of her guns.
(NHHC NH 87235)

Colmar (ex-*Kolberg*) in the Yangtse, between 1922 and 1924, when she was French flagship in the Far East. *(NHHC NH 68988)*

ined at Toulon, before being stripped of her guns[23] and used for underwater explosion and bombing tests, during which she sank in shallow water in the Bay of Ciens in early 1922. Soon refloated, she was finally sunk by gunfire from the battleships *Paris*, *Jean Bart* and *France* off Cape Cépet in June 1922. Few of the other Austro-Hungarian ships allocated to the country were brought to France, most being sold to Italian companies to be broken up locally.

The first of the five ex-enemy light cruisers to be commissioned into French service was *Metz* (ex-*Königsberg*) in 1920, the remainder following in 1922. The renaming programme underscored French territorial gains following the First World War: just as the vessels had been ceded to France as war reparations under the Treaty of Versailles, they were all renamed after towns and cities annexed by Germany during the Franco-Prussian War of 1871 and returned to France under the same treaty. *Thionville* (ex-*Novara*)'s re-entry into service was delayed when she foundered in shallow water at Brindisi in March 1920 at the beginning of a tow to Bizerte. She was soon salved, and after five weeks' repairs was able to resume her tow to North Africa. In October 1921 she was towed to Toulon, where she received a refit and rearmament, entering French service, with French guns and serving primarily as a gunnery and torpedo training vessel.

The ex-German vessels kept their original main guns, the main armament changes being the fitting of 75mm weapons in lieu of their German 88mm pieces, directly replacing the original mountings, except in *Strasbourg* (ex-*Regensburg*), where they replaced the superimposed 150mm gun aft, and in *Colmar* (ex-*Kolberg*), where they were installed on a new

deckhouse aft of the mainmast); *Metz* also received new torpedo tubes.

Colmar sailed for the Far East on 19 June 1922 to become the flagship of the Division Navale de l'Extrême Orient (DNEO), relieving the armoured cruiser *Montcalm* and arriving on 7 September. In 1923 she was at Vladivostok when the Tokyo earthquake occurred, proceeding to provide aid at Yokohama. She left Indochina in November 1924, being relieved on station by the armoured cruisers *Jules Michelet* and *Victor Hugo*, arriving back in France on 11 February 1925. Repairs subsequently proved uneconomic and in 1926 she provided additional temporary accommodation for student officers at Brest.[24] Stricken in 1927 and condemned soon afterwards, *Colmar* was scrapped in 1929.

Metz served in the Atlantic from November 1921, before moving to the Mediterranean in the spring of 1922, where she served with *Mulhouse* (ex-*Stralsund*) and *Strasbourg* (and briefly also *Thionville*) in the 3rd Light Division, renamed the 2nd Light Division in December 1926. At first based in the Mediterranean, the squadron was transferred to the Atlantic in August 1928, but all ships went into reserve, first at Brest, and then at Landévennec, during 1929/30. The withdrawal of the ex-German ships from service coincided with the commissioning of French-built modern cruisers, beginning with the three *Duguay-Trouin*s in 1927 and the two big *Duquesne*s in 1929. *Thionville* was decommissioned on 1 May 1932; she was then hulked for the gunnery school at Toulon until broken up in 1941.

With yet more new cruisers joining the fleet as the 1930s progressed, there was soon no need to retain the older ships,

23. One main gun went to Gavres for trials; the other eleven went into storage at Tarbes, where they remained until seized by the Germans after 1940, but there is no evidence that they were subsequently used by them and were presumably scrapped.

24. *Le Figaro*, 11 (11 January 1926), p 4; *Armée et Marine*, 15/1 (13 June 1926), p 4.

Mulhouse (ex-Stralsund). (AD collection)

even in reserve. *Mulhouse* was condemned on 15 February 1933, *Metz* on 18 August; they were sold for scrap that September and in the autumn of 1934 respectively. Partially dismantled – her after funnels had been cut down and the mainmast removed even prior to being moved to Landévennec – *Metz* caught fire in the scrapyard in December 1933. *Strasbourg* was renamed *Strasbourg II* in early 1934 to free her name for the new battleship, and was moved to Landévennec in November. However, on 15 January 1936 she arrived under tow at Lorient to become

Strasbourg II (ex-Strasbourg, ex-Regensburg) while laid up at Landévennec during 1935, seen with Japanese-built Arabe class destroyers alongside, and the battleships Voltaire and Diderot just ahead. (AD collection)

the depot ship for the 6th Destroyer Division, being stricken in June but retained as a hulk.

The ten destroyers taken into French service joined the fleet between 1920 and 1922, the big *Amiral Sénès* (ex-*S113*) spending much of her career as leader of Atlantic destroyers, *Mogador* being first approved as her replacement in the 1932 naval budget. *Sénès* was reduced to special reserve on 1 November 1935, and sunk as a target in July 1938. The remaining ships had rather shorter careers, *Pierre Durand* (ex-*V79*), *Chastang* (ex-*S133*), *Deligny* (ex-*S139*), *Rageot de la Touche* (ex-*H146*) and *Delage* (ex-*H147*) being stricken in 1933, *Vesco* (ex-*S134*) and *Mazaré* (ex-*S135*) in 1935, and, finally, the ex-Austro-Hungarian *Matelot Leblanc* (ex-*Dukla*) in May 1936. Their new French names had honoured French seamen of all ranks who had died for their country during the recent war and were characteristic of a commemorative melancholy that also extended to new civilian builds from French shipyards.[25]

Of the submarines transferred to France from the UK in 1919 (and had not been lost on passage – see p 24, above), *U56*, *U79*, *U105*, *U108*, *U113*, *U119*, *U139*, *U151*, *UB24*, *UB73*, *UB94*, *UB126*, *UC58*, *UC103* and *UC104* had been received in a serviceable condition, *U121*, *U153*, *U157*, *U160*, *UB6*, *UB84*, *UB97*, *UB100*, *UB142*, *UB154*, *UB155* and

25. S Cant, 'Diary of the War: March 1917: Mousse Le Moyec', *Wreck of the Week* published online March 2017 <https://thewreckoftheweek.wordpress.com/tag/mousse-le-moyec/>.

Amiral Sénès (ex-*S113*), still on trials at the end of the First World War, and commissioned into the German navy in August 1919. *(AD collection)*

Matelot Leblanc (ex-*Dukla*), the one ex-Austro-Hungarian destroyer taken by France. *(AD collection)*

UC100 in an 'unmaintained' state, with *U25*, *U36*, *U71*, *U136*, *U166*, *UC22*, *UC27* and *UC107* having major components missing. Most were scrapped during 1921/22, some after being used in underwater explosion tests.[26] Two (*U121* and *U151*) were sunk as targets off Cherbourg in early July 1921.

Nine were, however, selected under the French concession that allowed ten to be commissioned into service, with the 'British' *U162* transferred at Portsmouth to make-up the full permitted number in May 1920, on completion of her trials programme.[27] In exchange for her, the French offered *U151*, *U153* or *U157*, with *U153* finally selected by the British, the boat proceeding to Portsmouth under her own power, her crew then taking *U162* back to France, the exchange occurring on 25 June 1920.

Commissioned into the French navy during 1922/23,

Buino (ex-V130). (AD collection)

most passed into reserve early in the 1930s, *Victor Reveille* (ex-*U79*), *Jean Autric* (ex-*U105*), *Léon Mignot* (ex-*U108*), *Halbronn* (ex-*U139*), *Pierre Marrast* (ex-*U162*), *Jean Roulier* (ex-*U166*), *Trinité-Schillemans* (ex-*UB94*) and *Carissan*

26. As noted above, there are discrepancies between published sources over the fates of a number of the German submarines handed over to France.

27. ADM 1/8576/337, dated 19 March 1920.

Delage (ex-H147); like S113, she was still running builders' trials when the war ended, and was only commissioned into the German navy for her voyage to Cherbourg. (AD collection)

Top: Jean Autric (ex-U105). **Middle:** the big *U139,* shown in 1919. She would become the French *Halbronn* in October 1920, serving from February 1923 to July 1935. **Bottom:** *Victor Reveille (ex-U79). (AD; NHHC NH 104658; AD)*

(ex-*UB99*) all being stricken in 1935. *Jean Corre* (ex-*UB155*) was hulked that year and stricken in October 1937, as was *René Audry* (ex-*U119*), the last ex-German submarine on the effective list. Again, their names had honoured those recently *morts pour la France*, principally those who had died at sea, but also commemorating airmen and soldiers.

ITALY

As with the other Allies in receipt of ex-Austro-Hungarian warships for disposal, those allocated to Italy were rapidly sold for scrap. Of her 'propaganda' vessels, the only one of any interest was the battleship *Tegetthoff*, the destroyers allocated all being older than those that Italy was being allowed to commission; the ten submarines also rapidly went for scrap. From the outset, it appears that there were hopes that, notwithstanding her 'propaganda' status and her resulting defined – and short – lifespan, it might be possible for *Tegetthoff* to be kept explicitly as a replacement for *Leonardo da Vinci*, which had been destroyed by an internal explosion in 1916. As already noted (p 40), Italy's official opinion was that her loss (and that of the battleship *Benedetto Brin* the previous year) was the result of Austrian sabotage, although it is clear that her allies had their doubts. This line was continued into the discussions leading up to the Washington Naval Treaty in 1922, under the terms of which Italy had the right to retain *Leonardo*, a ship that, although salved, was never recommissioned, leaving a possibility for her retrospective replacement – potentially with *Tegetthoff*.

Accordingly, nothing was done about her disposal until it became clear that insufficient funding would in any case be available for her refitting and recommissioning. By this time, it was necessary to request a concession to delay her 'incapable' date from 1 January 1923 to 1 July, which was granted in view of a similar request from the British over *Posen*

(pp 55–56, above), but only on the condition that if she had not been rendered 'incapable' by then, she should immediately be sunk in deep water.[28] However, it was not actually until 1924 that *Tegetthoff* was in the hands of breakers, and not until 1925 that she had actually been scrapped.

On the other hand, the five light cruisers granted to the Italian navy were soon taken in hand for refit and eventual recommissioning, all renamed after ports on Italy's Adriatic coastline facing the former Austro-Hungarian territories on the other side of the Adriatic. *Helgoland*, at Bizerte, and *Saida*, at Pola, were incorporated into the Italian navy on 19 September 1920 as *Brindisi* and *Venezia*, the former being transferred to La Spezia during 22/26 October. Both were refitted, with their 66mm AA guns replaced by 37mm weapons, triple 450mm torpedo tubes substituted for their original twin 533mm mountings, and minelaying equipment added.

28. TNA ADM 1/8641/119.

Tegetthoff being broken up at La Spezia during 1924/25, long after her 'due' date. *(AD collection)*

Commissioned in June 1923 as a 'scout', *Brindisi* then joined the Italian Levant Squadron, relieving the armoured cruiser *San Giorgio* as flagship, returning to Italy in January 1924. The following year she transferred to Libyan waters until going into reserve in July 1926. Recommissioned on 1 June 1927 as a flagship of the 1st Destroyer Squadron, she paid off for the last time on 26 November 1929. *Brindisi* was then employed as a depot ship, successively at Ancona, Pola and Trieste, before being stricken in March 1937 and broken up. *Venezia* joined the Italian fleet at the same time as her sister, being paid off on 4 July 1930 at Genoa, where she became an accommodation ship in March 1935; later moved to La Spezia, she was also stricken in 1937.

The ex-German cruisers were slower to complete their refits, the first into service being *Bari* (ex-*Pillau*), commissioned as a scout (as would all the ex-enemy light cruisers) at Taranto in January 1924. She was followed by *Ancona* (ex-*Graudenz*) in May 1925 and by *Taranto* (ex-*Straßburg*) in June 1925; all had 76mm AA guns fitted in lieu of their 88mm German outfit. *Bari* had been otherwise little altered,

but the other two vessels initially had their after superimposed 150mm guns (reclassified as 149mm/43 by the Italian navy) moved amidships, but then moved back again in 1926 when a platform for an aircraft (initially a Macchi M.7, later a CANT 25AR) was fitted in that location, handled by a derrick stepped from the mainmast.

Taranto was in the Red Sea as flagship from May 1926 to January 1927, while in 1929 all three ex-German cruisers joined with *Premuda* (ex-*V116*; see just below) to form the Scout Division of the 1st Squadron, based at La Spezia; later that year they were reclassified from scouts to cruisers. During 1928/29 *Ancona* had been refitted with a catapult on the forecastle, requiring the stem to be extended forward in a graceful clipper shape; the intention was to trial this arrangement, which was being incorporated into the new generation of Italian cruisers. However, difficulties were now emerging in the maintenance of the ex-German ships, and following an August 1932 deployment, *Ancona*, judged to be in the poorest condition, was laid up in reserve at Taranto as a source of spares for *Bari* and *Taranto*.

Early in the 1930s, *Bari* had a temporary extension made to the rear of her bridge and the forefunnel cut down to the same height as the remainder, this combination indicating that her six coal-fired forward boilers were no longer in use. They (and the funnel) were removed during a refit during the summer of 1934, the remaining funnels being cut down to the top of their casings. The remaining four oil-fired boilers gave *Bari* 21,000shp, for a speed of 24.5 knots, In September she sailed for the Red Sea, remaining there until

Venezia (ex-*Saida*), one of the two ships of her class that were taken over by Italy; the third went to France. *(AD collection)*

Taranto (ex-*O*, ex-*Straßburg*), at her namesake port in 1936. *(AD collection)*

Ancona (ex-*E*, ex-*Graudenz*) in June 1929, after the extension of her stem to support a catapult. *(AD collection)*

Taranto in July 1937, after her reconstruction and trunking of her forward funnels. *(AD collection)*

relieved by the new sloop *Eritrea*[29] in May 1938. She was joined there in September 1935 by *Taranto*, which remained in the Red Sea for a year before returning home for refit. During this period, *Taranto* lost her foremost pair of boilers, the uptakes of the remaining pair in the boiler room being trunked back into the second funnel; the fourteen remaining mixed-fired units gave 13,000shp for 21 knots.

Proposals were put forward in 1936 to also refit *Ancona* for colonial service, with her after boiler room converted to bunkerage, new oil-fired boilers exhausting into a single funnel, and three single 76mm/40 added.[30] Another option, put forward earlier that year, had been to transform her into

an anti-aircraft vessel for the defence of emergency bases. This would have involved removing all but six of her existing boilers, giving a speed of 21 knots, dismantling all the super-structure abaft the first funnel, and installing no fewer than thirteen 100mm/47 twin mountings plus three HA directors (plus a fourth reserve director); she would also have retained a minelaying capability of 100 mines.[31] However, the cost of the reconstruction was regarded as excessive (17,469,300 Lire, compared to 10 million Lire for an *Oriani* class destroyer); an alternative scheme, which involved new machinery, giving the ship a fleet escort capability, was even less affordable. The colonial cruiser option was also ruled out on cost grounds, and *Ancona* was stricken on 11 March 1937 (along with *Venezia* and *Brindisi*), and broken up the following year

Following Italy's entry into the Second World War, *Bari* and *Taranto* were based at Taranto for service in the Adriatic and Aegean, including mining and bombardment opera-tions. The two ex-German cruisers were intended to lead the landing force for the projected occupation of Malta in 1942, while *Bari* was flagship for the Italian landings in Corsica in November 1942.

Both had their light AA batteries enhanced during the war, and both were earmarked for conversion to anti-aircraft cruisers in 1943.[32] Work actually began at Leghorn on

---

29. See M Cosentino, 'The Colonial Sloop *Eritrea*', *Warship* [XXXVIII] (2016), pp 30–41.
30. Cosentino, *Warship* [XXXVIII], p 37.

31. E Bagnasco and E Cernuschi, 'La Regia Marina e l'incrociatore antiaerei', *Storia Militaire* 40 (1997), pp 24–34.
32. Cf. Bagnasco and Cernuschi, *Storia Militare* 40.

Bari (ex-*U*, ex-*Pillau*) was also reconstructed in the late 1930s; she is shown here in February 1942, with a characteristically Italian camouflage scheme. *(AD collection)*

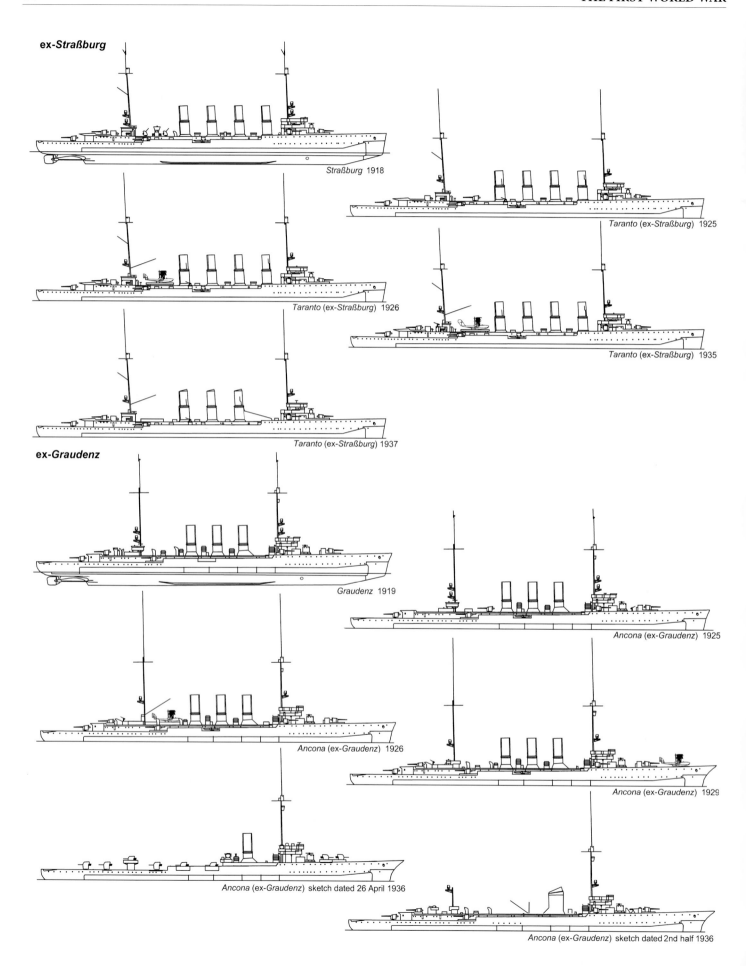

ex-Straßburg

Straßburg 1918

Taranto (ex-Straßburg) 1925

Taranto (ex-Straßburg) 1926

Taranto (ex-Straßburg) 1935

Taranto (ex-Straßburg) 1937

ex-Graudenz

Graudenz 1919

Ancona (ex-Graudenz) 1925

Ancona (ex-Graudenz) 1926

Ancona (ex-Graudenz) 1929

Ancona (ex-Graudenz) sketch dated 26 April 1936

Ancona (ex-Graudenz) sketch dated 2nd half 1936

ex-*Pillau*

Modifications to ex-German ships in Italian hands.
(AD graphic)

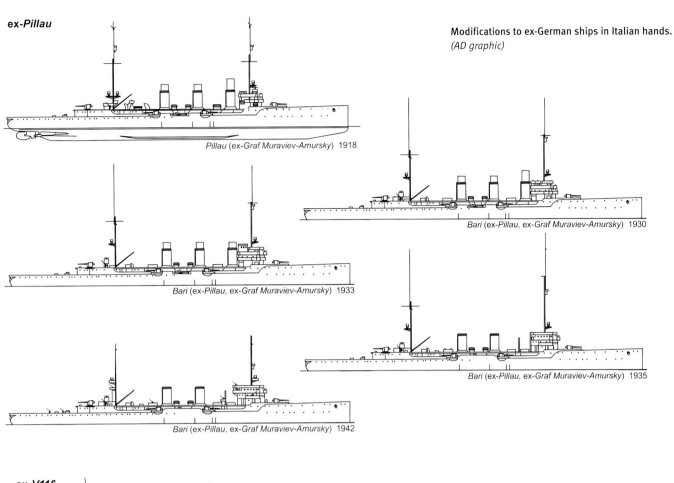

Pillau (ex-*Graf Muraviev-Amursky*) 1918

Bari (ex-*Pillau*, ex-*Graf Muraviev-Amursky*) 1930

Bari (ex-*Pillau*, ex-*Graf Muraviev-Amursky*) 1933

Bari (ex-*Pillau*, ex-*Graf Muraviev-Amursky*) 1935

Bari (ex-*Pillau*, ex-*Graf Muraviev-Amursky*) 1942

ex-*V116*

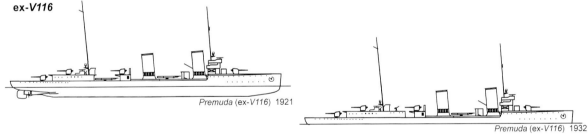

Premuda (ex-*V116*) 1921

Premuda (ex-*V116*) 1932

ex-*B97*

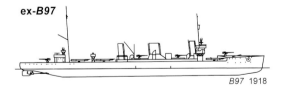

B97 1918

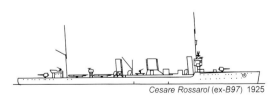

Cesare Rossarol (ex-*B97*) 1925

ex-*S63*

S63 1918

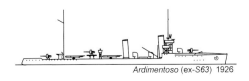

Ardimentoso (ex-*S63*) 1926

0   20 metres

rearming *Bari* with eight single 90mm/50, eight 37mm/54 and eight 20mm weapons, but on 28 June 1943 she was sunk by American bombs. Salvage work was interrupted by the Italian armistice, and the wreck was sabotaged to prevent German recovery of the vessel. The hulk was partially demolished by German forces during 1944, the remains (which had been formally stricken on 27 February 1947) being refloated on 13 January 1948 and broken up.

Taranto had transferred to Leghorn on 26 February 1942 as a seagoing training ship, but had then been placed in reserve at La Spezia in December, where she was scuttled on 9 September 1943 following the Italian Armistice. Soon refloated by the Germans, she was sunk again on 23 October 1943 during an Allied air raid, and although refloated yet again during January/April 1944 the hulk was finally sunk by bombs that September and broken up after the war.

In contrast to the long careers of some of the cruisers, the ex-enemy destroyers had relatively short front-line lives, except for the big *Premuda* (ex-*V116*), named for an Italian battle of 1918 on the Dalmatian coast against Austria-Hungary; she served extensively, classified as a scout, until 1938, when she was reclassified as a destroyer, shortly before she was stricken. Initial modifications were limited to the addition of 40mm AA guns, but owing to a shortage of German 533mm torpedoes, her forward torpedo tubes were replaced by 450mm Italian examples in 1932; the aft mounting was replaced by a 120mm/15 starshell gun. *Cesare Rossarol* (ex-*B97*) was entirely rearmed, three 120mm guns replacing the original four 105mm weapons, two 76mm/40 AA added, the forward torpedo tubes removed to allow the forecastle to extended aft, and the bridge and forefunnel heightened. Entering service as a light scout in 1924, she served as a scout during the 1920s, before being reclassified as a destroyer in October 1926. She was rebuilt as a trials ship in 1931, having the forward boiler replaced by a gyroscopic stabiliser, and all armament but the forward twin

120mm mounting removed, but two twin 450mm torpedo tubes added.

The other ex-German destroyer, *Ardimentoso* (ex-*S63*) was also rearmed before entering service, in October 1925, her three 105mm guns being replaced by the same number of 100mm weapons, two 40mm AA guns added, and the number of torpedo tubes reduced to two, the well-deck between the bridge and forecastle being filled in. From 1931, *Ardimentoso* became a torpedo training ship at Pola, two 450mm tubes replacing her existing aft 533mm examples in 1933. She was paid off in 1938 and stricken in February 1939.

Of the seven ex-Austro-Hungarian vessels, two, *Fasana* (ex-*Tátra*) and *Zenson* (i, ex-*Balaton*), never became operational, and were instead cannibalised for spares, being then stricken in July 1923 and broken up. As with the French vessels, the ships ceded from a former enemy were assigned names that either reflected similar cessations of territory from the same enemy to Italy, or marked the location of significant battles between Italy and Austria-Hungary during the war. The five vessels actually commissioned were modified by replacing their original torpedo tubes by four Italian 450mm examples, and two/four 6.5mm machine guns added. *Grado* (ex-*Triglav*), *Cortellazzo* (ex-*Lika*), *Pola* (ex-*Orjen*) and *Monfalcone* (ex-*Uszok*) were mainly employed on patrol duties off the Libyan coast and training duties out of Taranto and Venice, but *Muggia* (ex-*Csepel*) was much more wide-ranging in her operations. During her first three years, she ventured into the Aegean and Black Sea, before leaving for the Far East in 1926, arriving at Shanghai on 10 March 1927. However, on 26 March 1929, en route from Amoy to Shanghai at night and in thick fog, she ran onto rocks and sank.

The survivors were reclassified as torpedo boats in 1929, and on 9 April 1931 *Pola* was renamed *Zenson* (ii). She became part of the naval engineering school on 1 July 1932,

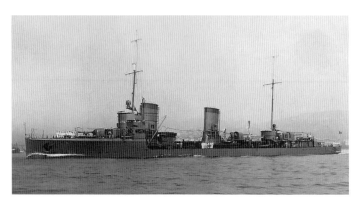

Unlike her French half-sister *S113*, the Italian *Premuda* (ex-*V116*) had actually served in the German Imperial navy. Like her, however, she was handed over to the Allies in 1920. *(AD collection)*

Ardimentoso (ex-*S63*) was the only member of her class not to be scuttled at Scapa Flow, and served in the Italian navy from 1925 to 1939. *(AD collection)*

The former Austro-Hungarian *Orjen* was originally commissioned into the Italian navy as *Pola*, but was renamed *Zenson* in 1931 to free her name for a new cruiser. She was one of the seven ships of her class to be taken over by Italy (an eighth went to France and two were war losses), one of which had previously been named *Zenson*, but had been stricken back in 1923. *(NHHC NH 47758)*

alongside the cruiser *Taranto*, including cruises between the ports of the Italian Adriatic, Albania, Greece and Libya. She was joined by her sister *Cortellazzo* a year later. *Zenson* (ii) was stricken in 1937, along with *Monfalcone*, the remaining pair in January 1939.

A range of auxiliary vessels also fell to Italy. The depot ship *Gäa*, originally built as a liner, was soon handed over to Italian Railways, and leased to the Cosulich Line as an Atlantic liner, but was damaged in heavy weather and scrapped. Various old hulked battleships and frigates were also taken over; most were soon disposed of, but *Feuerspeier* (ex-*Erzherzog Albrecht*) served as *Buttafuoco* until 1950.

JAPAN

None of the 'propaganda' surface vessels given to Japan (the battleship *Oldenburg*, the light cruiser *Augsburg* and the destroyers *S60*, *V80* and *V127*) were taken up, and were sold for scrap at Rosyth along with those allocated to her for disposal (the battleship *Nassau* and the destroyers *T181* and torpedo boat *A70*). However, the seven submarines handed over in 1919, and retrospectively designated part of Japan's 'propaganda' allocation, were all taken to Japan.

U46, *U55*, *U125*, *UB125*, *UB143*, *UC90* and *UC99* had been handed over at Harwich on 19 December 1918, and departed from Devonport in two groups, on 18 February

and 6 March 1919. They were towed via the Mediterranean and the Suez Canal by Japanese destroyers that had previously been deployed to European waters, escorted by the armoured cruisers *Izumo* and *Nisshin*, and the depot ship *Kwanto*. Both groups arrived at Yokosuka on 18 June 1919, and were made available for inspection by the Japan-accredited attachés of the Allied powers on the 25th. All boats were taken into service (but not formally taken into the Japanese fleet) in 1920, with the temporary designations *O1* to *O7*, and used for trials. Due to be rendered 'ineffective' by the middle of 1921, the seven vessels were dismantled during the first half of the year, with armament, machinery and conning towers all removed.[33]

O5 (ex-*UC99*) was expended as a target in October, although others were retained for a time for auxiliary purposes, *O1* (ex-*U125*) enduring as a test object for submarine salvage operations into the 1930s. Her engines also survived, powering the outer shafts of the minelayer *Itsukushima* (1929; the centre shaft had a similar Japanese-built motor). Her design would also be perpetuated in the new Type-KRS (*I21* class) submarines, near-copies of *U125*, of which six ordered in 1924, and four completed during 1927/28; the other pair were cancelled.

USA

Of the American 'propaganda' fleet, a key purpose of bringing the submarines across the Atlantic was to support the US government's Victory Bond drive. An ex-German submarine had already been used in 1917 during the precursor Liberty Loan campaign, when *UC5*, captured by the British after running aground on 27 April 1916, and exhibited around UK ports, was transported to the USA and

33. S Dent and I Johnston, 'Japan's U-boats, Sasebo, 1921', *Warship* [XL] (2018), pp 220–4.

U111 and the cruiser *Rochester* at Brooklyn Navy Yard in April 1919. *(AD collection)*

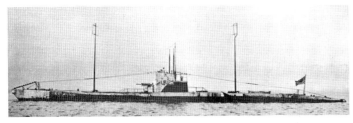

O6 (ex-*UB125*) at Yokosuka 23 June 1919, soon after arriving from Europe, flying the Japanese ensign, but with her German number still painted-up. *(AD collection)*

U117 and *U140* on 18 June 1921, en route to their destruction off Virginia
Capes. *(NMUSN Lot-6080-4)*

displayed in New York's Central Park in October 1917. On
the basis of the success of this, it was proposed that the US
prizes be sent on tours of the American coast to drum up
support for bond sales, starting on the 29 April 1919.[34]

For this purpose, the country was divided into five zones,
each with its own submarine (the engineless *U140* was not
used). *U111* visited ports along the New England coast,
completing her itinerary in the late summer of 1919. *U117*
toured the Atlantic coast, while *UB88* started there, before
proceeding southwards to the Gulf of Mexico (including a
voyage up the Mississippi), and then via the Panama Canal
to the West Coast, ending up at San Pedro, CA, on
8 November. *UC97* went from New York to the Great Lakes,
via Halifax and St Lawrence, with *UB148* spending her time
in the New York area, sailing up the Hudson, and finishing
at New London.

UC97 finished her tour at Chicago on 21 August. Hopes
were expressed that she might be preserved, but this was
excluded by the terms of the inter-Allied agreements, and
she was dismantled over the next few weeks, leaving a largely
empty hull. *UB88* underwent a similar process, beginning in
April 1920, and was decommissioned on 1 November. *U117*,
which had finished her tour at Washington, DC on 23 June,
was more carefully dissected at Philadelphia Navy Yard, to
learn technical lessons that could be applied to future US
submarines. One of her engines was used the following year
to re-engine the submarine tender *Fulton*, but it was
removed when the latter was decommissioned in 1925.
Another ex-German engine of 1,750bhp, but of apparently
unrecorded origin, was installed in *Fulton* when she was
recommissioned as a gunboat in 1930.[35] On the other hand,
U111 (tour ended at New London on 9 May) and *UB148*
(New London, 12 May) remained active for performance
trials, the former in competition with the new USS/M *S3*.

All the boats were subject to the 1 July 1921 deadline for
their destruction, and thus all were expended as targets
during 1921. First to go was *UB88*, sunk by the destroyer
Wickes in January, followed by *UC97*, dispatched by the
gunboat *Wilmette* in Lake Michigan on 7 June. Of the
remaining four boats, *U117* was bombed and sunk on
21 June, with *U140* and *UB148* facing destroyer gunfire the

next day. However, *U111* foundered en route to the target
area, in water too shallow (12m) to meet the USA's disposal
obligations, which also constituted a hazard to navigation.
She was accordingly salved the following summer by
USS *Falcon*, patched up at Norfolk Navy Yard, and definitively sunk in deep water further out to sea off the Winter
Quarter Shoal, Virginia.[36] The sinkings were formally notified to the Conference of Ambassadors on 12 August 1922.

Of the United States' surface-ship prizes, *Frankfurt* was
commissioned into the US navy on 4 June 1920, followed by
Ostfriesland on 7 June. Escorted by the transport
USS *Hancock*, the battleship left Rosyth on the 17th,

36. *New York Herald*, (LXXXVII, 3), 2 September 1922, p 15.

S132 in tow to the USA, her engines having being ruined at Scapa Flow.
However, four of her sisters, *S133*, *S134*, *S135* and *S139* served in the
French navy under the names *Chastang*, *Vesco*, *Mazaré* and *Deligny*,
respectively. *(NHHC NH 111341)*

Ostfriesland under the US flag. *(NHHC NH 43706)*

34. On the careers of the boats transferred to the USA, see C Dubbs, *America's U-
Boats: Terror Trophies of World War I* (Lincoln & London: University of Nebraska
Press, 2014), pp 76–187, noting that '*U161*' is consistently misprinted as '*U164*'.
35. C C Wright, 'Re: Mystery Photo No. 176 (*W.I.* 46, no. 3:240)', *Warship
International* XLVII/1 (2010), p 75.

V43, *G102* and *S132* at New York, showing the much greater size of *G102*. (*LoC LC-B2- 5278-1*)

Ostfriesland sinking around 1240hrs on 21 July 1921. (NHHC NH 43718)

Frankfurt sinking on 18 July 1921. (NHHC NH 44026)

accompanied by *Frankfurt*, *V43*, *G102* and *S132*, under the tow of the minesweepers *Redwing*, *Rail* and *Falcon*. Calling at Brest until 13 July, the convoy then sailed for the USA via the Azores, *Frankfurt* now being towed by *Ostfriesland* and just the torpedo boats by the minesweepers; they arrived off Sandy Hook on 9 August, the battleship being decommissioned on 20 September.[37]

All were, like the final four submarines, destined for sinking as targets off the Virginia coast,[38] having been prepared at New York Navy Yard by both stripping and also sealing bulkheads to maximise watertight integrity. On 13 July 1921, *G102* was sunk by bombs, as was *S132* on 15 July, when *V43* was also sent to the bottom by the battleship *Florida*. On the 18th, *Frankfurt* was the target for Army Air Force and Navy aircraft with bombs of increasing size. Initial minor damage culminated in two 600lb (270kg) weapons striking the ship between the funnels and the mainmast, and a third, abreast the bridge, causing such underwater damage that *Frankfurt* sank at 1825hrs. *Ostfriesland* met her fate on 20/21 July 1921, about 100km off the Virginia Capes. After a first phase of bombing, during which five bombs hit (out of fifty-two dropped), the ship was taking on water via a split seam, the flooding being exacerbated by pre-trial vandalism that had led to the opening or even removal of watertight doors. Thus, by the morning, she was both listing to port and settling by the stern. Then, three

37. For a US assessment of the ship, see K F Smith, 'The Ex-German Battleship *Ostfriesland*', *Journal of the American Society of Naval Engineers* 32 (1920), pp 652–87.
38. T Wildenberg, *Billy Mitchell's War with the Navy: The Interwar Rivalry Over Naval Air Power* (Annapolis, MD: Naval Institute Press 2013), pp 73–80.

Right: The post-war odyssey of SMS *G102*, ordered from Germania as the Argentine *San Luis*, but requisitioned by Germany and commissioned in April 1915. From top to bottom: beached at Scapa Flow; in tow of the minesweeper USS *Falcon* across the Atlantic; during her final moments, as a bombing target off Cape Henry, VA, on 13 July 1921. (*Burrows*, Scapa with a Camera, p 126; NHHC NH 45786; NH 111347)

more hits were scored, near-misses causing additional flooding, the ship finally foundering after two more hits and two more near-misses. The sinkings were formally notified to the Conference of Ambassadors on 12 August.

POLAND

As noted above (pp 45–46), Brazil and Poland negotiated a swap that allowed the latter to acquire two large torpedo boats, rather than the one allocated, enhancing the value of her force of six boats. *V105* was thus commissioned into the Polish navy in 1921 as *Mazur*, alongside her sister *Kaszub* (ex-*V108*), and the smaller *Ślązak* (ex-*A59*), *Krakowiak* (ex-*A64*), *Kujawiak* (ex-*A68*) and *Góral* (*A80*, renamed *Podhalanin* in 1922). The names of the first three commemorated the regions of Mazuria, Kashubia and Silesia that had either seen direct conflict during the First World War or continued to be a flashpoint between Germany and the Second Polish Republic of the interwar years. *Kaszub*, *Krakowiak* and *Kujawiak* were refitted at Rosyth Dockyard between December 1920 and August 1921. It was envisaged that they should proceed under their own power to Poland; however, breakdowns en route meant that all eventually arrived at Danzig under tow, *Kaszub* on 3 October 1921. *Mazur*, *Ślązak* and *Góral* had already been delivered to Poland under tow in September 1921.

Delivered fit only for police duties, the ships received proper armament only in 1925, when they were fitted with two 75mm guns, two 450mm torpedo tubes and mine rails. On 20 July 1925 *Kaszub* was broken in half by the explosion

of her forward boiler while lying in the Neufahrwasser at Danzig; the forepart sank but the after part of the ship remained afloat. The bow was refloated a week later and the whole ship docked; she was subsequently broken up.

The other ships survived into the 1930s, *Mazur* being extensively rebuilt during 1935–37 and still in service as a gunnery training ship at the time of the German invasion. She was then bombed and sunk at Oksywie on 1 September 1939. *Krakowiak* had been stricken in October 1936 and broken up, but *Ślązak* had become a target ship for aircraft in 1937; captured by the Germans in 1939, she subsequently sank while under tow. *Kujawiak* and *Podhalanin* had been stricken and converted to oil hulks in 1939; they were sunk, respectively, by bombs at Oksywie on 3 September, and in tow between Jastarnia and Hel on 24 September.

BELGIUM

The Belgian navy was short-lived, being abolished in 1927. Nevertheless, during its short life the ex-German torpedo boats went through a series of renumberings, a number receiving names: for example, *A14* joined the Belgian navy

The Belgian *A2PC* (ex-German *A12*), later renamed *A2 Prince Charles*. *(AD collection)*

The training ship *West Diep*, formerly the torpedo boat *20* (ex-*A20*, ex-*A9*, ex-*A9PC*, ex-German *A20*). She would survive to return to German service in 1940. *(AD collection)*

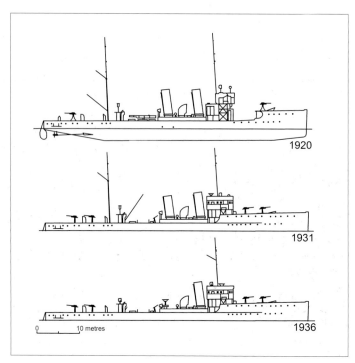

The modifications carried out to the Polish *Mazur* (ex-*V105*). *(AD graphic)*

as *A1PC*, was later renumbered and named as *A1 Prince Leopold*, and finally as *A12*. As the primary offensive vessels of the now-defunct navy, most of the torpedo boats were sold for scrap in 1931. On the other hand, four lasted longer as civilian training vessels: two, *Wielingen* (ex-*A43*, ex-*A24*, ex-*A24PC*, ex-*A43*) and *West Diep* (ex-*A20*, ex-*A9*, ex-*A9PC*, ex-*A20*) being still in service in 1940 and seized by Germany.[39] The latter served in the German navy, surviving to re-enter service with her former owners, and be broken up post-war.

PORTUGAL

The Turkish gunboat awarded to Portugal was never delivered following the abrogation of the Treaty of Sèvres; however, six ex-Austro-Hungarian torpedo boats were handed over, but two of them never reached Portugal, *Zêzere* (ex-*85F*) and *Cávado* (ex-*88F*) being wrecked in tow off Bône, Tunisia, in December 1921. The other four, however, remained in service into the 1930s: *Liz* (ex-*90F*) being stricken in 1934 and *Mondego* (ex-*91F*) in 1938; the last two, *Ave* (ex-*86F*) and *Sado* (ex-*89F*) were stricken in 1940.

GREECE

The destroyer and torpedo boats ceded to Greece all came from the Austro-Hungarian fleet, the first being one of the older *Huszár* class, rather than one of the modern *Tátras* given to France and Italy. The service of *Smyrni* (ex-*Ulan*) with the Greek navy was fairly brief, being stricken in 1928. However, the six *82F/98M*-type torpedo boats all continued in service through the 1930s, except for *Panormos* (ex-*92F*),

---

39. One other A-boat served during the Second World War. This was the former *A32*, which had been wrecked off the Baltic island of Saaremaa in October 1917, salvaged by Estonia in October 1923, and commissioned as their *Sulev* in August 1924. She became the Soviet *Ametist* in 1940, following the annexation of the Baltic States, and survived as a patrol vessel and finally a tender until scrapped in the 1950s.

The Greek torpedo boat *Panormos*, the former Austro-Hungarian *92F*. *(AD collection)*

sunk after a collision in the Gulf of Aegina during a gale on 11 March 1928, her captain going down with his ship.

The others were all lost during the Axis attack on Greece in April 1941. *Proussa* (ex-*94F*) was bombed at Corfu on the 4th by Italian Ju 87 dive bombers, *Kios* (ex-*99M*) scuttled off Athens on the 23rd, *Pergamos* (ex-*95F*) and *Kyzikos* (ex-*98M*) at Salamis on the 25th; finally, *Kidoniai* (ex-*100M*), was bombed south of the Peloponnese on the 26th.

YUGOSLAVIA

Yugoslavia finally received her much-reduced allocation of ships in March 1921, with the final evacuation of the Cattaro area – the future Yugoslav naval hub – by the French. The largest was the old battleship *Kronprinz Erzherzog Rudolf*, which had spent the war as guardship at Cattaro. Nominally brought into Yugoslav service as *Kumbor*, she was, however, sold to a Dutch shipbreaker the following year.

Although twelve torpedo boats had been allocated to Yugoslavia, only one of the four vessels of the *Kaiman* class (*T9–T12*), and three of the eight *74T/82T* class (*T1–T8*) were commissioned at first. The remaining *Kaiman*s were soon disposed of, in 1924, but the more modern boats remained core elements of the Yugoslav fleet for many years. *T4* (ex-

The Austro-Hungarian destroyer *Ulan*, later the Greek *Smyrni*. *(AD collection)*

Erzherzog Kronprinz Rudolf at Cattaro around 1915; as *Kumbor*, she would become the largest warship granted to the Yugoslav navy by the Allies. *(NHHC NH 87063)*

The Yugoslav torpedo boat *T3*, built as the Austro-Hungarian *78T*. She would in 1941 pass under Italian control, and end her career under the German flag. *(AD collection)*

The river monitor *Drava* (ex-Austro-Hungarian *Enns*), one of the few vessels taken over by Yugoslavia at the end of 1918 to be formally allocated to her by the Allies. *(AD collection)*

79T) was wrecked on the Dalmatian coast in 1932 and *T2* (ex-*77T*) was scrapped in 1939, but the others were still in service when Yugoslavia was invaded by the Axis in April 1941. All were taken over by Italy, retaining their Yugoslav names, *T1* (ex-*76T*) and *T5* (ex-*87F*) being handed back to the Yugoslav navy in December 1943, after the Italian armistice. Both continued in service post-war, as the patrol vessels *Golešnica* and *Cer*, respectively, until broken up at the beginning of the 1960s. *T6* (ex-*93F*) was scuttled, and *T8* (ex-*97F*) bombed, on 10/11 September 1943 while attempting to escape from the Adriatic, but both *T3* (ex-*78T*) and *T7* (ex-*96F*) fell into German hands, serving as *TA48* and *TA34* (i) until the summer of 1944, when they were passed on to the Croats, under their original names. *T7* was lost shortly afterwards to British MTBs, and *T3* was taken back by the Germans in December, being bombed at Trieste in February 1945.

As noted above, three of the four minesweepers (ex-torpedo boats) *D1–D4* of the *Kibitz* class that were taken over by Yugoslavia were scrapped in 1924, but *D2* (ex-*36*,

The Yugoslav minesweeper *Galeb*, built as the German *M100* and purchased in 1921. *(AD collection)*

ex-*Uhu*) survived to be captured by the Italians in 1941 (becoming *D10*) and the Germans in 1943, sinking while in their hands. They were replaced by ex-German minesweepers bought from the civil market in July 1921 (cf. pp 80–81), while the old German cruiser *Niobe* was acquired as the training ship *Dalmacija* in 1925 (p 83). A series of small *MT130* class mine tenders on the stocks fell into Yugoslav hands at Kraljevica (formerly Porto Ré), which were finally completed in 1931; two had been completed by the Italians in 1920. They had been excluded from the requirement that all unfinished warships be destroyed on the basis that they could be used for commercial purposes – although all actually ended up as naval units.

Of the Danube monitors provisionally taken over by Yugoslavia in December 1918, three had been allocated to Romania, but the remaining four, *Sava* (ex-*Bodrog*), *Vardar* (ex-*Bosna*), *Drava* (ex-*Enns*) and *Morava* (ex-*Körös* – originally excluded) were ultimately allowed to be kept. Formally handed over to the Yugoslavs by the NACDEV on 15 November 1920, they served until the Axis invasion in April 1941, when they were sunk by bombing or scuttling.

Among subsidiary vessels handed over was the old ironclad *Kaiser Max*, which continued serving as an accommodation hulk at Tivat in the Bay of Cattaro. She was renamed *Tivat*, and later *Neretva* at Sebenico. Captured by Italy in April 1941, she became their *San Marco*, and was seized by the Germans on 11 September 1943, after which her fate is unknown.

ROMANIA

Romania's share of ex-enemy tonnage had been fixed at seven torpedo boats for potential operational employment, plus a further six for police duties if desired. However, only the former were actually taken over, being further ex-

Marx, ex-*Újvidék*, ex-*Inn*). Formally handed over at Novi Sad on 14 December 1920, they would also serve through the Second World War and beyond.

The Romanian torpedo-boat *Năluca* (ex-Austro-Hungarian *82F*). *(AD collection)*

Austro-Hungarian *74T/82F* class vessels, six of which, with two Italian-built destroyers repurchased after wartime service with the Italian navy, would form the core of the Romanian navy until new tonnage was delivered from 1930 onwards. The seventh torpedo boat, *Fulgerul* (ex-*84F*) was lost in a storm shortly after entering the Black Sea on her delivery voyage.

Half the remaining vessels (*Viforul* [ex-*74T*], *Vârtejul* [ex-*75T*] and *Vijelia* [ex-*80T*]) were stricken in 1932, but the others survived to be active during the Second World War. One (*Năluca* [ex-*82F*]) was sunk by bombing in August 1944, but the other pair (*Sborul* [ex-*81T*] and *Smeul* [ex-*83F*]), after a year in Soviet hands during 1944/45 (see pp 162-63) returned to serve the Romanian navy through the 1950s.

As already noted, three ex-Austro-Hungarian monitors were allocated to Romania, becoming *Bucovina* (ex-*Soca*, ex-*Sava*), *Ardeal* (ex-*Drina*, ex-*Temes*) and *Basarabia* (ex-

THE NEW GERMANY

With the handover of the last vessels demanded by the Versailles Treaty and the subsequent protocol, Germany was in a position to begin to rebuild a navy, such as was allowed by Article 181 of the treaty:

> After the expiration of a period of two months from the coming into force of the present Treaty the German naval forces in commission must not exceed:
> 6 armoured ships of the Deutschland or Lothringen type; 6 light cruisers; 12 destroyers; 12 torpedo boats; or an equal number of ships constructed to replace them as provided in Article l90.
> No submarines are to be included.
> All other warships, except where there is provision to the contrary in the present Treaty, must be placed in reserve or devoted to commercial purposes.

All had to come from vessels currently within the navy, as Versailles Article 186 required 'the breaking up of all the German surface warships now under construction'.

Swords to Ploughshares?

However, on 13 February 1920 the German Foreign Office wrote to the NIACC asking for a ruling on the definition of 'breaking up'. Germany proposed that it be understood as 'so stripping such vessels of their characteristics as war vessels that re-construction of war vessels would be impossible', the intention being that such vessels could be used as the basis for merchant ships. This was referred to the Allied

Odin, shown before and after her rebuilding from a coast defence vessel to a mercantile locomotive transport. Although converted to the same basic concept, *Odin* differed from her sister *Aegir* and half-sister *Frithjof* in having a single mast, rather than their two. *(NHHC NH 47884; Drüppel)*

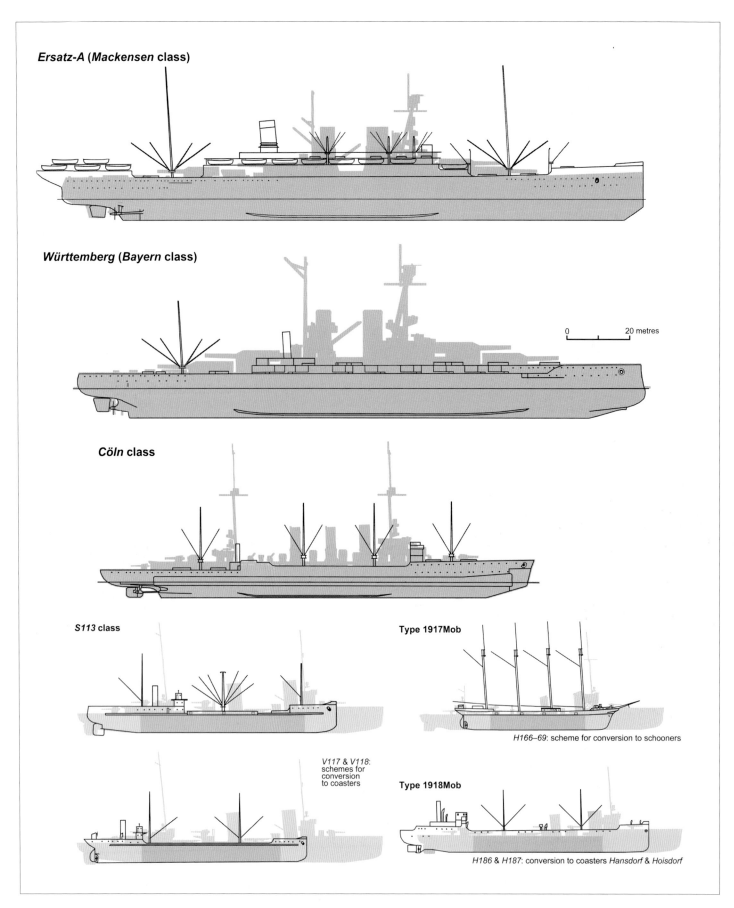

Ersatz-A (Mackensen class)

Württemberg (Bayern class)

0   20 metres

Cöln class

S113 class

Type 1917Mob

H166–69: scheme for conversion to schooners

V117 & V118:
schemes for
conversion
to coasters

Type 1918Mob

H186 & H187: conversion to coasters *Hansdorf* & *Hoisdorf*

Schemes for the completion of unfinished German warships into merchantmen. *(AD graphic)*

Conference of Ambassadors with a recommendation for acceptance, as it achieved the objectives of the clause while also meeting a requirement under Article 189 that material arising from the breaking up of warships must be used for industrial or commercial purposes.

Article 181 allowed for surplus German warships to be devoted to commercial purposes, and a considerable number of minesweepers were sold for conversion to ferries or small cargo ships (see pp 80–81, below). In addition, a handful of larger vessels were rebuilt as merchantmen. The coast defence ships *Frithjof*, *Odin* and *Aegir* became vehicle transporters, the boiler rooms and magazines being stripped out to provide cargo space, the original engines being replaced by a pair of 550bhp ex-submarine diesels. They appear to have been successful in the new role, as *Frithjof* lasted until 1930 and *Odin* was not scrapped until 1935 (*Aegir* had been wrecked in 1929).

Also, the old cruisers *Gefion* and *Victoria Louise*, lying at Danzig, were purchased by a local consortium to be converted to cargo ships, to provide employment in the former Danzig Imperial Dockyard and act as symbols of Danziger commerce, work being authorised by the local Allied authorities in May 1920. *Gefion* (renamed *Adolf Sommerfeld*) received a pair of 2,400bhp diesels from the

unfinished submarines *U115* and *U116* (building at Danzig), fitted in what had been her after engine room. Some components were salvaged from the battleship *Brandenburg*, also bought by the consortium, additionally donating material for *Victoria Louise*'s conversion to the similar, but steam-powered SS *Flora Sommerfeld*; the battleship was then scrapped. Neither of the *Sommerfeld*s lasted long in mercantile service, both ships being broken up in 1923.

As for the unfinished ships, these ranged from battleships and battlecruisers down to destroyers and torpedo boats, and when details of ships to be converted were requested by the NIACC, a fairly long list was submitted.[40] This included the battleships *Sachsen* and *Württemberg*, four *Mackensen*-class battlecruisers, *Cöln*-class light cruisers and a range of destroyers. The state of the ships ranged from the all but finished cruiser *Wiesbaden* through to the in-frame on the slip cruiser *Ersatz-Karlsruhe* and various destroyers.

40. For further detail on individual categories of vessel, see A Dodson, *The Kaiser's Battlefleet: German Capital Ships* (Barnsley: Seaforth, 2016), pp 149–53; A Dodson, 'After the Kaiser: The Imperial German Navy's Light Cruisers after 1918', *Warship* [XXXIX] (2017), pp 143–4; A Dodson and D Nottelmann, *The Kaiser's Cruisers, 1871–1918* (Barnsley: Seaforth, in preparation); A Dodson, 'Beyond the Kaiser: The Imperial German Navy's Destroyers and Torpedo Boats after 1918', *Warship* [XLI] (2019), pp 129–44; much of the data for these sources is derived from TNA ADM 116/1994, ADM 116/1992 and ADM 116/2113.

The incomplete *Ersatz-Freya* and *Württemburg* being broken up in the Roßhaven at Hamburg in late 1921. *(AD collection)*

Sketches were provided of them as dry cargo vessels with armour and protective bulkheads and decks removed (where structurally possible – which it was not for the belts of the light cruisers), and magazines and most machinery spaces given over to cargo. Most, including the ex-light cruisers, were to be diesel-powered, the engines coming from incomplete submarines. By the autumn of 1920, options on the cruisers and big ships had been taken by the Deutsches Petroleumgesellschaft, now with a view to them becoming oil tankers, but although the plans were approved by the NIACC, nothing was done to implement the conversions. By the spring of 1921 the NIACC was becoming increasingly concerned that not enough was being done in the meantime to gut the ships of their military features, culminating in a demand (enshrined in a protocol dated 27 June 1921) that all unfinished warships should have all side armour removed and all machinery, armament, armour decks and torpedo bulkheads destroyed by 31 July 1921 (see Appendix 3.1). All the larger vessels were soon after sold for scrap.

It was only in the case of the destroyers that actual adaptations were put in hand, and of those, only four were completed. Two basic schemes were drawn up and approved by the NIACC: one for a conventional coaster with a diesel engine aft, and one for a four-masted schooner with auxiliary diesel propulsion. Both schemes involved cutting off the bow at the forward boiler room and the stern at the after engine room bulkhead, and adding new ends to this midship section. The latter comprised principally the machinery spaces, which would be emptied of boilers and turbines and would now accommodate the holds of the new merchantman, whose propulsion machinery would be housed in the brand-new stern section.

The removal of the original bow and stern was in any case necessary to meet a key Allied requirement that the hull-form of any converted vessel be no longer suitable for high speeds: '[i]n the case of Torpedo Craft a complete reconstruction of the Bow and Stern would do away with the character of a fast warship.'[41] It was on this basis that a design for the mercantile completion of the large S113-type G119–G121 was rejected on 7 September 1920 as retaining the whole original underwater form. However, a modified scheme, apparently including the requisite truncation, was approved at the beginning of October for G119–G121, together with the very similar S114–S115, V117–V118 and B122–B124 (of which B122 was then being employed as a fuel hulk for the generators at the Blohm & Voss shipyard at Hamburg). Plans for converting the four A-III type torpedo boats fitting out at the Armistice (A67 and A83–A85) were also approved, but none of these even got as far as finding a potential mercantile converter.

The concern to remove any chance of the ships ever being completed or rebuilt as warships led to demands by the NIACC that bows and sterns be cut from all unfinished destroyer hulls that were not being scrapped immediately, whether or not a contract yet existed for a mercantile conversion to be carried out. Eventually, a compromise was reached in July 1921 whereby the bow and stern of still-extant unfinished destroyers could be cut off, but only as far

41. ADM 116/1994, 7 February 1920.

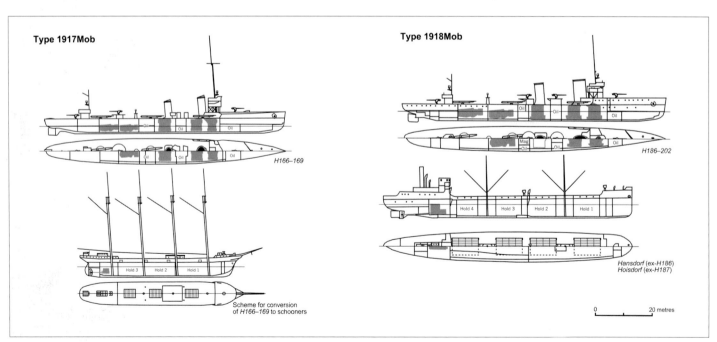

The conversion of destroyers to merchantmen. (AD graphic)

as the waterline, to allow the hulks to be stored afloat until they could be converted; shaft brackets had also to be cut away and all original machinery cleared from the hull to fully meet NIACC requirements.

By the summer of 1921, however, while various unfinished destroyers had had their bow and/or stern cut away and their machinery removed, substantive conversions had been restricted to four ships, all belonging to the 1918Mob type. Two (S178 and S179) had been building at Schichau, Elbing: following the removal of their bows, they had been moved successively to Danzig, then to Bremen, where they were both completed according to the schooner scheme, and entered service with the Bremerhaven firm of F Kimme in 1921. The former S178 became *Franziska Kimme*, passing through various hands until sold for scrap in Brazil in 1935. The ex-S179 entered service as *Georg Kimme*, coming under the French flag in 1928 as *Zazpiakbat*, by 1932 adapted as a refrigerated trawler for employment off the Grand Banks of Newfoundland.[42] Laden with cement, she was scuttled at Martigues, near Marseilles, on 21 August 1944; attempts to refloat her in 1945 failed.

The remaining pair were the Howaldtswerke (Kiel) H186 and H187, which were completed as coasters in early 1921, under the names of *Hansdorf* and *Hoisdorf* respectively. Both went to a Brazilian owner in 1930; the former H186 was sold for scrap in 1935, but her sister passed under the Newfoundland (1931) and British Honduran (1933) flags before being broken up in 1933.

The same basic coaster drawings were approved for the conversion of both the large S113-type and the smaller 1917 Mob-type S152–S157, V158–V163 and H166–H169. Schooner drawings were also provided for H166–H169, but neither coaster nor schooner conversions were taken forward in these cases. A proposal of 5 March 1921 (approved 12 March) was that H166–H169 be converted to oil lighters without propulsion engines but with auxiliary boilers to drive oil pumps and to warm oil. Although bows and sterns had been removed by April, work was then suspended following the receipt of additional requirements from Germanischer Lloyd (the national maritime classification society). This proved to be the end of the vessels, the hulks being scrapped at Kiel before the end of the year. Scrap also proved to be the ultimate destiny of all the remaining potential mercantile conversions from the summer of 1921 onwards, since although a further handful had been sold for conversion, a shipping slump meant that the reconstructions were simply no longer economically viable.

In addition to surface vessels, a large number of submarines had been under construction at the Armistice, and even these were considered for mercantile use after being so stripped 'that re-construction of war vessels would be impossible'. The approach taken was to employ the pressure hulls as oil containers, and use them as the basis for oil lighters and self-propelled tankers (see Appendix 3.1). A dozen hulls were acquired by the firm of Hugo Stinnes, two hulls from U127 class boats being converted into four shore-based oil tanks, and two examples from UB-IIIs were joined together to make an oil-lighter; four more UB-III hulls were turned into oil tanks.

Four larger pressure-hulls were used to build self-propelled tankers at Germania's Kiel yard, although the costs appear to have been high. They employed the hulls of U183, U184, U187 and U188, which they had been building at the yard, the first two forming the basis for *Ostpreussen* (1921), with her engines from another unfinished Germania submarine, U129. The other two hulls went into her sister *Oberschlesien*, whose engines came from U130. Of 3900 GRT (2070 BRT), the resulting vessels were 87.5 metres long overall, with a beam of 12.3 metres, and capable of 10kt. As with the warships entering service in several Allied countries, the mercantile names of these vessels had significance in the post-Versailles geopolitical world of the new German state. East Prussia (Ostpreussen) was now divided from Germany proper by the so-called 'Polish Corridor', while Upper Silesia (Oberschlesien) was partitioned along German-Polish community lines, with the final settlement of the region in 1922. They entered service with the Hamburg-based Hugo Stinnes-Rübeck Montan & Oelwerke AG, but were sold to Italian owners in 1927, *Ostpreussen* becoming *Caucaso* and her sister *Nautilus*. Both ships were lost during the Second World

The tanker *Ostpreussen*, constructed around the pressure hulls of the unfinished submarines U183 and U184. (AD collection)

42. M Boury, 'Le froid appliqué à la conservation du poisson', *Révue générale du froid*, 20/4 (April 1939), pp 103–19; *Le Petit Journal*, 25,480 (20 October 1932), p 4.

War, *Caucaso* (ex-*Ostpreussen*) being beached after being bombed by British aircraft off the Tunisian coast in December 1942, and *Nautilus* (ex-*Oberschlesien*), returned to the German flag as a naval replenishment oiler in July 1942 as *Languste*, was sunk by a British submarine off Sardinia that October.

Surplus to Requirements

Beyond the ships that Germany was explicitly permitted to retain armed under the treaty, the latter placed no limit on what could be kept in disarmed reserve. After the subsequent agreement of an allowance for armed reserve vessels (see p 81, below), however, a wholesale disposal programme was embarked upon regarding the remainder. Although the formal record of the authorisation of armed reserve vessels

M140 was completed as a ferry, ending her career as the restaurant ship *Concord* in Sicily, where she was broken up in 2008. *(AD collection)*

made no reference to such, the Germans later stated that these scrappings were a quid pro quo for this concession.[43] In any case, however, without guns, such vessels would have been of little use, and given the poor financial state of the country, were of far more value as realisable scrap assets.

As well as scrapping surplus vessels in the treaty-controlled categories, the minesweeper force was massively reduced once Germany's obligation to clear minefields under Article 193 of the treaty[44] had been fulfilled, pursuant to which minesweepers had been excluded from the prohibition of completing unfinished ships. The small FM-type coastal vessels had never been particularly satisfactory, and most were stricken during 1919/20, only three being kept for a few years as pilot boats. Some were part of bulk sales to German and foreign interests, making tracing subsequent careers on occasion problematic. The majority became ferries or small cargo vessels, but others found their way into foreign navies, and a few ultimately back to the German navy during the Second World War.

Some seventy-five of the larger M-type minesweepers were stricken during 1920–22, many being sold via intermediate purchasers for further service as merchantmen, some of considerable duration, one lasting as a floating restaurant until 2008. As with the *FM*-boats, a number found their way back into naval service around the world, four being immediately acquired by the Yugoslavian navy, two by that of Italy and ten by that of Argentina, while *M59* ended up in the Latvian navy, and *M42*, after long French mercantile service,

The minesweeper *FM36* was not completed until 1919, and the following year was one of a number of similar vessels sold to a Romanian bank. She then served as the mercantile ferry *Socrates*, until 1941, when she returned to German service as the *Xanten*, numbered *UJ116* the following year. She was finally scuttled in the Black Sea in August 1944. *(AD collection)*

M147 was altered on the stocks as an engines-aft cargo vessel, serving under six names before being renamed *Korrigan IV* in 1938. As such she served until November 1966, when she foundered in the Gulf of California. *(AD collection)*

43. UK–GE conversation, 22 February 32 (TNA ADM 116/2945, p 6).
44. This required that:
Germany will forthwith sweep up the mines in the following areas in the North Sea to the eastward of longitude 4° 00' E. of Greenwich:
(1) Between parallels of latitude 53° 00' N. and 59° 00' N.;
(2) To the northward of latitude 60° 30' N.
Germany must keep these areas free from mines.
Germany must also sweep and keep free from mines such areas in the Baltic as may ultimately be notified by the Governments of the Principal Allied and Associated Powers.

was requisitioned first by the French, and then the German, navy during the Second World War. This left around thirty-five in German navy service, nineteen still being afloat at the end of the Second World War.

Rebuilding

As noted above, Versailles Article 181 allowed Germany six battleships, six light cruisers, a dozen destroyers and a dozen torpedo boats. However, following representations from the German authorities that her ability to deploy her full allowance of ships would be impossible without a reserve of vessels with guns on board to cover for refits or losses, in March 1920 the Allies permitted the retention of an extra pair of battleships and extra cruisers, together with four more destroyers and four torpedo boats. The additional pair of battleships were *Preußen* and *Lothringen*, although no attempt was actually made to replace the guns removed during the war, or the fittings added when they had been converted into minesweeper support ships in 1919. Thus they were, at best, spare-parts reserves for their sisters and half-sisters.

In any case, resources were never sufficient to have more than four battleships fully operational at one time.[45] *Hannover*, the only one of the permitted vessels that had still

Of the six battleships allowed to Germany by the Treaty of Versailles, all but one had been disarmed during the war; this is *Braunschweig*, shown as an accommodation ship at Kiel in 1919. *(US NA 165-WW-330B-034)*

The extensively modernised *Schlesien* passes *Zähringen*, converted to a radio-controlled target, with *Hannover* in the background, at the beginning of the 1930s. *(AD collection)*

been a combatant warship at the Armistice (she had been guardship in the Øresund), was the first battleship to return to service, recommissioning after refit in February 1921. She was followed by *Braunschweig*, a disarmed accommodation ship since 1917, which was recommissioned in December 1921, although not actually rejoining the fleet until 1 March 1922; she became fleet flagship in 1923. *Elsaß* followed her back into service in February 1924, *Hessen* being recommissioned at the beginning of 1925. In addition to the operational battleships, the older *Wittelsbach*-class *Zähringen* survived as a hulk into the 1920s, being then rebuilt as a radio-controlled target during 1926–28.

On 31 January 1926, *Braunschweig* was relieved as fleet flagship by an extensively refitted *Schleswig-Holstein* and paid off for the very last time. The last ship to be reactivated, *Schlesien*, also underwent a major reconstruction before recommission on 1 March 1927, relieving *Hannover*, which went into refit. On her return in February 1930, *Hannover* replaced *Elsaß* on active service, but was herself retired in September 1932, in anticipation of the commissioning of the new armoured ship *Deutschland* the following spring. Although the remaining three old battleships were retired to

Schleswig-Holstein, fleet flagship, leads *Hessen*, *Schlesien*, *Elsaß*, *Nymphe* and *Amazone* during 1928/29. *(AD collection)*

training or target duty over the next few years, all would survive to serve during the Second World War, and down to final dissolution of the German navy.

As far as the cruisers were concerned,[46] the first back in operational service was *Medusa*, which was recommissioned in July 1920, followed by *Hamburg* in September 1920, *Arcona* in May 1921, and *Thetis* in April 1922. The fifth ship to be recommissioned, *Berlin*, re-entered service as a cadet training ship in July 1922. *Amazone* relieved *Arcona* in December 1923, and *Nymphe*, one of the two vessels nominated as a reserve ship, came back into the fleet

45. On the careers of the Reichsmarine's ex-Imperial battleships, see Dodson, *Kaiser's Battlefleet*, pp 157–67.

46. See Dodson, *Warship* [XXXIX] (2017), pp 140–60.

Nymphe as flagship of Flag Officer Light Naval Forces Baltic in the mid-1920s. *(AD collection)*

The first new major German warship, *Emden* (iii), as completed. *(AD collection)*

The last of the old generation of cruisers, *Amazone*, transfers her crew to the new *Köln*. *(AD collection)*

in November 1924, replacing *Thetis*. *Medusa* had paid off two months earler.

The oldest cruiser retained by Germany, *Niobe*, was never to be recommissioned in German service. Under Article 190 of the Treaty of Versailles, cruisers could be replaced twenty years after their launch. As *Niobe* had entered the water on 18 July 1899, her scheduled replacement date almost coincided with the signing of the treaty; thus the 1920 budget included 200 million Marks for *Ersatz-Niobe*. On 3 May 1920, before work began, the German authorities approached the Allies seeking permission to utilise the hull of *Magdeburg*, then being dismantled under Article 186 (see above), for reasons of economy. The request was turned down on the 11th by the NIACC as incompatible with terms of the treaty, but the Germans then appealed to the Commission of Guarantees on the grounds that this decision was economically illogical. The Commission of Guarantees declared itself incompetent in the matter, the issue going to the Allied Conference of Ambassadors in January 1922. The British were in favour of granting the request on economic grounds, but this was opposed by France and Italy on the basis that this would set a precedent for nullifying the letter of the treaty; the request was thus refused on 22 August. The Germans had, however, long since given up on the idea, since *Magdeburg*, as already noted, had been sold for scrap on 28 October 1921, and by August 1922 *Ersatz-Niobe* had been on the building-slip at Wilhelmshaven for some nine months! She was, nevertheless, in most essentials a modernised unit of the *Cöln* class. The new ship having been launched on 7 January 1925 as *Emden* (iii), the old *Niobe* was stricken in June. However, rather than being disposed of for scrap, she was sold to Yugoslavia for further service as a training cruiser under the name *Dalmacija* (cf. p 74, above).

Emden was commissioned on 15 October 1925, and during 1929/30 she was joined by the new K-class cruisers *Königsberg*, *Karlsruhe* and *Köln*, which progressively

Amazone was dismantled as an accommodation hulk, here shown at Kiel alongside *Admiral Hipper* fitting out in the summer of 1939. *(NHHC NH 81934)*

replaced the old ships, the last one left in commission being *Amazone*, paid off in 1931 on her relief by *Köln*. Although stricken, she and some of the others survived in immobile roles into the Second World War, *Medusa* and *Arcona* as anti-aircraft batteries, *Berlin*, *Hamburg* and *Amazone* as accommodation ships.

To provide the Reichsmarine's flotilla craft, the operational torpedo boats were initially to be *T99*, *T101*, *T102*,

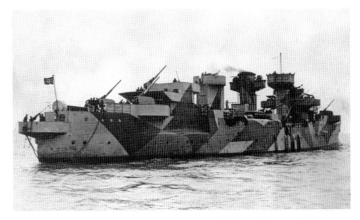

Arcona (shown here) and *Medusa* also became hulks, and were rebuilt as immobile anti-aircraft batteries during the Second World War. *(AD collection)*

Part of the Reichsmarine's destroyer force in the late 1920s, with *S19* and *T185* in the foreground, with three of the *T151–T158* series beyond them. *S19* was the second newest destroyer left to the German navy after the First World War, commissioned in 1913. Despite this, *S19* was stricken in 1931 and broken up in 1935, while the older (but larger) *T185* survived to be allocated to the Soviet Union in 1945. *(AD collection)*

T103, *T104*, *T105*, *T106*, *T107*, *T108*, *T109*, *T110* and *T113*, with *T88* and *T89* (Kiel) and *T86* and *T85* (Wilhelmshaven) as reserve vessels. However, it was then agreed with the Allies early in 1921 that, given the limited military value of the latter ancient vessels, sixteen ships of the *T132–T168* series would become the Reichsmarine's 'torpedo boat' allocation. The vessels selected were *T139*, *T141*, *T143*, *T146*, *T149* and *T168* (Baltic operational), *T144* and *T155* (Kiel reserve), *T151*, *T153*, *T154*, *T156*, *T157* and *T158* (North Sea) and *T148* and *T152* (Wilhelmshaven reserve).

The dozen operational 'destroyers' were originally to be *T185*, *T190*, *T196*, *V2*, *V3*, *V5*, *V6*, *G8*, *G10*, *G11*, *S18* and

S19. However, the list was subsequently adjusted to take into account the state of the various ships, with ships swapped with others from a pool of 'alternates' that initially comprised *S23*, *T151–T156*, *T158*, *T167*, *T168*, *T170* and *T175*. Thus, in March 1920, *G7* was swapped for *V6*, and *S23* for *S19*, the latter joining the group of four ships that were by the summer listed as the four allowed long-term reserves (*S19* and *T175* at Kiel; *V6* and *T170* at Wilhelmshaven). Further changes then occurred, *V1* being withdrawn from the scrap pool to replace *T185* on the 'active' list, the latter going into the reserve pool in place of *T170* at Wilhelmshaven, which was now joined there by *T175*, *V6* going to the 'active' list and replaced by *T190*, which went to the Kiel reserve alongside *S19*. *T170* was stricken on 22 March 1921, along with many of the remaining old torpedo craft in excess of the Versailles allocations (others had already been stricken during 1920). The surviving modern Type A-I boats were stricken in May 1922, and the few remaining older vessels were gone by the end of that year.

Although divided between 'destroyers' and nominally smaller 'torpedo boats' by the Versailles Treaty (which also limited replacement 'destroyers' to 800 tons and 'torpedo boats' to 200 tons), most of the ships listed as 'destroyers' were actually smaller than some of the 'torpedo boats'. This had at its root a decision that torpedo boats built under the 1911 programme should be smaller than those of the 1910 programme, meaning that the most modern vessels were the smaller ones. In allocating ships to treaty headings, a key criterion also seems to have been propulsion, all the

The original *Blitz* was the former *T141*, seen here in 1928, soon after her conversion. *(NHHC NH 88048)*

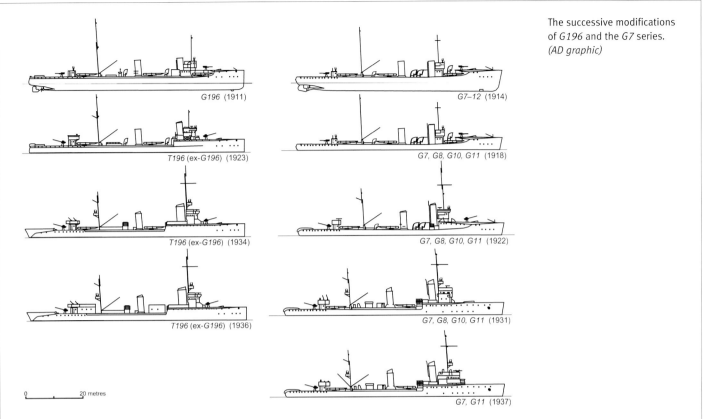

The successive modifications of *G196* and the *G7* series. *(AD graphic)*

G196 (1911)

G7–12 (1914)

T196 (ex-*G196*) (1923)

G7, G8, G10, G11 (1918)

T196 (ex-*G196*) (1934)

G7, G8, G10, G11 (1922)

T196 (ex-*G196*) (1936)

G7, G8, G10, G11 (1931)

0   20 metres

G7, G11 (1937)

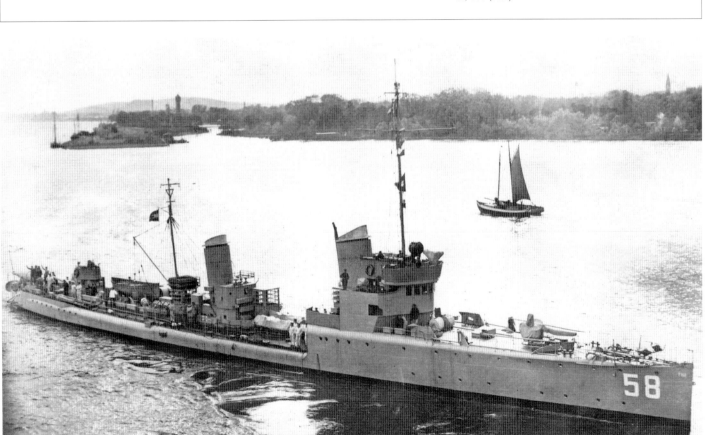

T158 as rebuilt during the 1920s, showing changes typical of the modernised pre-First World War destroyers and torpedo boats. She served through to the end of the Second World War, then operating under the Soviet flag until 1961 (see p 230). *(AD collection)*

T156, sister of *T158*, as built, and showing the scale of the post-war modifications to such boats. *(NHHC NH 65793)*

'destroyers' being turbine-powered, while of the 'torpedo boats' only *T168* had turbines. Nevertheless, in practice, the 'destroyers' and 'torpedo boats' were managed as a single pool, all units of which continued to be designated *Torpedoboot* by the Reichsmarine: it was not until the 1930s that the formal classification of *Zerstörer* was introduced into the German navy.

The first 'destroyers' to be recommissioned were *G7*, *G8* and *G11* on 22 March 1921, after thorough refits,[47] joining *Hannover*, commissioned as the first ship of the Reichsmarine on 10 February. They were followed on 25 May by *S18* and *S23*, and later in the year by *V5* and *G10*. By the beginning of

1923, *G7*, *G8*, *G10*, *G11*, *S18* and *S23* were allocated as the Baltic 'destroyers', with *T139*, *T141*, *T143*, *T144*, *T146* and *T149* as the 'torpedo boats', supporting *Hannover* and the cruisers *Medusa*, *Berlin* and *Thetis*. Attached to the North Sea station were *V1*, *V2*, *V3*, *V5*, *V6* and *T196* as 'destroyers' and *T151*, *T153*, *T154*, *T156*, *T157* and *T158* as 'torpedo boats', alongside *Elsaß*, *Hamburg* and *Arcona*.

Under the Versailles Treaty, destroyers and torpedo boats could be replaced fifteen years after launch, and as the oldest ships had been launched back in 1907, new ships could be begun in 1922. However, these should have been 200-ton 'torpedo boats', so in the event the first ships to be 'replaced' were the smallest 'destroyers', launched in 1911, and thus replaceable in 1926.

47. On these and later refits, see Dodson, *Warship* [XLI], pp 138–44.

Twelve new vessels of the *Möwe/Wolf* (Types 1923/24) were thus built and commissioned between October 1926 and August 1929, although of the ships actually stricken in compensation, only six (*T175*, *V1*, *V2*, *V3*, *V5* and *V6*) were from the declared 'destroyers' list, the other six being nominally 'torpedo boats'. Evidently it was a case of clearing out the least capable vessels rather than strict adherence to the letter of the Versailles Treaty, particularly since further replacements would be subject to the 200-ton 'torpedo boat' replacement limit, a figure that was less than a third of the displacement of the ships that would need to be taken out of service in exchange.

Doubtless it was for this reason that the building of the *Möwe/Wolf* classes was accompanied by the rebuilding of *G7*, *G8*, *G10* and *G11* during 1928–31, including being lengthened amidships, and the extensive refitting of *T185*,

T190 and *T196*. These seven vessels thus represented the most effective of the old destroyers available to the Reichsmarine at the beginning of the 1930s and, with the exception of *T185*, would remain in front-line service until the latter part of the decade.

Again in view of the excessive restriction on 'torpedo boat' tonnage, the next 'replacement' ships were to be for the four 'reserve' destroyers. These were, however, planned as much larger ships, in view of the hope that Versailles limits would in due course be lifted; they emerged as the 2,500-ton Type 1934 (*Z1/Leberecht Maas* class) in 1937. The latter, and the follow-on Type 1934A allowed the old ships to finally be retired. Nevertheless, all were retained in subsidiary roles, some to survive to be distributed among the Allies at the end of the Second World War, one serving into the 1960s (see p 230).

Appendix 3.1[1]

REPORT ON WORK CARRIED OUT ON SURFACE WAR VESSELS UNDER ART.186, PEACE TREATY. AUGUST 1920 AUGUST 1921.

1. <u>CAPITAL SHIPS.</u>

<u>Battleships.</u>

Under construction at the Armistice were two Battleships, "SACHSEN" and "WURTEMBERG".

<u>"SACHSEN".</u> Was building by Krupps at the Germania Werft, Kiel, and was in a very advanced stage nearing completion. Turrets were complete (ex Guns). Main Machinery was complete except a special large 12,000 H.P. Diesel Engine for the middle shaft which was in the Erecting Shop. Casemates for secondary armament were practically complete.

A proposal was sent in to convert this vessel to an Oiler which was approved on 4th September 1920, but apparently owing to difficulties in finding a purchaser owing to the high cost involved no progress was made for months. Eventually the vessel was removed from Germania Werk to the Nord Mole, Kiel, and work proceeded slowly in the direction of demilitarisation.

Subsequent to the decision of the Supreme Council regarding completing the work by 31st July 1921, a visit was paid to the vessel by a combined Committee and definite instructions were outlined in a Protocol date the 27th June as to N.I.A.C.C.'s requirements.

This work involved removal of all armour, destruction of all main machinery on board, destruction of all turrets, destruction of torpedo and splinter protection and armour decks, destruction of all torpedo tubes.

This work has been completed and the vessel is no more than a hulk cut in all directions and her future can only be in the direction of complete breaking up.

<u>"WURTTEMBURG."</u> Sister ship to "Sachsen" (except for machinery). Building at Vulkan Werk, Hamburg. Not so far advanced as "Sachsen" when taken in hand. Her turrets were not complete and her turbines were not installed.

The proposal for conversion of "Sachsen" covered "Wurtemburg" also.

At first the removal of armour turrets proceeded slowly and it was obvious that the firm were anxious to get rid of the vessel. Within the last few months she was shifted to the Abwrackt Werf, Rosshaven, and after the final decisions given on the 13th June at an inspection, and which decisions were subsequently approved in the Protocol, the work has gone on expeditiously and the vessel now has no military value. Her present condition is as follows: All armour has been removed and destroyed, a large quantity being allowed to remain on board for the time being in the destroyed condition owing to the difficulty of transport.

All turrets and their machinery have been destroyed.

The boilers have been destroyed in place.

The armour and protection bulkheads are destroyed.

Secondary gun rings and supports, Conning Tower and supports, and all other military characteristics have been destroyed in a manner similar to that described for "Sachsen".

Although proposals have been approved for the conversion of this vessel for mercantile use, it is practically certain that owing to the high cost of such conversion the final disposal of "Wurtemburg" will be for scrapping.

<u>Battle Cruisers.</u>

At Armistice there were five large Cruisers of one type[2] building:

1.   Graf Spee, at Danzic.
2.   Mackensen, Blohm & Voss, Hamburg.
3.   Erz. Freya, -do.- -do.-
4.   Erz. A, Wilhelmshaven.
5.   Erz. Yorck, Vulkan, Hamburg.

<u>Ersatz "Yorck"</u> had only proceeded to a small extent and the structure erected was destroyed at an early date in 1920.

<u>"Graf Spee"</u>, was removed from Danzic to the Reichwerf, Kiel subsequent to the Armistice and the removal of her military characteristics was begun in a dilatory manner. Her side armour and casemates was removed in an early stage and also the turrets were removed and parts destroyed.

The Boiler Room installation was complete but turbines had not been installed and were allowed to remain in Danzic.

There were no torpedo tubes on board.

Proposals were submitted for the conversion of all Battle Cruisers into Oil Tank steamers and approved by N.I.A.C.C. in September 1902. None of these projects, however, materialised.

In view of the Supreme Council's decision regarding the demilitarisation by 31st July 1921, a detailed list of requirements was made in the Protocol dated 27th June. These instructions were to destroy the boilers remaining in the vessel by cutting. To destroy the Anti-Torpedo and Splinter Bulkheads by cutting large holes. Destroy armour deck by cutting large areas away. Cut out armour bulkheads remaining in vessel. This work has been satisfactorily completed and the vessel has no further value as a warship.

"Mackensen", when first inspected had no armour fitted . Her boilers were said to have been cut up 3 months previously by the builders, Blohm & Voss. There were no torpedo tubes aboard. Proposals for conversion were approved but at present the project has not materialised.

Her present condition is in the form of a hulk in which the only entire parts are the Inner and Outer Bottoms. All military characteristics have been destroyed and the vessel is littered with large areas of plating cut from her thick decks and bulkheads.

Ersatz "Freya". Had only been launched previous to the Armistice and was practically only a hull. She is now being cut to pieces at the Aburackwerk, Rosshaven. Her stern has been cut away and the side plating from the Forecastle to Main Deck at side is hanging loose.

Ersatz "A". This vessel was only half built and not ready for launching. Two Boiler Rooms had Boilers installed and temporarily roofed in. Various projects have been put forward for her conversion, the latest being to use her as an oil hulk with square ends.

Her bow has been cut away for about 100 ft. and her stern is cut right through about 100 feet from the stern post. Torpedo Bulkheads have been destroyed by cutting 40 large holes in them. All boilers have been removed from the vessel.

Light Cruisers. Vessels under construction were as under.:-

Leipsic.	)	
Emden.[3]	)	Building at Weser Werk, Bremen.
Cöln.[4]	)	
Magdeburg.		Building at Howaldtswerk, Kiel.
Frauenlob.		Building at Reichwerft, Kiel.
Wiesbaden.	)	
Rostock.	)	Building at Vulkan, Stettin.

These vessels are of very lightweight construction with a water line belt of Nickel steel plate of 60 mm. thickness which forms the outer bottom and cannot be removed without the vessel collapsing. Proposals were submitted for conversion of these vessels into oilers but at present in no case has the project been taken up.

"Leipzic". Was approaching completion when stopped having had her machinery installed and decked in. Her Torpedo Tubes were laying on the Upper Deck and were destroyed as directed. After proposals for conversion was approved a start was made with the removal of all machinery. The boilers were cut up on board and the turbines lifted ashore. A final list of requirements was drawn up on 14th June but a few days later the vessel was sold to Neugebauer of Lemwerder for breaking up completely. Which work is being carried out very expeditiously.

"Köln." Was not so far advanced as "Leipsic", but the general remarks as regards progress apply to the two vessels, which were sold together to the purchaser.

"Emden." Had not been launched very long when her progress was stopped. Subsequently she was sold to a firm at Hamburg, to be broken up completely at the Kohlen Brand Werk.

"Magdeburg". Was approaching completion when stopped and was removed from Howaldtswerk to the Reichwerk, Kiel. All her spare parts, etc, were laid on the Upper Deck for transport. A first start was made by destroying the Torpedo Tubes and Gun Rings. Her machinery installation was fairly complete with the exception of the L.P. Turbines and Condensers.

The progress with this ship was consistently slow until a sharp letter had been sent by N.I.A.C.C. referring to a proposal to be allowed to retain the vessel. After that progress has been rapid and the whole of the requirements to regard to demilitarisation are complete. Her main bulkheads are cut into pieces in a number of cases and the armour deck cut to pieces forward and aft. In addition a large number of small bulkheads are cut out. This is in addition to the removal of all engines and the destruction of the boilers. Eventual future of the vessel is unsettled but most probably with be complete destruction.

"Weisbaden" and "Rostock", were nearly complete at Stettin, Wiesbaden being further advanced with funnels up and bridges erected. She was towed to a new yard at Lübeck where all machinery destroyed and cleared. Main Bulkheads broken as directed and armour deck destroyed. She is now awaiting a purchaser but the hull is ruined and she is almost certain to be broken up.

"Rostock". The above remarks apply also.

Torpedo Boat Destroyers

There were two classes of destroyers building at the Armistice, "Leaders" and a late type of destroyer, of about 950 tons displacement.

The Leaders were building at:

(a)	Hamburg, Blohm & Voss.	B.122, 123, 124.
(b)	Germania, Kiel.	G.119, 120, 121.
(c)	Vulkan, Stettin.	V.117, 118.
(d)	Schieau, Danzig.	S.114, 115.

G.N.P.C. submitted plans for conversion of these vessels into merchant craft for coastal work, and these were approved on 1st October 1920. In no case has a conversion been carried out and it is anticipated that all vessels will eventually be broken up.

B.122. Was launched as a hulk her after part being unfinished. She has been used as an oil tank by Blohm & Voss for their Electric Engines and will be broken up.

B.123 and 124. Were just beyond launching stage without any machinery on board. After laying for months in an extremely bad condition they were towed to Harburg to have their bows cut off and shafts brackets broken. Of no further use.

G.119, 120, 121. G.119 was launched at Armistice and had only boilers on board. G.120 and 121 were on the slips and were launched to clear the slips.

Present condition: Vessels bought for breaking up at Kiel. Their bows cut off abaft break or forecastle. Boilers in G.119 are destroyed. All Gun supports destroyed. Vessels of no further value except scrap.

V.117, 118. These vessels particularly V.117 were practically complete. V.117 has run trials and was presumably ready for sea. It is understood that the Reichtreuhandgesellschaft have been making efforts for months to see these vessels for conversion but only recently (end of June) had any success been obtained, when the vessels were sold to the shipbreaking firm of Naugebauer for destruction. The cutting away of the bow and destruction of boilers &c was completed by 31st July 1921 and the vessels are now in course of demolition.

S.115, 115. Were towed from Danzic and after various movements eventually were brought to Olltmanns Werk at Ronnebeck, near Bremen. Their bows are cut away as directed, machinery has all been removed, bridges and gun supports destroyed, and shaft brackets cut at the upper arm. Understood that buyer will cut them up as the cost of conversion is too high.

Destroyers.

A large number of these vessels in all stages of construction were in hand at the Armistice:

Howaldtswerke, Kiel, had 6 destroyers under construction.

H.186–7, were approved to be converted in Coasting vessels (motor driven). Their conversion was speedily taken in hand and the vessels proved very serviceable. They were completed in early 1921.

H.166-7-8-9, were bought by a Trading Company for conversion. When last inspected the bows and sterns had been removed together with the forecastles. N.I.A.C.C. therefore have no further interest in them and they were released.

Vulkan, Stettin. Eleven destroyers were building by this Firm.

V.163-3, were on the slips and were cut up in place.

V.160, was damaged in towing away. Was salved and is now converted into a coaster at Hamburg.

V.140, was lost on the Coast of Denmark and is stated to be a complete wreck.

V.141-2-3-4, were bought by a firm and are converting at Wewelsfleth. All work required by N.I.A.C.C. has been carried out. Vessels will be built into lighters or scrapped.

V.158-9-161, are still at Stettin. They have been bought by Shipbreaking firm Neugebauer for scrapping.

Boats built by Schieau, Danzic.

S.152 and S.157, were towed at first to Glueckstadt for conversion. Eventually the option expired and the vessels are being converted by a new firm at Wewelsfleth, near Hamburg.

S.154-5, are at Otto Werk Harburg. Their bows are cut off, Gun supports destroyed, all machinery removed or destroyed, or shaft brackets cut away.

A Boats.

4 vessels were building at the Armistice and all were in an advanced stage. Apparently it has been impossible to sell any for conversion although plans were submitted and approved. The whole number are now sold for destruction.

A.83-4-5, building at Howaldtswerke, were moved down Kiel Haven to a new Aburackwerft for destruction and when last inspected the bows were cut off, shaft brackets destroyed, machinery destroyed or removed, and the mining arrangements at the stern burnt away.

A.67, building at Stettin. Remarks as above. Has been bought for scrap by Neugebauer firm.

From the above reports it will be seen that the whole of the Surface War Vessels have been dealt with in a matter which will effectively prevent their use in any military capacity whatever. And, in addition, it can be seen that in general the proposals for conversion have not been sincere, the ships being unsuitable and too costly to convert. On occasion it has been the duty of the N.I.A.C.C. to call attention to the dilatory methods adopted by the G.N.P.C. and Associated Departments to get progress made, and these dilatory methods have only resulted in a loss off money to the German Government as the prices of metals and even vessels has been continually falling for the last year.

Only a firm ultimatum given at the Conference on 6th June and followed by an approved Protocol of requirements have had the necessary effect of bringing the matter to a satisfactory conclusion.

Submarine Pressure Hulls.

Twelve pressure hulls of various sizes were bought by the firm of Stinnes from the German Government. They had no internal fittings and no outer hull excepting the Regulating Tanks. The disposal of these has been carefully inspected by Officers of the N.I.A.C.C. from time to time and the present condition of these Hulls is given below.

Four hulls 80.00 metres long were brought to Germania Werk, Kiel. Approval was given to convert them into motor oilers by joining together 2 hulls by a ship-shape structure. This work has been carried out, is understood to be satisfactory, but very expensive.

The first vessel, the "Ost Preussen" was completed at the end of June and is on her first voyage.

The second vessel, the "Ober Schliesen" is nearly complete and should leave Kiel early in August 1921.

The vessels are propelled by two Diesel motors of 900 HP. each and have a speed of about 11? knots.

2 hulls of 65.00 metres length lay at Rendsburg for months. They are now at Harburg where they are being cut into two pieces to be lifted ashore as fixed oil tanks.

6 smaller pressure hulls 41.5 metres long.

2 are being built together into an oil tank lighter at the Wolkau Works, Hamburg. As the work is far advanced no further interest is taken in them, as the possibilities of future use in submarines is out of the question.

4 others of similar size are at Otto Werk, Harburg. They are to be used as tank-lighters and sufficient cutting has been done before 31st July 1921 to prevent their use in submarine form at any future date.

Submarine U.1, was inspected at München. She is to be used for exhibition purposes, and this has received the approval of the N.I.A.C.C.

U.B.3. An old small coastal boat was found at Neugebauer Works. G.N.P.C. made repeated efforts to obtain permission to use the vessel for various purposes, but the demolition was insisted on by N.I.A.C.C. and carried out.

[signed]
29/7/21

Notes
[1] From TNA ADM 116/1994; spellings and typography as found in the original document.
[2] Actually, *Ersztz-Yorck* was being built to a considerably modified design.]
[3] Actually *Ersatz-Emden*.]
[4] Actually *Ersatz-Cöln*.]

Appendix 3.2 THE REUSE OF EX-GERMAN SUBMARINE ENGINES IN THE UK

The recycling of parts from German submarines made a contribution to the post-war British industrial landscape, which has been very little studied and one that ensured they were distributed far and wide. The hulls were to be simply broken up for scrap; Cohen's were the only firm whose representative spoke to the press about their plans for the submarines purchased on 3 March 1919. They stressed that steel plates would go to patch up 'torpedoed British boats' and envisaged that, as was characteristic of shipbreaking activity in British yards throughout the nineteenth and twentieth centuries, some souvenirs might be made available to the public.[5]

As may be seen from Table 1/1, the boats' diesel engines had a significant commercial value in their own right, especially in view of the perceived superiority of German engineering (cf. below). Thus, in the first wave of sales of boats for scrap in early 1919, they were sold separately from the hulls, albeit often to the same purchaser (the breaker who had to separate them from the hull in the first place). These engines regularly changed hands at prices close to those of the hulls to which they had originally belonged: for example, the Tyneside-based breaker Hughes Bolckow paid £2,000 for two engines from U9, while the rest of the boat only went for £475 more.

The engines were then widely cascaded from the breakers' yards to specialist engineering subcontractors for refurbishment, which also provided employment for former naval crew with experience of working with diesels.[6] They were then sold on at some profit, with £9,000 realised from the sale of four engines, two from U100 and two from U164, to Southend Corporation.

Although Article 189 of the Treaty of Versailles (see p 33) enjoined that machinery salvaged from the breaking of warships or submarines in Germany should not be reused in a military context, but only for industrial or commercial purposes, this did not, of course, apply to Britain. The repurposing of material from the German submarines surrendered to Britain was, however, parallel to, and consistent with, the principles articulated in that clause. It also extended over a similar period of time. An initial deadline of 31 March 1921 for the conversion of submarine engines remaining in Germany to civil purposes was not met and was therefore extended to December 1921. From the British point of view, it is clear that their interest in these engines was likewise primarily commercial and technical, and that the former German submarine engines had largely found their new homes by the end of 1921.

Nevertheless, and despite the at times virulent anti-submarine rhetoric expressed on the part of the press and public, there were some 'mingled feelings' over the 'wholesale destruction' of 'the wonderful amount of scientific and technical ingenuity' of the ex-German submarines, particularly by those who had taken the opportunity to see them for themselves while on tour.[7] The proposed reuse of their engines and other components in 'peaceful industries', was, however, regarded as a 'consolation' by some. The only exception to the otherwise civil and commercial repurposing of German submarine engines in the UK were

apparently the two recycled from U126 in 1923 into the Royal Navy's HMS/M X1, commissioned in 1925 (see p 56). These are also the only two engines whose post-war history appears to be securely recorded in a maritime context.

Even so, the Admiralty presented 'several British firms who make a speciality of building internal combustion engines' with examples from surrendered U-boats for technical examination. Contemporaries recognised that this was not necessarily a 'benevolent' act but one of outsourcing 'for the Navy's benefit',[8] with applications for future capital ship development.

Some engines found ready buyers among engine specialists, either for immediate use or for reconditioning purposes and onward sale, one engine from UB67 going to the National Fuel Oil Co. while UB120's engines were purchased by Wick Diesel Oil Engines Ltd for £500 each. The Disposal Board ordered the sale of two engines from unnamed German submarines, one developing 3,000bhp and a smaller engine of 300bhp at Newcastle in December 1921, with engines still available by March 1922.[9] On the other hand, the majority of the ex-submarine diesel engines whose subsequent commercial history can be traced had already been installed at the premises of their new owners – on land. Another set of engines were used in a cement works in the Medway (see p 101). It is unclear how long they were retained at the cement works, but it was certainly no longer extant by 1982.

Engines were often conveniently purchased from a local shipbreaking yard or other business, clearly keeping both transportation and installation costs down.[10] In other cases, the engines travelled some distance from breaker to buyer, sometimes via an intermediary. Southend Corporation received some of their engines from Swansea, via reconditioning at Belliss & Morcom of Birmingham, who ultimately supplied six engines to the corporation.[11]

Southend's acquisition of these six engines for three sites at London Road, Southend, Leigh-on-Sea and Thorpe Bay, formally opened in May 1922, received widespread publicity. Together, the three sites generated electricity to service the local tramway system, with the Leigh and Thorpe Bay termini at either end and the London Road depot at the centre of the system.[12] Southend was by no means the only local authority to invest in diesel engines from German submarines, and recycling of engines in similar contexts appeared to be a popular option for purchasers which also generated interest among engineering societies for examination on days out.

Reuse of German submarine engines among local authorities to generate power is also attested elsewhere, at Guildford, Harrogate, Wisbech and York in England, and Larne in Northern Ireland. In the case of Guildford, Larne, and Wisbech, their respective source submarines were not identified in the press: the news of the two latter purchases actually comes from a Lancashire newspaper, suggesting that

---

5 For example, *Chelmsford Chronicle*, 8,060 (7 March 1919), p 5.

6 Grand Fleet Fund, advertisement, *Western Morning News* 18,985 (10 January 1921), p 1.

7 *Western Daily Press*, 18,992 (30 April 1919), p 5.

8 *Hampshire Telegraph*, 3,747 (13 April 1920), p 7.

9 *Yorkshire Post*, 23,224 (3 December 1921), p 3; *Worthing Gazette*, XXXIX/35 (1 March 19 22), p 6.

10 P O'Driscoll, 'WW1 Medway U-boats', *After the Battle* 36 (1982), p 36.

11 'Diesel Engines at Southend on Sea', *The Engineer* 133 (1922), 21, p 578.

12 As depicted on Ordnance Survey 1:2500 Epoch 4 mapping (1919–39) for Southend-on-Sea.

their origins might have been in one of the submarines broken up by Ward at Morecambe or Preston, an easily accessible source for Northern Ireland.[13] The two sets of engines for Yorkshire were, however, named, despite the characteristic press conflation of the *U-/UB-* prefixes which occasionally obscure submarine identities in contemporary news articles (and did so in this case).

Thus, Harrogate is said to have received its engine from *U25*, but this attribution must be incorrect, since *U25* was surrendered directly to France and broken up at Cherbourg. It is more likely to have been sourced from *UB25*, which was sold to Cohen's in its entirety and dismantled by them, including the deck gun still mounted on the submarine.[14] From Cohen's the engines were re-sold to H G Nicholson at £8 per ton. The two engines were then purchased by Harrogate Corporation for £15,000.[15] York sourced theirs for the Foss Islands Road generating station from *U63*, broken up at Blyth.

The chief advantage of ex-submarine engines for electricity supply was their ready availability at a time when domestic plant was difficult to obtain owing to the exigencies of the war. This exacerbated the issues faced by local authorities of inadequate power generation from the existing plant in the face of increasing local demand. For Harrogate the submarine engines 'offered for sale by the Government' were 'just the very thing'. The ambitions of Harrogate's electricity generation scheme went beyond adequate capacity to meet local demand. The Borough Engineer aimed to harness the hot water that was a waste by-product of the generating process and distribute it to spas and hotels in the town, and thereby benefit its tourist industry.

There was public disappointment in Worthing in March 1922 that a domestically produced plant had been chosen over a former German engine to supply electricity, but the local council had preferred to stick with the existing supplier on grounds of proven reliability.[16] Other authorities turned them down as not fit for their projected purpose: 'the second-hand submarine Diesel engines up [to] 1500 B.H.P which are advertised for sale, are quite unsuitable for continuous running' was the reason given at Kirkcaldy.[17] There were also warnings against employing ex-German engines in electricity generation, a possible future difficulty in sourcing of spares being cited as an issue (cf. the experience of running the ex-German diesels in HMS/M *X1*: p 56, above).

Such was the interest generated by the reconditioning and installation of these engines that day trips to examine them proved a popular attraction for local engineering societies during the early 1920s. On 19 July 1921 members of the Gloucestershire Engineering Society visited Belliss & Morcom in Birmingham where they were 'engrossed' in examining a German submarine engine currently being refurbished, probably one of those later installed at Southend.[18] They had wide academic and technical appeal and the Admiralty presented the Applied

Science Department of Sheffield University with the starboard engine from a German submarine in 1920, albeit one that was from a captured (presumably *UB110* [p 24]), rather than surrendered, vessel. A further engine was promised to the Belfast Technical Institute in the same year.[19]

Elsewhere, some former German diesel engines were put to use in modern media, for example in powering radio transmission.[20] Another engine was reported by its owners in October 1921 to have gone to one of the two Gaumont-British film studios (Lime Grove or Islington, both since demolished). Although footage was shot of the engine *in situ*, its stated provenance appears unlikely: it was attributed to *Deutschland/ U155*, which may be a piece of studio publicity,[21] given the explosion in *Deutschland*'s engine room as the engines were being stripped in September that year. An engine from a different submarine would appear more plausible.

Among the more unusual recipients of ex-enemy diesel engines was the brewing trade. An unidentified set of engines is reported as being put to use in a similarly unidentified Midlands brewery in 1920.[22] In the same year a submarine engine installed at the Stag Brewery premises of Watney, Combe, Reid Ltd. at Pimlico, London, attracted some publicity. Their engine was said to have been sourced from *U35* and seems, in common with many, to have travelled a significant distance to London from the breaking yard at Blyth, although as a coal port Blyth offered the facilities for easy onward transportation as an additional cargo aboard a collier. The extraction of *U35*'s Krupp two-stroke engines caused some difficulties, as the submarine heeled over and filled over the course of three tides before the engine could be got out.[23] It is not known how long the engine remained in use with Watney's, but it was certainly no longer extant by 1959 when they left the site: only the street name of Stag Lane, SW1, remains to commemorate the site where once their brewery stood.

Other engines are said to have provided power for the British Empire Exhibition at Wembley in 1924, therefore having a connection with one of London's more iconic structures. Again, no trace now remains of these engines, with some buildings demolished after the exhibition closed in 1925 and the entire structure torn down in 2002. One set of engines is reported as having been exported to New Zealand,[24] not only dispersing components far and wide but also to a part of the world that had, during the war itself, been beyond the reach of German submarines.

Smaller components were sometimes rapidly extracted and cascaded for public sale shortly after acquisition: for example, by mid-April 1919, within weeks of their purchase of twenty-five submarines, Cohen's were advertising 'several hundred' accumulator cells from 'enemy submarines' for sale 'cheap to clear'.[25] Other parts such as ventilation systems also

13 Both evidently press releases, widely reproduced verbatim in many different publications at home and abroad; for Guildford, see, for example, *Pall Mall Gazette*, 17,196 (3 July 1920), p 3; for Wisbech and Larne, the *Lancashire Evening Post*, 10,520 (12 March 1920), p 3, has been identified as the primary text.

14 British Pathé, *Old Iron*, c.1919.

15 *Yorkshire Evening Post*, 9,205 (19 March 1920), p 5.

16 *Worthing Gazette*, XXXIX/35 (1 March 1922), p 6.

17 *Fife Free Press*, 2,617 (19 March 1921), p 3.

18 *Gloucester Journal*, 10,373 (23 July 1921), p 8.

19 *Sheffield Daily Telegraph*, 30 April 1920, p 4; *Belfast News-Letter*, 32,728 (26 March 1920), p 8.

20 Attributed to the '2LO transmitter at Daventry' in O'Driscoll, *After the Battle* 36. 2LO is probably correct, as it was opened in 1922, but this was in London. Daventry was opened in 1925, which seems too late for the incorporation of a former U-boat engine. Its code was 5XX.

21 *Around the Town Cinemagazine*, 100 (27 October 1921), leading with footage of generating plant at the studio: this edition discussed in detail in *Shields Daily News*, 19,563 (11 November 1921), p 2.

22 *Lancashire Evening Post*, 10,520 (12 March 1920), p 3.

23 *Daily Herald*, 26 February 1920, p 3.

24 O'Driscoll, *After the Battle* 36, p 41.

25 *Sheffield Daily Telegraph*, 19,903 (23 April 1919), p 3.

found buyers: a system extracted from a former German submarine found 'therapeutic use' in a medical context and survives in the collections of the Wellcome Trust.[26]

There is therefore a well-attested record of engines and other components from former German submarines contributing in various ways to Britain's industrial, commercial and civic needs – widely

---

26 A625562, Science Museum, London, on loan from the Wellcome Trust <https://collection.sciencemuseum.org.uk/objects/co143054/part-of-u-boat-ventilation-system-german-1910-19-ventilation-systems>.

dispersed in location and in ultimate function. The part they played was, however, an impermanent one. They served industries that were either very much of their time and long-since defunct in a British context, such as tramways, or industries that have developed and closed down over the course of time, such as the early film industry in Britain, when they were no longer fit for purpose. Their exact disposal under new ownership remains untraced, but it would appear that little or nothing survives of these components in a British industrial archaeology context. The maritime archaeology, however, is a different story.

Appendix 3.3 AN ARCHAEOLOGY OF FORGOTTEN SHIPS

The events of 21 June 1919, when the major part of the German High Seas Fleet was so dramatically scuttled at Scapa Flow, dominated contemporary headlines and have since come to overshadow the wider post-war narrative of the German fleet. The outrage expressed by the British press and public, and to some extent by the Admiralty, at the mass scuttling and its subsequent impact on the peace negotiations, did not quite eclipse the previous contemporary interest in the German navy's submarines, but their far less dramatic fates generally attracted little attention. Thus, while the archaeological remains at Scapa Flow are well known today, a more obscure heritage of tangible remains of German naval craft lies scattered around the English coastline.

Public sentiment had been coloured by wartime events such as the torpedoing of the *Lusitania* (1915) by *U20*, although strict censorship over shipping losses and naval operations, particularly from 1917 onwards, ensured that details of many casualties would only emerge in the immediate post-war era. Official histories and naval memoirs published throughout the 1920s, and films such as *Q-Ships* (1928), thus kept wartime shipping casualties high in the public consciousness until well into the 1930s. Nevertheless, public interest largely dwindled away following the submarine tours of winter 1918/19 (see pp 19–21), although the occasional submarine could make the news. Officialdom also exhibited a similar weariness of the subject: given that the boats were in any case intended for destruction, if that destruction came about accidentally rather than through the officially sanctioned course, it was of no great moment.

This factor has contributed to the fact that, despite their relatively recent date, size, steel construction and formal reporting procedures, not all wartime and related post-war sinkings (of warships, submarines or indeed any type of vessel) have been definitively located, with significant scope for confusion in both the archaeological and documentary

German submarines laid up at Harwich. (*Abrahams*)

evidence. Similarly, as has been previously noted, the surviving record is sometimes incomplete, and published sources riddled with inaccuracies. Indeed, the archaeology of the German fleet after 1918 is a case study in how difficult it can be to ascertain fully what happened to a number of ships that did not make it as far as the breakers, and their locations today. This appendix considers the topic of such lost vessels collectively, and the way in which a given set of archaeological remains can shed light on others; some of this evidence is presented here for the first time.

By 1 December 1918 there were 122 German submarines moored several abreast along 'U-boat Avenue' at Harwich, becoming a temporary feature of the river landscape, thinned out by the more robust submarines immediately going on tour, followed by the sales from March 1919 onwards. By 12 September 1919 'U-boat Avenue' had dwindled to twenty-four hulks, stripped of their engines and periscopes.[27]

A clue to the temporary landscape of the winter of 1918/19 is clearly charted even today southeast of Erwarten Ness, off the northern bank of the Stour. With so many submarines lying several abreast, it was an accident waiting to happen: *UB117* sank at her moorings, triggering a

German submarines laid up at Harwich. (*Abrahams*)

---

27 *Chelmsford Chronicle* 8,087 (12 Sep 19), p 6.

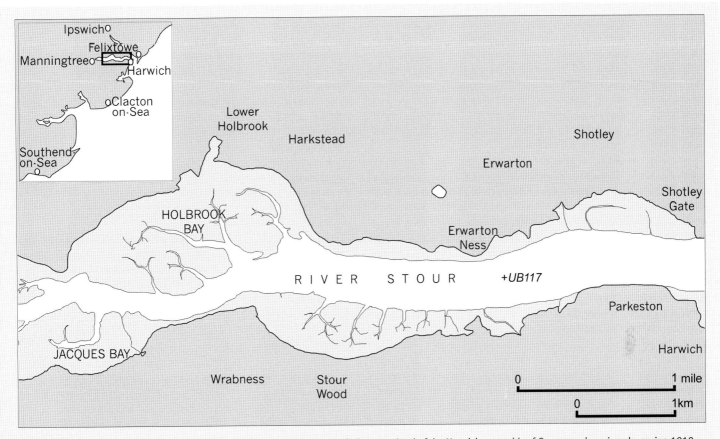

The wreck of *U117* as charted, illustrating the approximate seaward limit of what remained of the Harwich assembly of German submarines by spring 1919, based on wreck records, documentary evidence, and aerial photographs. *(AD Graphic)*

chain reaction, as *UB105* then fouled the wreck and capsized, in turn taking down *UB101* with her. By 14 September 1920 both *UB101* and *UB105* had been cleared as navigational hazards, but a buoy still marked the wreck of *UB117*.

UB105 had in fact been sold to George Cohen, Sons & Co. for £1,900 on 3 March 1919, following the acceptance of their tender for twenty-five submarines.[28] This sum was later refunded, suggesting that she sank after the time of purchase, and demonstrating that she was considered the most badly damaged of the three submarines, having been in contact with *UB117* and *UB101* on either side. Yet it would not be until 1 April 1920 that *UB101* and *UB117* were finally sold, suggesting that the expense of salvage was a difficulty for both current owner and prospective purchasers. Eventually all were sold on for much lower sums: *UB101* and *UB117* at £200 each on 1 April 1920, and the more severely damaged *UB105* on 14 May for £100 to the Stanlee Shipbreaking & Salvage Company of Dover, to be broken up at their site on the Stour at nearby Felixstowe, which at least minimised transportation costs.

By 14 September 1920 Stanlee had cleared *UB101* and *UB105*, but in the end it would be *UB117* that remained *in situ* until at least 1926, when her wreck buoy was removed. There is sufficient uncertainty over the extent of dispersal for her to remain charted by the United Kingdom Hydrographic Office (UKHO) at the time of writing, revealing the location of at least one of the vessels formerly moored along 'U-boat Avenue'.[29]

Such vestigial survivals post-dispersal are reasonably common in riverine environments in a UK-wide context, even for vessels cleared by explosives operations, such as those undertaken by the Mersey Docks and Harbour Board between the mid-nineteenth to mid-twentieth centuries. Even though no longer posing a hazard to navigation, reduced vessels may survive several feet proud of the seabed.[30]

UB117's fate illuminates that of the old *U3* – the most elderly boat to be surrendered (cf. pp 17–18) – whose history remains the most obscure of all the surrendered submarines. On 1 December 1918 *U3* arrived at Harwich, where she was sold on 3 March 1919 for £2,050 to T W Ward for breaking. The Admiralty Sales Ledger notes '[s]ank in tow; purchase price refunded + £10-2-2 interest'. The latter represented 0.5 per cent of the purchase price, together with a similar refund of the £2 13s 6d insurance premium. However, the details of her loss cannot be identified from the admittedly scant surviving records. On the other hand, the scale of the refunds, unique among the surrendered submarines, has a bearing on *U3*'s possible location. A potential search area between Harwich and Preston initially appears near impossible to resolve with any one of a number of natural hazards en route, but, despite the sparse documentary evidence, it may be possible to suggest where she might now lie.

Her very sale in March 1919 indicates that she was then regarded by both seller and purchaser as capable of removal, despite being the oldest submarine surrendered, yet the premium refund was accompanied by a note in Ward's archives that stated *U3* 'sank before delivery',[31] in other

---

28 *Sheffield Daily Telegraph*, 19,858 (4 March 1919), p 8.

29 As at 2019: UKHO No.14678.

30 Based on observation and analysis of the National Record of the Historic Environment (NRHE) shipwreck database, Historic England.

words, she did not undertake the voyage for which she had been insured. This would otherwise have attracted a payout rather than a refund under the terms of the Marine Insurance Act, 1906, which further stipulated that '[w]here the consideration for the payment of the premium totally fails, and there has been no fraud or illegality … the premium is thereupon returnable to the assured.'[32] Ward's were understandably keen to insure *U3*, having very nearly lost the also elderly *U9* under the tow of a government tug while putting into Dover on 13 March, although that vessel ultimately made it to the yard in May.

Ward's then began to remove some of their other submarine purchases out of Harwich to their yards at Preston and Morecambe during May/June 1919. Attempts were made, though not systematically, to record removal dates against a list of submarines sold, an attempt apparently abandoned after 12 June 1919, when the last addition to the document marked the foundering of *UB60* (see next page). *U3* was thus implicitly still at Harwich on that date.[33] Ward's then commissioned a now-untraced report from Lloyd's during 20–25 July 1919,[34] which at least provides a *terminus ante quem* for the date of the wreck event, and probably confirmed the grounds for refund. This implies that she was sufficiently close inshore to be accessible for inspection by Lloyd's surveyor, making the scenario of foundering significantly offshore rather less probable.[35]

The July report suggests that her condition was discovered as Ward's began removing their purchases from Harwich. Surrounded by other submarines, any pre-sale inspection is likely to have been cursory at best, and her condition would only have become apparent when no longer supported by neighbouring submarines, so in this respect her fate differs from *UB101*, *UB105* and *UB117*. It seems likely that she was among the twenty-four hulks remaining at Harwich by September 1919, as no record has been traced for her onward sale or disposal, suggesting that she was by now also irrecoverable, joining *UB117* as tangible, albeit as yet unlocated, remains at Harwich. The apparent lack of surviving records for the *U3's* demise is in particularly marked contrast to a number of well-recorded submarine wreck events on the English Channel coast around this time, although, again, some attracted little attention (official or otherwise) and no others would result in a refund.

Submarines that were driven ashore by force of weather were more likely to come to public notice and be better documented than those that disappeared into mud and obscurity or foundered under tow. For example, on 15 April 1919, *U118* and *UB121*, both allocated to France, went ashore on the Sussex coast while under tow to Brest escorted by the French destroyer *Francis Garnier*. *U118* went ashore at Hastings just in time for the Easter weekend commencing 18 April, presenting an opportunity to raise money for the local mayor's Fund for the Welcome

Home of the Troops.[36] She was, however, clearly a nuisance for a public beach for the forthcoming high season and was sold a month later. She would be broken up *in situ* over the next two years, with her purchasers, the south coast firm of James Dredging Co., well placed to carry the material away by sea.

By contrast, *UB121* drove ashore in a less accessible location under the cliffs near Birling Gap, striking the recent wreck of the SS *Oushla* under Bailey's Brow, and being wrecked in her turn. Her relative inaccessibility failed to deter contemporary souvenir hunters, who were summonsed for taking what was not theirs.[37] Like *U118*, *UB121* was subsequently broken up *in situ* for scrap, but fragments survive beside the remains of the *Oushla* and may still be discerned today,[38] and in this respect *UB121* is typical of wrecks in cliffside locations and one of a select group of 'wreck-on-wreck' remains.

UB121 provides an interesting case-study in the history of the mis-identification of ex-German submarines over the years. Although contemporary press reports, and the Admiralty Sales Ledger make clear that the boat that went aground at Birling Gap was indeed *UB121*, the 'standard sources' list *UB121* as surrendered to France, used in underwater explosion tests, and broken up at Toulon in July 1921. As a result her wreck has been confused with that of *UB21*, resulting in a complicated theory of salvage and re-sinking.[39]

Breaking tow on their final voyages to the shipbreakers became something of a theme for former German submarines lost around the English coast, a fate they shared with their British counterparts (starting with *Holland 5*, in 1912), disposed of pre-war, and can be regarded as a characteristic of the archaeology of early twentieth-century submarines in English waters. With engines inoperable, or with these missing entirely (cf p 24), they were simply helpless if inclement weather or rough seas broke their tow ropes.

The remains of a submarine that could not be retrieved under such circumstances almost certainly lie off the Devon coast after foundering very suddenly under tow on 12 June 1919. This wreck has been attributed to both *U60* and *UB60* (both boats being recorded in the Admiralty Sales Ledger as lost in tow) but, while the sinking of *UB60* is clearly recorded, the loss of *U60* is, like that of *U3*, much more obscure. The fates of *U60* and *UB60* are intertwined and quite genuinely coincidental beyond their similar numbers: they were indubitably sold to the same shipbreaker (Cohen's) at the same location (Chatham), whence both were consigned to Cohen's premises at Swansea. It is therefore a question of whether the two vessels were also lost at the same time and place or sequentially in separate incidents. The contemporary press reported that *U60* foundered under tow from Chatham to Swansea 9 miles southeast of Berry Head, Devon, on 12 June 1919, while *UB60* is recorded as lost under tow off Start Point, Devon, on 12 June 1919.[40] As *U118* and *UB121* attest, it was not uncommon for submarines to be towed together on the same voyage, but there is no evidence that this was the case here.

Sources for wreck events typically vary by details originating perhaps

31 Ward's records on insurances, Shipbreaking Archive, Marine Technology Special Collections, University of Newcastle.

32 *Marine Insurance Act, 1906*, 6 Ed 7, Ch.41 <www.legislation.gov.uk/ukpga/ 1906/41/pdfs/ukpga_19060041_en.pdf>, with specific reference to s.84(i).

33 ADM 116/1975.

34 Personal communication with Ian Buxton, Marine Technology Special Collections, University of Newcastle, 29 October 2018.

35 The only source for her foundering under tow, perhaps implicitly at sea, is the Admiralty Sales Ledger. Examination of T W Ward's company records (Sheffield Archives) has yielded no further information concerning the event or place of loss: similarly, the event appears to be unrecorded in the contemporary press, suggesting that a dramatic foundering event was less likely (although even those could escape press attention).

36 *Hastings and St Leonard's Observer*, 3,209 (19 April 1919), p 2.

37 *Sussex Agricultural Express*, 8,188 (26 March 1920), p 3.

38 CITiZAN, *UB121* Sketchfab model,<sketchfab.com/models/75b416510a 26498f8850f06640df81b6> 2016. Not charted by UKHO.

39 McCartney, *Lost Patrols*, pp 104–5.

40 For example, in the *Sheffield Daily Telegraph*, 19,944 (13 June 1919), p 4. *UB60* is reported lost the same day off Start Point in TNA ADM 116/1975.

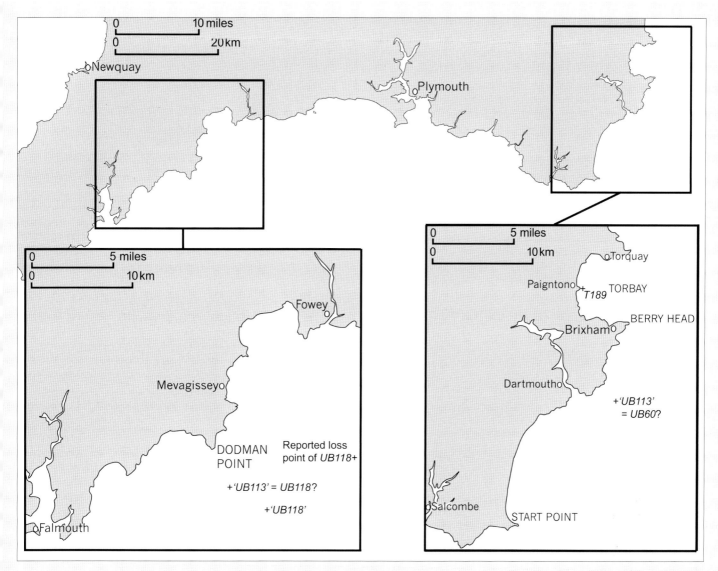

Map of the Berry Head/New Stone/Start Point area, showing the wreck-points of *U113*, *U118* and '*U60*'. *(AD graphic)*

from different locations or witnesses, suggesting multiple wrecks, but which can normally be reconciled into a fully fleshed account of a single casualty, which seems to be the case in this instance. The same detailed report from a direct witness, the towing tug *Knight Templar*, with a very distinctive manner of loss, and clearly in the singular, was widely cited in the press for *U60* on 12 June 1919: 'the submarine foundered unexpectedly, going down stern first nine miles south-east of Berry Head.' This more specific position approximates to a point east of Start Point and therefore corresponds well to the official location, albeit for *UB60*, as lost 'off Start Point'.

That *U60* was lost after *UB60* is implied by the aforementioned (p 96) annotated list of submarines sold. Notes were apparently added as removals progressed, with the last annotation being the loss of *UB60* off Start Point on 12 June 1919: at this point *U60* remained unannotated and thus presumably still, as listed, at Chatham. The characteristic interchangeability of U-boat prefixes in documentary sources has therefore played its part in obscuring the respective fates of the two submarines, and *UB60* must be the vessel to which press reports, ostensibly regarding *U60*, refer.

It would thus appear that *U60* was, after all, not lost on the same occasion as *UB60*, but on a similar subsequent voyage, for which no records up to the cut-off date for disposal at the end of June 1921 have survived. In any case, given the coverage of *U118* and *UB121* just a couple of months earlier, the foundering of two former German submarines under the same circumstances is likely to have been newsworthy in its own right, circumstantially supporting a consecutive loss event for *U60*.

Indeed, the case of *U60* and *UB60* illustrates a key difficulty of locating shipwreck archaeology. Even the most carefully recorded wreck positions are subject to variables such as the weather, tidal conditions, instrumental accuracy and the sheer struggle to survive, which may throw them out by some miles. It is common for wrecks to be identified at some distance from the position recorded in contemporary reports, a difficulty shared by other submarines in the post-war disposals group.

UB60 can at least be identified with some certainty in the right area, and off the Mew Stone has been mapped a wreck labelled 'UB113 POSSIBLY'. While it cannot be *UB113*, which was sunk off Zeebrugge (and may be a copying-error for *UB118* – see just below), the identification suggests that the wreck might be that of UB-III type vessel – as was *UB60*. The location, between Berry Head and Start Point, would appear to reconcile the two reported loss-locations of UB60, and thus be characteristic of wreck sites lying some distance from the originally-reported position of loss.

There are no similarly obvious candidates for *U60* among these or any other wreck sites so far discovered off the coast of Devon, the one tempting wreck, 7 miles to the southeast of the potential *UB60*, proving (by its possession of four bow torpedo tubes) to be of the wrong (*U81*) class.[41] On the other hand, off the Kent coast there lie a number of unidentified submarines of the First World War era that remain so far unmatched with reported submarine losses. Any one of these, such as a site off the South Foreland formerly believed to be *U11*, would similarly lie on the route from Chatham to Swansea, its fate obscured by lying in a submerged landscape with a high concentration of wartime losses, and have a claim to be considered as a candidate for *U60*.[42]

The remains of *U90*, which foundered under tow to Belgium on 29 November 1919 off St Catherine's Point, Isle of Wight, form a perfect example of a submarine wreck positively identified at some distance from the reported position, after two previous 'false starts'. Such initial mis-identifications are not only characteristic of wreck archaeology as a whole, but apply particularly to wrecks of the First World War and the immediate post-war period, which lie in a landscape of war.

A hydrographic report of 1919 for the *U90* specifies a position of loss '12 miles SE x E 0.5 E of St. Catherine's Light'. The three sites successively attributed to the *U90* illustrate a wide search area, with two discarded sites further east at 7.7 miles and 8.2 miles southeast of Dunnose Point, respectively.[43] The site now definitively identified as *U90*,[44] with a towing hawser still attached to her bows after a century, lies much closer to St Catherine's Point at just over 6.5 miles distant than the position quoted in the original hydrographic report.[45]

To date, however, despite undergoing a similar process of successive attributions as *U90*, the site of *UB118* has not been positively identified on the seabed. She is recorded as having foundered off Dodman Point, south Cornwall, where two potential wrecks exist. One has been, like the potential *UB60*, been labelled by the UKHO as 'UB113' since its discovery in 1977;[46] this label may have its origins in a misreading of 'UB118'. The location of 'UB113' is within 5½ miles of the recorded position of *UB118*'s sinking on her voyage between Devonport and Falmouth and has been identified by divers as a type UB-III vessel,.[47] although not relocated in a 2014 survey, the ground being classified currently as 'foul'. There is, however, a second candidate, also off the Dodman, two miles further out to sea, which has actually been labelled by the UKHO as 'UB118'.[48] However, its status as a submarine wreck remains unclear, the UKHO currently classifying the 'UB118 wreck' as 'dead'. This may not, however, exclude the presence of archaeological material, perhaps completely buried; the remains of a tug in any case seem to lie nearby. .

T189 on the rocks at Roundham Head, near Torbay; her remains still lie there. *(AD collection)*

On 12 December 1920 the German destroyers *S24* and *T189* broke tow while en route from Cherbourg to Teignmouth for breaking, as their tug attempted to put into Torbay for shelter in the teeth of a snowstorm, going ashore in different locations in the same general vicinity, like *U118* and *UB121*. Their subsequent fates were a result of the different terrain at their respective stranding sites. *S24* went ashore on Preston Sands, and as she was 'high and dry' at low water, despite being badly damaged, salvage was a viable proposition and she was recovered within days.[49] On the other hand, *T189* went ashore 'on a rocky bottom' under Roundham Head, and was predicted to become a total wreck. The wreck was sold on, and although salved *in situ* and today uncharted, was more difficult to access and salvage, so that some remains persist to the present day.

Overlapping with accidents at sea en route to the breakers during 1919/20 was a subsequent phase of planned experiments and trials at sea over the course of 1920–22, likewise represented in a legible submerged archaeological landscape. The submarine trials at Falmouth (see pp 51–53) between November 1920 and February 1921 have resulted in a significant assemblage of submarine wrecks with some surviving remains. This assemblage might have been even larger had *UB118* and *UB131* not been lost en route to the same trials. Even so, this submarine graveyard represents possibly the largest group outside Scapa Flow of surviving remains of Germany's First World War fleet. These boats' remains are scattered within the intertidal zone of Castle Beach, off Pendennis Point. Consideration of the archaeological, documentary and photographic evidence suggests that the locations of the submarines can still be identified, despite the largely vestigial nature of the extant remains. Five submarines, excluding *UC92*, are visible in official photographs and unofficial snapshots of the trials, dating these images before 7 March, the date of the experiments on *UC92*.

Despite the lack of photographs of her, *UC92* has been the easiest submarine of this 'trials' group to identify, and was located in the centre of the post-trial dumping area just off Castle Beach in 2013.[50] Some vestigial remains lie as charted, although labelled as a 'lift' or recovered vessel. As we have seen with the dispersal of *UB117* (see p 95) this would be consistent with the minor remains that are still *in situ*. Examination of these vestiges has revealed mine tubes, which must originate from *UC92* as she was the only submarine of minelaying type among this assemblage.[51]

41 McCartney, *Lost Patrols*, p 61.

42 UKHO No 13603.

43 UKHO No 19585 and UKHO No 19907 respectively.

44 UKHO No 61784.

45 Maritime Archaeology Trust, *Forgotten Wrecks*; McCartney, *Lost Patrols*, pp 113–14.

46 UKHO No.17583.

47 McCartney, *Lost Patrols*, pp 56–57.

48 UKHO No.17568.

49 *Lloyd's List* reports, reprinted in *Shields Daily News*, 19,292 (14 December 1920), p 4; 19,295 (17 December 1920), p 4.

50 Wessex Archaeology, *U-boat off Castle Beach, Falmouth: Photographic Survey* unpublished report for Historic England (Salisbury, 2013); position of submarine noted as 50° 08.818'N, 005° 03.335'W, 100m southeast of the charted site, UKHO No.17311 in 50° 08.819'N, 005° 03.429'W, Wessex.

51 Ibid.

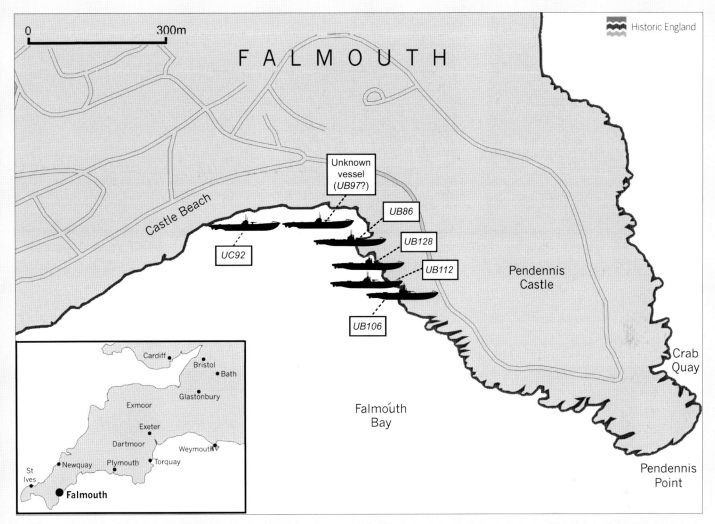

Location map of the largest known assemblage of German submarines on UK coasts, off Falmouth. Their final resting places have been identified by correlating contemporary photographs *in situ* with the archaeological remains. *(Modern Ordnance Survey mapping: © Crown Copyright and database right 2019. All rights reserved. Ordnance Survey Licence number 100024900. © Historic England)*

The remains of the five all-but-identical UB-III-type boats have understandably been more difficult to assign with confidence to individual vessels. *UB112*, the first to be expended during the trials is, however, identifiable as the submarine at the westernmost edge of the group.[52] *UB106*, the second 'trials' submarine, is likewise identifiable as the easternmost set of remains.[53] The photographic record and the charted position for *UB86* coincide and the fragmentary remains reported from that site can therefore be assigned with confidence to *UB86*.[54]

UB112 and *UB106* therefore delimit the dumping area for the submarines after their respective trials. *UB97* has been proposed as the identity of the fragmentary remains within the centre of the UB-III group.[55] The submarines flanking them have been less positively and interchangeably identified. To the east of '*UB97*', and just west of *UB106*, lie the remains of another boat that may be identified with some confidence as *UB86*, but *UB128* is not impossible.[56] Similarly, the wreckage to the east of *UB112* has been identified as either *UB86* or *UB128*.[57] Thus, even where the remains form a significant and well-documented assemblage relatively close inshore, it can be difficult to convincingly attribute an identity to individual remains or to precisely fix their locations, particularly where two sets of remains lie close to one another. Even photographic evidence may be deceptive, exaggerating or minimising a distance between complete features which is harder to establish against minimal wreck remains.

52 M Milburn, 'The U-Boat Coast', *Diver* 63/7 (2018) pp 20–3; Jack Casement collection, Historic England. UB112 charted in position for filing only, UKHO No.16346 in 50° 08.685'N, 005° 03.396'W, but broadly reflecting its position as the westernmost submarine of the group.

53 Milburn, *Diver* 63/7; Jack Casement collection, Historic England. UB106 charted in position for filing only, UKHO No.16345 in 50° 08.685'N, 005° 03.096 'W, but, again, as the easternmost set of remains.

54 Milburn, *Diver* 63/7; UKHO No.16344 in 50° 08.702'N, 005° 03.013'W.

55 UB97 charted in position for filing only as UKHO No.16341 in 50° 08.744'N, 005° 03.096'W at the broad centre of the group.

56 Identification as *UB86*: Wessex Archaeology, *U-boat off Castle Beach*; UKHO No.16344 in 50° 08.702'N, 005° 03.013'W, a broadly indicative position; identification as UB128: Milburn, *Diver*, 63/7.

57 Identification as *UB128*: assigned a position for filing only, UKHO No.16343 in 50° 08.785'N, 005° 03.329'W. Identified as UB86 in Milburn, *Diver* 63/7, and within the Jack Casement collection, Historic England.

The German submarine hulk in East Hoo Creek, Medway. The size and the layout of the wreck are consistent with it being the remains of a type UB-III, and thus all-but-certainly one of *UB144*, *UB145* or *UB150*, recorded as 'dumped' in 1922. *(Historic England 27196-026)*

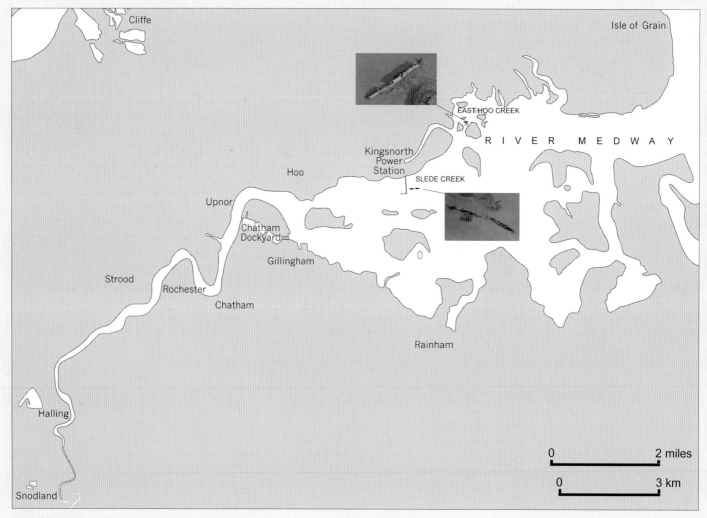

Map of the Medway, showing the locations of the three ex-German submarine hulks. *(AD map)*

U86 was one of the 'left-over' group due to be sunk by 1 July 1921 (see pP 54–55) and had been positively identified in mid-Channel some 18 miles southeast of Selsey Bill, very close to her reported position, unlike many of the other submarines dealt with in this chapter.[58] Her scuttling took place concurrently with pre-trial witness statements in London against two of her former officers, who were about to undergo war crimes trials at Leipzig for sinking the hospital ship *Llandovery Castle* and firing on the survivors on 27 June 1918, but the scuttling passed largely without comment or exploitation for political capital.[59]

During July and September 1920, M Lynch & Son had purchased the ex-German submarines, *U112, UB76, UB93, UB133, UB136, UB144, UB145* and *UB150*. All were apparently moored off Rochester, close to the bridge across the Medway. *U112, UB76* and *UB93* had been acquired on behalf of Albert Bachelor, owner of the Clinkham Cement Works, of Halling, near Rochester, and the diesel engines of all eight boats were removed for eventual reuse, two at the Halling works, two at the Holborough cement works at Snodland, two at Southend municipal power station (joining six from *U100, U164* and *UB149*), two to provide power for the 1924 Wembley Exhibition, two to a radio transmitter at Daventry 2LO, and two exported to New Zealand (see further Appendix 3.2).

UB76, UB93 and *UB133* had presumably been sufficiently mutilated through the removal of their machinery to meet their 'due' dates, although enough remained of each for the first two to be re-sold to the Upnor Shipbreaking Company, and the third to Ward's, during 1922. Of the others, which were among those deemed 'overdue', Upnor bought *U112*, along with *UB76* and *UB93*, while *UB133* and *UB136* also went to Ward's. However, the Admiralty Sales Ledger records that the hulls of *UB144, UB145* and *UB150* were simply 'dumped' during 1922.

Indeed, the remains of at least three submarines still lie among the Medway mudflats, one substantially preserved in East Hoo (Humble Bee) Creek, and two well cut-down (apparently done in 1940) in Slede Creek.[60] An estimate of the length of the latter hulk, approximately 50 metres, would certainly fit with the 56-metre length of a UB-III type boat,[61] as do the visible structural details. Accordingly, the three hulks are almost certainly those of *UB144, UB145* and *UB150*.[62] That they were dumped, rather than sold on for breaking-up, as had been the case for the other 'Medway' boats, may have been due to their incomplete

state when surrendered, with accordingly less of the non-ferrous material that made much shipbreaking an economic proposition.

The hulks of destroyers *V44* and *V82* have recently been identified at Whale Island, Portsmouth, beached after the trials they respectively underwent on 8 December and 13 October 1920 (p 49, above).[63] For both vessels it is clear that the wrecking process over the intervening century has both protracted and varied. Both vessels were, in a sense, 'veterans' of the mass scuttling at Scapa Flow and had been beached and recovered within weeks, so were already somewhat battered. Both then underwent firing trials, but instead of a second scuttling as gunnery targets, as might have been expected, their fate was not dissimilar to the Pendennis group of submarines. After the trials they were then beached, before being partially broken up *in situ* in one or possibly two phases in the 1920s. They, too, suffered some vandalism during that phase, not unlike *UB121*, before finally being abandoned and forgotten to rot away in the inter-tidal zone, as seems to have been the case with *U3, U117*, and *UB122*.

The fate of these warships therefore encompasses all phases of the story of the post-war disposals of submarines and other vessels within English waters. They represent a discrete subset of wrecks of First World War vintage, the submarines joining those of their numerous sisters lost in action around the English coastline, but generally wrecked in the inter-tidal zone, rather than foundering offshore due to war causes. The group is further differentiated from wartime losses by including a handful of German warships, none of which were sunk in English waters during the war but yet would not have been lost had it not been for the war. The wreck processes for many of the vessels concerned have incorporated a long forgetting of physical remains, paralleling their obscurity in the century since Britain began to break up the naval craft of her former enemy. Their wrecking paradoxically preserves them as a maritime archaeological heritage which is nearly as extensive, albeit much more widely dispersed, than the unique assemblage at Scapa Flow, and one which deserves to be much better known.

---

58 UKHO No.63321: in 50° 26.628'N, 0° 33.954'W.

59 *Pall Mall Gazette*, [17,503] (4 July 1921), p 7.

60 O'Driscoll, *After the Battle* 36, pp 39–42., with erroneous speculations as the boats' identities; K E Walker and S J Webster, *Strategic Assessment of Submarines in English Waters* (Cirencester: Cotswold Archaeology, 2014), pp 30, 39, 40, [111], [174], [175].

61 Walker and Webster, *Strategic Assessment*, p [109].

62 Walker and Webster, *Strategic Assessment*, p 40. There have, however, been a wide range of identifications in the past, the one enshrined in Google Maps being *UB122* which, however, was certainly one of the boats scuttled off the Isle of Wight in 1921 (p 54). A popular candidate has been *U112*, but her length of 72 metres is well in excess of the aforementioned estimate of the size of the wreck (Walker and Webster, *Strategic Assessment*, p [109]), while the layout is also not consistent; in any case, the hulk's resting place, far below Upnor, sits uneasily with a stranding on passage from Rochester to Upnor, the only obvious reason for her not being broken up there. In addition, had *U112 not* been broken up, one would have expected a reference in the Admiralty ledger.

63 See S Fisher and J Whitewright, 'Hidden Heritage: The German Torpedo Boats in Portsmouth Harbour', *Warship* [XXXIX] (2017), pp 166–70.

Ships and fates

1. The German Navy: 11 November 1918

Table 1.1/1. Capital Ships

Class	Disp.	Length	Beam	Machinery	Power/speed	Main gun(s)
Bayern	28,500t	180.0m	30.0m	14 x boilers, 3 x Tu	35,000shp=22.0kt	8 x 38cm/45
Braunschweig	13,208t	127.7m	22.2m	14 x boilers, 3 x VTE	16,000ihp=18.0kt	[4 x 28cm/40]
Derfflinger	26,600t	210–213m	29.0m	18 x boilers, 4 x Tu	63–72,000shp=26.5kt	8 x 30.5cm/50
Deutschland	13,191t	127.6m	22.2m	12 x boilers, 3 x VTE	16–17,000ihp=18.0kt	4 x 28cm/40
Ersatz Yorck	33,500t	227.8m	30.4m	32 x boilers, 4 x Tu	90,000shp=27.3kt	8 x 38cm/45
Fürst Bismarck	10,690t	127.0m	20.4m	12 x boilers, 3 x VTE	13,500ihp=18.7kt	[4 x 24cm/40]
Helgoland	22,808t	167.2m	28.5m	15 x boilers, 3 x VTE	28,000ihp=20.5kt	12 x 30.5cm/50
K Augusta	6065t	123.2m	15.6m	8 x boilers, 3 x VTE	12,000ihp=21.0kt	1 x 15cm + 4 x 10.5cm
K F Wilhelm	10,013t	115.7m	19.5m	12 x boilers, 2 x VTE	10,000ihp=16.5kt	[6 x 28cm/35–40]
K Friedrich III	11,100t	125.3m	20.4m	12/10 x boilers, 3 x VTE	13,000ihp=17.5kt	[4 x 24cm/40]
Kaiser	24,724t	172.4m	29.0m	16 x boilers, 2/3 x Tu	28,000shp=21.0kt	10 x 30.5cm/50
König	25,798t	175.4m	29.5m	15 x boilers, 3 x Tu	31,000shp=21.0kt	10 x 30.5cm/50
König Wilhelm	9574t	109.0m	18.3m	8 x boilers, 1 x HSE	8000ihp=14.0kt	[22 x 24cm/20]
Mackensen	31,000t	223.0m	30.4m	32 x boilers, 4 x Tu	90,000shp=28.0kt	8 x 35cm/45
Moltke	22,979t	186.6m	29.4m	24 x boilers, 4 x Tu	52,000shp=25.5kt	10 x 28cm/50
Nassau	18,873t	146.1m	26.9m	12 x boilers, 3 x VTE	22,000ihp=19.0kt	12 x 28cm/45
Odin	4100t	86.2m	15.4m	8 x boilers, 2 x VTE	5000ihp=15.0kt	[3 x 24cm/35]
Prinz Heinrich	8887t	126.5m	19.6m	14 x boilers, 3 x VTE	15,000ihp=20.0kt	[2 x 24cm/40]
Roon	9533t	127.8m	20.2m	16 x boilers, 3 x VTE	19,000ihp=21.0kt	[4 x 21cm/40]
Sachsen	7635t	93.0m	18.4m	8 x boilers, 2 x HSE	5600ihp=14.0kt	6 x 26cm/22
Seydlitz	24,998t	200.6m	28.5m	27 x boilers, 4 x Tu	63,000shp=26.5kt	10 x 28cm/50
Siegfried	4000t	86.1m	14.9m	8 x boilers, 2 x VTE	5000ihp=15.0kt	[3 x 24cm/35]
Victoria Louise	5,700t	110.5m	17.5m	8 x boilers, 3 x VTE	10,000ihp=18.5kt	[2 x 21cm/40]
Von der Tann	19,370t	171.7m	26.6m	18 x boilers, 4 x Tu	42,000shp=24.8kt	8 x 28cm/45
Wittelsbach	11,774t	126.8m	22.8m	12 x boilers, 3 x VTE	14,000ihp=18.0kt	[4 x 24cm/40]

Name	[1]	Class	Builder	Launch	Comp/comm	Int (I)/surr (S)	Alloc[2]	Fate.
Aegir	[D]	*Odin*	Kiel DYd	3 Apr 95	15 Oct 96	–	–	Stricken 17 Jun 19; sold Schleswig-Holstein Wirtschaftgemeinschaft 1919; re-sold Arnold Bernstein (Hamburg) and mercantile 1919; stranded off Karlsö (Gotland) 8 Dec 29; salved 1930 and BU Kiel
Baden		*Bayern*	Schichau (Danzig)	30 Oct 15	19 Oct 16	9 Jan 19 (I) Scapa Flow	UK (P)	Foundered Smoogro Bay 25 Jun 19 after being scuttled Scapa Flow 21 Jun 19; salved 11 Jul 19; foundered off Portsmouth after use as target 3 Feb 21; salved 21 May 21; target and scuttled NNE of Guernsey (49° 50' 20" N, 2° 21' 20" W) 16 Aug 21
Bayern.		*Bayern*	Howaldt (Kiel)	18 Feb 15	18 Mar 16	26/27 Nov 18 (I) Scapa Flow	UK (sunk)	Scuttled Scapa Flow 21 Jun 19; sold Metal Industries 3 Nov 33 (£750); salved 1 Sep 34; arrived Rosyth 30 Apr 35; BU 5 Jun 35–11 Mar 36
Beowulf	[D]	*Siegfried*	AG Weser (Bremen)	8 Nov 90	1 Apr 92	–	–	Stricken 17 Jun 19; sold Norddeutsche Tiefbaugesellschaft (Berlin) 1919; re-sold Schleswig-Holstein Wirtschaftgemeinschaft 1919; arrived Emden Jul 19 to BU by Abbruchbetrieb 'Kaiserin Augusta'; BU 1921
Brandenburg	[D]	*Brandenburg*	AG Vulcan (Stettin)	21 Sep 91	19 Nov 93	–	–	Stricken 13 May 19; sold Norddeutches Tiefbaugesellschaft (Berlin) 1919; re-sold Danziger Hoch- und Tiefbau GmbH 20 May 19; BU Danzig 1920
Braunschweig	[D]	*Braunschweig*	Germania (Kiel)	20 Dec 02	15 Oct 04	–	–	Stricken 31 Mar 31; BU Bremerhaven c.1935 (?)
Derfflinger		*Derfflinger*	Blohm & Voss (Hamburg)	12 Jul 13	1 Sep 14	25 Nov 18 (I) Scapa Flow	UK (sunk)	Scuttled Scapa Flow 21 Jun 19; sold Metal Industries 30 Mar 36 (£750); salved 25 Jul 39; arrived Faslane 15 Nov 46; BU to Jun 48
Deutschland	[D]	*Deutschland*	Germania (Kiel)	19 Nov 04	3 Aug 06	–	–	Stricken 25 Jan 20; BU Seliger Werke, Rüstringen 1921–22
Elsaß	[D]	*Brauschweig*	Schichau (Danzig)	26 May 03	29 Nov 04	–	–	Stricken 31 Mar 31; sold Techisches Betrieb des Norddeutschen Lloyd 31 Oct 35; BU Bremerhaven 1936

[1] [D] = Disarmed.

[2] (P) = Propaganda vessel.

Name	Class	Builder	Launch	Comp/comm	Int (I)/surr (S)	Alloc	Fate.
Ersatz-Freya	Mackensen	Blohm & Voss (Hamburg)	30 Mar 20	–	–	–	Stricken 17 Nov 19; BU Hamburg by F Kubatz 1920–22
Ersatz-Friedrich Carl/Ersatz-A	Mackensen	Wilhelms-haven DYd	–	–	–	–	Stricken 17 Nov 19; BU on stocks to 1922
Ersatz-Gneisenau	Ersatz-Yorck	Germania (Kiel)		–	-.-	–	Stricken 17 Nov 19; BU on stocks
Ersatz-Scharnhorst	Ersatz-Yorck	Blohm & Voss (Hamburg)		–	-.-	–	Stricken 17 Nov 19; BU on stocks
Ersatz-Yorck	Ersatz-Yorck	AG Vulcan (Hamburg)	–	–	–	–	Stricken 17 Nov 19; BU on stocks early 1920
Freya	[D] Victoria Louise	Danzig DYd	27 Apr 97	20 Oct 98	–	–	Stricken 25 Jan 20; BU Securitas Werke, Harburg 1921
Friedrich der Große	Kaiser	AG Vulcan (Hamburg)	10 Jun 11	15 Oct 12	26/27 Nov 18 (I) Scapa Flow	UK (sunk)	Scuttled Scapa Flow 21 Jun 19; sold Metal Industries 27 Jun 34 (£750); salved 29 Apr 37; arrived Rosyth 5 Aug 37; BU 25 Aug 37–18 May 38
Frithjof	[D] Siegfried	AG Weser (Bremen)	21 Jul 91	23 Feb 93	–	–	Stricken 17 Jun 19; sold Schleswig-Holstein Wirtschaftgemeinschaft 1919; sold F Oltmann & stripped Rönnebeck; re-sold Arnold Bernstein, Hamburg, and mercantile 1919; BU Danzig 1930
Fürst Bismarck	[D] Fürst Bismarck	Kiel DYd	25 Sep 97	1 Apr 00	–	–	Stricken 17 Jun 19; sold Schleswig-Holstein Wirtschaftgemeinschaft 1919; re-sold Brandt & Sohn, Audorf; BU Audorf-Rendsburg 1919–20
Graf Spee	Mackensen	Schichau (Danzig)	15 Sep 17	–			Stricken 17 Nov 19; sold 28 Oct 21; BU Kiel-Nordmole by Deutsche Werke 1921–22
Großer Kurfürst	König	AG Vulcan (Hamburg)	5 May 13	30 Jul 14	26/27 Nov 18 (I) Scapa Flow	UK (sunk)	Scuttled Scapa Flow 21 Jun 19; sold Metal Industries 27 Jun 34 (£750); salved 26 Apr 38; arrived Rosyth 27 Jul 38; BU 24 Aug 38–24 Jan 40
Hagen	[D] Siegfried	Kiel DYd	21 Oct 93	2 Oct 94	–	–	Stricken 17 Jun 19; sold Norddeutsche Tiefbaugesellschaft (Berlin) 1919; re-sold Schleswig-Holstein Wirtschaftgemeinschaft 1919; arrived Emden 1919 to BU by Abbruchbetrieb 'Kaiserin Augusta'; BU Emden 1920–21
Hannover	Deutschland	Wilhelms-haven DYd	29 Sep 05	1 Oct 07	–	–	Stricken 1935; BU Bremerhaven 1944/46
Hansa	[D] Victoria Louise	AG Vulcan (Stettin)	12 Mar 98	20 Apr 99	–	–	Stricken 6 Dec 19; BU Brandt & Sohn, Audorf-Rendsburg 1920
Heimdall	[D] Siegfried	Wilhelms-haven DYd	27 Jul 92	7 Apr 94	–	–	Stricken 17 Jun 19; sold Schleswig-Holstein Wirtschaftgemeinschaft 1919; re-sold and BU F Oltmann, Rönnebeck 1921
Helgoland = K (1920)	Helgoland	Howaldts-werke (Kiel)	25 Sep 09	23 Aug 11	5 Aug 20 (S) Rosyth	UK	Stricken 5 Nov 19; sold T W Ward 23 May 21 (£36,000, with Westfalen); arrived Birkenhead 29 Jan 22 for stripping and Morecambe 16 Nov 22 to BU
Hertha	[D] Victoria Louise	AG Vulcan (Stettin)	14 Apr 97	23 Jul 98	–	–	Stricken 6 Dec 19; BU Brandt & Sohn, Audorf-Rendsburg 1920
Hessen = Tsel (1946)	[D] Brauschweig	Germania (Kiel)	18 Sep 03	19 Sep 05	–	–	Stricken 31 Mar 35; target ship; see Table 2.1/2
Hildebrand	[D] Siegfried	Kiel DYd	6 Aug 92	28 Oct 93	–	–	Stricken 17 Jun 19; sold A Wijenschenk (Amsterdam) 1919; stranded north of IJmuiden 21 Dec 19; wreck blown up 1933 and BU
Hindenburg	Derfflinger	Wilhelms-haven DYd	1 Aug 15	10 May 17	25 Nov 18 (I) Scapa Flow	UK (sunk)	Scuttled Scapa Flow 21 Jun 19; sold Cox & Danks 25 Jan 24 (£3,000); salved 22 Jul 30; sold Metal Industries 1930 (£75,000); arrived Rosyth 27 Aug 30 to BU
Kaiser	Kaiser	Kiel DYd	22 Mar 11	1 Aug 12	26/27 Nov 18 (I) Scapa Flow	UK (sunk)	Scuttled Scapa Flow 21 Jun 19; sold Cox & Danks 11 Apr 28 (£1,000); salved 20 Mar 29; sold Alloa Shipbreaking (£75,000); arrived Rosyth 23 Jul 29; BU 11 Sep 29–23 Dec 31
Kaiser Barbarossa	[D] Kaiser Friedrich III	Schichau (Danzig)	21 Apr 00	10 Jun 01	–	–	Stricken 6 Dec 19; BU Seeliger Werke, Rüstringen 1919–20
Kaiser Friedrich III	[D] Kaiser Friedrich III	Wilhelms-haven DYd	1 Jul 96	7 Oct 98	–	–	Stricken 6 Dec 19; BU Kiel 1920
Kaiser Karl der Große	[D] Kaiser Friedrich III	Blohm & Voss (Hamburg)	18 Oct 99	4 Feb 02	–	–	Stricken 6 Dec 19; BU F Oltmann, Rönnebeck 1920
Kaiser Wilhelm der Große	[D] Kaiser Friedrich III	Germania (Kiel)	1 Jun 99	5 May 01	–	–	Stricken 6 Dec 19; BU Kiel 1920
Kaiser Wilhelm II	[D] Kaiser Friedrich III	Wilhelms-haven DYd	14 Sep 97	13 Feb 00	–	–	Stricken 17 Mar 21; BU Hamburg-Altenwärder 1922

Name		Class	Builder	Launch	Comp/comm	Int (I)/surr (S)	Alloc	Fate.
Kaiserin		Kaiser	Howaldtswerke (Kiel)	11 Nov 11	14 May 13	26/27 Nov 18 (I) Scapa Flow	UK (sunk)	Scuttled Scapa Flow 21 Jun 19; sold Metal Industries 1 Nov 34 (£750); salved 14 May 36; arrived Rosyth 31 Aug 36; BU 18 Nov 36–13 Dec 37
Kaiserin Augusta	[D]	Kaiserin Augusta	Germania (Kiel)	15 Jan 92	17 Nov 92	–	–	Stricken 1 Oct 19; sold Norddeutches Tiefbaugesellschaft (Berlin); BU by Abbruchbetrieb 'Kaiserin Augusta', Emden 1920
König		König	Wilhelmshaven DYd	1 Mar 13	9 Aug 14	6 Dec 18 (I) Scapa Flow	UK (sunk)	Scuttled Scapa Flow 21 Jun 19; sold Metal Industries 30 Mar 36 (£750); re-sold Nundy Marine Metals Ltd c.1956; re-sold Scapa Flow Salvage Ltd 1970; re-sold Undersea Associates 1978, sold Clark's Diving Services Ltd 1981; wreck designated 23 May 2001; sold Middle Eastern interests 9 Jul 2019 (£25,000)
König Albert		Kaiser	Schichau (Danzig)	27 Apr 12	31 Jul 13	26/27 Nov 18 (I) Scapa Flow	UK (sunk)	Scuttled Scapa Flow 21 Jun 19; sold Metal Industries 1 Nov 34 (£750); salved 31 Jul 35; arrived Rosyth 4 May 36; BU to 1937
König Wilhelm (ex-Wilhelm I, ex-Fatikh)	[D]	König Wilhelm	Thames Iron Works (Blackwall)	25 Apr 68	20 Feb 69	–	–	Stricken 4 Jan 21; BU F Oltmann, Rönnebeck 1921
Kronprinz Wilhelm (ex-Kronprinz)		König	Germania (Kiel)	21 Feb 14	8 Nov 14	26/27 Nov 18 (I) Scapa Flow	UK (sunk)	Scuttled Scapa Flow 21 Jun 19; sold Metal Industries 30 Mar 36 (£750); re-sold Nundy Marine Metals Ltd c.1956; re-sold Scapa Flow Salvage Ltd 1970; re-sold Undersea Associates 1978, sold Clark's Diving Services Ltd 1981; wreck designated 23 May 2001; sold Middle Eastern interests 9 Jul 2019 (£25,000)
Lothringen	[D]	Brauschweig	Schichau (Danzig)	27 May 04	18 May 06	–	–	Stricken 31 Mar 31; sold 1931; BU Blohm & Voss, Hamburg
Mackensen		Mackensen	Blohm & Voss (Hamburg)	21 Apr 17	–	–	–	Stricken 17 Nov 19; sold Oct 21 and BU Hamburg by F A Kubatz
Markgraf		König	AG Weser (Bremen)	4 Jun 13	1 Oct 14	26/27 Nov 18 (I) Scapa Flow	UK (sunk)	Scuttled Scapa Flow 21 Jun 19; sold Metal Industries 30 Mar 36 (£750); re-sold Nundy Marine Metals Ltd c.1956; re-sold Scapa Flow Salvage Ltd 1970; re-sold Undersea Associates 1978, sold Clark's Diving Services Ltd 1981; wreck designated 23 May 2001; sold Middle Eastern interests 9 Jul 2019 (£25,000)
Mecklenburg	[D]	Wittelsbach	AG Vulcan (Stettin)	9 Nov 01	25 May 03	–	–	Stricken 25 Jan 20; sold Deutsche Werke 16 Aug 21; BU Kiel-Nordmole
Moltke		Moltke	Blohm & Voss (Hamburg)	7 Apr 10	30 Sep 11	25 Nov 18 (I) Scapa Flow	UK (sunk)	Scuttled Scapa Flow 21 Jun 19; sold Cox & Danks 28 Aug 26 (£1,000); salved 10 Jun 27; sold Alloa Shipbreaking Mar 28 (£40,000); arrived Rosyth 21 May 28; BU 16 Jun 28–20 Mar 29
Nassau = B (1920)		Nassau	Wilhelmshaven DYd	7 Mar 08	1 Oct 09	5 Apr 20 (S) Rosyth	JP	Stricken 5 Nov 19; sold Hughes Bolckow Jun 20 and stripped Derwenthaugh; re-sold Frank Rijsdijk 1922 and BU Dordrecht
Odin	[D]	Odin	Danzig DYd	3 Nov 94	22 Sep 96	–	–	Stricken 6 Dec 19; sold Arnold Bernstein (Hamburg) and mercantile 1919; BU 1935
Oldenburg = M (1920)		Helgoland	Schichau (Danzig)	30 Jun 10	1 May 12	12 May 20 (S) Rosyth	JP (P)	Stricken 5 Nov 19; sold British shipbreaker Jun 20; re-sold Frank Rijsdijk and BU Dordrecht 1921
Ostfriesland = H (1920)		Helgoland	Wilhelmshaven DYd	30 Sep 09	1 Aug 11	5 Apr 20 (S) Rosyth	US (P)	Stricken 5 Nov 19; sunk as bombing target off Cape Henry VA (37° 9' 8" N, 74° 34' 3" W) 21 Jul 21
Posen = G (1920)		Nassau	Germania (Kiel)	12 Dec 08	31 May 10	12 May 20 (S) Rosyth	UK	Stricken 5 Nov 19; sold T W Ward 27 Jul 21 (£15,000; sale cancelled); sold N/V 'Holland' 31 Aug 21 (£8,000); departed for Rotterdam 8 Oct 21; BU Dordrecht 1922
Preußen	[D]	Brauschweig	AG Vulcan (Stettin)	30 Oct 03	12 Jul 05	–	–	Stricken 5 Apr 29; sold 25 Feb 31; BU Wilhelmshaven
Prinz Heinrich	[D]	Prinz Heinrich	Kiel DYd	23 Mar 00	11 Mar 02	–	–	Stricken 25 Jan 20; BU Brandt & Sohn, Audorf-Rendsburg 1920
Prinzregent Luitpold		Kaiser	Germania (Kiel)	17 Feb 12	31 Jul 13	26/27 Nov 18 (I) Scapa Flow	UK (sunk)	Scuttled Scapa Flow 21 Jun 19; sold Cox & Danks 25 Jun 29 (£1,000); salved 22 Jul 31; beached Cava 16 Jul 31; re-sold Metal Industries Feb 33 (£38,000); arrived Rosyth 11 May 33; BU 13 Jun 33–14 Mar 34
Rheinland = F (1920)	[D]	Nassau	AG Vulcan (Stettin)	26 Sep 08	30 Apr 10	–	UK	Stricken 5 Nov 19; sold Frank Rijsdijk 22 Jun 20 (£32,100); arrived Dordrecht 29 Aug 20 to BU
Roon	[D]	Roon	Kiel DYd	27 Jun 03	5 Apr 06	–	–	Stricken 25 Nov 20; BU Kiel-Nordmole 1921
Sachsen		Bayern	Germania (Kiel)	21 Nov 16	–	–	–	Stricken 3 Nov 19; sold 1920; BU Kiel-Arsenalmole 1921–23
Schlesien	[D]	Deutschland	Schichau (Danzig)	28 May 06	5 May 08	–	–	See Table 2.1/1

Name	Class	Builder	Launch	Comp/comm	Int (I)/surr (S)	Alloc	Fate.
Schleswig-Holstein	[D] *Deutschland*	Germania (Kiel)	17 Dec 06	6 Jul 08	–	–	See Table 2.1/1
Schwaben	[D] *Wittelsbach*	Wilhelms-haven DYd	19 Aug 01	13 Apr 04	–	–	Stricken 8 Mar 21; sold 1921; BU Kiel-Nordmole 1921
Seydlitz	*Seydlitz*	Blohm & Voss (Hamburg)	30 Nov 12	22 May 13	25 Nov 18 (I) Scapa Flow.	UK (sunk)	Scuttled Scapa Flow 21 Jun 19; sold Cox & Danks 10 Oct 24 (£3,000); salved 2 Nov 28; sold Alloa Shipbreaking Nov 28 (£65,000); arrived Rosyth 11 May 29; BU 12 Jun 29–30 Dec 31
Siegfried	[D] *Siegfried*	Germania (Kiel)	10 Aug 89	29 Apr 90	–	–	Stricken 17 Jun 19; sold Schleswig-Holstein Wirtschaftgemeinschaft 1919; re-sold Peters (Wewelsfleth); BU Wewelsfleth 1920
Thüringen = L (1920)	*Helgoland*	AG Weser (Bremen)	27 Nov 09	1 Jul 11	25 Apr 20 Cherbourg	FR (P)	Stricken 5 Nov 19; target Gâvres Jul–Aug 21; beached 47° 41' 20" N, 03° 18' 37" W; sold Société ouest des Métaux de Paris 18 Feb 23; partly BU in situ to 1933
Victoria Louise = Flora Sommer-feld (1920)	[D] *Victoria Louise*	AG Weser (Bremen)	29 Mar 97	20 Feb 99	–	–	Stricken 1 Oct 19; sold Norddeutches Tiefbaugesellschaft 1919; re-sold Danziger Hoch- und Tiefbau GmbH 20 May 19 and mercantile 1920; BU Danzig 1923
Vineta	[D] *Victoria Louise*	Danzig DYd	9 Dec 97	13 Sep 99	–	–	Sricken 6 Dec 19; BU Securitas Werke, Harburg 1920
Von der Tann	*Von der Tann*	Blohm & Voss (Hamburg)	20 Mar 09	1 Sep 10	25 Nov 18 (I) Scapa Flow	UK (sunk)	Scuttled Scapa Flow 21 Jun 19; sold Cox & Danks 25 Jun 29 (£1,000); salved 7 Dec 30; beached Cava 8 Dec 30; sold Metal Industries Feb 33 (£30,500); arrived Rosyth 9 Jul 33; BU 12 Jul 33–23 May 34
Westfalen = D (1920)	*Nassau*	AG Weser (Bremen)	1 Jul 08	16 Nov 09	5 Aug 20 (S) Rosyth.	UK	Stricken 5 Nov 19; sold T W Ward 23 May 21 (£36,000, with *Helgoland*); arrived Birkenhead 3 Sep 21 for lightening, and Barrow 18 May 22 to BU
Wettin	[D] *Wittelsbach*	Schichau (Danzig)	6 Jun 01	1 Oct 02	–	–	Stricken 1 Mar 20; stripped Rüstringen 1920–21; sold 21 Nov 21 and BU Rönnebeck 1922
Wittelsbach	[D] *Wittelsbach*	Wilhelms-haven DYd	3 Jul 00	15 Oct 02	–	–	Stricken 8 Mar 21; sold 7 Jul 21; BU Wilhelmshaven
Wörth	[D] *Brandenburg*	Germania (Kiel)	6 Aug 92	31 Oct 93	–	–	Stricken 13 May 19; sold A Wijenschenk (Amsterdam) 1919; BU Netherlands
Württemberg (i)	*Sachsen*	AG Vulcan (Stettin)	9 Nov 78	9 May 81	–	–	Stricken 20 Oct 20; sold Hattinger; BU Wilhelmshaven
Württemberg (ii)	*Bayern*	AG Vulcan (Hamburg)	20 Jun 17	–	–	–	Stricken 3 Nov 19; sold 1921; BU Hamburg by F A Kubatz
Zähringen	[D] *Wittelsbach*	Germania (Kiel)	12 Jun 01	25 Oct 02	–	–	Stricken 11 Mar 20; target ship 1927; bombed Gdynia 18 Dec 44; salved and scuttled as blockship 26 Mar 45; see Table 2.1/2

Table 1.1/2. German Cruisers

Class	Disp.	Length	Beam	Machinery	Power/speed	Guns	TT
Gefion	3746t	110.4m	13.2m	6 x boilers, 2 x VTE	9000ihp=19.0kt	[10 x 10.5cm/35	2 x 45cm]
Gazelle	~2650t	~105.0m	11.8m	8/10 x boilers, 2 x VTE	8000ihp=21.5kt	10 x 10.5cm/40	2 x 45cm
Frauenlob	2706t	105.0m	12.3m	9 x boilers, 2 x VTE	8000ihp=21.5kt	10 x 10.5cm/40	2 x 45cm
Bremen	3278t	111.1m	13.3m	10 x boilers, 2 x VTE	10,000ihp=22.0kt	10 x 10.5cm/40	2 x 45cm
Lübeck	3265t	111.1m	13.3m	10 x boilers, 2 x Tu	11,500shp=22.5kt	10 x 10.5cm/40	2 x 45cm
Danzig	3278t	111.1m	13.3m	10 x boilers, 2 x Tu	10,000ihp=22.0kt	10 x 10.5cm/40	2 x 45cm
Stettin	3480t	117.4m	13.3m	11 x boilers, 2 x Tu	13,500shp=24.0kt	10 x 10.5cm/40	2 x 45cm
Stuttgart	3469t	117.4m	13.3m	11 x boilers, 2 x VTE	13,200ihp=23.0kt	4 x 10.5cm/40	2 x 45cm
Kolberg	4362t	130.5m	14.0m	15 x boilers, 4 x Tu	19,000shp=25.5kt	6 x 15cm/45	2 x 45cm
Magdeburg	4564t	138.7m	13.5m	16 x boilers, 2/3 x Tu	25,000shp=27.0kt	7 x 15cm/45	2/4 x 50cm
Graudenz	4912t	142.7m	13.8m	10 x boilers, 2 x Tu	26,000shp=27.5kt	7 x 15cm/45	4 x 50cm
Pillau	4390t	135.3m	13.6m	6 x boilers, 2 x Tu	30,000shp=27.5kt	8 x 15cm/45	2 x 50cm
Wiesbaden	5180t	145.3m	13.9m	12 x boilers, 2 x Tu	31,000shp=27.5kt	8 x 15cm/45	4 x 50cm
Brummer	4385t	140.4m	13.2m	6 x boilers, 2 x Tu	33,000shp=28.0kt	4 x 15cm/45	2 x 50cm
Königsberg (ii)	5440t	151.4m	14.3m	10 x boilers, 2 x Tu	31,000shp=27.5kt	8 x 15cm/45	4 x 50cm
Cöln	5620t	155.5m	14.2m	14 x boilers, 2 x Tu	31,000shp=27.5kt	8 x 15cm/45	4 x 60cm

Name	Class	Builder	Launch	Comp/comm	Int (I)/surr (S)	Alloc	Fate.
Amazone	(D) *Gazelle*	Germania (Kiel)	6 Oct 00	15 Nov 01	–	–	Stricken 31 Mar 31; accommodation hulk; see Table 2.1/2
Arcona	(D) *Frauenlob*	AG Weser (Bremen)	22 Apr 02	13 May 03	–	–	Stricken 15 Jan 30; accommodation hulk; see Table 2.1/2
Augsburg = Y (1920)	*Kolberg*	Kiel DYd	10 Jul 09	1 Oct 10	3 Sep 20 (S) Rosyth	JP (P)	Stricken 5 Nov 19; BU Dordrecht 1922
Berlin	*Bremen*	Danzig DYd	22 Sep 03	4 Apr 05	–	–	Stricken 1 Oct 35; accommodation ship; see Table 2.1/2

Name		Class	Builder	Launch	Comp/comm	Int (I)/surr (S)	Alloc	Fate.
Bremse		Brummer	AG Vulcan (Stettin)	11 Mar 16	1 Jul 18	26 Nov 18 (I) Scapa Flow	UK (sunk)	Scuttled Scapa Flow 21 Jun 19; sold Cox & Danks 28 Oct 25; salved 27 Nov 29; arrived Lyness 30 Nov 29; BU to May 31
Brummer		Brummer	AG Vulcan (Stettin)	11 Dec 15	2 Apr 16	26 Nov 18 (I) Scapa Flow	UK (sunk)	Scuttled Scapa Flow 21 Jun 19; salvage rights sold Nundy Marine Metals (£200) 6 Nov 62; salvage work Sep/Oct 70; re-sold Scapa Flow Salvage Ltd 21 Oct 77; re-sold Undersea Associates 1978; sold Clark's Diving Services 20 Nov 81; rights reverted to MoD Dec 82; sold Orkney Islands Council (£1) 3 Nov 86; wreck designated 23 May 2001
Cöln (ii)		Cöln	Blohm & Voss (Hamburg)	5 Oct 16	17 Jan 18	23 Nov 18 (I) Scapa Flow	UK (sunk)	Scuttled Scapa Flow 21 Jun 19; salvage rights sold Nundy Marine Metals (£200) 6 Nov 62; salvage work Sep/Oct 70; re-sold Scapa Flow Salvage Ltd 21 Oct 77; re-sold Undersea Associates 1978; sold Clark's Diving Services 20 Nov 81; rights reverted to MoD Dec 82; sold Orkney Islands Council (£1) 3 Nov 86; wreck designated 23 May 2001
Danzig = R (1920)		Danzig	Danzig DYd	23 Sep 05	1 Dec 07	15 Sep 20 (S) Rosyth	UK	Sold George Clarkson 17 Feb 21 (£5,525); BU Whitby 1921–28
Dresden (ii)		Cöln	Howaldts-werke (Kiel)	25 Apr 17	28 Mar 18	16 Dec 18 (I) Scapa Flow	UK (sunk)	Scuttled Scapa Flow 21 Jun 19; salvage rights sold Nundy Marine Metals (£200) 6 Nov 62; salvage work Sep/Oct 70; re-sold Scapa Flow Salvage Ltd 21 Oct 77; re-sold Undersea Associates 1978; sold Clark's Diving Services 20 Nov 81; rights reverted to MoD Dec 82; sold Orkney Islands Council (£1) 3 Nov 86; wreck designated 23 May 2001
Emden (ii)		Königsberg (ii)	AG Weser (Bremen)	1 Feb 16	16 Dec 16	26 Nov 18 (I) Scapa Flow	FR (P)	Scuttled Scapa Flow 21 Jun 19; beached Smoogro Bay; salved 28 Jun 19; to FR 11 Mar 20; BU Caen 1926
Ersatz-Cöln		Cöln	AG Weser (Bremen)	c.Nov 19	–	–	–	Stricken 17 Nov 19; sold Neugebauer (Lemwerder) 21 Jun 21 (~400,000M); BU Hamburg-Kohlbrandwerft
Ersatz-Emden		Cöln	AG Weser (Bremen)	c.Nov 19	–	–	–	Stricken 17 Nov 19; sold 25 Jun 21 (~400,000M); BU Hamburg-Altenwärter by P Berendsohn
Ersatz-Karlsruhe		Cöln	Kiel DYd	–	–	–	–	Stricken 17 Nov 19; BU 1920
Frankfurt.		Wiesbaden	Kiel DYd	20 Mar 15	20 Aug 15	26 Nov 18 (I) Scapa Flow	US (P)	Scuttled Scapa Flow 21 Jun 19; beached Smoogro Bay; salved 12 Jul 19; to US; commissioned 4 Jun 20; expended as aircraft bombing target off Cape Henry VA 18 Jun 21
Frauenlob (iii)		Cöln	Kiel DYd	26 Sep 18	–	–	–	Stricken 17 Nov 19; BU Deutsche Werke, Kiel 1921
Gazelle	(D)	Gazelle	Germania (Kiel)	31 Mar 98	15 Jun 01	–	–	Stricken 28 Aug 20; BU Wilhelmshaven
Gefion = Adolf Sommer-feld (1920)	(D)	Gefion	Schichau (Danzig)	31 May 93	27 Jun 94	–	–	Stricken 5 Nov 19; sold Norddeutsche Tiefbaugesellschaft (Berlin) 1919; sold Danziger Hoch- und Tiefbau (Danzig) 1919 (freighter); BU Danzig 1923
Graudenz = E (1920) = Ancona (1920)		Graudenz	Kiel DYd	25 Oct 13	10 Aug 14	1 Jun 20 (S) Cherbourg	IT	Stricken 10 Mar 20; IT commission 6 May 25; stricken 11 Mar 37; BU 1938
Hamburg		Bremen	AG Vulcan (Stettin)	25 Jul 03	8 Mar 04	–	–	Stricken 31 Mar 31; accommodation ship; bombed Hamburg 1944; BU 1949–56
Karlsruhe		Königsberg (ii)	Wilhelms-haven DYd	31 Jan 16	23 Dec 16	26 Nov 18 (I) Scapa Flow	UK (sunk)	Scuttled Scapa Flow 21 Jun 19; sold Metal Industries 1955; re-sold Nundy Marine Metals c.1956; salvage work Sep/Oct 70; re-sold Scapa Flow Salvage Ltd 21 Oct 77; re-sold Undersea Associates 1978; sold Clark's Diving Services 20 Nov 81; wreck designated 23 May 2001; sold UK interests 9 Jul 2019 (£8,500)
Kolberg = W (1920) = Colmar (1920)		Kolberg	Schichau (Danzig)	14 Nov 08	21 Jun 10	25 Apr 20 (S) Cherbourg	FR	Stricken 5 Nov 19; FR commission 1922; stricken 21 Jul 27; BU 1929
Königsberg (ii) = A (1920) = Metz (1920)		Königsberg (ii)	AG Weser (Bremen)	18 Dec 15	12 Aug 16	20 Jul 20 (S) Cherbourg	FR	Stricken 31 May 20; FR commission 6 Oct 20; stricken 18 Aug 33; sold late 1934; BU
Leipzig (iii)		Cöln	AG Weser (Bremen)	28 Jan 18	–	–	–	Stricken 17 Nov 19; sold Neugebauer (Lemwerder) 21 Jun 21; BU Hamburg 1921
Lübeck = P (1920)		Lübeck	AG Vulcan (Stettin)	26 Mar 04	26 Apr 05	3 Sep 20 (S) Rosyth	UK	Sold Anders J Anderson 12 Mar 21 (£4,600); re-sold and BU in Germany
Magdeburg (ii)		Cöln	Howaldts-werke (Kiel)	17 Nov 17	–	–	–	Stricken 17 Nov 19; sold 28 Oct 21 (1,300,000M); BU Kiel-Nordmole 1922
Medusa	(D)	Gazelle	AG Weser (Bremen)	5 Dec 00	26 Jul 01	–	–	Stricken 27 Mar 29; accommodation ship; see Table 2.1/2
München = Q (1920)		Bremen	AG Weser (Bremen)	30 Apr 04	10 Jan 05	5 Jul 20 (S) Rosyth	UK	Expended as torpedo target Firth of Forth (56° 07' 00" N, 02° 45' 50" W) 28 Oct 21

Name	Class		Builder	Launch	Comp/comm	Int (I)/surr (S)	Alloc	Fate.
Niobe = *Dalmacija* (1925) = *Cattaro* (Apr 41) = *Niobe* (Sep 43)	(D) *Gazelle*		AG Weser (Bremen)	18 Jul 99	25 Jan 00	–	–	Stricken 26 Jun 25; YU; IT 17 Apr 41; see Table 2.2/3
Nürnberg (ii)	*Königsberg* (ii)		Howaldts-werke (Kiel)	14 Apr 16	15 Feb 17	26 Nov 18 (I) Scapa Flow	UK (P)	Scuttled Scapa Flow 21 Jun 19; beached off Cava; salved 3 Jul 19; target 5 Nov 20; gunfire target HMS *Repulse* S of Poole (50° 08' 172 N, 01°41' 738 W) 7 Jul 22
Nymphe	(D) *Gazelle*		Germania (Kiel)	21 Nov 99	20 Sep 00	–	–	Stricken 31 Mar 31; sold 29 Aug 31; BU Hamburg 1932
Pillau (ex *Muravev-Amurskiy*) = *U* (1920) = *Bari* (1920)	*Pillau*		Schichau (Danzig)	11 Apr 14	14 Dec 14	20 Jul 20 (S) Cherbourg	IT	Stricken 5 Nov 19; IT commission 23 Jan 24; see Table 2.3/3
Regensburg = *J* (1920) = *Strasbourg*	*Graudenz*		Kiel DYd	25 Apr 14	3 Jan 15	4 Jun 20 (S) Cherbourg	FR	Stricken 10 Mar 20; FR commission May 22; stricken 14 Jun 36; hulked Lorient; sunk 1944
Rostock (ii)	*Cöln*		AG Vulcan (Stettin)	6 Apr 18	–	–	–	Stricken 17 Nov 19; stripped Lübeck; sold 1921; BU Hamburg
Stettin = *T* (1920)	*Stettin*		AG Vulcan (Stettin)	7 Mar 07	29 Oct 07	15 Sep 20 (S) Rosyth	UK	Sold Petersen & Albeck 15 Feb 21 (£6,350); BU Copenhagen
Stralsund = *Z* (1920) = *Mulhouse* (1920)	*Magdeburg*		AG Weser (Bremen)	4 Nov 11	10 Dec 12	3 Aug 20 (S) Cherbourg	FR	Stricken 10 Mar 20; FR commission 3 Aug 22; stricken 15 Feb 33; sold to BU 2 Nov 33
Straßburg = *O* (1920) = *Taranto* (1920)	*Magdeburg*		Wilhelms-haven DYd	24 Aug 11	9 Oct 12	20 Jul 20 (S) Cherbourg	IT	Stricken 10 May 20; IT commission 26 Jun 25; see Table 2.2/3
Stuttgart = *S* (1920).	*Stuttgart*		Danzig DYd	22 Sep 06	1 Feb 08	20 Jul 20 (S) Cherbourg	UK	Sold Channel Shipbreaking Company (Teignmouth) 22 Oct 20 (£9,500); BU Dartmouth to 1922
Thetis	(D) *Gazelle*		Danzig DYd	3 Jul 00	14 Sep 01	–	–	Stricken 27 Mar 29; sold Blohm & Voss; BU Hamburg 1930
Wiesbaden (ii)	*Cöln*		AG Vulcan (Stettin)	3 Mar 17	–	–	–	Stricken 17 Nov 19; stripped Lübeck; BU 1921

Table 1.1/3. Torpedo Boats/Destroyers

Class[3]	Disp.	Length	Beam	Machinery	Power/speed	Main gun(s)	TT
S7	86t	37.7m	4.9m	1 x boilers, 1 x VTE	725ihp=20.4kt	1 x 5cm/40	3 x 35cm
S24	83t	37.7m	4.8m	1 x boilers, 1 x VTE	840ihp=19.1kt	1 x 5cm/40	3 x 35cm
S33	94t	39.9m	4.8m	1 x boilers, 1 x VTE	900ihp=20.0kt	1 x 5cm/40	3 x 35cm
S42	123t	44.2m	5.0m	1 x boilers, 1 x VTE	1420ihp=22.2kt	1 x 5cm/40	3 x 35cm
S43	127t	44.2m	5.0m	1 x boilers, 1 x VTE	1571ihp=21.5kt	1 x 5cm/40	3 x 35cm
S58	132t	44.3m	5.0m	1 x boilers, 1 x VTE	1232ihp=20.2kt	1 x 5cm/40	3 x 35cm
S67	137t	47.9m	5.4m	1 x boilers, 1 x VTE	1610ihp=21.9kt	1 x 5cm/40	3 x 45cm
S74	157t	49.9m	5.5m	2 x boilers, 1 x VTE	2500ihp=23.7kt	1 x 5cm/40	3 x 45cm
S75	152t	49.0m	5.3m	2 x boilers, 1 x VTE	1744ihp=22.3kt	1 x 5cm/40	3 x 45cm
S82	142t	48.2m	5.1m	2 x boilers, 1 x VTE	2146ihp=25.3kt	1 x 5cm/40	3 x 45cm
S88	147t	48.7m	5.0m	2 x boilers, 1 x VTE	2468ihp=26.0kt	1 x 5cm/40	3 x 45cm
S90	310t	63.0m	7.0m	3 x boilers, 2 x VTE	5900ihp=27.0kt	2 x 8.8cm/35	3 x 45cm
S102	315t	63.2m	7.0m	3 x boilers, 2 x VTE	5900ihp=28.0kt	2 x 8.8cm/35	3 x 45cm
G108	330t	65.8m	6.7m	3 x boilers, 2 x VTE	6600ihp=28.0kt	2 x 8.8cm/35	3 x 45cm
S114	315t	63.2m	7.0m	3 x boilers, 2 x VTE	5900ihp=27.0kt	2 x 8.8cm/35	3 x 45cm
S120	391t	64.7m	7.0m	3 x boilers, 2 x VTE	6400ihp=27.5kt	2 x 8.8cm/35	3 x 45cm
S125	355t	64.7m	7.0m	3 x boilers, 3 x Tu	6600shp=28.0kt	2 x 8.8cm/35	3 x 45cm
S126	371t	64.7m	7.0m	3 x boilers, 2 x VTE	6400ihp=28.0kt	2 x 8.8cm/35	3 x 45cm
G132	412t	65.7m	7.0m	3 x boilers, 2 x VTE	7000ihp=28.0kt	2 x 8.8cm/35	3 x 45cm
G137	580t	71.5m	7.7m	3 x boilers, 3 x Tu	10,800shp=30.0kt	2 x 8.8cm/35	3 x 45cm
S138	533t	70.7m	7.8m	4 x boilers, 2 x VTE	11,000ihp=30.0kt	2 x 8.8cm/35	3 x 45cm
V150	558t	72.5m	7.8m	4 x boilers, 2 x VTE	10,900ihp=30.0kt	2 x 8.8cm/45	3 x 45cm

[3] Larger German torpedo craft were designated by a serial number, prefixed by a letter denoting the builder. This series was re-started with the ordering of *V1*, with earlier vessels having their prefix changed to *T* (sometimes with an additional leading digit to the serial number) to avoid duplication of names. This list of such classes, and the table of ships itself, is therefore ordered by serial number, not the letter-prefix. The exceptions are the *D* and *A* series boats, which were numbered in separate sequences.

Class	Disp.	Length	Beam	Machinery	Power/speed	Main gun(s)	TT
V161	596t	72.5m	7.8m	4 x boilers, 2 x Tu	14,800shp=32.0kt	2 x 8.8cm/45	3 x 45cm
V162	639t	73.9m	7.9m	4 x boilers, 2 x Tu	15,100shp=32.0kt	2 x 8.8cm/45	3 x 45cm
S165	665t	74.2m	7.9m	4 x boilers, 2 x Tu	17,500shp=32.0kt	2 x 8.8cm/45	3 x 45cm
G173	700t	74.0m	7.9m	4 x boilers, 2 x Tu	15,000shp=32.0kt	2 x 8.8cm/45	4 x 50cm
S176	566t	74.2m	7.9m	4 x boilers, 2 x Tu	17,600shp=32.0kt	2 x 8.8cm/45	4 x 50cm
V180	650t	73.9m	7.9m	4 x boilers, 2 x Tu	18,000shp=32.0kt	2 x 8.8cm/45	4 x 50cm
V186	666t	73.9m	7.9m	4 x boilers, 2 x Tu	18,000shp=32.0kt	2 x 8.8cm/45	4 x 50cm
G192	660t	74.0m	7.9m	4 x boilers, 2 x Tu	18,200shp=32.0kt	2 x 8.8cm/45	4 x 50cm
V1	569t	71.1m	7.6m	4 x boilers, 2 x Tu	17,000shp=32.0kt	2 x 8.8cm/45	4 x 50cm
G7	573t	71.5m	7.6m	4 x boilers, 2 x Tu	16,000shp=32.0kt	2 x 8.8cm/45	4 x 50cm
S13	568t	71.5m	7.4m	4 x boilers, 2 x Tu	15,700shp=32.5kt	2 x 8.8cm/45	4 x 50cm
						2 x 10.5cm/45 (S18)	
V25 (Mob)	812t	78.5m	8.3m	4 x boilers, 2 x Tu	23,500shp=33.5kt	3 x 10.5cm/45	6 x 50cm
S31 (Mob)	802t	79.6m	8.3m	4 x boilers, 2 x Tu	24,000shp=33.5kt	3 x 10.5cm/45	6 x 50cm
G37 (Mob)	822t	79.5m	8.4m	4 x boilers, 2 x Tu	24,000shp=34.0kt	3 x 10.5cm/45	6 x 50cm
V43 (Mob)	852t	79.6m	8.3m	4 x boilers, 2 x Tu	24,000shp=34.5kt	3 x 10.5cm/45	6 x 50cm
S49 (Mob)	802t	79.6m	8.4m	4 x boilers, 2 x Tu	24,000shp=34.0kt	3 x 10.5cm/45	6 x 50cm
S53 (Mob)	919t	83.1m	8.4m	4 x boilers, 2 x Tu	24,000shp=34.0kt	3 x 10.5cm/45	6 x 50cm
V67 (Mob)	924t	82.0m	8.3m	4 x boilers, 2 x Tu	24,000shp=34.0kt	3 x 10.5cm/45	6 x 50cm
G85 (Mob)	960t	83.0m	8.4m	4 x boilers, 2 x Tu	24,000shp=33.5kt	3 x 10.5cm/45	6 x 50cm
B97	1374t	98.0m	9.4m	4 x boilers, 2 x Tu	40,000shp=36.5kt	4 x 10.5cm/45	6 x 50cm
V99	1350t	99.0m	9.4m	4 x boilers, 2 x Tu	40,000shp=36.5kt	4 x 10.5cm/45	6 x 50cm
V105	340t	62.6m	6.2m	2 x boilers, 2 x Tu	5500shp=28.0kt	2 x 8.8cm/45	2 x 45cm
S113	2060t	106.0m	10.2m	4 x boilers, 2 x Tu	45,000shp=34.5kt	4 x 15cm/45	4 x 60cm
V116	2060t	107.5m	10.4m	4 x boilers, 2 x Tu	45,000shp=34.5kt	4 x 15cm/45	4 x 60cm
G119	2060t	108.0m	10.3m	4 x boilers, 2 x Tu	46,000shp=34.5kt	4 x 15cm/45	4 x 60cm
B122	2060t	108.0m	10.3m	4 x boilers, 2 x Tu	46,000shp=34.5kt	4 x 15cm/45	4 x 60cm
V125 (1916Mob)	924t	82.0m	8.3m	3 x boilers, 2 x Tu	23,500shp=34.0kt	3 x 10.5cm/45	6 x 50cm
S131 (1916Mob)	919t	83.1m	8.3m	3 x boilers, 2 x Tu	24,000shp=32.0kt	3 x 10.5cm/45	6 x 50cm
V140 (1916Mob)	924t	82.0m	8.3m	3 x boilers, 2 x Tu	23,500shp=32.0kt	3 x 10.5cm/45	6 x 50cm
H145 (1916Mob)	990t	84.5m	8.4m	3 x boilers, 2 x Tu	24,500shp=32.0kt	3 x 10.5cm/45	6 x 50cm
G148 (1917Mob)	1020t	85.1m	8.4m	3 x boilers, 2 x Tu	24,500shp=32.5kt	3 x 10.5cm/45	6 x 50cm
S152 (1917Mob)	1020t	83.0m	8.3m	3 x boilers, 2 x Tu	22,000shp=32.5kt	3 x 10.5cm/45	6 x 50cm
V158 (1917Mob)	1030t	83.0m	8.3m	3 x boilers, 2 x Tu	26,500shp=32.5kt	3 x 10.5cm/45	6 x 50cm
H166 (1917Mob)	1061t	85.1m	8.4m	3 x boilers, 2 x Tu	26,000shp=32.5kt	3 x 10.5cm/45	6 x 50cm
V170 (1918Mob)	1268t	92.5m	9.1m	3 x boilers, 2 x Tu	36,000shp=35.0kt	4 x 10.5cm/45	4 x 60cm
S178 (1918Mob)	1268t	99.4m	9.1m	3 x boilers, 2 x Tu	38,000shp=35.0kt	4 x 10.5cm/45	4 x 60cm
H186 (1918Mob)	1268t	92.5m	9.1m	3 x boilers, 2 x Tu	38,000shp=35.0kt	4 x 10.5cm/45	4 x 60cm
D1	249t	56.1m	6.6m	2 x boilers, 1 x VTE	2200ihp=20.6kt	3 x 5cm/40	3 x 35cm
D3	249t	57.6m	6.8m	2 x boilers, 1 x VTE	2200ihp=20.3kt	3 x 5cm/40	3 x 35cm
D5	300t	59.6m	7.4m	2 x boilers, 1 x VTE	3200ihp=22.6kt	3 x 5cm/40	3 x 35cm
D7	320t	59.7m	7.4m	2 x boilers, 1 x VTE	2600ihp=22.5kt	3 x 5cm/40	3 x 45cm
D9	350t	63.0m	7.7m	2 x boilers, 1 x VTE	2600ihp=23.5kt	3 x 5cm/40	3 x 45cm
D10	310t	66.1m	5.6m	2 x boilers, 2 x VTE	5783ihp=27.2kt	5 x 5cm/40	3 x 45cm
RU Novik	1110t	98m	9.3m	5 x boilers, 2 x Tu	23,000shp=29.0kt	3 x 10.2cm/60	10 x 45cm
RU Leitnant Schestakov	605t	73.4m	7.5m	4 x boilers, 2 x VTE	7300ihp=25.0kt	2 x 12cm/45	3 x 45cm
RU Bespokoiny	350t	64m	6.4m	4 x boilers, 2 x VTE	6000ihp=26.0kt	2 x 7.5cm/50	3 x 45cm
A-I	109t	41.6m	4.6m	1 x boiler, 1 x VTE	1200ihp=20.0kt	1 x 5cm/40	2 x 45cm
A-II (A26)	227t	50.0m	5.3m	1 x boiler, 1 x Tu	3250shp=25.0kt	2 x 8.8cm/30	1 x 45cm
A-II (A50)	229t	50.0m	5.6m	1 x boiler, 1 x Tu	3250shp=25.0kt	2 x 8.8cm/30	1 x 45cm
A-III (A56)	330t	61.1m	6.4m	2 x boilers, 2 x Tu	6000shp=28.0kt	2 x 8.8cm/30	1 x 45cm
A-III (A68)	335t	60.0m	6.4m	2 x boilers, 2 x Tu	6000shp=28.0kt	2 x 8.8cm/30	1 x 45cm
A-III (A80)	330t	60.4m	6.4m	2 x boilers, 2 x Tu	5700shp=26.0kt	3 x 8.8cm/30	-
A-III (A81)	330t	60.4m	6.4m	2 x boilers, 2 x Tu	5700shp=26.0kt	2 x 8.8cm/30	1 x 45cm
A-III (A92)	335t	61.2m	6.4m	2 x boilers, 2 x Tu	5700shp=26.5kt	2 x 8.8cm/30	1 x 45cm
A-III (A96)	330t	60.4m	6.4m	2 x boilers, 2 x Tu	5700shp=26.0kt	2 x 8.8cm/30	1 x 45cm

Name	Class	Builder	Launch	Comp/comm	Int (I)/surr (S)	Alloc	Fate.
T11 (ex-S11)	S7	Schichau (Elbing)	18 Jun 85	31 Jul 85	–	–	Stricken 3 Apr 20; sold 28 Aug 20 (26,000M); BU Lübeck
T13 (ex-S13)	S7	Schichau (Elbing)	7 Jul 85	28 Aug 85	–	–	Stricken 3 Apr 20; sold 28 Aug 20 (26,000M); BU Lübeck
T14 (ex-S14)	S7	Schichau (Elbing)	15 Jul 85	3 Sep 85	–	–	Stricken 3 Apr 20; sold 28 Aug 20 (42,000M); BU Kiel
T15 (ex-S15)	S7	Schichau (Elbing)	29 Jul 85	14 Oct 85	–	–	Stricken 3 Apr 20; sold 12 Oct 20 (25,000M); BU Hamburg
T16 (ex-S16)	S7	Schichau (Elbing)	1 Aug 85	14 Oct 85	–	–	Stricken 3 Apr 20; sold 28 Aug 20 (26,000M); BU Lübeck
T20 (ex-S20)	S7	Schichau (Elbing)	8 Sep 85	11 Nov 85	–	–	Stricken 3 Apr 20; sold 28 Aug 20 (26,000M); BU Lübeck
T22 (ex-S22)	S7	Schichau (Elbing)	1 Oct 85	27 Nov 85	–	–	Stricken 3 Apr 20; sold 21 May 20 (20,000M); BU Wilhelmshaven

Name	Class	Builder	Launch	Comp/comm	Int (I)/surr (S)	Alloc	Fate.
T24 (ex-S24)	S24	Schichau (Elbing)	30 Jul 86	24 Oct 86	–	–	Stricken 3 Apr 20; sold 28 Aug 20 (42,000M); BU Kiel
T27 (ex-S27)	S24	Schichau (Elbing)	24 Sep 86	15 Nov 86	–	–	Stricken 3 Apr 20; sold 28 Aug 20 (42,000M); BU Kiel
T28 (ex-S28)	S24	Schichau (Elbing)	6 Oct 86	3 Dec 86	–	–	Stricken 3 Apr 20; sold 12 Oct 20 (25,000M); BU Hamburg
T29 (ex-S29)	S24	Schichau (Elbing)	19 Oct 86	23 Dec 86	–	–	Stricken 3 Apr 20; sold (40,000M); BU Wilhelmshaven
T30 (ex-S30)	S24	Schichau (Elbing)	22 Nov 86	15 Jan 87	–	–	Stricken 3 Apr 20; sold 12 Oct 20 (25,000M); BU Hamburg
T31 (ex-S31)	S24	Schichau (Elbing)	4 Dec 86	13 Apr 87	–	–	Stricken 3 Apr 20; sold 12 Oct 20 (25,000M); BU Hamburg
T33 (ex-S33)	S33	Schichau (Elbing)	3 May 87	20 Jun 87	–	–	Stricken 3 Apr 20; sold 12 Oct 20 (25,000M); BU Hamburg
T34 (ex-S34)	S33	Schichau (Elbing)	7 May 87	24 Jun 87	–	–	Stricken 3 Apr 20; sold 12 Oct 20 (25,000M); BU Hamburg
T35 (ex-S35)	S33	Schichau (Elbing)	25 May 87	26 Jun 87	–	–	Stricken 3 Apr 20; sold 12 Oct 20 (25,000M); BU Hamburg
T36 (ex-S36)	S33	Schichau (Elbing)	25 Jun 87	15 Jul 87	–	–	Stricken 3 Apr 20; sold (40,000M); BU Wilhelmshaven
T37 (ex-S37)	S33	Schichau (Elbing)	9 Jul 87	12 Apr 87	–	–	Stricken 3 Apr 20; sold 12 Oct 20 (25,000M); BU Hamburg
T38 (ex-S38)	S33	Schichau (Elbing)	27 Jul 87	29 Jul 87	–	–	Stricken 3 Apr 20; sold 12 Oct 20 (25,000M); BU Hamburg
T39 (ex-S39)	S33	Schichau (Elbing)	16 Aug 87	19 Sep 87	–	–	Stricken 3 Apr 20; sold 12 Oct 20 (25,000M); BU Hamburg
T40 (ex-S40)	S33	Schichau (Elbing)	27 Aug 87	28 Sep 87	–	–	Stricken 3 Apr 20; sold 12 Oct 20 (25,000M); BU Hamburg
T42 (ex-S42)	S42	Schichau (Elbing)	29 May 87	27 Jun 89	–	–	Stricken 26 Oct 20; sold (40,000M); BU Wilhelmshaven
T44 (ex-S44)	S43	Schichau (Elbing)	30 Oct 89	6 Dec 89	–	–	Stricken 26 Oct 20; BU Hamburg
T45 (ex-S45)	S43	Schichau (Elbing)	12 Jul 89	2 Nov 89	–	–	Stricken 10 May 22; steam supply boat Kiel
T49 (ex-S49)	S43	Schichau (Elbing)	30 Jan 90	20 Aug 90	–	–	Stricken 26 Oct 20; BU Hamburg
T53 (ex-S53)	S43	Schichau (Elbing)	18 Jun 90	25 Sep 90	–	–	Stricken 26 Oct 20; BU Wilhelmshaven
T55 (ex-S55)	S42	Schichau (Elbing)	19 Feb 90	22 Nov 90	–	–	Stricken 26 Oct 20; sold 23 Apr 21 (110,000M); BU Kiel
T59 (ex-S59)	S58	Schichau (Elbing)	9 Dec 91	29 May 92	–	–	Stricken 3 Apr 20; sold 12 Oct 20 (25,000M); BU Hamburg
T60 (ex-S60)	S58	Schichau (Elbing)	26 Mar 92	11 Jul 92	–	–	Stricken 26 Oct 20; BU Hamburg
T61 (ex-S61)	S58	Schichau (Elbing)	6 Apr 92	23 Jul 92	–	–	Stricken 26 Oct 20; sold 23 Apr 21 (110,000M); BU Kiel
T62 (ex-S62)	S58	Schichau (Elbing)	7 May 92	29 Jul 92	–	–	Stricken 26 Oct 20; sold 23 Apr 21 (110,000M); BU Kiel
T63 (ex-S63)	S58	Schichau (Elbing)	28 May 92	12 Aug 92	–	–	Stricken 26 Oct 20; BU Hamburg
T69 (ex-S69) = WHz1 (1920)	S67	Schichau (Elbing)	20 Apr 93	15 Aug 93	–	–	Stricken 26 Oct 20; steam supply boat Wilhelmshaven
T70 (ex-S70)	S67	Schichau (Elbing)	6 Jun 93	9 Sep 93	–	–	Stricken 26 Jan 21; sold 23 Apr 21 (110,000M); BU Wilhelmshaven
T71 (ex-S71)	S67	Schichau (Elbing)	2 Aug 93	6 Oct 93	–	–	Stricken 23 Mar 21; sold 14 Jul 21 (110,000M); BU Wilhelmshaven
T72 (ex-S72)	S67	Schichau (Elbing)	20 Jun 93	23 Nov 93	–	–	Stricken 26 Jan 21; sold 23 Apr 21 (110,000M); BU Wilhelmshaven
T73 (ex-S73)	S67	Schichau (Elbing)	23 Jun 93	9 Jan 94	–	–	Stricken 26 Jan 21; sold 18 May 21 (112,000M); BU Wilhelmshaven
T74 (ex-S74)	S67	Schichau (Elbing)	7 Nov 94	25 Oct 95	–	–	Stricken 26 Jan 21; sold 23 Apr 21 (110,000M); BU Wilhelmshaven
T75 (ex-S75)	S75	Schichau (Elbing)	22 Jan 95	26 Apr 95	–	–	Stricken 26 Jan 21; sold 23 Apr 21 (110,000M); BU Wilhelmshaven
T76 (ex-S76)	S75	Schichau (Elbing)	13 Mar 95	29 May 95	–	–	Stricken 26 Jan 21; sold 16 Apr 21 (125,000M); BU Wilhelmshaven
T77 (ex-S77)	S75	Schichau (Elbing)	6 May 95	10 Jul 95	–	–	Stricken 26 Jan 21; sold 23 Apr 21 (110,000M); BU Wilhelmshaven
T79 (ex-S79)	S75	Schichau (Elbing)	6 Jul 95	1 Sep 95	–	–	Stricken 22 Mar 21; sold May 21 (110,000M); BU Kiel
T80 (ex-S80)	S75	Schichau (Elbing)	14 Jun 95	11 Aug 95	–	–	Stricken 26 Jan 21; sold 23 Apr 21 (110,000M); BU Wilhelmshaven
T81 (ex-S81)	S75	Schichau (Elbing)	30 Sep 95	28 Mar 96	–	–	Stricken 26 Jan 21; sold 16 Apr 21 (125,000M); BU Wilhelmshaven
T82 (ex-S82)	S82	Schichau (Elbing)	15 Apr 97	29 Oct 97	–	–	Stricken 26 Jan 21; sold 13 May 21 (112,000M); BU Hamburg-Moorburg
T83 (ex-S83)	S82	Schichau (Elbing)	26 Jun 97	26 Nov 97	–	–	Stricken 26 Jan 21; sold 13 May 21 (85,000M); BU Hamburg-Moorburg
T84 (ex-S84)	S82	Schichau (Elbing)	27 Sep 97	28 Dec 97	–	–	Stricken 26 Jan 21; sold 23 Apr 21 (110,000M); BU Wilhelmshaven
T85 (ex-S85)	S82	Schichau (Elbing)	9 Sep 97	20 Mar 98	–	–	Stricken 22 Mar 21; sold May 21 (110,000M); BU Kiel
T86 (ex-S86)	S82	Schichau (Elbing)	8 Nov 97	15 Apr 98	–	–	Stricken 22 Mar 21; sold May 21 (110,000M); BU Kiel
T87 (ex-S87)	S82	Schichau (Elbing)	10 Dec 97	15 Apr 98	–	–	Stricken 26 Jan 21; sold 23 Apr 21 (110,000M); BU Wilhelmshaven
T88 (ex-S88)	S88	Schichau (Elbing)	10 Jul 97	2 May 98	–	–	Stricken 22 Mar 21; sold May 21 (110,000M); BU Kiel
T89 (ex-S89)	S88	Schichau (Elbing)	19 Feb 98	18 Aug 98	–	–	Stricken 22 Mar 21; sold May 21 (110,000M); BU Kiel
T91 (ex-S91)	S90	Schichau (Elbing)	25 Sep 99	24 Apr 00	–	–	Stricken 22 Mar 21; sold .... (Dusseldorf) 26 May 21; BU
T92 (ex-S92)	S90	Schichau (Elbing)	15 May 00	27 Jun 00	–	–	Stricken 22 Mar 21; sold .... (Dusseldorf) 26 May 21; BU
T93 (ex-S93)	S90	Schichau (Elbing)	24 Mar 00	14 Jul 00	–	–	Stricken 22 Mar 21; sold .... (Dusseldorf) 26 May 21; BU
T94 (ex-S94)	S90	Schichau (Elbing)	23 Apr 00	27 Jul 00	–	–	Stricken 26 Oct 20; sold 13 Jul 21 (160,000M); BU Wilhelmshaven
T95 (ex-S95)	S90	Schichau (Elbing)	20 Feb 00	29 Aug 00	–	–	Stricken 22 Mar 21; sold 13 May 21 (180,000M); BU Kiel

Name	Class	Builder	Launch	Comp/comm	Int (I)/surr (S)	Alloc	Fate.
T96 (ex-*S96*)	S90	Schichau (Elbing)	31 Jan 00	27 Sep 00	–	–	Stricken 22 Mar 21; sold .... (Dusseldorf) 26 May 21; BU
T97 (ex-*Sleipner*, ex-*S97*)	S97	Schichau (Elbing)	16 Dec 99	28 May 00	–	–	Stricken 22 Mar 21; sold .... (Dusseldorf) 26 May 21; BU
T98 (ex-*S98*)	S90	Schichau (Elbing)	28 Jul 00	4 Nov 00	–	–	Stricken 22 Mar 21; sold .... (Dusseldorf) 26 May 21; BU
T99 (ex-*S99*)	S90	Schichau (Elbing)	4 Sep 00	13 Dec 00	–	–	Stricken 22 Mar 21; sold .... (Dusseldorf) 26 May 21; BU
T101 (ex-*S101*)	S90	Schichau (Elbing)	22 Dec 00	30 May 01	–	–	Stricken 22 Mar 21; sold 13 May 21 (180,000M); BU Kiel
T102 (ex-*S102*)	S102	Schichau (Elbing)	18 Apr 01	18 Jul 01	–	–	Stricken 22 Mar 21; sold 13 May 21 (180,000M); BU Kiel
T103 (ex-*S103*)	S102	Schichau (Elbing)	15 May 01	17 Sep 01	–	–	Stricken 22 Mar 21; sold .... (Dusseldorf) 26 May 21; BU
T104 (ex-*S104*)	S102	Schichau (Elbing)	22 Jun 01	7 Oct 01	–	–	Stricken 22 Mar 21; sold .... (Dusseldorf) 26 May 21; BU
T105 (ex-*S105*)	S102	Schichau (Elbing)	7 Aug 01	17 Nov 01	–	–	Stricken 22 Mar 21; sold .... (Dusseldorf) 26 May 21; BU
T106 (ex-*S106*)	S102	Schichau (Elbing)	7 Sep 01	9 Dec 01	–	–	Stricken 22 Mar 21; sold .... (Dusseldorf) 26 May 21; BU
T107 (ex-*S107*)	S102	Schichau (Elbing)	17 Oct 01	27 Jan 02	–	–	Stricken 22 Mar 21; sold 13 May 21 (180,000M); BU Kiel
T108 (ex-*G108*)	G108	Germania (Kiel)	7 Sep 01	26 Mar 02	–	–	Stricken 22 Mar 21; BU Hamburg
T109 (ex-*G109*)	G108	Germania (Kiel)	9 Nov 01	19 Jun 02	–	–	Stricken 22 Mar 21; sold 13 May 21 (180,000M); BU Kiel
T110 (ex-*G110*)	G108	Germania (Kiel)	9 Sep 02	21 Jan 03	–	–	Stricken 22 Mar 21; BU Hamburg
T111 (ex-*G111*)	G108	Germania (Kiel)	2 Apr 02	21 Jul 02	–	–	Stricken 22 Mar 21; sold 13 Jun 21 (200,000M); BU Kiel
T112 (ex-*G112*)	G108	Germania (Kiel)	19 Jun 02	6 Sep 02	–	–	Stricken 22 Mar 21; sold 13 Jun 21 (200,000M); BU Kiel
T113 (ex-*G113*)	G108	Germania (Kiel)	9 Aug 02	16 Oct 02	–	–	Stricken 22 Mar 21; sold 8 Jun 21 (260,000M); BU Wilhelmshaven
T114 (ex-*S114*)	S114	Schichau (Elbing)	9 Aug 02	25 Oct 02	–	–	Stricken 9 Nov 20; sold 7 Jul 21 (170,000M); BU Kiel
T120 (ex-*S120*)	S120	Schichau (Elbing)	10 Feb 04	7 May 04	–	–	Stricken 22 Mar 21; sold 28 May 21 (210,000M); BU Wilhelmshaven
T121 (ex-*S121*)	S120	Schichau (Elbing)	3 Mar 04	17 Jun 04	–	–	Stricken 22 Mar 21; sold 13 Jun 21 (200,000M); BU Kiel
T125 (ex-*S125*)	S125	Schichau (Elbing)	19 May 04	4 Apr 05	–	–	Stricken 26 Oct 20; sold 13 May 21 (215,000M); BU Hamburg-Moorburg
T126 (ex-*S126*)	S126	Schichau (Elbing)	26 Nov 04	30 Apr 05	–	–	Stricken 22 Mar 21; sold 13 Jun 21 (200,000M); BU Kiel
T127 (ex-*S127*)	S126	Schichau (Elbing)	15 Jan 05	7 Jun 07	–	–	Stricken 22 Mar 21; sold 28 May 21 (210,000M); BU Wilhelmshaven
T128 (ex-*S128*)	S126	Schichau (Elbing)	25 Feb 05	8 Jul 05	–	–	Stricken 22 Mar 21; sold 13 Jun 21 (200,000M); BU Kiel
T130 (ex-*S130*)	S126	Schichau (Elbing)	27 Apr 05	17 Apr 05	–	–	Stricken 22 Mar 21; sold 28 May 21 (210,000M); BU Wilhelmshaven
T131 (ex-*S131*)	S126	Schichau (Elbing)	25 May 05	6 Oct 05	–	–	Stricken 22 Mar 21; sold 28 May 21 (210,000M); BU Wilhelmshaven
T132 (ex-*G132*)	G132	Germania (Kiel)	12 May 06	22 Aug 06	–	–	Stricken 22 Mar 21; sold 28 May 21 (210,000M); BU Wilhelmshaven
T133 (ex-*G133*)	G132	Germania (Kiel)	30 Jun 06	10 Dec 06	–	–	Stricken 22 Mar 21; sold 28 May 21 (210,000M); BU Wilhelmshaven
T134 (ex-*G134*)	G132	Germania (Kiel)	23 Jul 06	6 Mar 07	–	–	Stricken 9 Nov 20; sold 13 May 21 (185,000M); BU Hamburg-Moorburg
T135 (ex-*G135*)	G132	Germania (Kiel)	7 Sep 06	24 Jan 07	–	–	Stricken 25 May 21; sold 10 Oct 21; BU Wilhelmshaven
T136 (ex-*G136*)	G132	Germania (Kiel)	25 Aug 06	16 Mar 07	–	–	Stricken 21 Jul 21; sold 20 Aug 21; BU Wilhelmshaven
T137 (ex-*G137*)	G137	Germania (Kiel)	24 Jan 07	24 Jul 07	–	–	Stricken 22 Mar 21; sold 28 May 21 (210,000M); BU Wilhelmshaven
T139 (ex-*S139*) = *Pfiel* (Aug 27)	S138	Schichau (Elbing)	12 Nov 06	6 Jul 07	–	–	Not traced after 1944
T141 (ex-*S141*) = *Blitz* (i) (Aug 27)	S138	Schichau (Elbing)	7 Feb 07	9 Sep 07	–	–	Stricken 3 Aug 27; sold 28 Apr 33; BU Wilhelmshaven
T143 (ex-*S143*)	S138	Schichau (Elbing)	6 Apr 07	12 Oct 07	–	–	Stricken 10 May 27; sold 25 Mar 30 (61,500M); BU Hamburg-Moorburg
T144 (ex-*S144*)	S138	Schichau (Elbing)	27 Apr 07	7 Dec 07	–	–	Stricken 8 Oct 28; sold .... (Essen) 10 Apr 29 (81,000M); BU
T146 (ex-*S146*)	S138	Schichau (Elbing)	27 Jun 07	20 Nov 07	–	–	Stricken 8 Oct 28; sold .... (Essen) 10 Apr 29 (81,000M); BU
T149 (ex-*S149*)	S138	Schichau (Elbing)	19 Oct 07	27 Jul 08	–	–	Stricken 16 May 27; BU
T151 (ex-*V151*)	V150	AG Vulcan (Stettin)	19 Sep 07	29 Feb 08	–	–	See Table 2.1/3
T152 (ex-*V152*)	V150	AG Vulcan (Stettin)	11 Oct 07	10 Apr 08	–	–	Stricken 31 Mar 31; BU 1935
T153 (ex-*V153*) = *Eduard Jungmann* (29 Aug 38)	V150	AG Vulcan (Stettin)	13 Nov 07	9 May 08	–	–	See Table 2.1/3
T154 (ex-*V154*)	V150	AG Vulcan (Stettin)	19 Dec 07	5 Jun 08	–	–	Stricken 8 Oct 28; BU 1935
T155 (ex-*V155*)	V150	AG Vulcan (Stettin)	28 Jan 08	25 Jun 08	–	–	See Table 2.1/3
T156 (ex-*V156*) = *Bremse* (1944)	V150	AG Vulcan (Stettin)	29 Feb 08	21 Jul 08	–	–	See Table 2.1/3
T157 (ex-*V157*)	V150	AG Vulcan (Stettin)	29 May 08	27 Aug 08	–	–	Mined Danzig Neufahrwasser 22 Oct 43
T158 (ex-*V158*)	V150	AG Vulcan (Stettin)	26 Jun 08	8 Oct 08	–	–	See Table 2.1/3
T159 (ex-*V159*)	V150	AG Vulcan (Stettin)	18 Jul 18	2 Nov 08	19 Aug 20 (S) Rosyth	UK	Sold Granton Shipbreaking 15 Feb 21 (£600); BU Granton

Name	Class	Builder	Launch	Comp/comm	Int (I)/surr (S)	Alloc	Fate.
T160 (ex-V160)	V150	AG Vulcan (Stettin)	12 Sep 08	15 Dec 08	19 Aug 20 (S) Rosyth	UK	Sold Granton Shipbreaking 15 Feb 21 (£600); BU Granton to 1922
T161 (ex-V161)	V161	AG Vulcan (Stettin)	21 Apr 08	17 Sep 08	2 Sep 20 (S) Rosyth	UK	Sold W Duguid 15 Feb 21 (£1,010); BU
T163 (ex-V163)	V162	AG Vulcan (Stettin)	24 May 09	22 Jul 09	2 Sep 20 (S) Rosyth	UK	Sold N/V 'Holland' 19 Feb 21 (£1,030); BU Dordrecht
T164 (ex-V164)	V162	AG Vulcan (Stettin)	27 May 09	20 Aug 09	5 Aug 20 (S) Rosyth	UK	Sold W Duguid 15 Feb 21 (£1,000); BU Bo'ness to 1922
T165 (ex-S165 [ii])	S165	Schichau (Elbing)	26 Nov 10	27 Apr 11	19 Sep 20 (S) Rosyth	UK	Sold J W Houston 22 Feb 21 (£756); BU Montrose
T166 (ex-S166 [ii])	S165	Schichau (Elbing)	27 Dec 10	7 Jul 11	5 Aug 20 (S) Rosyth	UK	Sold T C Pas 15 Feb 21 (£1,030); BU Dordrecht (Nieuw Lekkerland) by 6 Jul 22
T167 (ex-S167 [ii])	S165	Schichau (Elbing)	15 Feb 11	26 Aug 11	–	–	Stricken 3 Sep 21 (250,000M); BU Kiel
T168 (ex-S168 [ii])	S165	Schichau (Elbing)	16 Mar 11	1 Sep 11	–	–	Stricken 8 Jan 27 (63,000M); BU Hamburg
T169 (ex-S169)	S165	Schichau (Elbing)	29 Dec 08	29 Apr 09	5 Aug 20 (S) Rosyth	UK	Sold T C Pas 15 Feb 21 (£1,030); BU Dordrecht-Nieuw Lekkerland by 6 Jul 22
T173 (ex-G173)	G173	Germania (Kiel)	28 Jul 09	24 Jan 10	2 Sep 20 (S) Rosyth	UK	Sold to N/V 'Holland' 28 Feb 21 (cancelled); sold J W Houston 11 Mar 21 (£700); BU Montrose by 3 Feb 22
T174 (ex-G174)	G173	Germania (Kiel)	8 Jan 10	6 Jul 10	19 Aug 20 (S) Rosyth	UK	Sold J W Houston 1 Mar 21 (£750); BU Montrose
T175 (ex-G175, ex-Sleipner, ex-G175)	G173	Germania (Kiel)	24 Feb 10	4 Dec 10	–	–	Stricken 23 Sep 26; sold (63,000M); BU Hamburg
T176 (ex-S176)	S176	Schichau (Elbing)	12 Apr 10	23 Sep 10	19 Sep 20 (S) Rosyth	UK	Sold J W Houston 1 Mar 21 (£750); BU Montrose
T178 (ex-S178)	S176	Schichau (Elbing)	14 Jul 10	9 Dec 10	5 Aug 20 (S) Rosyth	UK	Sold T C Pas 28 Feb 21 (£3,000); transferred to C H C Sunderman; BU Dordrecht-Nieuw Lekkerland by 6 Jul 22
T179 (ex-S179)	S176	Schichau (Elbing)	27 Aug 10	8 Mar 11	5 Aug 20 (S) Rosyth	UK	Sold T C Pas 28 Feb 21 (£3,000); transferred to C H C Sunderman; BU Dordrecht-Nieuw Lekkerland by 6 Jul 22
T180 (ex-V180)	V180	AG Vulcan (Stettin)	15 Oct 09	4 Jan 10	5 Aug 20 (S) Rosyth	UK	Sold T C Pas 28 Feb 21 (£3,000); transferred to C H C Sunderman; BU Dordrecht-Nieuw Lekkerland by 6 Jul 22
T181 (ex-V181)	V180	AG Vulcan (Stettin)	6 Nov 09	11 Mar 10	19 Aug 20 (S) Rosyth	JP	BU Dordrecht 1922
T182 (ex-V182)	V180	AG Vulcan (Stettin)	1 Dec 09	4 May 10	5 Aug 20 (S) Rosyth	UK	Sold T C Pas 28 Feb 21 (£3,000); transferred to C H C Sunderman; BU Dordrecht by 6 Jul 22
T183 (ex-V183)	V180	AG Vulcan (Stettin)	23 Dec 09	12 May 10	5 Aug 20 (S) Rosyth	UK	Sold T C Pas 15 Feb 21 (£1,030); BU Dordrecht-Nieuw Lekkerland
T184 (ex-V184)	V180	AG Vulcan (Stettin)	26 Feb 10	29 Jun 10	5 Aug 20 (S) Rosyth	UK	Sold C H C Sunderman 15 Feb 21 (£1,025); BU Dordrecht-Nieuw Lekkerland
T185 (ex-V185) = Blitz (ii) (Oct 32) = Vystrel (1946)	V180	AG Vulcan (Stettin)	9 Apr 10	20 Sep 10	–	–	See Table 2.1/3
T186 (ex-V186)	V180	AG Vulcan (Stettin)	28 Nov 10	21 Apr 11	5 Aug 20 (S) Rosyth	UK	Sold N/V 'Holland' 19 Feb 21 (£1,030); BU Dordrecht
T189 (ex-V189)	V180	AG Vulcan (Stettin)	14 Mar 11	30 Jun 11	25 Apr 20 (S) Cherbourg	UK	Sold Channel Shipbreaking Co (Teignmouth) 22 Oct 20 (£1,800); wrecked in tow Roundham Head (Torquay) 12 Dec 20; wreck sold Mr Shaw (Brixham)
T190 (ex-V190) = Claus von Bevern (29 Aug 38)	V180	AG Vulcan (Stettin)	12 Apr 11	5 Aug 11	–	–	See Table 2.1/3
T192 (ex-G192)	G192	Germania (Kiel)	5 Nov 10	8 May 11	25 Apr 20 (S) Cherbourg	UK	Sold G A Ryland (Cradley Heath) 22 Oct 20 (£5,000); transferred to T Oakley (Luton); BU begun Holywell; re-sold back to Ryland; transferred to Barking Shipbreaking Co; BU Chatham
T193 (ex-G193)	G192	Germania (Kiel)	10 Dec 10	25 Jun 11	25 Apr 20 (S) Cherbourg	UK	Sold G A Ryland (Cradley Heath) 22 Oct 20 (£5,000); transferred to T Oakley (Luton); BU begun Holywell; re-sold back to Ryland; transferred to Barking Shipbreaking Co; BU Chatham
T195 (ex-G195)	G192	Germania (Kiel)	8 Apr 11	8 Sep 11	25 Apr 20 (S) Cherbourg	UK	Sold G A Ryland (Cradley Heath) 22 Oct 20 (£5,000); transferred to T Oakley (Luton); BU begun Holywell; re-sold back to Ryland; transferred to Barking Shipbreaking Co; BU Chatham
T196 (ex-G196)	G192	Germania (Kiel)	25 Apr 11	24 May 11	–	–	See Table 2.1/3
T197 (ex-G197)	G192	Germania (Kiel)	23 Jun 11	10 Nov 11	25 Apr 20 (S) Cherbourg	UK	Sold T W Ward 22 Oct 22 (£1,850); BU Briton Ferry
V1	V1	AG Vulcan (Stettin)	11 Sep 11	12 Jan 12	–	–	Stricken 27 Mar 29; BU Wilhelmshaven

Name	Class	Builder	Launch	Comp/comm	Int (I)/surr (S)	Alloc	Fate.
V2	V1	AG Vulcan (Stettin)	14 Oct 11	28 Mar 12	–	–	Stricken 18 Nov 29; sold 25 Mar 30 (61,000M); BU Wilhelmshaven
V3	V1	AG Vulcan (Stettin)	15 Nov 11	2 May 12	–	–	Stricken 18 Nov 29; sold 25 Mar 30 (71,000M); BU Wilhelmshaven
V5	V1	AG Vulcan (Stettin)	25 Apr 13	17 Jul 13	–	–	Stricken 18 Nov 29; sold 25 Mar 30 (61,000M); BU Wilhelmshaven
V6	V1	AG Vulcan (Stettin)	28 Feb 13	17 May 13	–	–	Stricken 27 Mar 29; BU Wilhelmshaven
G7 = T107 (23 Apr 39)	G7	Germania (Kiel)	7 Nov 11	30 Apr 12	–	–	See Table 2.1/3
G8 = T108 (23 Apr 39)	G7	Germania (Kiel)	21 Dec 11	6 Aug 12	–	–	See Table 2.1/3
G10 = T110 (23 Apr 39)	G7	Germania (Kiel)	15 Mar 12	28 Aug 12	–	–	Scuttled Travemünde 5 May 45
G11 = T111 (23 Apr 39)	G7	Germania (Kiel)	23 Apr 12	8 Aug 12	–	–	See Table 2.1/3
S18	S13	Schichau (Elbing)	10 Aug 12	12 Jan 13	–	–	Stricken 31 May 31; BU Wilhelmshaven 1935
S19	S13	Schichau (Elbing)	17 Oct 12	29 Mar 13	–	–	Stricken 31 May 31; sold 4 Feb 35; BU Deutsche Werke, Kiel.
S23 = T123, Komet (23 Apr 39)	S13	Schichau (Elbing)	29 Mar 13	1 Nov 13	–	–	See Table 2.1/3
S24	S13	Schichau (Elbing)	28 Jun 13	27 Aug 13	25 Apr 20 (S) Cherbourg	UK	Sold Channel Shipbreaking Co (Teignmouth) 22 Oct 20 (£1,700); stranded in tow Preston Beach (Torquay) 12 Dec 20; salved; re-sold Mr Shaw (Brixham); BU
V26	V25	AG Vulcan (Stettin)	21 Feb 14	1 Aug 14	14 Jun 20 (S) Cherbourg	UK	Sold T W Ward 22 Oct 22 (£2,250); BU Portishead
V28	V25	AG Vulcan (Stettin)	9 May 14	22 Sep 14	23 May 20 (S) Cherbourg	UK	Sold T W Ward 22 Oct 22 (£2,350); BU Portishead
S32	S31	Schichau (Elbing)	28 Feb 14	10 Sep 14	23/25 Nov 18 (I) Scapa Flow	UK (sunk)	Scuttled Scapa Flow 21 Jun 19; sold Cox & Danks (£200) 25 Jan 24; raised 19 Jun 25;.re-sold Granton Shipbreaking; arrived Granton 8 Jul 25 to BU
S36	S31	Schichau (Elbing)	17 Oct 14	4 Jan 15	23/25 Nov 18 (I) Scapa Flow	UK (sunk)	Scuttled Scapa Flow 21 Jun 19; sold Cox & Danks 12 Sep 24 (£200); salved 18 Apr 25; salvage pontoon for Hindenburg 1926; BU 21 Mar–30 May 26
G38	G37	Germania (Kiel)	23 Dec 14	30 Jul 15	23/25 Nov 18 (I) Scapa Flow	UK (sunk)	Scuttled Scapa Flow 21 Jun 19; sold Cox & Danks 12 Sep 24 (£200); salved 27 Sep 24; salvage pontoon for Moltke and Seydlitz 1928; BU Lyness 1929
G39	G37	Germania (Kiel)	16 Jan 15	20 Aug 15	23/25 Nov 18 (I) Scapa Flow	UK (sunk)	Scuttled Scapa Flow 21 Jun 19; sold Cox & Danks 12 Sep 24 (£200); salved 3 Jul 25; BU Lyness to 7 Feb 27
G40	G37	Germania (Kiel)	27 Feb 25	16 Sep 15	23/25 Nov 18 (I) Scapa Flow	UK (sunk)	Scuttled Scapa Flow 21 Jun 19; sold Cox & Danks 12 Sep 24 (£200); salved 29 Jul 25; sold T W Ward; left for Inverkeithing 18 Jun 25; BU 1926
V43	V43	AG Vulcan (Stettin)	27 Jan 15	28 May 15	23/25 Nov 18 (I) Scapa Flow	US (P)	Scuttled Scapa Flow 21 Jun 19; salved Jul/Aug 19; to US 9 Oct 20; gunfire target USS Florida off Cape Henry VA 15 Jul 21
V44	V43	AG Vulcan (Stettin)	24 Feb 15	22 Jun 15	23/25 Nov 18 (I) Scapa Flow	UK (P)	Scuttled Scapa Flow 21 Jun 19; salved Jul/Aug 19; target 8 Dec 20; beached Portsmouth; sold T W Ward 30 Mar 21 (£1,250, reduced to £900); re-sold H Pound (Porchester) 1927; remains extant south side of Whale Island, Portsmouth, visible at low tide
V45	V43	AG Vulcan (Stettin)	29 Mar 15	30 Sep 15	23/25 Nov 18 (I) Scapa Flow	UK (sunk)	Scuttled Scapa Flow 21 Jun 19; sold Scapa Flow Salvage & Shipbreaking 26 Apr 23 (£100); salved Oct 24; re-sold J J King & Sons to BU
V46	V43	AG Vulcan (Stettin)	23 Dec 14	31 Oct 15	23/25 Nov 18 (I) Scapa Flow	FR (P)	Scuttled Scapa Flow 21 Jun 19; salved Jul/Aug 19; to FR 1920; BU Cherbourg 1924
S49	S49	Schichau (Elbing)	10 Apr 15	12 Jul 15	23/25 Nov 18 (I) Scapa Flow	UK (sunk)	Scuttled Scapa Flow 21 Jun 19; sold Scapa Flow Salvage & Shipbreaking (£100) 24 Apr 23; salved Dec 24; re-sold Granton Shipbreaking 10 Mar 25; BU
S50	S49	Schichau (Elbing)	24 Apr 15	15 Aug 15	23/25 Nov 18 (I) Scapa Flow	UK (sunk)	Scuttled Scapa Flow 21 Jun 19; sold Scapa Flow Salvage & Shipbreaking (£100) 26 Apr 23; salved Nov 24; re-sold Granton Shipbreaking 10 Mar 25; BU Luce Bay, Stranraer
S51	S49	Schichau (Elbing)	29 Apr 15	7 Sep 15	23/25 Nov 18 (I) Scapa Flow	UK (sunk)	Scuttled Scapa Flow 21 Jun 19; salved Jul/Aug 19; beached Grangemouth; sold James A White (£750) 2 Feb 21; re-sold James Kelly?; arrived Tayport Jul 21 to BU?[4]

[4] Possibly to be identified with the 'German destroyer' broken up by Kelly's at Tayport; that company certainly undertook the scrapping of G92 and G95 (see I Buxton, 'Shipbreaking on the East Coast of Scotland – Some Corrections', Warships 184 (2016), pp 42–3.

Name	Class	Builder	Launch	Comp/comm	Int (I)/surr (S)	Alloc	Fate.
S52	S49	Schichau (Elbing)	15 Jun 15	28 Sep 15	23/25 Nov 18 (I) Scapa Flow	UK (sunk)	Scuttled Scapa Flow 21 Jun 19; sold Cox & Danks 12 Sep 24 (£200); salved 14 Oct 24; re-sold T W Ward; left for Inverkeithing 16 Dec 24 to BU
S53	S53 (Mob)	Schichau (Elbing)	18 Sep 15	17 Dec 15	23/25 Nov 18 (I) Scapa Flow	UK (sunk)	Scuttled Scapa Flow 21 Jun 19; sold Cox & Danks 12 Sep 24 (£200); salved 14 Aug 24; BU Scapa 1926/27
S54	S53 (Mob)	Schichau (Elbing)	11 Oct 15	30 Jan 16	23/25 Nov 18 (I) Scapa Flow	UK (sunk)	Scuttled Scapa Flow 21 Jun 19; salved Jul/Aug 19; foundered E of Flotta 12 Feb 20; re-sold Cox & Danks 30 Nov 27 (£200); blown up Oct 31
S55	S53 (Mob)	Schichau (Elbing)	6 Nov 15	6 Mar 16	23/25 Nov 18 (I) Scapa Flow	UK (sunk)	Scuttled Scapa Flow 21 Jun 19; sold Cox & Danks 12 Sep 24 (£200); salved 29 Aug 24; re-sold Granton Shipbreaking; arrived Granton 11 Feb 25 to BU
S56	S53 (Mob)	Schichau (Elbing)	11 Dec 15	16 Apr 16	23/25 Nov 18 (I) Scapa Flow	UK (sunk)	Scuttled Scapa Flow 21 Jun 19; sold Cox & Danks 12 Sep 24; salved 5 Jun 25; BU Mill Bay 25 Oct 25–Mar 28
S60	S53 (Mob)	Schichau (Elbing)	3 Apr 16	15 Aug 6	23/25 Nov 18 (I) Scapa Flow	JP (P)	Scuttled Scapa Flow 21 Jun 19; salved Jul/Aug 19; to JP; arrived Hughes Bolckow, Tyne Oct 1920 to BU
S63 = Ardimentoso (1920)	S53 (Mob)	Schichau (Elbing)	25 May 16	18 Dec 16	23 May 20 (S) Cherbourg	IT	IT commission Oct 25; stricken 4 Feb 39
S65	S53 (Mob)	Schichau (Elbing)	14 Oct 16	22 Apr 17	23/25 Nov 18 (I) Scapa Flow	UK (sunk)	Scuttled Scapa Flow 21 Jun 19; sold Cox & Danks 12 Sep 24 (£200); salved 16 May 25; re-sold Granton Shipbreaking; arrived Granton 3 Jun 25 to BU
V70 = Salvage Unit No. 3 (Sep 28)	V67 (Mob)	AG Vulcan (Stettin)	14 Oct 15	6 Jan 16	23/25 Nov 18 (I) Scapa Flow	UK (sunk)	Scuttled Scapa Flow 21 Jun 19; sold Cox & Danks 10 May 24 (£200); salved 1 Aug 24; part-BU Sep 28; salvage hulk; BU Lyness May 33
V71	V67 (Mob)	AG Vulcan (Stettin)	1 Sep 15	10 Mar 16	12 May 20 (S) Rosyth	UK	Sold John Jackson 25 May 21 (£750); BU Bo'ness
V73	V67 (Mob)	AG Vulcan (Stettin)	24 Sep 15	16 Feb 16	23/25 Nov 18 (I) Scapa Flow	UK (sunk)	Scuttled Scapa Flow 21 Jun 19; salved Jul/Aug 19; to Grangemouth; sold G & W Brunton 15 Feb 21 (£400); BU Grangemouth to 1922
V78	V67 (Mob)	AG Vulcan (Stettin)	19 Feb 16	18 May 16	23/25 Nov 18 (I) Scapa Flow	UK (sunk)	Scuttled Scapa Flow 21 Jun 19; sold Cox & Danks 12 Sep 24 (£200); salved 7 Sep 25; re-sold Granton Shipbreaking; left for Granton 7 Oct 25 to BU
V79 = Pierre Durand (1920)	V67 (Mob)	AG Vulcan (Stettin)	18 Apr 16	11 Jul 16	14 Jun 20 (S) Cherbourg	FR	FR commission 1922; stricken 15 Feb 33; sold 1934.
V80	V67 (Mob)	AG Vulcan (Stettin)	28 Apr 16	6 Jul 16	23/25 Nov 18 (I) Scapa Flow	JP (P)	Scuttled Scapa Flow 21 Jun 19; salved Jul/Aug 19; sold Jun 20; BU 1922
V81	V67 (Mob)	AG Vulcan (Stettin)	27 May 16	29 Jul 16	23/25 Nov 18 (I) Scapa Flow	UK (sunk)	Scuttled Scapa Flow 21 Jun 19; salved Jul/Aug 19; foundered in tow Sinclair's Bay (58° 30' N, 3° 7' E) Feb 20; wreck sold J Mowatt (Stromness) 23 Sep 37 (£60); part-BU to Aug 38
V82	V67 (Mob)	AG Vulcan (Stettin)	5 Jul 15	30 Aug 16	23/25 Nov 18 (I) Scapa Flow	UK (sunk)	Scuttled Scapa Flow 21 Jun 19; salved Jul/Aug 19; target 8 Dec 20; beached Portsmouth; sold T W Ward 30 Mar 21 (£1,250, reduced to £900); re-sold H Pound (Porchester) 1927; remains extant south side of Whale Island, Portsmouth, visible at low tide
V83	V67 (Mob)	AG Vulcan (Stettin)	10 Jun 16	3 Oct 16	23/25 Nov 18 (I) Scapa Flow	UK (sunk)	Scuttled Scapa Flow 21 Jun 19; sold East Coast Wrecking Co 1920 (£150); re-sold Peter Kerr (Aberdeen) 1925; part-BU to 1928
G86	G85	Germania (Kiel)	24 Aug 15	11 Jan 16	23/25 Nov 18 (I) Scapa Flow	UK (sunk)	Scuttled Scapa Flow 21 Jun 19; sold Cox & Danks 12 Sep 24 (£200); salved 14 Jul 25; re-sold Granton Shipbreaking; arrived Granton 17 Aug 25 to BU
G89	G85	Germania (Kiel)	11 Dec 15	10 May 16	23/25 Nov 18 (I) Scapa Flow	UK (sunk)	Scuttled Scapa Flow 21 Jun 19; sold A Young (Stromness) 1920 (£500); salved Dec 22; part-BU Stromness; re-sold Cox & Danks Aug 28; BU Lyness Sep 28–c.1931
G91	G85	Germania (Kiel)	16 Nov 15	22 Jul 16	23/25 Nov 18 (I) Scapa Flow	UK (sunk)	Scuttled Scapa Flow 21 Jun 19; sold Cox & Danks (£200) 25 Jan 25; salved 12 Sep 24; re-sold T W Ward; left for Inverkeithing 15 Dec 24 to BU
G92	G85	Germania (Kiel)	15 Feb 16	25 Aug 16	23/25 Nov 18 (I) Scapa Flow	UK (sunk)	Scuttled Scapa Flow 21 Jun 19; salved 15 Aug 19; to Grangemouth; sold B Fryer (£3,750 (with G95)) 28 Feb 21; re-sold James Kelly; arrived Arbroath 17 Mar 21 to BU
G95	G85	Germania (Kiel)	29 Aug 16	25 Nov 16	5 Aug 20 (S) Rosyth	UK	Sold B Fryer 28 Feb 21 (£3,750 (with G92)); re-sold James Kelly; arrived Arbroath 4 Apr 21 to BU
B97 = Cesare Rossarol (1920)	B97	Blohm & Voss (Hamburg)	15 Dec 14	13 Feb 15	23 May 20 (S) Cherbourg	IT	IT 19 Sep 20; commissioned 1 Dec 24; stricken 17 Jan 39
B98	B97	Blohm & Voss (Hamburg)	2 Jan 15	24 Mar 15	Seized 21 Jun 19	UK (wreck)	Stranded in tow Lopness Bay (59° 16' 46" N, 2° 26' 50" W) 17 Feb 20; sold East Coast Wrecking 25 Jun 20 (£700); partly BU 1940s

Name	Class	Builder	Launch	Comp/comm	Int (I)/surr (S)	Alloc	Fate.
V100	V99	AG Vulcan (Stettin)	8 Mar 15	17 Jun 15	23/25 Nov 18 (I) Scapa Flow	FR (P)	Scuttled Scapa Flow 21 Jun 19; salved Aug 19; BU 1921
G101 (ex-Santiago)	G101	Germania (Kiel)	12 Aug 14	4 Mar 15	23/25 Nov 18 (I) Scapa Flow	UK (sunk)	Scuttled Scapa Flow 21 Jun 19; sold Cox & Danks 12 Sep 24 (£200); salved 13 Apr 26; re-sold Alloa Shipbreaking; left for Charlestown 17 Jun 26; BU 26 Jun 26–26 Mar 29
G102 (ex-San Luis)	G101	Germania (Kiel)	16 Sep 14	8 Apr 15	23/25 Nov 18 (I) Scapa Flow	US (P)	Scuttled Scapa Flow 21 Jun 19; salved Jul/Aug 19; aircraft bombing target off Cape Henry VA 13 Jul 21
G103 (ex-Santa Fe)	G101	Germania (Kiel)	14 Nov 14	11 May 15	23/25 Nov 18 (I) Scapa Flow	UK (sunk)	Scuttled Scapa Flow 21 Jun 19; sold Cox & Danks 12 Sep 24 (£200); salved 30 Sep 25;.re-sold Granton Shipbreaking; stranded in tow off Rosehearty (57° 41' 55" N, 2° 7' 25" W) 25 Nov 25; BU
G104 (ex-Tucuman)	G101	Germania (Kiel)	28 Nov 14	5 Jun 15	23/25 Nov 18 (I) Scapa Flow	UK (sunk)	Scuttled Scapa Flow 21 Jun 19; sold Cox & Danks 12 Sep 24 (£200); salved 30 Apr 26;.re-sold Alloa Shipbreaking (£600); arrived Charlestown 13 Jul 26; BU 4 Aug 26–19 Mar 29
V105 (ex-Z1) = Mazur (1920)	V105	AG Vulcan (Stettin)	26 Aug 14	5 Jan 15	19 Aug 20 (S) Rosyth	BR	Sold James A White 13 Jun 21 (£550); exchanged with A69; PL 1920; bombed Oksywie 1 Sep 39
V106 (ex-Z2)	V105	AG Vulcan (Stettin)	26 Aug 14	25 Jan 15	19 Aug 20 (S) Rosyth	BR	Sold James A White 13 Jun 21 (£610); BU
V108 (ex-Z4) = Kaszub (1920)	V105	AG Vulcan (Stettin)	12 Dec 14	23 Mar 15	5 Aug 20 (S) Rosyth	PL	Internal explosion Danzig 20 Jul 25; salved 29 Jul 25 and BU.
B109	B109	Blohm & Voss (Hamburg)	11 Mar 15	8 Jun 15	23/25 Nov 18 (I) Scapa Flow	UK (sunk)	Scuttled Scapa Flow 21 Jun 19; sold Cox & Danks 25 Jan 24 (£200); salved 27 Mar 26; sold Alloa Shipbreaking (£600); arrived Charlestown 25 Jun 26; BU 10 Jul 26–18 Jun 29
B110	B109	Blohm & Voss (Hamburg)	31 Mat 15	26 Jun 15	23/25 Nov 18 (I) Scapa Flow	UK (sunk)	Scuttled Scapa Flow 21 Jun 19; sold Cox & Danks 25 Jan 24 (£200); salved 10 Dec 25; sold Granton Shipbreaking; arrived Granton 21 Jan 26 to BU
B111	B109	Blohm & Voss (Hamburg)	8 Jun 15	10 Aug 15	23/25 Nov 18 (I) Scapa Flow	UK (sunk)	Scuttled Scapa Flow 21 Jun 19; sold Cox & Danks 25 Jan 24 (£200); salved 8 Mar 26; sold Granton Shipbreaking; left for Granton 8 Apr 26 to BU
B112	B109	Blohm & Voss (Hamburg)	17 Jun 15	3 Sep 15	23/25 Nov 18 (I) Scapa Flow	UK (sunk)	Scuttled Scapa Flow 21 Jun 19; sold Cox & Danks 25 Jan 24 (£200); salved 11 Feb 26; sold Granton Shipbreaking; arrived Granton to BU Mar 26
S113 = Amiral Sénès (1920)	S113	Schichau (Elbing)	31 Jan 18	5 Aug 19	23 May 20 (S) Cherbourg	FR	FR commission May 22; sunk as target 19 Jul 38.
S114	S113	Schichau (Elbing)	11 Apr 18	–	–	–	Stricken 3 Nov 19; stripped F Oltmann (Rönnebeck); BU Bremerhaven
S115	S113	Schichau (Elbing)	20 Jul 18	–	–	–	Stricken 3 Nov 19; stripped F Oltmann (Rönnebeck); BU Bremerhaven
V116 = Premuda (1920)	V116	AG Vulcan (Stettin)	2 Mar 18	31 Jun 18	23 May 20 (S) Cherbourg	IT	IT commission 1 Jun 20; stricken 1 Jan 39; BU La Spezia
V117	V116	AG Vulcan (Stettin)	4 May 18	–	–	–	Stricken 3 Nov 19; sold Neugebaur 4 Jul 21; BU Hamburg
V118	V116	AG Vulcan (Stettin)	6 Jul 18	–	–	–	Stricken 3 Nov 19; sold Neugebaur 4 Jul 21; BU Hamburg
G119	G119	Germania (Kiel)	8 Oct 18	–	–	–	Stricken 3 Nov 19; sold 8 Jul 21 (95,000M); BU Kiel
G120	G119	Germania (Kiel)	1920	–	–	–	Stricken 3 Nov 19; sold 8 Jul 21 (95,000M); BU Kiel
G121	G119	Germania (Kiel)	30 Dec 20	–	–	–	Stricken 3 Nov 19; sold 8 Jul 21 (95,000M); BU Kiel
B122	B122	Blohm & Voss (Hamburg)	16 Oct 17	–	–	–	Stricken 3 Nov 19; oil hulk at builder's yard; sold 4 Jul 21; BU Hamburg
B123	B122	Blohm & Voss (Hamburg)	26 Oct 18	–	–	–	Stricken 3 Nov 19; sold 4 Jul 21; BU Harburg
B124	B122	Blohm & Voss (Hamburg)	6 Jun 19	–	–	–	Stricken 3 Nov 19; sold 4 Jul 21; BU Harburg
V125	V125 (1916Mob)	AG Vulcan (Stettin)	18 May 17	29 Aug 17	23/25 Nov 18 (I) Scapa Flow	UK (sunk)	Scuttled Scapa Flow 21 Jun 19; salved Jul 19; to Portsmouth; sold John Cashmore 20 Jul 21 (£1,010); BU Newport 1922
V126	V125 (1916Mob)	AG Vulcan (Stettin)	30 Jun 17	25 Sep 17	23/25 Nov 18 (I) Scapa Flow	FR (P)	Scuttled Scapa Flow 21 Jun 19; salved Jul/Aug 19; BU Lorient 1925
V127	V125 (1916Mob)	AG Vulcan (Stettin)	28 Jul 17	23 Oct 17	23/25 Nov 18 (I) Scapa Flow	JP (P)	Scuttled Scapa Flow 21 Jun 19; salved Jul/Aug 19; BU Dordrecht 1922
.V128	V125 (1916Mob)	AG Vulcan (Stettin)	11 Aug 17	15 Nov 17	23/25 Nov 18 (I) Scapa Flow	UK (sunk)	Scuttled Scapa Flow 21 Jun 19; salved Jul/Aug 19; to Grangemouth; sold G & W Brunton 15 Feb 21 (£700); BU Grangemouth to 1922
V129	V125 (1916Mob)	AG Vulcan (Stettin)	19 Oct 17	20 Dec 17	23/25 Nov 18 (I) Scapa Flow	UK (sunk)	Scuttled Scapa Flow 21 Jun 19; sold Cox & Danks 25 Jan 24 (£200); salved 11 Aug 25; re-sold T W Ward; left for Inverkeithing 28 Aug 25 to BU

Name	Class	Builder	Launch	Comp/comm	Int (I)/surr (S)	Alloc	Fate.
V130 = Buino (1920)	V125 (1916Mob)	AG Vulcan (Stettin)	20 Nov 17	2 Feb 18	3 Aug 20 (S) Cherbourg	IT	IT 1920; stricken 15 Feb 33
S131	S131 (1916Mob)	Schichau (Elbing)	3 Mar 17	2 Oct 17	23/25 Nov 18 (I) Scapa Flow	UK (sunk)	Scuttled Scapa Flow 21 Jun 19; sold Scapa Flow Salvage & Shipbreaking 26 Apr 23 (£400); salved 29 Aug 24; re-sold Granton Shipbreaking; BU Granton
S132	S131 (1916Mob)	Schichau (Elbing)	19 May 17	2 Oct 17	23/25 Nov 18 (I) Scapa Flow	US (P)	Scuttled but not sunk Scapa Flow 21 Jun19; US 17 Feb 20; aircraft bombing target off Cape Henry VA 15 Jul 21
S133 = Chastang (1920)	S131 (1916Mob)	Schichau (Elbing)	1 Sep 17	21 Feb 18	20 Jul 20 (S) Cherbourg	FR	FR 1920; stricken 17 Aug 33
S134 = Vesco (1920)	S131 (1916Mob)	Schichau (Elbing)	25 Aug 17	4 Jan 18	14 Jun 20 (S) Cherbourg	FR	FR 1920; stricken 24 Jul 35; BU 1936
S135 = Mazaré (1920)	S131 (1916Mob)	Schichau (Elbing)	27 Oct 17	15 Mar 18	20 Jul 20 (S) Cherbourg	FR	FR 1920; stricken 24 Jul 35; BU 1936
S136	S131 (1916Mob)	Schichau (Elbing)	1 Dec 17	30 Apr 18	23/25 Nov 18 (I) Scapa Flow	UK (sunk)	Scuttled Scapa Flow 21 Jun 19; sold Cox & Danks 25 Jan 24 (£200); salved 3 Apr 25; BU Lyness 1928–29
S137	S131 (1916Mob)	Schichau (Elbing)	9 Mar 18	14 Jun 18	23/25 Nov 18 (I) Scapa Flow	UK (sunk)	Scuttled Scapa Flow 21 Jun 19; beached; salved 27 Jun 19; sold W Duguid 28 Feb 21 (£920); BU
S138	S131 (1916Mob)	Schichau (Elbing)	22 Apr 18	29 Jul 18	23/25 Nov 18 (I) Scapa Flow	UK (sunk)	Scuttled Scapa Flow 21 Jun 19; sold Cox & Danks 25 Jan 24 (£200); salved 1 May 25; sold T W Ward; arrived Inverkeithing 16 Jun 25 to BU
S139 = Deligny (1920)	S131 (1916Mob)	Schichau (Elbing)	24 Nov 17	15 Apr 18	20 Jul 20 (S) Cherbourg	FR	FR 1920; stricken 17 Aug 1933, BU 1934
V140	V140	AG Vulcan (Stettin)	22 Dec 17	18 Nov 18	–	–	Stricken 3 Nov 19; stranded in tow off DK coast 8 Dec 20 en route to BU
V141	V140	AG Vulcan (Stettin)	26 Mar 18	–	–	–	Stricken 3 Nov 19; sold and stripped Wewelsfleth 1920; sold 27 Oct 21; BU Kiel
V142	V140	AG Vulcan (Stettin)	25 Sep 18	–	–	–	Stricken 3 Nov 19; sold and stripped Wewelsfleth 1920; sold 27 Oct 21; BU Kiel
V143	V140	AG Vulcan (Stettin)	10 Oct 18	–	–	–	Stricken 3 Nov 19; sold and stripped Wewelsfleth 1920; sold 27 Oct 21; BU Kiel
V144	V140	AG Vulcan (Stettin)	1919	–	–	–	Stricken 3 Nov 19; sold and stripped Wewelsfleth 1920; sold 27 Oct 21; BU Kiel
H145	H145 (1917Mob)	Howaldtswerke (Kiel)	11 Dec 17	4 Aug 18	23/25 Nov 18 (I) Scapa Flow	UK (sunk)	Scuttled Scapa Flow 21 Jun 19; sold Cox & Danks (£200) 25 Jan 24; salved 14 Mar 25; BU Lyness 15 Jan–21 Sep 28
H146 = Rageot de la Touche (1920)	H145 (1917Mob)	Howaldtswerke (Kiel)	23 Jan 18	3 Oct 18	23 May 20 (S) Cherbourg	FR	FR 1920; stricken 15 Feb 1933, BU 1934
H147 = Delage (1920)	H145 (1917Mob)	Howaldtswerke (Kiel)	13 Mar 18	13 Jul 20	20 Jul 20 (S) Cherbourg	FR	FR 1920; stricken 15 Feb 1933, BU 1934
G148, G149	G148 (1917Mob)	Lübeck Maschinenbau (Lübeck)	–	–	–	–	Stricken 3 Nov 19; BU
G150	G148 (1917Mob)	Lübeck Maschinenbau (Rendsburg)	–	–	–	–	Stricken 3 Nov 19; BU
Ww151	G148 (1917Mob)	Wilhelmshaven DYd	–	–	–	–	Stricken 3 Nov 19; BU 1920
S152	S152 (1917Mob)	Schichau (Elbing)	1918	–	–	–	Stricken 3 Nov 19; sold 1920; to Glückstadt; to Wewelsfleth for stripping; BU
S153	S152 (1917Mob)	Schichau (Elbing)	1918	–	–	–	Stricken 3 Nov 19; BU 1920/21
S154–S155	S152 (1917Mob)	Schichau (Elbing)	1918	–	–	–	Stricken 3 Nov 19; sold 1920; to Otto Werk (Harburg) for stripping; BU 1920/21
S156	S152 (1917Mob)	Schichau (Elbing)	1918	–	–	–	Stricken 3 Nov 19; BU 1920/21
S157	S152 (1917Mob)	Schichau (Elbing)	1918	–	–	–	Stricken 3 Nov 19; sold 1920; to Glückstadt; to Wewelsfleth for stripping; BU
V158, V159	V158 (1917Mob)	AG Vulcan (Stettin)	1 Nov 18	–	–	–	Stricken 3 Nov 19; sold Naugebauer 4 Jul 21; BU Hamburg
V160	V158 (1917Mob)	AG Vulcan (Stettin)	11 Mar 21	–	–	–	Stricken 3 Nov 19; damaged in tow; conversion to coaster at Hamburg not carried out; BU Sassnitz

Name	Class	Builder	Launch	Comp/comm	Int (I)/surr (S)	Alloc	Fate.
V161	V158 (1917Mob)	AG Vulcan (Stettin)	1919?	–	–	–	Stricken 3 Nov 19; sold Naugebauer 4 Jul 21; BU Hamburg
V162, V163	V158 (1917Mob)	AG Vulcan (Stettin)	–	–	–	–	Stricken 3 Nov 19; BU on slip
V164, V165	V158 (1917Mob)	AG Vulcan (Stettin)	–	–	–	–	Cancelled
H166	H166 (1917Mob)	Howaldtswerke (Kiel)	25 Oct 19	–	–	–	Stricken 3 Nov 19; sold for mercantile conversion 1920 and stripped; BU Kiel
H167	H166 (1917Mob)	Howaldtswerke (Kiel)	26 Oct 18	–	–	–	Stricken 3 Nov 19; sold for mercantile conversion 1920 and stripped; BU Kiel
H168	H166 (1917Mob)	Howaldtswerke (Kiel)	8 Nov 19	–	–	–	Stricken 3 Nov 19; sold for mercantile conversion 1920 and stripped; BU Kiel
H169	H166 (1917Mob)	Howaldtswerke (Kiel)	19 Oct 18	–	–	–	Stricken 3 Nov 19; sold for mercantile conversion 1920 and stripped; BU Kiel
V170–V177	V170 (1918Mob)	AG Vulcan (Stettin)	–	–	–	–	Stricken 3 Nov 19; BU
S178 = Franziska Kimme (1921) = Kapitän J Frobeen (1926) = Capitan Alfredo Kling II (1926) = Ajuricaba (1927) = Gonza (1931)	S170 (1918Mob)	Schichau (Elbing)	1919	[1921]	–	–	Stricken 3 Nov 19; sold Friedrich Kimme, (Bremerhaven) 1920; sold Bremerhavener Reederei AG 1922; sold Atlantic-Rhederei (Hamburg) 1926; sold H Kling (Hamburg) 1926; sold Luiz Oliveira (Porto Alegre); 1927; sold Luiz de Almeida (Rio de Janeiro) 1931; sold Banco de Brasil 1931; sold Companhia 'Serras' de Navegação e Comércio 1935; BU 1935
S179 = Georg Kimme (1921) = Anneliese Rathjen (1927) = Zazpiakbat (1928)	S170 (1918Mob)	Schichau (Elbing)	1919	[1921]	–	–	Stricken 3 Nov 19; sold .... (Bremen) 1919; sold .... (Danzig) 1920; sold F Kimme (Bremerhaven) (schooner); sold Addieks (Bremen) 1927; sold La Morue Français (St Pierre-Miquelon) 1928; scuttled Martigues 21 Aug 44
S180–S185	S170 (1918Mob)	Schichau (Elbing)	–	–	–	–	Stricken 3 Nov 19; BU
H186 = Hansdorf (1921) = Dietrich Bohnekamp (1924) = Peryneas II (1929)	H170 (1918Mob)	Howaldtswerke (Kiel)	1920	[1921]	–	–	Stricken 3 Nov 19; sold Howaldtswerke (Kiel) 24 Nov 19 (81,000M); sold Baltishe Reederei (Hamburg) 1921 (coaster); sold H Bohnekamp (Hamburg) 1924; sold Handel & Transport (Hamburg) 1928; sold Comp Salinas Peryneas (Rio de Janeiro) 1931; BU 1935
H187 = Hoisdorf (1921) = Hermann Bohnekamp (1924) = Peryneas (1929)	H170 (1918Mob)	Howaldtswerke (Kiel)	1920	[1921]	–	–	Stricken 3 Nov 19; sold Howaldtswerke (Kiel) 24 Nov 19 (81,000M); sold Baltishe Reederei (Hamburg) 1921 (coaster); sold H Bohnekamp (Hamburg) 1924; sold Handel & Transport (Hamburg) 1928; sold W Ogilvie (St John's) 1931; sold P L Ogilvie (Belize) 1933; BU 1933
V203–V210	V170 (1918Mob)	AG Vulcan (Stettin)	–	–	–	–	Cancelled
S211–S223	S170 (1918Mob)	Schichau (Elbing)	–	–	–	–	Cancelled
R01 (ex-Schastliviy)	Novik	Putilov (St Petersburg)/ Vaddon (Kherson)	29 Mar 14	RU: May 15 GE: 7 Aug 18	24 Nov 18		Sevastopol – Foundered Mudros 1919

Name	Class	Builder	Launch	Comp/comm	Int (I)/surr (S)	Alloc	Fate.
R04 (ex-Kapitan Saken, ex-Leitnant Pushchin) = R2 (Nov 18) = Kapitan Saken (1919)	RU Leitnant Schestakov	Naval (Nikolaev)	Sep 07	RU: Oct 09 GE: 12 Oct 18	24 Nov 18		Sevastopol – To FR 1919 Nov 18; to White Russia 1919; interned Bizerte 29 Dec 20; BU 1930
R10 (ex-Zorkiy)	Bespokoiny	Naval (Nikolaev)	Oct 04	RU: Oct 05 GE: 7 May 18	24 Nov 18		Sevastopol – To White Russia 1919; interned Bizerte 29 Dec 20; BU 1930
R11 (ex-Zvonkiy)	Bespokoiny	Naval (Nikolaev)	Oct 04	RU: Aug 05 GE: Jul 18	24 Nov 18		Sevastopol – Decommissioned 1 Oct 18; to GR Nov 18; to White Russia 1919; interned Bizerte 29 Dec 20; BU 1930
R12 (ex-Zivoy)	Bespokoiny	Admiralty (Nikolaev)	1904	RU: 1905 GE: 22 Oct 18	24 Nov 18		Sevastopol – Decommissioned 1 Oct 18; to White Russia 1919; interned Bizerte 29 Dec 20; BU 1930
D1 (ex-Carmen, ex-D1, ex-D2)	D1	Schichau (Elbing)	19 Dec 86	27 Apr 87	–	–	Stricken 2 Aug 21; sold (142,000M); BU Wilhelmshaven
D2 (ex-Alice Roosevelt, ex-D2, ex-D1)	D1	Schichau (Elbing)	11 Sep 86	1 May 87	–	–	Stricken 7 Dec 20; BU 1921
D3	D3	Schichau (Elbing)	1 Oct 87	3 May 88	–	–	Stricken 7 Dec 20; BU Wilhelmshaven 1921
D4	D3	Schichau (Elbing)	9 Nov 87	15 Oct 88	–	–	Stricken 7 Dec 20; BU Hamburg 1921
D5	D5	Schichau (Elbing)	20 Oct 88	17 Apr 89	–	–	Stricken 7 Dec 20; BU Hamburg 1921
D6	D5	Schichau (Elbing)	9 Feb 89	28 Jun 89	–	–	Stricken 7 Dec 20; BU 1921
D7	D7	Schichau (Elbing)	6 May 91	25 Jul 91	–	–	Stricken 7 Dec 20; BU Hamburg 1921
D8	D7	Schichau (Elbing)	8 Jun 91	25 Oct 91	–	–	Stricken 7 Dec 20; BU Hamburg 1921
D9	D9	Schichau (Elbing)	3 Sep 94	29 Dec 94	–	–	Stricken 7 Dec 20; BU Hamburg 1921
D10	D10	Thornycroft (Chiswick)	24 Mar 98	13 Oct 98	–	–	Stricken 28 Jul 22; BU Wilhelmshaven 1922
A1	A-I	AG Vulcan (Hamburg)	16 Jan 15	29 Jan 15	–	–	Stricken 10 May 22; sold (1,900,000M); BU Kiel 1922
A4 = A3PC (1920) = A3 Princess Marie-José	A-I	AG Vulcan (Hamburg)	26 Jun 15	30 Jun 15	–	–	Scuttled Antwerp 11 Nov 18; salved; BE 25 Jun 19; sold 1931; BU
A5 = A4PC (1920) = A4 (1927) = 5 (1927)	A-I	AG Vulcan (Hamburg)	5 May 15	10 May 15	–	–	Interned Hellevoetsluis 15 Nov 18; BE 25 Jun 19; sold 1931; BU
A8 = A5PC (1920) = A5 (1927) = 8 (1927) = Oever (1931)	A-I	AG Vulcan (Hamburg)	25 Apr 15	21 May 15	–	–	Interned Hellevoetsluis 15 Nov 18; BE 25 Jun 19; training boat 1931; sold 1939
A9 = A6PC (1920) = A6 (1927) = 9 (1927)	A-I	AG Vulcan (Hamburg)	4 Aug 15	6 Aug 15	–	–	Interned Hellevoetsluis 15 Nov 18; BE 25 Jun 19; sold 1931; BU
A11 = A7PC (1920) = A7 (1927) = 11 (1927)	A-I	AG Vulcan (Hamburg)	4 Jun 15	7 Jun 15	–	–	Interned Hellevoetsluis 15 Nov 18; BE 25 Jun 19; sold 1931; BU
A12 = A2PC (1920) = A2 Prince Charles	A-I	AG Vulcan (Hamburg)	28 Apr 15	2 May 15	–	–	Interned Hellevoetsluis 15 Nov 18; BE 25 Jun 19; sold 1930; BU
A14 = A1PC (1920) = A1 Prince Leopold = 14 (1927)	A-I	AG Vulcan (Hamburg)	22 Jul 15	27 Jul 15	–	–	Interned Hellevoetsluis 15 Nov 18; BE 25 Jun 19; sold 1931; BU
A16 = A8PC (1920) = A8 (1927) = 16 (1927)	A-I	AG Vulcan (Hamburg)	16 Jun 15	19 Jun 15	–	–	Interned Hellevoetsluis 15 Nov 18; BE 25 Jun 19; sold 1931; BU
A17	A-I	AG Vulcan (Hamburg)	8 Jun 15	6 Jul 15	–	–	Scuttled off Kiel during Kapp Putsch 13 Mar 20; salved; stricken 6 Jan 21; BU 1922
A18	A-I	AG Vulcan (Hamburg)	2 Jul 15	20 Jul 15	–	–	Stricken 21 Jan 22; BU Kiel 1922

Name	Class	Builder	Launch	Comp/comm	Int (I)/surr (S)	Alloc	Fate.
A20 = A9PC (1920) = A9 (1927) = 20 (1927) = West Diep (1931) = Reiher (1940) = Warendorp (Oct 43)	A-I	AG Vulcan (Hamburg)	27 Aug 15	1 Sep 15	–	–	Interned Hellevoetsluis 15 Nov 18; BE 25 Jun 19; training boat 1931; GE 1940; US 1945; BE 1945; BU 1948
A21	A-I	AG Vulcan (Hamburg)	1 Jun 15	29 Jun 15	–	–	Scuttled off Kiel during Kapp Putsch 13 Mar 20; salved; stricken 6 Jan 21; BU 1922
A22	A-I	AG Vulcan (Hamburg)	22 May 15	8 Jun 15	–	–	Stricken 15 May 22; steam supply vessel Kiel
A23	A-I	AG Vulcan (Hamburg)	5 May 15	29 May 15	–	–	Stricken 15 May 22; target after 1924
A24	A-I	AG Vulcan (Hamburg)	12 Jun 15	6 Aug 15	–	–	Stricken 15 May 22; steam supply vessel Swinemünde; target after 1924
A25	A-I	AG Vulcan (Hamburg)	13 Jul 15	27 Jul 15	–	–	Stricken 15 May 22; steam supply vessel Kiel
A26	A-II [A26]	Schichau (Elbing)	20 May 16	22 Jul 16	–	–	Stricken 23 Mar 21; BU
A27	A-II [A26]	Schichau (Elbing)	27 May 16	12 Aug 16	19 Aug 20 (S) Rosyth	UK	Sold John Jackson & Co 10 Mar 21 (£120); BU Bo'ness
A28	A-II [A26]	Schichau (Elbing)	10 Jun 16	26 Aug 16	19 Aug 20 (S) Rosyth	UK	Sold John Jackson & Co 10 Mar 21 (£120); BU Bo'ness
A29	A-II [A26]	Schichau (Elbing)	15 Jun 16	9 Sep 16	19 Aug 20 (S) Rosyth	UK	Sold John Jackson & Co 10 Mar 21 (£120); BU Bo'ness
A30 = A29PC (1920)	A-II [A26]	Schichau (Elbing)	15 Jul 16	28 Sep 16	–	–	Interned Hellevoetsluis 15 Nov 18; to BE 25 Jun 19; sold 1927; BU
A31	A-II [A26]	Schichau (Elbing)	1 Jul 16	30 Sep 16	19 Aug 20 (S) Rosyth	UK	Sold John Jackson & Co 10 Mar 21 (£120); BU Bo'ness
A33	A-II [A26]	Schichau (Elbing)	29 Jul 16	8 Nov 16	19 Sep 20 (S) Rosyth	UK	Sold John Jackson & Co 10 Mar 21 (£120); BU Bo'ness
A34	A-II [A26]	Schichau (Elbing)	20 Jul 16	8 Nov 16	19 Sep 20 (S) Rosyth	UK	Sold John Jackson & Co 10 Mar 21 (£120); BU Bo'ness
A35	A-II [A26]	Schichau (Elbing)	19 Aug 16	1 Dec 16	19 Aug 20 (S) Rosyth	UK	Sold John Jackson & Co 21 Mar 21 (£150)
A36	A-II [A26]	Schichau (Elbing)	14 Aug 16	24 Nov 16	19 Aug 20 (S) Rosyth	UK	Sold John Jackson & Co 21 Mar 21 (£150)
A37	A-II [A26]	Schichau (Elbing)	12 Aug 16	24 Nov 16	19 Sep 20 (S) Rosyth	UK	Sold John Jackson & Co 10 Mar 21 (£120); BU Bo'ness
A38	A-II [A26]	Sachsenberg (Rosslau)/ Schichau (Elbing)	17 Nov 16	14 Mar 17	19 Sep 20 (S) Rosyth	UK	Sold John Jackson & Co 10 Mar 21 (£120); BU Bo'ness
A39	A-II [A26]	Schichau (Elbing)	12 Sep 16	16 Dec 16	19 Aug 20 (S) Rosyth	UK	Sold John Jackson & Co 28 Feb 21 (£150); BU Bo'ness
A40 = A22PC (1920) = A22 (1926) = 40 (1927)	A-II [A26]	Schichau (Elbing)	2 Sep 16	8 Dec 16	–	–	Interned Hellevoetsluis 15 Nov 18; to BE 25 Jun 19; sold to private person 1934
A41	A-II [A26]	Sachsenberg (Rosslau)/Schichau (Elbing)	8 Dec 16	16 Mar 17	19 Aug 20 (S) Rosyth	UK	Sold John Jackson & Co 10 Mar 21 (£120); BU Bo'ness
A42 = A23PC (1920) = A23 (1926) = Zavel (1927)	A-II [A26]	Schichau (Elbing)	1 Nov 16	5 Jan 17	–	–	Interned Hellevoetsluis 15 Nov 18; to BE 25 Jun 19; training boat 1927; BU 1934
A43 = A24PC (1920) = A24 (1926) = 43 (1927) = Wielingen (1930)	A-II [A26]	Schichau (Elbing)	25 Dec 16	2 Apr 17	–	–	Interned Hellevoetsluis 15 Nov 18; to BE 25 Jun 19; training boat 1931; GE 18 May 40; BU 1943
A44	A-II [A26]	Schichau (Elbing)	10 Mar 17	30 Apr 17	19 Sep 20 (S) Rosyth	UK	Sold John Jackson & Co 10 Mar 21 (£120); BU Bo'ness
A45	A-II [A26]	Schichau (Elbing)	8 Nov 16	15 Jun 17	2 Sep 20 (S) Rosyth	UK	Sold John Jackson & Co 28 Feb 21 (£150); BU Bo'ness
A46	A-II [A26]	Schichau (Elbing)	24 Mar 17	22 May 17	2 Sep 20 (S) Rosyth	UK	Sold John Jackson & Co 28 Feb 21 (£150); BU Bo'ness

Name	Class	Builder	Launch	Comp/comm	Int (I)/surr (S)	Alloc	Fate.
A47 = A25PC (1920) = A25 (1926) = 47 Caporal Trésignies (1926) = Varouni (1938)	A-II [A26]	Schichau (Elbing)	23 Apr 17	22 Jun 17	–	–	Interned Hellevoetsluis 15 Nov 18; to BE 25 Jun 19; sold as pleasure craft 1938
A48	A-II [A26]	Schichau (Elbing)	9 Jun 17	31 Jul 17	2 Sep 20 (S) Rosyth	UK	Sold John Jackson & Co 10 Mar 21 (£120); BU Bo'ness
A49	A-II [A26]	Schichau (Elbing)	19 May 17	9 Jul 17	19 Sep 20 (S) Rosyth	UK	UK 1920; sold John Jackson & Co 10 Mar 21 (£120); BU Bo'ness
A52	A-II [A50]	Schichau (Elbing)	18 Jan 17	1 Apr 17	30 Sep 20 (S) Rosyth	UK	Sold John Jackson & Co 10 Mar 21 (£120); BU Bo'ness
A53	A-II [A50]	Schichau (Elbing)	3 Feb 17	7 Apr 17	19 Sep 20 (S) Rosyth	UK	Sold John Jackson & Co 10 Mar 21 (£120); BU Bo'ness
A54	A-II [A50]	Schichau (Elbing)	22 Feb 17	14 Apr 17	30 Sep 20 (S) Rosyth	UK	Sold John Jackson & Co 10 Mar 21 (£120); BU Bo'ness
A55	A-II [A50]	Schichau (Elbing)	10 Mar 17	27 Apr 17	30 Sep 20 (S) Rosyth	UK	Sold John Jackson & Co 10 Mar 21 (£120); BU Bo'ness
A59 = Ślązak (1920)	A-III [A56]	AG Vulcan (Stettin)	13 Apr 17	9 Jun 17	30 Sep 20 (S) Rosyth	PL	Target ship 1937
A61	A-III [A56]	AG Vulcan (Stettin)	15 May 17	11 Jul 17	19 Sep 20 (S) Rosyth	UK	Sold John Jackson & Co 10 Mar 21 (£120); BU Bo'ness
A62	A-III [A56]	AG Vulcan (Stettin)	8 Jun 17	25 Jul 17	19 Sep 20 (S) Rosyth	UK	Sold John Jackson & Co 10 Mar 21 (£120); BU Bo'ness
A63	A-III [A56]	AG Vulcan (Stettin)	16 Jun 17	11 Aug 17	30 Sep 20 (S) Rosyth	UK	Sold John Jackson & Co 10 Mar 21 (£120); BU Bo'ness
A64 = Krakowiak (1920)	A-III [A56]	AG Vulcan (Stettin)	30 Mar 18	8 Aug 18	30 Sep 20 (S) Rosyth	PL	Stricken Oct 36; BU
A65	A-III [A56]	AG Vulcan (Stettin)	30 Mar 18	24 Aug 18	2 Sep 20 (S) Rosyth	BR (ex-UK)	Sold James A White 13 Jun 21 (£170); BU Queensferry
A66	A-III [A56]	AG Vulcan (Stettin)	23 Jun 18	20 Sep 18	30 Sep 20 (S) Rosyth	UK	Sold John Jackson & Co 10 Mar 21 (£120); BU Bo'ness
A67	A-III [A56]	AG Vulcan (Stettin)	23 Jun 18	–	–	–	Stricken 3 Nov 19; sold Neugebauer 1920; BU
A68 = Kujawiak (1920)	A-III [A68]	Schichau (Elbing)	11 Apr 17	12 Jun 17	2 Sep 20 (S) Rosyth	PL	Bombed Oksywie 3 Sep 39
A69	A-III [A68]	Schichau (Elbing)	28 Apr 17	4 Jul 17	2 Sep 20 (S) Rosyth	PL	Exchanged with V105; BU Queensferry by James A White 1921
A70	A-III [A68]	Schichau (Elbing)	19 May 17	23 Jul 17	30 Sep 20 (S) Rosyth	UK	Sold John Jackson & Co 28 Feb 21 (£150); BU Bo'ness
A74	A-III [A68]	Schichau (Elbing)	4 Aug 17	9 Oct 17	2 Sep 20 (S) Rosyth	BR	Sold James A White 13 Jun 21 (£170); BU Queensferry
A75	A-III [A68]	Schichau (Elbing)	11 Aug 17	26 Oct 17	30 Sep 20 (S) Rosyth	UK	Sold John Jackson & Co 10 Mar 21 (£96)
A76	A-III [A68]	Schichau (Elbing)	1 Sep 17	12 Nov 17	30 Sep 20 (S) Rosyth	UK	Sold John Jackson & Co 10 Mar 21 (£120); BU Bo'ness
A78	A-III [A68]	Schichau (Elbing)	13 Oct 17	15 Dec 17	2 Sep 20 (S) Rosyth	BR	Sold James A White 13 Jun 21 (£150); BU Queensferry
A80 = Góral (1920) = Podhalanin (1922)	A-III [A80]	AG Vulcan (Stettin)	24 Oct 17	21 Dec 17	30 Sep 20 (S) Rosyth	PL	Bombed between Jastarnia and Hel 24 Sep 39
A81	A-III [A80]	AG Vulcan (Stettin)	27 Nov 17	10 Jan 18	30 Sep 20 (S) Rosyth	UK	(ex-BR) Sold Thomas Round 30 Mar 21 (£150); BU Sunderland 1922
A83	A-III [A83]	Howaldtswerke (Kiel)	28 May 18	–	–	–	Stricken 3 Nov 19; BU Kiel
A84	A-III [A83]	Howaldtswerke (Kiel)	19 Apr 18	–	–	–	Stricken 3 Nov 19; BU Kiel
A85	A-III [A83]	Howaldtswerke (Kiel)	6 Jun 18	–	–	–	Stricken 3 Nov 19; BU Kiel
A86	A-III [A86]	AG Vulcan (Stettin)	5 Feb 18	16 Mar 18	30 Sep 20 (S) Rosyth	UK	Sold John Jackson & Co 10 Mar 21 (£96)
A87	A-III [A86]	AG Vulcan (Stettin)	21 Feb 18	8 Apr 18	19 Sep 20 (S) Rosyth	UK	Sold John Jackson & Co 10 Mar 21 (£96)
A88	A-III [A86]	AG Vulcan (Stettin)	2 Mar 18	27 Apr 18	30 Sep 20 (S) Rosyth	UK	Sold John Jackson & Co 10 Mar 21 (£120); BU Bo'ness

Name	Class	Builder	Launch	Comp/comm	Int (I)/surr (S)	Alloc	Fate.
A89	A-III [A86]	AG Vulcan (Stettin)	22 Mar 18	14 May 18	30 Sep 20 (S) Rosyth	UK	Sold John Jackson & Co 10 Mar 21 (£120); BU Bo'ness
A90	A-III [A86]	AG Vulcan (Stettin)	6 Apr 18	6 Jun 18	30 Sep 20 (S) Rosyth	UK	Sold John Jackson & Co 10 Mar 21 (£120); BU Bo'ness
A91	A-III [A86]	AG Vulcan (Stettin)	27 Apr 18	22 Jun 18	30 Sep 20 (S) Rosyth	UK	Sold John Jackson & Co 10 Mar 21 (£120); BU Bo'ness
A92	A-III [A92]	Schichau (Elbing)	16 Mar 18	24 May 18	19 Sep 20 (S) Rosyth	UK	Sold John Jackson & Co 10 Mar 21 (£120); BU Bo'ness
A93	A-III [A92]	Schichau (Elbing)	9 Apr 18	18 Jun 18	30 Sep 20 (S) Rosyth	BR	Sold W Duguid 13 Jun 21
A94	A-III [A92]	Schichau (Elbing)	27 Apr 18	19 Jul 18	30 Sep 20 (S) Rosyth	UK	Sold John Jackson & Co 10 Mar 21 (£120); BU Bo'ness
A95	A-III [A92]	Schichau (Elbing)	25 May 18	19 Aug 18	30 Sep 20 (S) Rosyth	UK	Sold John Jackson & Co 10 Mar 21 (£120); BU Bo'ness
A96–A113	A-III [A96]	AG Vulcan (Stettin)	–	–	–	–	Stricken 3 Nov 19; BU

Table 1.1/4. Submarines

Class[5]	Disp.[6]	Length	Beam	Machinery	Power/speed	TT	Gun(s)	Mines
U1	238/283t	42.4m	3.8m	1 x oil 2 x electric	400bhp=10.8kt 400bhp=8.7kt	1 x 45cm	–	–
U2	341/430t	45.4m	5.5m	2 x oil 2 x electric	600bhp=13.2kt 630bhp=9.0kt	4 x 45cm	–	–
U3	421/510t	51.3m	5.6m	2 x oil 2 x electric	600bhp=11.8kt 1030bhp=9.4kt	4 x 45cm	1 x 37mm	–
U9	493/611t	57.4m	6.0m	4 x oil 2 x electric	1000bhp=14.2kt 1160bhp=8.1kt	4 x 45cm	1 x 37mm	–
U16	489/627t	57.8m	6.0m	4 x oil 2 x electric	1200bhp=15.6kt 1160bhp=10.7kt	4 x 45cm	1 x 37mm	–
U17	564/691t	62.3m	6.0m	2 x diesel 2 x electric	1400bhp=14.9kt 1120bhp=9.5kt	4 x 45cm	1 x 37mm	–
U19	650/837t	64.1m	6.1m	2 x diesel 2 x electric	1700bhp=15.4kt 1200bhp=9.5kt	4 x 50cm	1 x 10.5cm/45 (*U19*) 2 x 8.8cm/30 (*U21, U22*)	– –
U23	669/864t	64.7m	6.3m	2 x diesel 2 x electric	1800bhp=16.7kt 1200bhp=10.3kt	4 x 50cm	1 x 8.8cm/30	–
U27	675/867t	64.7m	6.3m	2 x diesel 2 x electric	2000bhp=16.7kt 1200bhp=9.8kt	4 x 50cm	2 x 8.8cm/30	–
U31	685/878t	64.7m	6.3m	2 x diesel 2 x electric	1850bhp=16.4kt 1200bhp=9.7kt	4 x 50cm	1 x 10.5cm/45	–
U43 (Mob)	725/940t	65.0m	6.2m	2 x diesel 2 x electric	2000bhp=15.2kt 1200bhp=9.7kt	4 x 50cm	1 x 10.5cm/45	–
U51 (Mob)	715/902t	65.2m	6.4m	2 x diesel 2 x electric	2400bhp=17.1kt 1200bhp=9.1kt	4 x 50cm	1 x 10.5cm/45 (*U52*) 1 x 10.5cm/45 + 1 x 8.8cm/30	–
U57 (Mob)	786/954t	67.0m	6.3m	2 x diesel 2 x electric	1800bhp=14.7kt 1200bhp=8.4kt	4 x 50cm	1 x 10.5cm/45 + 1 x 8.8cm/30	–
U60 (Mob)	768/956t	67.0m	6.3m	2 x diesel 2 x electric	2400bhp=16.5kt 1200bhp=8.4kt	4 x 50cm	1 x 10.5cm/45 + 1 x 8.8cm/30	–
U63 (Mob)	810/927t	68.4m	6.3m	2 x diesel 2 x electric	2200bhp=16.5kt 1200bhp=9.0kt	4 x 50cm	1 x 10.5cm/45 + 1 x 8.8cm/30	–
U66 (Mob)	791/933t	69.5m	6.3m	2 x diesel 2 x electric	2300bhp=16.8kt 1240bhp=10.3kt	5 x 45cm	1 x 10.5cm/45	–
U71 (UE-I)	755/832t	56.8m	5.9m	2 x diesel 2 x electric	900bhp=10.6kt 900bhp=7.9kt	2 x 50cm	1 x 8.8cm/30	38
U75 (UE-I)	755/832t	56.8m	5.9m	2 x diesel 2 x electric	900bhp=9.9kt 900bhp=7.8kt	2 x 50cm	1 x 10.5cm/45	38

[5] Designations in parentheses are those for overarching series of boats, within which there were individual classes.
[6] Surfaced/submerged.

Class	Disp.	Length	Beam	Machinery	Power/speed	TT	Gun(s)	Mines
U81 (MS)	808/946t	70.1m	6.3m	2 x diesel 2 x electric	2400bhp=16.8kt 1200bhp=9.1kt	4 x 50cm	1 x 10.5cm/45	–
U87 (MS)	757/998t	65.8m	6.2m	2 x diesel 2 x electric	2400bhp=15.6kt 1200bhp=8.6kt	6 x 50cm	1 x 10.5cm/45 + 1 x 8.8cm/30	–
U93 (MS)	838/1000t	71.6m	6.3m	2 x diesel 2 x electric	2400bhp=16.8kt 1200bhp=8.6kt	6 x 50cm	1 x 10.5cm/45 + 1 x 8.8cm/30	–
U96 (MS)	837/998t	71.6m	6.3m	2 x diesel 2 x electric	2300bhp=16.9kt 1200bhp=8.6kt	6 x 50cm	1 x 10.5cm/45 + 1 x 8.8cm/30	–
U99 (MS)	750/952t	67.6m	6.3m	2 x diesel 2 x electric	2400bhp=16.5kt 1200bhp=8.8kt	4 x 50cm	1 x 10.5cm/45 + 1 x 8.8cm/30	–
U105 (MS)	798/1000t	71.6m	6.3m	2 x diesel 2 x electric	2300bhp=16.4kt 1200bhp=8.4kt	6 x 50cm	1 x 10.5cm/45 + 1 x 8.8cm/30	–
U111 (MS)	798/996t	71.6m	6.3m	2 x diesel 2 x electric	2300bhp=16.4kt 1200bhp=8.4kt	6 x 50cm	1 x 10.5cm/45 + 1 x 8.8cm/30	–
U115 (MS)	882/1233t	72.3m	6.5m	2 x diesel 2 x electric	2400bhp=16.0kt 1200bhp=9.0kt	6 x 50cm	1 x 10.5cm/45 + 1 x 8.8cm/30	–
U117 (UE-II)	1164/1512t	81.5m	7.4m	2 x diesel 2 x electric	2400bhp=14.7kt 1200bhp=7.0kt	4 x 50cm	1 x 15cm/45 + 1 x 8.8cm/30	200
U122 (UE-II)	1163/1468t	82.0m	7.4m	2 x diesel 2 x electric	2400bhp=14.7kt 1235bhp=7.2kt	4 x 50cm	2 x 10.5cm/45	200
U127 (Pr. 42)	1221/1649t	82.0m	7.5m	4 x diesel 2 x electric	4400bhp=17.0kt 1690bhp=8.1kt	6 x 50cm	1 x 15cm/45	–
U131 (Pr 42)	1160/1527t	82.5m	7.5m	4 x diesel 2 x electric	4400bhp=17.0kt 1690bhp=8.1kt	6 x 50cm	1 x 15cm/45	–
U135 (Pr 42)	1175/1534t	83.5m	7.5m	4 x diesel 2 x electric	4400bhp=17.0kt 1690bhp=8.1kt	6 x 50cm	1 x 15cm/45	–
U139 (Pr. 36)	1930/2483t	92.0m	9.1m	4 x diesel 2 x electric	3750bhp=15.3kt 1780bhp=7.6kt	6 x 50cm	2 x 15cm/45 + 2 x 8.8cm/30	–
U140 (Pr. 36)	1930/2483t	92.0m	9.1m	4 x diesel 2 x electric	3950bhp=15.8kt 1780bhp=7.6kt	6 x 50cm	2 x 15cm/45 + 2 x 8.8cm/30	–
U142 (Pr. 36)	2158/2785t	97.5m	9.1m	4 x diesel 2 x electric	6450bhp=17.5kt 2600bhp=8.5kt	6 x 50cm	2 x 15cm/45 + 2 x 8.8cm/30	–
U145 (Pr. 36)	2173/2789t	97.5m	9.1m	4 x diesel 2 x electric	6450bhp=17.5kt 2600bhp=8.5kt	6 x 50cm	2 x 15cm/45 + 2 x 8.8cm/30	–
U148 (Pr. 36)	2153/2766t	97.5m	9.1m	4 x diesel 2 x electric	6450bhp=17.5kt 2600bhp=8.5kt	6 x 50cm	3 x 15cm/45	–
U151	1512/1875t	65.0m	8.9m	2 x diesel 2 x electric	800bhp=12.4kt 800bhp=5.2kt	2 x 50cm	2 x 15cm/45 + 2 x 8.8cm/30	–
U158 (MS)	811/1034t	71.2m	6.2m	2 x diesel 2 x electric	2400bhp=16.0kt 1200bhp=9.0kt	6 x 50cm	1 x 10.5cm/45	–
U160 (MS)	821/1002t	71.6m	6.3m	2 x diesel 2 x electric	2400bhp=16.2kt 1200bhp=8.2kt	6 x 50cm	2 x 10.5cm/45	–
U161 (MS)	821/1002t	71.6m	6.3m	2 x diesel 2 x electric	2400bhp=16.2kt 1200bhp=8.2kt	6 x 50cm	1 x 10.5cm/45	–
U173 (Pr. 36)	2115/2790t	97.5m	9.1m	4 x diesel 2 x electric	6450bhp=17.5kt 2600bhp=8.5kt	6 x 50cm	2 x 15cm/45 + 2 x 8.8cm/30	–
U177 (Pr. 36)	2175/2791t	97.5m	9.1m	4 x diesel 2 x electric	6450bhp=17.5kt 2600bhp=8.5kt	6 x 50cm	2 x 15cm/45 + 2 x 8.8cm/30	–
U179 (Pr. 36)	2153/2766t	97.5m	9.1m	4 x diesel 2 x electric	6450bhp=17.5kt 2600bhp=8.5kt	6 x 50cm	2 x 15cm/45 + 2 x 8.8cm/30	–
U181 (Pr. 36)	2119/2790t	97.5m	9.1m	4 x diesel 2 x electric	6450bhp=17.5kt 2600bhp=8.5kt	6 x 50cm	2 x 15cm/45 + 2 x 8.8cm/30	–
U183 (Pr. 36)	2115/2790t	97.5m	9.1m	4 x diesel 2 x electric	6450bhp=17.5kt 2600bhp=8.5kt	6 x 50cm	3 x 15cm/45	–

Class	Disp.	Length	Beam	Machinery	Power/speed	TT	Gun(s)	Mines
U191 (Pr. 36)	2119/2790t	97.5m	9.1m	4 x diesel 2 x electric	6450bhp=17.5kt 2600bhp=8.5kt	6 x 50cm	2 x 15cm/45 + 2 x 8.8cm/30	–
U195 (Pr. 36)	2153/2766t	97.5m	9.1m	4 x diesel 2 x electric	6450bhp=17.5kt 2600bhp=8.5kt	6 x 50cm	3 x 15cm/45	–
U201 (MS)	820/1000t	71.6m	6.3m	2 x diesel 2 x electric	2400bhp=16.0kt 1200bhp=9.0kt	6 x 50cm	1 x 10.5cm/45	–
U213 (Pr. 42A)	1335/1830t	88.1m	7.9m	4 x diesel 2 x electric	4100bhp=18.0kt 1200bhp=9.0kt	6 x 50cm	1 x 15cm/45	
U219 (Pr. 42A)	1400/1900t	87.6m	7.9m	4 x diesel 2 x electric	4100bhp=18.0kt 1200bhp=9.0kt	6 x 50cm	1 x 15cm/45	
U229 (MS)	908/1192t	74.0m	6.7m	2 x diesel 2 x electric	2900bhp=16.5kt 1230bhp=9.0kt	6 x 50cm	1 x 10.5cm/45	–
U247 (MS)	940/1205t	74.0m	6.7m	2 x diesel 2 x electric	2400bhp=16.0kt 1230bhp=9.0kt	6 x 50cm	1 x 10.5cm/45	–
U251 (MS)	940/1205t	74.0m	6.7m	2 x diesel 2 x electric	2900bhp=16.5kt 1230bhp=9.0kt	6 x 50cm	1 x 10.5cm/45	–
U263 (MS)	882/1233t	72.3m	6.5m	2 x diesel 2 x electric	2400bhp=16.0kt 1230bhp=9.0kt	6 x 50cm	1 x 10.5cm/45	–
U268 (MS)	940/1205t	74.0m	6.7m	2 x diesel 2 x electric	2900bhp=16.5kt 1230bhp=9.0kt	6 x 50cm	1 x 10.5cm/45	–
UA	270/342t	46.7m	4.8m	2 x diesel 2 x electric	700bhp=14.2kt 380bhp=7.3kt	3 x 45cm	1 x 8.8cm/30	–
UB1 (UB-I)	127/142t	28.1m	3.2m	1 x diesel 1 x electric	60bhp=6.5kt 120bhp=5.5kt	2 x 45cm	–	–
UB9 (UB-I)	127/141t	27.9m	3.2m	1 x diesel 1 x electric	60bhp=7.5kt 120bhp=6.2kt	2 x 45cm	1 x 37mm (*UB14*)	–
UB18 (UB-II)	263/292t	36.1m	4.4m	2 x diesel 2 x electric	284bhp=9.1kt 280bhp=5.8kt	2 x 50cm	1 x 5cm/40	–
UB24 (UB-II)	265/291t	36.1m	4.4m	2 x diesel 2 x electric	270bhp=8.9kt 280bhp=5.7kt	2 x 50cm	1 x 5cm/40	–
UB30 (UB-II)	274/303t	36.9m	4.4m	2 x diesel 2 x electric	270bhp=9.0kt 280bhp=5.7kt	2 x 50cm	1 x 8.8cm/30	–
UB42 (UB-II)	279/305t	36.9m	4.4m	2 x diesel 2 x electric	270bhp=9.0kt 280bhp=5.7kt	2 x 50cm	1 x 8.8cm/30	–
UB48 (UB-III)	516/651t	55.3m	5.8m	2 x diesel 2 x electric	1100bhp=13.6kt 788bhp=8.0kt	5 x 50cm	1 x 10.5cm/45	–
UB54 (UB-III)	516/646t	55.8m	5.8m	2 x diesel 2 x electric	1060bhp=13.4kt 788bhp=7.8kt	5 x 50cm	1 x 10.5cm/45	–
UB60 (UB-III)	508/639t	55.5m	5.8m	2 x diesel 2 x electric	1100bhp=13.3kt 788bhp=8.0kt	5 x 50cm	1 x 10.5cm/45	–
UB66 (UB-III)	513/647t	55.8m	5.8m	2 x diesel 2 x electric	1100bhp=13.2kt 788bhp=8.0kt	5 x 50cm	1 x 10.5cm/45	–
UB75 (UB-III)	516/648t	55.3m	5.8m	2 x diesel 2 x electric	1100bhp=13.6kt 788bhp=7.8kt	5 x 50cm	1 x 10.5cm/45	–
UB88 (UB-III)	510/640t	55.5m	5.8m	2 x diesel 2 x electric	1100bhp=13.0kt 788bhp=7.4kt	5 x 50cm	1 x 10.5cm/45	–
UB103 (UB-III)	519/649t	55.3m	5.8m	2 x diesel 2 x electric	1100bhp=13.3kt 788bhp=7.5kt	5 x 50cm	1 x 10.5cm/45	–
UB118 (UB-III)	512/643t	55.8m	5.8m	2 x diesel 2 x electric	1060bhp=13.9kt 788bhp=7.6kt	5 x 50cm	1 x 10.5cm/45	–
UB133 (UB-III)	533/656t	55.8m	5.8m	2 x diesel 2 x electric	1100bhp=13.5kt 788bhp=7.6kt	5 x 50cm	1 x 10.5cm/45	–
UB142 (UB-III)	523/653t	55.8m	5.8m	2 x diesel 2 x electric	1060bhp=13.5kt 788bhp=7.5kt	5 x 50cm	1 x 10.5cm/45	–

Class	Disp.	Length	Beam	Machinery	Power/speed	TT	Gun(s)	Mines
UB154 (UB-III)	539/656t	55.5m	5.8m	2 x diesel 2 x electric	1100bhp=13.5kt 788bhp=7.5kt	5 x 50cm	1 x 10.5cm/45	–
UB170 (UB-III)	533/656t	56.8m	5.8m	2 x diesel 2 x electric	1060bhp=13.5kt 788bhp=7.5kt	5 x 50cm	1 x 10.5cm/45	–
UB178 (UB III)	555/684t	56.8m	5.8m	2 x diesel 2 x electric	1060bhp=13.5kt 788bhp=7.5kt	5 x 50cm	1 x 10.5cm/45	–
UB188 (UB-III)	539/656t	57.8m	5.8m	2 x diesel 2 x electric	1060bhp=13.5kt 788bhp=7.5kt	5 x 50cm	1 x 10.5cm/45	–
UC16 (UC-II)	417/493t	49.4m	5.2m	2 x diesel 2 x electric	500bhp=11.6kt 460bhp=7.0kt	3 x 50cm	1 x 8.8cm/30 or 1 x 10.5cm/45	18
UC25 (UC-II)	400/480t	49.5m	5.2m	2 x diesel 2 x electric	500bhp=11.6kt 460bhp=6.7kt	3 x 50cm	1 x 8.8cm/30 or 1 x 10.5cm/45	18
UC34 (UC-II)	427/509t	50.4m	5.2m	2 x diesel 2 x electric	600bhp=11.6kt 460bhp=6.8kt	3 x 50cm	1 x 8.8cm/30 or 1 x 10.5cm/45	18
UC40 (UC-II)	400/480t	49.5m	5.2m	2 x diesel 2 x electric	520bhp=11.7kt 460bhp=6.7kt	3 x 50cm	1 x 8.8cm/30 or 1 x 10.5cm/45	18
UC46 (UC-II)	420/502t	51.8m	5.2m	2 x diesel 2 x electric	600bhp=11.7kt 460bhp=6.9kt	3 x 50cm	1 x 8.8cm/30 or 1 x 10.5cm/45	18
UC49 (UC-II)	434/511t	52.7m	5.2m	2 x diesel 2 x electric	600bhp=11.8kt 620bhp=7.2kt	3 x 50cm	1 x 8.8cm/30 or 1 x 10.5cm/45	18
UC55 (UC-II)	415/498t	50.5m	5.2m	2 x diesel 2 x electric	600bhp=11.6kt 620bhp=7.3kt	3 x 50cm	1 x 8.8cm/30 or 1 x 10.5cm/45	18
UC65 (UC-II)	427/508t	50.4m	5.2m	2 x diesel 2 x electric	600bhp=12.0kt 620bhp=7.4kt	3 x 50cm	1 x 8.8cm/30 or 1 x 10.5cm/45	18
UC74 (UC-II)	410/493t	50.5m	5.2m	2 x diesel 2 x electric	600bhp=11.8kt 620bhp=7.3kt	3 x 50cm	1 x 8.8cm/30 or 1 x 10.5cm/45	18
UC87 (UC-III)	474/560t	56.1m	5.5m	2 x diesel 2 x electric	600bhp=11.5kt 770bhp=6.6kt	3 x 50cm	1 x 8.8cm/30 or 1 x 10.5cm/45	14
UC90 (UC-III)	491/571t	56.5m	5.5m	2 x diesel 2 x electric	600bhp=11.5kt 770bhp=6.6kt	3 x 50cm	1 x 8.8cm/30 or 1 x 10.5cm/45	14
UC119 (UC-III)	511/582t	57.1m	5.5m	2 x diesel 2 x electric	600bhp=11.5kt 770bhp=6.6kt	3 x 50cm	1 x 8.8cm/30 or 1 x 10.5cm/45	14
UD1 (Pr. 50)	~3800/4500t	125m	10.5m	2 x turbine 2 x electric	24,000shp=25.0kt 3800bhp=9.5kt	3 x 50cm	1 x 8.8cm/30 or 1 x 10.5cm/45	–
UF	380/410t	44.6m	4.4m	2 x diesel 2 x electric	600bhp=11.0kt 620bhp=7.0kt	5 x 50cm	1 x 8.8cm/30	–

Name	Class	Builder	Launch	Comp/comm	Surrendered	Alloc	Fate.
U1	U1	Germania (Kiel)	4 Aug 06	14 Dec 06	–	–	Stricken 19 Feb 19; sold Germania (Kiel) and museum exhibit, Deutsches Museum, Munich; still extant
U2	U2	Danzig DYd	18 Jun 08	18 Jul 08	–	–	Stricken 19 Feb 19; BU
U3	U3	Danzig DYd	27 Mar 09	29 May 09	Harwich 1 Dec 18	UK	Sold at Harwich to T W Ward 3 Mar 19 (£2,050); foundered uncertain location after 12 Jun 19 (purchase price refunded + £10-2-2 interest)
U4	U3	Danzig DYd	18 May 09	1 Jul 09	–	–	Stricken 27 Jan 19; BU Kiel DYd; pressure hull sold Hugo Stinnes (Hamburg)
U9	U9	Danzig DYd	22 Feb 10	18 Apr 10	Harwich 26 Nov 18	UK	Sold at Harwich to T W Ward 3 Mar 19 (£2,050 + £250 for engines); foundered Dover 13 Mar 19; salved 2 Apr 19; dep Harwich 19 May 19; arrived Morecambe 30 May 1919 to BU
U16	U16	Germania (Kiel)	23 Aug 11	28 Dec 11	–	–	Foundered Elbe estuary (58° 59' N, 08° 29' W) 8 Feb 19
U17	U17	Danzig DYd	16 Apr 12	3 Nov 12	–	–	Stricken 27 Jan 19; BU Kiel DYd; hull sold Hugo Stinnes (Hamburg) 3 Feb 20
U19	U19	Danzig DYd	10 Oct 12	6 Jul 13	Harwich 24 Nov 18	UK	Sold at Harwich to Hughes Bolckow 3 Mar 19 (£2,475 + 2 engines @ £1,000 each); dep Harwich 19 Apr 19; arrived Blyth by 25 Apr 19 to BU to 1922
U21	U19	Danzig DYd	8 Feb 13	22 Oct 13	–	–	Foundered North Sea (54° 15' N, 04° 03' E) 22 Feb 19
U22	U19	Danzig DYd	6 Mar 13	25 Nov 13	Harwich 1 Dec 18	UK	Sold at Harwich to Hughes Bolckow 3 Mar 19 (£2,475 + £500 for 1 engine); dep Harwich 10 Apr 19 to BU Blyth
U24	U23	Germania (Kiel)	24 May 13	6 Dec 13	Harwich 22 Nov 18	UK	Sold at Chatham to George Cohen 3 Mar 19 (£2,400 + £756 for port engine); dep Chatham 12 May 19 to BU Swansea. Starboard engine retained at Chatham

Name	Class	Builder	Launch	Comp/comm	Surrendered	Alloc	Fate.
U25	*U23*	Germania (Kiel)	12 Jul 13	9 May 14	Harwich 23 Feb 19	FR	BU Cherbourg 1921–22
U30	*U27*	Danzig DYd	15 Nov 13	26 Aug 14	Harwich 22 Nov 18	UK	Sold at Harwich to Hughes Bolckow 3 Mar 19 (£2,475 + 2 engines @ £1,000 each); dep Harwich 29 Mar 19 to BU Blyth to 1922
U33	*U31*	Germania (Kiel)	19 May 14	27 Sep 14	Harwich 16 Jan 19	UK	Sold at Harwich to Hughes Bolckow 3 Mar 19 (£2,475 + 2 engines @ £500 each); dep Harwich 21 May 19 to BU Blyth
U35	*U31*	Germania (Kiel)	18 Apr 14	3 Nov 14	Harwich 26 Nov 18	UK	Sold at Harwich to Hughes Bolckow 3 Mar 19 (£2,475 + 2 engines @ £500 each; latter re-sold Watney, Combe, Reid, Ltd, brewers, Pimlico); BU Blyth to 1922
U38	*U31*	Germania (Kiel)	9 Sep 14	15 Dec 14	Harwich 23 Feb 19	FR	BU Brest 1921
U39	*U31*	Germania (Kiel)	26 Sep 14	13 Jan 15	Toulon 24 Mar 19	FR	Interned Cartagena 18 May 18; BU Toulon Dec 23
U43	*U43* (Mob)	Danzig DYd	26 Sep 14	30 Apr 15	Harwich 20 Nov 18	UK	Sold at Chatham to George Cohen 3 Mar 19 (£2,400); dep Chatham 20 May 19 to BU Swansea. 2 engines sold to H G Nicholson @ £8/ton
U46 = *O2* (1919)	*U43* (Mob)	Danzig DYd	18 May 15	17 Dec 15	Harwich 26 Nov 18	JP	JP commission 1920; BU Kure 1922 or foundered 21 Apr 25; salved; scuttled on or after 5 Aug 27
U52	*U51* (Mob)	Germania (Kiel)	8 Dec 15	16 Mar 16	Harwich 21 Nov 18	UK	Sold at Chatham to George Cohen 3 Mar 19 (£2,400); BU Swansea. Engines sold with those of *U53*, *UB77* & *UB79* to Cohen for total of £4,000
U53	*U51* (Mob)	Germania (Kiel)	1 Feb 16	22 Apr 16	Harwich 1 Dec 18	UK	Foundered Harwich; salved; sold at Chatham to George Cohen 3 Mar 19 (£2,400); BU Swansea. Engines sold with those of *U52*, *UB77* & *UB79* to Cohen for total of £4,000
U54	*U51* (Mob)	Germania (Kiel)	22 Feb 16	22 May 16	Harwich 24 Nov 18	IT	Exhibited Dover Dec 18; to IT 1919; BU Taranto May 19
U55 = *O3* (1919) = *Tokumukan No. 2538* (1923)	*U51* (Mob)	Germania (Kiel)	18 Mar 16	8 Jun 16	Harwich 20 Nov 18	JP	JP commission 1920; dismantled by Jun 21; BU Sasebo after 1923
U57	*U57* (Mob)	AG Weser (Bremen)	29 Apr 16	6 Jul 16	Harwich 24 Nov 18	FR	BU Cherbourg 1921
U60	*U60* (Mob)	AG Weser (Bremen)	5 Jul 16	1 Nov 16	Harwich 21 Nov 18	UK	Sold at Chatham to George Cohen 3 Mar 19 (£2,410); foundered in tow after 12 Jun 19 en route to BU Swansea
U62	*U60* (Mob)	AG Weser (Bremen)	2 Aug 16	30 Dec 16	Harwich 21 Nov 18	UK	Exhibited Dundee Dec 18; sold at Rosyth to Forth Shipbreaking Co 3 Mar 19 (£3,060); BU Bridgeness Works, Bo'ness. Engines sold with those of *U70*, *U94*, *UB96* & *UB111* to Forth Shipbreaking for total of £10,000; re-sold to unidentified factory
U63	*U63* (Mob)	Germania (Kiel)	8 Feb 16	11 Mar 16	Harwich 16 Jan 19	UK	Sold at Harwich to Hughes Bolckow 3 Mar 19 (£2,475 + 2 engines @ £500 each: installed in Foss Islands Road generating station, York); dep Harwich 3 May 19 to BU Blyth
U67 (ex-AH *U7*)	*U66* (Mob)	Germania (Kiel)	15 May 15	4 Aug 15	Harwich 20 Nov 18	UK	Exhibited Southampton Dec 18; sold at Portsmouth to Maden & McKee 17 Jun 20 (£1,700); BU Fareham
U70 (ex-AH *U11*)	*U66* (Mob)	Germania (Kiel)	20 Jul 15	22 Sep 15	Harwich 20 Nov 18	UK	Exhibited Firth of Forth Dec 18; sold at Rosyth to Forth Shipbreaking Co 3 Mar 19 (£3,230); BU Bo'ness to 1922. Engines sold with those of *U62*, *U94*, *UB96* & *UB111* to Forth for total of £10,000
U71	*U71* (UE-I)	AG Vulcan (Stettin)	31 Oct 15	10 Dec 15	Harwich 23 Feb 19	FR	BU Cherbourg 1921
U79 = *Victor Reveille* (1 Jun 22)	*U75* (UE-I)	AG Vulcan (Stettin)	9 Apr 16	25 May 16	Harwich 21 Nov 18	FR	FR commission 1 Jun 22; reserve 1930; stricken 27 Jul 35; condemned 29 Jul 35; sold L'Hermitte (Brest) 6 Aug 36 (FF 70,642)
U80	*U75* (UE-I)	AG Vulcan (Stettin)	22 Apr 16	6 Jun 16	Harwich 16 Jan 19	UK	Sold at Harwich to George Cohen 3 Mar 19 (£2,300); dep Harwich 23 Mar 19 to BU Swansea. Engines sold to H G.Nicholson @ £8/ton
U82	*U81* (MS)	AG Vulcan (Stettin)	1 Jul 16	16 Sep 16	Harwich 16 Jan 19	UK	Sold at Harwich to Hughes Bolckow 3 Mar 19 (£2,475 + 2 engines @ £500 each); dep Harwich 29 May 19; BU Blyth
U86	*U81* (MS)	Germania (Kiel)	7 Nov 16	30 Nov 16	Harwich 20 Nov 18	UK	Exhibited Bristol Dec 18; scuttled English Channel (50° 26.628" N, 0° 33.954? W) 30 Jun 21
U90	*U87* (MS)	Danzig DYd	12 Jan 17	2 Aug 17	Harwich 20 Nov 18	BE	Foundered in tow off St Catherine's Point (50° 30' 56" N, 01° 09' 51" W) 29 Nov 19; wreck sold Martin Woodward 1995
U91	*U87* (MS)	Danzig DYd	14 Apr 17	17 Sep 17	Harwich 26 Nov 18	FR	BU Brest Jul 21
U94	*U93* (MS)	Germania (Kiel)	5 Jan 17	3 Mar 17	Harwich 20 Nov 18	UK	Exhibited Newcastle and Hartlepool Dec 18; sold at Rosyth to Forth Shipbreaking Co 3 Mar 19 (£3,230); BU Bridgeness Works, Bo'ness to 1922. Engines sold with those of *U62*, *U70*, *UB96* & *UB111* to Forth for total of £10,000

Name	Class	Builder	Launch	Comp/comm	Surrendered	Alloc	Fate.
U96	U96 (MS)	Germania (Kiel)	15 Feb 17	11 Apr 17	Harwich 20 Nov 18	UK	Sold at Campbeltown to Forth Shipbreaking Co 3 Mar 19 (£2,140); laid up Greenock; BU Bo'ness. Engines sold 21 Mar 21 to Scott's, Greenock for £250 all
U97	U96 (MS)	Germania (Kiel)	4 Apr 17	16 May 17	–	–	Foundered North Sea (53° 25' N, 93° 10' E) 21 Nov 18
U98	U96 (MS)	Germania (Kiel)	28 Feb 17	31 May 17	Harwich 20 Nov 18	UK	Exhibited Whitby Dec 1918; sold at Middlesborough to Hughes Bolckow 3 Mar 19 (£1,900 + 2 engines @ £500 each); BU Blyth
U100	U99 (MS)	AG Weser (Bremen)	25 Feb 17	16 Apr 17	Harwich 21 Nov 18	UK	Exhibited Blyth Dec 18: sold at Blyth to George Cohen 3 Mar 19 (£2,250); BU Swansea. Engines sold to Southend Corporation with those of U164 for £9,000 for the 4 (reconditioned and installed by Belliss & Morcom, Birmingham)
U101	U99 (MS)	AG Weser (Bremen)	1 Apr 17	15 May 17	Harwich 21 Nov 18	UK	Sold at Devonport to T W Ward 17 Jun 20 (£1,550); arrived Morecambe c.11 Aug 20 to BU to 1922
U105 = Jean Autric (1920)	U105 (MS)	Germania (Kiel)	16 May 17	4 Jul 17	Harwich 20 Nov 18	FR	FR commission 1922; reserve 1932; stricken 27 Aug 35; BU 1938
U107	U105 (MS)	Germania (Kiel)	28 Jun 17	18 Aug 17	Harwich 20 Nov 18	UK	Exhibited Portland, Weymouth and Poole Dec 18–Jan 19; sold at Portland to George Cohen 3 Mar 19 (£2,425); dep Portland 26 Apr 19 to BU Swansea. 1 engine sold to G E T Smithson & Co for £1,250; 1 sold to H G Nicholson @ £8/ton
U108 = Léon Mignot (1922)	U105 (MS)	Germania (Kiel)	11 Oct 17	5 Dec 17	Harwich 20 Nov 18	FR	At Brest 1 Jan 19; FR commission 13 Feb 22; reserve Aug 32; condemned 24 Jul 35; sold Gosselin-Duruez (Brest) 14 May 36 (FF 108,212)
U111	U111 (MS)	Bremer Vulcan (Vegesack)/ Germania (Kiel)	5 Sep 17	30 Dec 17	Harwich 20 Nov 18	US (ex-UK)	Exhibited Liverpool and Manchester Dec 18; exchanged for U164; US commission Mar 19; exhibited New England ports to May 19; decommissioned Apr 20; foundered off Cape Henry VA 17 Jul 21; salved 19 Aug 22; scuttled in deep water 29 Aug 22
U112	U111 (MS)	Bremer Vulcan (Vegesack)/ Germania (Kiel)	26 Oct 17	30 Jun 18	Harwich 22 Nov 18	UK	Sold at Pembroke to M Lynch & Son for Clinkham Cement Works (Albert Batchelor Ltd), Halling, nr Rochester 27 Sep 20 (£1,000); re-sold Upnor Shipbreaking 25 Oct 22
U113	U111 (MS)	Bremer Vulcan (Vegesack)/ Germania (Kiel)	29 Sep 17	23 Feb 18	Harwich 20 Nov 18	FR	At Brest 1 Jan 19; BU Brest Jul 21
U114	U111 (MS)	Bremer Vulcan (Vegesack)/ Germania (Kiel)	27 Nov 17	19 Jun 18	Harwich 26 Nov 18	IT	BU La Spezia May 19
U115	U115 (MS)	Schichau (Danzig)	1918 (95% complete)		–	–	BU; engines used in conversion of cruiser Gefion to merchantman (see p.77)
U116	U115 (MS)	Schichau (Danzig)	1918 (95% complete)		–	–	BU; engines used in conversion of cruiser Gefion to merchantman (see p.77)
U117	U117 (UE-II)	AG Vulcan (Hamburg)	10 Dec 17	23 Mar 18	Harwich 21 Nov 18	US	US commission Mar 19; exhibited US Atlantic ports to Jun 19; decommissioned 1920; sunk as bombing target off Cape Charles VA 21 Jun 21
U118	U117 (UE-II)	AG Vulcan (Hamburg)	23 Feb 18 23 Feb 19	20 Jun 18	Harwich	FR	Wrecked after breaking tow Hastings 15 Apr 19 en route Brest (with UB121); sold James Dredging Co 21 May 19 (£2,200); BU in situ 1919–21
U119 = René Audry (6 Jan 22)	U117 (UE-II)	AG Vulcan (Hamburg)	4 Apr 18	20 Jun 18	Harwich 24 Nov 18	FR	FR commission 6 Jan 22; reserve 21 Dec 31; condemned 6 Sep 37; stricken 7 Oct 37; sold Toussant Gosselin-Duruez 2 Sep 38 (FF 168,500); BU Orchies
U120	U117 (UE-II)	AG Vulcan (Hamburg)	20 Jun 18	31 Aug 18	Harwich 22 Nov 18	IT	BU La Spezia Apr 19
U121	U117 (UE-II)	AG Vulcan (Hamburg)	20 Sep 18	–	Harwich 10 Mar 19	FR	Expended as gunnery target off Cherbourg 1 Jul 21
U122	U122 (UE-II)	Blohm & Voss (Hamburg)	9 Dec 17	4 May 18	Harwich, 26 Nov 18	UK	Scuttled English Channel (50°° 30' N, 1° 24' 00" W) 1 Jul 21
U123	U122 (UE-II)	Blohm & Voss (Hamburg)	26 Jan 18	20 Jul 18	Harwich 22 Nov 18	UK	Exhibited Portsmouth Dec 18; scuttled English Channel (50° 11' 10" N, 1° 18' 50" W) 28 Jun 21
U124	U122 (UE-II)	Blohm & Voss (Hamburg)	28 Mar 18	13 Jul 18	Harwich 1 Dec 18	UK	Interned Karlskrona 13 Nov 18; sold at Portland to James Dredging Co 3 Mar 19 (£3,300); re-sold George Cohen; foundered Swansea Oct 20; salved; BU; engines sold to Cohen
U125 = O1 (1919) = Tokumukan No. 2900 (19 Aug 31)	U122 (UE-II)	Blohm & Voss (Hamburg)	26 May 18	4 Sep 18	Harwich 26 Nov 18	JP	JP commission 1920; dismantled Yokosuka Jan–Mar 21; jetty Kure Mar 24–Jan 25; test object for submarine salvage operations from 1925; BU after 1935
U126	U122 (UE-II)	Blohm & Voss (Hamburg)	16 Jun 18	7 Oct 18	Harwich 22 Nov 18	UK	Exhibited Devonport Dec 18; sold at Portsmouth C A Beard & Son 10 Feb 23 (£1,700, with U141); BU Upnor. Engines used in HMS/M X1

Name	Class	Builder	Launch	Comp/comm	Surrendered	Alloc	Fate.
U127	U127 (Proj. 42)	Germania (Kiel)	8 Jan 19 (80–85% complete)	–	–	–	BU Oslebhausen 1921; engines surrendered
U128	U127 (Proj. 42)	Germania (Kiel)	1918 (80–85% complete)	–	–	–	BU Oslebhausen 1921; engines surrendered
U129	U127 (Proj. 42)	Germania (Kiel)	1918 (80–85% complete)	–	–	–	BU Oslebhausen 1921; engines to *Ostpreussen* (see *U183*, *U184*)
U130	U127 (Proj. 42)	Germania (Kiel)	1918 (80–85% complete)	–	–	–	BU Oslebhausen 1921; engines to *Oberschlesien* (see *U187*, *U188*)
U131	U131 (Proj. 42)	AG Weser (Bremen)	1918 (80–85% complete)	–	–	–	BU 1919–20
U132	U131 (Proj. 42)	AG Weser (Bremen)	1918 (80–85% complete)	–	–	–	BU 1919–20
U133	U131 (Proj. 42)	AG Weser (Bremen)	1918 (80–85% complete)	–	–	–	BU 1919–20
U134	U131 (Proj. 42)	AG Weser (Bremen)	1918 (80–85% complete)	–	–	–	BU 1919–20
U135	U135 (Proj. 42)	Danzig DYd	8 Sep 17	20 Jun 18	Harwich 20 Nov 18	UK	Scuttled English Channel 30 Jun 21
U136	U135 (Proj. 42)	Danzig DYd	7 Nov 17	15 Aug 18	Harwich 24 Feb 19	FR	BU Cherbourg 1921
U137	U135 (Proj. 42)	Danzig DYd	8 Jan 18 (90% complete)	–	–	–	BU 1919; engines surrendered in part-compensation for loss of *UC48*
U138	U135 (Proj. 42)	Danzig DYd	26 Mar 18 (90% complete)	–	–	–	BU 1919; engines surrendered in part-compensation for loss of *UC48*
U139 = *Halbronn* (6 Oct 20)	U139 (Proj. 36)	Germania (Kiel)	3 Dec 17	18 May 18	Harwich 24 Nov 18	FR	At Brest 1 Jan 19; FR commission 10 Feb 23; paid off 24 Jul 35; stricken 27 Aug 35; sold Gosselin-Duruez 14 May 36 (FF 206,504) and BU Brest
U140	U140 (Proj. 36)	Germania (Kiel)	4 Nov 17	28 Mar 18	Harwich 23 Feb 19	US	US commission Mar 19; decommissioned summer 1919; gunfire target USS *Dickerson* off Cape Charles VA 22 Jul 21
U141	U140 (Proj. 36)	Germania (Kiel)	9 Jan 18	24 Jun 18	Harwich 26 Nov 18	UK	Exhibited Portsmouth Dec 18; target 7 Oct 20; sold at Portsmouth C A Beard & Son 10 Feb 23 (£1,700, with *U126*); BU Upnor
U142	U142 (Proj. 36)	Germania (Kiel)	4 Mar 18	10 Nov 18	–	–	BU Oslebhausen 1919; engines surrendered
U143	U142 (Proj. 36)	Germania (Kiel)	20 Apr 18 (80% complete)	–	–	–	BU Oslebhausen 1920; engines surrendered
U144	U142 (Proj. 36)	Germania (Kiel)	25 May 18 (80% complete)	–	–	–	BU Lemwerder 1920; engines surrendered
U145	U145 (Proj. 36)	AG Vulcan (Hamburg)	1 Nov 18 (75% complete)	–	–	–	BU Hamburg 1919–20; engines surrendered
U146– U149	U145 (Proj. 36)	AG Vulcan (Hamburg)	(70–75% complete)	–	–	–	– BU 1919–20
U150	U145 (Proj. 36)	AG Vulcan (Hamburg)	–	–	–	–	BU 1919–20; engines surrendered in part-compensation for loss of *UC48*
U151 (ex-*Oldenburg*)	U151	Flensburger (Flensburg)/ Germania (Kiel)	4 Apr 17	12 Jul 17	Harwich 24 Nov 18	FR	Gunfire target *Gueydon* off Cherbourg 7 Jul 21
U152	U151	Reihersteig (Hamburg)/ Germania (Kiel)	20 May 17	20 Oct 17	Harwich 24 Nov 18	UK	Exhibited Tower Bridge, Thames Dec 18; scuttled English Channel (50°' 00" N, 1° 17' 45" W) 30 Jun 21
U153	U151	Reihersteig (Hamburg)/ Germania (Kiel)	19 Jul 17	17 Nov 17	Harwich 24 Nov 18	FR	Exhibited Greenwich Pier Dec 18; to UK (in exchange for *U162*) 17 Jun 20; scuttled English Channel (50° 15' 00" N, 1° 14' 10" W) 30 Jun 21
U155 (ex-*Deutschland* [*U200*])	U151	Flensburger (Flensburg)/ Germania (Kiel)	28 Mar 16	19 Feb 17	Harwich 24 Nov 18	UK	Exhibited St Katherine's Dock, Thames Dec 18, then to Liverpool; sold at Rosyth to James Dredging Co 3 Mar 19 (£3,500); re-sold Noel Pemberton-Billing (£17,000); re-sold John Bull Ltd Apr 19 (£15,000); explosion in engine-room during dismantling at Clover, Clayton & Co, Birkenhead 10 September 1921; re-sold R Smith & Son (Birkenhead) 22 Jun 22 (£200); BU Rock Ferry
U157	U151	Stülcken (Hamburg)/ Germania (Kiel)	23 May 17	22 Sep 17	Harwich 8 Feb 19	FR	Interned Trondheim 11 Nov 18; BU Brest Jul 21
U158	U158 (MS)	Danzig DYd	16 Apr 18 (95% complete)	–	–	–	BU 1919
U159	U158 (MS)	Danzig DYd	16 Apr 18 (95% complete)	–	–	–	BU 1919
U160	U160 (MS)	Bremer Vulcan (Vegesack)	27 Feb 18	26 May 18	Harwich 24 Nov 18	FR	BU Cherbourg 1922
U161	U161 (MS)	Bremer Vulcan (Vegesack)	23 Mar 18	29 Jun 18	Harwich 20 Nov 18	UK	Exhibited Devonport Dec 18; scuttled English Channel (49°' 397" N, 4° 46' 305" W) 30 Jun 21

Name	Class	Builder	Launch	Comp/comm	Surrendered	Alloc	Fate.
U162 = Pierre Marrast (1920)	U161 (MS)	Bremer Vulcan (Vegesack)	20 Apr 18	31 Jul 18	Harwich 20 Nov 18	UK	To FR (in exchange for U153) 17 Jun 1920; FR commission 21 Jan 22; reserve 20 Oct 31; condemned 27 Jan 37; sold at Cherbourg to L'Hermitte Frères (Brest) 21 Apr 38 (FF 223,333)
U163	U161 (MS)	Bremer Vulcan (Vegesack)	1 Jul 18	21 Aug 18	Harwich 22 Nov 18	IT	BU La Spezia Aug 19
U164	U161 (MS)	Bremer Vulcan (Vegesack)	7 Aug 18	17 Oct 18	Harwich 22 Nov 18	UK (ex-US)	Exchanged for U111; sold at Portland to George Cohen 3 Mar 19 (£2,425); dep Portland 29 Apr 19 to BU Swansea. Engines sold to Southend Corporation with those of U100 for £9,000 for the 4
U165	U161 (MS)	Bremer Vulcan (Vegesack)	21 Jun 18	6 Nov 18	–	UK	Foundered Weser (53° 10' N, 08° 35' E) 18 Nov 18; raised 21 Feb 19; stricken and BU
U166 = Jean Roulier (1920)	U161 (MS)	Bremer Vulcan (Vegesack)	6 Sep 18	–	Harwich 21 Mar 19	FR	FR commission 1922; condemned 24 Jul 35; stricken 27 Aug 35; sold Gosselin-Durriez (FF 113,225) and BU Brest
U167	U161 (MS)	Bremer Vulcan (Vegesack)	28 Sep 18	–	Harwich 18 Apr 19	UK	Sold at Harwich to T W Ward 17 Jun 20 (£1,550); BU Grays
U168	U161 (MS)	Bremer Vulcan (Vegesack)	19 Oct 18	(75% complete)	–	–	BU 1919; engines surrendered (one to USS/M T-3)
U169	U161 (MS)	Bremer Vulcan (Vegesack)	15 Nov 18	–	–	–	BU 1919; engines surrendered
U170	U161 (MS)	Bremer Vulcan (Vegesack)	1918	–	–	–	BU 1919; engines surrendered
U171	U161 (MS)	Bremer Vulcan (Vegesack)	1918	–	–	–	BU 1919; engines surrendered
U172	U161 (MS)	Bremer Vulcan (Vegesack)	1918	–	–	–	BU 1919; engines surrendered
U173	U173 (Proj. 36)	Germania (Kiel)	1918 (?)	–	–	–	BU; engines surrendered
U174– U176	U173 (Proj. 36)	Germania (Kiel)	1918 (?)	–	–	–	BU
U177, U178	U173 (Proj. 36)	AG Vulcan (Hamburg)	1919	–	–	–	BU Lemwerder 1919–20; engines surrendered
U179, U180	U173 (Proj. 36)	AG Weser (Bremen)	1919	–	–	–	BU Lemwerder 1919–20; engines surrendered
U181	U173 (Proj. 36)	Blohm & Voss (Hamburg)	19 Oct 18	–	–	–	BU Lemwerder 1919–20; engines surrendered
U182	U173 (Proj. 36)	Blohm & Voss (Hamburg)	1919	–	–	–	BU Lemwerder 1919–20; engines surrendered
U183, U184 [= Ost-preussen (1921) = Caucaso (1927)]	U173 (Proj. 36)	Germania (Kiel)	1919 -	[Jun 21]	–	–	Engines surrendered; hulls incorporated into tanker Ostpreussen; IT 1927; beached 2km N of Sousse after bombing UK aircraft 14 Dec 42
U185, U186	U173 (Proj. 36)	Germania (Kiel)	1919	–	–	–	BU Lemwerder 1919–20; engines surrendered
U187, U 188 [= Obser-schlesien (1921) = Nautilus (1927) = Languste [M7023] (1942)]	U173 (Proj. 36)	Germania (Kiel)	1919 -	[30 Jul 21] - –		–	Engines surrendered; hulls incorporated into tanker Oberschlesien; IT 1927; GE Jul 42; torpedoed HMS/M Utmost 4nm SSW of Cape Figari 13 Oct 42
U189, U190	U173 (Proj. 36)	Germania (Kiel)	1919	–	–	–	BU Lemwerder 1919–20; engines surrendered
U191– U194	U173 (Proj. 36)	Blohm & Voss (Hamburg)	1919	–	–	–	BU Lemwerder 1919–20; engines surrendered
U195, U199	U173 (Proj. 36)	AG Weser (Bremen)	1919	–	–	–	BU Lemwerder 1919–20; engines surrendered
U201– U209	U201 (MS)	Bremer Vulcan (Vegesack)	–	–	–	–	BU on slips
U210– U212	U201 (MS)	Bremer Vulcan (Vegesack)	–	–	–	–	Cancelled 1918/19

Name	Class	Builder	Launch	Comp/comm	Surrendered	Alloc	Fate.
U213–U218	U213 (Proj. 42A)	Danzig DYd	–	–	–	–	Cancelled 1918/19
U219–U224	U219 (Proj. 42A)	AG Weser (Bremen)	–	–	–	–	Cancelled 1918/19
U225–U228	U213 (Proj. 42A)	Blohm & Voss (Hamburg)	–	–	–	–	Cancelled 1918/19
U229–U246	U229 (MS)	Germania (Kiel)	–	–	–	–	Cancelled 1918/19
U247–U250	U247 (MS)	Bremer Vulcan (Vegesack)	–	–	–	–	Cancelled 1918/19
U251–U262	U251 (MS)	Bremer Vulcan (Vegesack)	–	–	–	–	Cancelled 1918/19
U263–U267	U263 (MS)	Schichau (Danzig)	–	–	–	–	Cancelled 1918/19
U268–U276	U268 (MS)	Schichau (Danzig)	–	–	–	–	Cancelled 1918/19
UA (ex-U0, ex-A5)	UA	Germania (Kiel)	9 May 14	14 Aug 14	Harwich 24 Nov 18	FR	Foundered in tow on passage to FR off Folkestone (51° ' 29" N, 01° 15' 63" E) Apr 19
UB2	UB1 (UB-I)	Germania (Kiel)	18 Feb 15	20 Feb 15	–	–	Stricken 19 Feb 19; sold Hugo Stinnes (Hamburg) 3 Feb 20 and BU
UB5	UB1 (UB-I)	Germania (Kiel)	1915	25 Mar 15	–	–	Stricken 19 Feb 19; sold Dräger (Lübeck) 1919 and BU
UB6	UB1 (UB-I)	Germania (Kiel)	1915	8 Apr 15	Harwich 25 Feb 19	FR	Interned Hellevoetsluis Mar 17; to FR 1919; BU Brest Jul 21
UB9	UB9 (UB-I)	AG Weser (Bremen)	6 Feb 15	18 Feb 15	–	–	Stricken 19 Feb 19; sold Dräger (Lübeck) 1919 and BU
UB11	UB9 (UB-I)	AG Weser (Bremen)	2 Mar 15	4 Mar 15	–	–	Stricken 19 Feb 19; sold Hugo Stinnes (Hamburg) 3 Feb 20 and BU
UB14 (ex-U26, ex-UB14)	UB9 (UB-I)	AG Weser (Bremen)	15 Mar 15	15 Mar 15	Sevastopol 25 Nov 18	–	Scuttled off Sevastopol early 1919
UB21	UB18 (UB-II)	Blohm & Voss (Hamburg)	26 Sep 15	20 Feb 16	Harwich 24 Nov 18	UK	Exhibited Ramsgate Dec 18; expended as gunnery target HMS Terror Solent (50° 44' 28" N, 01° 01' 6" W) 30 Sep 20; wreck sold 1970; BU by 1998
UB23	UB18 (UB-II)	Blohm & Voss (Hamburg)	9 Oct 15	13 Mar 16	Brest 25 Mar 19	FR	Interned Lá Coruña 29 Jul 17; to Ferrol Nov 18; BU Brest Jul 21
UB24	UB24 (UB-II)	AG Weser (Bremen)	18 Oct 15	11 Dec 15	Harwich 24 Nov 18	FR	To FR 1919; BU Brest Jul 21
UB25	UB24 (UB-II)	AG Weser (Bremen)	22 Nov 15	11 Dec 15	Harwich 26 Nov 18	UK	Sold at Harwich to George Cohen 3 Mar 19 (£750); BU Canning Town; engines sold to H G Nicholson @ £8/ton
UB28	UB24 (UB-II)	AG Weser (Bremen)	20 Dec 15	27 Dec 15	Harwich 24 Nov 18	UK	Exhibited Great Yarmouth Dec 18; sold at Rosyth to Forth Shipbreaking Co 3 Mar 19 (£1,350, including engines); BU Bo'ness
UB34	UB30 (UB-II)	Blohm & Voss (Hamburg)	28 Dec 15	10 Jun 16	Harwich 26 Nov 18	UK	Sold at Harwich to George Cohen 3 Mar 19 (£750); engines sold to H Bachelor @ £250 each
UB42	UB42 (UB-II)	AG Weser (Bremen)	4 Mar 16	23 Mar 16	Sevastopol 25 Nov 18	UK	Sold at Malta to Emmanuel Grimeo 24 Dec 19 (£1,310, with UC37); BU
UB49	UB48 (UB-III)	Blohm & Voss (Hamburg)	6 Jan 17	28 Jun 17	Harwich 16 Jan 19	UK	Sold at Harwich to George Cohen 3 Mar 19 (£1,900); dep Harwich 3 May 19 to BU Swansea. Engines sold to H Bachelor @ £500 each
UB50	UB48 (UB-III)	Blohm & Voss (Hamburg)	6 Jan 17	12 Feb 17	Harwich 16 Jan 19.	UK	Sold at Harwich to George Cohen 3 Mar 19 (£1,900); dep Harwich 13 May 19 to BU Swansea to 1922. Engines sold to H Bachelor @ £500 each
UB51	UB48 (UB-III)	Blohm & Voss (Hamburg)	8 Mar 17	26 Jul 17	Harwich 16 Jan 19	UK	Sold at Harwich to George Cohen 3 Mar 19 (£1,900); dep Harwich 23 May 19 to BU Swansea to 1922. Engines sold to H Bachelor @ £500 each
UB60	UB60 (UB-III)	AG Vulcan (Hamburg)	14 Apr 17	6 Jun 17	Harwich 26 Nov 18	UK	Sold at Chatham to George Cohen 3 Mar 19 (£1,850); foundered between Berry Head and Start Point 12 Jun 19
UB62	UB60 (UB-III)	AG Vulcan (Hamburg)	11 May 17	9 Jul 17	Harwich 21 Nov 18	UK	Sold at Harwich to George Cohen 3 Mar 19 (£1,900); dep Harwich 1 Jun 19 to BU Swansea to 1922. Engines sold to H Bachelor @ £500 each
UB64	UB60 (UB-III)	AG Vulcan (Hamburg)	9 Jun 17	5 Aug 17	Harwich 21 Nov 18	UK	Exhibited off House of Commons, Thames Dec 18; sold at Portsmouth to Maden & McKee 17 Jun 20 (£1,300); BU Fareham
UB67	UB66 (UB-III)	Germania (Kiel)	6 Jun 17	23 Aug 17	Harwich 24 Nov 18	UK	Sold at Harwich to George Cohen 3 Mar 19 (£1,900); dep Harwich 11 Jun 19 to BU Swansea. 1 engine sold to National Fuel Oil Co @ £670; 1 @ £600
UB73	UB60 (UB-III)	AG Vulcan (Hamburg)	11 Aug 17	2 Oct 17	Harwich 21 Nov 18	FR	To FR 1919; BU Brest Jul 21

Name	Class	Builder	Launch	Comp/comm	Surrendered	Alloc	Fate.
UB76	*UB75* (UB-III)	Blohm & Voss (Hamburg)	5 May 17	23 Sep 17	Harwich 12 Feb 19	UK	Sold at Harwich to M Lynch & Son for Clinkham Cement Works (Albert Batchelor Ltd), Halling, nr Rochester 7 Sep 20 (£1,500); re-sold Upnor Shipbreaking 25 Oct 22
UB77	*UB75* (UB-III)	Blohm & Voss (Hamburg)	5 May 17	2 Oct 17	Harwich 16 Jan 19	UK	Sold at Harwich to George Cohen 3 Mar 19 (£1,900); BU Swansea. Engines sold with those of *U52*, *U53* & *UB79* to Cohen for total of £4,000
UB79	*UB75* (UB-III)	Blohm & Voss (Hamburg)	3 Jun 17	27 Oct 17	Harwich 26 Nov 18	UK	Sold at Harwich to George Cohen 3 Mar 19 (£1,900); BU Swansea to 1922. Engines sold with those of *U52*, *U53* & *UB77* to Cohen for total of £4,000
UB80	*UB54* (UB-III)	AG Weser (Bremen)	4 Aug 17	8 Sep 17	Harwich 26 Nov 18	IT	BU La Spezia May 19
UB84	*UB54* (UB-III)	AG Weser (Bremen)	3 Oct 17	31 Oct 17	Harwich 26 Nov 18	FR	Foundered in tow Cherbourg–Brest 2 October 1919
UB86	*UB54* (UB-III)	AG Weser (Bremen)	10 Oct 17	10 Nov 17	Harwich 24 Nov 18	UK	Expended explosion trials Falmouth 14 Jan 21; beached; sold R H.Roskelly & Rogers 19 Apr 21 (£110)
UB87	*UB54* (UB-III)	AG Weser (Bremen)	10 Nov 17	27 Dec 17	Harwich 20 Nov 18	FR	BU Brest Jul 21
UB88	*UB88* (UB-III)	AG Vulcan (Hamburg)	11 Dec 17	26 Jan 18	Harwich 26 Nov 18	US	US commission Mar 19; exhibited southern States and West Coast to Nov 19; decommissioned 1 Nov 20; scuttled off San Pedro after gunfire USS *Wickes* 1 Mar 21
UB89	*UB88* (UB-III)	AG Vulcan (Hamburg)	22 Dec 17	25 Feb 18	–	–	Broke tow off course en route Harwich 7 Mar 19 and to IJmuiden; BU Dordrecht 1920
UB91	*UB88* (UB-III)	AG Vulcan (Hamburg)	6 Mar 18	11 Apr 18	Harwich 21 Nov 18	UK	Exhibited Cardiff Dec 18; sold T W Ward; BU Briton Ferry 1921
UB92	*UB88* (UB-III)	AG Vulcan (Hamburg)	25 Mar 18	27 Apr 18	Harwich 21 Nov 18	UK	Exhibited Firth of Forth Dec 18; Montrose, Aberdeen and Peterhead Jan 19; sold at Rosyth to Forth Shipbreaking Co 3 Mar 19 (£2,050 including engines); BU Bridgeness Works, Bo'ness to 1922
UB93	*UB88* (UB-III)	AG Vulcan (Hamburg)	12 Apr 15	15 May 18	Harwich 21 Nov 18	UK	Exhibited Dún Laoghaire Jan 19; sold at Pembroke M Lynch & Son for Clinkham Cement Works (Albert Batchelor Ltd), Halling, nr Rochester 7 Sep 20 (£1,000); re-sold Upnor Shipbreaking 25 Oct 22
UB94 = *Trinité-Schillemans* (1920)	*UB88* (UB-III)	AG Vulcan (Hamburg)	26 Apr 18	1 Jun 18	Harwich 22 Nov 18	FR	FR commission 1922; reserve 31 Sep 31; hulked 24 Aug 32; condemned 24 Jul 35; stricken 27 Aug 35; sold Van Acker 10 Dec 36 (FF 12,000) to BU Toulon
UB95	*UB88* (UB-III)	AG Vulcan (Hamburg)	10 May 18	20 Jun 18	Harwich 21 Nov 18	IT	BU La Spezia Aug 19
UB96	*UB88* (UB-III)	AG Vulcan (Hamburg)	2 Feb 18	4 Mar 18	Harwich 24 Nov 18	UK	Sold at Campbeltown to Forth Shipbreaking Co 3 Mar 19 (£1,480); BU Bo'ness. Engines sold with those of *U62*, *U70*, *U94* & *UB111* to Forth for total of £10,000
UB97	*UB88* (UB-III)	AG Vulcan (Hamburg)	13 Jun 18	25 Jul 18	Harwich 21 Nov 18.	UK	Expended explosives trials Falmouth 25 Feb 21; sold R H.Roskelly & Rogers 19 Apr 21 (£50)
UB98	*UB88* (UB-III)	AG Vulcan (Hamburg)	1 Jul 18	8 Aug 18	Harwich 21 Nov 18	UK	Sold at Queenstown to J W Ellis & Co 7 Sep 20 (£550); BU Portmadoc 1922
UB99 = *Carissan* (1920)	*UB88* (UB-III)	AG Vulcan (Hamburg)	29 Jul 18	4 Sep 18	Harwich 26 Nov 18	FR	FR commission 1921; reserve 1932; condemned 24 Jul 35; stricken 28 Aug 35; sold 2 Jun 36 to BU Toulon
UB100	*UB88* (UB-III)	AG Vulcan (Hamburg)	13 Aug 18	17 Sep 18	Harwich 22 Nov 18	UK	Expended explosion trials Spithead 23 Mar 21; sold at Portsmouth C A Beard 29 Jun 21 (£350); to be mutilated by 1 Aug 21; BU Dordrecht 1922
UB101	*UB88* (UB-III)	AG Vulcan (Hamburg)	27 Aug 18	26 Nov 18	Harwich 26 Nov 18	UK	Foundered Harwich (with *UB105* & *UB117*) Mar 19; wreck sold Stanlee Shipbreaking Co 1 Apr 20 (£200); salved by 14 Sep 20 and BU Felixstowe
UB102	*UB88* (UB-III)	AG Vulcan (Hamburg)	13 Sep 18	17 Oct 18	Harwich 22 Nov 18	IT	BU La Spezia Jul 19
UB105	*UB103* (UB-III)	Blohm & Voss (Hamburg)	7 Jul 17	14 Jan 18	Harwich 16 Jan 19	UK	Sold at Harwich to George Cohen 3 Mar 19 (£1,900); foundered Harwich (with *UB101* & *UB117*) Mar 19 and money refunded; wreck sold Stanlee Shipbreaking Co 14 May 20 (£100); salved by 14 Sep 20 and BU Felixstowe to 1922
UB106	*UB103* (UB-III)	Blohm & Voss (Hamburg)	21 Jul 17	7 Feb 18	Harwich 26 Nov 18	UK	Expended explosion trials Falmouth 13/17 Jan 21; beached; sold R H.Roskelly & Rogers 19 Apr 21 (£125)
UB111	*UB103* (UB-III)	Blohm & Voss (Hamburg)	1 Sep 17	5 Apr 18	Harwich 21 Nov 18.	UK	Sold at Campbeltown to Forth Shipbreaking Co 3 Mar 19 (£1,480); BU Bo'ness/Troon to 1922. Engines sold with those of *U62*, *U70*, *U94* & *UB96* to Forth for total of £10,000
UB112	*UB103* (UB-III)	Blohm & Voss (Hamburg)	15 Sep 17	16 Apr 18	Harwich 24 Nov 18	UK	Expended explosion trials Falmouth 20 Nov/1 Dec 20; beached; sold R H.Roskelly & Rogers 19 Apr 21 (£125)
UB114	*UB103* (UB-III)	Blohm & Voss (Hamburg)	23 Sep 17	4 May 18	Harwich 26 Nov 18	FR	To FR 1919; foundered in tow off Brighton (50° 25' 00" N, 00° 12' 30" W) on passage Apr 19
UB117	*UB103* (UB-III)	Blohm & Voss (Hamburg)	21 Nov 17	6 May 18	Harwich 22 Nov 18	UK	Foundered Harwich (with *UB101* & *UB105*) 1919; wreck sold Stanlee Shipbreaking Co 1 Apr 20 (£200); possibly removed by 1926 (uncertain)

Name	Class	Builder	Launch	Comp/comm	Surrendered	Alloc	Fate.
UB118	UB118 (UB-III)	AG Weser (Bremen)	13 Dec 17	22 Jan 18	Harwich 20 Nov 18	UK	Took water on passage Devonport/Falmouth and sunk HMS *Kennet* off Dodman (50° 12' 30" N, 04° 36' W) 21 Nov 20
UB120	UB118 (UB-III)	AG Weser (Bremen)	23 Feb 18	23 Mar 18	Harwich 24 Nov 18	UK	Exhibited Belfast Dec 18; sold at Buncrana George Cohen 3 Mar 19 (£1,625). Engines sold to Wick Diesel Oil Engines Ltd @ £500 each
UB121	UB118 (UB-III)	AG Weser (Bremen)	6 Jan 18	10 Feb 18	Harwich 20 Nov 18	FR	To FR 1919; wrecked Birling Gap after breaking tow (with *U118*) on passage to Brest 15 Apr 19; sold R Longmate 3 May 19 (£500: 'Guns, torpedoes to remain property of the Admiralty, it seems'); BU in situ, fragmentary remains extant
UB122	UB118 (UB-III)	AG Weser (Bremen)	2 Feb 18	4 Mar 18	Harwich 24 Nov 19	UK	Exhibited Southampton Dec 18; scuttled English Channel (50° ' 53" N, 1° 10' 00" W) 1 Jul 21
UB125 = O6 (1919)	UB118 (UB-III)	AG Weser (Bremen)	16 Mar 18	18 May 18	Harwich 20 Nov 18	JP	JP commission 1920; BU Kure 1921
UB126	UB118 (UB-III)	AG Weser (Bremen)	12 Mar 18	20 Apr 18	Harwich 24 Nov 18	FR	Expended underwater explosion tests; BU Toulon Jul 21
UB128	UB118 (UB-III)	AG Weser (Bremen)	10 Apr 18	11 May 18	Harwich 3 Feb 19	UK	Expended explosion trials Falmouth 1 Feb 21; beached; sold R H.Roskelly & Rogers 19 Apr 21 (£120)
UB130	UB118 (UB-III)	AG Weser (Bremen)	27 May 18	28 Jun 18	Harwich 26 Nov 18	FR	Foundered in tow off Hastings (50° ' 54" N, 00° 15' 21" E) 1919
UB131	UB118 (UB-III)	AG Weser (Bremen)	4 Jun 18	4 Jul 18	Harwich 24 Nov 18	UK	Wrecked in tow near Bulverhythe 9 Jan 21; sold F Ray & Sons 23 May 21 (£655) and BU in situ
UB132	UB118 (UB-III)	AG Weser (Bremen)	22 Jun 18	25 Jul 18	Harwich 21 Nov 18	UK	Sold at Buncrana to George Cohen 3 Mar 19 (£1,625); BU Swansea to 1922. Engines sold to H G Nicholson @ £8/ton
UB133	UB133 (UB-III)	Germania (Kiel)	27 Sep 18	–	Harwich 20 Apr 19	UK	Sold at Harwich to M Lynch & Sons 22 Jul 20 (£1,000); hull re-sold T W Ward 1922; BU Rochester
UB134	UB133 (UB-III)	Germania (Kiel)	1918	–	–	–	BU 1919
UB135	UB133 (UB-III)	Germania (Kiel)	1918	–	–	–	BU 1919
UB136	UB133 (UB-III)	Germania (Kiel)	1918 No engines		Harwich 20 Apr 19	UK	Sold at Harwich to M Lynch & Sons 22 Jul 20 (£1,000); hull re-sold T W Ward 1922; BU Rochester
UB137	UB133 (UB-III)	Germania (Kiel)	2 Nov 18	–	–	–	BU 1919
UB138	UB133 (UB-III)	Germania (Kiel)	2 Nov 18	–	–	–	BU 1919
UB139	UB133 (UB-III)	Germania (Kiel)	2 Nov 18	–	–	–	BU 1919
UB140	UB133 (UB-III)	Germania (Kiel)	2 Nov 18	–	–	–	BU 1919
UB141	UB133 (UB-III)	Germania (Kiel)	2 Nov 18	–	–	–	BU 1919
UB142	UB142 (UB-III)	AG Weser (Bremen)	23 Jul 18	31 Aug 18	Harwich 22 Nov 18	FR	To FR 1919; BU Landerneau Jul 21
UB143 = O7 (1919)	UB142 (UB-III)	AG Weser (Bremen)	21 Aug 18	3 Oct 18	Harwich 1 Dec 18	JP	Interned Karlskrona 13 Nov 18; JP commission 1920; BU Yokosuka 1921
UB144	UB142 (UB-III)	AG Weser (Bremen)	5 Oct 18	–	Harwich 27 Mar 19	UK	Sold at Chatham to M Lynch & Sons 22 Jul 20 (£2,000); hull dumped Slede Creek (Medway) 1922
UB145	UB142 (UB-III)	AG Weser (Bremen)	Oct 18	–	Harwich 27 Mar 19	UK	Sold at Chatham to M Lynch & Sons 22 Jul 20 (£2,000); hull dumped Slede Creek (Medway) 1922
UB146	UB142 (UB-III)	AG Weser (Bremen)	1918	–	–	–	BU 1919
UB147	UB142 (UB-III)	AG Weser (Bremen)	1918	–	–	–	BU 1919
UB148	UB142 (UB-III)	AG Weser (Bremen)	7 Aug 18	19 Sep 18	Harwich 1 Dec 18	US	Interned Karlskrona 13 Nov 18; US commission Mar 19; exhibited New York region to May 19; decommissioned 1920; gunfire target USS *Sicard* off Cape Henry VA 22 June 21
UB149	UB142 (UB-III)	AG Weser (Bremen)	19 Sep 18	22 Oct 18	Harwich 22 Nov 18	UK	Sold at Portland to George Cohen 3 Mar 19 (£1,900); dep Portland 13 May 19 to BU Rochester to 1922. Engines sold to Southend Corporation for £2,120
UB150	UB142 (UB-III)	AG Weser (Bremen)	19 Oct 18	–	Harwich 27 Mar 19	UK	Sold at Chatham to M Lynch & Sons 22 Jul 20 (£2,000); hull dumped Slede Creek (Medway) 1922
UB151– UB153	UB142 (UB-III)	AG Weser (Bremen)	1918	–	–	–	BU 1919
UB154	UB154 (UB-III)	AG Vulcan (Hamburg)	7 Oct 18	14 Dec 18	Harwich 10 Mar 19	FR	BU Brest 1921
UB155 = *Jean Corre* (Oct 20)	UB154 (UB-III)	AG Vulcan (Hamburg)	26 Oct 18	26 Feb 19	Harwich 9 Mar 19.	FR	FR commission 24 Jan 23; reserve 18 Apr 31; training hulk 17 Apr 35; condemned and stricken 7 Oct 37; sold Van Acker 5 May 38 (FF 117,815) and BU Toulon

Name	Class	Builder	Launch	Comp/comm	Surrendered	Alloc	Fate.
UB156–UB169	UB154 (UB-III)	AG Vulcan (Hamburg)	1919	–	–	–	BU 1919
UB170–UB175	UB170 (UB-III)	Germania (Kiel)	1919	–	–	–	BU 1919
UB176, UB177	UB170 (UB-III)	Germania (Kiel)	–	–	–	–	Cancelled 1918/19
UB178–UB183	UB178 (UB-III)	AG Weser (Bremen)	1919	–	–	–	BU 1919
UB184–UB187	UB178 (UB-III)	AG Weser (Bremen)	–	–	–	–	Cancelled 1918/19
UB188, UB189	UB188 (UB-III)	AG Vulcan (Hamburg)	–	–	–	–	BU 1919
UB190–UB195	UB188 (UB-III)	AG Vulcan (Hamburg)	–	–	–	–	Cancelled 1918/19
UB196–UB205	UB188 (UB-III)	AG Vulcan (Hamburg)	–	–	–	–	BU 1919
UB206–UB219	UB178 (UB-III)	AG Weser (Bremen)	–	–	–	–	Cancelled 1918/19
UB220–UB249	UB188 (UB-III)	AG Vulcan (Hamburg)	–	–	–	–	Cancelled 1918/19
UC17	UC16 (UC-II)	Blohm & Voss (Hamburg)	19 Feb 16	23 Jul 16	Harwich 26 Nov 18	UK	Sold at Harwich to T W Ward 3 Mar 19 (£1,500); BU Preston. Engines among 14 sold to Ward for £4,000
UC20	UC16 (UC-II)	Blohm & Voss (Hamburg)	1 Apr 16	8 Sep 16	Harwich 16 Jan 19	UK	Sold at Harwich to T W Ward 3 Mar 19 (£1,500); dep Harwich 4 Jun 19 to Morecambe; BU Preston after Jun 19. Engines among 14 sold to Ward for £4,000
UC22	UC16 (UC-II)	Blohm & Voss (Hamburg)	1 Feb 16	1 Jul 16	Harwich 3 Feb 19	FR	BU Landerneau Jul 21
UC23 (ex-U77, ex-UC23)	UC16 (UC-II)	Blohm & Voss (Hamburg)	19 Feb 16	28 Jul 16	Sevastopol 25 Nov 18	FR	BU Bizerte Aug 21
UC27	UC25 (UC-II)	AG Vulcan (Hamburg)	28 Jun 16	25 Jul 16	Harwich 3 Feb 19	FR	BU Landerneau Jul 21
UC28	UC25 (UC-II)	AG Vulcan (Hamburg)	8 Jul 16	6 Aug 16	Harwich 12 Feb 19	FR	Foundered in tow to FR 1919
UC31	UC25 (UC-II)	AG Vulcan (Hamburg)	7 Aug 16	2 Sep 16	Harwich 26 Nov 18	UK	Sold at Chatham to George Cohen 3 Mar 19 (£1,125); dep Chatham 20 May 19 to BU Canning Town. Engines sold to H G Nicholson @ £8/ton
UC37	UC34 (UC-II)	Blohm & Voss (Hamburg)	5 Jun 16	13 Oct 16	Sevastopol 25 Nov 18	UK	Sold at Malta to Emmanuel Grimeo 24 Jan 20 (£1,310, with UC42)
UC40	UC40 (UC-II)	AG Vulcan (Hamburg)	5 Sep 16	1 Oct 16	–	–	Foundered North Sea (54° 55' N, 04° 47' E) on passage to Harwich 21 Jan 19
UC45	UC40 (UC-II)	AG Vulcan (Hamburg)	20 Oct 16	18 Nov 16	Harwich 24 Nov 18	UK	Sold at Harwich to T W Ward 3 Mar 19 (£1,500); BU Preston. Engines among 14 sold to Ward for £4,000
UC48	UC46 (UC-II)	AG Weser (Bremen)	27 Sep 16	6 Nov 16	–	–	Interned Ferrol 20 Mar 18; scuttled off Ferrol (43° 31' N, 08° 25' 21" W) 15 Mar 19
UC52	UC49 (UC-II)	Germania (Kiel)	23 Jan 17	15 Mar 17	Harwich 16 Jan 19	UK	Sold at Harwich to T W Ward 3 Mar 19 (£1,500); arrived Morecambe 16 May 19 to BU. Engines among 14 sold to Ward for £4,000
UC56	UC55 (UC-II)	Danzig DYd	26 Aug 16	18 Dec 16	Rochefort 27 Mar 19	FR	To FR 1919; BU Rochefort 1923
UC58	UC55 (UC-II)	Danzig DYd	21 Oct 16	12 Mar 17	Harwich 24 Nov 18	FR	To FR 1919; BU Cherbourg 1921
UC59	UC55 (UC-II)	Danzig DYd	28 Sep 16	12 May 17	Harwich 21 Nov 18	UK	Exhibited Hull, Immingham, Grimsby and Goole Dec 18; sold at Rosyth to Forth Shipbreaking Co 3 Mar 19 (£1,880 including engines); BU Bridgeness Works, Bo'ness
UC60	UC55 (UC-II)	Danzig DYd	8 Nov 16	25 Jun 17	Harwich 23 Feb 19	UK	Sold at Harwich to T W Ward 17 Jun 20 (£750); BU Rainham
UC67	UC65 (UC-II)	Blohm & Voss (Hamburg)	6 Aug 16	10 Dec 16	Harwich 16 Jan 19	UK	Sold at Harwich to T W Ward 3 Mar 19 (£1,500); BU Briton Ferry. Engines among 14 sold to Ward for £4,000
UC71	UC65 (UC-II)	Blohm & Voss (Hamburg)	12 Aug 16	28 Nov 16	–	–	Foundered North Sea (54° 10' N, 04° 54' E) on passage to Harwich 20 Feb 19
UC73	UC65 (UC-II)	Blohm & Voss (Hamburg)	26 Aug 16	24 Dec 16	Harwich 16 Jan 19	UK	Sold at Harwich to T W Ward 3 Mar 19 (£1,500); BU Briton Ferry. Engines among 14 sold to Ward for £4,000
UC74	UC74 (UC-II)	AG Vulcan (Hamburg)	19 Oct 16	26 Nov 16	Toulon 6 Apr 19	FR	Interned Barcelona 2 Nov 18; BU Toulon Jul 21
UC76	UC74 (UC-II)	AG Vulcan (Hamburg)	25 Nov 16	17 Dec 16	Harwich 1 Dec 18	UK	Interned Karlskrona 13 Nov 18; sold at Harwich T W Ward 3 Mar 19 (£1,500); BU Briton Ferry/Milford Haven to 1922. Engines among 14 sold to Ward for £4,000
UC80–UC86	UC74 (UC-III)	Danzig DYd	–	–	–	–	BU Helling 1919.

Name	Class	Builder	Launch	Comp/comm	Surrendered	Alloc	Fate.
UC87–UC89	UC87 (UC-III)	AG Weser (Bremen)	1918	–	–	–	BU 1919
UC90 = O4 (1919)	UC90 (UC-III)	Blohm & Voss (Hamburg)	19 Jan 18	15 Jul 18	Harwich 1 Dec 18	JP	Interned Karlskrona 13 Nov 18; JP commission 1920; dismantled 1921; ASW target, 1924–26; BU
UC91	UC90 (UC-III)	Blohm & Voss (Hamburg)	19 Jan 18	31 Jul 18	–	–	Foundered North Sea (54° 15' N, 03° 56' E) 10 Feb 19
UC92	UC90 (UC-III)	Blohm & Voss (Hamburg)	19 Jan 18	24 Nov 18	Harwich 24 Nov 18 UK	[BE]	Exhibited Bristol Dec 18; expended explosion trials Falmouth 7 Mar 21; sold R H.Roskelly & Rogers 19 Apr 21
UC93	UC90 (UC-III)	Blohm & Voss (Hamburg)	19 Feb 18	22 Aug 18	Harwich 26 Nov 18	IT	BU La Spezia Aug 19
UC94	UC90 (UC-III)	Blohm & Voss (Hamburg)	19 Feb 18	31 Aug 18	Harwich 26 Nov 18	IT	BU Taranto Apr 19
UC95	UC90 (UC-III)	Blohm & Voss (Hamburg)	19 Feb 18	16 Sep 18	Harwich 22 Nov 18	UK	Exhibited Westminster Pier Dec 18; sold at Portsmouth Maden & McKee 17 Jun 20 (£3,000); BU Fareham to 1922
UC96	UC90 (UC-III)	Blohm & Voss (Hamburg)	17 Mar 18	25 Sep 18	Harwich 24 Nov 18	UK	Sold at Harwich to T W Ward 3 Mar 19 (£1,650); arrived Morecambe 16 May 19 to BU. Engines delivered to Admiralty Machinery Department: sold to H G Nicholson @ £8/ton
UC97	UC90 (UC-III)	Blohm & Voss (Hamburg)	17 Mar 18	6 Sep 18	Harwich 22 Nov 18	US	US commission Mar 19; exhibited Great Lakes to Aug 19; decommissioned 1920; sunk as gunfire target USS Willmette Lake Michigan 7 Jun 21
UC98	UC90 (UC-III)	Blohm & Voss (Hamburg)	17 Mar 18	10 Sep 18	Harwich 24 Nov 18	IT	BU La Spezia Apr 19
UC99 = O5 (1919)	UC90 (UC-III)	Blohm & Voss (Hamburg)	17 Mar 18	20 Sep 18	Harwich 22 Nov 18	JP	JP commission 1920; dismantled Yokosuka Mar–Jun 21; expended as target Oct 21
UC100	UC90 (UC-III)	Blohm & Voss (Hamburg)	14 Apr 18	1 Oct 18	Harwich 22 Nov 18	FR	To FR 1919; BU Cherbourg 1921
UC101	UC90 (UC-III)	Blohm & Voss (Hamburg)	14 Apr 18	8 Oct 18	Harwich 24 Nov 18	UK	Expended explosion trials Spithead 26 Mar 21; sold at Portsmouth C A Beard 29 Jun 21 (£350); to be mutilated by 1 Aug 21; BU Dordrecht 1922
UC102	UC90 (UC-III)	Blohm & Voss (Hamburg)	17 Apr 18	15 Oct 18	Harwich 22 Nov 18	UK	Expended explosion trials Spithead 30 Mar 21; sold at Portsmouth C A Beard 18 Aug 21 (£50); to be mutilated by 18 Oct 21; BU Dordrecht 1922
UC103	UC90 (UC-III)	Blohm & Voss (Hamburg)	14 Apr 18	21 Oct 18	Harwich 24 Nov 18	FR	To FR; at Brest 1 Jan 19; BU Cherbourg 1921
UC104	UC90 (UC-III)	Blohm & Voss (Hamburg)	25 May 18	18 Oct 18	Harwich 24 Nov 18	FR	BU Brest Jul 21
UC105	UC90 (UC-III)	Blohm & Voss (Hamburg)	25 May 18	28 Oct 18	Harwich 22 Nov 18	UK	Sold at Portland to George Cohen 3 Mar 19 (£1,800); dep Portland 7 May 19 to BU Swansea to 1922. Engines, incomplete, sold to Cohen for £150
UC106	UC90 (UC-III)	Blohm & Voss (Hamburg)	25 May 18	18 Mar 19	Harwich 1919	UK	Sold at Harwich to Stanlee Shipbreaking Co 17 Jun 20 (£650); BU Felixstowe 1921
UC107	UC90 (UC-III)	Blohm & Voss (Hamburg)	2 Jun 18	18 Mar 19	Harwich 1919	FR	BU Brest 1921
UC108	UC90 (UC-III)	Blohm & Voss (Hamburg)	2 Jun 18	18 Mar 19	Harwich 1919	UK	Sold at Harwich to Stanlee Shipbreaking Co 17 Jun 20 (£650); BU Felixstowe 1921
UC109	UC90 (UC-III)	Blohm & Voss (Hamburg)	2 Jun 18	–	Harwich 24 Apr 19.	UK	Sold at Harwich to Stanlee Shipbreaking Co 17 Jun 20 (£650); BU Felixstowe 1921
UC110	UC90 (UC-III)	Blohm & Voss (Hamburg)	6 Jul 18	18 Mar 19	Harwich 1919	UK	Scuttled English Channel (50° 11' 30" N, 1° 24' 00" W) 1 Jul 21
UC111	UC90 (UC-III)	Blohm & Voss (Hamburg)	6 Jul 18	18 Mar 19	Harwich 29 Mar 19	UK	Sold at Harwich to Stanlee Shipbreaking Co 17 Jun 20 (£650); BU Felixstowe 1921
UC112	UC90 (UC-III)	Blohm & Voss (Hamburg)	6 Jul 18	18 Mar 19	Harwich 1919	UK	Sold at Harwich to Stanlee Shipbreaking Co 17 Jun 20 (£650); BU Felixstowe 1921
UC113	UC90 (UC-III)	Blohm & Voss (Hamburg)	6 Jul 18	18 Mar 19	Harwich 27 Mar 19	UK	Sold at Harwich to George Sharpe 17 Jun 20 (£700); BU Derwenthaugh 1921–22
UC114	UC90 (UC-III)	Blohm & Voss (Hamburg)	11 Aug 18	18 Mar 19	Harwich 1919	UK	Sold at Harwich to George Sharpe 17 Jun 20 (£700); BU Newcastle 1921
UC115–UC118	UC90 (UC-III)	Blohm & Voss (Hamburg)	11 Aug 18	–	–	–	BU Hamburg 1919
UC119–UC121	UC119 (UC-III)	Blohm & Voss (Hamburg)	1918	–	–	–	BU Hamburg-Moorburg 1919
UC122–UC124	UC119 (UC-III)	Blohm & Voss (Hamburg)	1 Oct 18	–	–	–	BU Hamburg-Moorburg 1919
UC125–UC128	UC119 (UC-III)	Blohm & Voss (Hamburg)	8 Dec 18	–	–	–	BU Hamburg 1919
UC129–UC138	UC119 (UC-III)	Blohm & Voss (Hamburg)	–	–	–	–	BU on slips

Name	Class	Builder	Launch	Comp/comm	Surrendered	Alloc	Fate.
UC139–UC152	*UC139* (UC-III)	Danzig DYd	–	–	–	–	Cancelled 1918/19
UC153–UC192	*UC119* (UC-III)	Blohm & Voss (Hamburg)	–	–	–	–	Cancelled 1918/19
UD1	*UD1*	Kiel DYd	–	–	–	–	Material BU 1918/19
UF1–UF20	UF	Schichau (Elbing)	–	–	–	–	Cancelled 1918/19
UF21–UF32	UF	Tecklenborg (Geestemünde)	–	–	–	–	Cancelled 1918/19
UF33–UF38	UF	Atlas-Werke (Bremen)	–	–	–	–	Cancelled 1918/19
UF39–UF44	UF	AG Neptun (Rostock)	–	–	–	–	Cancelled 1918/19
UF45–UF48	UF	Seebeck (Geestemünde)	–	–	–	–	Cancelled 1918/19
UF49–UF60	UF	Tecklenborg (Geestemünde)	–	–	–	–	Cancelled 1918/19
UF61–UF72	UF	Seebeck (Geestemünde)	–	–	–	–	Cancelled 1918/19
UF73–UF76	UF	Atlas-Werke (Bremen)	–	–	–	–	Cancelled 1918/19
UF77–UF80	UF	AG Neptun (Rostock)	–	–	–	–	Cancelled 1918/19
UF81–UF92	UF	Schichau (Elbing)	–	–	–	–	Cancelled 1918/19

Table 1.1/5. Minelayers

Class	Disp.	Length	Beam	Machinery	Power/speed	Main gun(s)	Mines
Nautilus	1975t	100.9m	11.2m	4 x boilers, 2 x VTE	6600ihp=20kt	2 x 8.8cm	200

Name	Class	Builder	Launch	Comp/comm	Fate.
Nautilus = *Hulk I* (1 Jan 23) = *Hulk A* (1 Apr 28)	*Nautilus* (Bremen)	AG Weser	28 Aug 06	19 Mar 07	Stricken 21 Mar 19; hulked Bremen 1921; sold (180,000M) 18 Aug 28; BU Copenhagen
Albatros	*Nautilus* (Bremen)	AG Weser	23 Oct 07	19 May 08	Returned from internment Jan 19; stricken 21 Mar 21; sold (900,000M) 1921; BU Hamburg

Table 1.1/6. Minesweepers

Class	Disp.	Length	Beam	Machinery		Power/speed	Main gun(s)	Mines
M1914	425t	55.1m	7.3m	2 x boilers,	2 x VTE	1400–1600ihp=16.3kt	2 x 8.8cm	30
M1915	480t	58.4m	7.3m	2 x boilers,	2 x VTE	1800ihp=16.5kt	3 x 8.8cm/2 x 10.5cm	30
M1916	506t	59.3m	7.3m	2 x boilers,	2 x VTE	1750–1860ihp=16kt	3 x 8.8cm/2 x 10.5cm	30
FM1	170t	43.0m	6.0m	1 x boiler,	2 x VTE	600ihp=14kt	1 x 8.8cm	–
FM37	185t	45.5m	6.0m	1 x boiler,	2 x VTE	750ihp=14.3kt	1 x 8.8cm	–

Name	Class	Builder	Launch	Comp/comm	Fate.
M1	M1914	G Seebeck (Geestemünde)	26 May 15	17 Jul 15	Stricken 17 Mar 20; sold 28 Jun 22; BU Wilhelmshaven
M2	M1914	G Seebeck (Geestemünde)	3 Jun 15	8 Aug 15	Stricken 24 Oct 21; sold Victor Boitin (Berlin) 29 Mar 22 for mercantile conversion and foreign re-sale; further fate unknown.[7]
M3	M1914	G Seebeck (Geestemünde)	19 Sep 15	28 Sep 15	Stricken 24 Oct 21; sold Victor Boitin (Berlin) 29 Mar 22 for mercantile conversion and foreign re-sale; further fate unknown
M4	M1914	G Seebeck (Geestemünde)	19 Sep 15	2 Oct 15	Stricken 24 Oct 21; sold Victor Boitin (Berlin) 29 Mar 22 for mercantile conversion and foreign re-sale; further fate unknown
M5	M1914	G Seebeck (Geestemünde)	19 Sep 15	25 Oct 15	Stricken 24 Oct 21; sold Victor Boitin (Berlin) 29 Mar 22 for mercantile conversion and foreign re-sale; further fate unknown
M7	M1914	AG Neptun (Rostock)	1915	29 Jul 15	Stricken 24 Oct 21; sold 28 Jun 22; BU Wilhelmshaven
M8	M1914	AG Neptun (Rostock)	18 Jun 15	15 Aug 15	Stricken 24 Oct 21; sold 28 Jun 22; BU Wilhelmshaven
M10 = *Aktion* (1922) = *Prince William* (1930)	M1914	AG Neptun (Rostock)	1915	24 Sep 15	Stricken 17 Mar 20; sold Hellenic Co of Maritime Enterprises (Athens) 19 Mar 20; sold Canadian National Steamship Co (Halifax) 1930; sold Armour Salvage & Towing Co (Halifax); untraced after 1945
M13	M1914	Nordseewerke (Emden)	26 May 15	23 Nov 15	Stricken 17 Mar 20; sold Victor Boitin (Berlin) 28 Apr 22 for mercantile conversion and foreign re-sale; further fate unknown
M17	M1914	G Seebeck (Geestemünde)	19 Dec 15	29 Jan 16	Stricken 17 Mar 20; sold Victor Boitin (Berlin) 28 Apr 22 for mercantile conversion and foreign re-sale; further fate unknown
M18	M1914	AG Neptun (Rostock)	25 Aug 15	18 Nov 15	Stricken 13 Jul 21; sold 30 Jun 22; BU Wilhelmshaven
M19	M1914	AG Neptun (Rostock)	10 Sep 15	15 Dec 15	Stricken 13 Jul 21; sold 4 Apr 22; BU Wilhelmshaven
M20	M1914	AG Neptun (Rostock)	30 Sep 15	23 Dec 15	Stricken 13 Jul 21; sold Victor Boitin (Berlin) 28 Apr 22 for mercantile conversion and foreign re-sale; further fate unknown
M21	M1914	J Frerichs (Einswerden)	Oct 15	17 Dec 15	Stricken 17 Mar 20; sold 22 Jun 22; BU Wilhelmshaven

[7] A number of ex-German minesweepers whose original names remain unknown are known to have been active in mercantile service during the inter-war period: see Gröner, *German Warships 1815–1945*, vol. 2, p. 114.

Name	Class	Builder	Launch	Comp/comm	Fate.
M25	M1914	J C Tecklenborg (Geestemünde)	28 Aug 15	8 Oct 15	Stricken 13 Jul 21; sold 29 Apr 22; BU Wilhelmshaven
M28 = *Pelikan* (11 Mar 29), = *M528* (1 Oct 40)	M1915	AG Neptun (Rostock)	6 May 16	24 Jun 16	See Table 2.1/7
M29	M1915	AG Neptun (Rostock)	27 May 16	15 Jul 16	Stricken 24 Oct 21; sold Victor Boitin (Berlin) 29 Mar 22 for mercantile conversion and foreign re-sale; further fate unknown
M30	M1915	AG Neptun (Rostock)	17 Jun 16	4 Aug 16	Stricken 24 Oct 21; sold Victor Boitin (Berlin) 29 Mar 22 for mercantile conversion and foreign re-sale; further fate unknown
M32	M1915	G Seebeck (Geestemünde)	14 May 16	29 Jun 16	Stricken 17 Mar 20; sold Paul Selinger (Dortmund) 1922; BU
M33	M1915	G Seebeck (Geestemünde)	25 Jun 16	20 Jul 16	Stricken 17 Mar 20; sold .... (Berlin) 1922; BU
M34	M1915	G Seebeck (Geestemünde)	25 Jun 16	10 Aug 16	Stricken 17 Mar 20; sold Paul Selinger (Dortmund) 1922; BU
M35	M1915	J C Tecklenborg (Geestemünde)	18 May 16	18 Jun 16	Stricken 24 Oct 21; sold .... (Berlin) 1922; BU
M37	M1915	J C Tecklenborg (Geestemünde)	24 Jun 16	6 Aug 16	Stricken 17 Mar 20; sold 10 May 22; BU Wilhelmshaven
M38 = *K103Wb* (1922)	M1915	J C Tecklenborg (Geestemünde)	13 Jul 16	20 Aug 16	Stricken 20 Feb 22; accommodation hulk; SU 25 Apr 46
M42 = *La Nymphe* (1922) = *Nymphe* (1923) = *AD 204* (1939) = *Nymphe* (1940)	M1915	Bremer Vulcan (Vegesack)	11 Aug 16	22 Sep 16	Stricken 17 Mar 20; sold .... (Berlin) 11 Aug 20; sold Vicomte de Gualès de Mezaubran (Nice) 1922; sold Norddeutscher Lloyd 1923; sold SA des Bains der Mer et du Cercle des Etrangers de Monaco 1928; FR Navy 1939; GE 1940; sunk Apr 45
M43	M1915	Bremer Vulcan (Vegesack)	7 May 16	28 Jun 16	Stricken 24 Oct 21; sold 5 May 22; BU
M44	M1915	Atlas-Werke (Bremen)	4 Jun 16	8 Aug 16	Stricken 24 Oct 21; sold .... (Berlin) 1922; BU
M45	M1915	AG Neptun (Rostock)	8 Jul 16	27 Aug 16	Stricken 24 Oct 21; sold .... (Berlin) 1922; fate unknown
M46	M1915	AG Neptun (Rostock)	19 Aug 16	16 Sep 16	Stricken 1 Dec 22; for disposal 10 Sep 23; fate unknown
M48 = *Maria* (Mar 22) = *M1* (1922) = *Bathurst* (1936)	M1915	AG Neptun (Rostock)	9 Sep 16	28 Oct 16	Stricken 24 Sep 21; sold Hugo Stinnes (Hamburg) 18 Mar 22; sold AR 1922; stricken 16 Dec 46; target; BU 1951
M50 = *Brommy* (1937) = *M550* (1 Oct 40)	M1915	G Seebeck (Geestemünde)	16 Aug 16	19 Sep 16	Bombed UK aircraft Boulogne 15 Jun 44
M51 = *Martha* (Mar 22) = *M2* (1922) = *Fourner* (1936)	M1915	G Seebeck (Geestemünde)	10 Sep 16	12 Oct 16	Stricken 24 Sep 21; sold Hugo Stinnes (Hamburg) 18 Mar 22; sold AR 1922; stricken 5 Apr 37; sold as hulk Yacimientos Petroliferos Fiscales; BU 1943
M52 = *M3* (1922) = *Jorge* (1936) = *Cormoran* [ii] (26 Jan 40)	M1915	G Seebeck (Geestemünde)	22 Nov 16	26 Nov 16	Stricken 24 Sep 21; sold Hugo Stinnes (Hamburg) 18 Mar 22; sold AR 1922; stricken 26 Aug 46
M53 = *Minna* (Mar 22) = *M4* (1922) = *King* (1936) = *Teniente de la Sota* (Nov 41)	M1915	G Seebeck (Geestemünde)	22 Nov 16	16 Dec 16	Stricken 24 Sep 21; sold Hugo Stinnes (Hamburg) 18 Mar 22; sold AR 1922; stricken 27 Jul 37; reinstated as training ship Nov 41; stricken 16 Dec 46; sold to BU 1948
M54	M1915	Bremer Vulcan (Vegesack)	14 Sep 16	14 Oct 16	Stricken 13 Jul 21; sold .... (Hamburg) 29 Apr 22; fate unknown
M57	M1916	G Seebeck (Geestemünde)	1 Jul 17	16 Sep 17	Accommodation hulk Kiel 1 Dec 22; fate unknown
M58	M1916	G Seebeck (Geestemünde)	4 Aug 17	23 Oct 17	Stricken 13 Jul 21; sold 10 May 22; BU Wilhelmshaven
M59 = *Prezidentas Smetona* (1927) = *Primunas* (Jun 40) = *Korall* (Aug 40) = *T-76 Korall* (19 Aug 41)	M1916	G Seebeck (Geestemünde)	31 Oct 17	30 Nov 17	Stricken 24 Oct 21; sold .... (Paris) 2 Aug 22; sold LT 1927; commissioned 2 Aug 35; SU 22 Jun 40; mined or torpedoed *U745* off Helsinki 11 Jan 45

Name	Class	Builder	Launch	Comp/comm	Fate.
M60 = Hecht (29 Aug 38) = M560 (1 Oct 40) = Hille (21 Jan 43)	M1916	G Seebeck (Geestemünde)	28 Nov 17	15 Jan 18	See Table 2.1/7
M61	M1916	G Seebeck (Geestemünde)	13 Apr 18	20 Apr 18	Mined off Hook of Holland 26 Jul 40
M65	M1916	J C Tecklenborg (Geestemünde)	12 May 17	10 Jun 17	Stricken 13 Jul 21; sold 5 Jul 22; BU Wilhelmshaven
M66 = Störtebeker (Nov 37) = M566 (1 Oct 40)	M1916	J C Tecklenborg (Geestemünde)	2 Jul 17	Jul 17	See Table 2.1/7
M69	M1916	AG Neptun (Rostock)	16 Aug 17	3 Nov 17	Stricken 24 Oct 21; sold Moinet (Paris) 2 Aug 22; fate unknown
M70	M1916	AG Neptun (Rostock)	28 Sep 17	7 Dec 17	Stricken 23 Jun 21; sold .... (Hamburg) 1922; fate unknown
M71	M1916	Bremer Vulcan (Vegesack)	11 Jan 18	14 Apr 18	Stricken 23 Jun 21; sold .... (Dortmund) 1922; fate unknown
M72 = M572 (1 Oct 40)	M1916	Bremer Vulcan (Vegesack)	20 Feb 18	28 Apr 18	See Table 2.1/7
M73	M1916	Bremer Vulcan (Vegesack)	20 Feb 18	18 Jul 18	Stricken 24 Oct 21; sold B Plage (Berlin) 1 May 22; fate unknown
M74 = Meta (Mar 22) = M5 (1922) = Murature (1936) = Cormoran [i] (1938)	M1916	Bremer Vulcan (Vegesack)	26 Apr 18	18 Jun 18	Stricken 13 Jun 21; sold Hugo Stinnes (Hamburg) 18 Mar 22; sold AR 1922; museum 1940
M75 = M575 (1 Oct 40)	M1916	J C Tecklenborg (Geestemünde)	21 Jul 17	16 Aug 17	Capsized off Øresund 2 Mar 45
M76	M1916	J C Tecklenborg (Geestemünde)	15 Aug 17	9 Sep 17	Stricken 13 Jul 21; sold 5 May 22; BU
M77 = Luwen 3 (1922) = Reichspräsident (1928) = Kranich (1935)	M1916	J C Tecklenborg (Geestemünde)	4 Sep 17	30 Sep 17	Stricken 13 Jul 21; sold .... (Berlin) 1922 (tug on Rhein); sold Hafen-Dampfschiffahrt (Hamburg) 1928 (ferry); sold Blohm & Voss (Hamburg) 1935 (aircraft recovery vessel); GE Luftwaffe 1941; UK 1945; sold Alex Schmidt (Hamburg) (salvage vessel); BU Bremerhaven 1961/62
M78	M1916	J C Tecklenborg (Geestemünde)	20 Nov 17	13 Dec 17	Stricken 13 Jul 21; sold B Plage (Berlin) 1 May 22; fate unknown
M79 = Melittam (Mar 22) = M6 (1922) = Pinedo (1936)	M1916	G Seebeck (Geestemünde)	15 Jan 19	18 Mar 19	Stricken 24 Sep 21; sold Hugo Stinnes (Hamburg) 18 Mar 22; sold AR 1922; stricken 25 Jul 51; sold Club Nautico Azoparto (San Nicolas) (accommodation ship); sold Escuela de Gremetos 'Juan Bautista Azopardo' (Santa Fe) 1956; sold Fa Alfredo S Mularrege 1969
M80 = Margot (Mar 22) = M7 (1922) = Py (1936)	M1916	G Seebeck (Geestemünde)	15 Jan 19	1 Apr 19	Stricken 12 Sep 21; sold Hugo Stinnes (Hamburg) 18 Mar 22; sold AR 1922; constructive total loss 1936; stricken 13 Jan 37; floating jetty La Plata
M81 = Nautilus (Mar 29) = M581 (1 Oct 40)	M1916	G Seebeck (Geestemünde)	8 Sep 19	13 Oct 19	See Table 2.1/7
M82 = Jagd (Mar 29) = M582 (1 Oct 40)	M1916	G Seebeck (Geestemünde)	8 Sep 19	8 Nov 19	See Table 2.1/7
M84 = M584 (1 Oct 40)	M1916	Atlas-Werke (Bremen)	10 Oct 17	16 Dec 17	Mined Kattegat 30 Nov 44
M85	M1916	Nordseewerke (Emden)	10 Apr 18	3 Aug 18	Mined NE of Heisternest 1 Oct 39
M86	M1916	Nordseewerke (Emden)	10 Oct 17	21 Mar 18	Stricken 13 Jul 21; sold 5 May 22 to BU Kiel
M87	M1916	J C Tecklenborg (Geestemünde)	30 Oct 17	23 Nov 17	Stricken 13 Jul 21; sold .... (Berlin) 1922; fate unknown
M89	M1916	J C Tecklenborg (Geestemünde)	11 Dec 17	1 Jan 18	Mined off Hook of Holland 26 Jul 40
M90 = Marianne (Mar 22) = M8 (1922) = Segui (1936)	M1916	J C Tecklenborg (Geestemünde)	29 Dec 17	23 Jan 18	Stricken 24 Sep 21; sold Hugo Stinnes (Hamburg) 18 Mar 22; sold AR 1922; diving tender 1934; stricken 29 Apr 50; diving club hulk 1951; foundered Rio Uruguay 18 Aug 63
M93	M1916	AG Neptun (Rostock)	18 Jan 18	14 Mar 18	Stricken 24 Oct 21; sold Paul Diete (Kiel) 15 Aug 22; fate unknown
M94	M1916	AG Neptun (Rostock)	20 Feb 18	15 Apr 18	Stricken 17 Mar 21; sold B Plage (Berlin) 1 May 22; fate unknown

Name	Class	Builder	Launch	Comp/comm	Fate.
M96	M1916	Atlas-Werke (Bremen)	22 Feb 18	15 Apr 18	Hospital ship 1920; capsized Stettin 15 Mar 20; salved 21 Aug 22; stricken 29 Aug 22; BU
M97 = Orao (1921) = Vergada (Apr 41) = Orao (Nov 43) = Pionir (Aug 45)	M1916	J C Tecklenborg (Geestemünde)	28 Mar 18	21 Apr 18	Stricken 24 Oct 21; sold YU 20 Jul 21; IT Apr 41; see Table 2.2/8
M98 = M598 (1 Oct 40)	M1916	J C Tecklenborg (Geestemünde)	16 Apr 18	7 May 18	See Table 2.1/7
M99	M1916	J C Tecklenborg (Geestemünde)	8 May 18	16 Jun 18	Stricken 24 Oct 21; sold .... (Berlin) 1922; BU Hamburg-Moorburg
M100 = Galeb (1921) = Selve (22 May 41)	M1916	J C Tecklenborg (Geestemünde)	23 May 18	16 Jun 18	Stricken 3 Mar 21; sold YU 20 Jul 21; IT Apr 41; see Table 2.2/7
M101 = M9 (1922) = Thorne (1936)	M1916	Atlas-Werke (Bremen)	20 Apr 18	19 Jun 18	Stricken 13 Jul 21; sold Hugo Stinnes (Hamburg) 18 Mar 22; sold AR 1922; stricken 16 Dec 46; hulked Rio Santiago; sold Idoeta, Reboratti & Cia 20 Jul 59; fate unknown
M102 = M502 (1 Oct 40)	M1916	Atlas-Werke (Bremen)	31 May 18	24 Jul 18	See Table 2.1/7
M103	M1916	AG Neptun (Rostock)	27 Mar 18	25 May 18	Stricken 24 Oct 21; sold B Plage (Berlin) 1 May 22; fate unknown
M104 = M504 (1 Oct 40)	M1916	AG Neptun (Rostock)	27 Apr 18	29 Jun 18	Bombed UK aircraft Kiel 9 Apr 45
M105 = Mecha (Mar 22) = M10 (1922) = Golondrina (1925)	M1916	Reihersteig (Hamburg)	6 Jul 18	10 Oct 18	Stricken 9 Feb 21; sold Hugo Stinnes (Hamburg) 18 Mar 22; sold AR 1922; state yacht 1925; stricken 20 Aug 58; sold Arenera 'Yapeyu'; fate unknown
M106 = Gavran (1921) = Labud (1923) = Zuri (29 May 41) = Oriole (1 Jun 42)	M1916	Reihersteig (Hamburg)	8 Jul 18	21 Mar 19	Stricken 24 Oct 21; sold YU 20 Jul 21; IT Apr 41; see Table 2.2/8
M107 = Von der Groeben (15 Apr 39) = M507 (1 Oct 40)	M1916	J C Tecklenborg (Geestemünde)	3 Jul 18	30 Jul 18	Bombed Boulogne 15 Jun 44
M108 = M508 (1 Oct 40)	M1916	J C Tecklenborg (Geestemünde)	17 Jul 18	10 Aug 18	See Table 2.1/7
M109 = Johan Wittenborg (29 Aug 38) = Sundevall (2 Dec 38) = M509 (1 Oct 40)	M1916	J C Teckleborg (Geestemünde)	7 Aug 18	29 Aug 18	See Table 2.1/7
M110 = M510 (1 Oct 40)	M1916	J C Tecklenborg (Geestemünde)	27 Aug 18	19 Sep 18	See Table 2.1/7
M111 = M511 (1 Oct 40)	M1916	J C Tecklenborg (Geestemünde)	17 Sep 18	11 Oct 18	Mined Kolberg 3 Nov 41
M112 = Jastreb (1921) = Irona (20 May 41)	M1916	J C Tecklenborg (Geestemünde)	12 Nov 18	31 Oct 19	Stricken 24 Oct 21; sold YU 20 Jul 21; IT Apr 41; see Table 2.2/8
M113 = Acheron (8 Oct 36) = M513 (1 Oct 40)	M1916	Stülcken Sohn (Hamburg)	27 May 19	31 Oct 19	See Table 2.1/7
M114 = Leopold David (1920)	M1916	Stülcken Sohn (Hamburg)	28 Sep 20	–	Sold incomplete .... (Hamburg) 26 Jun 19; Leopold David Shipping 1920; internal explosion Cuxhaven 9 Jan 22
M115 = M515 (1 Oct 40)	M1916	Atlas-Werke (Bremen)	12 Jul 18	19 Sep 18	Mined W of Fehmarin 22 May 44
M116 = W1Wb	M1916	Atlas-Werke (Bremen)	10 Aug 18	15 Oct 18	Transport vessel 1920; accommodation ship 1922; still in existence 1934
M117 = M517 (1 Oct 40)	M1916	Atlas-Werke (Bremen)	20 Sep 18	1919	Table 2.1/7
M118	M1916	Atlas-Werke (Bremen)	12 Oct 18	1 Apr 19	Stricken 13 Jul 21; sold .... (Berlin) 1922
M119 = Meteo (Dec 21) = Vieste (1925)	M1916	AG Neptun (Rostock)	22 Jun 18	17 Aug 18	Stricken 9 Mar 21; sold IT 15 Dec 21; see Table 2.2/8
M120 = Abastro (Dec 21) = Crotone (1925) = Kehrwieder (Sep 43)	M1916	AG Neptun (Rostock)	24 Jul 18	20 Sep 18	Stricken 9 Mar 21; sold IT 15 Dec 21; see Table 2.2/7

Name	Class	Builder	Launch	Comp/comm	Fate.
M121 = *Kobac* (1921) = *Unie* (30 Nov 41)	M1916	AG Neptun (Rostock)	10 Sep 18	25 Oct 18	Stricken 13 Jul 21; sold YU 20 Jul 21; IT Apr 41; see Table 2.2/8
M122 = *M522* (1 Oct 40)	M1916	AG Neptun (Rostock)	21 Sep 18	27 Feb 19	See Table 2.1/7
M125 = *W2Wb* (1922)	M1916	Flensburger Schiffbau (Flensburg)	26 Oct 18	24 Apr 19	Transport vessel 1920; accommodation ship 1922; still in existence 1934
M126 = *M526* (1 Oct 40) = *Alders* (27 Apr 43)	M1916	Flensburger Schiffbau (Flensburg)	21 Dec 18	1 Jul 19	See Table 2.1/7
M129 = *Otto Braun* (29 Aug 38)	M1916	Reihersteig (Hamburg)	15 Jan 19	20 May 19	Mined off Kolberg 2 Dec 41
M130 = *Fuchs* (12 May 28) = *M530* (1 Oct 40) = *M3800* (1944)	M1916	Reihersteig Schiffswerke (Hamburg)	19 Feb 19	29 Jul 29	See Table 2.1/7
M131	M1916	Reihersteig Schiffswerke (Hamburg)	7 Jun 19	–	Stricken 24 Jun 19; sold incomplete Alberto A Dodero (Montevideo) 4 Nov 19 (to be passenger vessel); fate unknown
M132	M1916	Reihersteig Schiffs- werke (Hamburg)	14 Jan 19	14 Nov 19	Sunk depth charge accident Lister Tief 13 Nov 39
M133 = *Wacht* (11 Mar 29) = *Raule* (24 Aug 39) = *M533* (1 Oct 40)	M1916	Frerichs (Eiswerden)	1919	15 Dec 19	Collision *R45* NW of Boulogne 9 May 42
M134 = *Frauenlob* (11 Mar 29) = *M534* (1 Oct 40) = *Jungingen* (27 Sep 43)	M1916	Frerichs (Eiswerden)	28 Jul 19	31 Oct 19	See Table 2.1/7
M135 = *Hela* (5 Feb 23) = *Gazelle* (2 Jan 39) = *M535* (1 Oct 40)	M1916	Frerichs (Eiswerden)	15 Mar 19	31 Oct 19	See Table 2.1/7
M136 = *Havel* (1939)	M1916	Frerichs (Eiswerden)	1919	15 Nov 19	Mined off Hook of Holland 26 Jul 40
M137	M1916	J C Tecklenborg (Geestemünde)	15 Jan 19	20 Mar 19	Stricken 5 Jul 21; sold to BU 10 May 22
M138 = *Zieten* (11 Sep 24) = *Nettelbeck* (10 May 39) = *M538* (1 Oct 40)	M1916	J C Tecklenborg (Geestemünde)	17 Feb 19	21 Mar 19	Stranded off Hela 26 Jan 45; stricken 3 Feb 45
M139 = *Helgoland* (1919) = *Tönsberg I* (1922) = *Bogota* (1931)	M1916	J C Tecklenborg (Geestemünde)	12 Mar 19	–	Stricken 24 Jun 19; sold incomplete Hapag 19 Jun 19 (ferry); sold Tonsberg & Hortens 1922; sold CO 1931; sunk 1946
M140 = *Hörnum* (1919) = *St Elian* (1922) = *Partenope* (1927) = *Ischia* (1949) = *Concord* (1972)	M1916	J C Tecklenborg (Geestemünde)	15 Apr 19	–	Stricken 24 Jun 19; sold incomplete Hapag 19 Jun 19 (ferry); sold Liverpool & North Wales Steamship Co (Liverpool) 1922; sold Soc. Partenopea Anon. di Nav (Naples) 1927; sold Carmine Lauri & Giuseppe Martino (Salerno) 1972 (restaurant ship); BU 5 Sep 2008
M144 = *Sokol* (Jul 21) = *Eso* (1 Feb 42)	M1916	Stülcken Sohn (Hamburg)	19 Mar 19	20 Jun 19	Stricken 17 Jun 21; sold YU 20 Jul 21; IT Apr 41; see Table 2.2/8
M145 = *M545* (1 Oct 40)	M1916	AG Neptun (Rostock)	22 May 19	20 Jun 19	See Table 2.1/7
M146 = *Taku* (26 Aug 33) = *M146* (28 Oct 35) = *M546* (1 Oct 40) = *Von der Lippe* (29 Aug 41)	M1916	Flensburger Schiffbau (Flensburg)	21 Dec 18	11 Aug 19	Bombed Boulogne 15 Jun 44
M147 = *Erna David* (1920) = *Principio* (1922) = *Zaragoza* (1928) = *Appollo* (c.1930) = *Principio* (c.1931) = *Tooya* (1932) = *Korrigan IV* (1938)	M1916	Flensburger Schiffbau (Flensburg)	May 20	–	Stricken 24 Jun 19; sold incomplete .... (Hamburg) 26 Jun 19; Leopold David Shipping 1920; sold T Lechelt (Hamburg) 1922; sold Occidental (Papeete) 1935; sold Boleo-Estudios e Inversiones Transportation (Manzanillo) 1928; sold South SeaTraders (St John's) 1932; sold E Rougier Mineas (Santa Rosalia) 1938; sold Impulsora Minera e Industrial de Baja California (SantaRosalia) 1956; foundered Gulf of California 28 Nov 66

Name	Class	Builder	Launch	Comp/comm	Fate.
M150 = *Julius* (1920)	M1916	Hansawerft (Tönning)	May 1920	–	Stricken 24 Jun 19; sold incomplete H Klinck (Kiel) 11 Aug 20 (motor vessel); stranded and sunk off Farö Island 14 Nov 20
M151 = *Kosmos I* (1920) = *Kosmos* (1925) = *Kosmos I* (1930) = *Baranquilla* (1941) = *Presidente Madero* (1945) = *Florida* (1948)	M1916	Hansawerft (Tönning)	Sep 20	–	Stricken 24 Jun 19; sold incomplete Krull & Mais (Hamburg) 26 Jun 19 (motor vessel); sold W M P Angione (Cortino) 1925; sold Standard Fruit & Steamship Co (Ceiba) 1930; sold Cia de Navigacion y Tierras … 'Elliot' (Panama) 1941; sold Cia Continental de Navigacion (Mexico) 1945; sold Hermanos Ayo (Puerto Limon) 1948; stranded and sunk Quita Sueno Bank
M152 = *Silbo* (1920)	M1916	Hansawerft (Tönning)	Jun 20	–	Stricken 24 Jun 19; sold incomplete ……… (Hamburg) 26 Jun 19; W Boelister (Hamburg) (motor vessel); foundered Scharfhorn 19 Jan 23
M157 = *M557* (28 Jun 41)	M1916	Nordseewerke (Emden)	9 Apr 19	8 Dec 19	Mined NE of Rugen 27 Dec 41
M158 = *Grille* (1920) = *Dinard* (1922) = *Cordova* (1933)	M1916	Nordseewerke (Emden)	1920	–	Stricken 24 Jun 19; sold ………… (Berlin) 11 Aug 20; sold Vicomte de Gualès de Mezaubran (Nice) 1922; sold CO 1933; sunk 1946
FM1 = *Tepscora* (1922) = *Siegfried* (1925) = *H521* (1939) = *Nordpol* (27 Jun 42) = *Siegfried* (1947)	FM1	G Seebeck (Geestemünde)	15 Jun 18	18 Jul 18	Stricken 7 Dec 20; sold 16 Jan 22; J B Hermann (Elbing) 1924; O Karczinowsky (Königsberg) 1925 (ferry); bombed Gdynia 9 Oct 43; salved and O Karczinowsky (Kappeln) 3 Mar 47; BU after 1960
FM2 = *Finlandia I* (1920) = *Czajka* (1921)	FM1	G Seebeck (Geestemünde)	6 Jul 18	24 Aug 18	Stricken 10 Mar 20; PL 20 Nov 20; stricken 1935; mercantile; scuttled Gdynia Sep 39; salved and BU
FM3 = *Cecedena IV* (1920s) = *Minna* (late 1920s)	FM1	J C Tecklenborg (Geestemünde)	17 Jan 18	13 Feb 18	Stricken 8 May 19; sold ………… (Berlin); sold Cie Continentale Belge de Navigation (Antwerp) 1920s; sold Leonhardt & Blumberg (Hamburg) 1925 (tug); sold G Joos; sold J Knaak 1930; sold F Mützfeld 1931; sold to BU Hamburg 1935
FM4	FM1	J C Tecklenborg (Geestemünde)	23 Feb 18	27 Feb 18	Stricken 10 Mar 20; sold ……… Bank (Bucharest); fate uncertain.[8].
FM5 = *Giorgios Galeos* (1919) = *Maria K* = *Maria Kalydon* = *10V1* (1941)	FM1	Frerichs (Eiswerden)	1918	5 Aug 18	Stricken 8 May 19; sold Greek interests 14 Oct 19 (ferry); GE 1941; sunk
FM6	FM1	Frerichs (Eiswerden)	1918	21 Oct 18	Stricken 31 Dec 19; sold Luwen (Duisburg-Ruhrort) 22 Jul 20; fate unknown
FM7	FM1	Frerichs (Eiswerden)	1918	–	Stricken 8 May 19; sold Gerhard Hulskens (Wesel); fate unknown
FM8	FM1	Stülcken Sohn (Hamburg)	26 Jul 18	19 Oct 18	Stricken 8 May 19; sold Gerhard Hulskens (Wesel); fate unknown
FM9	FM1	Stülcken Sohn (Hamburg)	3 Dec 18	14 Jan 19	Stricken 8 May 19; sold ………… (Berlin); fate unknown
FM10	FM1	Stülcken Sohn (Hamburg)	16 Jan 19	1 Apr 19	Stricken 26 Nov 19; sold Bieber (Memel); fate unknown
FM11	FM1	Gebrüder Sachsenberg (Rosslau)	1918	13 Sep 18	Stricken 8 May 19; sold ………… (Berlin); fate unknown
FM12	FM1	Gebrüder Sachsenberg (Rosslau)	1918	–	Stricken 8 May 19; sold Fentsch & Laeisz (lighter); fate unknown
FM13	FM1	Union-Giesserei (Königsberg)	20 Jul 18	7 Oct 18	Stricken 8 May 19; sold Antwerper Schiffs- & Maschinenbau (Hamburg); fate unknown
FM14	FM1	Union-Giesserei (Königsberg)	28 Oct 18	23 Jan 23	Stricken 26 Nov 19; sold Bieber (Memel); fate unknown
FM15	FM1	Übigau (Dresden)	1918	1918	Stricken 8 May 19; sold 14 Oct 19; fate unknown
FM16 = *Shqipnja* (1925)	FM1	Übigau (Dresden)	1919	–	Stricken 10 Mar 20; sold ……… Bank (Bucharest); AL Dec 25; constructive total loss 1935/36
FM17	FM1	Jos L Mayet (Papenburg)	8 May 18	10 Sep 18	Stricken 8 May 19; sold ………… (Berlin); fate unknown
FM18	FM1	Jos L Mayet (Papenburg)	1918	1918	Stricken 8 May 19; sold Antwerper Schiffs- & Maschinenbau (Hamburg); fate unknown
FM19 = *Tönning* (1922) = *Raul Cascais* (Oct 22)	FM1	J C Tecklenborg (Geestemünde)	23 Feb 18	14 Mar 18	PT 26 Oct 22; stricken 4 Sep 36; BU 1937
FM20	FM1	J C Tecklenborg (Geestemünde)	9 Mar 18	27 Mar 18	Stricken 10 Mar 20; sold ……… Bank (Bucharest); fate uncertain

[8] Fates of individual vessels sold to Romanian interests are often unclear, although most served throughout the 1930s; one (either ex-*FM4*, *FM20* or *FM23*) became the Hungarian minesweeper *Körös* in 1928, and was allocated to the USA in 1945, being BU at Passau after 1951.

Name	Class	Builder	Launch	Comp/comm	Fate.
FM21 = *Peilboot III* (1920)	FM1	G Seebeck (Geestemünde)	14 Dec 18	1 Apr 19	Stricken 1 Oct 28; sold F Mützelfeld 7 Aug 30; sold SA Bremerhaven 1936; bombed UK aircraft Bremerhaven 24 Oct 44
FM22 = *Peilboot IV* (1920)	FM1	G Seebeck (Geestemünde)	19 Feb 19	9 May 19	Stricken 22 Jul 27; BU Hamburg-Moorburg 1928
FM23 = *Skënderbeg* (1925)	FM1	Frerichs & Co (Eiswerden)	1918	25 Dec 18	Stricken 31 Dec 19; sold .... Bank (Bucharest); AL Dec 25; constructive total loss 1935/36
FM24 = *Fatiya* (1923) = *Pahlavi* (1926) = *Shahin* (1935)	FM1	Frerichs & Co (Eiswerden)	1918	15 Mar 19	Stricken 29 Apr 22; sold .... (Hamburg) 7 Apr 22; IR 1923; BU early 1940s
FM25 = *Bismarck* (1925) = *Ålands Express* (1927) = *Express* (1930) = *S Costanzo Express* (1933) = *Gianpaolo I* (1935) = *F97* (1941) = *Gianpaolo I* (1946)	FM1	Unterweser (Rostock) (Bremerhaven)	10 May 18	3 Aug 18	Stricken 29 Apr 22; sold .... (Hamburg) 7 Apr 22; sold P Mestermann 1925 (ferry); sold Ålands Angbaat (Åbo) 1927; sold Åbolands Angf 1930; sold Natale Giuffrè di Sorrento 1933; sold Navigazione a Vapore Municipalizzata (Trieste) 1935; BU 1954
FM26 = *Peilboot VII* (1920)	FM1	Unterweser (Bremerhaven)	19 Jul 18	1 Oct 18	Stricken 22 Jul 27; BU Hamburg-Moorburg 1928
FM27 = *Finlandia II* (1920) = *Jaskolka* (1921)	FM1	Caesar Wollheim (Breslau)	1918	1918	Stricken 10 Oct 19; PL 20 Nov 20; stricken 1935; BU
FM28 = *Finlandia III* (1920) = *Mewa* (1921) = *Pomorzanin* (1935)	FM1	Caesar Wollheim (Breslau)	1918	1918	Stricken 10 Oct 19; PL 20 Nov 20; bombed German aircraft Jastarnia 14 Dep 39; salved and BU 1946
FM29 = *Westfalen* (1926) = *Montijense* (1932)	FM1	Nobiskrug (Rensdburg)	1919	1919	Stricken 8 Jun 25; sold Heidmann (Stettin) (ferry); sold C Wollheim (Stettin) 1928; sold Soc Maritima de Transportes (Barriero) 1932; sunk after 1958
FM30	FM1	Lübecker Machin- enbau (Lübeck)	1919	1919	Stricken 26 Nov 19; sold Breslauer Dampfer 3 May 21; fate unknown
FM31 = *Finlandia IV* (1920) = *Rybitwa* (1921)	FM1	Lübecker Machinenbau (Lübeck)	1919	11 Jun 19	Stricken 10 Mar 20; PL 20 Nov 20; stricken 1935; BU
FM32	FM1	Gebrüder Sachs- enberg (Rosslau)	1919	1919	Stricken 26 Nov 19; sold Breslauer Dampfer 3 May 21; fate unknown
FM33	FM1	Nordseewerke (Emden)	1919	18 Jun 19	Stricken 10 Oct 19; sold .... Bank (Bucharest); fate unknown
FM34	FM1	Nordseewerke (Emden)	1919	1919	Stricken 31 Dec 19; sold Luwen (Duisburg-Ruhrort) 22 Jul 20; fate unknown
FM35 = *Baltic* (1922)	FM1	Union-Giesserei (Königsberg)	1919	1919	Stricken 10 Oct 19; sold .... (Memel) 23 Feb 20; sold Otwiwerke (Bremen) 1922; fate unknown
FM36 = *Socrates* (1920) = *Xanten* (18 Oct 41) = *UJ116* (1942)	FM1	Stettiner Oderwerke (Stettin)	1919	1919	Stricken 31 Dec 19; sold .... Bank (Bucharest); (Danube ferry); GE 5 Oct 41; scuttled S of Cape Kaliakra 30 Aug 44
FM37 = *Fiumana I* (1923) = *Arco Azurro* (1939)	FM37	Unterweser (Bremerhaven)	1919	1919	Stricken 22 Aug 21; sold .... (Berlin); sold Costiera SA di Navigazione Marittima (Fiume) 1923; sold Soc Fiumana di Navigazione 1939; bombed Genoa 23 Oct 42; BU
FM38 = *Fiumana II* (1923) = *Lurana* (1939) = *Fiumana II* (1945)	FM37	Unterweser (Bremerhaven)	1919	1919	Stricken 22 Aug 21; sold .... (Berlin); sold Costiera SA di Navigazione Marittima (Fiume) 1923; sold Soc Fiumana di Navigazione 1939; fate unknown
FM39	FM37	Unterweser (Bremerhaven)	1918	1918	Stricken 16 Sep 19; sold .... (Berlin); sold .... (Regensburg); fate unknown
FM40, FM41	FM37	Unterweser (Bremerhaven)	–	–	Cancelled; BU
FM42 = *Pionier* (1922)	FM37	Rickmers (Geestemünde)	1918	18 Nov 19	Stricken 29 Apr 22; sold Aug Bolten (Hamburg); sold SU
FM43	FM37	Rickmers (Geestemünde)	1919	–	Fate unknown
FM44	FM37	Rickmers (Geestemünde)	–	–	Cancelled; BU
FM45–FM47	FM37	Henry Koch (Lübeck)	–	–	Cancelled; BU
FM48	FM37	Jos L Meyer (Papenburg)	1919	1919	Stricken 29 Aug 21; sold .... (Berlin) Nov 21

Name	Class	Builder	Launch	Comp/comm	Fate.
FM49 = Fiumana III (1923) = Albona (1939) = Fiumana III (1945)	FM37	Jos L Meyer (Papenburg)	1919	–	Stricken 8 May 19; sold .... (Berlin) 14 Oct 19; sold Costiera SA di Navigazione Marittima (Fiume) 1923; sold Soc Fiumana di Navigazione 1939; fate unknown
FM50 = Eliene	FM37	Jos L Meyer (Papenburg)	1919	–	Stricken 8 May 19; sold .... (Berlin) 14 Oct 19; sold Smyrna International Ferry Services; fate unknown
FM51–FM53	FM37	Janssen & Schmilinski (Hamburg)	–	–	Cancelled; BU
FM54 = Freiheit (17 Apr 20) = Vestjyden (1922) = Memelland (1925) = Brunhilde (1930) = Carmen (1935)	FM37	D W Kremer (Elmshorn)	1919	–	Sold B Plage (Berlin) Mar 20 (ferry); sold Rinkjöbing Dampskip 1922; sold Seebäderdienst Memel 1925; sold G Hermann (Elbing) 1927; sold O Karczinowsky (Königsberg) 1930; sold Polska Zegluga Rzeczna Vistula (Gdynia) 1935; sunk Sep 39
FM55 = King Albert (1922) = Wilhelmina (1930) = Miramar (1931) = Eider (1940)	FM37	D W Kremer (Elmshorn)	1918	–	Sold .... 1922 (ferry); sold D Dekker (Wildervink) 1930; sold SA des Bateaux Belges (Antwerp) 1931; GE 1940; fate unknown
FM56	FM37	Caesar Wollheim (Breslau)	1918	1918	Stricken 16 Sep 19; sold .... (Berlin); sold .... (Regensburg); fate unknown
FM57	FM37	Caesar Wollheim (Breslau)	1918	1918	Stricken 16 Sep 19; sold .... (Berlin); sold .... (Regensburg); fate unknown
FM58, FM59	FM37	Ubigau (Dresden)	–	–	Cancelled; BU
FM60, FM61	FM37	Nobiskrug (Rendsburg)	–	–	Cancelled; BU
FM62 = Vaterland = Ribatejo Primeiro (1935)	FM37	Thormählen (Elmshorn)	1919	–	Stricken 6 Jun 19; sold .... (Bremerhaven) (ferry); sold Soc Maritima de Transportes (Barriero) 1935; still in existence 1947
FM63, FM64	FM37	Klawitter (Danzig)	–	–	Cancelled; BU
FM65, FM66	FM37	Nüscke (Stettin)	–	–	Cancelled; BU

Table 1.1/7. Major Auxiliaries

Submarine Salvage Vessels

	Disp.	Length	Beam	Machinery	Power/speed	Main gun(s)
Vulcan	2595t	85.3m	17.0m	4 x boilers, 2 x TE	1340shp=12kt	–
Cyclop	4010t	94.0m	19.6m	4 x boilers, 2 x VTE	1800ihp=9kt	–

Name	Builder	Launch	Comp/comm	Alloc	Fate.
Vulcan	Howaldtswerke (Kiel)	28 Sep 07	4 Mar 08	–	Foundered North Sea (54° 54.16' N, 06° 18.12' E) 6 Apr 19; wreck demolished by depth charges Apr 19
Cyclop = Cyklop (1920)	Danzig DYd/ Bremer Vulcan (Vegesack)	1916	1 Jul 18	UK	UK commission by Dec 1920; sold Alfred Kubatz (Berlin) 29 May 22; BU GE

▓ 2. The Austro-Hungarian Navy: 4 November 1918

Table 1.2/1. Capital Ships

Class	Disp.	Length	Beam	Machinery	Power/speed	Main gun(s)	TT
Erzherzog Karl	10,640t	125.0m	21.8m	16 x boilers, ? x VTE	18,000ihp=20.5kt	4 x 24cm/40	2 x 45cm
Habsburg	8250t	115.0m	19.8m	16 x boilers, 2 x VTE	15,000ihp=19.5kt	3 x 24cm/40	2 x 45cm
Kaiser Karl VI	6166t	120.0m	17.3m	18 x boilers, 2 x VTE	12,300ihp=20.0kt	[2 x 24cm/40]	2 x 45cm
K Erz Rudolf	6900t	95.0m	19.2m	10 x boilers, 2 x VC	6500ihp=16.0kt	3 x 30.5cm/35	4 x 40cm
KuK Maria Theresia	5330t	113.7m	16.3m	6 x boilers, 2 x HTE	9000ihp=19.0kt	[two 7.6in/42]	4 x 45cm
Mars	7431t	92.5m	21.8m	8 x boilers, 2 x VTE	8160ihp = 15.5kt	6 x 24cm/35	2 x 35cm
Monarch	5645t	97.0m	16.9m	8/16 x boilers, 2 x VTE	8500ihp=17.5kt	4 x 24cm/40	2 x 45cm
Radetzky	14,508t	138.8m	24.6m	12 x boilers, 2 x VTE	19,800ihp=20.5kt	4 x 30.5cm/45	3 x 45cm
Sankt Georg	7289t	124.3m	19.0m	12 x boilers, 2 x VTE	12,300ihp=21.0kt	[2 x 24cm/40]	2 x 45cm
Tegetthoff	20,014t	152.2m	27.3m	12 x boilers, 4 x Tu	26,400shp=20.0kt	12 x 30.5cm/45	4 x 53.3cm

Name	Class	Builder	Launch	Comp/comm	Location at Jan 20	Alloc	Fate.
Arpád	Habsburg	Stab Tecnico Triestino (Trieste)	11 Sep 01	15 Jun 03	Pola	UK	Sold Ceneva & G Vaccaro 21 Aug 20 (5,000,000L, with Kaiser Karl VI, Budapest, Habsburg & Babenerg); BU Cantiere navale di scoglio olive, Pola
Babenberg	Habsburg	Stab Tecnico Triestino (Trieste)	4 Oct 02	24 May 04	Pola	UK	Sold Ceneva & G Vaccaro 21 Aug 20 (5,000,000L, with Kaiser Karl VI, Budapest, Habsburg & Arpád); BU Cantiere navale di scoglio olive, Pola
Budapest	Monarch	Stab Tecnico Triestino (Trieste)	27 Apr 96	12 May 98	Pola	UK	Sold Ceneva & G Vaccaro 21 Aug 20 (5,000,000L, with Kaiser Karl VI, Habsburg, Arpád & Babenberg); BU
Erzherzog Ferdinand Max	Erzherzog Karl	Stab Tecnico Triestino (Trieste)	21 May 05	21 Dec 07	Cattaro	UK	Sold Count Taverna & Alessandro Piaggio 12 Aug 20 (1,600,000L, with Monarch & Sankt Georg); BU Genoa
Erzherzog Franz Ferdinand	Radetzky	Stab Tecnico Triestino (Trieste)	30 Sep 08	6 Jul 10	Venice	IT	BU Ancona 1921
Erzherzog Friedrich	Erzherzog Karl	Stab Tecnico Triestino (Trieste)	30 Apr 05	31 Jan 07	Cattaro	FR	BU La Spezia 1920
Erzherzog Karl	Erzherzog Karl	Stab Tecnico Triestino (Trieste)	4 Oct 03	17 Jun 06	Bizerte	FR	Stranded off Bizerte in tow to Toulon 1920; BU 1921
Habsburg	Habsburg	Stab Tecnico Triestino (Trieste)	9 Sep 00	31 Dec 02	Pola	UK	Sold Ceneva & G Vaccaro 21 Aug 20 (5,000,000L, with Kaiser Karl VI, Budapest, Arpád & Babenberg); BU Cantiere navale di scoglio olive, Pola
Kaiser Karl VI	Kaiser Karl VI	Stab Tecnico Triestino (San Rocco)	4 Oct 98	23 May 00	Pola	UK	Sold Ceneva & G Vaccaro 21 Aug 20 (5,000,000L, with Habsburg, Budapest, Arpád & Babenberg); BU Naples to 1922
Kaiserin und Königin Maria Theresia	KuK Maria Theresia	Stab Tecnico Triestino (San Rocco)	29 Apr 93	24 Mar 95	Pola	UK	Sold Fiat Motor Co (Turin) 27 Aug 20 (1,081,473L, with Aspern & Szigetvár); re-sold Vaccaro & Co; BU Portoferraio (Elba)
Kronprinz Erzherzog Rudolf = Kumbor (Mar 21)	K Erz Rudolf	Pola DYd	6 Jul 87	1889	Pola	YU	BU 1922
Mars (ex-Tegetthoff)	Mars	Stab Tecnico Triestino (San Rocco)	15 Oct 78	Oct 81	Pola	IT	BU 1920
Monarch	Monarch	Pola DYd	9 May 95	11 May 98	Cattaro	UK	Sold Count Taverna & Alessandro Piaggio 12 Aug 20 (1,600,000L, with E Ferdinand Max & Sankt Georg); BU
Prinz Eugen	Tegetthoff	Stab Tecnico Triestino (Trieste)	30 Nov 12	17 Jul 14	Pola	FR	Expended as gunfire target Paris, Jean Bart & France off Toulon 28 Jun 22
Radetzky	Radetzky	Stab Tecnico Triestino (Trieste)	3 Jul 09	15 Jan 11	Spalato	IT	BU 1920
Sankt Georg	Sankt Georg	Pola DYd	8 Dec 03	21 Jul 05	Taranto	UK	Sold Count Taverna & Alessandro Piaggio 12 Aug 20; re-sold Vaccaro & Co; BU Taranto
Tegetthoff	Tegetthoff	Stab Tecnico Triestino (Trieste)	31 Mar 12	21 Jul 13	Venice	IT (P)	BU La Spezia 1924–25
Zrinyi	Radetzky	Stab Tecnico Triestino (Trieste)	12 Apr 10	6 Jul 10	Spalato	IT	BU 1920

Table 1.2/2. Light Cruisers

Class	Disp.	Length	Beam	Machinery	Power/speed	Main gun(s)
K Franz Joseph I	3967t	104.0m	14.8m	4 x boilers, 2 x HTE	8000ihp=19.5kt	2 x 15cm/40
Panther	1582t	75.0m	10.0m	6 x boilers, 2 x VTE	6000ihp=18.0kt	4 x 6.6cm/45
Zenta	2350t	97.0m	11.8m	8 x boilers, 2 x VTE	8000ihp=20.0kt	8 x 12cm/40
Admiral Spaun	3500t	130.6m	12.8m	16 x boilers, 4 x Tu	25,130shp=27.0kt	7 x 10cm/50
Mod Admiral Spaun	3500t	130.6m	12.8m	16 x boilers, 2 x Tu	30,178shp=27.0kt	9 x 10cm/50

Name	Class	Builder	Launch	Comp/comm	Location at Jan 20	Alloc	Fate.
Admiral Spaun	*Admiral Spaun*	Pola DYd	30 Oct 09	15 Nov 10	Venice	UK	Sold Cavaliere Luigi Stanita (Naples) Nov 20 (613,000L); BU Venice
Aspern	*Zenta*	Pola DYd	3 May 99	29 May 00	Pola	UK	Sold Fiat Motor Co (Turin) 27 Aug 20 (1,081,473L, with *KuK Maria Theresia* & *Szigetvár*); re-sold Vaccaro & Co; BU Venice
Helgoland = *Brindisi* (Jun 23)	Mod *Admiral Spaun*	Danubius (Fiume)	23 Nov 12	29 Aug 14	Bizerte	IT	IT commission 7 Jun 23; paid off 25 Nov 29; stricken 11 Mar 37; BU Trieste(?)
Kaiser Franz Joseph I	*K Franz Joseph I*	Stab Tecnico Triestino (San Rocco)	18 May 89	2 Jul 90	–	–	Foundered off Kumbor, Cattaro Bay, 17 Oct 19; salvage work 1922, 1967
Leopard	*Panther*	Armstrong (Elswick)	10 Sep 85	26 Mar 86	Pola	UK	Sold Battaglia, Battari & Serrao 20 Aug 20 (744,146L, with *Panther, Chamaleon, Salamander, 8, 9, 10, 14* & *18*); re-sold Vaccaro & Co; BU Messina
Novara = *Thionville*	Mod *Admiral Spaun*	Danubius (Fiume)	15 Feb 13	10 Jan 15	Cattaro	FR	Foundered Brindisi Jan 20; salved; FR commission 1922; paid off 17 Aug 33; accommodation hulk; sold 1 Feb 41 to BU Toulon
Panther	*Panther*	Armstrong (Elswick)	13 Jun 85	31 Dec 86	Pola	UK	Sold Battaglia, Battari & Serrao 20 Aug 20 (744,146L, with *Leopard, Chamaleon, Salamander, 8, 9, 10, 14* & *18*); re-sold Vaccaro & Co; BU Messina
Saida = *Venezia* (Jul 21)	Mod *Admiral Spaun*	Cantiere Naval Triestino (Monfalcone)	26 Oct 12	1 Aug 14	Pola	IT	IT commission 5 Jul 21; paid off 4 Jul 30; accommodation ship 16 Mar 35; stricken 11 Mar 37; BU Genoa(?)
Szigetvár	*Zenta*	Pola DYd	29 Oct 00	30 Sep 01	Pola	UK	Sold Fiat Motor Co (Turin) 27 Aug 20 (1,081,473L, with *KuK Maria Theresia* & *Aspern*); re-sold Vaccaro & Co; BU Portoferraio (Elba)

Table 1.2/3. Destroyers/Torpedo Boats

Class	Disp.	Length	Beam	Machinery	Power/speed	Main gun(s)	TT
Ersatz Tátra	880t	84.6m	7.8m	6 x boilers, 2 x Tu	22,360shp=32.6kt	2 x 10cm/50	4 x 45cm
Huszár	389t	68.4m	6.3m	4 x boilers, 2 x VTE	6000ihp=28.0kt	1 x 6.6cm + 7 x 47mm	2 x 45cm
Kaiman	210t	56.9m	5/4m	2 x boilers, 1 x VTE	3000ihp=26.2kt	4 x 47mm/33	3 x 45cm
Kibitz	80t	40.0m	4.8m	2 x boilers, 1 x VTE	1800ihp=24.0kt	2 x 47mm/33	2/3 x 45cm
Komet	418t	59.0m	6.9m	2 x boilers, 1 x VTE	2600ihp=21.0kt	8 x 47mm	2 x 35/45cm
Magnet	477t	67.5m	8.2m	4 x boilers, 2 x VTE	6000ihp=26.0kt	6 x 47mm	3 x 45cm
Meteor	428t	57.0m	6.8m	2 x boilers, 1 x VTE	2600ihp=21.0kt	8 x 47mm	2 x 45cm
Natter	166t	46.0m	5.3m	2 x boilers, 1 x VTE	2300ihp=26.5kt	2 x 47mm/33	2 x 45cm
Planet	498t	67.1m	7.0m	4 x boilers, 2 x VTE	3500ihp=19.6kt	8 x 6.6cm	2 x 45cm
Python	132t	46.6m	4.6m	2 x boilers, 1 x VTE	1800ihp=24.0kt	2 x 47mm/33	3 x 45cm
Satellit	606t	67.2m	8.1m	3 x boilers, 2 x VTE	4000ihp=21.0kt	1 x 6.6cm + 6 x 47mm	2 x 45cm
Sebenico	890t	58.0m	8.2m	... x boilers, 1 x VTE	900ihp=14.0kt	1 x 6.6cm/30	–
Tátra	850t	83.5m	7.8m	6 x boilers, 2 x Tu	20,640shp=32.6kt	2 x 10cm/50	4 x 45cm
Trabant	532t	67.0m	8.0m	4 x boilers, 2 x VTE	3800ihp=20.0kt	2 x 6.6cm/30	2 x 45cm
Viper	124t	45.0m	4.5m	2 x boilers, 1 x VTE	1800ihp=24.0kt	2 x 47mm/33	3 x 45cm
Warasdiner	389t	68.4m	6.3m	4 x boilers, 2 x VTE	6000ihp=30.0kt	6 x 6.6cm	4 x 45cm
Zara	840t	55.0m	8.2m	... x boilers, 1 x VTE	850ihp=14.0kt	1 x 6.6cm/30	2 x 35cm
73T	262t	57.8m	5.8m	2 x boilers, 2 x Tu	5000shp=28.0kt	2 x 6.6cm/30	2 x 45cm
82F	244t	58.8m	5.8m	2 x boilers, 2 x Tu	5000shp=28.0kt	2 x 6.6cm/30	4 x 45cm
98M	250t	60.4m	5.6m	2 x boilers, 2 x Tu	5000shp=29.5kt	2 x 6.6cm/30	4 x 45cm
I	116t	44.2m	4.3m	2 x boilers, 1 x VTE	2500ihp=28.0kt	2 x 47mm/44	2 x 45cm
VII	132t	44.2m	4.3m	2 x boilers, 1 x VTE	2400ihp=26.5kt	2 x 47mm/44	2 x 45cm

Name	Class	Builder	Launch	Comp/comm	Location at Jan 20	Alloc	Fate.
Balaton = *Zenson* [i] (Sep 20)	*Tátra*	Danubius (Porto Ré)	16 Nov 12	3 Nov 13		IT	To IT 26 Sep 20; stricken 5 Jul 23
Blitz	*Komet*	Schichau (Elbing)	7 Jul 88	Jan 88	Pola	IT	BU 1920
Csepel = *Muggia* (Sep 20)	*Tátra*	Danubius (Porto Ré)	30 Dec 1	29 Dec 13		IT	To IT 26 Sep 20; wrecked off Shang Hsu (Xia Yu) 25 Mar 29
Csikós	*Huszár*	Danubius (Fiume)	24 Jan 09	16 Nov 09		IT	BU 1920
Dinara	*Huszár*	Danubius (Fiume)	16 Oct 09	31 Dec 09	Pola	IT	BU 1920
Dukla = *Matelot Leblanc* (Sep 20	*Ersatz Tátra*	Danubius (Porto Ré)	18 Jul 17	7 Nov 17		FR	To FR Sep 20; stricken 30 May 36; sold Societé Klaguine 5 Oct 36; BU Bizerte
Huszár	*Huszár*	Pola DYd	20 Dec 10	8 Feb 11	Pola	IT	BU 1920
Komet	*Komet*	Schichau (Elbing)	18 Aug 88	Feb 89	Pola	IT	BU 1920
Lika = *Cortellazzo* (Sep 20)	*Ersatz Tátra*	Danubius (Porto Ré)	8 May 17	6 Sep 17		IT	To IT 26 Sep 20; stricken 5 Jan 39
Magnet	*Magnet*	Schichau (Elbing)	31 Mar 96	Dec 96	Pola	IT	BU 1920
Meteor	*Meteor*	Schichau (Elbing)	17 Aug 87	1887	Pola	IT	BU 1920

Name	Class	Builder	Launch	Comp/comm	Location at Jan 20	Alloc	Fate.
Orjen = *Pola* (Sep 20) − *Zenson* [ii] (9 Apr 31)	*Tátra*	Danubius (Porto Ré)	26 Aug 13	Jul 14		IT	IT commission Mar 22; stricken 1 May 37
Pandur	*Huszár*	Danubius (Fiume)	25 Oct 08	31 Jan 09	Cattaro	FR	Foundered en route Toulon
Planet	*Planet*	Palmers (Newcastle)	25 Sep 89	1890	Pola	IT	BU 1920
Reka	*Huszár*	Danubius (Fiume)	28 Apr 09	31 Dec 09	Bizerte	FR	BU 1920
Satellit	*Satellit*	Schichau (Elbing)	21 Sep 92	Jun 93	Bizerte	FR	BU 1920
Scharfschutze	*Huszár*	Stab Tecnico Triestino (Trieste)	5 Dec 06	15 Sep 07		IT	BU 1920
Sebenico	*Sebenico*	Pola DYd	28 Feb 82	1882	Pola	IT	BU 1920
Spalato	*Zara*	Stab Tecnico Triestino (Trieste)	30 Aug 79	1881	Pola	IT	BU 1920
Tátra = *Fasana* (Sep 20)	*Tátra*	Danubius (Porto Ré)	4 Nov 12	18 Oct 13		IT	To IT 26 Sep 20; stricken 5 Jul 23
Trabant	*Trabant*	Stab Tecnico Triestino (San Rocco)	21 May 90	20 Oct 90	Pola	IT	BU 1920
Triglav = *Grado* (Sep 20)	*Ersatz Tátra*	Danubius (Porto Ré)	24 Feb 17	21 Jul 17		IT	To IT 26 Sep 20; stricken 30 Sep 37
Turul	*Huszár*	Danubius (Fiume)	9 Aug 08	31 Dec 08	Pola	IT	BU 1920
Ulan = *Smyrni* (1920)	*Huszár*	Stab Tecnico Triestino (Trieste)	8 Apr 06	12 Sep 06		GR	Discarded 1928; sold c.1931
Uskoke	*Huszár*	Stab Tecnico Triestino (Trieste)	20 Jul 07	31 Dec 07		IT	BU 1920
Uszok = *Monfalcone* (Sep 20)	*Ersatz Tátra*	Danubius (Porto Ré)	16 Sep 17	25 Jan 18		IT	To IT 26 Sep 20; stricken 5 Jan 39
Velebit	*Huszár*	Danubius (Fiume)	24 Jul 09	31 Dec 09	Pola	IT	BU 1920
Warasdiner (ex-*Lung Tuan*)	*Warasdiner*	Stab Tecnico Triestino (Trieste)	1912	10 Sep 14	Pola	IT	BU 1920
Zara	*Zara*	Pola DYd	13 Nov 79	1881	Pola	IT	BU 1920
1 (ex-*I*)	*I*	Stab Tecnico Triestino (Trieste)	12 Aug 09	31 Dec 09	Pola	IT	BU
2 (ex-*II*)	*I*	Stab Tecnico Triestino (Trieste)	27 Sep 09	31 Dec 09	Pola	IT	BU
3 (ex-*III*)	*I*	Stab Tecnico Triestino (Trieste)	8 Nov 09	31 Dec 09		IT	To IT Customs; BU 1925
4 (ex-*IV*)	*I*	Stab Tecnico Triestino (Trieste)	2 Dec 09	31 Dec 09	Pola	IT	BU
5 (ex-*V*)	*I*	Stab Tecnico Triestino (Trieste)	30 Dec 09	24 Feb 10		IT	BU
6 (ex-*VI*)	*I*	Stab Tecnico Triestino (Trieste)	Jan 10	31 Nov 10	Pola	UK	BU
7 (ex-*VII*)	*VII*	Danubius (Fiume)	30 Jan 10	29 Jul 10		IT	BU
8 (ex-*VIII*)	*VII*	Danubius (Fiume)	24 Feb 10	20 May 10	Pola	UK	Sold Battaglia, Battari & Serrao 20 Aug 20 (744,146L, with *Leopard, Panther, Chamaleon, Salamander, 9, 10, 14 & 18*); BU Messina
9 (ex-*IX*)	*VII*	Danubius (Fiume)	22 Mar 10	20 May 10	Pola	UK	Sold Battaglia, Battari & Serrao 20 Aug 20 (744,146L, with *Leopard, Panther, Chamaleon, Salamander, 8, 10, 14 & 18*); BU Messina
10 (ex-*X*)	*VII*	Danubius (Fiume)	14 May 10	13 Jul 10	Pola	UK	Sold Battaglia, Battari & Serrao 20 Aug 20 (744,146L, with *Leopard, Panther, Chamaleon, Salamander, 8, 9, 14 & 18*); BU Messina
11 (ex-*XI*)	*VII*	Danubius (Fiume)	24 May 10	31 Dec 10		IT	BU
12 (ex-*XII*)	*VII*	Danubius (Fiume)	31 May 10	23 May 11	Spalato	IT	Stranded off Spalato Dec 18; BU 1922
13 (ex-*Python*)	*Python*	Yarrow (Poplar)	11 Apr 99	12 Oct 99	Cattaro	FR	BU
14 (ex-*Kigyo*)	*Python*	Yarrow (Poplar)	11 Apr 99	31 Jan 00	Pola	UK	Sold Battaglia, Battari & Serrao 20 Aug 20 (744,146L, with *Leopard, Panther, Chamaleon, Salamander, 8, 9, 10 & 18*); BU Messina
15 (ex-*Boa*)	*Python*	Yarrow (Poplar)	Sep 98	1898	Cattaro	FR	BU
16 (ex-*Cobra*)	*Python*	Yarrow (Poplar)	1898	1898	Cattaro	FR	BU
17 (ex-*Viper*)	*Viper*	Yarrow (Chiswick)	1896	Oct 96	Cattaro	FR	BU
18 (ex-*Natter*)	*Natter*	Schichau (Elbing)	1896	Nov 96	Pola	UK	Sold Battaglia, Battari & Serrao 20 Aug 20 (744,146L, with *Leopard, Panther, Chamaleon, Salamander, 8, 9, 10 & 14*); BU Messina
19 (ex-*Kibitz*) = *D4* (1920)	*Kibitz*	Pola DYd	1891	1891		YU	To YU 1920; minesweeper; BU 1924
20 (ex-*Kukuk*)	*Kibitz*	Schichau (Elbing)	1889	1889		IT	BU
21 (ex-*Staar*) = *D1* (1920)	*Kibitz*	Schichau (Elbing)	May 89	1889		YU	To YU 1920; minesweeper; BU 1924

Name	Class	Builder	Launch	Comp/ comm	Location at Jan 20	Alloc	Fate.
22 (ex-Krähe)	Kibitz	Schichau (Elbing)	1889	1889		IT	To IT Customs Sep 20; BU 1925
23 (ex-Rabe)	Kibitz	Schichau (Elbing)	1888	1888		IT	BU
24 (ex-Elster)	Kibitz	Schichau (Elbing)	1888	1888		IT	To IT Customs Sep 20; BU 1925
25 (ex-Gaukler)	Kibitz	Stab Tecnico Triestino (Trieste)	1889	1890		IT	To IT Customs Sep 20; BU 1925
27 (ex-Secretär)_	Kibitz	Stab Tecnico Triestino (Trieste)	1889	1889		IT	BU
29 (ex-Marabou)	Kibitz	Stab Tecnico Triestino (Trieste)	12 Dec 89	Dec 89		IT	To IT Customs Sep 20; BU 1925
30 (ex-Harpie)	Kibitz	Stab Tecnico Triestino (Trieste)	1890	1890		IT	BU
31 (ex-Sperber)	Kibitz	Schichau (Elbing)	1886	1886		IT	BU
32 (ex-Habicht)	Kibitz	Schichau (Elbing)	1886	1886		IT	To IT Customs Sep 20; BU 1925
33 (ex-Bussard)	Kibitz	Pola DYd	30 Sep 86	1886		IT	BU
34 (ex-Condor)	Kibitz	Pola DYd	17 Sep 86	1886		IT	BU
35 (ex-Geier)	Kibitz	Pola DYd	17 Nov 86	1886		IT	BU
36 (ex-Uhu) = D2 (1920) = D10 (Apr 41)	Kibitz	Pola DYd	7 Dec 86	1886		YU	To YU 1920; minesweeper; to IT Apr 41; to GE Sep 43; sank off Kumbor
37 (ex-Würger)	Kibitz	Pola DYd	1887	1887		IT	BU
38 (ex-Kranich) = D3(1920)	Kibitz	Pola DYd	1887	1887		YU	To YU 1920; minesweeper; BU 1924
39 (ex-Reiher)	Kibitz	Pola DYd	1887	1887		IT	BU
40 (ex-Ibis)	Kibitz	Pola DYd	1886	1887		IT	BU
50E (ex-Kaiman)	Kaiman	Yarrow (Poplar)	3 Jun 05	14 Sep 05	Pola	UK	Sold Count Taverna & Alessandro Piaggio 21 Aug 20 (14,000L= £200); BU Cantiere navale di scoglio olive, Pola
51T (ex-Anaconda)	Kaiman	Stab Tecnico Triestino (Trieste)	8 May 06	21 Sep 06	Pola	UK	Sold Count Taverna & Alessandro Piaggio 21 Aug 20 (14,000L = £200); BU Cantiere navale di scoglio olive, Pola
52T (ex-Alligator)	Kaiman	Stab Tecnico Triestino (Trieste)	30 Jun 06	31 Dec 06	Spalato	IT	Stranded off Spalato Dec 18; BU 1922
53T (ex-Krokodil)	Kaiman	Stab Tecnico Triestino (Trieste)	25 Jul 06	31 Dec 06	Pola	UK	Sold Count Taverna & Alessandro Piaggio 21 Aug 20 (14,000L = £200); BU Cantiere navale di scoglio olive, Pola
54T (ex-Wal) = T12 (1920)	Kaiman	Stab Tecnico Triestino (Trieste)	10 Sep 06	15 Jun 07		YU	To YU 1920; BU 1924
55T (ex-Seehund)	Kaiman	Stab Tecnico Triestino (Trieste)	15 Sep 06	15 Jun 07	Pola	UK	Sold Count Taverna & Alessandro Piaggio 21 Aug 20 (14,000L = £200); BU Cantiere navale di scoglio olive, Pola
56T (ex-Delphin)	Kaiman	Stab Tecnico Triestino (Trieste)	29 Nov 06	15 Jun 07	Pola	UK	Sold Count Taverna & Alessandro Piaggio 21 Aug 20 (14,000L = £200); BU Cantiere navale di scoglio olive, Pola
57T (ex-Narwal)	Kaiman	Stab Tecnico Triestino (Trieste)	17 Dec 06	15 Jun 08	Pola	UK	Sold Count Taverna & Alessandro Piaggio 21 Aug 20 (14,000L = £200); BU Cantiere navale di scoglio olive, Pola
58T (ex-Hai)	Kaiman	Stab Tecnico Triestino (Trieste)	24 Mar 07	15 Jun 08	Pola	UK	Sold Count Taverna & Alessandro Piaggio 21 Aug 20 (14,000L = £200); BU Cantiere navale di scoglio olive, Pola
59T (ex-Möve)	Kaiman	Stab Tecnico Triestino (Trieste)	30 Mar 07	15 Jun 08	Pola	UK	Sold Count Taverna & Alessandro Piaggio 21 Aug 20 (14,000L = £200); BU Cantiere navale di scoglio olive, Pola
60T (ex-Schwalbe) = T9 (1920)	Kaiman	Stab Tecnico Triestino (Trieste)	8 Apr 07	20 Mar 09		YU	BU 1924
61T (ex-Pinguin) = T10 (1920)	Kaiman	Stab Tecnico Triestino (Trieste)	18 Apr 07	20 Mar 09		YU	BU 1924
62T (ex-Drache)	Kaiman	Stab Tecnico Triestino (Trieste)	13 Jul 07	20 Mar 09	Pola	UK	Sold Count Taverna & Alessandro Piaggio 21 Aug 20 (14,000L= £200); BU Cantiere navale di scoglio olive, Pola
63T (ex-Greif)	Kaiman	Stab Tecnico Triestino (Trieste)	8 Jul 07	20 Mar 09	Pola	UK	Sold Count Taverna & Alessandro Piaggio 21 Aug 20 (14,000L = £200); BU Cantiere navale di scoglio olive, Pola
64F (ex-Triton)	Kaiman	Danubius (Fiume)	18 Jul 08	31 Dec 08	Pola	UK	Sold Count Taverna & Alessandro Piaggio 21 Aug 20 (14,000L = £200); BU Cantiere navale di scoglio olive, Pola
65F (ex-Hydra)	Kaiman	Danubius (Fiume)	11 Oct 08	19 Jan 09	Pola	UK	Sold Count Taverna & Alessandro Piaggio 21 Aug 20 (14,000L = £200); BU Cantiere navale di scoglio olive, Pola
66F (ex-Skorpion)	Kaiman	Danubius (Fiume)	15 Nov 08	22 Jan 09	Pola	UK	Sold Count Taverna & Alessandro Piaggio 21 Aug 20 (14,000L = £200); BU Cantiere navale di scoglio olive, Pola
67F (ex-Phönix)	Kaiman	Danubius (Fiume)	10 Jan 09	3 Aug 09	Pola	UK	Sold Count Taverna & Alessandro Piaggio 21 Aug 20 (14,000L = £200); BU Cantiere navale di scoglio olive, Pola
68F (ex-Krake)	Kaiman	Danubius (Fiume)	7Feb 09	15 Sep 09	Pola	UK	Sold Count Taverna & Alessandro Piaggio 21 Aug 20 (14,000L = £200)
69F (ex-Polyp) = T11 (1920)	Kaiman	Danubius (Fiume)	17 Apr 09	15 Sep 09		YU	BU 1926
70F (ex-Echse)	Kaiman	Danubius (Fiume)	8 May 09	15 Jun 10	Pola	UK	Sold Count Taverna & Alessandro Piaggio 21 Aug 20 (14,000L = £200); BU Cantiere navale di scoglio olive, Pola

Name	Class	Builder	Launch	Comp/ comm	Location at Jan 20	Alloc	Fate.
71F (ex-Molch)	Kaiman	Danubius (Fiume)	14 Jul 09	15 Jun 10	Pola	UK	Sold Count Taverna & Alessandro Piaggio 21 Aug 20 (14,000L = £200); BU Canticre navale di scoglio olive, Pola
72F (ex-Kormoran)	Kaiman	Danubius (Fiume)	31 Jul 09	5 Mar 10	Pola	UK	Sold Count Taverna & Alessandro Piaggio 21 Aug 20 (14,000L = £200); BU Cantiere navale di scoglio olive, Pola
73F (ex-Alk)	Kaiman	Danubius (Fiume)	2 Oct 09	15 Jun 10	Pola	UK	Sold Count Taverna & Alessandro Piaggio 21 Aug 20 (14,000L = £200); BU Cantiere navale di scoglio olive, Pola
74T = Viforul (Jul 20)	74T	Stab Tecnico Triestino (Trieste)	28 Aug 13	1Feb 14		RO	Stricken 1932
75T = Vartejul (Jul 20)	74T	Stab Tecnico Triestino (Trieste)	20 Nov 13	11 Jul 14		RO	To RO Jul 20; stricken 1932
76T = T1 (Mar 21) = Golešnica (1945)	74T	Stab Tecnico Triestino (Trieste)	15 Dec 13	20 Jul 14		YU	To YU Mar 21; see Table 2.2/4
77T = T2 (Mar 21)	74T	Stab Tecnico Triestino (Trieste)	30 Jan 14	11 Aug 14		YU	To YU Mar 21; BU 1939
78T = T3 (Mar 21) = TA48 (Sep 43)	74T	Stab Tecnico Triestino (Trieste)	4 Mar 14	23 Aug 14		YU	To YU Mar 21; see Table 2.2/4
79T = T4 (Mar 21)	74T	Stab Tecnico Triestino (Trieste)	30 Apr 14	30 Sep 14		YU	To YU Mar 21; wrecked Drvenik Mali island 1932
80T = Vijelia (Jul 20)	74T	Stab Tecnico Triestino (Trieste)	3 Aug 14	8 Nov 14		RO	To RO Jul 20; stricken 1932
81T = Sborul (Jul 20) = Musson (Oct 44) = E2 (Oct 45)	74T	Stab Tecnico Triestino (Trieste)	6 Aug 14	1 Dec 14		RO	To RO Jul 20; see Table 2.4/3
82F = Năluca (Jul 20)	82F	Danubius (Fiume)	11 Aug 14	16 Aug 16		RO	To RO Jul 20; bombed SU aircraft Constanza 20 Aug 44
83F = Smeul (Jul 20) = Toros (Oct 44) = E1 (Oct 45)	82F	Danubius (Fiume)	7 Nov 14	7 Aug 15		RO	To RO Jul 20; see Table 2.4/3
84F = Fulgerul (Jul 20)	82F	Danubius (Fiume)	21 Nov 14	2 Nov 16		RO	To RO Jul 20; foundered 3nm W of Kilyos 8 Feb 22
85F = Zêzere (1921)	82F	Danubius (Fiume)	5 Dec 14	19 Dec 15		PT	Wrecked in tow tug Patrao Lopez off Bône 29 Dec 21
86F = Ave (1921)	82F	Danubius (Fiume)	19 Dec 14	23 May 16		PT	Discarded 1940
87F = T5 (Mar 21) = Cer (1945)	82F	Danubius (Fiume)	20 Mar 15	25 Oct 15		YU	To YU Mar 21; see Table 2.2/4
88F = Cávado (1921)	82F	Danubius (Fiume)	24 Apr 15	30 Nov 15		PT	Wrecked in tow tug Patrao Lopez off Bône 29 Dec 21
89F = Sado (1921)	82F	Danubius (Fiume)	12 May 15	1 Mar 16		PT	Stricken Jul 40
90F = Liz (1921)	82F	Danubius (Fiume)	28 May 15	8 Aug 16		PT	Discarded 1934
91F = Mondego (1921)	82F	Danubius (Fiume)	21 Jun 16	11 Jul 16		PT	Discarded 1938
92F = Panormos (1920)	82F	Danubius (Fiume)	29 Sep 16	23 Mar 16		GR	Collision off Aegina 11 Mar 28
93F = T6 (Mar 21)	82F	Danubius (Fiume)	25 Nov 15	16 Apr 16		YU	To YU Mar 21; see Table 2.2/4
94F = Proussa (1920)	82F	Danubius (Fiume)	8 Mar 16	17 Jun 16		GR	Bombed IT aircraft Dafnila Bay, Corfu 4 Apr 41; salved; foundered
95F = Pergamos (1920)	82F	Danubius (Fiume)	24 Jun 16	27 Sep 16		GR	Scuttled Salamis 25 Apr 41
96F = T7 (Mar 21)	82F	Danubius (Fiume)	7 Jul 16	23 Nov 16		YU	To YU Mar 21; see Table 2.2/4
97F = T8 (Mar 21)	82F	Danubius (Fiume)	20 Aug 16	22 Dec 16		YU	To YU Mar 21; see Table 2.2/4
98M = Kyzikos (1920)	98M	Cantiere Navale Triestino (Monfalcone)	18 Nov 14	19 Aug 15		GR	Scuttled Salamis 25 Apr 41
99M = Kios (1920)	98M	Cantiere Navale Triestino (Monfalcone)	17 Dec 14	29 Oct 15		GR	Scuttled off Athens 23 Apr 41
100M = Kidoniai (1920)	98M	Cantiere Navale Triestino (Monfalcone)	15 Jan 15	13 Mar 16		GR	Bombed GE aircraft S of Peloponnese 26 Apr 41

Table 1.2/4. Submarines

Class	Disp.	Length	Beam	Machinery	Power/speed	Main gun(s)	TT
U1	223/278t	30.8m	6.8m	2 x diesel 2 x electric	720bhp=10.3kt 200shp=6.0kt	1 x 37mm	3 x 45cm
U3	240/300t	42.3m	4.5m	2 x oil 2 x electric	600bhp=12.0kt 320shp=8.5kt	–	2 x 45cm
U5	240/273t	32.1m	4.2m	2 x petrol 2 x electric	500bhp=10.75kt 230shp=8.5kt	–	2 x 45cm
FR Brumaire	397/551t	52.2m	5.2m	2 x diesel 2 x electric	840bhp=12.6kt 660shp=9.0kt	1 x 8.8cm/30	7 x 53.3cm
U20	173/210t	38.8m	4.0m	1 x diesel 1 x electric	450bhp=12.0kt 160shp=11.0kt	1 x 6.6cm/26	2 x 45cm
U27 (mod GE UB-II)	264/301t	36.9m	4.4m	2 x diesel 2 x electric	270bhp=9.0kt 280shp=7.5kt	1 x 75mm/30	2 x 45cm
U48	818/1184t	73.3m	6.7m	2 x diesel 2 x electric	2400bhp=16.25kt 1200shp=8.5kt	2 x 90mm/35	6 x 45cm
U50	840/1100t	73.5m	6.3m	2 x diesel 2 x electric	2300bhp=16.5kt 1200shp=8.5kt	2 x 10cm/35	6 x 45cm
U52	849/1200t	76.0m	7.0m	2 x diesel 2 x electric	2400bhp=15.75kt 1480shp=9.0kt	2 x 10cm/35	6 x 45cm
U101	428/620t	53.5m	5.8m	2 x diesel 2 x electric	1060bhp=13.25kt 788shp=8.25kt	1 x 10cm/35	5 x 45cm
U107	791/933t	69.5m	7.0m	2 x diesel 2 x electric	2300bhp=?kt 1260shp=?kt	1 x 10cm/35	5 x 45cm

Name	Class	Builder	Launch	Comp/comm	Alloc	Fate
U1	U1	Pola DYd	2 Oct 09	15 Apr 11	IT	BU Pola 1920
U2	U1	Pola DYd	3 Apr 09	22 May 11	IT	BU Pola 1920
U4	U3	Germania (Kiel)	20 Nov 08	19 Aug 09	FR	BU 1920
U5	U5	Whitehead (Fiume)	10 Feb 09	1 Apr 10	IT	BU Venice 1920
U10 (ex-UB1)	GE UB1 (UB-I)	Germania (Kiel)	19 Jan 15	15 Jul 15	IT	BU Trieste 1920
U11 (ex-UB15)	GE UB9 (UB-I)	AG Weser (Bremen)	4 Apr 15	20 Jun 15	IT	BU Pola 1920
U14	FR Brumaire	Toulon DYd	18 Jul 12	FR: 18 Jul 13 A-H: 1 Jun 15	–	Retroceded FR 17 Jul 19; stricken 29 Mar 28; sold M Caselli 26 Nov 30 (91,113FF)
U15	GE UB9 (UB-I)	AG Weser (Bremen)	Apr 15	12 Sep 15	IT	BU Pola 1920
U17	GE UB9 (UB-I)	AG Weser (Bremen)	21 Apr 15	10 Oct 15	IT	BU Pola 1920
U21	U20	Pola DYd	15 Aug 16	15 Aug 17	IT	BU Venice 1920
U22	U20	UBAG (Fiume)	27 Jan 17	23 Nov 17	FR	BU 1920
U27	U27 (mod GE UB-II)	Cantiere Navale Triestino (Pola)	19 Oct 16	24 Feb 17	IT	BU Fiume 1920
U28	U27 (mod GE UB-II)	Cantiere Navale Triestino (Pola)	8 Jan 17	26 May 17	IT	BU Venice 1920
U29	U27 (mod GE UB-II)	Danubius (Fiume)	21 Oct 16	21 Jan 17	IT	BU 1920
U31	U27 (mod GE UB-II)	Danubius (Fiume)	28 Mar 17	24 Apr 17	FR	BU 1920
U32	U27 (mod GE UB-II)	Danubius (Fiume)	11 May 17	29 Jun 17	IT	BU Venice 1920
U40	U27 (mod GE UB-II)	Cantiere Navale Triestino (Pola)	21 Apr 17	4 Aug 17	IT	BU Venice 1920
U41	U41 (mod GE UB-II)	Cantiere Navale Triestino (Pola)	11 Nov 17	19 Feb 18	FR	BU 1920
U43 (ex-UB43)	GE UB42 (UB-II)	AG Weser (Bremen)	8 Apr 16	30 Jul 17	FR	BU 1920
U47 (ex-UB47)	GE UB42 (UB-II)	AG Weser (Bremen)	17 Jun 16	30 Jul 17	FR	BU 1920
U48 (ex-U85)	U48	Cantiere Navale Triestino (Pola)	–	–	–	BU 1920
U49 (ex-U86)	U48	Cantiere Navale Triestino (Pola)	–	–	–	BU 1920
U50 (ex-U87)	U50	Danubius (Fiume)	–	–	–	BU 1920
U51	U50	Danubius (Fiume)	–	–	–	BU 1920
U52	U52	UBAG (Fiume)	–	–	–	BU 1920
U53	U52	UBAG (Fiume)	–	–	–	BU 1920
U54, U55	U52	UBAG (Fiume)	–	–	–	Not laid down
U56, U57	U50	Danubius (Fiume)	–	–	–	Not laid down
U58, U59	U48	Cantiere Navale Triestino (Pola)	..		–	Not laid down
U101–U103 (ex-U88–U90)	U101	Cantiere Navale Triestino (Pola)	–	–	–	BU 1920
U104–U106 (ex-U91–U93)	U101	Cantiere Navale Triestino (Monfalcone)	–	–	–	BU 1920
U107–U110 (ex-U94–U97)	U101	Danubius(Fiume)	–	–	–	BU 1920

Table 1.2/5. Minelayers

Class	Disp.	Length	Beam	Machinery	Power/speed	Main gun(s)	Mines
Basilisk	314t	46.0m	7.9m	1 x boiler, 1 x VTE	550ihp=11.0kt	2 x 47mm/33	145
Chamaeleon	1100t	30.8m	9.2m	4 x boilers, 2 x VTE	5500ihp=20.8kt	2 x 90mm/44	300
Dromedar	175t	32.0m	5.4m	1 x boiler, 1 x VTE	350ihp=10.0kt	2 x 47mm/33	50
MT130	128t	30.1m	6.7m	1 x boiler, 2 x VTE	280ihp=11.6kt	1 x 47mm/44	39
Salamander	268t	39.6m	8.1m	1 x boiler, 1 x VTE	350ihp=10.0kt	2 x 47mm/33	90

Name	Class	Builder	Launch	Comp/comm	Alloc	Fate.
Basilisk	Basilisk	Martinolich (Lussinpiccolo)	28 Nov 02	21 Feb 02	FR	BU 1920
Chamaeleon	Chamaeleon	Pola DYd	15 Dec 13	2 Dec 14	UK	Sold Battaglia, Battari & Serrao 20 Aug 20 (744,146L, with *Leopard, Panther, Salamander, 8, 9, 10, 14 & 18*); BU Messina
Dromedar	Dromedar	Pola DYd	25 Nov 90	1891	FR	BU 1920
MT130 (ex-*MTXXIX*) = *RD58* (1920) = *Albona* (1921) = *Netztender 57* (Sep 43)	MT130	Danubius (Porto Ré)	20 Jul 18	31 Jan 20	–	Sold IT 1919; see Table 2.2/8
MT131 (ex-*MTXXX*) = *RD59* (1920) = *Laurana* (1921)	MT130	Danubius (Porto Ré)	24 Aug 18	7 Feb 20	–	Sold IT 1919; see Table 2.2/8
MT132 (ex-*MTXXXI*) = *RD60* (1920) = *Rovigno* (1921) = *Netztender 56* (Sep 43)	MT130	Danubius (Porto Ré)	28 Sep 18	16 Jul 20	–	Sold IT 1919; see Table 2.2/8
MT133 (ex-*MTXXXII*) = *Marjan* (1931) = *Ugliano* (Apr 41) = *M2* (1945) = *M202* = *M32*	MT130	Danubius (Porto Ré)	YU: 1931	YU: 1931	–	Completed YU; IT 17 Apr 41; see Table 2.2/8
MT134 (ex-*MTXXXIII*) = *Mosor* (1931) = *Pasman* (Apr 41)	MT130	Danubius (Porto Ré)	YU: 1931	YU: 1931	–	Completed YU; IT 17 Apr 41; see Table 2.2/8
MT135 (ex-*MTXXXIV*) = *Malinska* (1931) = *Arbe* (Apr 41)	MT130	Danubius (Porto Ré)	YU: 1931	YU: 1931	–	Completed YU; IT 17 Apr 41; see Table 2.2/8
MT136 (ex-*MTXXXV*) = *Meljine* (1931) = *Solta* (Apr 41) = *M1* (1945) = *M201* = *M31*	MT130	Danubius (Porto Ré)	YU: 1931	YU: 1931	–	CompletedYU; IT 17 Apr 41; see Table 2.2/8
MT137 (ex-*MTXXXVI*) = *Mljet* (1931) = *Meleda* (Apr 41) = *M3* (1945) = *M203* = *M33*	MT130	Danubius (Porto Ré)	YU: 1931	YU: 1931	–	Completed YU; IT 17 Apr 41; Table 2.2/8
MT138–MT143 (ex-*MTXXXVII–MTXLII*)	MT130	Danubius (Porto Ré)	–	–	–	Cancelled
Salamander	Salamander	Stab Tecnico Triestino (Trieste)	9 May 91	1892	UK	Sold Battaglia, Battari & Serrao 20 Aug 20 (744,146L, with *Panther, Chamaleon, Leopard, 8, 9, 10, 14 & 18*); BU Messina

Table 1.2/6. River Monitors

Class	Disp.	Length	Beam	Machinery	Power/speed	Main gun(s)
Enns	541t	62.0m	10.5m	2 x boilers, 2 x VTE	1600ihp=13.0kt	2 x 120mm/45
Körös	448t	54.0m	9.0m	2 x boilers, 2 x VTE	1200ihp=10.0kt	2 x 120mm/35
Leitha	310t	50.6m	8.0m	2 x boilers,; 2 x TE	700ihp=8.0kt	1 x 120mm/35 or 1 x 66m/45
Sava	580t	62.0m	10.3m	2 x boilers, 2 x VTE	1750ihp=13.5kt	2 x 120mm/42
Temes	440t	57.7m	9.5m	2 x boilers, 2 x VTE	1400ihp=13.0kt	2 x 120mm/35

Name	Class	Builder	Launch	Comp/ comm	Location Jan 20	Alloc	Fate
Bodrog = *Sava* (Dec 18)	*Temes*	H Schönischen (Budapest)	12 Apr 04	10 Nov 04	Visnitsa	YU	To YU 31 Dec 18; scuttled Belgrade 12 Apr 41; salved; HR; gunfire YU shore artillery Bosanski-Brod 9 Sep 44; salved; stricken 1962; barge; preserved Belgrade Dec 2015; opened as museum 2019
Bosna (ex-*Temes*) = *Vardar* (Jan 19)	*Sava*	Stab Tecnico Triestino (Linz)	1915	9 Jul 15	Belgrade	YU	To YU 31 Dec 18; scuttled Belgrade 12 Apr 41
Enns = *Drava* (Jan 19)	*Enns*	Stab Tecnico Triestino (Linz)	Sep 14	17 Oct 14	Belgrade	YU	To YU 31 Dec 18; bombed GE aircraft Sip 12 Apr 41; salved and BU
Inn = *Ujvidek* (13 Mar 19) = *Marx* (Jul 19) = *Basarabia* (Apr 20) = *Kerch* (Sep 44) = *M206* (Jul 51)	*Enns*	Danubius (Budapest)	25 Feb 15	11 Apr 15	Novi Sad (since Nov 19)	RO	To HU 13 Mar 19; to RO 14 Dec 20; see Table 2.4/6
Körös = *Morava* (Dec 18) = *Bosna* (1941)	*Körös*	H Schönischen (Budapest)	1892	1892.		YU	To YU 31 Dec 18; scuttled River Sava 12 Apr 41; salved; HR; mined Bosanski-Novi Jun 44
Leitha = *József Lajos* (1928) = *FK-201* (1949) = *Leitha* (2005)	*Leitha*	Elso Magyar Pest-Fiumei Hajógyár Rt (Budapest)	17 May 71	13 Oct 72	–	CID	To YU 31 Dec 18; sold A Fleichmann (Budapest) as dredger Jan 21; sold Delmár and Tsai (Budapest) 1938; to FOKA 1948; museum 20 Aug 2010
Maros	*Leitha*	Elso Magyar Pest-Fiumei Hajógyár Rt (Budapest)	20 Apr 71	13 Oct 72	–	CID	BU Jan 21
Sava = *Soca* (Dec 18) = *Bucovina* (Apr 20) = *Izmail* (Sep 44) = *M205* (Jul 51)	*Sava*	Stab Tecnico Triestino (Linz).	31 May 15	15 Sep 15	Novi Sad	RO	To YU 31 Dec 18; to RO 14 Dec 20; see Table 2.4/6
=*Szamos* = *Tivadar* (1920) = *FK 202* (1949)	*Körös*	H Schönischen (Budapest)	25 Aug 92	1893	–	CID	To YU 31 Dec 18; sold A Fleichmann (Budapest) as dredger Jan 21; sold Delmár and Tsai (Budapest) 1938; to FOKA 1948; withdrawn 1962; sold YU shipbreaker 1989
Temes = *Drina* (Dec 18) = *Ardeal* (Apr 20)	*Temes*	H Schönischen (Budapest)	26 Apr 04	10 Nov 04	Novi Sad	RO	To YU 31 Dec 18; to RO 14 Dec 20; see Table 2.4/6

Table 1.2/7. Depot Ship

Class	Disp.	Length	Beam	Machinery	Power/speed	Main gun(s)
Gäa	12,130t	153.2m	17.6m	9 x boilers, 2 x VTE	14,743ihp=18.7kt	4 x 12cm/35

Name	Class	Builder	Launch	Comm	Alloc	Fate.
Gäa (ex-*Don*, ex-*Moskva*, ex-*Fürst Bismarck*) = *San Giusto* (1920)	*Gäa*	AG Vulcan (Stettin)	1891	15 May 10	IT	To IT; BU 1923–24

Table 1.2/8. Admiralty Yacht (ex-Cruiser)

Class	Disp.	Length	Beam	Machinery	Power/speed	Main gun(s)
Lacroma	1680t	71.0m	10.5m	4 x boilers, 2 x VTE	6000ihp=18kt	6 x 4.7cm/44

Name	Builder	Launch	Comm	Alloc	Fate
Lacroma (ex-*Tiger*)	Stab Tecnico Triestino (Trieste)	28 Jun 87	14 Mar 88	IT	To IT; BU.

3. The Bulgarian Navy: 30 September 1918

Table 1.3/1. Torpedo Gunboat

Class	Disp.	Length	Beam	Machinery	Power/speed	Main gun(s)	TT
Nadezhda	715t	67.0m	8.3m	4 x boilers, 2 x VTE	2600ihp=18.0kt	1 x 100mm/40	2 x 381mm

Name	Builder		Launched	Comp/ comm	Fate.
Nadezhda	Chantiers & Ateliers de la Gironde(Bordeaux)		10 Sep 98	Oct 98	Abandoned Sevastopol Apr 19; seized SU 2 Dec 20; condemned 23 Jun 23; handed over to BU Sevastopol 27 Sep 24; BU to 1925

Table 1.3/2. Torpedo Boats

Class	Disp.	Length	Beam	Machinery	Power/speed	Main gun(s)	TT
Druzki	97.5t	38.0m	4.4m	2 x boilers, 1 x VTE	1900ihp=26kt	2 x 37mm	3 x 450mm
Vasil Levski	20t	18.3m	2.3m	1 x boiler, 1 x VC	220ihp=13kt	MGs	–

Name	Class	Builder	Launched	Comp/comm	Fate.
Druzki = Ingul (Sep 44) = Druzki (Jul 45)	Druzki	Schneider (Chalons-sur-Saône)	10 Aug 07	Jan 08	See Table 2.5/1
Smeli	Druzki	Schneider (Chalons-sur-Saône)	10 Aug 07	Jan 08	Foundered between Varna and Burgas 19 May 43
Khrabri = Vychegda (Sep 44) = Khrabri (Jul 45)	Druzki	Schneider (Chalons-sur-Saône)	10 Aug 07	Jan 08	See Table 2.5/1
Strogi	Druzki	Schneider (Chalons-sur-Saône)	6 Apr 08	Aug 09	See Table 2.5/1
Letyashchi	Druzki	Schneider (Chalons-sur-Saône)	6 Apr 08	Aug 09	Wrecked off Varna 28 Nov 18
Vasil Levsk (ex-Bychok)	Vasil Levsk	Baird (St Petersburg)	1877	RU: 1877	BG: Jun 84 Stricken 1938
Khristo Botev (ex-Cherepakha)	Vasil Levsk	Baird (St Petersburg)	1877	RU: 1878	BG: Jun 84 Stricken 1938

Table 1.3/3. Submarine

Name	Class	Builder	Launched	Comp/comm	Surrendered	Fate.
Podvodnik No 18.(ex-UB8)	GE UB1	(UB-I) Germania (Kiel)	1915	GE: 23 Apr 15 BG: 25 May 16	c.23 Jan 19 Varna	Sold Harry Vere (Constantinople) (£200) 4 Mar 21; scuttled off Varna

4. The Ottoman Navy: 27 October 1918

Table 1.4/1. Capital Ships

Class	Disp.	Length	Beam	Machinery	Power/speed	Main gun(s)	TT
Asar-i Şevket	2047t	64.4m	12.9m	4 x boilers, 1 x HC	1750ihp=12kt	1 x 9in MLR	–
İclaliye	2228t	66.0m	12.8m	2 x boilers, 1 x HC	1800ihp=12kt	[2 x 278mm]	–
Avnillah	2362t	71.9m	10.9m	2 x boilers, 1 x HC	2200ihp=12kt	[4 x 150mm/40]	–

Name	Class	Builder	Launch	Comp/comm	Alloc	Fate.
İclaliye.	İclaliye	Stabilimento Tecnico Triestin (San Rocco)	1869	Feb 71	UK	Accommodation ship; training ship Feb 19; accommodation ship 1923; decommissioned 1928; BU Gölcük
Muin-i Zafer	Avnillah	Thames Iron Works (Blackwall)	Jun 69	1870	UK	Torpedo training ship; accommodation ship 1920; submarine depot ship 1928; decommissioned 1932;. BU Erdek from 1934
Necm-i Şevket	Asar-i Şevket	Forges et Chantiers de la Méditerranée (La Seyne)	1868	3 Mar 1870	UK	Accommodation ship; decommissioned 1929; BU
Turgut Reis (ex-Weißenburg)	GE K F Wilhelm (Table 1.1/1)	AG Vulcan (Stettin)	14 Dec 91	GE: 5 Jun 1894 TU: 31 Aug 10	JP	(P) Training hulk Gölcük 1924; accommodation ship 1933; BU Gölcük from 1950
Yavûz Sultân Selîm (ex-Goeben) = Yavûz Selîm (1930) = Yavûz (1936)	GE Moltke (Table 1.1/1)	Blohm & Voss (Hamburg)	28 Mar 11	GE: 2 Jul 12 TU: 16 Aug 14	UK	Decommissioned 20 Dec 50; stricken 14 Nov 54; sold MKE (Seyman) 7 Jun 73; BU Seyman Jul 73–Feb 76

Table 1.4/2. Cruisers

Class	Disp.	Length	Beam	Machinery	Power/speed	Main gun(s)	TT
Peyk-i Şevket	775t	80.1m	8.4m	4 x boilers, 2 x VTE	5100ihp=18.0kt	2 x 105mm/40	2 x 450mm
Mecidiye	3485t	102.4m	12.8m	16 x boilers, 2 x VQE	12,500ihp=18.0kt	2 x 152mm/45	2 x 457mm
Hamidiye	3904t	112.0m	14.5m	16 x boilers, 2 x VTE	12,000ihp=22.0kt	2 x 150mm/45	2 x 457mm

Name	Class	Builder	Launch	Comp/comm	Alloc	Fate.
Berk-i Satvet = Berk (1924)	Peyk-i Şevket	Germania AG (Kiel)	1 Dec 06	Nov 07	?	Decommissioned 1944; BU İsmit 1953/55
Hamidiye (ex-Abdül Hamid)	Hamidiye	Armstrong (Elswick)	25 Sep 03	Apr 04	UK	Training hulk 1945; decommissioned Mar 47; naval museum Istanbul-Kabataş 1949–51; sold 10 Sep 64; BU Istanbul-Paşabahçe to 1966
Mecidiye (ex-Prut, ex-Mecidiye, ex-Abdül Mecid).	Mecidiye	Cramp (Philadelphia)	26 Jul 03	TU: 19 Dec 03 RU: 29 Oct 15 TU: 13 May 18	UK	Training hulk 1940; decommissioned 1 Mar 47; sold 1952; BU Istanbul-Kasimpaşa 1952/56
Peyk-i Şevket = Peyk (1924)	Peyk-i Şevket	Germania AG (Kiel)	15 Nov 06	Nov 07	?	Decommissioned 1944; BU Gölcük 1953/54

Table 1.4/3. Destroyers and Torpedo Boats

Class	Disp.	Length	Beam	Machinery	Power/speed	Main gun(s)	TT
Berk Efşân	230t	59.9m,	6.6m	2 x boilers, 2 x VTE	3500ihp=21.0kt	2 x 47mm/50	2 x 428mm
Hamidiye	145t	50.6m	5.6m	3 x boilers, 2 x VTE	2400ihp=26.0kt	1 x 47mm	1 x 450mm
Akhisar	165t	50.6m	5.6m	2 x boilers, 2 x VTE	2400ihp=24.0kt	1 x 47mm	1 x 450mm
Antalya	165t	51.0m	5.7m	2 x boilers, 2 x VTE	2700ihp=26.0kt	1 x 57mm	1 x 450mm
Demirhisar	97t	40.2m	4.4m	2 x boilers, 1 x VTE	2200ihp=26.0kt	2 x 37mm	3 x 450mm
Samsun	284t	58.2m	6.3m	2 x boilers, 2 x VTE	5950ihp=28.0kt	1 x 65mm/50	2 x 450mm

Name	Class	Builder	Launch	Comp/comm	Alloc	Fate.
Akhisar	Akhisar	Ansaldo (Sestri Ponete)	24 Apr 04	Jun 04	UK*	Decommissioned 1930; BU 1935
Basra	Samsun	Chantiers et Ateliers de la Gironde (Bordeaux)	1907	1907	UK	Decommissioned 1932; BU Gölcük 1949
Berk Efşân	Berk Efşân	Germania (Kiel)/ Constantinople DYd.	1892	1894	UK	Decommissioned 1928; BU 1932
Draç	Antalya	Ansaldo (Sestri Ponete)	Apr 04	8 Jan 07	UK*	Decommissioned 1924; hulked as work barge Gölcük 1926; BU 1936
Muâvenet-i Millîye (ex-S165)	GE S165 (Table 1.1/3)	Schichau (Elbing)	20 Mar 09	17 Aug 10	UK	Hulked Tsakizak Tersane, Istanbul, 1919; BU 1953
Mûsul	Antalya	Ansaldo (Sestri Ponete)	1904	8 Jan 07	UK*	Decommissioned 1929; BU 1936
Nümûne-i Hamiyet (ex-S167)	GE S165 (Table 1.1/3)	Schichau (Elbing)	3 Jul 09	17 Aug 10	UK	Hulked Tsakizak Tersane, Istanbul, 1919; BU 1953
Samsun	Samsun	Chantiers et Ateliers de la Gironde (Bordeaux)	1907	3 Sep 07	UK	Decommissioned 1932; BU Gölcük 1949
Sivrihisar	Demirhisar	Schneider (Chalons-sur-Saone)	1907	1907	UK*	Decommissioned 1928; BU 1935
Sultanhisar	Demirhisar	Schneider (Chalons-sur-Saone)	1907	1907	UK*	Decommissioned 1928; BU 1935
Taşoz	Samsun	Chantiers et Ateliers de la Gironde (Bordeaux)	1907	1907	UK	Decommissioned 1932; BU Gölcük 1949
Yûnus (ex-Abdül Mecid)	Hamidiye	Ansaldo (Genoa)	1901	1902	UK*	Dispatch vessel 1926; decommissioned 1929; BU 1935

* Listed in Treaty of Sévrès for retention by Turkey.

Table 1.4/4. Submarine

Class	Disp.	Length	Beam	Machinery	Power/speed	Main gun(s)	TT
FR Émeraude	393/425t	44.9m	3.9m	2 x diesel	600bhp=11.0kt	–	6 x 450mm

Name	Class	Builder	Launch	Comp/comm	Alloc	Fate
Müstecip Onbaşı (ex-Turquoise)	FR Émeraude	Toulon DYd	3 Aug 08	FR: 10 Dec 10 TU: 10 Nov 15	–	Retroceded FR 1 Jul 19; BU Istanbul

Table 1.4/5. Sloops and Gunboats

Class	Disp.	Length	Beam	Machinery	Power/speed	Main gun(s)
Zuhaf	643t	57.9m	7.3m	2 x boilers, 1 x VTE	640ihp=14.0kt	[1 x 120mm/25]
Aydin Reis	503t	54.5m	8.2m	3 x boilers, 2 x VTE	1025ihp=14.0kt	2 x 76mm
İsa Reis	413t	47.0m	7.9m	3 x boilers, 2 x VTE	850ihp=14.0kt	2 x 76mm
Taşköprü	212t	47.0m	6.2m	1 x boiler, 1 x VTE	480ihp=12.0kt	1 x 47mm
Nasr-ü Hüda	198t	38.6m	5.4m	1 x boiler, 1 x VTE	400ihp=10.0kt	1 x 57mm

Name	Class	Builder	Launch	Comp/comm	Alloc	Fate.
Zuhaf	Zuhaf	Constantinople DYd	31 Aug 1894	Oct 1896	UK	Decommissioned 1932; BU Gölcük 1936
Malatya	Taşköprü	Schneider (Chalons-sur-Saone	1907	Jan 08	UK	Accommodation ship; BU 1921
Barika-i Zafer	Nasr-ü Hüda	Constantinople DYd	1904	1908	UK	Guard ship Istanbul Mar 22; decommissioned 1926; BU
Aydin Reis.	Aydin Reis	Chantiers & Ateliers de St Nazaire	Jun 12	13 Jun 14	–	Interned Novorossiysk Sep 20; TU 16 May 21; training ship 1925; survey vessel 1926; decommissioned 1949; sold 1954 to BU
Bürak Reis	Aydin Reis	Chantiers & Ateliers de St Nazaire	May 12	13 Jun 14	–	Survey vessel 1932; capsized Heybeliada 1953; salved; sold 1955 to BU
Sakiz.	Aydin Reis	Chantiers & Ateliers de St Nazaire	1912	13 Jun 14	–	Submarine HQ hulk Gölcük 1930; decommissioned 1935; BU
Preveze.	Aydin Reis	Chantiers & Ateliers de St Nazaire	Jan 12	13 Jun 14	–	Interned Novorossiysk Sep 20; TU 16 May 21; decommissioned 1926
Hizir Reis = Emin (1960) = Murut Ayanoglu (1981) = Kaptan Cavit (1982) = Miktat Kalkavan (Oct 95)	İsa Reis	Forges & Chantiers de la Mediterranée (Granville)	10 Apr 12	13 Jun 14	–	Seized GR 6 Jul 19; retroceded 1922; minesweeper 1932; pilot hulk 1948; decommissioned 1952; sold as mercantile 1958; still in service (2018)
Kemal Reis (ex-Durac Reis).	İsa Reis	Forges & Chantiers de la Mediterranée (Granville)	Feb 12	13 Jun 14	–	Customs vessel 1926; minesweeper 1932; survey vessel 1948; decommissioned 1955; sold MKE 1964; BU Seyman
İsa Reis	İsa Reis	Forges & Chantiers de la Mediterranée (Granville)	10 Apr 12	13 Jun 14	–	Customs vessel 1926; minesweeper 1932; survey vessel 1948; decommissioned 1955; sold MKE 1964; BU Seyman

Table 1.4/6. Minelayer

Class	Disp.	Length	Beam	Machinery	Power/speed	Main gun(s)	Mines
Nusret	365t	40.2m	7.5m	2 x boilers, 2 x VTE	1200ihp=15kt	2 x 47mm	40

Name	Builder	Launch	Comp/comm	Alloc	Fate
Nusret = Yardin (1937) = Nusret (1939) = Kaptan Nusret (1966)	Germania (Kiel)	4 Dec 11	1913	UK	Diving tender 1937; decommissioned 1955; sold mercantile 1962; foundered Mersin Apr 89; salved 2002; museum Tarsus 2008

4

Endgame: Italy, Romania, Bulgaria and Finland 1943–45

ITALY
Armistice

By May 1943, the Axis position was rapidly deteriorating, their forces in North Africa surrendering on 13 May 1943, and Rome received its first aerial bombardment on 16 May. On 10 July, Allied forces landed in Sicily, Palermo being entered on the 22nd. The following day, a meeting of the Fascist Grand Council began, which ran into the following morning and approved an Order of the Day that requested King Vittorio Emanuele III to resume supreme command – effectively removing Mussolini from power. On the 25th, the King did just that, replacing Mussolini as head of government with Marshal Pietro Badoglio, the former Duce being arrested.

Although the new government pledged to continue the war, contacts were initiated with a view to securing an armistice with the Allies, discussions being carried out in Lisbon, and the Italian delegate returned to Italy on 27 August to brief Badoglio. He was then sent to Sicily to continue discussions, culminating in the signature of the Armistice of Cassibile on 3 September. The agreement remained secret, although the Germans were already aware that an armistice was in the offing. The timing of implementation was in the hands of the Allies, and although the Italians had been working on the basis of it coming into effect on 12 September, the announcement was made by the Allies on the 8th. Accordingly, German forces were able to take advantage of Italian disorganisation and confusion to turn on their erstwhile allies, with the result that the majority of mainland Italy, save parts of Apulia and Calabria (including Taranto), had been occupied by them by the 12th, although a month later Allied advances had driven them from the southern quarter of the peninsula.

Clause 4 of the Armistice dealt with the Italian navy,

Roma in June 1943. *(AD collection)*

requiring 'Immediate transfer of the Italian Fleet and Italian aircraft to such points as may be designated by the Allied Commander in Chief, with details of disarmament to be prescribed by him'.[1] During the days leading up to the Armistice, plans were drawn up for a suicide attack by the fleet on the Allied invasion forces assaulting Salerno – an 'honour-saving' act akin to the plan for the German High Seas Fleet in October 1918. This was assumed by the CinC, Vice-Admiral Carlo Bergamini (leading the main body of the fleet, at La Spezia), and Rear-Admiral Alberto Da Zara (commanding forces at Taranto) to be the reason (as it initially indeed was) for an instruction on the 7th from the chief of staff, Admiral Raffaele de Courten, to maintain their ships at six hours' notice for sea.

On the evening of the 8th, the Armistice was finally announced, and Italian warships and submarines were ordered to cease all hostilities, the latter to go to either Bône (Annaba) in Algeria or Augusta in Sicily. Bergamini's force, already preparing to attack the Salerno beachhead, was redi-

---

1 On the Italian navy and the events surrounding and following the Armistice, see V O'Hara and E Cernuschi, *Dark Navy: The Italian Regia Marina and the Armistice of 8 September 1943* (Ann Arbor, MI: Nimble Books, 2009); J Caruana, *Destination Malta: The Surrender of the Italian Fleet, September 1943* (Rabat: Wise Owl Publications, 2010); Z Freivogel and A Rastelli, *Adriatic Naval War 1940–1945* (Zagreb: Despot Infinitus, 2015), pp 154–77.

rected towards La Maddelena at the north end of Sardinia – rather than following the Allied requirement that all ships sail towards Cap de Garde, near Bône, where, flying black pennants, they would be met by a British force, and conducted to an as-yet-unknown final destination. The fleet only finally sailed on the direct orders of de Courten, many of its senior officers being minded to scuttle following the news of the Armistice; Bergamini was reassured that if the supreme command of the Italian navy, Supermarina, became aware that the ships were to be seized by the Allies, a coded instruction to scuttle would be transmitted, and individual commanders were authorised to scuttle if seizure were attempted.

The torpedo boats *Impetuoso*, *Orione*, *Orsa* and *Pegaso* were the first to leave La Spezia, at 0200hrs, followed by the 9th Division battleships *Roma* (fleet flag) *Vittorio Veneto* and *Italia* (ex-*Littorio*), the 7th Division light cruisers *Eugenio di Savoia* (flag), *Emanuele Filberto Duca d'Aosta* and *Raimondo Montecuccoli*, the 12th Destroyer Division's *Mitragliere*, *Fuciliere*, *Carabiniere* and *Velite* and the 14th Destroyer Division's *Legionario*, *Oriani*, *Artigliere* and *Grecale*. They rendezvoused at 0630 with the light cruisers of the 8th Division, *Luigi di Savoia Duca Degli Abruzzi*, *Giuseppe Garibaldi* and *Attilo Regolo*, which had sailed from Genoa at 0315, together with the torpedo boat *Libra*.

However, La Maddelena was already falling to a German commando attack, forcing Bergamini to reverse course at 1445 that afternoon when already approaching the port. He was then ordered to sail for Bône as agreed with the Allies – but never acknowledged this thrice-repeated order, as the fleet proceeded on a westerly heading. Nothing is known of Bergamini's intentions at this point, as he would shortly be dead: at 1537 came an initial (unsuccessful) attack by German aircraft, followed at 1550 by eleven Dornier Do 217Ks from III Gruppe/Kampfgeschwader 100, armed with Ruhrstahl FX 1400 radio-controlled glider bombs. *Roma* was hit twice and set on fire, the forward magazines blowing up at 1605; the ship then broke in two and sank at 1611. Command of the

fleet devolved onto Vice-Admiral Romeo Oliva, FO 7th Division, who was, however, unaware both of Bergamini's intentions and the orders to sail towards Bône.

Regolo, *Carabiniere*, *Fuciliere*, *Mitragliere*, *Impetuoso*, *Orsa* and *Pegaso* were detached to rescue survivors, but lacking the CinC's special cypher, Oliva was unable to decode the orders from Supermarina, and for the time being could do no more than continue the fleet's current westerly progress. Shortly afterwards, a further German attack hit *Italia* with an FX 1400, although with relatively minor damage.

In the meantime, surface actions had been taking place between Italian and German forces, the corvettes *Ape*, *Cormorano* and *Folaga* sinking German barges off Terracina, another barge being sunk by the light cruiser *Scipione* in the area of Taranto. Off Leghorn, the Italian vidette boat *VAS234* was sunk by German light forces, while further Italian losses occurred off Corsica late in the afternoon. The destroyers *Antonio Da Noli* and *Ugolino Vivaldi* had been sent from to Civitavecchia, near Rome, to evacuate the King and government to La Maddalena, but had been frustrated by the German seizure of the road from Rome to the west coast (the King was eventually evacuated via the east coast). They had thus sailed west to join the main fleet, but were then directed to interdict German transfers of troops from Sardinia to Corsica. In doing so, they were fired on by shore artillery and German surface vessels, *Da Noli* striking a mine and sinking in the Strait of Bonifacio. *Vivaldi* managed to limp away, but was then attacked by German aircraft, including a hit from a Henschel Hs 293 guided bomb. The damage was such that she had to be scuttled northwest of Sardinia in the early hours of the 10th, following a complete machinery breakdown.

In the Aegean, the destroyers and torpedo boats *Turbine*, *Francesco Crispi*, *Calatafimi* and *San Martino* were trapped in Piraeus harbour by a minefield laid by the German minelayer *Drache* (ex-Yugoslav seaplane tender *Zmaj*), German shore batteries, and the threat of German air attack if they by some means got out; the destroyers thus surrendered on the orders of the Italian army. At Suda Bay on Crete, the torpedo boats *Castelfidardo* and *Solferino* and a number of FPBs were seized. All were soon incorporated into the German navy (see pp 161–62, below).

Back with the main fleet, Oliva informed Supermarina of the loss of *Roma* at 1700 on the 9th (with some initial confusion over whether the attacking aircraft had been British or German), and requested orders in a cypher he could read. Further German air attacks over the next 130 minutes failed to make further hits, while the fleet continued westwards, Oliva ignoring an order at 1840 to head for Bône. Around 2000 the order was re-transmitted, with the same reassur-

Roma sinking on 9 September 1943; 'B' turret has already been blown over the side by the magazine explosion that followed two hits by German FX 1400 guided bombs launched by Dornier Do 217K-2. She broke in two and sank five minutes later. *(AD collection)*

ances previously given to Bergamini over the fate of the ships, and confirmation that the Armistice had been authorised by the King. Thus, after nightfall, at 2107, the fleet changed course, towards the rendezvous point.

Black pennants were finally hoisted at 0702 on the 10th, and forty-five minutes later an Allied squadron was sighted, comprising the British battleships *Warspite* and *Valiant*, the destroyers HMS *Echo*, *Faulknor*, *Fury*, *Intrepid*, *Raider*, together with the French *Le Terrible* and Greek *Vasilissa Olga*. Informed that their destination was Malta, the Italian battleships and cruisers took station in line ahead astern the British battleships, with the destroyers abeam. At 1000, *Libra* and *Orione* left for Bône to refuel, while *Impetuoso* was detached to Bizerte with boiler defects; all three later proceeded on to Malta.

In the meantime, the ships that had detached to search for survivors of *Roma*, having completed their task, headed back towards La Spezia to land the wounded. However, around 1900 on the 9th they were informed that the base was now in German hands, so their intended destination was changed to Leghorn. *Impetuoso*, *Orsa* and *Pegaso* had now become separated from the rest of the group owing to shortages of fuel, which was now so severe that they were incapable of making Leghorn; as a result, they changed course for the Balearic Islands around 2030. They were followed 140 minutes later by the remainder of the group, frustrated in their objective by ongoing occupation activities by the Germans. A faulty message from Supermarina ordering the ships to the Bône rendezvous was ignored, by which time all vessels were so short of fuel that no other destination than the Balearics was possible.

Thus, at 0800 on the 10th, *Regolo*, *Carabiniere*, *Fuciliere* and *Mitragliere* moored at Port Mahon, Menorca. Later that morning, *Impetuoso*, *Orsa* and *Pegaso* arrived at Pollensa; the next day, fearing that the Spanish authorities might hand their ships to the Germans or the Allies, the commanders of *Impetuoso* and *Pegaso* took their ships out of harbour and scuttled them. By doing so, they violated the terms of the Armistice; they were court-martialled, after the war, although acquitted. Although never formally interned, the surviving Italian ships had insufficient fuel to leave the Balearics, and would remain there until 15 January 1945. Subsequent;y, *Regolo*, *Carabiniere*, *Fuciliere*, *Mitragliere* and *Orsa* proceeded to Taranto via Algiers, arriving back in Italy on the 23rd.

At Taranto, Da Zara commanded the 5th Division, comprising the battleships *Caio Duilio* (flag) and *Andrea Doria*, together with light cruisers *Luigi Cadorna*, *Scipione Africano* and *Pompeo Magno* and the destroyer *Nicoloso da Recco*. At 0642 on the 9th, the ships were ordered to Malta, except for *Scipione*, which was sent to Pescara, along with the corvettes *Baionetta* and *Scimitarra* from Brindisi, to evacuate the King and government to the latter port, which would now act as the temporary capital. *Scipione* and *Baionetta* remained there until it was clear that the city was secure from German attack.

The rest of the Taranto ships sailed at 1700, after a decision to follow orders, rather than scuttle, as had been proposed by some elements. As they were departing, they passed an Allied force comprising the cruisers HMS *Aurora*, *Dido*, *Penelope* and *Sirius* and USS *Boise*, the minelayer *Abdiel* and the destroyer *Javelin* on its way to occupy the naval base and its hinterland. This operation was successful, except for the loss of *Abdiel*, sunk by a mine laid by the German FPBs *S54* and *S61* prior to their evacuation a few hours earlier.

Attilo Regolo, Mitragliere, Carabiniere and *Fuciliere* at Port Mahon in the spring of 1944, and en route to Taranto on 23 January 1945. *(AD collection)*

Boise, Abdiel, Aurora and *Penelope*, viewed from *King George V*, proceeding to occupy Taranto on 9 September 1943. *(NHHC UA 451.21.21)*

Guilio Germanico in May 1943; although still incomplete, she defended Castellammare di Stabia against the Germans directly after the Armistice. (AD collection)

At Castellammare di Stabia, the unfinished cruiser *Giulio Germanico* contributed gunfire that initially held off a German attempt at taking the base. However, once the cruiser had run out of ammunition, the dockyard would fall under their control on the 13th. Another example of ultimately futile resistance was the attempted escape of the brand-new corvette *Berenice* at Trieste, which was sunk in the act of doing so by German artillery.

At 1400 on the 11th, the battleship *Guilio Cesare* arrived at Taranto to refuel. Although nominally part of the 5th Division, she had been in reduced commission as a training ship since 1942, most recently at Pola, alongside other training vessels, such as the sail training ships *Cristoforo Colombo* and *Amerigo Vespucci*, and the ex-prime ministerial yacht *Aurora*. With Pola threatened by imminent German occupation, the first two vessels left on the morning of the 9th, arriving at Brindisi on the 13th. The battleship was ordered to Cattaro to await further orders, departing at 1600 on the 9th, escorted by the torpedo boat *Sagittario* and the corvette *Urania*. However, at 1655 her ultimate destination was changed to Malta, with a stop at Taranto to top up her bunkers. *Aurora* also left in the afternoon, en route to Sebenico, via a refuelling stop at Zara. Redirected to Taranto following the German seizure of Sebenico, she was, however, intercepted off Ancona by *S54* and *S61*, continuing their withdrawal from Taranto, and sunk by torpedo at dawn on the 11th.

Although such vessels attempted to escape, lack of fuel prevented the old cruiser *Cattaro* (ex-Yugoslav *Dalmacija*, ex-German *Niobe*: cf. p 74, above) from leaving Pola, being taken over and recommissioned back into German service. Also seized in Adriatic ports were the destroyers *Antonio Pigafetta* (at Fiume) and *Sebenico* (ex-Yugoslav *Beograd*, under refit at Venice) and the torpedo boats *Pugnale*, *Spada* and *Audace* (at Venice), *Giuseppe Dezza* and *T3* (at Fiume), and *T7* (at Gruz).

During the early hours of the 10th, *Cesare* had suffered a mutiny by members of her crew who wished to scuttle the ship, rather than place her into Allied custody. However, her commanding officer managed to regain control, and at 1215 on the 10th the seaplane tender *Giuseppe Miraglia*, which had sailed from Venice, joined the group. Also now heading for Taranto from the Adriatic was the destroyer *Augusto Riboty*, which had departed Bari at 1700 that day, and the submarines *Fratelli Bandiera* and *Jalea*, from the Gulf of Taranto; another submarine, *Atropo*, was already at Taranto at the time of the Armistice. Also at Taranto when the British arrived were the destroyers *FR23* (ex-French *Tigre*) and *Granatiere*, and the torpedo boats *Sirio*, *Clio* and *Aretusa*.

At 1345 on the 11th, German aircraft attacked *Cesare* and her companions, without success, and at 1400 they arrived at Taranto, *Riboty* also safely making harbour at 2300. On the other hand, around the same time, the destroyer *Quintino Sella*, escaping from Venice, was sunk by the deadly *S54–S61* pairing about 25nm south of the city. Also sunk in the Adriatic were the torpedo boats *T8*, hit by German bombs off Punta Olipa, and *T6*, scuttled off Rimini for lack of fuel. The Italo-German conflict was not, however, one-sided, as the previous day the German torpedo boat *TA11* (formerly the French *L'Iphegenie*) had been destroyed by Italian shore fire during an initial attempt to take the port of Piombino.

Malta

Duilio, *Doria*, *Cadorna*, *Pompeo* and *Da Recco* were attacked by German aircraft without success on the evening of the 9th, and at 0930 the next morning were met northeast of Cape Passero (the southern tip of Sicily) by the escort destroyer HMS *Hursley*, which was to lead them through the swept channel to Malta. Around 1100, they met the battleship *King George V* and six destroyers, detached from the covering force for the occupation of Taranto, and began to anchor off the northeast coast of the island on the evening of the 10th.

Contrary to the terms of the Armistice, British guards were posted aboard the Italian ships, overseeing the removal of radio-valves and breechblocks. Although some officers argued for immediate scuttling, Da Zara demurred, and the following evening had a meeting with Admiral Andrew Cunningham, the British CinC, at which the terms of the internment were agreed. These also applied to the ships of the main fleet, which had arrived at Malta that morning, and which now came under the command of Da Zara, as he was senior to Oliva.

Cunningham and Da Zara agreed that the ships were *interned*, rather than surrendered, and as such had their British guards removed, and radio-valves and breechblocks restored. In addition, when the submarine *Menotti*, intercepted by HMS/M *Unshaken* south of the Strait of Otranto on

Italian warships at Malta on 11 September 1943. *Aosta* is in the foreground, with *Duilio*, *Doria* and *Cadorna* behind her; beyond the latter, to the left, is *Pompeo*, with *Da Recco* to the right. *(IWM NA6592)*

the 9th, arrived on the 12th carrying the British submarine's prize crew, they were immediately removed. The two admirals also agreed that smaller Italian vessels could be used for escort duties – and that the 'disarmament to be prescribed by' Cunningham under Clause 4 of the Armistice would be 'nil'. However, wider issues to do with the ships would need to be dealt with between Cunningham and De Courten at a meeting that would take place ten days later. The Cunningham–Da Zara meeting was followed by the rather theatrical signal from Cunningham to the Admiralty: 'Be pleased to inform their Lordships that the Italian Battle Fleet now lays at anchor under the guns of the fortress of Malta.'

At 0723 on the 13th, *Cesare* and *Miraglia*, which had left Taranto the previous afternoon, were met by *Warspite* (which had hit *Cesare* at a range of some 13nm during the Battle of Calabria in July 1940) and four destroyers off Cape Passero, arriving at Malta around 1100. They were joined that afternoon by *Riboty*, *Atropo*, *Bandiera* and *Jalea*, and that evening by the oiler *Nettuno*, which had originally left Bari with *Riboty*. *Cesare*'s originals escorts, *Sagittario* and *Urania*, were diverted to rescue Italian personnel on Corfu, and never went to Malta.

Also on the 13th, it was agreed that, to ease concerns over potential German attacks on the Italian ships, a number should be transferred to Alexandria, *Italia*, *Vittorio Veneto*, *Aosta*, *Cadorna*, *Eugenio*, *Montecuccoli*, *Artigliere*, *Da Recco*, *Grecale* and *Velite* departing the next morning, escorted by *King George V*, *Howe*, *Echo*, *Eclipse*, *Faulknor*, *Fury*, *Intrepid* and *Vasilissa Olga*; they arrived off the Egyptian coast on the 16th. At the same time, *Legionario* and *Oriani* sailed for Bizerte, to transport American troops to Corsica to reinforce Italian and French forces there, before returning to Malta on the 29th.

Of the submarines ordered to Bône and Augusta on the 8th, *Alagi* (after a daring escape from German captivity on the 9th), *Brin*, *Galatea*, *Giada*, *Marea* and *Platino* went to Bône, whence they were escorted to Malta by the destroyer *Isis*, arriving on 16 September. *Marcantonio Bragadin*, *Onice*, *Luigi Settembrini*, *Squalo*, *Vorticei* and *Zoea* arrived at Augusta on the night of 10/11 September, leaving on the 16th, to arrive at Malta the following afternoon.

Turchese was damaged by a German aircraft on the 11th while on passage to Bône, arriving there early on the 13th under tow; she then suffered engine defects that meant she did not reach Malta until 4 October, under tow via Bizerte. *Diaspro*, directed to Bône, diverted to Cagliari in Sardinia owing to defects, arriving on the 11th, while *Nichelio* was diverted to Palermo on the orders of a British MTB on the 13th. Unfortunately, *Topazio* was sunk in error by a British aircraft on the 12th while en route to Bône. *Filippo Corridoni* was en route to La Spezia at the Armistice, and was intercepted on the 10th by the Dutch submarine *Dolfijn* and directed to Portoferraio on Elba to refuel before proceeding to Bône, arriving there shortly before *H1*, *H2* and *H4*, from Ajaccio.

A considerable number of vessels, originally ordered to La Maddalena, assembled at Portoferraio following the German occupation of their original destination. These included a dozen torpedo boats: *Ardimentoso* and *Antonio Mosto* (from La Spezia); *Indomito* and *Impavido* (from Lerici, the former carrying the Duke of Aosta, sometime titular King of Croatia); *Animoso* and *Ariente* (from Genoa); *Calliope*, *Nicola Fabrizi* and *Fortunale* (on passage from Puzzuoli to La Spezia); and *Aliseo*, *Ardito* and *Giacinto Carini* (from Bastia: *Aliseo* had sunk the German *UJ2203* and *UJ2219* on leaving); five corvettes: *Ape* (already at Portoferraio); *Folaga* (from La Spezia); *Cormorano* (from Bastia); and *Danaide* and *Minerva* (from La Maddalena); the submarine *Axum* (from Gaeta); and two FPBs, *MS55* (from Gaeta) and *MAS551* (from Lerici). In addition, two auxiliary gunboats (one from Genoa, one from near La Spezia), a tug (from La Spezia) and a dozen vedette boats (from La Spezia) had made their way to Elba, although a further five MLs had been lost en route and three captured by the Germans off Leghorn. Together with the five submarines, all but *Ardito* (damaged by German gunfire while escaping from Bastia), *Impavido* (machinery defects), *MAS551*, the tug and three MLs, sailed for Palermo, arriving on the 12th. The vessels left behind were subsequently captured by the Germans.

As well as *Axum* and *MS55*, three corvettes (*Gabbiano*, *Gru* and *Pellicano*), the FPB *MS64* and the hospital ship *Toscana* had escaped from Gaeta, the latter making Palermo on the 10th, *Gru* and *MS64* sailing via Ponza, where they picked up *MS35* (from Capri), and arrived on the 11th. The other two corvettes spent the next few days escorting a pair of merchantmen and participating in the unsuccessful defence of Montecristo, before making their way to Palermo, *Gabbiano* on the 14th, and *Pelicano* on the 16th. Seven FPBs from Capri (*MS21*, *MS24*, *MS35*, *MS52*, *MS54*, *MS56*, *MS61* and *MS72*) arrived at Palermo on the 10th, but all left again on the 12th, to operate in support of Allied operations off Salerno, during which *MS21* was lost.

Toscana left for Malta on the 13th, to carry the wounded from the bombing of *Italia* to Taranto; the auxiliary gunboat *Zagabria*, carrying the Duke of Aosta, went to Taranto via Augusta on the 19th, escorted by *Gru* and *Folaga*, arriving on the 21st. The rest were sent to Malta on the 19th, arriving between that evening and the 21st, joined on the 23rd by three of the Capri FPBs (*MS54*, *MS56* and *MS61*), no longer required at Salerno.

Although, as noted above, various vessels were surrendered intact to the Germans, many ships that were unable to sail or were otherwise trapped in captured ports were scuttled. In particular, at La Spezia, vessels sunk during the afternoon of the 9th included the light cruiser *Taranto*, the destroyers *Corazziere*, *Maestrale*, *Nicoló Zeno*, *FR21* and *FR22* (ex-French *Lion* and *Panthère*), the torpedo boats *Generale Antonio Cascino*, *Ghibli*, *Lira*, *Generale Carlo Montanari* and *Procione*, the submarines *Ambra*, *Aradam*, *Murena*, *Sirena*, *Sparide* and *Volframio*, and the corvettes *Euterpe* and *Persefone*.

Apart from those deployed in the Mediterranean, a number of Italian vessels were operating further afield, in particular submarines on transport duty to and from Japan under the 'Aquila' programme.[2] This was a German initiative under which, in exchange for receiving ten German Type VIIC submarines (to be *S1–S10*), a similar number of bigger Italian boats would be adapted to carry high-strategic-value cargoes between Europe and Japan. Five boats (*Aquila I* [*Enrico Tazzoli*], *Aquila II* [*Reginaldo Giuliani*], *Aquila III* [*Commandante Cappelini*], *Aquila V* [*Barbarigo*] and *Aquila VI* [*Luigi Torelli*]) left Bordeaux in May/June 1943, but *Tazzoli* and *Barbarigo* were both lost before leaving European waters. Two were at Singapore when the Armistice came into effect, while *Cappelini* had got as far as Sabang, Indonesia. They were all taken over by the Japanese, who then gave them to Germany, and it numbered them *UIT23–UIT25*. *Aquila IV* [*Giuseppe Finzi*] and *Aquila IX* [*Alpino Bagnolini*] were due to sail from Bordeaux in July, but were delayed following the fall of Mussolini, and were seized by the Germans at the

Armistice (see further p 162, below). Also in the Far East was *Ammiraglio Cagni*, on a raiding cruise that was intended to finish in Japan, whence a cargo of rubber and tin would be brought back to Europe. On 8 September, she was 1,600nm west of Singapore; she immediately reversed course to surrender at Durban, South Africa, on 20 September, escorted by the British corvette *Jasmine*. *Cagni* left for Taranto on 8 November, arriving on 2 January 1944.

Operating in support of the transport boats was the colonial sloop *Eritrea*, which had been sent from Italian East Africa to Japan, along with the auxiliary cruisers *Ramb I* and *Ramb II*, in early 1941 to avoid loss or capture in the impending Italian defeat in this theatre of war.[3] *Eritrea* was in the Malacca Strait, in transit between Singapore and Sabang, to meet *Cappellini*, newly arrived from Europe, when she received the news of the Armistice, and immediately turned to head for Ceylon, arriving at Colombo on 14 September. She remained there for a year, acting as a training and support ship for Allied submarines, until she sailed for Italy on 11 September 1944, arriving at Taranto on 23 October.

Of the auxiliary cruisers, *Ramb I* was sunk en route to Japan by the New Zealand cruiser *Leander*, but *Ramb II* reached Kobe on 23 March 1941, and subsequently reverted to mercantile status, under the name *Calitea II*; she was chartered to the Japanese government in December, and to its navy in September 1942. Following the Italian Armistice, the still-Italian crew scuttled the ship at Kobe, although she was later salved and returned to service as the Japanese *Ikutagawa Maru*, being bombed and sunk southeast of Saigon on 12 January 1945. Based at Shanghai were the river gunboat *Ermanno Carlotto* and minelayer *Lapanto*; both were scuttled there on 9 September. The ships were soon refloated and commissioned into the Japanese navy, passing to China at the end of the Pacific War.

Changing Sides

Although the Armistice of Cassibile had been signed on 3 September, it was a sketchy document, covering only the military imperatives, with a final, twelfth, clause stating that 'Other conditions of a political, economic and financial nature with which Italy will be bound to comply will be transmitted at a later date.'[4] Such conditions had still been in early draft when it became necessary to provide the Italians with terms in mid-August, and although they were ready in advance of the signing date, they were held back by General Dwight D Eisenhower, Allied Supreme Commander, for fear that they would delay signature of the key military ('short')

2 E Rössler, *The U-boat: The Evolution and Technical History of German Submarines* (London: Arms & Armour Press, 1981), p 206.

3 Cosentino, *Warship* [XXXVIII] (2016).

4 For the full tortuous story of the Armistice conditions, see Caruana, *Destination Malta*, pp 59–72.

armistice document. Only then would the 'long' document be submitted, under the cover of Clause 12 on the 'short' version. Apparently not anticipating the nature of the document heralded by Clause 12 (although one general had inadvertently been given sight of it), the Italians signed.

The draft 'long' armistice, presented to the Italians on 4 September was far more harsh than presaged by the 'short' version, Clause 1 declaring the 'unconditional surrender' of all Italian forces – a term not present in the 'short' version, which had merely provided for the 'immediate cessation of all hostile activity by the Italian armed forces'. It also contained various commitments on behalf of Italy that were made impossible to fulfil soon after the Armistice came into effect by the rapid occupation of three-quarters of the country by German forces, as well as the declaration of Mussolini's new Italian Social Republic (RSI) on 16 September. In view of the situation, both Eisenhower and President Roosevelt were minded to discard the 'long' armistice, but Churchill would not agree, Eisenhower being ordered both to retain it and get it signed.

Meanwhile, on 23 September, Admirals Cunningham and De Courten held a meeting at Taranto at which the modus vivendi for the future role of the Italian navy was agreed. Under the 'Cunningham–De Courten Accord':[5]

(A) Such ships as can be employed to assist actively in the Allied effort will be kept in commission and will be used under the orders of the Commander-in-Chief, Mediterranean, as may be arranged between the Allied Commander-in-Chief and the Italian Government.

(B) Ships which cannot be so employed will be reduced to a care and maintenance basis and be placed in designated ports, measures of disarmament being undertaken as may be necessary.

As regards specific categories of ship:

(a) All battleships will be placed on a care and maintenance basis in ports to be designated and will have such measures of disarmament applied as may be directed. These measures of disarmament will be such that the ships can be brought into operation again if it so seems desirable. Each ship will have on board a proportion of Italian Naval personnel to keep the ships in proper condition and the Commander-in-Chief, Mediterranean, will have the right of inspection at any time.

(b) *Cruisers*. Such cruisers as can be of immediate assistance will be kept in commission. At present it is visualised that one squadron of four cruisers will suffice and the remainder will be kept in care and maintenance as for the battleships but at a rather greater degree of readiness to be brought into service if required.

(c) *Destroyers and Torpedo Boats*. It is proposed to keep these in commission and to use them on escort and similar duties as may be requisite. It is proposed that they should be divided into escort groups working as units and that they should be based on Italian ports.

(d) *Small Craft*. M.A.S., Minesweepers, auxiliaries and similar small craft will be employed to the full, detailed arrangements being made with the Flag Officer (Liaison) by the Italian Ministry of Marine for their best employment.

(e) *Submarines.* In the first instance submarines will be immobilised in ports to be designated and at a later date these may be brought into service as may be required to assist the Allied effort.

The Italian navy's status would be as follows:

Under this modification of the armistice terms, all the Italian ships will continue to fly their flags. A large proportion of the Italian Navy will thus remain in active commission operating their own ships and fighting alongside the forces of the United Nations against the Axis Powers.

The requisite Liaison officers will be supplied to facilitate the working of the Italian ships in co-operation with allied forces. A small Italian liaison mission will be attached to the Headquarters of the Commander-in-Chief, Mediterranean, to deal with matters affecting the Italian Fleet.

Thus, the Italian navy would operate as co-belligerents (*not* as allies) of the Allied powers, under conditions similar to those applicable to the Allied Polish, Free French, Greek, Dutch and Norwegian naval forces. Vessels from these forces were operationally under the control of the British navy, but remained under their own national flag, and with a national crew. On the other hand, British discussions during late September[6] mulled over the possibility of taking over Italian ships for manning by Allied crews.

Linked with this, and in contrast to the pragmatic approach being taken by the operational commanders, at the Allied political level signature of the 'long' armistice was still being insisted on. Badoglio objected in particular to the term 'unconditional surrender' at meetings begun on 27 September; the following day it was agreed that he would

5 Essentially a 'gentlemen's agreement', albeit endorsed by not only the two admirals, but also by Marshal Badoglio.

indeed sign, subject to the issue of a letter relieving the Italians from the execution of 'impossible' clauses, and that a request be passed to Eisenhower that 'unconditional surrender' would be removed. Accordingly, later that day, Badoglio embarked in *Scipione* for Malta, where he signed the 'long' armistice on 29 September aboard the battleship *Nelson*, having received oral assurances from Eisenhower over the release from 'impossible' conditions and that he would try to get the objectionable 'unconditional surrender' term removed. A letter to the former effect was handed over immediately after the signature, and on 8 October Badoglio was informed that the document's title had been changed from 'Instrument of Surrender of Italy' to 'Additional conditions of Armistice with Italy', and the objectionable Clause 1 amended to read: 'The Italian land, sea and air forces wherever located hereby surrender.' On 13 October, Italy declared war on Germany. The amendments, and some other changes, including adding the Soviet Union to the agreement, were enshrined in a protocol dated 9 November, and signed on the 12th.

Most of the ships at Malta had now already returned to Italy, and on the 16th the majority of those previously sent to Alexandria left Egypt for home, arriving on the 18th. The exceptions were the battleships, not required for immediate service under the Cunningham–De Courten Accord. *Cesare*, *Duilio* and *Doria* remained at Malta until the summer of 1944, *Doria* leaving for Taranto on 8 June, escorted by two torpedo boats, followed by *Cesare* on the 17th, escorted by *Artigiere* and *Fortunale*, and finally *Duilio* on the 27th, under escort from *Aliseo* and *Siria*. Back in Italian waters, the three battleships were employed as stationary training ships. On the other hand, *Italia* and *Vittorio Veneto* were kept in Egypt, sailing with reduced crews on the 16th towards Port Said, arriving there the next morning and passing through the Suez Canal into the Great Bitter Lake. In response to a spring 1944 query from the British prime minister as to whether the ships might have a role in the war against Japan, manned by US crews, the response[7] estimated that ships would first require some nine months' refitting. Nothing was taken forward, and the two battleships would remain laid up in Egypt until they returned to Italy on 5 February 1947.

Co-Belligerence

The largest Italian warships actually used operationally subsequent to the Armistice were light cruisers, *Abruzzi* and *Aosta* serving on trade protection and anti-blockade runner duties in the South Atlantic, based at Freetown in Sierra Leone from November 1943 to April 1944. They joined on the duty the French cruisers *Montcalm*, *Georges Leygues*, *Gloire* and *Suffren*, *Garibaldi* being added to the squadron from the end of March. *Cadorna* and *Pompeo* were used as fast troop carriers in the Mediterranean, although *Cadorna* was in poor condition, and went into refit at Taranto at the beginning of 1944; *Montecuccoli* was also used in a transport role. Smaller vessels were employed on a range of duties in the Mediterranean theatre, in particular the escort of convoys, transport of high-priority material, and the landing and retrieval of personnel from German-held coasts. Losses included the submarine *Axum*, stranded off the coast of Morea while attempting to extract agents, and a number of FPBs.

The long-standing Italian expertise in clandestine harbour attacks was harnessed on a number of occasions, with the destroyers *Granatiere*, *Grecale* and *Geniere*, plus FPBs, used as parent ships for Anglo-Italian human torpedo teams. One of the most notable attacks was on La Spezia on 22 June 1944, to sink the hulks of the damaged heavy cruisers *Bolzano* and *Gorizia*, which it was feared would be used as blockships by the Germans. *Bolzano* was sunk, but the other cruiser remained afloat, albeit waterlogged. Also not wholly successful was a similar attack on the carrier *Aquila* at Genoa in April 1945.[8]

The conventional submarine force was largely employed on training duties, acting as targets for Allied anti-submarine training activities. One group operated out of Bermuda, Guantanamo Bay, Key West, Port Everglades, New London and Casco Bay, as part of the US navy's SubRon7, between February 1944 and the end of 1945, comprising *Onice*, *Mameli* (the last on station, leaving in November 1945), *Da Procida*, *Speri*, *Dandolo*, *Atropo*, *Vortice* and *Marea*

8 For the latter see A Rastelli and E Bagnasco, 'The Sinking of the Italian Aircraft Carrier Aquila – A Controversial Question', *Warship International* XXVII/1 (1990), pp 55–70; M Grossman, 'The Allied Assault on *Aquila* – Operation Toast', *Warship International* XXVII/2 (1990), pp 166–73.

The hulk of *Gorizia* at La Spezia in 1945. *(AD collection)*

6 TNA 1/14893, dated 28 September 1943.
7 TNA 1/14383.

(*Settembrini* was accidentally rammed and sunk by the US destroyer *Fremont*, in November 1944 while on passage from Gibraltar to Bermuda); seven French boats[9] were also part of the group. In addition, *Giada* and *Brin* operated out of Colombo, *Bragadin*, *Corridoni*, *Alagi*, *Galatea* and *Menotti* out of Haifa, *H1* from Malta, and *Cagni* did so based at Palermo.[10] It was also proposed at the end of 1943 that Italian cruisers be employed as aircraft targets, at Rosyth, Invergordon, Ceylon and Suez,[11] but this was not taken forward after the British First Sea Lord made his objections known, although *Eugenio* did act as such at Suez for a period.

In the background to this co-operation was – luckily unknown to the Italians – the spectre of a Soviet demand for the immediate cession of the share of the Italian fleet that

they regarded their due. At the Moscow conference of foreign ministers in October 1943, the Soviet delegation requested that the USSR be granted immediately one battleship, one cruiser, eight destroyers, four submarines, and 40,000t of merchant shipping. The principle was accepted, and endorsed at the subsequent Tehran conference of heads of government, but the UK and US naval authorities were concerned that any attempt at implementing such a transfer at this stage in the war could have a disastrous effect on the increasingly smooth collaboration between the Italian navy and the Allies. In addition to the likely impact on Italian willingness to play the roles now being allocated to them, and which they were carrying out to a high standard, it was pointed out that the handing over of ships would not enhance Soviet naval power in the short term, as the ships could not in the current state of the war access the Black Sea and, designed for Mediterranean conditions, were totally unfitted, without major modifications, for service with the Northern Fleet, the only Soviet formation they could practically join.

Accordingly, it was proposed that the Soviets be loaned

---

9 *Argo, Amazone, Antiope, Archimede, Casabianca, Le Centaure* and *Le Glorieux*.
10 While employed in British-controlled waters, many boats were given UK pennant numbers: N31 (*Atropo*); N36 (*Cagni*); N49 (*Bragadin*); N55 (*Corridoni*); N58 (*Alagi*); N66 (*Menotti*); N71 (*Galatea*); N82 (*Zoea*); N88 (*Giada*); N96 (*Brin*); and P56 (*H1*). Also on the British pennant list were the cruiser *Abruzzi* (D04) and the destroyers *Carabinere* (H81) and *Velite* (H59).
11 TNA ADM 1/13650.

Archangelsk (ex-*Royal Sovereign*), soon after being transferred to the Soviet navy in lieu of Italian tonnage on 30 May 1944. *(AD collection)*

ships equivalent to those claimed from UK and US resources, until replacements from the Italian fleet could be made available. Thus, the UK provided the battleship *Royal Sovereign* (to become *Archangelsk*), eight ex-US destroyers (*St Albans* [*Dostoiny*]; *Brighton* [*Zharky*]; *Richmond* [*Zhyvuchy*]; *Chelsea* [*Derzky*]; *Leamington* [*Zhguchy*]; *Roxborough* [*Doblestny*]; *Georgetown* [*Zhostky*]; *Churchill* [*Dveyatelny*]), and four submarines (*Sunfish* [*B-1*]; *Unbroken* [*B-2*]; *Unison* [*B-3*]; *Ursula* [*B-4*]). From the USA came the light cruiser *Milwaukee* (*Murmansk*), 'temporarily loaned to the Naval Command, Union of Soviet Socialist Republics, until a replacement from the Italian fleet can be placed at the disposal of the Soviet Union'.

Milwaukee was handed over at Murmansk on 20 April 1944, having sailed with convoy JW 58 in late March from Loch Ewe, while *Royal Sovereign* was formally transferred in UK waters on 30 May 1944, the submarines on 26 June and the destroyers on 16 July. The submarines sailed from Dundee in July, *B1* being sunk in error by a British aircraft on the 27th, although the other arrived safely. The battleship and destroyers left Scapa Flow as escort to convoy JW 59 on 17 August, and made the Kola Inlet intact on the 25th, in spite of being attacked by *U711* en route. A further destroyer, *Lincoln*, was allocated for cannibalisation, being handed over on 26 August; she was, however, commissioned as *Druzhny* on 23 September. Apart from *Dveyatelny*, sunk by *U997* in January 1945, the ships would remain with the Soviet navy until after 1947, when the Italian vessels finally became available (see p 211).

Under German and Italian Fascist Flags

In spite of the widespread scuttlings of ships left behind by the Italian navy following the Armistice, many of those under heavy repair or still under construction were taken over more or less intact. These included two battleships, two aircraft carriers, two heavy cruisers and five light cruisers, but these were of little value to the Germans, requiring resources to complete far in excess of what could ever be made available; they were in any case of no use in the Mediterranean war that the Germans were now having to fight. On the other hand, vessels suitable for minelaying and escort were in huge demand: refit and fitting-out were thus pushed ahead for destroyers, torpedo boats and corvettes, plus smaller vessels. The resulting ships joined those operational vessels successfully seized following the Armistice, plus the existing small German torpedo boat force, made up of ex-French tonnage.[12]

In addition, although most of the Italian navy obeyed government orders, some senior officers and crews preferred to remain allied with the Germans.[13] The Italian Social Republic (RSI) was established under Mussolini on 23 September, with its own Marina Nazionale Repubblicana (MNR), albeit under German operational control. In the period between the Armistice and the institution of the RSI, a number of vessels in the Adriatic remained under the Italian flag through local agreements to co-operate with German authorities. These included the torpedo boats *T7* (at Gravosa), *Pilo* and *Missori* (at Durazzo), plus a number of FPBs and other small vessels. However, *Pilo*'s crew mutinied on the 21st, rejoining the main Italian navy at Brindisi on the 26th; *MAS433* would do something similar on 19 November. As a result of such events, Germany took over most of the ships in question, adding a number to her navy. On the other hand, vessels from other parts of Italy began the build-up of the MNR, focussed initially on light forces, three scuttled submarines also being allocated for salvage and refitting (which was never completed). Plans for the salvage of the destroyer *Maestrale* and the torpedo boat *Ghibi* were dropped by the Germans in January 1944, although the unfinished cruisers *Etna* and *Vesuvio* were handed over to the MNR for post-war completion in September 1944.

However, the vast majority of Italian vessels in Axis service after September 1943 were under the German flag. Thirty destroyers and torpedo boats were commissioned into the German navy, thirteen being members of the *Ariete* class that were completed under German auspices.[14] The rest

13 For German–allied Italian naval activities, see V P O'Hara and E Cernuschi, *Black Phoenix: History and Operations of the Marina Repubblicana 1943–1945* (Chula Vista, CA: Propeller Press, 2014).

14 P Hervieux, 'German TA Torpedo Boats at War', *Warship XXI* (1997–98), pp 133–48; Z Freivogel, *Beute-Zerstörer und Torpedoboote der Kriegsmarine*, Marine-Arsenal 48 (Wölfersheim-Brstadt: Podzun-Pallas-Verlag, 2000); Freivogel and Rastelli, *Adriatic Naval War 1940–1945*, pp 178–483.

The German torpedo boat *TA24*, formerly the Italian *Arturo*. *(AD collection)*

12 Seized by the Italians at Toulon in November 1942 and Bizerte in December, and transferred to the Germans in April 1943.

TA21 (ex-*Insidioso*), sunk at Fiume by a US aerial torpedo in November 1944; the 'balkan cross' on the ship's side was a recognition symbol painted on most German warships deployed in the Adriatic. *(Geirr Haar collection)*

ranged in age from the 1913-vintage *TA21* (ex-*Insidioso*), through 1930s vessels of Italian and Yugoslav origin, to the 1942/3 *Ariete* class. They bore the brunt of German surface warfare in the Mediterranean, Aegean and Adriatic, most being lost in action, with the few survivors scuttled during the closing days of the war.

Six FPBs were formed into a new German formation in the Aegean, the 24th, *S511* (ex-*MAS557*, with a part-Italian crew), *S512* (ex-*MAS553*), and four ex-Yugoslav boats (*S601* [ex-*MS42*, ex-*Velebit*], *S602* [ex-*MS43*, ex-*Dinara*], *S603* [ex-*MS 44*, ex-*Triglav*] and *S604* [ex-*MS46*, ex-*Rudnik*]; two sisters had been scuttled by the Italians). Other FPBs seized incomplete were finished off and later joined the flotilla.

It was intended by the Germans that the transport submarines taken over at Bordeaux and in the Far East should continue in their 'Aquila' role (although the programme was now renamed 'Merkator'). With German officers, but with mixed German/Italian crews, the first voyage back to Europe was begun by *UIT24* (ex-*Cappellini*) at the beginning of 1944, but she was forced to return to Penang for lack of fuel, exacerbated by machinery defects, when her intended tanker *Charlotte Schliemann*, and the latter's replacement *Brake*, were both sunk in the Indian Ocean on 12 February and 12 March respectively, prior to their rendezvous with the submarine. *UIT23* (ex-*Giuliani*) was next to make the attempt, leaving Singapore for Penang on 13 February, but was sunk by HMS/M *Tally-ho* the following day.

The first post-Italian Armistice eastbound voyage had begun on 26 January around the same time by *UIT22* (ex-*Bagnolini*), but she was first damaged by air attack off Ascension Island, and then sunk by South African aircraft off the Cape of Good Hope on 11 March. Coupled with the Allied destruction of the tanker network intended to facilitate the voyages, the whole scheme was now suspended. *UIT24* and *UIT25* (ex-*Torelli*), following refits at Kobe, were henceforth used for local transport missions between Japan and Borneo and other German bases in the region. They survived to be seized by the Japanese on the German

surrender in May 1945 (see p 172); the final 'Aquila' boat, *UIT21* (ex-*Finzi*), remained at Bordeaux in poor mechanical condition and was scuttled by the Germans in August 1944.

ROMANIA

The fourth largest navy in the Axis was that of Romania, which had joined in November 1940, taking part in the invasion of the Soviet Union the following June, and playing an important role in the war in the Black Sea.[15] However, beginning in December 1943, a Soviet offensive began that had pushed Axis forces back to the pre-war Soviet–Romanian border by April 1944, a further offensive in August resulting in an Axis collapse. Against this background, on 23 August, King Mihai I staged a coup, removing the pro-Axis Marshal Ion Antonescu, accepting an armistice (formally signed on 12 September), and declaring war on Germany. An attempted counter-coup by the Germans was defeated, and for the rest of the war the Romanian army fought alongside the Soviets throughout eastern and central Europe.

The Romanian navy had been involved in the evacuation of Axis forces from Crimea in April/May 1944, but had subsequently remained at Constanţa, facing heavy air attacks. By September, only two destroyers (*Regina Maria* and *Mărăşeşti*), two minesweepers/gunboats (*Dumitrescu* and *Ghiculescu*), the minelayer *Amiral Murgescu* and three motor torpedo boats were still fully operational.

Although initially left in Romanian hands after the country's reversal of alliances, the sinking of the Soviet minesweeper *T-410 Vzryv* by the German *U19*[16] on 2 September, while in company with *Amiral Murgescu*, was used by the Soviets as a pretext for the seizure of the vessels at Constanţa and the Romanian Danube Flotilla at Izmail on 5 September. However, the submarine *Delfinul*, in dockyard hands at Galaţi, was not seized until the 12th, when most Romanian ships were sailed from Constanţa by Soviet crews. Also taken over at Constanţa were the wrecks of the German submarines *U9*, *U18* and *U24*, the first of which had been bombed there on 20 August, the others scuttled on the 25th. All were salved by the Soviets and taken to the USSR, but proved beyond repair and were scrapped (*U9*) or expended as targets during 1947. Following their arrival in Soviet waters, most seagoing vessels were formally commissioned on 20 October, followed by the river monitors on the 30th.

15 On the Romanian navy's role in the war, see C Crăciunoiu and M Axworthy, 'Romanian Minelaying Operations in the Second World War', *Warship* XV (1991), pp 146–59; C Crăciunoiu and M Axworthy, 'Romanian Submarine Operations in the Second World War', *Warship* XVI (1992), pp 142–59; P Hervieux, 'The Royal Romanian Navy at War, 1941–1944', *Warship* XXIV (2001–02), pp 70–88.
16 Which subsequently scuttled herself off the Turkish port Zonguldak on the 10th, together with her sisters *U20* and *U23*.

Regele Ferdinand as the Soviet *Likhoi*. (AD collection)

Mărăşti under the Soviet flag as *Lovkyi*, seen behind the Type 7U destroyer *Soobrazitelnyi*. (AD collection)

The submarine *TS-2* (ex-*Marsouinul*) was badly damaged by a torpedo explosion at Poti in February 1945.

Older vessels, comprising the destroyers ex-*Mărăşeşti* and ex-*Mărăşti*, the former Austro-Hungarian torpedo boats ex-*Sborul* and ex-*Smeul*, the submarine *Delfinul*, six FPBs, three patrol boats and two surveying vessels were returned to Romania at Galaţi on 12 October 1945. However, the newer destroyers ex-*Regina Maria* and ex-*Regele Ferdinand I*, together with the submarine ex-*Requinul* and the river monitors, were kept until the summer of 1951, and the minelayer ex-*Amiral Murgescu* retained indefinitely (she was eventually scrapped in 1988). The Soviets scrapped the damaged submarine ex-*Marsouinul* during 1950/51.

The returned ships remained in service until the end of the 1950s, although the terms of the peace treaty, signed in Paris in 1947, prevented Romania from operating submarines, meaning that the two submarines never again became operational. The four destroyers were all discarded in April 1961.

BULGARIA

The reversal of alliances by Romania opened the way to a Soviet advance across its territory to Bulgaria, which announced its neutrality in the German–Soviet war on 26 August 1944, ordering German troops to leave the country. Nevertheless, the USSR declared war on Bulgaria on 5 September, and three days later occupied the north-eastern part of the country unopposed, together with the ports of Varna and Burgas by the following day. The Bulgarian navy was seized, the vessels being incorporated into the Soviet navy (two of the three surviving torpedo boats becoming training vessels) until returned in July 1945.

The government having been overthrown on the 8th, the new regime declared war on Germany. Bulgarian troops thenceforward aided the Soviets in expelling German forces from both Bulgaria and southern Yugoslavia, continued through Hungary and reached Austria by the German surrender.

FINLAND

Finland had been invaded by the Soviet Union on 30 November 1939, the so-called 'Winter War' being ended by the Treaty of Moscow in March 1940, under which Finland's Hangö Peninsula was 'leased' to the Soviet Union. However, with Germany's invasion of the Soviet Union in June 1941, Finland resumed hostilities against the latter. A stable advanced front line was established in 1942, but a major Soviet offensive was launched on 9 June 1944, a month later pushing Finnish forces back to lines approximating those at the end of the Winter War. The Finnish navy was active during the summer campaigns, the submarines operating against Soviet shipping, with *Vetehinen* and *Vesihiisi* also laying minefields. Attempts by the Soviets to neutralise the coast defence ship *Väinämöinen* were unsuccessful, although a mistaken sighting resulted in the sinking by Soviet bombs of the German anti-aircraft ship *Niobe* (ex-*Gelderland*) on 16 July at Kotka.

Although the front then stabilised, few resources remained to resist a further offensive, and as the Soviets were keen to divert resources to their push into Germany, a ceasefire was agreed on 4 September 1944. Under the Moscow Armistice, signed on 19 September, Finland was obliged to expel German troops from her territory, the resulting Lapland War effectively being concluded in November, although a few German elements remained on Finnish soil until April 1945, and in January 1945 the German submarine *U370* sank the Finnish minelayer *Louhi* in the Gulf of Bothnia.

Four FPBs captured by the Finns from the Soviet Union in 1941 and 1944 were returned to their owners, as were seven minesweepers, ordered by the USSR as tugs and seized and converted by the Finns. The biggest ship of the Finnish navy, *Väinämöinen*, had, like the rest of the fleet, retired to her base on 22 September 1944, in accordance with the Moscow Armistice. She remained at Turku under care and maintenance for the next two years.

5

Endgame 1945 – Germany

During the last six months of the Second World War, the steadily shrinking German navy was the subject of an onslaught of Allied aircraft bombing and mining: between August 1944 and March 1945, some 10,000 (out of a planned total of 27,000) sea mines were sown by British aircraft. The effectiveness of air attack was enhanced by the belated introduction of the Mark VII radar, and the widespread use of high-performance Bristol Beaufighter and de Havilland Mosquito aircraft in anti-shipping roles. This was aimed especially at blunting any resurgence of the German submarine threat, particularly in light of the introduction of *Schnorchels*, allowing diesels to be run underwater, as well as the revolutionary high-underwater-speed boats of Types XXI and XXIII, and the potential of the air-independent-propulsion systems under development.

Rocket-projectile-firing Hawker Typhoon aircraft began to be used in anti-shipping roles in March 1945, while the tempo of Soviet anti-shipping aircraft sorties stepped up over the winter. Nevertheless, although significant losses were imposed, the German navy managed to maintain operations up to May. Likewise, although extensive raids struck

naval bases and shipbuilding yards, the progressive construction of reinforced concrete bunkers since 1940 allowed submarines to receive significant protection, both during construction and when in port. Smaller surface combatants could also seek refuge. The prefabrication of sections of the Type XXI and XXIII submarines in remote locations lessened the direct effect of bombing on the construction process, but damage to the railway network made their transport to assembly yards increasingly problematic.

Air attacks against specific units included the damage to *Tirpitz* at Trondheim by British 12,000lb 'Tallboy' bombs in September, and her capsize at Tromsø by further such bombs in November. Near misses by similar projectiles sank *Lützow* in shallow water at Swinemünde on 16 April 1945, leaving her resting with a 56° list, although she was later brought back on an even keel.

As with the other surviving German big ships, *Lützow* had, since the latter half of 1944, been employed in supporting the army, retreating before the Red Army advance. Even the long-laid-up *Admiral Hipper* was to be brought forward for duty, but she was still under refit at Kiel

The wreck of *Lützow*, with 30m of her starboard side opened up by a near-miss by a 12,000lb 'Tallboy' bomb on 16 April 1945. She was also struck by three 1,000lb bombs: one of which had penetrated three decks; another two decks (albeit without exploding); and one that created a 6 x 1.5m hole in the upper deck. Righted from her heavily listed post-attack state, her forward turret remained in action until the hulk was further damaged by demolition charges by the retreating Germans on 3 May, including wrecking her main turrets. *(AD collection)*

The Deutsche Werke, Kiel, in May 1945: view from the north, with the empty Dock VI on the right, *Hipper* in Dock V in the centre, and the suspended Type XIV submarine tankers *U491*, *U492* and *U493* on the slip on the left. *(AD collection)*

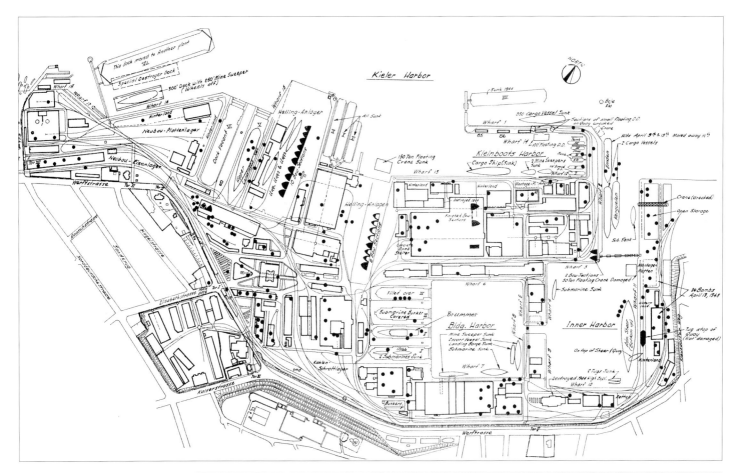

Above: Map of Kiel, as in May 1945, showing locations of bomb-hits. (*Adapted from* US Strategic Bombing Survey, Report 95: Deutsche Werke Kiel, *Exhibit C*)

Right: Wilhelmshaven in 1945, with the wreck of *Köln* on the right: she had been bombed on 30 March, and subsequently used as a battery – hence the staging around her turrets. (*AD collection*)

The Deutsche Werke, Kiel, in May 1945: view from the west, with, from the left: the partly filled-in Dock IV; the 'Konrad' submarine construction and repair bunker, built over the former Dock III; the wreck of *Brummer* in Dock II; and *U1166* in the adjacent Dock I. The capsized wreck of *Scheer* is visible in the background, in the Innerhafen. The partly-scrapped remains of *Brummer* and *Scheer* were subsequently buried when the docks were filled in, although that of the former was exposed again when the new Howaldtswerke yard was being built directly to the west in the early 1960s; during this time the 'Konrad' bunker was finally demolished. *(AD collection)*

when severely damaged by bombs while in the yard's Dock V on 3 May (the minelayer *Brummer*, in Dock II, suffered similarly), further damage being caused by subsequent scuttling activities. Also at Kiel, on 9/10 April *Admiral Scheer* had been capsized by bombing on the west side of the inner harbour, and *Emden* reduced to a wreck on the 13th, and beached in Heikendorfer Bay the following day; both had been under refit by the Deutsche Werke.

The bombing of Wilhelmshaven on 30 March had already sunk *Köln* in harbour, much as a raid on Gotenhafen (Gdynia) had done to *Schleswig-Holstein* by three hits on 18/19 December 1944; the latter raid had also sunk the submarine depot ship *Waldemar Kophamel* and the target ship (ex-battleship) *Zähringen*. The hulk of *Gneisenau*, also at Gdynia, was not hit, but was scuttled there as a blockship on 27 March 1945, having been towed into position across the southern entrance to the harbour by *Z31*. *Zähringen*, sunk in the December raid, was temporarily salved for a similar duty, but was not actually placed across the channel.

The light cruiser *Nürnberg* had been assigned to minelaying duties at the beginning of 1945, but lack of fuel meant that she was immobilised at Copenhagen from 24 January onwards. Her half-sister *Leipzig* had been badly damaged in collision with *Prinz Eugen* on 14 October 1944, and had subsequently been used a training hulk at Gdynia. She then sailed to the Hela Peninsula in March, whence she departed on the 24th, laden with German refugees, finally reaching Åbenrå in Denmark on 29 April. In the interim she had been attacked repeatedly, but had survived in spite of a maximum speed of only 6kt, achieved on her diesel engine, her steam plant having been wrecked in the aforementioned collision. Also by then at Copenhagen was *Prinz Eugen*, withdrawn from Swinemünde after the sinking of *Lützow*, arriving at the Danish capital on 20 April.

Thus, as the war entered its last weeks, the only vessel above destroyer size still operational was the ancient battleship *Schlesien*, which continued bombardments off what was left of Germany's Baltic coast. But even the old ship's days

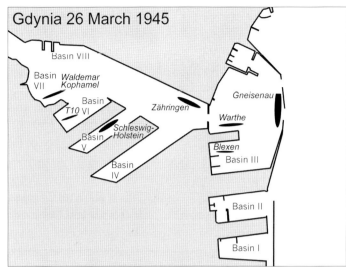

Gdynia 26 March 1945

Basin VIII

Basin VII

Waldemar Kophamel

Basin VI

T10

Basin V

Schleswig-Holstein

Zähringen

Gneisenau

Warthe

Blexen

Basin III

Basin IV

Basin II

Basin I

Zähringen (top), *Schleswig-Holstein* (middle) and *Gneisenau*, sunk at Gdynia. The first two (with *T10*, the depot ship *Waldemar Kophamel*, the tanker *Blexen* and the steamer *Warthe* [ex-*Bratland*]) had been sunk by bombing on 18 December 1944, *Schleswig-Holstein* by three bombs, two of which penetrated the engine rooms. *Gneisenau* had been scuttled to block the southern entrance to the harbour on 27 March 1945, having been towed into position by *Z31*. The hulk of *Zähringen* had been salved with a view to blocking the entrance to the inner harbour, but came to rest parallel with the channel. *(AD graphic/AD collection/ Drüppel/NHHC NH 83613)*

were numbered: on 3 May she struck a mine off Peenemünde, and grounded while in tow towards Swinemünde by the destroyer *Z39*, escorted by *Z38*. For a short while she was used as an anti-aircraft battery, but when the port was evacuated the following day she was scuttled and settled in shallow water.

Like the larger ships, the destroyers and torpedo boats remained active, primarily in the east, laying minefields, undertaking shore bombardments, escorting big ships and convoys – particularly those carrying refugees – and themselves carrying refugees westwards, all hampered by a chronic shortage of fuel oil. Numbers also dwindled through loss and serious damage, especially as Soviet air superiority

became total. Thus, *Z28* was on 6 March broken in two and sunk in Sassnitz Bay by bombs, and a week later *T3* and *T5* were sunk by mines off Hela. On 9 April *Z43* was first damaged by a bomb and then struck a mine the following day, leaving her with a broken back and flooded boiler rooms. *Z34* was torpedoed by a Soviet MTB off Hela on 16 April, being towed by *T36* and *M204* to Swinemünde with a flooded engine room.

As April drew to a close, vessels began to be withdrawn westwards, including *Z5 Jacobi* (at Flensburg from 2 May), *Z31* (at Brunsbüttel from 30 April), *Z33* (at Cuxhaven from 28 April) and the makeshift-repaired *Z43*, which limped to Warnemünde and then to Kiel on 2 May. The last vessels

Left: *Schlesien*, soon after having been mined off Peenemünde on 3 May 1945; she was blown up while aground off Greifswalder Oie the following day (right). *(Dirk Nottelmann collection/AD)*

operational in the east were *Z38*, *Z39*, *T33* and *T36*, plus the patched-up *Z34*. All left Swinemünde for Copenhagen on 4 May, laden with refugees, although *T36* did not make the open sea before being bombed and sunk. The previous day, *Z43* had been scuttled in Geltinger Bay, off Flensburg, a day after most of the disabled ships at Kiel, including *Hipper* and *Emden*, had been scuttled with demolition charges.

The 4th had also seen all submarines ordered to break off operations, and proceed to Norwegian ports. Nevertheless, they continued to come under Allied attack, a number being sunk over the next few days. On the 5th, at 0800, all German forces in northwest Germany, the Netherlands and Denmark surrendered unconditionally to the British, the terms including the non-destruction of equipment and ships. However, on 30 April, President Karl Dönitz had ordered that the entire fleet should be scuttled, save fishing, trans-

port and mine clearance vessels, with the associated codeword *Regenbogen* to signal the order to scuttle the ships.

Thus, shortly before the surrender formally came into effect, all vessels in German and Danish waters, or otherwise south of 55° 10′ N at 0800 that day were ordered to execute *Regenbogen*. There remains some dispute over whether this was formally withdrawn, but at 1514 that afternoon Generaladmiral Hans-Georg von Friedeburg, CinC of the German navy, emphasised that submarines in Norway were not to be scuttled or destroyed. Nevertheless, 218 submarines had been scuttled elsewhere by the end of the 5th. On the other hand, other vessels in the area, including nineteen submarines (sixteen in Germany, three in Denmark), remained afloat and were surrendered to British forces (all with a nominal surrender date of the 5th). A final unconditional surrender of German forces throughout

Bremen after its capture in May 1945, showing Type XXI submarines on the slips of the Deschimag yard. *(NHHC 80-G-333672)*

Europe was signed on 7 May, which came into effect at 2301 CET on the next day.

Already captured intact, albeit incomplete, were the incomplete destroyer *Z45* and sixteen Type XXI submarines at the Deschimag yard in Bremen. The city had been surrendered on 26 April to a British naval force, the 30th Assault Unit, which was charged with gathering intelligence and acquiring enemy equipment, and was in some cases the first to enter German ports, with a particular brief to forestall any destruction. Hamburg had also fallen intact into British hands on 3 May.

On the 5th, prior to the surrender, *Z10 Lody*, *Z14 Ihn*, *Z6 Riedel*, *Z25*, *T17*, *T19*, *T23*, *T28* and *T35* had departed Copenhagen for Hela for a further refugee run. At the end of this, they had returned once more to Hela, the final evacuation voyage comprising *Lody*, *Ihn*, *Riedel*, *Galster*, *Z25*, *Z33*, *Z38*, *Z39*, *T17*, *T19*, *T23* and *T28*, plus FPBs and the depot ship *Tsingtau*, reaching Glücksberg in peacetime, on the 8th.

Original plans for the occupation of Germany had placed all the western ports in British hands, although a Combined Chiefs of Staff meeting at the Quebec conference in September 1944 had agreed that the USA would occupy Bremen and Bremerhaven as an enclave in the prospective British Zone. However, there were major issues over the US manpower available to disarm the two ports – and also over the adequacy of UK resources to manage activities even in their now-reduced portfolio (the latter exacerbated by the creation of the British Pacific Fleet).

Nevertheless, the occupation of the German naval ports was successfully implemented, Wilhelmshaven being taken over on the 6th, Cuxhaven (with *Z15 Steinbrink* and *Z33* [immediately transferred to Wilhelmshaven], a number of submarines and various auxiliary vessels) and Brunsbüttel on the 7th, and Kiel on the 8th. Working relationships were soon established between the British and the German naval authorities, with the latter allowed to continue to manage day-to-day tasks, subject to the absolute authority of the British. At Kiel, the hulk of *Admiral Hipper* was removed from her original location and dumped in Heikendorfer Bay in July, close to *Emden* and other derelicts. Also at Kiel, the depot ship *Hermann von Wissmann* was taken over as headquarters ship, taking the name *Royal Harold* as formal depot ship for the so-named British naval command at the port in August. Paid off in February 1948, the ship was later handed over to Belgium (see pp 234–235, below). The hulked cruiser *Amazone* was also employed by the British as an accommodation ship at Kiel; *Berlin* was also present in the harbour.

A considerable number of German vessels were in Danish waters at the time of the surrender, in particular those involved in the Baltic evacuations. Considerable friction

Admiral Hipper dumped in Heikendorfer Bay during the summer of 1945. *Hipper* had been damaged by bombing in Dock V at Kiel on 3 and 9 April 1945, and by demolition charges around 0425hrs on 3 May. The hulk was then patched up and removed from the dock the following month. Behind is just visible the hulk of *Emden*, damaged by bombing while lying against Wharf 2 on 9 and 13 April, and grounded in Heikendorfer Bay soon afterwards, where the wreck was blown up on 3 May. *(AD collection)*

resulted when Danish elements attempted to board German vessels, the latter's crews not recognising the Danes as victors – only the British, to whom they had been formally surrendered under the 5 May agreement. Apart from the big ships, the replenishment ship *Nordmark*, together with *T47*, *T107*, *T108* and *T151* and other smaller vessels, had been at Copenhagen on the 7th. Larger vessels also in Danish waters were the target ship (ex-battleship) *Hessen*, the anti-aircraft ships *Undine* and *Ariadne* (ex-Dutch ex-*IJmuiden*, ex-*Jacob van Heemskerk*, and *Vliereede*, ex-*Hertog Hendrik*) and target control-ship *Blitz* at Nyborg, and *T153*, *T158*, *T190* and *T196* at Køge. At Frederikshaven was the hulk of *T16*.

Matters improved at Copenhagen with the arrival of the cruiser *Birmingham*, accompanied by the destroyers *Zephyr*, *Zodiac*, *Zest* and *Zealous* on the 9th, with the Danes taking over formal responsibility for the port of Copenhagen and the security of the German ships. *Prinz Eugen* and *Nürnberg*

The anti-aircraft ship *Nymphe* (ex-Norwegian coast defence ship *Tordenskjold*), wrecked at Moldøra while on passage from Svolvær to Narvik, with 180 German military personnel aboard, to surrender to Norwegian forces on 17 May 1945, allegedly due to the inebriation of the crew. *(Lofotmuseet)*

were escorted to Wilhelmshaven by the cruisers *Devonshire* and *Dido*, together with the destroyers *Savage* and *Iroquois*, on 27 May. *Leipzig* arrived at Wilhelmshaven in June.

Allied forces began moving into Norway on the 13th, *Devonshire*, with the minelayers *Apollo* and *Ariadne*, escorted by *Savage*, *Iroquois*, *Arendal* and *Campbell*, also carrying the Norwegian crown prince and naval CinC. Norwegian waters actually contained the largest number of surviving German warships, including around a hundred submarines (thirty-four of which were at Bergen alone), sent there during the last days of hostilities. Given the vast area involved, and a shortage of manpower, all remaining service-able German submarines and merchantmen were ordered to British ports on the 24th, in part to forestall any potential Soviet demand that vessels (especially submarines) be sent to Murmansk or nearby ports.[1] Work also began on concen-trating German personnel and vessels from remote loca-tions, the anti-aircraft ship *Nymphe* (ex-Norwegian coast defence ship *Tordenskjold*) running aground on the 17th while on passage to Narvik to surrender to Norwegian forces.

Fifteen ex-Norwegian boats were already in the UK by the 24th. *U294*, *U295*, *U312*, *U313*, *U363*, *U427*, *U481*, *U668*, *U716*, *U968*, *U997* and *U1165* had been in harbour at Narvik, their base, on 9 May, *U278* and *U318* arriving during the day and *U992* on the 10th.[2] On the 12th, all had been

moved to Skjomenfjord on Allied orders, and then on the 15th directed to Trondheim, having landed all ammunition. However, while en route on the 19th, the boats had been diverted to Loch Eriboll, a sheltered deep-water anchorage in Scotland between Cape Wrath and the Pentland Firth, although the two depot ships, an accommodation ship and a tanker accompanying them had been permitted to continue to their original destination of Trondheim. The boats arrived in Scotland on the 19th.

Fifteen German destroyers and eleven modern torpedo boats were still afloat, but by no means all were in a seagoing condition. *Z15 Steinbrinck* and *Z33* lay at Cuxhaven, the former unrepaired after bomb damage in November 1944, and the latter paid off since April, having been damaged by grounding off the Norwegian coast in February, and later by air attack. *Z29* was at Bremerhaven, a refit begun in December being still incomplete. Larger vessels also at the latter port included the damaged and partly dismantled *T21* and *T156*. Nearby, in the Deschimag yard at Bremen, were the sunken hulks of the unfinished destroyer *Z44* and the torpedo boats *T7* and *T37*, the latter evacuated from Elbing. *Z4 Beitzen* and *Z30* were in a damaged condition at Oslo, having respectively been damaged by a near-miss on 24 April, and by a mine on 20 October 1944. Also at Oslo were the torpedo boats *T20* and *Panther*; all were placed under the control of the Norwegian navy on 15 July. At Trondheim lay the former yacht and submarine headquar-ters ship *Grille*, which was transferred to the UK along with the repair ships *Huascarian*, *Kamerun* and *Neumark*, and the supply ship *Kärnten*, on 16 July.

The remaining destroyers and torpedo boats had been involved in the evacuation of East Prussia, during which *Z34* had been torpedoed by a Soviet MTB, but remained afloat. They, and all but the three vessels laid up at Oslo, were grad-ually transferred to Wilhelmshaven, where they were reduced to care and maintenance regimes with reduced complements. Refits were then carried out where possible to make the ships fit for handing over to the victors – and also to keep the yard employed. *Z38*, *Z39*, *T28* and *T35* sailed to the UK on 6 July 1945.

A number of FPBs were in the Mediterranean area at the surrender. Several (*S30*, *S36*, *S61*, *S151*, *S152*, *S155* and *S156*) surrendered at Ancona, were towed to Malta in the late summer of 1945, and laid up off Valetta harbour. They were towed to sea two years later and sunk with explosive charges, one of which detonated prematurely while the boat was still in tow.

Surrender instructions for all submarines were broadcast on the 8 May, with immediate effect. On the 9th, ninety-three boats surrendered in Norwegian ports, as did one

1 D Waller, 'U-boats in Norway, post 08 May 1945 (Part 2)', *Warships* 179 (2015), pp 8–17.
2 D Waller, 'U-boats in Norway, post 08 May 1945 (Part 1)', *Warships* 178 (2015), pp 25–30.

(*U510*) at St Nazaire in France. Submarines still at sea were to surface, hoist a black flag, and burn navigation lights at night. They should then radio their positions and await directions to a surrender point, with all weapons made safe and ammunition dumped. The first such boat to surrender was *U1105*, to British aircraft at 0907 on the 9th.

British ports received twenty-one submarines, beginning with *U249* and *U1023* at Portland on the 10th (where *U776* would also surrender, on the 16th), two more surrendering at Gibraltar on the 12th, while other vessels did so in German ports. Amongst the more unusual surrenders, on 14 May *U2326* was given up at Dundee to the local base-ship *Cressy* – the 1824-vintage sailing frigate ex-*Unicorn*.[3] The majority of surrenders in British waters, however, were at Loch Eriboll, which received *U244*, *U255*, *U293*, *U516*, *U532*, *U764*, *U802*, *U825*, *U826*, *U956*, *U1009*, *U1010*, *U1058*, *U1105*, *U1109*, *U1231* and *U1305* between 10 and 17 May. The aforementioned Dundee-surrendered *U2326* was moved to Loch Eriboll on the 18th, while fifteen boats came from Norway (see below).

In more distant waters, *U889*, outbound to operate off New York, formally surrendered off Nova Scotia, after having been under Canadian escort since the 10th; *U190* had also surrendered to Canadian forces the previous day. Further south, *U805* and *U858* passed into US hands on the 14th, followed over the next five days by *U873*, *U1228* and *U234*.[4] Two boats tried to avoid Allied captivity by sailing for Argentina, *U530* and *U977* arriving at Mar del Plata on 10 July and 17 August; both were, however, handed over to the USA by the Argentine authorities (on 17 July and 6 September, respectively), and sailed for the USA in September (see p 219).[5]

A number of commanders ignored the terms of the German surrenders and scuttled their boats after the 5th. Thus, on the morning of the 8th, *U2538* was sunk off Ærø east of Flensburg, *U3030* was scuttled in Eckerförder Bay, *U3503* in the Kattegat west of Gothenburg, Sweden, and *U2365* nearby, northwest of Anholt island, Denmark.[6] In addition, four submarines returning from distant waters were also scuttled rather than surrendered, *U287* in the Elbe Estuary on 16 May, *U963* off Nazaré, Portugal, on the 20th,

Lisahally on 14 May 1945, with Type VIIC submarines in the foreground, with a British 'Captain' class frigate and further boats beyond. *(IWM A 28894)*

U979 off Amrum in the Frisian Islands on the 24th, and *U1277* northwest of Porto on 3 June. A number of commanders were subsequently tried and convicted of disobeying orders by sinking their vessels.[7]

It had been agreed that surrendered submarines, with the exception of those in American ports, would be laid up in British waters. Accordingly, during May, Operation 'Pledge' was implemented, with all seaworthy vessels to be concentrated at Loch Ryan in Scotland, or Lisahally, in Northern Ireland. Loch Eriboll acted only as a transit stop en route to Lisahally:[8] once boarding parties had been put on board, the boats within twenty-four hours to Loch Alsh for final disarmament and reduction to skeleton crews with British guards, before proceeding to the Northern Irish port. One partial exception was *U532*, which went from Loch Alsh to Liverpool, and then Barrow, to unload cargo that she had been carrying back from Japan. Once this had been done, however, she proceeded to Lisahally. A formal 'surrender' ceremony had been staged at the latter on 14 May. The boats involved were *U293*, *U802*, *U826*, *U1009*, *U1058*, *U1105*, *U1109* and *U1305*.

The last boats to be processed at Loch Eriboll were *U312*, *U716*, *U992* and *U1165*, which arrived at Lisahally on 23 May. Scapa Flow then took over Loch Eriboll's role from the 28th, particularly for vessels from Norwegian ports. Four boats (*U170*, *U874*, *U975* and *U1108*) from Oslo and eight from Stavanger (*U637*, *U901*, *U1171*, *U2322*, *U2324*, *U2329*, *U2345* and *U2348*) arrived there on 30 May, ten from Trondheim (*U483*, *U773*, *U775*, *U861*, *U953*, *U978*, *U994*, *U1019*, *U1064* and *U1203*) and thirteen from Bergen (*U245*, *U298*, *U328*, *U868*, *U928*, *U930*, *U1002*, *U1022*, *U1052*,

3 Renamed from 1942 to 1959, during the service of the maintenance carrier *Unicorn* (1941); she remains in existence as a museum ship.

4 On the surrender of German submarines in northeast American waters, see D Waller, 'USCG Cutter ARGO: The Surrender of U-boats in North East USA in May 1945 (part 1)', *Warships* 185 (2016), pp 7–21.

5 V Frampton, V Toyka, D Waller, H Visser, 'U-boats Surrendered in Argentina', *Warship International* LI/2 (2014), pp 120–2; D Waller, 'U-boats Surrendered in Argentina', *Warship International* LII/2 (2015), pp 126–7.

6 She was salvaged in 1956, and commissioned into the West German navy as *Hai*.

7 C Madsen, *The Royal Navy and German Naval Disarmament 1942–1947* (London: Routledge, 1998), pp 180–1; for a case of vessels being scuttled after surrender, see p 189, below.

8 For the activities carried out at Loch Eriboll, see D M Hird, *The Grey Wolves of Eriboll*, new edition (Dubeath: Whittles Publishing, 2018).

U1061, U1104, U1272 and *UD5*) the following day. The start of June saw the arrival of fourteen boats from Kristansand-South on the 1st (*U281, U299, U369, U712, U1163, U2321, U2325, U2335, U2337, U2350, U2353, U2354, U2361* and *U2356*; a further boat from here, *U2334*, arrived on the 5th, having broken down en route, and been repaired at Dundee), the 2nd one from Stavanger (*U3035*), and the 4th thirteen from Bergen (*U218, U539, U778, U875, U907, U991, U1004, U1005, U1057, U1271, U1301, U1307* and *U2328*). All boats were almost immediately forwarded to Lisahally or Loch Ryan to lay-up. Ten boats proceeded direct from Norway to Lisahally, one arriving on 6 June (*U2529*, from Kristiansand-South), four on the 7th (*U2513, U2518, U3017* and *U3041* [Oslo]), one on the 8th (*U3514* [Bergen]), two on the 9th (*U2502* and *U3515* [Oslo]) and two on the 21st (*U2506* and *U2511* [Bergen]).

This left twenty-five submarines at Wilhelmshaven, where vessels from Danish and other north German ports had been concentrated. These transferred directly to Lisahally or Loch Ryan during June, being joined there by the boats surrendered at Gibraltar and Portland, and by another (*U760*) towed from Spanish internment. This gave a total of 138 boats at Lisahally or Loch Ryan, although one, *UD5*, was soon returned to her original owners, the Dutch. This left just ten other boats afloat, but unseaworthy, elsewhere – seven in Norway (*U310, U315* and *U995* [Trondheim], *U324, U926* and *U1202* [Bergen] and *U4706* [Kristiansand-South]), two in Germany (*U1406* and *U1407*: see pp 189–190, below) and one in France. Fifteen Type VIIC boats were moved from Lisahally to Loch Ryan in September 1945 to relieve congestion.[9] On the other hand, four sailed in the opposite direction at the end of October, as part of a concentration of boats at Lisahally earmarked for the Soviet Union.

In addition to vessels surrendered to the Allies, on 5 May the Japanese seized six German submarines that happened to be in the Far East at the time of the capitulation. *U181* had been one of the 33. ('Monsun') SF, operating against shipping out of Penang and, although scheduled to return to Europe early in 1945, had had to return to Jakarta owing to defects when she had reached South African waters. She then went to Singapore for repairs and was still there in May. Her sister *U862* had also been on offensive operations, and put into Singapore on the German surrender.

The other four boats were all transport submarines. *U219* and *U195* had arrived at Jakarta in December 1944, with cargoes including V-2 missiles. In January 1945 *U195* acted as support vessel for the attempted return of other members

of the 33. SF to Europe, before returning to Jakarta. *UIT24* and *UIT25* (see p 162, above) were both at Kobe in Japan at the German surrender. Crews having been interned, the boats hoisted the Japanese flag, with numbers in the *I501–I506* sequence.

The intent was that *I501* (ex-*U181*) and *I502* (ex-*U862*) should initially be used as transport vessels to the Andaman Islands, before heading for Japan for changes to their torpedo tubes to allow the use of Japanese torpedoes. *I505* (ex-*U219*) and *I506* (ex-*U195*) were intended for long-term transport use. However, all six were still at their ports of seizure at the end of the Pacific War.

The German naval hierarchy was maintained for the first weeks of May, in parallel with the continued existence of the government headed by Dönitz. However, on 23 May, the president and his government were arrested, and the Wehrmacht High Command disestablished by order of General Eisenhower. Navy CinC Friedeburg committed suicide during his arrest, but the Navy High Command continued to exist, with Admiral Walter Warzecha at its head, until finally disestablished on 22 July, the management of German naval affairs being taken over by an Allied control council. The only activity remaining under significant German administration was minesweeping, the principal operational activity for the German navy. This was placed under a new German Minesweeping Authority [Deutschen Minenräumdienst] (GM/SA).

MINESWEEPING

The GM/SA was established on 21 July 1945, under the authority of the British naval CinC Germany, Admiral Harold Burrough, although also reporting to an International Mine Clearance Board in London. While the USSR undertook minesweeping in waters controlled by it with its own units (no German minesweepers had remained intact in waters under Soviet control), the UK lacked the resources to do so in its own area, especially with the redeployment of many of its own vessels to the Far East. Although seen by the British as a pragmatic move, the Soviets viewed the establishment of the GM/SA as a sinister means of delaying the full disbandment of German armed forces, and continually pushed for the GM/SA's dissolution.

The German Konteradmiral Fritz Krauss served as administrator,[10] based at Glücksburg. Personnel were vetted by the British, both to guarantee expertise in minesweeping, and to avoid the danger of creating a cadre capable of forming the core of a resurgent German navy. Initially,

---

9 On boats at Loch Ryan, see D Waller, 'U-boats in Loch Ryan – May to December 1945', *Warships* 190 (2018), pp 24–35.

10 For the GM/SA, see Madsen, *Disarmament*, pp 127–34, 143–5; D C Peifer, *The Three German Navies: Dissolution, Transition, and New Beginnings, 1945–1960* (Gainesville, FL: University Press of Florida), pp 67–73.

German naval uniforms were worn (less eagle and swastika), replaced by new dedicated uniforms in May 1946. Involving initially some 27,000 personnel and 840 vessels, it had six operational divisions: 1. Kiel; 2. Cuxhaven; 3. Denmark; 4. Norway; 5. Netherlands; 6. Bremen (see Appendix 5.1). Numbers of men and vessels had halved by late 1946, as the minefields were progressively made safe, a number of vessels also having been handed over to the USSR in October 1945 (see pp 188–189, below). By early 1947, the vessels involved comprised eighty-four M-boats, sixty-three R-boats, sixty-seven trawlers, six *Sperrbrecher* and 110 miscellaneous auxiliaries.

Meanwhile, in French waters, vessels of the former 4. M-boat Group (*M34*, *M38*, *M275*, *M277*, *M404*, *M408*, *M432*, *M452*, *M454*, *M475* and *M476*) formed, together with *M9*, *M12*, *M21*, *M24*, *M28*, *M85*, *M254*, *M424*, *M442* and *M495*, and twenty-two trawlers, a force with the vessels' officers replaced by Frenchmen, but with the rest of their German crews retained.[11] The latter had POW status – thus making their employment contrary to the Geneva Convention – and were kept in confinement when ashore. They were repatriated after the completion of this part of the work in February 1946.

As already noted, the Soviet Union was suspicious of the GM/SA as contrary to agreements over the demilitarization of Germany, and in spite of British-implemented cosmetic measures to make the force appear less like a continuation of the Kriegsmarine, opposition persisted, and in March 1947 it was announced that the GM/SA would be wound up by the end of the year. The 3. and 5. Divisions were disestablished in October 1947, and the other flotillas and the central staff in early 1948 (except for the 4. Division, which had already been disestablished in October 1946). The residual vessels were then handed over to the power to which they had been allocated by the Trinational Naval Commission back in 1945 (see p 188, below). During its existence, five minesweepers and five auxiliary ships had been lost by the GM/SA.

However, there were still mines in need of sweeping, and accordingly a small civilian-manned minesweeping unit was established under British auspices at Cuxhaven, as part of the local customs control unit (Minenräumverband des Zollgrenzschutzes Cuxhaven), funded by the German states of Hamburg and Lower Saxony. Under control of the British representatives of the Allied Control Commission (ACC), rather than the Royal Navy, it comprised twelve US-allocated R-boats (*R132–R138*, *R140*, *R142*, *R144*, *R146*, *R147*);

11 As of 15 October 1945, *M24*, *M28*, *M34*, *M38*, *M85*, *M254*, *M275*, *M277*, *M408*, *M432*, *M434*, *M442*, *M452* and *M454* were operational, with the rest in reserve.

M806, M323, M605, M612(?) and three unidentified sisters laid up in 1947, after the winding-up of the GM/SA. *M806*, *M612* and *M605* were broken up in the UK the following year, while *M323* was transferred to Norway, but broken up in 1950. *(AD collection)*

the support ship (ex-fisheries protection vessel) *Weser*; the *Sperrbrecher SPF212*; three naval trawlers (*KFK409*, *KFK531*, *KFK616*); and the tanker *Dievenow*. It operated from January 1948 until June 1951, when the R-boats were absorbed into the new US LSU(B), and the remaining ships into a new British Marinedienstgruppe (Naval Work Group, see p 238, below)

In addition to those serving in the GM/SA, other former German navy personnel were retained in care and maintenance roles for German warships held at Wilhelmshaven awaiting decisions on their fate. As usual, the British worked through a subordinate German hierarchy, but with an ongoing concern over leaving Germans in positions that could allow them to sabotage the vessels in their care, the spectre of Scapa Flow always hovering over the naval base – especially regarding ships destined for the Soviet Union. Accordingly, planning went forward for a three-stage operation ('Caesar'), to remove German crews to shore barracks, guard the ships in their berths, and then sail them to the countries of their new owners. In the event of resistance and/or attempts to scuttle, a show of force, with live ammunition used if necessary, would be used to secure vessels ('Caesar's Wife'). To keep the Germans in the dark, especially as to which ships would go to which nation, the British consistently refused Soviet requests to inspect 'their' ships before they were actually seized. Even after these ships were handed over to new owners , a rump of personnel was maintained to carry out technical tasks, including port clearance, demolitions and maintenance, from 1 May 1946 wearing the same new uniform as the GM/SA. These were dissolved during 1947, in August in the British Zone and in October in the US enclave, when many ships in the latter were handed over to the French.

Appendix 5.1
THE GERMAN MINE SWEEPING ADMINISTRATION (GM/SA) AS OF 1 OCTOBER 1945

1. Minenräumdivision (Kiel)

2. Minensuchflottille	*M371, M373, M374, M606, M607, M608, M609, M610, M611, M801*
12. Minensuchflottille	*M601, M602, M603, M604, M605, M612, M803, M812*
20. Minensuchflottille	12 trawlers
31. Minensuchflottille	*R25*, 1 naval trawler (KFK), 3 support vessels
Gruppe A:	8 naval trawlers (KFK)
Gruppe B:	8 naval trawlers (KFK)
Gruppe C:	8 naval trawlers (KFK), 1 support vessel
Gruppe D:	8 naval trawlers (KFK)
1. Räumflottille	*M566, R24, R43, R52, R67, R68, R76, R120, R127, R128, R150, R249*, 1 landing craft
8. Räumflottille	*R96, R98, R99, R100, R101, R117, R118, R130, R146, R147*, mine transport MT 2
1. Sperrbrecherflottille	*Minerva, Zeus, Martha, Templar, Strijpe*, 1 landing craft
KFK-Bewachungsverband	
1. Gruppe	7 naval trawlers (3 x KFK)
2. Gruppe	10 naval trawlers (KFK)
3. Gruppe	6 naval trawlers (KFK)
4. Gruppe	9 naval trawlers (8 x KFK)
5. Gruppe	13 naval trawlers (11 x KFK)
6. Gruppe	11 naval trawlers (10 x KFK)
7. Gruppe	9 naval trawlers (8 x KFK)
KFK-Sondergruppe	10 naval trawlers (9 x KFK)

2. Minenräumdivision (Cuxhaven)

Cuxhaven

7. Minensuchflottille	*M4, M23, M32, M33, M82, M102, M104, M131, M201, M256, TF7, TF8*
9. Räumflottille	*Alders* (ex *M526*), *R87, R103, R105, R107, R149, R414, R417, R412, R413, R415, R416, R419*
13. Räumflottille	*Nordsee, R22, R55, R71, R91, R102, R132, R133, R134, R135, R136, R137, R138, R140, R142, R144,* 2 support vessels
Netzräumverband	3 net-lighters
2. Sperrbrecherflottille	*Waltraud Horn, Cressida, Tantalus, Ophelia, Import, Prins Wilhelm IV*
2. Transportflottille	15 vessels

Wilhelmshaven

14. Minensuchflottille	
1. Gruppe	8 naval trawlers (7 x KFK)
2. Gruppe	8 naval trawlers (7 x KFK)
3. Gruppe	8 naval trawlers (7 x KFK)
4. Gruppe	8 naval trawlers (5 x KFK)
5. Gruppe	8 naval trawlers (4 x KFK)
6. Gruppe	5 naval trawlers (KFK)
7. Gruppe	7 naval trawlers (KFK)
16. Minensuchflottille	7 vessels

Bremerhaven

18. Minensuchflottille	
1. Gruppe	7 naval trawlers, 4 landing craft, 1 transport boat
2. Gruppe	1 landing craft, 12 naval trawlers (KFK)
Einsatzfahrzeuge:	*Eilenau, Kepler, TF15, TF17, RA102, RA110*, 5 air-sea rescue boats, 2 fishery protection vessels, 1 tug, 1 lighter, 1 lifeboat, 4 smokescreen vessels
Nebelträgergruppe:	18 smokescreen vessels

3. Minenräumdivision (Copenhagen)

HQ ship	*Reiher*
30. Minensuchflottille	
1. Gruppe:	6 naval trawlers (5 x KFK)
2. Gruppe:	5 naval trawlers (KFK)
3. Gruppe:	1 landing craft, 5 naval trawlers (KFK)
4. Gruppe:	1 tug, 1 landing craft, 5 naval trawlers (KFK)
40. Minensuchflottille	*M502, M509, M510, M517, M528, M545, M572, M581, M582, M588, M598,* 1 tug
25. Räumflottille	*R240, R241, R244, R245, R255,*
3. Sperrbrecherflottille	*Belgano, Tamo, Drau,* 1 trawler
Netzräumgruppe	2 netlayers, 4 net tenders, 1 trawler, 2 landing craft
Under Danish control	*R18, R26, R32, R143, R152, R153, R154, R155, R156, R157, R160, R167, R168, R173, R174, R175, R176, R181, R214, R225, R226, R229, R230, R231, R233, R236, R242, R259*

4. Minenräumdivision (Kristiansand)

Depot ship	*Adolf Lüderitz*
5. Minensuchflottille	*Aldebaran, M35, M81, M154, M202, M251, M252, M253, M295,*
9. Minensuchflottille	*M272, M306, M326, M364, M365*
22. Minensuchflottille	*M302, M321, M322, M361, M436*
4. Räumflottille	*Ente, R47, R48, R49, R83, R115, R121, R143, R168, R240, R244, R255, R268*
5. Räumflottille	*Elbe, R53, R58, R63, R90, R113, R122, R124, R238, R265, R260,* 3 naval trawlers (KFK)
7. Räumflottille	*Weser, R32, R152, R153, R154, R155, R156, R157, R160, R173*
16. Räumflottille	*Pollux, R253, R264, R266, R267, R401, R403, R404, R405, R406, R407, R408*
53. Vorposten-Flottille	2 pilot boats
1. Gruppe:	*RA201, RA202, RA203, RA204*
2. Gruppe:	5 whalers, 2 tenders, 10 auxiliary MMS
55. Vorposten-Flottille	1 tender
1. Gruppe:	9 naval trawlers (KFK)
2. Gruppe:	9 naval trawlers (KFK)
61. Vorposten-Flottille	1 tender, 3 naval trawlers (KFK), 8 whalers
65. Vorposten-Flottille	1 tender, 6 naval trawlers (KFK), 6 whalers
67. Vorposten-Flottille	2 whalers, 16 naval trawlers (KFK)
8. Landungsflottille	4 tenders, 8 landing craft, 3 naval trawlers
9. Landungsflottille	1 tender, 17 landing craft, 1 naval trawler (KFK)
KFK-Gruppe Oslo	6 naval trawlers (KFK)
KMA-Räumflottille Stavanger	8 naval trawlers (KFK)
KMA-Räumflottille Kristiansand-Süd	*R26,* 1 auxiliary minesweeper, 3 naval trawlers (KFK)

5. Minenräumdivision (IJmuiden, Borkum)

25. Minensuchflottille	*M278, M294, M328, M341, M375, M441, M453, M455, M460*
16. Räumflottille	*R264, R266, R267, R401, R403, R404, R405, R406, R407, R408, R424*
17. Räumflottille	*R31, R167, R170, R172, R174, R175, R176, R181, R246, R251, R252*
Dutch-manned	*R220, R240, R244, R246, R251, R252, R255, R268, R290, R424*

6. Minenräumdivision (Bremerhaven)

18. Minensuchflottille	
1. Gruppe:	13 trawler/whaler-type
2. Gruppe:	12 naval trawlers (KFK), 1 landing craft
Einsatzfahrzeuge:	2 *Sperrbrecher,* 2 escort boats, *RA102, RA110,* 14 support vessels

Endgame 1945 – Japan

THE LAST DAYS OF THE JAPANESE NAVY

The battles and other actions centring around the Philippines during the latter months of 1944 had resulted in the destruction, or crippling, of most of the Japanese navy's remaining big ships. Thus, as of the beginning of 1945, her battleship strength was down to *Yamato*, *Nagato* and *Haruna*. The remaining vessels were essentially divided between the waters around Malaya, Sumatra and Java, and home waters. Fuel was available in the former, although ammunition was scarce, but back in Japan, most vessels were immobilized by an ever-worsening oil-supply situation. Of these, only *Yamato* would see further action at sea – when she was sunk, along with the light cruiser *Yahagi* and four destroyers, during a suicidal attack on the US landings on Okinawa on 7 April.

Nagato had been immobilised in the area of Yokohama since 10 February through lack of fuel, initially as an anti-aircraft battery, and, although damaged by bombs and partially dismantled to aid camouflage, was still afloat at the Japanese surrender. However, *Haruna*, immobile in the Kure area, although surviving bomb attacks in June, sank in

Nagato, pictured here on 9 September 1945, had been reduced to an anti-aircraft battery at the beginning of the year, with the upper part of her funnel and mainmast cut away to clear sky arcs, and her secondary battery landed in two phases. Power was provided from ashore and a sub-chaser moored alongside. She was damaged by two 500lb bombs on 18 July, but remained afloat, the last Japanese battleship. *(AD collection)*

All the other Japanese battleships still afloat at the beginning of 1945 were sunk by bombing in late July: *Haruna*, shown here, on the 28th, following a number of hits and, in particular, near-misses. *(NHHC 80-G-490226)*

shallow water on 28 July. In addition, there were the hybrid battleship-carriers *Ise* and *Hyuga*, also stationary in home waters from February onwards, and also sunk by bombing, on 28 and 26 July, respectively.

The heavy cruiser force had by the beginning of 1945 been reduced to two operational vessels: *Haguro* and *Ashigara*, based on Singapore, plus *Tone* and *Aoba*, immobile in the Kure area from February. *Aoba*, with significant unrepaired damage from October 1944, was badly damaged by bombing on 24 April and finally sunk in shallow water on 24 July; the

wreck was further damaged on the 28th. *Tone*, which had been reduced to a stationary training ship, shared this fate. The other two vessels remained active, principally on transport duties, until sunk by British forces in Malay waters, *Haguro* by destroyers on 16 May, and *Ashigara* by HMS/M *Trenchant* on 7 June.

Still afloat was their sister *Myoko*, as was *Takao*; however, both had been laid up at Singapore as floating AA batteries following torpedo damage the previous year, in particular the loss of both ships' sterns. Unaware of the cruisers' true state and concerned at their possible use of their main batteries against any attempt to retake the base, the British launched a midget submarine attack on 31 July. *XE1* failed to reach *Myoko*, but *XE3* managed to cause underwater damage to *Takao*, though not enough to sink her.

Of the remaining light cruisers, *Isuzu* was still active, acting as a transport, when she was torpedoed and sunk by USS/M *Gabilan* and *Charr* on 7 April. *Oyodo* also acted as a transport, before becoming a stationary training ship at Kure on 1 March. As such, she was beached after bomb damage on the 19th, although soon refloated and patched up in dry dock. She was, however, further damaged by bombs on 24 July, and capsized after further hits on the 28th. Three further vessels, however, remained undamaged and afloat at the surrender: *Sakawa* at Maizuru; *Kashima*, which had remained active as an escort vessel, at Nanao; and *Kitakami* at Kure. There were also three old armoured cruisers, *Yakumo*, *Iwate* and *Izumo*, now used as training ships, and a

Takao at Singapore in 1945 after her surrender to the British. During the Battle of Leyte Gulf, on 23 October 1944, she had been hit by two torpedoes from USS/M *Darter*, which had blown off her stern (see p 199) and flooded three boiler rooms; she arrived at Singapore on 12 November. Since there was no possibility of getting her back to Japan for repairs, she was employed as a floating AA battery, with reduced crew and all 203mm ammunition landed; it was at this time that the ship was camouflaged. She was subsequently attacked by HMS/M *XE3* on 31 July 1945, which deposited a 1-ton mine and limpet mines below her, blowing a 7 x 3m hole in her bottom, flooding a number of compartments and unseating a number of turrets and rangefinders. *(AD collection)*

Wreck of *Oyodo*, sunk at Kure on 28 July 1945 by bombs, having already been badly damaged by others on the 24th. *(NHHC 80-G-490228)*

The minelayer (ex-armoured cruiser) *Tokiwa*, aground at Ominato, after being hit by one bomb, and near-missed by four others on 9 August 1945. *(AD collection)*

further example, *Tokiwa*, in use as a minelayer. While the last three were all aground or sunk in shallow water by the surrender, *Yakumo* remained operational to the end.

Ten aircraft carriers were afloat at the beginning of 1945, but of these, only *Amagi* and *Katsuragi* were commissioned fleet carriers, the construction of their sisters *Kasagi*, *Aso* and *Ikoma* all being suspended early in 1945 for want of materials. *Junyo* was under repair following torpedoing in December 1944, work which would never be completed. There were also the light carriers *Hosho* and *Ryuho*, plus the escort carrier *Kaiyo*. All were without air groups, and would never again leave home waters. The latter pair would be damaged or sunk in shallow water during the spring and summer air raids.

Around forty-five destroyers and torpedo boats were in service at the beginning of 1945, of which half were of the new lightweight 'emergency' *Matsu* and *Tachibana* classes, with more under construction. However, losses continued through the year, fuel shortages meaning that sea time was in any case limited. Escorts made use of what fuel oil was left, but sustained ongoing losses right up the surrender as they fought against the US submarine fleet.

Apart from old boats relegated to training in home waters, only a handful of submarines remained operational as 1945 began, the larger ones being fitted to carry midget suicide submarines (*Kaiten*), a few old vessels also being brought forward for this service. Other boats were being employed in transport roles, the *Ha101* class ordered by the navy specifically for this duty.[1] More fell victim to US anti-submarine activity as the year progressed, although on 29 July *I56* sank the US heavy cruiser *Indianapolis*, with heavy loss of life.

New boats being built included the vast *I400* class submarine aircraft carriers and the high-underwater-speed *I201* and *Ha201* classes, but none completed an operational voyage before the end of the war.

In terms of the broader Pacific conflict, the Allied advance towards the Japanese home islands had brought the latter within the range of land-based bombers based in the Marianas, with regular raids beginning in late 1944, and attacks by carrier-based aircraft beginning in February 1945, reducing most Japanese cities to rubble. In June, the emperor directed that a way out of the war be found, in the hope that the Soviet Union might be prepared to act as an intermediary – although the latter had, unknown of course to the Japanese, already committed themselves to fighting Japan within three months of the defeat of Germany. The occupation of Iwo Jima and Okinawa during the first half of 1945 was intended to presage the invasion of the home islands themselves in November, but before this could take place, the dropping of atomic bombs on Hiroshima on 6 August and Nagasaki on the 9th, combined with the Soviet declaration of war (and invasion of Japanese-dominated Manchuria) on the 8th, finally convinced the Japanese to surrender. An Imperial Rescript on 15 August accepted the Allied surrender terms, ending the Second World War.

A meeting was held in Manila on 19 August between Japanese officials and those of the prospective US occupation authorities, the first US personnel arriving in Japan on the 28th. General Douglas MacArthur arrived as Supreme Commander for the Allied Powers (SCAP) on the 30th, and the formal instrument of surrender was signed on board the battleship USS *Missouri* on 2 September (which also ended the new war with the USSR, which had not been covered by the 15 August surrender). The formal surrender of Japanese-occupied territory took some time, beginning in Penang on the 2nd itself (aboard HMS *Nelson* – the second time she had

---

[1] The Japanese army also built its own *Yu*-series transport boats, but little is now known about their service or fates: see M L Bailey, 'Imperial Japanese Army Transport Submarines: Details of the *YU-2* Class Transport Submarine *YU-3*', *Warship International* XXXV/1 (1998), pp 55–63; Y. Kunimoto, 'The Maruyu Submarines', *Warship International* XXXVI/3 (1999), pp 267–73.

The destroyer *Hatsuzakura* acted a pilot vessel for the arrival of the Allied fleet in Tokyo Bay on 27 August 1945: she is seen here rendezvousing with USS *Nicholas* (DD-449). *(NHHC 80-G-339801)*

Of the six *Unryu/Katsuragi* class aircraft carriers actually laid down, the *Unryu* was sunk by submarine torpedo in December 1944. *Amagi,* like many other of the Japanese big ships, was hit in the two big raids on Kure in late July 1945, rolling onto her port side on the 29th as a result of progressive flooding (top). The wreck is shown here in 1946, by the end of which work on salvage had begun, the ship being refloated for scrapping on 31 July 1947. However, her sister *Katsuragi* (bottom), although damaged by bombing at Kure on 24 and 28 July 1945, was still serviceable when shown here in October 1945. *(AD; NHHC 80-G-351362)*

Surrendered vessels at Kure around October 1945; they include the cruiser *Yakumo* (top right), destroyers *Hanatsuki*, *Natsutsuki*, *Harutsuki*, *Yoisuki*, *Kiri* and *Yukaze*, the submarines *I47*, *I36*, *I402*, *Ha203*, *Ha204*, *I203*, *Ha106*, *I58* and *I53*, and the transport *T22*. *(NHHC NH 94884)*

hosted a surrender [see p 159]), followed (inter alia) by Labuan on the 10th, Sarawak (aboard the corvette HMAS *Kapunda*) on the 11th, and 12th in Singapore; Taiwan was handed over to China on 25 October.

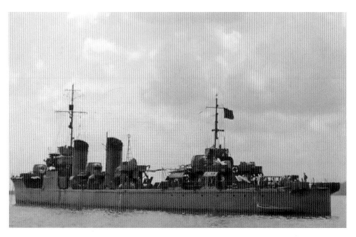

Based there since February 1945, *Kamikaze* was formally surrendered at Singapore to the British on 12 September. *(AD collection)*

SURRENDER

Most Japanese vessels surrendered at their bases, to which they had been directed following the announcement on the 15th. Others, ordered to hoist a black flag and black ball, surrendered at sea: for example, *I400*, en route to raid the US anchorage at Ulithi, received the order on the 26th and gave herself up to US destroyers the following day. Dates of ships being physically taken over by Allied personnel depended on location, those in home waters passing under US control in late August or early September, in some other locations later in the month. Most vessels in remote territories were small, although Singapore hosted the destroyer *Kamikaze*, the disabled cruisers *Myoko* and *Takao*, and the ex-German submarines *I501* and *I502*.[2] Another ex-German boat, *I505*, was in Indonesian waters, at Tanjong Priok, while yet another, *I506*, was at Surabaya. The latter would be used to provide local electric power after the destruction of the city's

[2] On the surrender of Japanese submarines, see D Waller, 'Japanese Submarines that Surrendered (Including ex U-Boats)', *Warships* 174 (2013), pp 21–6.

power station during the conflict between Indonesian nationalist and British occupation forces.

Ships generally retained at least some of their Japanese crews for the time being, although there were significant desertions at Yokosuka, Kure and Sasebo. SCAP Directive No 2 (3 September 1945) required that all vessels be demilitarised. However, some naval tasks could not be abandoned, in particular the sweeping of mines. This was carried out through to 1949 by a fleet that peaked at 328 vessels (some vessels were damaged or even sunk [e.g. the escort *Daito*]), under the control of the Second Demobilisation Ministry (from March 1946, Bureau), renamed from the Navy Ministry on 1 December 1945. This also directed a Repatriation Service, to return Japanese personnel from the far-flung areas still under Japanese occupation.

Such ad hoc voyages had begun soon after the surrender, but repatriation was put on a formal footing from 1 December, with a wide range of ships pressed into service. These ranged from the aircraft carriers *Hosho* and *Katsuragi*, whose hangars were fitted with bunks to provide extensive accommodation, through the cruisers *Kashima*, *Sakawa* and *Yakumo*, six destroyers, a minesweeper, fifty-six escorts and

Hosho on passage from Kure to the Marshall Islands, 13 October 1945 to pick up Japanese personnel for repatriation in conjunction with the cruiser *Kashima*; they arrived back in Japan on 2/3 November. *(NHHC 80-G-351904)*

the depot ship *Chogai*, as well as 188 Japanese merchantmen, supplemented by 100 US Liberty ships and Landing Ships (Tank), manned by Japanese crews. The cruiser *Kitakami* also acted as a repair ship for the repatriation fleet at Kagoshima.

All of these vessels had been stricken from the naval register in batches in September, October and November. On completion of repatriation duties in the summer of 1946,

Also surrendered at Singapore were the cruisers *Takao* (pp 177, 199) and *Myoko*, plus the ex-German submarines *I501* (ex-*U181*) and *I502* (ex-*U862*), the latter three vessels being shown here. *Myoko* had been laid up as an AA vessel since 25 December 1944, having been hit in her aft engine room by an aerial torpedo on 24 October and had her stern blown off by a submarine torpedo on 13 December. *(IWM A-30701)*

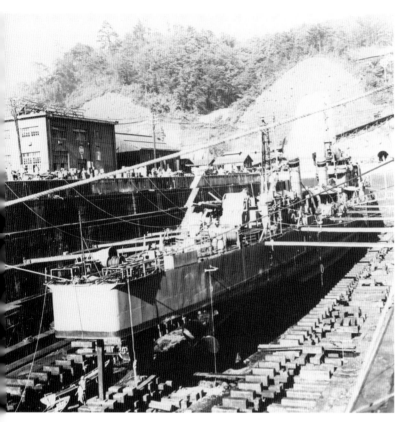

The destroyer *Odake* in dock at Maizuru undergoing modifications for repatriation duty, 13 October 1945. *(NHHC SC 216454)*

The installation of an additional deck into *Hosho*'s hangar to increase accommodation capacity. *(NHHC NHHC 80-G-351905)*

The cruiser *Sakawa* at Sasebo on 15 October 1945. *(US Navy)*

the ex-naval repatriation fleet was handed over to the Home Ministry for scrap, with the exception of a number of vessels judged fit for distribution to the USA, UK, USSR and China – and *Sakawa*, for which a more promethean fate was in store (see pp 198–199, below).

In addition, there were a handful of ex-Allied vessels that had been captured by the Japanese, served with their navy, and had survived the war. These included ex-US, ex-Portuguese and ex-Italian river gunboats (all soon gifted to China by their original owners), and larger patrol vessels (*Shōkaitei*), the biggest being the ex-destroyers *101* (ex-HMS *Thracian*, when surrendered *Renshu-Tei No. 1*), *102* (ex-USS

Stewart) and *106* (ex-HrMs *Banckert*). All of these were taken over by their original owners, except for *104* (ex-HrMs *Valk*) which was mined in late August.

Although nominally an independent state, Manchukuo (Manchuria) had been entirely under Japanese control. It had a small navy of light craft, including river gunboats on the River Amur. These were seized by the USSR on 24 September 1945, and served first in the Soviet navy into the mid-1950s.

7

Dividing the Spoils – 2

GERMANY

Planning for dealing with Germany after a victorious conclusion of the war had begun in the UK in the summer of 1942,[1] and a meeting of Allied foreign ministers in Moscow in November 1943 agreed to the setting up of a European Advisory Committee (EAC), to be based in London to work on potential armistice terms and other matters surrounding a German surrender. The UK played a leading role in this, producing memoranda in January 1944, covering the details of an armistice document, the disarmament of Germany and the country's division into three zones of occupation, with the UK taking the northwest, including the principal naval bases of Wilhelmshaven and Kiel – and thus the leading role in German naval disarmament. Although the EAC had agreed the basic surrender terms by the end of February, discussions dragged on over other issues. In this planning, it was anticipated that the German naval hierarchy would still exist as a conduit for the Allies' immediate post-surrender organisational and control purposes.

By the summer of 1944, the British intention was that major German warships should be transferred to Scapa Flow, a repetition of June 1919 being prevented by a drastic reduction of German crews on arrival, the confiscation of ships' boats, the emplacement of guns ashore covering the German anchorage – and possibly by grounding the biggest ships (e.g. *Tirpitz*) in shallow water by flooding a number of compartments. Submarines would be collected in Northern Irish ports.

As for the longer-term fate of the ex-German vessels,[2] the US view was that, with the exception of a few to be taken over for experimental purposes, all should be destroyed, initially preferring sinking in deep water. However, in view of the consequent loss of valuable scrap metal, the final US

recommendation in November 1944 envisaged scrapping in most cases. The British view was similar, neither nation having any use for surrendered tonnage in their own fleets. However, the British recognised that other powers, including the USSR, and nations such as France that had lost much of their navies during the war, would want a share, and accordingly did not endorse the US 'scrap the lot' approach, reserving the UK position for the time being, until other Allies' formal views emerged. That the USSR *would* want a share seemed likely, in view of their demands for a tithe of the Italian fleet directly after the Italian armistice (pp 160–61, above). Indeed, some British elements were initially fairly sanguine about the Soviet Union receiving all surviving German surface vessels, taking the view that the Western navies would be better off acquiring surplus British tonnage than difficult-to-maintain German ships (especially in view of the political and commercial advantages that would accrue to the UK as a result!).

The Soviet desiderata emerged in May 1945, Stalin stating his belief that the USSR could 'with all good reason and in all fairness count on a minimum of one third of Germany's navy and merchant marine', citing the precedent of the case of the Italian fleet, already admitted by the UK and USA. The original US position of total destruction had now been softened by the death of Roosevelt and the succession of President Truman, who was willing to be more flexible in pursuit of a settlement, and thus the partition of German warships and merchantmen was placed on the agenda of the three-power conference to be held at Potsdam, just outside Berlin, from 17 July to 2 August.

As almost all intact vessels were now in their hands, the British felt that they had some leverage in the upcoming negotiations, and while the ideal remained the destruction of all ex-German ships, they were agreeable to a distribution if necessary – but with an underlying aim of the destruction of most submarines. In pursuit of this, a July paper indicated that the UK would not object if the USSR were to be given *Nürnberg, Leipzig, Graf Zeppelin*, six destroyers, two FPBs,

---

[1] For much of the following, see Madsen, *Disarmament*; D C Peifer, *Three German Navies*.

[2] Madsen, *Disarmament*, pp 101–26.

ten submarines and fifty minesweepers, with *Prinz Eugen*, two more destroyers and two FPBs to be added after being used for British trials. The US position also preferred whole-sale destruction, with the fallback of an equal three-way division, of which the American share might be tradable with the USSR for assistance in the Far East against Japan. However, while both powers were willing to cede ships to the USSR, the British generosity was to be dependent on Soviet political concessions in other areas, in contrast to the Americans, whose quid pro quo concerned shorter-term operational assistance and was thus prospectively part of a 'softer' deal than that contemplated by the UK.

British trials

As the power in possession of all but a handful of the surviving tithe of ex-German warships, the UK took the opportunity to undertake trials with a number of vessels in advance of any formal allocations. These were perforce covert, as implicitly contrary to inter-Allied agreements – although condoned by the USA, who also wished to under-take such trials (see opposite). Thus, the destroyer *Z38*, the torpedo boat *T28*, the FPBs *S208*, *S212*, *S213* and *S221* and a number of smaller vessels had been brought to the UK in the summer of 1945, *Z38* leaving Wilhelmshaven on 6 July. A number of minesweepers were temporarily UK-manned for trials purposes, while the replenishment ships *Nordmark* and *Dithmarschen* were also taken over. Nevertheless, the UK was conscious that it was at this time 'acting as caretaker on behalf of the United Nations' and that 'the greatest care would have to be taken during trials that no damage was caused' to vessels evaluated.

A list of desiderata regarding the trialling and examination of German submarines had been drawn up back in October 1944: two Type XXI to commission; one Type XXIII to commission, one to cannibalise; one Type XIV to strip and examine; one Type IXD2 to strip and examine; one Type XB to commission, one to cannibalise; one Type IXC to commission, one to cannibalise; one Type IXD to strip and examine; one Type VIIC/42 to commission, one to canni-balise.[3] By the German surrender, however, the two surviving Type XBs were in distant waters (one about to fall into Japanese hands) and the Type XIV extinct, except for three incomplete hulks on the slipway at Kiel.[4] On the other hand, examples of all others were available amongst the mass of German boats laid up in British waters following the end of the war, while by March 1945 knowledge of the radical

Walter air-independent (high-test peroxide [HTP]-based) submarine propulsion system led to Types XVII and XXVI being added to the British desiderata (although no Type XXVI boats proved in the event ever to have been launched).

U1105, a Type VIIC, was of particular interest as having a rubber-coated ('Alberich') hull to reflect ASDIC pulses,[5] and was thus used for trials by the Royal Navy from July to October 1945, with *U1171*, a 'standard' sister, used as a comparator. Although not formally commissioned, both boats received the pennant numbers *N16* and *N19*, respec-tively, and were attached to the 3rd SF at Holy Loch for the duration of the initial trials with RAF Coastal Command aircraft off Tobermory and Londonderry. In October, they moved to the 5th SF at Gosport, although the trials were again carried out off Scotland, based at Rothesay on the Isle of Bute. *U1105* was transferred to the USA in December, with a view to similar trials (see p 219), while *U1171* returned to lay up at Lisahally on 3 February 1946. A further 'Alberich' boat, *U485*, had also fallen into Allied hands, but she and her covering were in poor condition, and no bid was made for her, even by the USSR, who had been excluded from the study of *U1105*.

Of the fast Type XXI and XXIII boats, *U2502* was selected for 'first of class' trials off the west coast of Scotland, being moved to Holy Loch on 6 July 1945. However, the boat proved to be riddled with defects, attempts being made to rectify them at Cammell Laird at Birkenhead, where she arrived on 22 July 1945. Unfortunately, the following day she suffered a machinery fire and was withdrawn from the proposed trials programme. *U3017* was then substituted, being given the pennant number *N41*, and taken to Barrow for docking – where she suffered a battery explosion on 29 August, injuring eight and causing significant damage, including fuel leaks and many other defects. *U3017* thus ignominiously returned to Lisahally on 21 October, all thoughts of trialling a Type XXI having been given up on the 14th. This decision was influenced by the fact that the US would be comprehensively trialling at least one of the two Type XXIs they were to receive, and that there was an informal agreement between the two nations to share expe-rience with trialling ex-German boats. As a result of this, the USA made no bid for Type XXIII boats, with a view to obtaining the research from the UK's work with such vessels.

U2326 had been selected by the UK as the Type XXIII trials vessel, arriving at Holy Loch on 6 July, where she joined the 3rd SF under the pennant number *N35*. However, the boat suffered from both engine and *Schnorchel* defects,

3 D Waller, 'The U-boats that Surrendered: U-boats in the Royal Navy Post-May 1945', *Warships* 168 (2012), pp 2–15; 169 (2012), pp 2–8; 170 (2012), pp 2–12.
4 All had been suspended on 23 September 1944.

5 For a full history of this boat, see A S Hamilton, *German Submarine U1105 'Black Panther': The Naval Archaeology of a U-boat* (Oxford: Osprey, 2019).

U1023 arriving at Plymouth, early in her tour of British west coast ports.
(AD collection)

with the result that she did not complete a dive until late July, and the trials between 27 and 31 August produced a disappointing speed. On completion of the trials at the beginning of October, *U2326* returned to Lisahally on 15 October. The Type VIIC *U249*, surrendered at Portland, was used in Weymouth Bay (wearing the pennant number *N86*) to evaluate her brand-new FuMB 35 'Athos' radar-warning equipment, not departing for Loch Ryan until 3 June.

As well as the vessels selected and manned for trials, the likewise-Portland-surrendered *U776* (*N65*) and *U1023* (*N83*) were taken on tours of British ports, reminiscent of those following the First World War, to raise funds for King George's Fund for Sailors. Both boats began at Weymouth, close to where they had surrendered, on 16 and 10 May respectively. From there, on 26 May, *U776* headed east,[6] with stops at London (ten days), Southampton, Dover, Chatham, Harwich, Great Yarmouth, Hull, Grimsby, Middlesbrough, Blyth, Newcastle, Sunderland, Edinburgh, Rosyth, Dundee, Aberdeen, Invergordon, Kirkwall and finally Lerwick, before sailing on to Loch Ryan on 21 August to lay up, arriving the next day, eighty-three days after leaving Portland. *U1023* went west for her eighty-one-day tour, visiting Plymouth, Brixham, Falmouth, Bristol, Cardiff, Swansea, Holyhead, Liverpool, Manchester, Fleetwood, Belfast, Rothesay, Glasgow, Greenock and Oban, before crossing back to Northern Ireland, via Loch Ryan, to lay up at Lisahally.

The USA was also keen to undertake early trials of German submarines, especially of Type XXIs, none of which had been among the boats surrendered in American waters. The US Submarine Mission to Europe (SubMisEu) arrived in the UK in May, and initially took control of one Type XXI

(*U2513*), one Type IXC (*U802*) and one Type VIIC (*U1305*).[7] The latter was soon relinquished and two more Type XXIs (*U2506* and *U3008*) taken over, with *U2513* and *U3008* selected for transfer across the Atlantic. Both required repairs to make them fit for the voyage, components being scavenged from other Type XXIs at Lisahally, the work resulting in a near-fatal fire on *U2511* while removing an item intended for *U2513*. In 'temporary' US custody, the two boats proceeded to the USA on 6 August, following inter-Allied agreement (see pp 189–191, below) that the UK, USA and USSR would get ten boats each for trials purposes. *U2506*, stripped for spares, and *U802* were at the same time returned to UK custody.

The Potsdam Agreement

From the outset, the Soviets insisted on the division of the German fleet, the initial British non-committal responses not being supported by the Americans. Thus, on 19 July a formal Soviet proposal envisaged the three-way split of all surviving German naval and merchant vessels, with an expert commission to manage the division. Without support from the US delegation, the British conceded the principle for surface vessels, but with the rider that all – ultimately 'a large proportion of' – submarines should be destroyed.

While the conference was in progress, the British delegation was changed by the Labour Party victory in the UK general election of that month. Nevertheless, it still tried to delay a final agreement on the fleet distribution in the hope that something substantive could be gained in exchange, with a further option of including the French in the share-out of surface vessels, and including shipping already seized by the USSR from Axis powers in any calculations. This was referred to a technical sub-committee, which came to be dominated by the Soviet CinC, Admiral Nikolai Kuznetsov. Thus, the idea of including France in the division was rejected by the Soviets, as was an informal French request that they might be granted sixteen incomplete submarines that currently lay in the Deschimag/AG Weser yard at Bremen.[8] For their own part, the Soviets demanded that they receive at least thirty submarines, with no firm agreed tripartite recommendations.

Thus, it was the foreign ministers' meeting on 1 August that produced the eventual agreement, which indeed excluded France from a share of surrendered naval tonnage, but restricted the submarine division to ten boats per nation, the British plea that any larger number would be unaccept-

---

6 With a crew including a significant number of those who had served in her sister, HMS/M *Graph* (ex-*U570*), captured in 1941 and disposed of in 1944.

7 D Waller, 'The Secret US Navy Submarine Mission in Europe in 1945', *Warships* 181 (2016), pp 9–22; 182 (2016), pp 5–18.

8 On the French aspirations for surrendered vessels, see D Waller, 'The French Connection (Part 1)', *Warships* 183 (2016), pp 6–19; 184 (2016), pp 4–16.

able to the UK public being accepted.[9] In addition, it was recorded that any claims from France, the Netherlands, Norway, Greece and Belgium would be fulfilled from the British share, and any from Poland by the USSR. This deal was endorsed by the heads of government within the overall 'Potsdam Agreement':

IV. Disposal Of The German Navy And Merchant Marine.

A. The following principles for the distribution of the German Navy were agreed:

(1) The total strength of the German surface navy, excluding ships sunk and those taken over from Allied Nations, but including ships under construction or repair, shall be divided equally among the U.S.S.R., U.K., and U.S.A.

(2) Ships under construction or repair mean those ships whose construction or repair may be completed within three to six months, according to the type of ship. Whether such ships under construction or repair shall be completed or repaired shall be determined by the technical commission appointed by the Three Powers and referred to below, subject to the principle that their completion or repair must be achieved within the time limits above provided, without any increase of skilled employment in the German shipyards and without permitting the reopening of any German ship building or connected industries. Completion date means the date when a ship is able to go out on its first trip, or, under peacetime standards, would refer to the customary date of delivery by shipyard to the Government.

(3) The larger part of the German submarine fleet shall be sunk. Not more than thirty submarines shall be preserved and divided equally between the U.S.S.R., U.K., and U.S.A. for experimental and technical purposes.

(4) All stocks of armament, ammunition and supplies of the German Navy appertaining to the vessels transferred pursuant to Articles (1) and (3) hereof shall be handed over to the respective powers receiving such ships.

(5) The Three Governments agree to constitute a tripartite naval commission comprising two representatives for each government, accompanied by the requisite staff, to submit agreed recommendations to the Three Governments for the allocation of specific German warships and to handle other detailed matters arising out of the agreement between the Three Governments regarding the German fleet. The Commission will hold its first meeting not later than 15th August, 1945, in Berlin, which shall be its headquarters. Each Delegation on the Commission will have the right on the basis of reciprocity to inspect German warships wherever they may be located.

(6) The Three Governments agreed that transfers, including those of ships under construction and repair, shall be completed as soon as possible, but not later than 15th February, 1946. The Commission will submit fortnightly reports, including proposals for the progressive allocation of the vessels when agreed by the Commission.

B. The following principles for the distribution of the German Merchant Marine were agreed:-

(1) The German Merchant Marine, surrendered to the Three Powers and wherever located, shall be divided equally among the U.S.S.R., the U.K., and the U.S.A. The actual transfers of the ships to the respective countries shall take place as soon as practicable after the end of the war against Japan. The United Kingdom and the United States will provide out of their shares of the surrendered German merchant ships appropriate amounts for other Allied States whose merchant marines have suffered heavy losses in the common cause against Germany, except that the Soviet Union shall provide out of its share for Poland.

(2) The allocation, manning, and operation of these ships during the Japanese War period shall fall under the cognizance and authority of the Combined Shipping Adjustment Board and the United Maritime Authority.

(3) While actual transfer of the ships shall be delayed until after the end of the war with Japan, a Tripartite Shipping Commission shall inventory and value all available ships and recommend a specific distribution in accordance with Article (1).

(4) German inland and coastal ships determined to be necessary to the maintenance of the basic German peace economy by the Allied Control Council of Germany shall not be included in the shipping pool thus divided among the Three Powers.

9 On the submarine issue, see D Waller, 'The Potsdam Conference and Agreement: The Kriegsmarine's U-boats', *Warships* 192 (2018), pp 7–18.

(5) The Three Governments agree to constitute a tripartite merchant marine commission comprising two representatives for each Government, accompanied by the requisite staff, to submit agreed recommendations to the Three Governments for the allocation of specific German merchant ships and to handle other detailed matters arising out of the agreement between the Three Governments regarding the German merchant ships. The Commission will hold its first meeting not later than September 1st, 1945, in Berlin, which shall be its headquarters. Each delegation on the Commission will have the right on the basis of reciprocity to inspect the German merchant ships wherever they may be located.

Nevertheless, the lesser Allied powers continued to press for an allocation of tonnage, in particular Norway, which had huge quantities of German war material on its territory, including a significant number of warships.[10] Thus, at the beginning of October, a request was made on behalf of the Norwegian navy for most of the vessels and infrastructure in Norwegian waters.

However, the Tripartite Naval Commission (TNC), which began its deliberations on 15 August,[11] was only concerned with dividing vessels between the three principal allies. The objectives of the British element included the allocation of *Prinz Eugen* for technical examination, sufficient minesweepers for ongoing North Sea and Baltic clearance work, the best destroyers and torpedo boats for onward transfer to France, and also the Walter-powered submarines *U1406* and *U1407*. There was also an imperative to maximise the number of ships classified as merchantmen.

The first job for the TNC was to draw up an authoritative list of extant vessels, with minesweepers given priority, given the urgent need to push forward clearance work. In doing so, it was agreed that vessels should be classified under three heads:

Category A (serviceable)
Category B (capable of being made serviceable within 3–6 months)
Category C (irreparable in under 6 months)

Only the first two categories were to be subject to division, all Category C vessels being due for destruction.

Work began on 24 August, inspection parties visiting all the significant locations containing German ships, across all zones of occupation and countries – including the UK and USA. One issue that had been outstanding for some time concerned Danzig, captured by Soviet forces at the end of March. On 30 March the USSR had announced the capture there of '10,000 prisoners and 84 aircraft, 140 tanks and self-propelled guns, 358 field guns, 566 mortars, 1,397 machine-guns, 15 armored trains, 45 submarines, 306 steam engines, 6,675 railroad cars, 151 ships of various displacement and 214 depots with armament, ammunition and foodstuffs'.[12] The figure of '45' submarines was immediately queried in the West, and clarification requested, but never given.

However, interviews carried out by the TNC when they were finally given access to Danzig (now becoming the Polish Gdansk) in August indicated that at time of the surrender of the city there were 'between nine and twelve submarines either still on the ways or having been so recently launched as to be incapable of movement under their own power' and that '[a]fter capture of the city by the Russians, those vessels still on the ways were completed sufficiently for launching and launched' and subsequently removed 'to unknown destinations'. After some pointed questioning at the TNC, the Soviets admitted that 'on the docks unfinished submarine hulks were found … not equipped with any machinery', and that '[t]hese submarine hulks were towed to bases in the Soviet Union', but that as there were 'no plans for completing their construction nor any machinery they [were] going to be scrapped for the metal'.

Following further probing by Western members of the TNC, the Soviet position was changed, arguing on 19 September that as the boats in question (now confirmed as three Type VIIC and seven Type XXI, now at Libau) had been captured prior to the German surrender, and thus were straightforward 'spoils of war', they were beyond TNC consideration (as with *U505*, captured at sea by the USA in June 1944). They also argued that they were so incomplete that without full plans and parts completion was impossible, the hulks being only suitable for scrap. Nevertheless, the Western Allies were still unsatisfied, highlighting on the 24th the difference between the 'eleven' boats now stated and the '45' of 30 March; the Soviet response was that the response on the 19th was 'complete' and that there was 'no further information'.

The TNC visited Libau, now in the process of becoming Liepāja, on 8 October, and was able to identify the three Type VIICs as *U1174*, *U1176* and *U1177*, all suspended since late 1943, when about four months from completion.[13] Six

---

10 TNA ADM 1/18449.
11 For minutes, see TNA ADM 116/5564.

12 See D Waller, 'The U-boats Captured by the Red Army in Danzig – March 1945, *Warships* 175 (2014), pp 4–25.
13 *U1173, U1175* and *U1178–U1190* had also been suspended at the same time, with the last eleven cancelled in July 1944; the fate of the rest is unclear, presumably scrapped or sunk before the Soviet occupation of Danzig.

Type XXIs were present: *U3535* and *U3536* (two months from completion); *U3537* and *U3540* (three months); *U3542* (five months); and *U3538* (damaged and flooded forward, but completable within six months). Two more (*U3539* and *U3541*) were found to have been transferred to Tallinn for docking, allegedly three months from completion. All were well advanced, and fitted with at least some machinery, contradicting earlier Soviet assurances as to their being only fit for scrap. However, the UK and USA decided not to push further, as the boats all appeared to fit into the 'unallocated submarine category', and thus due for sinking in deep water by 15 February 1946. On the other hand, a suggestion was made by the USA that the eleven boats be substituted for the equivalent boats previously allocated to the USSR from those in the UK; this was, unsurprisingly, rejected by the Soviets. In addition to these nearly complete boats, many prefabricated sections of Type XXI vessels (*U3543–U3554*) were removed to the Soviet Union during 1946, along with most of the shipyard infrastructure at Danzig.

Other post-inspection debates included such matters as the correct classification of *Leipzig*, which, although in poor condition and requiring more than six months' work, was felt by the Soviet representatives to be a 'pity to waste'. There were also questions regarding the boilers of the destroyer *Z14 Friedrich Ihn*, harbour service hulks, and trawlers requisitioned by Germany for use as minesweepers. However, issues were progressively closed down, with the agreement that ships would be divided into broadly equal lots and allocated by drawing out of a hat.

There remained, however, the question of 'exchange rates' for unique ships – especially with the much-coveted *Prinz Eugen*: was she worth four or six Type 1936A destroyers? In addition, the British attempted to delay the draw in hope of getting an agreement that they receive *Prinz Eugen* in any case – something opposed by both the Soviet and American representatives. Nevertheless, three lots were agreed for the surviving major ships:

X: *Prinz Eugen*; one Type 1936A; five other destroyers/torpedo boats.
Y: *Nürnberg*; four Type 1936A; six other destroyers/torpedo boats.
Z: Eight Type 1936A; five other destroyers/torpedo boats.

In addition to the division of these major vessels, work also proceeded on lesser vessels, which were also divided by category into broadly equivalent lots. A particular discussion involved minesweepers, of which the USSR wished to receive their share early, to allow their use before the annual Baltic freeze. Thus, the TNC agreed its allocation of

minesweepers on 9 October, with a decision two days later to withdraw vessels now earmarked for the Soviet Union in stages from the GM/SA, for concentration at Travemünde.

The submarines at Loch Ryan were also subject to categorisation, although this was somewhat academic as the decision had already been made to sink the vast majority. However, of the seventy-eight boats inspected, forty-two were placed in Category A, thirty-one in B and eight (*U155*, *U249*, *U739*, *U760*, *U1102*, *U1163*, *U2329* and *U2335*) in C. There were discussions whether the latter could be sunk immediately, rather than as part of the final disposals following allocation of boats to be kept, but this was vetoed by the Soviet representatives. They were, however, segregated and were subject to no further maintenance whatever.

It was not until 29 October that the British were prepared to go ahead on the basis of the 'luck of the draw', and later that day the draw took place. To the consternation of the British and Soviets, both keen to get *Prinz Eugen*, lot X fell to the Americans; lot Y went to the USSR and Z to the UK. This result was enshrined in the final report of the TNC, which was signed on 6 December 1945.[14]

Under this, all vessels under construction afloat and damaged vessels afloat counting as part of Category C were to be sunk at a depth of no less than 100m, or destroyed for scrap metal by 15 August 1946. Those still on the slip had to be destroyed or scrapped by 15 May 1946. Vessels sunk in harbours or approach channels and obstructing shipping could be refloated, but then destroyed or sunk by 15 May 1947. Where the sunken vessel was not causing an obstruction, she had to be mutilated to a degree that precluded the possibility of salvage for full or partial use for naval purposes by 15 May 1946 (although cannibalisation was permitted). Responsibility for doing so lay with the power in whose zone of occupation or territorial waters the vessel lay (except for the carrier *Graf Zeppelin*, in to-be-Polish Stettin, for which the USSR agreed responsibility), with reports made to the three powers by the 'due' dates. Unallocated submarines afloat had to be sunk in the open sea at a depth of at least 100m by 15 February 1946.

Implementation
Minesweepers
It was intended that the minesweepers allocated to the USSR (forty-four M-boats, forty-nine R-boats, four R-boat headquarters ships, ninety-one KFKs, twenty-two trawlers, four *Sperrbrecher*, and four depot ships)[15] should be delivered by German crews, with consequent concerns that such crews

14 Full copies are in TNA ADM 116/5575 and 5564.
15 TNA 228/22.

might be detained by the Soviet authorities on arrival. Leaving aside any such moral issues, the British were in the case of minesweepers unwilling to lose expertise and manpower needed for the GM/SA. Accordingly, explicit assurances were given by the senior Soviet admiral that crews would be returned promptly, although not prevented from genuinely volunteering to work for the Soviets. A further issue was that a number of vessels allocated to the USSR were in French hands, with the French unwilling to release them. In the event, some swaps took place, with the 'French' boats reallocated to the USA and boats from the latter's pool reallocated to the Soviet Union. In this, the Soviets declined to recognise any standing on the part of France, who had been denied a share at Potsdam.

The minesweeper transfers took place in two phases (as parts of operations 'Scram' [the main transfer of ships to Soviet ports, with forty separate groups of vessels] and 'Bitumen'), beginning with each group sailing to Travemünde for formal handover, followed by proceeding to Bornholm or Swinemünde under Soviet escort. The first group (comprising the 23rd M-boat flotilla and 25th R-boat flotilla) sailed on 24 October, the last one (comprising the 5th R-boat flotilla) on 25 November. Inspections of vessels on arrival often revealed missing fittings, but shortages of spares made this difficult to resolve.

Submarines

As noted above, the UK had been keen to acquire Walter boats, something shared by the USA – which was coupled with a desire to deny such vessels to their erstwhile ally, the Soviet Union.[16] Thus, as British forces entered the northwest of Germany, to become the British Occupation Zone, including Kiel and Wilhelmshaven, measures were taken to secure – and deny Soviet access to – the Walterwerke at Kiel, where Dr Hellmuth Walter was developing the system (it was captured by the special 'T-Force' on 5 May). In addition, there was an imperative to secure the handful of completed Walter-boats – the Type Wa201/Wk202 U792, U793, U794 and U795 and Type XVIIB U1406 and U1407, while minimising Soviet access to them, in spite of their rights under the Potsdam Agreement. Of the vessels in question, the Type Wa201/Wk202s were known to be in poor condition, leading to the British position that only the XVIIBs should be considered for distribution – and that they should be reserved for the UK and USA. The USSR, perhaps surprisingly, agreed to this allocation – perhaps because they

had already captured plans and a mock-up of the larger Type XXVI Walter-boat.

There was, however, the issue of actually locating U1406 and U1407, last heard of leaving Kiel on or about 5 May. They had actually left Rendsburg on the Kiel Canal on 1 May for Cuxhaven, arriving on 3 May. There, they formally surrendered on 5 May, the German orders forbidding any acts of scuttling or sabotage. However, once their crews had been interned ashore and the boats towed to lay up in Cuxhaven's Neuer Fischereihafen – and in spite of being moored alongside the two guardships for the Cuxhaven submarines – on the night of 6/7 May a German officer based on one of the guardships boarded U1406 and U1407 and scuttled them both by opening the main vents and valves, and leaving the conning tower hatches open. He was subsequently tried by a British military court and sentenced to seven years' imprisonment.[17]

Meanwhile, two incomplete sisters, U1408 and U1409, had been located in a bomb-damaged condition at Blohm & Voss's Hamburg yard. A 30 May report that U1405, U1406 and U1407 had been found scuttled at Rendsburg proved to be a false alarm: the wrecks in question were actually U792 and U793, plus a Type VIIC boat (U428 or U748). The two Wa201s were nevertheless salvaged and transported to Kiel for examination and possible refitting.

In June, Konteradmiral Eberhard Godt, former head of the German submarine arm, was tasked by the British with tracking down the 'missing' boats, reporting on the 24th that U1406 and U1407 lay sunk at Cuxhaven, although U1405 remained as yet unlocated (she had actually been scuttled at Eckernförde on 5 May). Work began to salvage U1406 and U1407 on 29 June and, although U1406 had had to be re-sunk after a fire, by the beginning of July they were both in Kiel, at the Howaldtswerke.

By August, all the Walter-boats had thus been located, when an American report noted that both U792 and U793 were 'internally blown', with the latter in the worse condition; U794 was 'satisfactory';[18] U795 had a '10 foot hole in Walter engine room'; U1405 was 'still sunk in Kiel Canal'; U1406 was 'satisfactory', albeit 'sunk, raised, burned, sunk, raised'; U1407 was 'good'; U1408 was 'no good', but suitable for cannibalisation, as was U1409, 'blown in two'.

It had already been agreed between the UK and USA that U1406 would go to the USA, and U1407 to the UK, and that the remaining boats be placed beyond any possibility of a

16 For the following, see D Waller, 'The U-Boats that Surrendered: U-1407 (HMS Meteorite) in the Royal Navy – 1945 to 1949', <https://uboat.net/articles/97.html>; D Waller, 'The U-boats that Surrendered: U-boats in the Royal Navy Post-May 1945 (Part Four)', *Warships* 171 (2012), pp 2–3; 181, pp 20–2; 182, pp 5–9.

17 Madsen, *Disarmament*, p 180.

18 Curiously, the report implies that U794 was not a Walter-boat, but had some kind of 'closed cycle oxygen plant'; however, it is quite clear that she was indeed a Walter-boat, with the same specification as U793; the actual closed-cycle boat was the Type XVIIK U798, whose construction had been abandoned in February 1945

U1406 lifted from the water at Bremerhaven on 11 August 1945, prior to her transport to the USA as deck cargo on US cargo vessel *Shoemaker*, leaving on 14 September and arriving at Portsmouth Navy Yard on 11 October. The tug *Thor* is on the left. *(NHHC SC 210745)*

late Soviet claim. This was achieved by declaring them, like *U1405*, 'scuttled in shallow water', and thus falling into Potsdam Category C, to be broken up, and thus not candidates for distribution (the fact that *U792*, *U793*, *U794* and *U795* had already been raised was kept from the Soviets). Of course, *U1406* and *U1407* had also been scuttled, and even if this were ignored, it was clear that their repair timescales would exceed the six months allowable for Category B vessels.

It had been planned that *U1406* and *U1407* might be reconditioned in German yards, *U1406* at Deschimag, Bremen, and *U1407* at Blohm & Voss, but this contradicted the policy agreed at Potsdam that no naval work would in future be carried out in German shipyards. Accordingly, it was directed that *U1407* and a set of machinery found at the Walterwerke should be transported to Vickers at Barrow for reconditioning, the boat being towed to Sheerness by the ex-German tug *Fohn II*, and then on to Barrow by a British tug; she arrived there in the first week of September 1945. *U1406* was taken to the USA as deck cargo on the SS *Shoemaker* in September.

As for the remaining Walter-boats, a 12 August request for disposal instructions from the British Naval CinC Berlin resulted in advice that parts from *U792*, *U793*, *U1408* and *U1409* should be sent to the UK; *U1405* was demolished *in situ*, along with other submarines scuttled in the location. The final fate of the Wa201/Wk202 hulls remains obscure, but they were presumably broken up at Kiel. Work on breaking up *U1408* and *U1409* commenced in late November 1945.

The formal allocation of submarines at the 13th meeting of the TNC on 10 October 1945, gave *U712*, *U953*, *U975*, *U1108*, *U1171*, *U1407*, *U2326*, *U2348*, *U2518 and U3017* to the UK.[19] The USA was to receive *U234*, *U873*, *U889* (in Canadian hands – see p 171 above), *U1023*, *U1105*, *U1406*, *U2351*, *U2356*, *U3041* and *U3515*, and the USSR *U1057*, *U1058*, *U1064*, *U1231*, *U1305*, *U2353*, *U2502*, *U2529*, *U3035* and *U3514*. However, the final version of 6 December made adjustments, substituting *U530*, *U858*, *U873*, *U977*, *U2513* and *U3008* for *U873*, *U1023*, *U2351*, *U2356*, *U3041* and *U3515* in the US allocation, and *U3041* and *U3515* for *U2502* (in poor condition and now partially cannibalised) and *U3514* (damaged in a collision: see below) in the USSR's group. The final change, in late January 1946, was to delete *U975* in favour of the Canadian-surrendered *U190* in the UK list (see pp 222–223, below). Eight of the UK's boats were already in UK waters, as was one for the USA, and all

of the Soviet ones. The rest of the US boats had either surrendered in US waters, in Argentina (two) and one in Canada. A further adjustment resulted from the UK ceding *U190* to Canada, and *U1105* to the USA.

The USSR initially wished for its allocation of submarines to be collected from the UK by Soviet crews. Various problems arose over this, for example over defects and missing items, but the British made it clear that they would have to sail 'as lying', with spares to be provided later from stocks in Germany. In the end, the boats thus sailed from Lough Foyle in the UK for Liepāja (formerly Libau) on 24 November 1945 under Operation 'Cabal', with Royal Navy crews, and one Soviet officer as an observer.

Five (*U1057*, *U1058*, *U1064*, *U1305* and *U1231*) were under their own power, escorted by HMS *Garth*, *Eglinton* and *Zetland*, four under tow (*U2353* [towed by HMS *Riou*], *U2529* [*Zephyr*], *U3035* [*Tremadoc Bay*] and *U3041* [*Narborough*]).[20] A tenth boat (*U3514*) suffered a collision with *U3017* while being prepared for the tow; as she proved irreparable within the available time and resources, the boat was accordingly swapped with the hitherto-unallocated *U3515*, which left in the tow of HMS *Icarus* on 6 December.

The 'five', plus *U2353* and *U2529*, arrived at Liepāja on 4 December, but *U3041* and *U3035* were delayed by steering defects, arriving on 10th and 14th, respectively. *U3515* was delayed by both defects and bad weather, with the boat under repair at Rosyth from 14 December to 23 January, sailing again on the 26th and finally arriving at Liepāja on 2 February 1946.

OPERATION 'DEADLIGHT'

Of the unallocated boats that were still afloat, all were to be 'sunk in the open sea in a depth of not less than one hundred metres by 15 February 1946', which was also the deadline for handing over the remaining allocated boats. The deadline for the sinkings appears to have been fixed without regard to the weather around Northern Ireland and the east coast of Scotland, where the unallocated boats lay and thus defined the area in which they would have to be sunk. Thus, Operation 'Deadlight', which was carried out by the Royal Navy between 25 November 1945 and 12 February 1946, was marred by a quarter of the boats foundering en route to their planned scuttling/target sinking locations, 130nm into the Atlantic (see Map 2, page 314).[21]

Boats were towed out of Loch Ryan, and then Lisahally, in twenty-two batches, those from Loch Ryan dubbed 'Flights' and the first seven out of Lisahally, 'Lifts'. The plan had been

19 On the following, see D Waller, 'The Potsdam Conference and Agreement: The Kriegsmarine's U-boats', *Warships* 192 (2018), pp 7–18.

20 D Waller, 'Operation Cabal', *Warships* 186 (2017), pp 4–24.

21 D Miller, 'Operation "Deadlight"', *Warship* XXI (1997–98), pp 115–32.

that while the majority of the 116 boats would be sunk by pre-installed demolition charges, forty-two boats from Loch Ryan would be dispatched as air targets, while others would be torpedoed by submarines. However, of Flight 1, in spite of moderate weather, one boat of the six (*U2328*) foundered on passage, and the demolition charges failed in all but one (*U2345*) of the remaining vessels, which had to be sunk by gunfire. All of Flight 2 also had to be disposed of by gunfire, but they had at least reached their sinking positions – unlike Flight 3, five-sixths of which sank, although the surviving *U328* was one of the designated air targets, being missed by an aerial torpedo before being sunk by bombs.

This general pattern repeated itself throughout the operation, in spite of additional precautions being taken over the seaworthiness of the submarines, most of which had been laid up with minimal maintenance for some months, although in some cases all boats got through if the weather held. Thus, of Flight 8's five boats, two were torpedoed by HMS/M *Tantivy*, two by de Havilland Mosquitoes firing rocket projectiles, and one by bombing by a mixed unit of Consolidated Liberators, Short Sunderlands and Vickers Warwicks. On the other hand, none of the sixteen boats of Flights 12/14 reached their designated sinking area, three foundering, and the rest having to be sunk prematurely by gunfire.

Thirty boats were taken out from Lisahally, Lift 1 starting badly with five boats sunk by gunfire after tows parted, and one returned to Northern Ireland to try again alongside the following day's Lift 2. This was also ill-fated, as one boat foundered and the rest had to be sunk prematurely by gunfire. A number of boats were due to be sunk by HMS/M *Templar*, but in the end only *U1109*, in Lift 5, survived long enough to fall victim to one of her torpedoes.

After Lift 7 took three boats to sea – one to founder and two to be sunk prematurely by gunfire – there was then a hiatus before the final pair of 'unallocated' boats left in UK waters were sunk. These were *U975* and *U3514*, originally allocated respectively to the UK and the USSR, but subsequently swapped-out. The former was sunk by a mixture of gunfire and the Squid anti-submarine mortar on 10 February, the latter in a test of the Shark 4in anti-submarine projectile by the frigate *Loch Arkaig* on the 12th, ending 'Deadlight'.

The same month, the USA disposed of two of the four 'unallocated' boats in her control: *U805* and *U1228*, which had surrendered in US waters, were sunk by USS/M *Sirago* off Cape Cod. The other two unallocated boats, *U1197* and *U1232*, had been in the US Zone at the end of the war, both in a poor condition, having been decommissioned at Wesermünde in April, where they had been taken over by

US troops. *U1197* was scuttled in the Skagerrak in mid-February 1946,[22] while *U1232* foundered in the Heligoland Bight at the beginning of March, while in tow en route to the same area for scuttling.

Also counted as 'unallocated' German submarines were the boats that had been seized by Japan after Germany's surrender, and had subsequently fallen into Allied hands at the end of the war in the Far East. These were thus subject to the 15 February deadline, and were accordingly sunk by the British just in time (see p 199, below). The TNC report also noted a number of German submarines that had been scuttled in waters now under Soviet occupation, including *U18* and *U24* at Constanţa in the Black Sea. It was directed that they be destroyed, but this did not happen until May 1947, when the salvaged hulks were sunk as torpedo targets.

LEFT-OVERS

In addition to boats that were subject to the above tripartite agreements were fourteen vessels in Norway (in commission at the time of surrender: *U310*, *U315*, *U324*, *U926*, *U995*, *U1202* and *U4706*; decommissioned/damaged: *U92*, *U228*, *U256*, *U437*, *U622*, *U985* and *U993*), and one in France (*U510*), that were afloat but in too poor a condition to sail to the UK. In addition, there were fourteen boats sunk in shallow water in French harbours, of which four (*U178*, *U188*, *U466* and *U967*) were actually mentioned as Category C vessels in the TNC final report.[23]

The latter 'requested' that such ex-German submarines should be scrapped or sunk by the TNC transfer/destruction deadline, but this was ignored by the French (with tacit British support) and the Norwegians. Thus, although *U92*, *U228*, *U256*, *U310*, *U315*, *U324*, *U437*, *U622*, *U926*, *U985*, *U993*, *U995*, *U1202* and *U4706* were broken up, the other four were eventually commissioned into the Norwegian navy (see p 233, below). Similarly, although *U178*, *U188*, *U466* and *U967* and other wrecks were eventually broken up by the French, as beyond repair, *U510* and the sunken *U123*, *U471* and *U766* (none of which had been reported to the TNC) were all repaired and commissioned into French service, joined by *U2326* and *U2518*, handed over in February 1946 from the UK's allocation (see below, p 224).

In addition, France had salvaged the destroyer *Z37*, burnt out in the dock in Bordeaux in August 1944 while awaiting repair to severe collision damage suffered in January, with a potential view to recommissioning. She had not been included in the list of Category C vessels (she was on the list

---

22 Waller, 'Fact or Fiction – Did U-1197 Surrender in 1945?', <https://uboat.net/articles/86.html>.
23 D Waller, 'The French Connection (Part 2)', *Warships* 184 (2016), pp 4–22.

Z25 in dock at Wilhelmshaven in December 1945. Two of the old ex-Imperial torpedo boats are in the next dock, and a third in the one beyond, including *T151* and *T153*, while one Type 1939 and two Type 1935/1936 modern torpedo boats are moored to the right, together with two minesweepers, and what may be the old *T107* or *T108*. *(AD collection)*

of war losses in Appendix 3 of the TNA report), and although aware of the matter, the British omitted it from the Cabinet paper on the TNC report 'as we have not been officially informed of it and it would only confuse the issue when the Three Powers request the French Government to destroy German craft left in their hands'.[24] France would also consider the repair of *Z23*, beached off La Pallice, also in August 1944 (see p 224, below).

Surface vessels
Distribution
During the autumn of 1945, work was ongoing at Wilhelmshaven, under British supervision, to repair and refit vessels to make them fit for their new owners when taken over in the New Year. An October report stated that *Z5*, *Z10*, *Z15* and *T196* needed a minimum of six weeks' work, *Blitz*, *T107* and *T153* eight weeks, *T158* ten, *Z6*, *Z20*, *T4*, *T11*, *T12*, *T17*, *T19*, *T23* and *T108* thirteen, and *Z31* and *Z33* twenty.[25]

Although Operation 'Caesar',[26] to take over the ships from their German crews in preparation for handover, had been planned for 9 January 1946, on 4 December 1945 it was cancelled over fears that it presented an opportunity for sabotage to take place over Christmas, with a replacement plan that ships would be taken over at an earlier date the moment that Soviet skeleton crews could be made available. The shadow cast by Scapa Flow in 1919 was indeed long. Thus, Operation 'Silver' was launched in the early hours of 16 December, the task having been made easier by sending *Prinz Eugen* to Bremerhaven for dry-docking two days earlier.

The operation was a complete success: all vessels at

Wilhelmshaven had their entire crews removed, and two days later 700 Soviet officers and men arrived in the German depot ship *Otto Wünsche* to take over their prizes. Once these personnel were aboard, German crews were allowed back, to actually steam their ships to their final destinations. *T12* and *T196* sailed to Kiel on 25 December 1945, en route to the Soviet Union, and on 2 January 1946, *Nürnberg* (flying the flag of Soviet Vice-Admiral Yuri Rall), *Hessen*, *Blitz*, *T33*, *T107* and *Otto Wünsche* sailed via the Kiel Canal to Liepāja under Operation 'Scram'.

Further vessels departed over the next few weeks. *T158*, *F7* and fourteen FPBs (*S24*, *S50*, *S65*, *S82*, *S110*, *S113*, *S132*, *S175*, *S209*, *S211*, *S219*, *S704* *S707* and *S708*), escorted by *S168* and *S196* (under British flag), sailed on 15 January; thirteen more FPBs (*S11*, *S81*, *S86*, *S99*, *S101*, *S109*, *S118*, *S123*, *S135*, *S204*, *S214*, *S222* and *S227*) departed on 24 January 1946, escorted by *S210* and *S705*. Deliveries to the USSR were completed with Operation 'Scram 40', in September 1946, although all major vessels had gone by 6 February. Likewise, departing Wilhelmshaven were ships allocated to the USA, which proceeded to the Bremen/ Bremerhaven enclave under Operation 'Scoot', as well as vessels destined for the UK itself. Ongoing problems were experienced with the Soviets as a result of errors in the

24 TNA ADM 116/5564, dated 30 January 1946.

25 ADM 116/5513, dated 9 October 1945.

26 Not to be confused with the German mission so-codenamed of 1944–45, in which *U864* was to deliver supplies of war material to Japan!

Nürnberg and *Hessen* in the Wilhelmshaven locks on 2 January 1946, at the beginning of their voyage to the Soviet Union. *(AD collection)*

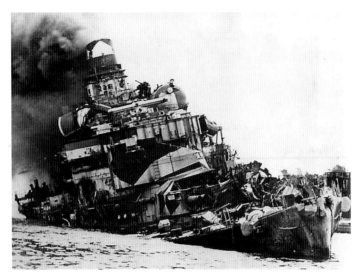

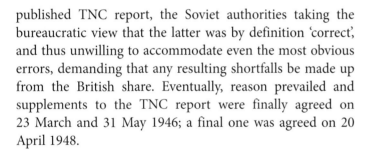

A sequence of views of *Hipper* being broken up in Heikendorfer Bay at Kiel between 1948 and 1952, in the upper view suffering from an accidental fire. Dumped in shallow water after removal from dry dock in June 1945 (see p 164-65, above), refloating was not permitted under the Potsdam Agreement, since she was not forming an obstruction to navigation. Rather, her hull (and that of the nearby *Emden*) was damaged beyond salvage by the detonation of depth charges in May 1946 (note the break aft of the turrets in the middle view), and finally scrapped *in situ*. (AD collection)

published TNC report, the Soviet authorities taking the bureaucratic view that the latter was by definition 'correct', and thus unwilling to accommodate even the most obvious errors, demanding that any resulting shortfalls be made up from the British share. Eventually, reason prevailed and supplements to the TNC report were finally agreed on 23 March and 31 May 1946; a final one was agreed on 20 April 1948.

Destruction

It had been agreed that unallocated submarines were to be sunk by 15 February 1946, and ships under construction and vessels sunk in shallow water destroyed by 15 May. In November 1945, an assessment was made of such vessels within UK jurisdiction:[27] this concluded that *Admiral Scheer* and *T15* were so badly damaged that no further demolition was required, but that *Emden, Admiral Hipper, Köln, Leipzig, T1, T111*, two unidentified torpedo boats, *M266, M504, M522, M802, M805, M809*, three unidentified minesweepers, *Sperrbrecher 25*, and ten torpedo recovery vessels required further demolition to meet TNC standards. As a minimum, engine rooms of larger units had to be wrecked, but smaller vessels could be wholly demolished by explosives. This was done with *T8* and *T9* on 10 December,

T111 and *M266* on the 14th, *M802* on the 15th, and *M805* on the 17th.

The UK made a start on detonating charges in engine rooms of various vessels at Kiel in January, *T1* being dealt with on the 8th, and *M504* and *M522* on the 9th. During the same month, the wrecks of the submarines *U350, U677, U747, U982, U1167, U1237, U1238, U2327, U2332, U2370, U2371, U2501, U2505, U2509, U3004, U3506* and two un-named boats (yard numbers 835 and 836) were destroyed at Hamburg, along with two unidentified Type VIICs and a Type XXIII. Salved and then destroyed were *U682, U1236, U2340, U2514* and *U2537*, while two unidentified floating Type VIICs were also destroyed. The scuttled wrecks of *U8, U14, U17, U60, U61, U62, U71, U137, U139, U140, U141, U142, U146, U148, U151, U152, U339, U382, U552, U554, U708, U777, U3006* and *U3504* were also destroyed, as was the sunken *U3532*.

Of vessels afloat, it was clear that facilities to scrap were insufficient to allow them to be reduced by 15 August 1946. Accordingly, the only option was to scuttle them in deep water. To find water of sufficient depth to fulfil their obligations when sinking vessels, the US identified an area just southwest of Kristiansand, and reported the sinking of *T190* on 17 March 1946 (sunk the previous day), *Z34* (sunk 26 March)[28] on 2 April, and the burning of *S22* and *S108* on the 10th.

---

27 TNA ADM 228/28.

The UK initially queried whether, to avoid long tows, it might be possible to gain tripartite dispensation to scuttle 'her' vessels in shallower water west of Heligoland, where the heavy seas would soon disperse the wrecks. However, in the end, an area in the Kattegat was chosen, the UK mounting a series of group scuttlings, the first convoy departing Kiel on 30 April 1946, including *S7*, *S9* and *S12*, led by the trawler *Cotillion*. The FPBs proved difficult to sink, *S9* being subject to gunfire and ramming by tugs, before finally sinking in two parts. On 7 May, the second scuttling convoy departed, including the unfinished hulls of *T38* and *T39*, the vessels being sunk on the 10th, *T39* requiring gunfire and additional charges before going down. The third convoy left Kiel on 16 May, its ships, including *M16* and *M522*, being sunk on the 18th. On the 28th, another convoy left Kiel, including the old cruiser *Berlin*[29] and a range of smaller vessels, including a pair of landing craft, one of which sank of her own volition on the 30th; *Berlin* was scuttled that evening, only one charge firing on the first attempt.

On 23 May, a British status report on vessels at Kiel noted that *T1* (lying in her side), *S201* and *M801*, had been blown up on 20 May, and on the following day depth charges had been detonated under the hulks of *Admiral Hipper* and *Emden*. This was judged enough to render them 'destroyed' by the deadline; the wrecks were broken up *in situ*[30] from 1948 onwards, the Eisen und Metall concern having quoted for their scrapping in April.

The US reported on 24 May that all vessels on slips or sunk in shallow waters in their Weser occupation area had been destroyed, and on 14 June that *Z29*, *T21* and *T156* had all been destroyed on the 10th. While one assumes that the intent had been to sink the last-named with the other two

(and *U1197*),[31] just off the Norwegian coast, hers may be the otherwise-unidentifiable wreck of an *S138* class vessel that has been located west of Denmark:[32] certainly, the wreck lies on the direct tow-route from Bremerhaven to the intended scuttling zone. The last Category C vessel afloat the Weser area, the unfinished *T37*, was scuttled at the end of July.

It had been agreed that Poland would have responsibility for the destruction of *Schleswig-Holstein*, *Schlesien*, *Gneisenau*, *Lützow*, *T5*, *T10*, *T41*, *T42*, *T43*, *T155*, and another torpedo boat on the stocks at Elbing (now Elbląg, Poland). Although also in Polish waters, the Soviet Union had taken responsibility for *Graf Zeppelin*, which she had refloated in April 1946. By the summer of 1946, however, in contrast to the regular US and UK progress reports on their destruction of Category C hulks, nothing had been received from the Soviet Union by any of the agreed deadlines. The only statement forthcoming was that 'in view of the great volume of work connected with the refloating and destruction of these ships [it] had been unable to complete the recommendations of the [TNC] by the specified date' and '[a]t the present time the Soviet naval authorities were taking steps towards implementation of these recommendations.'

In July 1946, a Polish newspaper published a report that an agreement had been reached by the Polish and Soviet governments to divide the wrecks at Gdynia between them: in particular, on the Soviet side, *Schleswig-Holstein* was to be

31 H L Arison III, *European Disposal Operations: The Sea Disposal of Chemical Weapons* (np: CreateSpace, 2013), pp 206, 362, lists a '*Bremse*' (the name given to *T156* in 1944) sunk at an unknown date at the location used for *Z29*, *T21* and *T190* (giving the wrong sinking date for the first two of these). Arison also separately lists *T156* as sunk on 3 May 1945 at an unknown location: here and elsewhere he displays problems with detail.

32 I McCartney, 'Scuttled in the Morning: The Discoveries and Surveys of HMS *Warrior* and HMS *Sparrowhawk*, the Battle of Jutland's Last Missing Shipwrecks', *International Journal of Nautical Archaeology* 47/2, pp 253-266 (2018) (doi: 10.1111/1095-9270.12302):.

28 Of this group, only *Z34* is charted at the time of writing, in the Skaggerak, UKHO No.33744.

29 While *Berlin* had been listed as sunk in shallow water, and thus placed in Category C, she was in fact still afloat at Kiel being used as an accommodation ship, and consideration was given to transferring her to the list of UK prizes. However, in the end she was left as Category C, and sunk.

30 The Potsdam Agreement did not allow any sunken Category C vessels to be refloated, even for scrapping, unless they were a hazard to navigation.

Leipzig shortly before scuttling charges were fired by British forces in December 1946. *(AD collection)*

At the end of the war, *T21* lay derelict at Bremerhaven; in June 1946, she was towed into the Skagerrak and sunk by gunfire from her US-controlled sister, *T19*; she is shown here just before sinking. *(NHHC SC 250112)*

repaired as a training ship, *Gneisenau* was to become a floating battery, and the recently refloated *Zähringen*[33] retained by the Poles. This was officially denied by the Polish naval authorities, who stated that all work on the wrecks was being done by the Soviets, to the firm exclusion of the Poles. However, the Poles' alleged desire to keep *Schleswig-Holstein* would have fitted well symbolically with the old battleship's role in firing the first shots of the war on 1 September 1939, her bombardment of Westerplatte heralding the Nazi invasion of Poland.

By January 1947, it was clear that neither the Poles nor the Soviets had carried out any destructions of Category C ships, nor 'unallocated' submarines (for the latter, see pp 187–188, above). *Schleswig-Holstein*, refloated by 29 August 1945 had been towed away, to Tallinn, on 22 May 1946, the incomplete ex-cruiser (to be carrier) *Seydlitz*, which had been scuttled at Königsberg in January 1945, had been photographed under tow in the Gulf of Finland on 10 October 1946, and *Lützow* was seen under salvage at Swinemünde in November. The issue was raised at the Council of Foreign Ministers (CFM) meeting in New York in December 1946, and followed up by an Anglo-American statement in the February report of the Allied Control Council. This noted that while the UK and US had, with one exception, disposed of all the Category C and 'unallocated' vessels under their control, 'no report has been made on the status of Category "C" ships and submarines' under Soviet control, and thus that 'it would appear that these craft have not been destroyed as agreed by the Tripartite Naval Commission.' An appendix recommended that the USSR be asked to explain itself, in particular querying:

- Why they did not destroy the vessels by the date specified?
- Why, if they were unable to fulfil their obligations, they did not report on the specified date that destruction had not been carried out?
- What progress in destruction has already been achieved, giving the names of all the ships disposed of and the dates of destruction?
- By what date the balance of the work will be completed?
- What truth is there in the rumour both completed submarines and sections of submarines in excess of the USSR allocation, have been and are being removed to the USSR?

The hulk of *Schleswig-Holstein* soon after her salvage. *(AD collection)*

At the next CFM, in Moscow, on 12 March 1946, the question was raised again by the UK, the Soviet response being that they were indeed making progress, and on the 27th issued a statement that 'the complete destruction of the ships of category C of the German Navy will be fully accomplished in August 1947', a decree to that effect having been issued by the USSR Council of Ministers on 10 March. A note stating that all ships involved had now been destroyed was sent to the western Allies on 1 October 1947, but no details were forthcoming as to their mode of disposal. It was not until the 1990s that the fates of the vessels began to emerge (see further pp 227–229 below).

DESTRUCTION OF CHEMICAL WEAPONS

A programme was drawn up during the summer of 1945 to dispose of the large stocks of German chemical munitions discovered by the Allies at the end of the war, with the intention that these munitions were to be loaded upon ships, which would then be sunk in deep water.[34] Each occupation zone had responsibility for the material within it, the UK sailing its first convoy of five ships, carrying 17,100 tons of material, on 30 September 1945: they were sunk 50nm NNW of Kristiansand on 4 October. By 6 June 1947, some 127,000 tons of munitions had been sunk by the UK in thirty-two vessels. The last to go down was the ex-Lufthansa mercantile catapult ship *Schwabenland*, the only ship of convoy CW 10.

As most appropriate for the disposal of bulk materials, the vast majority of the ships employed were former merchantmen. However, one warship, the incomplete *T63*, was used, being sunk on 21 December 1946 as part of convoy CW 8 – beyond the point at which such a Category C ship should have been destroyed. However, she and *Schwabenland* had been held back for potential use in chemical munitions disposal, and notified to TNC as such on 31 August 1946, with a note that all other 'UK' ships had now been destroyed.

---

33 Curiously, as late as the March 1946 supplement to the TNC report, *Zähringen*'s location was still listed as 'unknown' (as were *T110* [actually sunk 5 May 1945], *T123* [uncertain], *T157* [sunk 22 October 1943], *S112* [in French hands at Lorient], *S116* [in US hands at Bremerhaven], *S137* [sunk 29 July 1943], *S191* [sunk 7 May 1945], *S193* [sunk 22 February 1945], *S194* [uncertain], *S223* [sunk 8 April 1945], *S224* [sunk February 1945], *S341, S349, S354* [never completed], *S700* [non-existent] and various auxiliaries).

34 See Arison, *European Disposal Operations*.

While most published sources record that the sinking of *Leipzig* a few days earlier was also part of the programme, the surviving official documentation does not confirm this – and loading significant quantities of munitions into such a vessel would have been problematic (in contrast with *T63*, whose empty machinery spaces provided perfect stowage for such a cargo); in addition, *Leipzig* was sunk by scuttling charges, rather than by opening seacocks, as appears to have been the protocol with 'chemical munition' sinkings, to avoid any danger of disturbing their deadly cargoes or of dispersing them over a wide area. This is also true of various other warships that have been alleged in various publications to have been used in the programme, but which again do not feature in the official documentation of the chemical munitions disposal scheme.[35] Other chemical munitions were sunk by the UK in twenty-four merchant ships in the Atlantic between 2 July 1945 and September 1946, more following between 1949 and 1956.

The parallel US activity was Operation 'Davey Jones Locker', made up of nine convoys of a total of eleven ships. The only convoy with more than one vessel for scuttling was DJL 1 that, unlike the rest, was made up of ex-warships – or, rather, the unfinished hulks of intended warships. Thus, *Sperrbrecher KSB3*, submarine chaser *UJ305*, and torpedo boat *T65* were all sunk on 1/2 July 1946; *T63*, would be scuttled by the British in the same location five months later.

JAPAN
For Destruction

The Potsdam Declaration had determined that: 'The Japanese military forces shall be completely disarmed.' To implement this policy, the Supreme Commander for the Allied Powers (SCAP) issued on 21 September a 'US Initial Post-Surrender Policy for Japan', which stated that 'Japan's ground, air and naval forces shall be disarmed and disbanded', and the 'naval vessels shall be surrendered and shall be disposed of as required by [SCAP].'

As in Germany, it was agreed by the Allies that all submarines should be sunk[36] and, while destroyers and smaller vessels should be divided between the UK, USA, USSR and China, SCAP decreed on 2 April 1946 that all larger vessels should be destroyed, as should all wrecks in shallow waters. Of vessels condemned to destruction, the

T65 had been launched at Vlissingen in the Netherlands in July 1944, but in September the bare hull had been evacuated to Wesermünde, where she was found in May 1945. She is seen here (top) at Nordenham, just upriver from Bremerhaven, where she was loaded with 1,550 tonnes of chemical munitions; behind her is the likewise-unfinished Sperrbrecher *KSB3* (1944), which received 1,367 tonnes. Both formed part of convoy DJL 1, *KSB3* being sunk in the Skagerrak at 1555hrs on 1 July 1946 (bottom), *T65* at 2025 the same day; the third vessel of the convoy, the unfinished submarine chaser *UJ305*, was sunk at 1237 the next day, carrying 682 tonnes. The scuttling was overseen by *T19*, operating under the American flag. *(NHHC SC 250116; SC 250113)*

technically-interesting submarines *I14*, *I400* and *I401* had sailed under escort for Hawaii on 11 December 1945, arriving on 6 January 1946.[37] They were all subject to detailed examination, but initial plans to carry out extensive trials in US waters had already been dropped in November; rather, they were sunk as targets off Pearl Harbor in May/June. *I201* and *I203* had been trialled off Sasebo during 28 December 1945–8 January 1946, before sailing for

35 Cf. Arison, *European Disposal Operations*, p 206; P Lindström, *Vrak i Skagerrak: sammanfattning av kunskaperna kring miljöriskerna med läckande vrak i Skagerrak* (Uddevalla: Forum Skagerrak II, 2006), p 24, lists *Leipzig*, *Berlin*, *Z29*, *Z34*, *T21*, *T38*, *T156*, *T190*, *M16*, *M522*, *S7*, *S9* and *S12* as all carrying gas munitions without query, but no substantive references are given, only to Gröner's volumes. That wooden FPBs should be used seems highly unlikely, especially as all three were sunk by gunfire.

36 Waller, *Warships* 174, pp 22–6.

37 C C Wright, 'The U.S. Navy's Operation of the Former Imperial Japanese Navy Submarines *I-14*, *I-400* and *I-401* 1945 – 1946', *Warship International* XXXVII/4 (2000), pp 348–401.

I14 coming alongside *I400*, already moored outboard the submarine tender USS *Proteus*, in Sagami Bay on 29 August 1945. *(NHHC NH 50387)*

Hawaii on 13 January, arriving a month later. Like the other group of boats, they were examined, before being expended as targets in May. There had been thoughts that *I202* should be handed over to the UK for examination, but since this might have encouraged the USSR to request access to an *I201* class boat, she was scuttled in Japanese waters along with the rest of the surviving Japanese submarine fleet in April (see just below).

In addition, *Nagato* and *Sakawa* were also sent west. On 5 February 1946, the latter, withdrawn from repatriation duty, took on a US navy crew, and departed Yokosuka for Eniwetok on 18 March 1946. She was accompanied by *Nagato*, which had run trials in Tokyo Bay during the previous two weeks. On the 28th, both broke down 300nm from their destination, being taken in tow by tugs on the 30th. The cruiser arrived on 1 April, followed by the battle-

Sakawa at Bikini Atoll after Test Able on 1 July 1946; she had been moored 384 metres from the explosion and had most of her superstructure demolished; leaking badly, she sank the next day in spite of an attempt to tow her to a beach. Resting in some 60 metres of water, the wreck was further damaged in Test Baker, whose bomb was detonated underwater 150 metres away; the ship in the background is the battleship USS *Arkansas*, with her funnel demolished by the explosion. *(Office of the Historian, Operation Crossroads, pp 162–3)*

ship on the 4th. The pair were then sufficiently repaired to steam on to their final destination, Bikini Atoll, during May.

There, they became part of the fleet of unwanted vessels to be used as the targets for Operation 'Crossroads', a series of tests to explore the effect of nuclear explosions on ships. *Sakawa*, moored less than 400 metres from the explosion, was severely damaged during test 'Able' on 1 July, and foundered the next day. In contrast, *Nagato*, 1,500m from ground zero, suffered only superficial injuries during 'Able', but during 'Baker', on 24 July, the underwater explosion caused more damage. She was boarded and a boiler activated for thirty-six hours, but during the night of the 29th progressive flooding led to the battleship's capsize in 50 metres of water.

The direction to sink the submarines still afloat in Japanese waters was given on 26 March 1946, most of which had been concentrated at Sasebo during the last part of 1945. The four German-built vessels seized by Japan in May 1945 had by then already been sunk: regarded as still 'German', they were counted as 'unallocated' boats to be sunk by 15 February (cf. p 191, above). The UK was given the responsibility of sinking them,[38] *I505* (ex-*U219*) being sunk on the 3rd south of the Sunda Strait by the Dutch destroyer *Kortenaer*, *I501* (ex-*U181*) and *I502* (ex-*U862*) on the 15th (the last permissible day) in the Straits of Malacca by the British frigates *Loch Lomond* and *Loch Glendhu*, and *I506* (ex-*U195*, which had been used as a power station at Surabaya, and which local UK authorities had wished to retain for the time being) by the British cruiser *Sussex* in the Bali Sea, also on the 15th.

All remaining boats, whether completed, decommissioned or incomplete, were covered by the direction, with sinkings to take place in five main areas: Maizuru Bay; Kii Suido; Iyo Nada (the Inland Sea); off Sasebo Bay; and off the islands of Goto-retto, west of Nagasaki. First, on 1 April 1946, twenty-four boats (*I36, I47, I53, I58, I156, I157, I158, I159, I162, I366, I367, I402, Ro50, Ha103, Ha105, Ha106, Ha107, Ha108, Ha109, Ha111, Ha201, Ha202, Ha203* and *Ha208*) left Sasebo under their own power, and with skeleton Japanese crews arrived at the latter location ('Point Deep Six') as part of Operation 'Road's End'. There, they were sunk by demolition charges and/or by gunfire from submarine tender USS *Nereus* and the destroyer USS *Everett F Larson*.

Next, Operation 'Dead Duck' on 5 April 1946 towed *I202, Ha207, Ha210* and *Ha216* off Sasebo Bay, where they were

Takao's severed stern at Singapore. *(IWM)*

sunk by explosive charges. Ten days later, the ex-Italian *I503* and *I504*, captured respectively in the Mitsubishi and Kawasaki shipyards at Kobe, were sunk on 16 April at Kii Suido, between the islands of Honshu and Shikoku. At the end of the month, on the 30th, *I121, Ro68* and *Ro500* were scuttled off Maizuru. May saw the last sinkings of surrendered boats in home waters when, on the 9th, *I155, Ro62, Ro63* and *Ha205* were sunk by the Australian destroyer *Quiberon* and the Indian sloop *Sutlej* in the Inland Sea in Operation 'Bottom'. In addition, around sixty hulks and unfinished vessels were sunk and forty-two broken up.[39]

Also sunk at sea were the two heavy cruisers at Singapore. On 2 July 1946 *Myoko* was towed out, and on the 8th was

[39] Surviving data on these vessels is sometimes contradictory; even more sketchy is information on the fates of the army's thirty-four remaining transport submarines. Some were lost accidentally after the surrender, while the majority appear to have been scuttled by the US authorities off Hiroshima in the autumn of 1945 (see Kunimoto, *Warship International* XXXVI/3, p 271).

Oyodo being broken up in dry dock at Kure on 27 April 1948. *(NHHC NH 111636)*

[38] *Ro500* (ex-*U511*) was excluded, as having been sold to Japan back in 1943, as were *I503* (ex-*UIT24*, ex-*Commandante Capelli*) and *I504* (ex-*UIT25*, ex-*Luigi Torelli*), as ultimately of Italian origin. All were, however, covered by the decision to sink all Japanese submarines: the deadline was merely different.

The aircraft carriers *Kasagi* and *Ibuki* being broken up at Sasebo in early 1947. *Kasagi* was another ship of the *Unryu* class, and had been suspended when 84 per cent complete on 1 April 1945, while *Ibuki* has been laid down as a heavy cruiser, but converted to a carrier after launching; she was suspended when 80 per cent complete on 16 March 1945. *(NHHC NH 85887)*

Hyuga had been badly damaged in the 24 July 1945 raid on Kure (p 177); she had settled on the bottom on the 26th, and been abandoned on 1 September. The hulk was broken up from July 1946 to July 1947. *(NHHC 80-G-351364)*

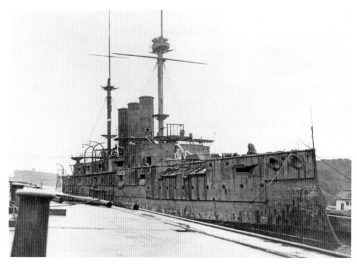

The battleship *Shikishima* had been dimilitarised in 1923 and subsequently used as a training ship; she is shown here on 28 April 1947, entering dock at Sasebo to be broken up. *(NHHC NH 111656)*

scuttled off Port Swettenham (Port Klang), close to where *I501* and *I502* already rested in water some 150m deep. They were joined nearby by *Takao* some three months later. She departed Singapore at 0730 on 19 October 1946, in tow of HM tugs *Gripper* annd *Assiduous*. At midday on the 27th the cruiser was scuttled, helped on her way by gunfire from the cruiser HMS *Newfoundland*.

The rest of the big ships, together with smaller vessels not judged fit to be included in the division between the victors, and various hulks, were all slated for scrapping. These were processed through a wide range of Japanese yards, joined by such vessels sunk in shallow water that could be refloated: of these, the last big ship to complete scrapping was *Tone*, in 1949. On the other hand, some were judged too difficult to raise, in particular the battleships *Haruna*, *Ise* and *Hyuga*, which were all broken up where they lay.

Drawing Lots

As had been the case with sharing the German fleet, decisions on the fate of the Japanese navy had been taken by the 'big three', the UK, USA and USSR, although in this case it had been agreed that China should also be a recipient of the division of ships. On 21 November 1945 Commander US 5th Fleet proposed that all vessels potentially fit for further service be divided into four near-equal lots and drawn for; this was agreed as the way ahead. An invitation was issued on 27 February 1947 for representatives to proceed to Tokyo to begin the draw, which would be carried out in phases, but with each nation receiving roughly the same number of each type of vessel at the end of the day. Vessels 'won' would be delivered by Japanese crews to nominated ports, accompanied by transports to repatriate Japanese personnel.

Powers such as the Netherlands and France, which had also suffered losses at the hands of the Japanese, were thus excluded, although, again as with the German division, the UK and USA made it known that they would meet such nations' claims from their shares. In practice, the Netherlands ultimately waived any claim in favour of something from Italy (see above p 203), as did France in November 1948. The British Dominions and Crown Colonies were also to claim from the UK share, but after a long trawl, only India showed firm interest in acquiring a fleet tug, New Zealand some transports and small craft, Hong Kong a crane ship, and Singapore a minelayer to serve as a reserve drillship.[40] Both the UK and the USA intended to scrap any vessels not taken by third parties.

In June, just as the first draw was to take place, Australia, with an eye to the provisions of the Italian Peace Treaty, protested to the USA over a division being made prior to a Japanese peace conference. However, UK legal opinion on 2 July was that the Japanese situation was analogous to the German one, with the complete dissolution of its armed forces, rather than the Italian example, where the fleet had remained under Italian control after their armistice.

By this time, the first draw had taken place, on 28 June, at the SCAP headquarters in the Dai-ichi Building, Tokyo. In this, China obtained the big destroyer *Yukikaze*, plus the smaller *Hatsuume* and *Kaede*, and the escorts *Kaibōkan Nos. 14, 67, 194* and *215*, and *Shisaka*. The USSR received the destroyers *Hibiki*, *Shii* and *Kaya*, together with the escorts *Kaibōkan Nos. 34, 105, 196* and *227*, and *Shimushu*, while the UK tithe was the destroyers *Kusunoki*, *Hagi* and *Take*, the escorts *Kaibōkan Nos. 8, 32* and *55*, and *Fukue* and *Habuto*. The US drew the destroyers *Kaki*, *Keyaki* and *Odake*, with the escorts *Kaibōkan Nos. 44, 106, 150* and *207*, and *Uku*.

The next draw, on 17 July, gave China the destroyers *Tsuta* and *Sugi*, and escorts *Kaibōkan Nos. 85, 118, 192, 198* and *205*, and *Tsushima*; the USSR the destroyers *Kiri* and *Hatsuzakura*, and the escorts *Kaibōkan Nos. 52, 78, 79, 142* and *221*, and *Ikuno*; the UK the destroyers *Sumire*, *Maki* and *Yukaze*, and the escorts *Kaibōkan Nos. 16, 27, 60* and *126*, and *Kanawa*; and the USA the destroyers *Kaba* and *Kashi*, and the escorts *Kaibōkan Nos. 36, 58, 87* and *158*, and *Hodaka* and *Etorofu*.

The third draw, on 15 August, completed the distribution of destroyers and escorts, and added 1st-class transports, the destroyers including for the first time the large anti-aircraft ships of the *Akizuki* class, one going to each country. China's destroyers were the old *Minekaze* and new *Yoizuki*, the escorts *Kaibōkan Nos. 40, 76, 81, 104* and *107*, and *Oki*,

Allocated to the UK, *Yukaze* leaves Sasebo for Singapore on 26 July 1947. *(AD collection)*

Tsushima and *Yashiro*, and the transport *16*; the USSR's final destroyer was *Harutsuki*, teamed with the escorts *Kaibōkan Nos. 48, 71, 77* and *102*, and *Kozu* and *Kiji*, and the transport *13*. The UK also received only one destroyer this time, *Natsusuki*, plus the escorts *Kaibōkan Nos. 29 154, 156, 160* and *217*, and *Amami* and *Kurahashi*, and the transport *19*; the USA drew the old destroyer *Harukaze* and the new *Hanazuki*, with the escorts *Habushi* and *Kaibōkan Nos. 12, 22, 26, 37* and *49*, and the transport *9*.

The fourth and final batch, drawn on 15 September 1947, included types not hitherto included in the range of vessels, from which China took the minelayer *Saishu* and the submarine chasers *9* and *49*, and the USSR the minelayer *Kamishima*, minesweeper *W-21* and the submarine chaser *38*. The UK received the torpedo boat *Hatsukari*, the minelayers *Kyosai* and *Wakataka*, the submarine chaser *21*, and the minesweeper *W-102* – a vessel that should have already been retroceded, as laid down for the UK at Hong Kong and completed by the Japanese. Finally, the USA received the minelayers *Ishizaki* and *Awashima*, the minesweeper *W-21* and the submarine chaser *47*. The batch also included a few auxiliaries, plus the destroyer *Kamikaze*, which had gone ashore while serving as a repatriation transport the previous year, and a total loss, fit only for scrap, by the time the draw took place.

All four nations had received an example of the most coveted vessels available, the *Akizuki*s, which were of sufficient interest for the USA to commission their *Hanazuki* for trials (see p 218, below). Otherwise, only China and the USSR had received examples of the big destroyers built by Japan from the 1930s onwards, ex-*Yukikaze* having a long career as the flagship of the Taiwanese fleet (see p 237, below). On the other hand, the USSR's ex-*Hibiki* only served for a year before being reduced to reserve.

The recipient nations' initial nominations for delivery were: Shanghai for China; Nakhodka, near Vladivostok, for the USSR; Singapore for the UK; the USA envisaged their vessels remaining in Japanese waters until scrapped or sunk. However, after the arrival of the first two batches in Singapore, it was decided that later 'British' vessels should in

40 See TNA ADM 116/5613 for this and much of the following.

most cases remain in Japan and be scrapped there. The key issue was that there was no meaningful ship-recycling industry in the Singapore area, and thus the harbour was becoming cluttered with Japanese hulks. There was also a concern expressed by the British Iron & Steel Board in August 1947 that breaking up in the Far East did nothing to resolve the acute shortage of scrap in the UK. Indeed, it was queried whether the vessels could be steamed or towed to the UK to break up there, or if they could be taken back to Japan, scrapped there, and the metal exported to the UK. In the end, vessels at Singapore were nevertheless broken up locally.

ITALY

A new Paris peace conference assembled in July 1946 to settle European affairs, and although nothing could as yet be agreed regarding Germany and Austria, treaties with Italy, Romania, Hungary, Bulgaria and Finland were drafted during sessions that ran through to October. All conforming to the same basic structure, with territorial, political, military and economic provisions, these were all signed on 10 February 1947.

The Italian treaty came into effect on 15 September.[41] Under its provisions, the Italian navy was permitted to retain only two battleships, four cruisers, four destroyers, thirteen torpedo boats, twenty corvettes, thirty-five minesweepers, eight vedette boats, and a range of auxiliaries. All permitted vessels were specifically named, except for 'one corvette to be salvaged, completed or constructed', and '16 YMS type [minesweepers] acquired from the United States of America'. Additional vessels could be kept for minesweeping duties until all work in this area was completed.

Excess vessels (again, all named) were to be 'placed at the disposal of the Governments of the Soviet Union, of the United Kingdom, of the United States of America, and of France', all to be 'fully equipped, in operational condition including a full outfit of armament stores, and complete with on-board spare parts and all necessary technical data', to be handed over 'within three months from the coming into force of the present Treaty, except that, in the case of naval vessels that cannot be refitted within three months, the time limit for the transfer may be extended by the Four Governments'. The treaty did not specify to whom individual ships would be allocated: this was the business of 'a Four Power Commission to be established under a separate protocol'.

Vessels not named in either group (including vessels under construction or non-operational) were to be scrapped or otherwise destroyed within nine months of the treaty's effective date, except for submarines afloat, which were to be 'sunk in the open sea in a depth of over 100 fathoms within three months'. Naval wrecks 'in Italian harbours and approach channels, in obstruction of normal shipping' were to be broken up within two years; those in shallow water, but not causing an obstruction, were to 'be rendered incapable of salvage' within a year. As far as the future was concerned, neither permitted battleship could be replaced, while aircraft carriers, submarines and MTBs were banned. Total tonnage (not counting the two retained battleships) was restricted to 67,500 tons and 25,000 officers and men, with no new vessels laid down before 1 January 1950.

The protocol setting up the Four Power Naval Commission (FPNC) also covered wider issues of the distribution of 'surplus' Italian vessels, and also the return of units loaned to the Soviet Union pending the allocation of Italian vessels.[42] Under it, the Italian government was held responsible for the security and maintenance of 'excess' units up to the time at which each transfer was completed, while, if an Allied nation decided not to take up a naval vessel from its allocation, Italy was obliged to scrap or sink that vessel within nine months of the effective date of the treaty.

Allocations, and arrangements for transfer, would be the responsibility of the FPNC to meet for the first time (in Paris) immediately after the signature of the treaty and protocol, and transfer to Rome once the treaty came into effect. Operating under the authority of the ambassadors of the USSR, UK, USA and France, it had the right to co-opt the representatives of Greece, Yugoslavia and Albania, where appropriate, and of Italy where necessary. The second part of the protocol dealt with the return of ships by the USSR, with the intent that they be co-ordinated with the handover of Italian vessels.

While the Soviet tithe of the Italian fleet had been fixed back in 1944, with the handover of UK and US ships in temporary lieu, there had been considerable discussion of what other nations should receive. For example, a UK Cabinet meeting in July 1945 recorded the country's then view that Greece should receive two light cruisers, with a damaged third example for cannibalisation, that France should not receive Italian ships, only German ones, and Yugoslavia 'only one or two torpedo boats'.[43] The two *Littorio*-class battleships should either both go to the UK, or be split with the USA – or potentially kept by the Italians, with the two *Duilio*s surrendered instead.

In the end, a rather different distribution was agreed, with

---

41 The full text of the naval clauses are given at Appendix 7.2.

42 For the full text of the protocol, see Appendix 7.3.
43 TNA ADM 116/5655, dated 12 July 1945.

France now taking a share. Thus, the two modern Italian battleships (which had returned to Italy from their Egyptian lay-up in February 1947) were granted to the UK and USA, the USSR having to be satisfied with the old *Cesare*. Also going to the USSR was the cruiser *Aosta*, her sister *Eugenio* being allocated to Greece; France was to receive *Attilio Regolo*, *Pompeo Magno*, *Scipione Africano* and the colonial sloop *Eritrea*. Of the Italian destroyer and torpedo boat fleet, the USSR was to get three of each, France four destroyers, and Yugoslavia three torpedo boats. The four principal powers were each to receive a pair of submarines, with the USSR getting ten MTBs, the UK and USA eight each, and France six; Yugoslavia would get five minesweepers, and the USSR and France three vedette boats each. A range of support vessels were also divided between the powers, ranging from landing craft, through the sail training ship *Cristoforo Columbo* (USSR), and the submarine salvage ship *Anteo* (UK), to tugs and water tankers. Numerically, the numbers of ships to be retained by Italy, and to be transferred to other powers, was as set out in the table at the bottom of the page.

The list of specific allocations remained 'Top Secret', and as a result the Italians, while aware of what ships they had to give up, had no idea as to where they were to go – and would not do so until long after the treaty was signed. A particular concern was whether attempts might be made to sabotage vessels allocated to a particular nation. The only 'leak' was by the Greeks, who made a public announcement that they were receiving *Eugenio* on 7 January 1947.

While the discussions were taking place, the Netherlands submitted a belated claim (in lieu of its claims against Japan: see p 201, above). Although this was turned down by the four-power Council of Ministers, the UK had sympathy for their position and, already aware that the USA had no interest in actually taking over *Italia* (see just below), there were musings as to whether the Dutch could be offered one of the *Littorios*.[44] However, this was soon dropped, both over the question of whether/how the Dutch could operate such a vessel, and the likely Soviet reaction, given their grudging agreement to take the old *Cesare*, rather than one of the two more modern battleships. On the other hand, there was no objection to letting the Netherlands have a tithe from anything not wanted by the UK or USA. Unfortunately, when the Dutch desiderata became known, little of what they wanted actually fell within the Anglo-American allocations. Although there was considerable discussion over handing over some vessels, and even making up the gaps from Anglo-American sources, in the end the Netherlands waived their claims on 2 March 1948.

The only real initial British interest was in *Vittorio Veneto*, and during the early months of 1947, discussions took place as to whether to actually take her, and if so to what purpose. Commissioning was not ruled out, especially as the cost of bringing her up to British standards was less than the potential outlay for modernising the 1920s-built battleships HMS *Nelson* and *Rodney*, which was still under consideration at

44 TNA ADM 116/5768.

ALLOCATION OF SHIPS OF THE ITALIAN NAVY, 1947

	Italy	USSR	UK	USA	France	Greece	Yugoslavia	Albania
Battleships	2	1	1	1	0	0	0	0
Cruisers	4	2	0	0	3	1	0	0
Sloops	0	0	0	0	1	0	0	0
Destroyers	4	3	0	0	4	0	0	0
Torpedo boats	16	3	0	0	0	0	3	0
Corvettes	20	0	0	0	0	0	0	0
Submarines	0	2	2	2	2	0	0	0
MTBs	0	11	8	8	6	0	0	0
Gunboats	0	0	0	0	0	0	0	1
Minesweepers	35	0	0	0	0	0	5	0
Vedettes	8	3	0	0	3	0	0	0
Landing craft	0	3	3	3	5	0	2	0
Tankers	2	1	0	1	2	0	0	0
Water carriers	12	4	2	2	4	1	1	0
Depot ships	1	0	1	0	0	0	0	0
Training ships	1	1	0	0	0	0	0	0
Aux minelayers	0	0	1	0	0	0	0	0
Transports	3	1	1	0	1	0	0	0
Tugs	50	12	11	8	12	0	4	0

this time.[45] Subsequently, the MTBs *MS72*, *MS73* and *MS74* were added to the list, for short-term use in trials, before being given to France.

From the moment of the signature of the treaty, Italy began a diplomatic offensive to undermine some of the naval terms (principally the competence of the FPNC) in general, and specific aspects of the surrender in particular, especially in the case of *Vittorio Veneto*.[46] However, unlike the case of some of the surrendered German vessels, whose high-pressure machinery was of technical interest, the Italian ships were of no particular interest to the UK or the USA, and both were prepared to waive their shares in exchange for the vessels in question being scrapped, or put to civilian use in the case of auxiliaries. There remained, however, some UK interest in using *Vittorio Veneto* as a target ship[47] (and then scrap), and three MTBs for trials purposes. On the other hand, France made it clear that she regarded her share as restitution for war losses, and would not be prepared to go without at least some actual ships during exchanges between the three powers in September 1947.

The USA made its announcement on 5 October, stating that it wished its allocation of vessels be scrapped and utilised 'as a contribution to the continued recovery of the Italian Economy'. However, at this point the list of which nation would receive what had not been made available to Italy, and while the British had now made a decision in principle to waive (for scrap) all but *Vittorio Veneto* and three of the MTBs, no announcement was yet forthcoming. One concern over giving up the battleship was that the Soviets might then raise the idea a swap of one of the now-to-be-scrapped *Littorio*s for their ancient *Cesare*.

Nevertheless, at the end of October, the British foreign secretary, Ernest Bevin, recommended to the prime minister that all but the three MTBs would be kept by the Italians and scrapped, with an equivalent to *Vittorio Veneto*'s scrap yield handed over to the UK. This was agreed with Italy on 31 October, the terms making it clear that all vessels involved were to be scrapped or sunk by 15 June 1948, and that Italy would not invoke the UK's decision in seeking any similar concession from France or Greece.[48] The agreement provided for the delivery of 20,000t of scrap steel, sold to the UK at cost price by 31 October (although deliveries did not

actually complete until January 1952). In May 1948 the take-over of the MTBs was also waived, meaning that the UK's entire allocation of Italian ships had now been renounced.

Negotiations also proceeded between France and Italy, with the latter proposing that, as would be also agreed with Greece, ships handed over should be regarded as restitution, rather than as war loot by treaty. These discussions also succeeded in reducing the number of vessels to be physically handed over, resulting in a protocol, dated 14 July, that left the cruiser *Pompeo*, the two submarines, the MTBs *MS54*, *MS55*, *MAS540*, *MAS545*, all the vedettes and landing craft, the oiler *Urano*, the water tanker *Sprugola*, and the tugs (except *Ercole* and *Nereo*) in Italy. In contrast to the UK and USA, the French did not insist that any of these waived vessels be broken up, giving Italy an excuse to keep them until a relaxation of treaty terms might allow the return of at least some to Italian service. Thus, the two submarines became 'battery charging vessels', and *Pompeo* was reclassified as a hulk, as was her salvaged unfinished sister *Guilio Germanico*, to await events.

Another negotiation concerned the disposal of submarines. Under Article 58 para 1(c), all boats other than those due to be surrendered were to be scuttled in deep water. In December 1947, Italy made representations that rather than sinking them by the 15th, as required, she should be permitted to scrap them instead.[49] Initial reactions were unenthusiastic, but the USA became supportive, in the face of which the UK followed suit, as did France. Only the Soviet Union remained opposed – and they nevertheless agreed on the 16th, subject to the concession being regarded by Italy neither as a revision of the treaty, nor as a precedent. Thus, the surplus Italian submarines were to be demolished by 15 April 1948 (although the Soviet Union originally pressed for a date a month earlier). The four UK/US-allocated boats, although excluded from sinking by the treaty, were also to be scrapped as part of the agreement for waiving their handover.

In spite of the clear timescales laid down by the treaty for the handover of vessels ceded to other nations, and for the destruction of surplus vessels, by the beginning of 1948 it was clear that Italy was dragging its heels badly over both. It was strongly suspected by the former Allies that Italy was hoping that France and/or the Soviet Union might be persuaded to renounce some or all of their prizes, and that some scrappings might also be waived. A note was thus sent at the end of January re-emphasising Italy's obligations, an annex specifying the minimum level of dismantling required in the case of the submarines by the 'due' date of 15 April.

45 Initial post-war British battleship plans were also to keep *Queen Elizabeth*, *Valiant* and *Renown*, along with the four surviving *King George V*s and *Vanguard*. However, all but the last five vessels were declared for disposal in early 1948, and even the modern ships rapidly passed into reserve, to be broken up a decade later.

46 TNA ADM 116/5768.

47 Although an aspiration to turn her into a radio-controlled target as a replacement for *Centurion* was unaffordable in resource terms.

48 TNA PREM 8/593.

49 TNA ADM 116/5768.

Pompeo Magno was originally allocated to France; her handover was waived, but she was nevertheless stricken in 1950. Reinstated the next year, she was rebuilt during 1951–55, with her original armament replaced by American twin 5in/38 mountings in A, X and Y positions and an anti-submarine mortar in B position. She also received twenty 40mm AA weapons, recommissioning as *San Giorgio* in 1956, shown here in 1961. She was further rebuilt as a cadet training ship during 1963–65, including re-engining with gas turbines and diesels and having her armament further modified (inset, in October 1969). Her sister *Guilio Germanico* (p 155), scuttled incomplete in September 1943, but salvaged in 1945, was rebuilt to the same design, entering service as *San Marco*, but was not further modified. (*A Nani; M Risolo*)

Vortice was allocated to France by the Italian peace treaty, and stricken in February 1948, but handover was waived and, after the nullification of the clauses banning submarines in December 1951, she was reinstated in November 1952, and recommissioned after an extensive refit, as shown here. (*AD collection*)

A further reminder was sent at the beginning of February, including the minimum standards applicable to surface vessels as well, a further note being sent on 7 February expressing four-power concerns at the tardiness of both scrapping and handover of ships.

Italy responded two days later, protesting that all the submarines had now been stripped and were in the process of being allocated to scrapyards. In September 1948 it was noted that while the minimum levels of destruction had been reached by 15 April, fittings such as guns and periscopes had gone into store, rather than having been destroyed as required.

Although *Italia* and *Vittorio Veneto* had been stricken on 1 June and 3 January 1948, respectively, a residual hope that they might be saved meant that only superficial dismantling, including AA batteries and funnels, was carried out at their berths at La Spezia during the early months of 1948. However, in June, with their 'scrapped or sunk' deadline imminent, the Soviets, who were hinting that they be allowed to swap one of the 'unwanted' modern battleships for their *Cesare*, pushed the Four Power Naval Commission to insist on the ships being at least fully demilitarised. A direction was thus issued requiring the immediate severing of the battleships' main guns, and the mutilation of their machinery by cutting steam pipes and wrecking reduction gearing. This having been carried out, the hulks remained at their berths until sold for scrap in 1951, breaking up being completed at La Spezia in 1954.

Although the destruction of *Italia* and *Vittorio Veneto* had been insisted upon on a four-power basis, the increasing

tensions between the Western powers and the USSR meant that the UK, USA and France looked increasingly favourably on nullifying many of the terms of the Treaty of Paris. This was done via an exchange of notes that resulted in an agreement that came into force on 21 December 1951. This released Italy from its political and military clauses, Articles 46–70 and their Annexes being withdrawn, the nullification of Article 59 meaning that aircraft carriers, submarines, MTBs and assault craft were again allowed, and the total tonnage limitation removed. Thus, the cruisers ex-*Pompeo* and ex-*Germanico*, the submarines ex-*Giada* and ex-*Vortice* were rebuilt and rejoined the fleet, and various FPBs re-shipped their torpedo tubes.

DELIVERING THE SPOILS

In preparation for handover, each ship received an alphanumeric designation. All those destined for the Soviet Union had a number prefixed by 'Z': *Cesare* was Z11; *Artigliere*, Z12; *Marea*, Z13; *Nichelo*, Z14; *Duca d'Aosta*, Z15; *Animoso*, Z16; *Fortunale*, Z17; *Colombo*, Z18; *Ardimentoso*, Z19; and *Rifiliere*, Z20. French vessels were designated by the initial letter of their name followed by a serial number: *Eritrea* was E1; *Oriani*, O3; *Regolo*, R4; and *Scipione*, S7. Yugoslav and Greek ships bore serial numbers prefixed by 'G' or 'Y': *Eugenio di Savoia* was G2; *Ariete*, Y8; *Aliseo*, Y9; and *Indomito*, Y10.

During the months that elapsed between the awards and the actual handing over of vessels, there was considerable anger in Italy at the prospect of cessions, in particular to the Soviet Union, which was refusing to confirm the fate of thousands of missing Italian prisoners of war. Accordingly, exceptional precautions were taken to avoid any sabotage attempts, including regular inspection of underwater hulls for explosive charges, given Italian wartime expertise in this area, displayed perhaps most famously in the crippling of the British battleships *Queen Elizabeth* and *Valiant* at Alexandria on 19 December 1941.

The delivery of the Soviet vessels began with the

destroyer *Artigliere*, which arrived at Odessa, with an Italian civilian crew, on 21 January 1949. Although the intent was that the majority of ships should similarly go direct from Italy to Odessa, the 1936 Montreux Convention Regarding the Regime of the Straits prohibited submarines and warships over 15,000 tons and/or 203mm guns from passing through the Dardanelles and Bosphorus Strait unless owned by a state possessing a Black Sea coast. Accordingly, *Cesare*, *Mare* and *Nicheio* were sailed to Valona (Vlorë) in Albania by Italian merchant crews, where they were formally handed over on 6 (*Cesare*) and 7 February and taken into Soviet service, before beginning their journey to the Black Sea. *Aosta*, *Colombo* and the torpedo boats arrived at Odessa on 28 February. All ammunition was sent separately in cargo ships, except for *Cesare*, which carried both her own ammunition and that for the two submarines. The USSR waived the delivery of the destroyer *Riboty*, the MTBs *MS53*, *MAS520* and *MAS521*, and the tugs *Lampedusa*, *Rapallo*, *N35*, *N37*, *N80* and *N94*, in view of their poor condition. In addition, *VAS246* was lost by fire at Venice on 21 August 1947.

Civilian crews were also employed for delivering ships to France at Toulon, beginning with *Eritrea* at the end of January 1948, followed by the two cruisers and four destroyers between June and August, *Scipione* and *Legionario* arriving on 15 August. Yugoslavia received her torpedo boats in April/May, but Greece did not receive her cruiser until July 1951, following the end of the Greek civil war, the ship being commissioned the following June. The gunboat allocated to Albania was never delivered.

FINLAND

The Finnish treaty contained minimal military clauses (Articles 13–21), the naval elements restricting the Finnish navy to 10,000 tons and 4,500 men, once regional minesweeping was complete. The country was also banned from possessing submarines and MTBs; as in Italy, the latter was achieved by removing the torpedo tubes from extant vessels, which thus became MGBs.

There was no requirement that any vessels be ceded, or any regulation of how surplus vessels should be dealt with. Indeed, the submarines *Vetehinen*, *Vesihiisi*, *Iku-Turso*, and *Saukko* were not sold for scrap until 1953, a residual hope that the submarine ban might be lifted meaning that *Vesikko* was kept until 1959, leading to her eventual preservation. However, the treaty did impose significant reparation payments, payable in commodities, including seagoing craft. Thus, the navy's biggest ship, the coast defence ship *Väinämöinen* was, at the suggestion of the Bank of Finland, offered in lieu of $1.98 million (265 million markka) of the $300 million reparation bill. She was accordingly commissioned as the Soviet *Vyborg* on 22 April 1947, and sailed to Kronstadt on 5 June 1947.

The treaty with Romania likewise contained minimal naval elements, which followed the pattern of the Finnish agreement, restricting the size of the force (Romania: 15,000 tons and 5,000 personnel; Bulgaria: 7,250 tons, 3,500 men), and banning submarines and MTBs. No cession of ships was included – not least because the USSR had already seized both navies back in 1944, although many ships had already been returned by the time of the treaties.

Appendix 7.1: SUMMARY OF TRIPARTITE NAVAL COMMISSION ALLOCATION OF EX-GERMAN NAVAL VESSELS

Category	USSR	UK	USA	Category	USSR	UK	USA
Cruisers	1	0	1	Minesweeper depot ships	16	9	9
Destroyers & torpedo boats	10	13	7	Tankers	7	1	3
Submarines	10	10	10	Aircraft crane ships	6	6	6
M-type minesweepers	44	44	44	Netlayers	3	4	3
Sperrbrechers	4	4	8	Catapult ships	1	2	1
Large torpedo recovery vessels & escort ships	6	5	6	Torpedo transporters & experimental ships	6	6	5
Anti-aircraft ships	3	2	3	Hydrographic vessels	1	4	2
R-type minesweepers	51	45	48	Miscellaneous vessels	7	9	5
Fast Patrol Boats	30	29	30	Despatch boats & launches	73	75	73
KFK-type naval trawlers	148	147	148	Training ships	2	0	2
Trawlers	42	36	40	Hulks	4	3	2
Landing craft	136	66	103	RA-type minesweepers	1	1	2
Naval seagoing tugs	37	18	26	**TOTALS**	**654**	**545**	**590**
Depot ships	5	6	3				**1,789**

Appendix 7.2: NAVAL CLAUSES OF ITALIAN PEACE TREATY

Section III-Limitation of the Italian Navy

ARTICLE 56

1. The present Italian Fleet shall be reduced to the units listed in Annex XIIA.

2. Additional units not listed in Annex XII and employed only for the specific purpose of minesweeping, may continue to be employed until the end of the mine clearance period as shall be determined by the International Central Board for Mine Clearance of European Waters.

3. Within two months from the end of the said period, such of these vessels as are on loan to the Italian Navy from other Powers shall be returned to those Powers, and all other additional units shall be disarmed and converted to civilian use.

ARTICLE 57

1. Italy shall effect the following disposal of the units of the Italian Navy specified in Annex XII B:

(a) The said units shall be placed at the disposal of the Governments of the Soviet Union, of the United Kingdom, of the United States of America, and of France;

(b) Naval vessels required to be transferred in compliance with sub-paragraph (a) above shall be fully equipped, in operational condition including a full outfit of armament stores, and complete with on-board spare parts and all necessary technical data;

(c) The transfer of the naval vessels mentioned above shall be effected within three months from the coming into force of the present Treaty, except that, in the case of naval vessels that cannot be refitted within three months, the time limit for the transfer may be extended by the Four Governments;

(d) Reserve allowance of spare parts and armament stores for the naval vessels mentioned above shall, as far as possible, be supplied with the vessels.

The balance of reserve spare parts and armament stores shall be supplied to an extent and at dates to be decided by the Four Governments, in any case within a maximum of one year from the coming into force of the present Treaty.

2. Details relating to the above transfers will be arranged by a Four Power Commission to be established under a separate protocol [Appendix 7.3].

3. In the event of loss or damage, from whatever cause, to any of the vessels in Annex XII B scheduled for transfer, and which cannot be made good by the agreed date for transfer of the vessel or vessels concerned, Italy under-takes to replace such vessel or vessels by equivalent tonnage from the list in Annex XII A, the actual vessel or vessels to be substituted being selected by the Ambassadors in Rome of the Soviet Union, of the United Kingdom, of the United States of America, and of France.

ARTICLE 58

1. Italy shall effect the following disposal of submarines and nonoperational naval vessels. The time limits specified below shall be taken as commencing with the coming into force of the present Treaty.

(a) Surface naval vessels afloat not listed in Annex XII, including naval vessels under construction afloat, shall be destroyed or scrapped for metal within nine months.

(b) Naval vessels under construction on slips shall be destroyed or scrapped for metal within nine months.

(c) Submarines afloat and not listed in Annex XII B shall be sunk in the open sea in a depth of over 100 fathoms within three months.

(d) Naval vessels sunk in Italian harbours and approach channels, in obstruction of normal shipping, shall, within two years, either be destroyed on the spot or salvaged and subsequently destroyed or scrapped for metal.

(e) Naval vessels sunk in shallow Italian waters not in obstruction of normal shipping shall within one year be rendered incapable of salvage.

(f) Naval vessels capable of reconversion which do not come within the definition of war material, and which are not listed in Annex XII, may be reconverted to civilian uses or are to be demolished within two years.

2. Italy undertakes, prior to the sinking or destruction of naval vessels and submarines as provided for in the preceding paragraph, to salvage such equipment and spare parts as may be useful in completing the on-board and reserve allowances of spare parts and equipment to be supplied, in accordance with Article 57, paragraph 1, for all ships specified in Annex XII B.

3. Under the supervision of the Ambassadors in Rome of the Soviet Union, of the United Kingdom, of the United States of America, and of France, Italy may also salvage such equipment and spare parts of a non-warlike character as are readily adaptable for use in Italian civil economy.

ARTICLE 59

1. No battleship shall be constructed, acquired or replaced by Italy.

2. No aircraft carrier, submarine or other submersible craft, motor torpedo boat or specialised types of assault craft shall be constructed, acquired, employed or experimented with by Italy.

3. The total standard displacement of the war vessels, other than battle-ships, of the Italian Navy, including vessels under construction after the date of launching, shall not exceed 67,500 tons.

4. Any replacement of war vessels by Italy shall be effected within the limit of tonnage given in paragraph 3. There shall be no restriction on the replacement of auxiliary vessels.

5. Italy undertakes not to acquire or lay down any war vessels before January 1, 1950, except as necessary to replace any vessel, other than a

battleship, accidentally lost, in which case the displacement of the new vessel is not to exceed by more than ten per cent the displacement of the vessel lost.

ARTICLE 60

1. The total personnel of the Italian Navy, excluding any naval air personnel, shall not exceed 25,000 officers and men.

ANNEX XII
(See Article 56)

The names in this Annex are those which were used in the Italian Navy on June 1, 1946.

A. LIST OF NAVAL VESSELS TO BE RETAINED BY ITALY
MAJOR WAR VESSELS

Battleships	Andrea Doria	*Torpedo Boats*	Rosalino Pilo
	Caio Duilio		Sagittario
Cruisers	Luigi di Savoia Duca		Sirio
	degli Abruzzi	*Corvettes*	Ape
	Giuseppe Garibaldi		Baionetta
	Raimondo Montecuccoli		Chimera
	Luigi Cadorna		Cormorano
Destroyers	Carabiniere		Danaide
	Granatiere		Driade
	Grecale		Fenice
	Nicoloso da Recco		Flora
Torpedo Boats	Giuseppe Cesare Abba		Folaga
	Aretusa		Gabbiano
	Calliope		Gru
	Giacinto Carini		Ibis
	Cassiopea		Minerva
	Clio		Pellicano
	Nicola Fabrizi		Pomona
	Ernesto Giovannini		Scimittara
	Libra		Sfinge
	Monzambano		Sibilia
	Antonio Mosto		Urania
	Orione		
	Orsa		

Together with one corvette to be salvaged, completed or constructed.

MINOR WAR VESSELS

Minesweepers R. D. Nos. 20, 32, 34, 38, 40, 41, 102, 103, 104, 105, 113, 114, 129, 131, 132, 133, 134, 148, 149, together with 16 YMS type acquired from the United States of America.

Vedettes VAS Nos. 201, 204, 211, 218, 222, 224, 233, 235

AUXILIARY NAVAL VESSELS

Fleet Tankers	Nettuno	*Tugs (large)*	San Pietro
	Lete		San Vito
Water Carriers	Arno		Ventimiglia
	Frigido	*Tugs (small)*	Argentario
	Mincio		Astico
	Ofanto		Cordevole
	Oristano		Generale Pozzi
	Pescara		Irene
	P0		Passero
	Sesia		Porto Rosso
	Simeto		Porto Vecchio
	Stura		San Bartolomeo
	Tronto		San Benedetto
	Vipacco		Tagliamento

Tugs (large)	Abbazia	N 1
	Asinara	N 4
	Atlante	N 5
	Capraia	N 9
	Chioggia	N 22
	Emilio	N 26
	Gagliardo	N 27
	Gorgona	N 32
	Licosa	N 47
	Lilibeo	N 52
	Linosa	N 53
	Mestre	N 78
	Piombino	N 96
	Porto Empedocle	N 104
	Porto Fossone	RLN 1
	Porto Pisano	RLN 3
	Porto Rose	RLN 9
	Porto Recanati	RLN 10

Training Ship	Amerigo Vespucci
Transports	Amalia Messina
	Montegrappa
	Tarantola
Supply Ship	Giuseppe Miraglia
Repair Ship	Antonio Pacinotti (after conversion from S/M Depot Ship)
Surveying Ships	Azio (after conversion from minelayer)
	Cherso
Lighthouse-Service Vessel	Buffoluto
Cable Ship	Rampino

B. LIST OF NAVAL VESSELS TO BE PLACED AT THE DISPOSAL OF THE GOVERNMENTS OF THE SOVIET UNION, OF THE UNITED KINGDOM, OF THE UNITED STATES OF AMERICA, AND OF FRANCE

MAJOR WAR VESSELS

Battleships	Giulio Cesare	*Torpedo Boats*	Aliseo
	Italia		Animoso
	Vittorio Veneto		Ardimentoso
Cruisers	Emanuele Filiberto		Ariete
	Duca d'Aosta		Fortunale
	Pompeo Magno		Indomito
	Attilio Regolo	*Submarines*	Alagi
	Eugenio di Savoia		Atropo
	Scipione Africano		Dandolo
Sloop	Eritrea		Giada
Destroyers	Artigliere		Marea
	Fuciliere		Nichelio
	Legionario		Platino
	Mitragliere		Vortice
	Alfredo Oriani		
	Augusto Riboty		
	Velite		

MINOR WAR VESSELS

M.T.Bs	MS Nos. 11, 24, 31, 35, 52, 53, 54, 55, 61, 65, 72, 73, 74, 75.
	MAS Nos. 433, 434, 510, 514, 516, 519, 520, 521,523, 538, 540, 543, 545, 547, 562.
	ME Nos. 38, 40, 41
Minesweepers	RD Nos. 6, 16, 21, 25, 27, 28, 29.

Gunboat	Illyria		
Vedettes	VAS Nos. 237, 240, 241, 245, 246, 248.		
Landing Craft	MZ Nos. 713, 717, 722, 726, 728, 729, 737, 744, 758, 776, 778, 780, 781, 784, 800, 831.		

AUXILIARY NAVAL VESSELS

Tankers	Prometeo	*Tugs (large)*	Arsachena
	Stige		Basiluzzo
	Tarvisio		Capod'Istria
	Urano		Carbonara
Water Carriers	Anapo		Cefalu
	Aterno		Ercole
	Basento		Gaeta
	Bisagno		Lampedusa
	Dalmazia		Lipari
	Idria		Liscanera
	Isarco		Marechiaro
	Istria		Mesco
	Liri		Molara
	Metauro		Nereo
	Polcevera		Porto Adriano
	Sprugola		Porto Conte
	Timavo		Porto Quieto
	Tirso		Porto Torres
Tugs (large)	Porto Tricase	*Tugs (small)*	N 2
	Procida		N 3
	Promontore		N 23
	Rapallo		N 24
	Salvore		N 28
	San Angelo		N 35
	San Antioco		N 36
	San Remo		N 37
	Talamone		N 80
	Taormina		N 94
	Teulada	*Depot Ship*	Anteo
	Tifeo	*Training Ship*	Cristoforo Colombo
	Vado	*Auxiliary Minelayer*	Fasana
	Vigoroso	*Transports*	Giuseppe Messina
Tugs (small)	Generale Valfre		Montecucco
	Licata		Panigaglia
	Noli		
	Volosca		

Appendix 7.3: PROTOCOL ON THE ESTABLISHMENT OF A FOUR POWER NAVAL COMMISSION, THE DISPOSAL OF EXCESS UNITS OF THE ITALIAN FLEET, AND THE RETURN BY THE SOVIET UNION OF WARSHIPS ON LOAN

PART I

Whereas the Treaty of Peace with Italy 1 provides that all the excess units of the Italian Fleet, as listed in Annex XII B of the said Treaty, shall be placed at the disposal of the Governments of the Union of Soviet Socialist Republics, the United Kingdom of Great Britain and Northern Ireland, the United States of America, and of France;

And whereas it is necessary to make provision for the final disposal among certain Allied and Associated Powers of the said excess units; The Governments of the Union of Soviet Socialist Republics, the United Kingdom of Great Britain and Northern Ireland, the United States of America, and of France have therefore agreed as follows:

1. The excess units of the Italian Fleet as listed in Annex XII B of the Treaty of Peace with Italy, and as finally verified on 1st January 1947, shall be allocated as set out in the Annex of this Protocol. No modification of the list of ships in Annex XII B will be accepted, irrespective of the date of any damage to or loss of such ships, the Italian Government being held responsible for the security and maintenance of such excess units up to the time at which each transfer is completed.

2. Upon transfer by the Italian Government, the vessels concerned shall respectively vest in full ownership in the States hereby becoming entitled thereto, subject to the following exceptions:

(*a*) The Governments of the Soviet Union and of France take note: that the Governments of the United Kingdom and of the United States of America have undertaken to meet, at least in part, and out of the tonnage at their disposal, the claims of certain other Powers for Italian naval vessels; furthermore, that in regard to any such Italian naval vessels as the Government of the United States of America may elect to transfer to other Powers, the Government of the United States of America will accept temporary custody only, and, upon transfer of custody by the United States Government to any such Power, full ownership will pass from the Italian Government to that Power.

(*b*) None of the Governments concerned shall be obliged to accept any ship assigned to it under this Protocol if such Government deems the ship unsuitable for its purpose, but in that case the Four Powers shall ensure that such ship, unless it is an auxiliary naval vessel, be scrapped or sunk by the Italian Government within nine months from the coming into force of the Treaty [15 September 1947].

3. A Commission, to be known as the Four Power Naval Commission, shall be set up, to meet for the first time immediately after the signature both of the Treaty of Peace with Italy and of this Protocol. This Commission shall make all detailed arrangements necessary to effect the transfer of the excess units of the Italian Fleet, together with their spare parts and armament stores, to the beneficiary Powers, in conformity with the naval clauses of the said Treaty.

4. By invitation of the French Government, the Commission will meet in Paris, where it will operate under the authority of the Council of Foreign Ministers, and carry out all preliminary work practicable prior to the coming into force of the Treaty.

5. Upon the coming into force of the Treaty, the Commission will move to Rome, where it will operate under the authority of the Ambassadors of the Soviet Union, the United Kingdom, the United States of America and of France.

6. All orders and instructions by the Commission shall be issued in the name of the Four Ambassadors, and shall be communicated by them to the Italian Government for execution.

7. The Commission shall have the right to co-opt the services of representatives of Greece, Yugoslavia and Albania, when matters affecting these States are under discussion, and to call for such Italian representation as may be found necessary to the execution of the work of the Commission.

8. The Annex to this Protocol will be published at a later date.

PART II

And whereas, by agreement between the Governments of the Union of Soviet Socialist Republics, the United Kingdom of Great Britain and Northern Ireland, and the United States of America, certain warships of the Royal Navy and of the United States Navy were, in 1944, transferred on loan to the Government of the Soviet Union; And whereas it is necessary to make provision for the return to the Governments of the United Kingdom and of the United States of America of the aforementioned warships now on loan; The Governments of the Union of Soviet Socialist Republics, the United Kingdom of Great Britain and Northern Ireland, and the United States of America have further agreed as follows:

9. The representatives of the abovementioned three Governments on the Commission shall coordinate the arrangements for the return to the Governments of the United States of America and of the United Kingdom of the vessels on loan to the Government of the Soviet Union, as listed in paragraph 10 below. The return of such vessels to United Kingdom and United States ports shall, as far as possible, be effected simultaneously with the transfer to the Soviet Union of the excess units of the Italian Fleet allocated to her.

10. List of Vessels on Loan from the United Kingdom

	British Name	Temporary Russian Name
Battleship	ROYAL SOVEREIGN	ARCHANGELSK
Destroyers	ST ALBANS	DOSTOINY
	BRIGHTON	ZHARKY
	RICHMOND	ZHYVUCHY
	CHELSEA	DERZKY
	LEAMINGTON	ZHGUCHY
	ROXBURGH	DOBLESTNY
	GEORGETOWN	ZHOSTKY
Submarines	UNBROKEN	B.2
	UNISON	B.3
	URSULA	B.4

Vessel on Loan from the United States

	United States Name	Temporary Russian Name
Cruiser	MILWAUKEE	MURMANSK

ANNEX
ALLOCATION OF UNITS OF THE ITALIAN FLEET SPECIFIED IN ANNEX XII B OF THE TREATY OF PEACE WITH ITALY

Type	USSR	UK	USA	France	Greece	Yugoslavia	Albania
Battleships	Giulio Cesare	Vittorio Veneto	Italia	–	–	–	–
Cruisers	Emanuele Filiberto		Attilio Regolo	Eugenio di Savoia	–	-	
	Duca d'Aosta			Pompeo Magno			
				Scipione Africano			
Sloop	–	–	–	Eritrea	–	–	–
Destroyers	Artigliere	–	–	Legionario	–	–	-
	Fuciliere			Mitragliere			
	Augusto Riboty			Alfredo Oriani			
				Velite			
Torpedo boats	Animoso	–	–	–	–	Aliseo	–
	Ardimentoso					Ariete	
	Fortunale					Indomito	
Submarines	Marea	Alagi	Dandolo	Giada	–	–	-
	Nichelio	Atropo	Platino	Vortice			
Motor torpedo Boats	MS52, 53, 61, 65, 75	MS72, 73, 74	MS11, 24, 31	MS35, 54, 55	–	–	–
	MAS516, 519, 520, 521	MAS.433, 434, 510, 514	MAS523,538, 547, 562	MAS540, 543, 545			
	ME40	ME41	ME38				
Gunboat	–	–	–	–	–	–	Illyria
Minesweepers	–	–	–	–	–	RD6, 16, 21, 25 27, 28, 29	-
Vedettes	VAS 245, 246, 248	–	–	VAS 237, 240, 241	–	–	–
Landing Craft	MZ778, 780, 781	MZ784, 800, 831	MZ744, 758, 776	MZ 722, 726, 728, 729,737	–	MZ 713, 717	-
Tankers	Stige	–	Prometheo	Tarvisio	–	–	–
				Urano			
Water Carriers	Basento	Metauro	Dalmazia	Anapo	Aterno	Isarco	-
	Istria	Timavo	Idria	Bisagno			
	Liri			Sprugola			
	Polcevera			Tirso			
Depot Ship	–	Anteo	–	–	–	–	–
Training Ship	Cristoforo Colombo	–	–	–	–	–	–
Auxiliary Minelayer	–	Fasana	–	–	–	–	–
Transports	Montecucco	Giuseppe Messina	–	Panigaglia	–	–	–
Tugs (Large)	Capo d'Istria	Carbonara	Arsachena	Ercole	–	Basiluzzo	-
	Lampedusa	Liscanera	Cefalu	Lipari	Molara		
	Porto Adriano	Mesco	Porto Torres	Nereo	Porto Conte		
	Rapallo	Procida	Teulaoa	Porto Quieto	San Remo		
	San Angelo	Salvore	Porto Tricase				
	Talamone	San Antioco	Promontore				
	Tifeo	Gaeta	Taormina				
	Vigoroso	Marechiaro		Vado			
Tugs (Small)	N35, 37, 80, 94	N2, 3, 24	Generale	Licata	–	–	–
	Valfre	N23, 28, 36					
	Noli						
	Volosca						

8

Under New Management – 2

UK

As already noted, the UK had no interest in the long-term employment of ex-enemy vessels, only wishing to run trials with a few of the more technically interesting examples. These comprised ships with high-pressure boilers, submarines with high underwater speeds, and minesweepers with Voith propulsors. Thus, most were intended for early scrapping or sinking. The exceptions were German units that the UK reallocated to France and other Allies excluded from the Potsdam share-out, such vessels being transferred as soon as possible after having been formally taken over by the UK.

In doing so, the Admiralty fell foul of UK Treasury procedures, since the ex-German ships had become British assets, and thus should have been written-off through Treasury Minutes – which did not occur.[1] Accordingly, a reprimand was issued by the Treasury in August 1947, when a similar re-transfer of surrendered Japanese tonnage was being considered.

Destroyers and Torpedo Boats
Ex-German
Of the UK's share of destroyers, *Z10 Lody*, *Z25*, *Z31*, *Z38* and *T108* were seaworthy (although *Z10* and *T108* had some minor defects), but *Z4 Beitzen*, *Z5 Jacobi*, *Z6 Riedel* and *Z30* all required significant work – the latter including a new stern. *Z38* was already in UK waters (see p 184), with *Z19*, *Z25*, *T23* and *T108* sailing for Portsmouth on 6 January 1946; *Jacobi* left for Rosyth on the 16th, in company with the escort vessel *F4*, the seaplane tender *Walter Holtzapfel* and the experimental torpedo-firing ship (ex-coaster) *Frieda Peters*;[2] they were followed a few days later by *Riedel*. The immobile *Z30* and *Z4* were towed from Oslo to Rosyth on 6 and 7 February, respectively.

Z38 was one of the first ex-German vessels brought to the UK, in July 1945, well before the formal division of the German fleet. After initial trials she was laid up until refitted for further experimental service under the name *Nonsuch* during the summer and autumn of 1947. She is shown here with the new pennant number D107 (of the fresh pattern introduced that year), replacing her original R40. *(AD collection)*

At the end of December 1945, the plan was that *Z10* and *Z38* would be used for long-term trials, to last up to two years, with *Z4* and *Z30* acting as spare-parts donors, to become targets after stripping. *T23* would be used for some more basic trials, and then join the remaining modern vessels in being given to France. However, *T23*'s condition was ultimately judged too poor, and she joined the main group heading for France (see pp 216–217, below).

Z4's dismal condition, including bottom damage from near-misses, was such that she had to be beached in December 1946 to avoid sinking; added to the disposal list the following month, she was scrapped in 1949. *Z30* was, however, fit to be taken to Loch Striven, where various surplus warships were being employed in trials to determine the effects of underwater explosions.[3] Thus, between May and September 1948, three charges were detonated at various depths below *Z30*'s hull; despite some damage, she remained basically intact, and was handed over for scrapping immediately after the completion of the tests.

The proposed trials on the remaining pair were soon cut

1 'Treasury Minutes' detail the value of UK government assets that are to be written off, and require approval by Parliament.
2 Later the UK *Sarepta*, employed at the Royal Naval Torpedo Factory, Greenock from 1946 until broken up in 1972.

3 D K Brown, 'Post War Trials: Test Against Destroyers', *Warship* XI (1987), pp 28–34.

213

back, *Z10* being used as a training hulk for high-pressure boilers until October 1946, when she became an accommodation ship at the Thornycroft yard at Southampton until declared for disposal in January 1949. *Z38* was actually used for initial trials in the Clyde, but then laid up at Portsmouth until brought forward for refit in November 1946. She was then renamed *Nonsuch* and in the summer of 1947 became both a trials ship for high-pressure machinery, and also an air-target ship, based on Rosyth. She was finally reduced to reserve in October 1948, and in March 1949 was, like *Z30*, employed in the Loch Striven underwater explosion trials series. These left her with a broken back and all boiler rooms flooded by October. Subsequently beached, she was sold in November, the vessel's stern being refloated for scrap in 1950, while the forepart was broken up *in situ*.

None of the Japanese destroyers allocated to the UK were of any technical interest, and those that were taken to Singapore simply cluttered up the harbour, until such time as arrangements could be made for them to be broken up by local contractors. As a result, it was decided to have *Natsuzuki*, the destroyer allocated to the UK during the last round of the lottery, broken up in Japan. In addition, *Sumire*, diverted to Hong Kong with boiler defects while en route to Singapore, was kept there and expended as a target off that colony.

Submarines

By the end of 1945, the UK had completed all her planned trials with Type VIIC, XXI and XXIII submarines (see pp 184–185, above) and thus, of the ten boats allocated to her by the TNC, three were immediately loaned to Canada and France, leaving just seven. Of these, by the end of February 1946, six were laid up at Lisahally, awaiting their fate. They were moved from Lisahally to Londonderry in the summer of 1947, placed on the disposal list in April 1949 and subsequently broken up.[4] None had seen any further employment by the British (indeed, *U712*, *U953*, *U1108* and *U2348* had not been used for *any* purpose in British hands), although at one point earmarked for potential target use. *U1407*, was, however, only just then beginning her British service.[5]

The Walter-boat had received a commanding officer and a pennant number on 25 September 1945, with a trials programme being devised to move forward the development of HTP-based propulsion for British service; indeed, a British-built trials vessel had already been included in the revised 1945 programme (to become HMS/M *Explorer*

The only ex-German Walter-boat actually to sail under an Allied flag, *Meteorite* (ex-*U1407*), being shown undergoing trials during the spring of 1949. *(AD collection)*

[1954]).[6] The former German boat was commissioned on 26 August 1947 as *Meteorite*, having received the completely new set of machinery retrieved from the Walterwerke. This was reconditioned under the supervision of Walter himself who, with a number of his team, began working under contract for the British government in January 1946; *Meteorite* also had her ventilation and electrical systems replaced. As a purely trials vessel, *Meteorite* had her torpedo tubes removed.

Trials did not begin until March 1948 – and even then her turbine had not yet been installed, the vessel running on diesel and electric propulsion only, to allow initial crew familiarisation. The turbine was finally installed during the summer and trialled on the surface over the next few months, completing in October. These trials proved promising, and led on to full operational trials during March/April 1949 off the west coast of Scotland.

Meteorite was adjudged a difficult vessel to handle on the surface, but with excellent underwater properties, and proven machinery, although the full evaluation of her potential was hampered by her only having one turbine, rather than the two she was designed for. The boat was towed back to Barrow at the end of April, and paid off on 8 July. Handed over to the British Iron & Steel Corporation (Salvage) (BISCO) for scrapping soon afterwards,[7] she was moved to T W Ward's Barrow yard on 7 September and broken up.

Patrol and Escort Vessels

Four of the F-type escorts (*F2*, *F4*, *F8* and *F10*) fell to the UK's share. None were employed, and were laid up until sold for breaking up, except for *F2*, which foundered in 15m of water during a storm at Scapa Flow in December 1946 (for

4 Waller, *Warships* 171, pp 8–9.

5 D Waller, 'The U-boats that Surrendered: U-boats in the Royal Navy Post-May 1945 (Part 4)', *Warships* 171 (2012), pp 2–7.

6 J Wise, 'The Royal Navy and the Evolution of the "True Submarine", 1945–1963', *Warship* XXXI (2009), pp 22–38.

7 In contrast to the earlier practice of the Admiralty selling surplus vessels direct to shipbreakers, the state-owned BISCO, established during the Second World War, now took over such vessels, allocated them to shipbreaking yards, which were paid their dismantling costs plus an amount per ton of steel recovered, surplus sums being remitted to the Treasury. Direct sales to breakers were resumed in 1962.

position, see p 35). Although sold for scrap in the late 1960s, work was abandoned when the salvage barge *YC21*, containing material thus far recovered, sank in a storm on 15 November 1968.

A vessel of anomalous type was the ex-state yacht *Grille*, which had been used as a minelayer and headquarters ship, ending the war at Narvik. Laid up at Hartlepool, she was sold in August 1946, with the intent that she be used to sail the world promoting British goods. However, this fell through and she was sold to a Lebanese businessman, acting on behalf of King Faruq of Egypt, who then decided that he did not want her by the time she had reached the eastern Mediterranean. Sailed to New York, the ship was touted for a range of new roles, but was sold for scrap in 1951.

Mine Warfare Vessels

Only one of the German minesweepers allocated to the UK ever served under the White Ensign. Almost all the rest were in use with the GM/SA or operating under French command at the time of allocation, and at the end of this duty they were either immediately disposed of, or transferred to other navies. The exceptions were examples of boats with Kort nozzles (*M23*) or Voith-Schneider propulsors (*M33* and *R115*), which were of some technical interest. However, the vessel to be actually operated and trialled under the British flag was *R115*, which became *ML6115* at Portsmouth, and survived until 1954.

A Japanese minelayer, *Wakataka*, was retained for onward transfer as a training ship to the new Singapore and Malayan Naval Force (Royal Malayan Navy in August 1952), raised by the Singapore government on 24 December 1948. She became HM Malayan Ship *Laburnum* in September 1949, symbolically taking the name and role of the former drill-ship at Singapore, HMS *Laburnum*, which had been scuttled on the fall of Singapore to the Japanese in February 1942. This second *Laburnum* was paid off in 1956, but continued as a drillship for the Singapore (Naval) Volunteer Force (SNVF), even after Singaporean secession from Malaysia in August 1965. She recommissioned as RSS *Singapura* on 5 May 1967 as the headquarters ship of the SNVF, but was stricken, sold and scrapped after the SNVF moved ashore in mid-1968.

Coastal Forces

As with other categories of vessels, the UK disposed of almost all the FPBs allocated to her, either by sale or as targets, with engines retained by the navy for trials or potential reuse. Three vessels, *S130* (replacing the originally earmarked *S221*), *S208* and *S212*, were, however, commissioned for further service. They were initially renamed

MTB5130, *5208* and *5212*, respectively, the prefix being changed to *FPB* in 1950. While ex-*S208* kept her original engines throughout, ex-*S212* had her outer engines replaced by Napier Deltic diesels for initial trials purposes, and ex-*S130* was wholly re-engined with Deltics. While ex-*S212* was employed in British waters until disposed of in 1956, in 1948 ex-*S208* was refitted for use in clandestine operations in Baltic waters, under British flag, but with a German crew picked from the GM/SA.[8] These began in April 1949, initially operating from Gosport, but later Finkenwerder, involving the landing and retrieval of agents, as well as monitoring Soviet transmissions via special collapsible masts.

From March 1951, following a refit by her original builders, ex-*S208* operated under the auspices of the British Baltic Fishery Protection Service (BBFPS), which from August 1952 also included ex-*S130*, also newly refitted by her designers, the Lürssen company, and from 1955 three new-build FPBs, *Silver Gull*, *Storm Gull* and *Wild Swan* (for which see p 239, below). The latter were all handed over to the new West German Bundesmarine on 28 March 1956, followed the next year by ex-*S130* and ex-*S208*, which became the training boats *UW10* and *UW11*. The latter ended up as a target during the 1960s, but ex-*S130* served on as the civilian-manned trials boat *EF3* until 1991, and was ultimately acquired for preservation in the UK.

Auxiliary Vessels

Most of the naval auxiliaries allocated to the UK were soon disposed of, including back into German service. However, some that were put into service under the White Ensign were retained for some time. In particular, the replenishment ship *Nordmark* (ex-*Westerwald*), taken over at Copenhagen, and which arrived at Rosyth on 8 June 1945, was then sent to Palmers at Hebburn for a refit, with a view to serving as a Royal Fleet Auxiliary tanker for the British Pacific Fleet; however, by the time that this was completed on 31 November the war was over.[9]

Accordingly, after a year in reserve at Milford Haven and Falmouth, it was decided to commission what was now known as HMS (not RFA) *Northmark* for under way replenishment trials. While under refit at Portsmouth from June to August 1947, she was renamed *Bulawayo*, and began operations out of Portland in October, fuelling a wide range of ships, from the battleship *Vanguard* to destroyers. During the first half of 1948 she also acted as a tanker, carrying oil

---

8 D Peifer, 'Forerunners to the West German Bundesmarine: The Klose Fast Patrol Group, the Naval Historical Team Bremerhaven, and the U.S. Navy's Labor Service Unit (B)', *International Journal of Naval History* 1/1 (2002).

9 G P Jones, *Under Three Flags: The Story of* Nordmark *and the Armed Supply Ships of the German Navy* (London: William Kimber, 1973).

In British hands, the replenishment ship *Nordmark* first became *Northmark* and then *Bulawayo*; she is seen here under the latter name at Malta on 3 November 1949. *(Wright & Logan)*

from Trinidad to the UK, before entering refit at Chatham at the beginning of July, which completed at the end of August. However, boiler problems led to a major refit at Portsmouth that lasted until October 1949, and she continued with trials and replenishment exercises until becoming headquarters ship for the Clyde reserve fleet in May, paying off in October 1950. Listed for disposal in 1955, she was handed over to the breakers that October.

The seaplane tender *Walter Holtzapfel* was commissioned as the diving tender *Deepwater* in March 1946, equipped with outdated diving equipment taken from her decommissioned predecessor in the role, the 'Hunt'-class minesweeper *Tedworth* (1917), sold for scrap in May. Thus, as soon as the new diving tender *Reclaim* became operational in 1949,

Deepwater was relegated to an 'alongside' training role at the *Vernon* training establishment at Portsmouth. Stripped during 1957/8, she was sold for scrap in 1960. A few small vessels were also kept for a while, in particular the boom defence tenders *Diver* (ex-*C28*) and *Dipper* (ex-*C30*), which served as mining tenders until 1959/60. There were also the tugs *Expeller* (ex-*Bora*) and *Exhorter* (ex-*Ostpreußen*) which were retained in service at Chatham and Devonport, respectively, until 1967 and 1962, although *Excluder* (ex-*Goldingen*) was sold out as early as 1950.

There was also initial interest in making use of the two catapult ships allocated to the UK, *Sperber* and *Friesenland*, the latter by the Royal Air Force, mirroring her former ownership: built for Deutsche Lufthansa from 1937, she had been requisitioned by the Luftwaffe on the outbreak of war in 1939. However, in the end *Sperber* became a floating crane at Wilhelmshaven and *Friesenland* was sold for conversion to a refrigerated cargo ship in 1950, serving under various names until broken up in 1969.

Passing On

As already noted, the UK had undertaken to pass unwanted vessels on to France, to make up for her being snubbed at Potsdam. Thus, on 31 December 1945 the Board of Admiralty approved the transfer of *Z5*, *Z6*, *Z25*, *Z31*, *T11*, *T20*, *T23*, *T28*, *T108*, *U2518* and *U2348* (the latter two nominally on loan; *U2326* was swapped for *U2348* before

10 TNA FO 371/57146.

The aircraft tender *Walter Holtzapfel* is seen here as the British diving tender *Deepwater* in June 1946. *(Wright & Logan)*

delivery)[10] to France. The formal offer was made on 3 January 1946, and with the exception of the old *T108*, which was rejected, all were handed over a few weeks later.

The French subsequently made specific requests for 'auxiliary' vessels, on 2 March asking for sixty landing craft, three hulks, five aircraft lighters, the aircraft tender *Immelmann*, the survey vessel *Paul Ulton*, the research ship *Strahl*, the diving tender *Taucherglockenfahrzug*, eight tugs, all available netlayers, two harbour water vessels, eight R-boats and four FPBs. Of these, the transfer of *Immelmann* (to become *Commandant Robert Giraud*), the netlayers *Netzleger IX* and *XIII* (*Retaire*), the hulk (ex-sail training ship) *Großherzogin Elisabeth* (*Duchesse Anne*), and the tugs *Polangen* (*Infatigable*), *Föhn II* (*Implacable*), *Nesserland* (*Imbattable*) and *Nordegünde* (*Intraitable*), was agreed on 17 May 1946, offered the following day, and the ships handed over in late July and August.[11] *Immelmann*'s sister, *Max Stinsky*, was later transferred by the USA from their share (to become *Paul Goffeny*).

However, the UK was less willing to respond positively to requests from such nations as the Netherlands, Denmark and Norway,[12] taking the view that they had all been provided with replacements for losses by Allied (mainly British) vessels transferred during the war, and that any further acquisitions should also be from Allied sources.[13] However, there was some willingness to provide such units as minesweepers and auxiliary vessels, although only after the completion of the ongoing GM/SA programme.

Indeed, a number of ex-German minesweepers had already been lent to the three nations for current work, and it had been the intent (albeit not made known to the recipients) that they should ultimately be gifted by the UK. In addition to these, various UK-allocated vessels now becoming surplus to GM/SA requirements were identified for potential transfer during 1947 – including those currently in Dutch and Danish hands.

Accordingly, it was agreed at the end of November 1946 that the French, Dutch, Danes and Norwegians should be offered the 'British' minesweepers currently in their hands, and that they, and the Belgians, be given a list of other units becoming surplus against which bids could be made. The

notification of this to the nations in question was delayed by wrangling with the UK Treasury over the approvals needed to gift UK assets to third parties (cf. p 213),[14] the eventual communications in October 1947 being caveated as 'subject to Parliamentary approval'. Six of the Danish vessels (R-boats) had previously been cannibalised, with UK permission, and these were to be swapped for serviceable vessels at the time of formal transfer. At one point, the Danes were interested in purchasing the 'British' depot ship *Tsingtau*, which had been working with them, but in the event she was scrapped in the UK in 1950. Thus, a total of twenty-one R-boats were given to Denmark and nine to the Netherlands, France receiving sixteen M-boats and Norway thirteen.

USA
Capital Ships and Cruisers

Although both *Nagato* and *Sakawa* sailed with US crews, both did so as part of their destruction process (p 197), and did not actually get commissioned. However, *Prinz Eugen* was commissioned under her original name, and the hull number IX-300, on 5 January 1946, with a composite American–German (40:574) crew. She sailed from Wesermünde for Boston on 13 January, arriving on the 22nd. The cruiser was examined on arrival, a number of components being removed for trial and further analysis, her passive sonar being installed in USS/M *Flying Fish*. The

Prinz Eugen leaving Philadelphia on 10 March 1946; note the removal of the guns from the forward 203mm turret. *(Naval Shipyard Philadelphia photo # 377-46-19)*

11 TNA ADM 116/5655.

12 Thus, in a list of such requests on TNA FO 1806/92, requests from Denmark and Norway for MTBs and submarines, and from Denmark for an F-type escort vessel are annotated as 'Contrary to Policy'.

13 TNA ADM 116/5655, dated 17 April 1946.

14 The valuations to be included in the Treasury Minutes were the subject of considerable debate, scrap values ultimately being accepted. As noted above (p 213), this had not been done for the destroyers, torpedo boats and auxiliaries handed over in 1946. This made the Treasury more difficult with the 1947 ships, especially as they were at the same time demanding that retrospective approval to

be sought regarding the 1946 vessels. Throughout the discussions, the Admiralty's position was that, in giving the ships away, the UK actually *saved* money: '[T]here were other advantages in making gift of them as early as possible. None of the ships were of value to the Royal Navy; most are fit only for scrapping, except in the eyes of the most impoverished navy; all were an incubus to the Admiralty. By disposing of them as promptly as possible a very considerable saving of the money and man power which would otherwise have been expended on their maintenance, was effected' (TNA ADM 116/5655, dated 3 October 1947).

15 For *Prinz Eugen*'s post-war history, see E F Sieche, 'The German Heavy Cruiser *Prinz Eugen*: A Career Under Two Flags', *Warship* 49 (1989), pp 44–8, *Warship International* XXVII (1990), pp 278–306.

The capsized wreck of *Prinz Eugen* at Kwajalein during the 2000s. The starboard screw was removed in August 1979, and is now at the Laboe Naval Memorial, near Kiel. *(AD collection)*

Hanazuki, shown on 16 October 1945. She was handed over to the USA in June 1947, and ran trials in Japanese waters as *DD-934*, before being sunk as a target in 1948. *(NHHC 80-G-351886)*

guns from the foremost turret were removed at Philadelphia in February, together with two 105mm mountings, a set of torpedo tubes, light AA guns and a number of range-finders.[15]

Allocated to join *Nagato* and *Sakawa* among the target ships for the Bikini Atoll atomic bomb tests, *Prinz Eugen* sailed for the Pacific, via the Panama Canal, on 3 March, arriving at San Diego on the 22nd. The German component of her crew departed in three phases, on 25 February, 9 April and 1 May; the Americans subsequently had significant problems with the cruiser's machinery, a breakdown of all but one boiler on passage from San Diego to Hawaii requiring *Prinz Eugen* to be towed into Honolulu.

She survived both test explosions in July with only superficial damage, but owing to her level of irradiation she was towed to Kwajalein, being decommissioned on 29 August 1946. She was now, however, leaking badly, and on 21 December developed a severe list; the hulk was beached in shallow water, but capsized the following day. One screw was removed in August 1979, for display at the Laboe Naval Memorial at Kiel.

Destroyers

Z39 was formally handed over to the USA at Devonport on 12 July 1945, and sailed for the USA on the 30th, in company

with *T35*, with mixed crews after docking at Falmouth. The two ships arrived at Boston on 7 August; *Z39* was commissioned into the US navy with a wholly American crew as *DD-939* on 14 September. She was then used for trials until November 1947, when she was handed over to France (see p 223).

One of the Japanese destroyers allocated to the USA, *Hanazuki,* was given a US hull number for brief trials, before being expended as a target off the Korean coast in early 1948, as had been *Kaki* and *Odake* in the late summer of 1947. Of the other two 'American' destroyers, *Kashi* was broken up in 1948 and *Harukaze* expended as a breakwater.

In addition, the USA also took over *Shōkaitei No. 102,* which had begun life as their own destroyer *Stewart.*[16] Recovered at Kure in October 1945, she was sailed by a Japanese crew to Hiro Wan, just west of Kure, where she was commissioned on 29 October, with just her hull number, as a new *Stewart* had been commissioned in 1943. She left for

16 J W Klar, 'USS *DD-224* (ex-*Stewart*)–The Voyage Home', *Warship International* XXVII (1990), pp 74–82; T Tamura, 'The Career of the Imperial Japanese Patrol Boat No. 102 (ex-USS *Stewart*, DD-224), *Warship International* LII (2015), pp 227–54.

Top: *Z39* running trials as the US *DD-939* off Boston, MA on 12 September 1945; **bottom:** *T35 (DD-935)* shown in the same area two days later; both were transferred to France in 1947 to be cannibalised for spares. *(NHHC 19-N-90595, NH 73335)*

The former *Shōkaitei No. 102*, originally the US destroyer *Stewart*, as reclaimed under the designation *DD-224*, on 29 October 1945, alongside the destroyer *Compton*. *(NHHC 80-G-356625)*

Okinawa on 8 November, arriving on the 10th after a breakdown en route, sailing on 11 November for Guam, but defects resulted in *DD-224* arriving under tow on the 17th. Leaving on 10 December, after repairs, she reached Eniwetok, in the Marshalls, the 20th, again under tow owing to constant defects. On 4 January 1946, the destroyer was towed out of Eniwetok, en route to Pearl Harbor, but subsequently diverted to Kwajalein, arriving on the 8th. *DD-224* finally made it to Hawaii under tow on 18 February, departing on the 21st in tow for San Francisco, finally arriving on 5 March. Moved to Oakland on the 26th, she was sunk as a target for rocket-firing naval aircraft on 24 May.

Submarines

Of the ten US ex-German submarines, *U530* and *U977* sailed from Rio Santiago on 11 September 1945, accompa-

U530 coming alongside *U977* at Rio de Janeiro on 16 September 1945, while on passage to the USA. *(AD collection)*

nied by the tug *Cherokee*, pausing at Rio de Janeiro from the 16th to 20th for machinery repairs, and then at Trinidad from 2 to 5 October, where they were inspected by the TNC on 3 October. Leaving Trinidad on 5 October, they arrived at New London on 12 October 1945. Like the German submarines ceded to the USA in 1919, the two boats were used to promote Victory Loan bonds, both departing New London on 5 November. *U530* undertook a seven-week tour of Texas ports, escorted by the destroyer-escort *Thomas*, returning on 22 December, while *U977* visited seven US East Coast ports in the company of the destroyer-escort *Baker*, finishing on 13 December.

The two boats were laid up at Boston in January 1946, the decision to dispose of them being taken in May. Stripping of useful material was completed in August, *U530* being sunk by USS/M *Toro* in a torpedo test on 13 November 1946 off Cape Cod; *U977* was sunk the same day by *Atule*.

U234, *U858* and *U873* were refitted late in 1945 for use in trials, which took place during the first half of 1946. They were subsequently laid up at Portsmouth, NH, until the first two were respectively sunk by USS/M *Greenfish* and *Sirago* during submarine torpedo tests in November 1947 off Cape Cod; *U873* was sold for scrap in March 1948.

U1105 had been employed by the British for trials before being allocated to the USA (see p 184, above), crossing the Atlantic between 19 December 1945 and 2 January 1946. While, like the British, the Americans were interested in her rubber coating, this had been badly affected by storm damage on passage, with the result that only samples were removed and the boat herself condemned for trials and target service. Laid up at Boston in February, she was moved to the Naval Gun Factory in Washington, DC in January 1947 in preparation for use at the Mine Warfare Test Station at Solomons Island, MD. It was not until August 1948 that trials began, and over the next thirteen months she was sunk by depth charges five times (the last time in September 1949) and raised four times in and around Chesapeake Bay and the Potomac River. The wreck was placed on the US National Register of Historic Places in 2001.[17]

Another vessel whose technical interest could not be fully exploited was *U1406*, which, although she arrived at Portsmouth, NH on 11 October 1945, proved to be beyond economic repair – unlike her 'British' sister *U1407*. Her HTP machinery was thus removed for study and the hulk authorised for disposal in February 1948, and for scrap in April. *U889*, previously trialled by the Canadians (see p 223, below), also had a short life in US hands, being in such a

17 National Register of Historic Places, 00001602, *U-1105 Black Panther*, located at Piney Point, Potomac River, Maryland.

U2513, *U3008* and a dilapidated Type IXC at New London in 1945. The latter boat may be *U505*, captured at sea in June 1944, and now a museum exhibit in Chicago. *(USN)*

poor condition when acquired that she was felt fit only to be cannibalized for spares. The hulk was then expended as a submarine torpedo target off Cape Cod by USS/M *Flying Fish* in November 1947.

On the other hand, the Type XXIs *U2513* and *U3008* both arrived secretly and in good condition from the UK in August 1945 (see p 185, above). Refitted at Portsmouth, NH, between September and the summer of 1946, both vessels were commissioned under their original names. *U3008*, which had her conning tower extensively modified, was used for a programme of trials off New England and Key West until paid off in June 1948. *U2513* spent most of her service in Florida waters, until paid off in July 1949; during her last year of service she was dependent on batteries taken from the laid-up *U3008*, stocks of German cells (mainly salvaged from Type IX boats) having become exhausted. She was then laid up at Portsmouth until August 1951, when she was towed back to Key West, and sunk as a rocket target by the destroyer *Robert A Owens* in October. *U3008* nevertheless survived as a test hulk until expended in explosives trials in May 1954 off Puerto Rico. She was salved the following year, dry docked at Ceiba, and sold for scrap locally.

Patrol and Escort Vessels

Of the various Japanese *Kaibōkan* allocated to the USA, almost all were broken up in Japanese yards. The only exceptions were *Kaibōkan Nos. 44*, *150* and *207*, expended as targets during August 1947.

Mine Warfare Vessels

Of the minesweepers allocated to the USA, most had been in

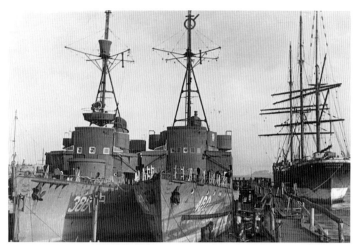

The US-allocated *M388* and *M460* laid up at Kiel in February 1949, with the Finnish barque *Winterhude*, serving as an accommodation ship, and soon to be broken up, in the background. Both minesweepers, together with *M294* and *M278* had been chartered to the local shipping company Paulsen & Ivers in April/June 1948 for conversion to ferries, but no work was ever done, and all four joined LSU(B) in February 1951 as *M201* (ex-*M294*), *M202* (ex-*M278*), *M203* (ex-*M388*) and *M204* (ex-*M460*). In 1956 they became respectively the Federal German navy *Seepferd*, *Seestern*, *Seehund* and *Seeigel* (cf. p 238). In lieu of *M278*, Ivers-Linie purchased the ex-*M607* in 1949, which became *Christian Ivers*; the former *M608* became *Harald Ivers* at the same time. Sold and rebuilt as roll-on-roll-off ferries in 1954, including re-engining with diesels, both were ultimately sold to Mediterranean owners, the former *M607* ending up as *Salvatore Lauro* in 1962 operating between Naples and Capri/Ischia. Re-engined in 1977, she survived until March 2006, when she sank in tow to the breakers. *(BA 183-2005-0715-510, AD)*

service with the GM/SA. Following its winding-up, a dozen R-boats went to the Minenräumverband Cuxhaven (see p 173, above) and thirteen M-type vessels were transferred to France in October 1947, nine (*M9*, *M24*, *M35*, *M81*, *M202*, *M205*, *M251*, *M252* and *M253*) seeing further active service, three (*M4*, *M12* and *M21*) being hulked, and one (*M495*) broken up for spares. The rest passed to the control of the Office of Military Government, United States (OMGUS) and were initially laid up. Most of these were then chartered out to the German authorities, with sub-charters to commercial concerns for mercantile use, for example as ferries, tugs or as accommodation vessels, the latter particularly in light of the damage to Germany's infrastructure caused by the war. However, some vessels proved unsuitable for their new roles, and most came back into US custody as their charters expired. Others, especially R-boats, were, however, sold outright for further service, two of the M-boats (*M607* and *M608*) having long careers as ferries in European and Mediterranean waters.

Some vessels were broken up without further service, in some cases after a period in US navy or US army custody, but three M-boats (*M328*, *M801* and *M803*) were sold to Italy in July 1949 by the US Surplus Stores Organisation as a commercial transaction under sealed bids. This was directly contrary to Article 52 of the six-month-old peace treaty with Italy, which forbade the 'acquisition of war material of German or Japanese origin or design, either from inside or outside Italy, or its manufacture' by Italy, but in this, and other similar matters, the US authorities turned a blind eye (or in this case, were allegedly unaware that the vessels were indeed ex-German).[18]

Around the same time an ex-German FPB had also been acquired by Italy – ex-*S67*, now the privately owned *Torüs*. No action was taken by US or UK agencies. Five M-boats and six R-boats were reactivated in 1951 for service with Labor Service Unit (B), with eleven further R-boats added in 1953 (see p 238, below).

Of the Japanese mine warfare vessels allocated to the USA, the minelayers *Awashima* and *Ishizaki* were broken up. The minesweeper *W-21* was, however, sunk as a target in the Yellow Sea in October 1947.

Coastal Forces[19]

The USA had previously acquired the hulk of *S144*, found sunk at Le Havre in February 1945, and brought to New York on a tank landing ship as *CEE #6527*. Unfit for testing without new engines, she was dismantled, wood samples taken, and a complete set of plans drawn before the remains were disposed of. The decision not to recondition this boat, as had previously been intended, was due to the availability of intact examples for trials.

Thus, while the majority of the FPBs allocated to the USA were transferred to Norway and Denmark (see pp. 233, 234), or disposed of in European waters, four serviceable vessels, *S116*, *S218*, *S228* and *S706*, were actually taken across the Atlantic. Of these, the last-named seems to have spent time at Philadelphia until transferred to Washington Navy Yard in

February 1947, apparently for disposal. A wreck (probably *S169*), found at Le Havre in February 1945, and salvaged the following month, had previously been taken to the USA in May as a potential trials vessel, but with the acquisition of the operational FPBs, any thoughts of refitting were dropped, although a thorough examination was undertaken before the hulk was scrapped in early 1946.

S116 was shipped across the Atlantic as deck-cargo on SS *Belgian Tenacity* under the auspices of the US army, and formally loaned by them to the navy at Fort Monroe, VA, being given the number *C-105179*. She then joined the recently arrived *S218* (*C-105180*) and *S225* (*C-105181*) at New York Navy Yard in November as a potential trials vessel. However, sufficient funding was only available to run one boat for tests, and *S218* was selected as being in the best condition, with work on the overhaul of the other two being suspended at the end of March 1946; they were, however, retained for the time being as reserves.

S218 was overhauled with a view to beginning her trials at the end of April, but work was not finished until the middle of May – when she was then damaged by striking a submerged object. Finally, on 31 July she ran a full power trial in conjunction with the American MTB *PT-620*, but on 12 August the centre engine suffered damage during a standardization and fuel economy trial off Long Island. It was not until a year later that trials were resumed, by which time *S218* had been transferred to Annapolis Naval Engineering Experiment Station. Here, trials were carried out in Chesapeake Bay during October/November 1947. Following their completion, *S218* was towed to Norfolk in January 1948 for disposal; stripped during February, the hulk was sold and handed over in July.

Of the two 'spare' boats, *S225* lay at New York until declared surplus on 12 April 1948; she was authorised for sale on 25 May 1948 and handed over to her purchaser at the beginning of September. *S116* also remained at New York Navy Yard, being definitively transferred to the navy in December 1947 and sold in July 1948. However, the 'sale' was for further government service in a clandestine role in a similar way to the British ex-*S130* and ex-*S208*, *S116* being accordingly shipped to Bremerhaven, to be manned by German nationals from LSU(B). Sold to the German Federal Frontier Guard in 1952 as a training vessel, she was subsequently transferred to the Federal German navy, becoming a hulk for the Damage Control Training Group (Lehrgruppe Schiffssicherung) at Neustadt in July 1957. She was burnt out there in 1965.

Auxiliary Vessels

As with the UK, few ex-enemy auxiliaries were taken into US

---

18 TNA FO 371/79492, dated 20 July 1949.

19 C Marshall, 'Easy Boats: Schnellboote in the US Navy' <www.prinzeugen.com/ USNSchnell.htm>, with *S144* identified at <http://s-boot.net/sboats-kriegsmarine-Losses.html>.

service, many being transferred to allies or passed back into German use, the latter including the hulked cruiser *Amazone*, which was used as an accommodation ship at Bremen until the mid-1950s, although a plan to turn her into a youth hostel was never realised. However, a sister of the British *Nordmark*, *Dithmarschen*, was likewise used by her captors for under way replenishment development purposes for some years.

Placed in US service on 2 May 1946 under her original name, and the hull number IX-301, she sailed from Bremerhaven on 8 May for Philadelphia to refit, arriving on 19 May. She was redesignated AO-110 and renamed *Conecuh* on 1 October 1946, but budgetary issues meant that she went into reserve on 24 October. Her hull number was changed to AOR-110 on 4 September 1952, the ship finally completing her refit and being commissioned on 16 February 1953.

Conecuh then served until transferred to the US Maritime Commission for preservation in the Reserve Fleet on 3 April 1956. Laid up in the James River, Lee Hall, VA, she was stricken on 1 June 1960 and sold for scrap that November.

Two sail training ships were allocated to the USA. One, *Horst Wessel*, was commissioned into the US Coast Guard as *Eagle*, replacing *Danmark*, loaned by the Danish government from 1942 to 1945; *Eagle* remains in active service at the time of writing. Her sister, *Albert Leo Schlageter*, was sold on to Brazil as *Guanabara*, becoming the Portuguese *Sagres* in 1961; she also remains in service with the Portuguese navy in her historic role of a sail training ship as of 2019.

CANADA
Submarines
As noted above, one of the UK 'ten' was formally loaned to Canada, although the vessel in question, *U190*, had actually surrendered there, and been commissioned into the RCN on 19 May 1945. She undertook a tour of ports around the St

Like the UK-allocated *Nordmark*, her sister *Dithmarschen* was also used for under way replenishment trials by her new owners, the US navy, serving as *Conecuh* until 1956. *(NHHC 80-G 678091)*

The sail training ship *Horst Wessel* became the US Coast Guard's *Eagle* in May 1946. *(NHHC NH 111356)*

The German sail training ship *Albert Leo Schlageter* was allocated to the USA after the Second World War, but was sold to Brazil for the nominal price of $US5,000 in 1948, becoming *Guanabara*; the ship was then purchased by Portugal in 1961, becoming *Sagres*, and is still active at the time of writing. She is shown here soon after the end of the war, with three other ex-German vessels moored ahead, the middle one being the escort *F7*, *F8* or *F10*, that on the right the aircraft tender *Grief*, later handed over by the USA to France in February 1948, to become *Marcel le Bihan*. *(NHHC NH 111357)*

Lawrence River and the Gulf of St Lawrence during the summer, along with *U889*, which has also surrendered in Canadian waters, and which was commissioned into the RCN on 14 May. Both boats were at Montreal on VJ-Day.

U889 was allocated to the USA by the TNC, paying off from Canadian service in December 1945, and sailing for Portsmouth, NH, on 11 January 1946, *U190* was initially an 'unallocated' boat and thus liable to sinking by 15 February 1946, but was added to the UK TNC allocation in January 1946 in exchange for *U975*, and immediately placed on two-year loan to Canada. *U190* was then employed as an anti-submarine training vessel, operating out of Halifax, NS until paid off in July 1947. She was sunk as a target off the Nova Scotian coast on 21 October (Trafalgar Day) under Operation 'Scuppered'.

FRANCE
Cruisers

Attilio Regolo arrived at Toulon on 31 July 1948, having been renamed *Châteaurenault*; her sister *Scipione Africano* became *Guichen* and arrived at Toulon a week later. They commissioned into the 2nd Light Division in September, which became the 2nd Destroyer Division in March 1951, but saw little sea time. The two ships were then rebuilt between 1951 and 1954 as fleet escorts, completely rearmed with three German-pattern twin 105mm mountings,[20] together with five twin 57mm, and four sets of triple anti-submarine torpedo tubes; new radar was also fitted. During 1956–58 they were again refitted, losing a 105mm mounting and two sets of torpedo tubes to become flotilla leaders. They served as such until 1961/62.

Destroyers and Escort Vessels

As noted above, nine of the UK's ex-German destroyers and

Alsacien (ex-*T23*), soon after entering French service. *(AD collection)*

torpedo boats were handed over to France, transfers taking place between 23 January and 4 February 1946, along with the ammunition from *Z4 Beitzen* and *Z10 Lody*. *Z5 Jacobi*, *Z6 Riedel*, *Z25*, *Z31*, *T11*, *T20*, *T23* and *T28* were renamed respectively *Desaix*, *Kléber*, *Hoche*, *Marceau*, *Bir Hacheim*, *Baccarat*, *Alsacien* and *Lorrain*. As with former German vessels allocated to France after the First World War, their new names had symbolic value: the first four were named after figures who had distinguished themselves in action along the German frontier during the Revolutionary/Napoleonic period; *Bir Hacheim* recalled a 1944 Free French victory in North Africa, as did *Baccarat* one in Western Europe the same year. *Alsacien* and *Lorrain*[21] of course referenced the inhabitants of the newly recovered provinces of Alsace and Lorraine.

The ex-American *Z39*, *T14*, and *T35* were also acquired in 1947, the latter two ships being handed over at Annapolis, MD on 10 November, and then towed, via Martinique, to Casablanca, arriving on 15 December; *T14* had languished at Bremerhaven since the end of the war. Although there had been thoughts of taking *Z39* into service as *Léopard*, she was instead hulked as a source of spares, and in spite of being

---

20 Possibly ex-*Graf Zeppelin* and *Gneisenau* (see P Schenk, 'German Aircraft Carrier Developments', *Warship International* XLV/2 [2008], p 159).

21 Not to be confused with the battleship *Lorraine*, named after the province itself.

The former *Scipione Africano* as first commissioned into the French navy as *Guichen* (top). Both she and her sister *Chateaurenault* (ex-*Attilio Regolo*) were rebuilt during 1951–54 as fleet escorts, with a completely new armament, *Chateaurenault* being shown here. This comprised three German-pattern twin 105mm/63, one forward and two aft, plus five twin 57mm/60 and four triple

550mm TT. They make an interesting comparison with the contemporary reconstructions of two of their sisters in Italy (see p 205). The French pair were further modified during 1956–58 as command ships, with the aftermost 105mm mounting and two sets of TT taken out to permit the installation of more accommodation. *(AD collection)*

Kléber (ex-Z6 Theodor Riedel) on 26 December 1951, soon after completion of an extensive refit, which included a new forefunnel cap and the replacement of no. 4 main gun by a pair of 40mm Bofors. Further pairs of the latter were installed in front of the bridge and amidships. *(AD collection)*

Hoche (ex-Z25) had already had no. 4 gun removed while in German service. She is shown here in 1948 before any substantive modifications, while serving in the 1st Destroyer Division at Cherbourg. She passed into reserve the following year, and was then extensively refitted during 1951–53, with her bridge enlarged, the twin turret forward replaced by a single mounting, eight 40mm guns installed in lieu of her original AA battery, and French 550mm TT replacing her German ones (see inset). *(AD collection)*

condemned in 1953, survived as a floating pier until 1969. *T14* was renamed *Dompaire* (commemorating a French victory of 1944 in the Vosges region), but *T35* did not even receive a new name, and was cannibalised for spares.

Three German aircraft tenders were acquired and classified as escorts. All were named for French heroes of the Second World War: *Commandant Robert Giraud* (a naval hero, ex-*Immelmann*); *O E Paul Goffeny* (an air ace, ex-*Max Stinsky*); and *Marcel le Bihan* (a prominent member of the Resistance, ex-*Grief*). The first came from the UK's allocation, and the latter two from that of the USA. Mainly employed on logistic duties in Indochina, *Goffeny* was condemned in 1969, but *Giraud* served as an oceanographic research vessel from 1962 to 1977, and *Bihan* an undersea operations vessel from 1959 to 1986, renamed *Gustave Zédé* in 1978. Other ex-German vessels taken over by France included a pair of retrocessions, the survivors of four French seaplane tenders seized in the slips in 1940, and taken forward as escorts. The two actually completed had become German war losses, but the others, still in the hands of the builder at the liberation, were finished as the survey vessels *Beautemps Beaupré* (ex-*SG3 Uranus*, ex-*Sans Souci*) and *Laperouse* (ex-*SG4 Merkur*, ex-*Sans Peur*).

In addition to vessels actually commissioned, the wreck of *Z23*, sunk off La Pallice in August 1944, was salved and taken to Brest, where she foundered. Refloated again, she was renamed *Léopard* in 1949, with a view to potential repair. However, she was condemned in 1951 and sold for scrap.

The four ex-Italian destroyers arrived during 1947–48, beginning with *Velite* (renamed *Duperré*) in June 1947, followed by *Mitragliere* (*Jurien de la Gravière*), *Alfredo Oriani* (*D'Estaing*) and *Legionario* (*Duchaffault*, arrived 15 August 1948). While all were commissioned for trials,

they soon passed into reduced commission and/or reserve, there being insufficient funds for refits.

Similarly, the ex-German *Bir Hacheim*, *Dompaire* and *Baccarat* were not taken into service, and condemned in 1951. On the other hand, after short refits, the other German ships (except for *Lorrain*, which remained in dockyard hands until 1949) entered service for short periods, before paying off, in most cases for more extensive alterations, although *Desaix*, paid off in November 1948, was cannibalised for spares until broken up in 1954.

Modifications to *Alsacien* and *Lorrain* were restricted to new light AA guns (four 40mm and twenty 20mm) and radars, together with the removal of the forward 105mm gun from the latter to make way for an ASDIC unit while acting as an anti-submarine and trials ship. On the other hand, during 1948–51, *Kléber* had one 127mm gun removed, her light AA battery replaced by six 40mm, her bridge enlarged, and new radar fitted. Having served in both the Atlantic and

Marceau (ex-Z31) had been acquired with a single 105mm gun forward, temporarily replacing a destroyed 150mm twin mounting. However, during her 1948–50 refit, this was replaced by a single 150mm weapon, and eight 40mm guns installed in lieu of her German AA battery. *(AD collection)*

Francis Garnier (ex-*Eritrea*) soon after being handed over by Italy. *(AD collection)*

Bouan (ex-*U510*), as refitted with a streamlined fin. *(AD collection)*

Mediterranean, she was reduced to reserve at Cherbourg on 20 December 1953. By 1957 in a poor condition, she was condemned in April and scrapped the following year.

Hoche spent 1949 in reserve before being taken in hand for her refit, which turned her into an anti-submarine escort. As such, she had new command spaces forward of the bridge, a main armament of three 150mm, a new AA battery and her torpedo tubes replaced by two triple sets of a new model 550mm tube. She was then used as an anti-submarine trials ship until 1956. *Marceau* also had her armament modified during her 1948–50 refit, the ship then serving until reduced to reserve in 1954.

The ex-Italian colonial sloop *Eritrea* was commissioned as *Francis Garnier* on 12 January 1950, and was immediately deployed to the Far East, undertaking hydrographic work and 'showing the flag' around French Polynesia. She was refitted at Toulon between October 1951 and September 1952, during which her main guns were replaced with more modern ones from ex-Italian destroyers in French hands, with the forward mounting reduced to a single. She then returned east, taking part in the war in Indochina, before spending much of the rest of her career as a support vessel for the French nuclear test facilities in the central Pacific. Paid off into reserve on 1 January 1966, she was expended as a target in October.

Submarines

The two submarines given to France by the UK, *U2326* and *U2518*, left Lisahally for Cherbourg on 5 February 1946 under Operation 'Thankful', arriving on the 13th, having been delayed for three days in the Irish Sea by bad weather.[22] *U2326* was used in the Mediterranean for *Schnorchel* trials, but was lost with all hands on 6 December 1946 off Toulon,

during diving trials: it was only subsequently that new calculations showed that the Type XXIII's safe depth limit was half that originally estimated.[23] Although both vessels had been nominally transferred only on two-year loan, that of *U2518* was extended by a further three years in February 1951, the boat becoming *Roland Morillot* (named for a French submarine commander of the First World War) in April 1951, and actually serving until the late 1960s.

She joined a number of 'left-behind' submarines that were refitted for further service: the derelicts *U123*, *U510* and *U766*, and the sunken *U471*, which were recommissioned as *Blaison*,[24] *Bouan*, *Laubie* and *Millé*, after French submarine and other naval officers who had perished in the late war. They remained in service into the late 1950s, all guns being removed; *Bouan* was rebuilt with a streamlined fin in the early 1950s. Four Type XXVIIB (Seehund) midgets (*S621* [ex-*U5074*], *S622* [ex-*U5090*], *S623* [ex-*U5107*] and *S624* [ex-*U5365*]) were also taken into French service in 1945, lasting until 1954/56.

In addition, two incomplete French submarines, *L'Africaine* and *L'Astrée*, which had been seized on the slip by the Germans in June 1940, and renamed *UF1* and *UF3* on 5 May 1941, had their construction resumed; they were launched (in the case of *L'Astrée*, re-launched) in 1946 and commissioned in 1949. Their sister *La Favorite* had been captured afloat and was commissioned in November 1941 as German *UF2*, serving as a training boat until paid off in July 1944; she was scuttled by the Germans at Gdynia in 1945.

Mine Warfare Vessels

As already noted (p 173), German minesweepers in French

22 See Hird, *Grey Wolves*, pp 258–9; Waller, *Warships* 184, pp 16–17.

23 Had she been commissioned into French service, she would apparently have been baptised *Lavallée*, after Jean Lavallée, a naval officer and resistance fighter, captured and shot in Buchenwald in 1940, and perhaps also the educationalist Alphonse Lavallée (1791–1873), given the omission of a Christian name.

24 Her refit utilising parts from the wreck of her sister *U129*, sunk at Lorient in August 1944: see <www.sous-mama.org/userfiles/files/Liste%20Sous-Marins%20Marc%20CASTEL.pdf>.

The minesweeper *Oise* (ex-*M38*) in 1947. She had been in French waters at the end of the war, and had operated with French officers, but a German crew, during 1945–47. Allocated to the UK by the TNC, she remained in French hands, being formally transferred in October 1947, when a number of minesweepers were handed over by the UK and USA. *(Drüppel)*

The submarine depot ship *Gustave Zédé* (ex-*Saar*). *(AD collection)*

waters were taken over and employed under French officers for local clearance work (to which were added *M432*, *M442* and *M452*, captured by the UK in Jersey). However, under the Potsdam Agreement, the dozen vessels involved were formally distributed to other powers at the beginning of 1946. Nevertheless, only in the case of the Soviet-allocated *M34* did this result in a ship being taken away from the French (to become the Black Sea-deployed *T-920* in August 1946). The rest were all immediately transferred to France by their new owners, to be joined by eighteen more in October 1947, once they had completed duty with the GM/SA.

Some of the ships were worn out and soon condemned after little, if any, further sea service, in particular ones from the former 4. Minesuchgruppe, although a few survived as hulks into the 1960s and 1970s. On the other hand, others served into the mid-1950s, when five (*Ailette* [ex-*M24*, which had been used as a fishery protection vessel], *Laffaux* [ex-*M81*], *Yser* [ex-*M85*], *Belfort* [ex-*M205*] and *Vimy* [ex-*M253*]) were transferred to the new West German navy.

Coastal Forces

France did not obtain any German FPBs, and of the six Italian vessels she was granted, only *MS35* and *MAS543* were actually taken over. Of these, *MS35* was only briefly used for trials, before being condemned and cannibalised to provide spares for the former *MAS543*, which was retained as *MAS782*, later *V782*, and still later *Y782*, until 1955.

Auxiliary vessels

Another vessel transferred on from the USA was the submarine depot ship *Saar*, originally taken over at Bremen. She was transferred to Cherbourg by a German crew, where she was commissioned in January 1948 as *Gustave Zédé*, named after the nineteenth-century French submarine designer. After a refit, which included a change of her AA armament,

she arrived at Toulon on 13 May 1949 to act as tender for the Groupe d'Action Sous-Marine. She continued in this role until 15 December 1970, being refitted in 1951, 1955 and 1958/59. Reduced to reserve in February 1971, the ship ended her days as a target ship for the development of the Exocet anti-ship missile, being finally sunk as a submarine torpedo target in February 1976.

Transferred by the UK was the sail training ship *Großherzogin Elisabeth*. She had not gone to sea since 1932 and, renamed *Duchesse Anne*, was used first as an accommodation ship at Lorient, and from 1951 to 1959 at Brest. Condemned in 1960 and stricken in 1966, after a number of false starts she became a museum ship at Dunkirk in 1981, and since 1992 has been classed as a *monument historique* on the French national register.

USSR
Capital ships

Guilio Cesare departed Augusta on 2 February 1949, arriving at Valona the following day, with the transfer formalised on

Novorossiysk (ex-*Guilio Cesare*) at Sevastopol in 1950, as yet without major modifications. *(AD collection)*

Above: The wreck of *Schleswig-Holstein*, grounded as long-term target off Osmussaar in the Gulf of Finland on 26 June 47, seen in 1961. The remains are now entirely submerged. *(Courtesy Dimitri Lemachko)*

Right: Salvage of the partly flooded hulk of *Lützow* (p 164) began in late 1946, and even when refloated the following summer required the constant running of pumps to remain so. During 20/22 July 1947, she was towed to Danzig Bay by the ice-breaker *Volynets* and the tug *MB-43*, with a number of bombs and shells placed on the ship for the upcoming trial. A 250kg bomb was detonated within the ship's conning tower at 0825hrs, blowing a hole in its floor, and throwing the rangefinder on top of it into the sea. At 1245hrs, a 500kg bomb was triggered below deck amidships, destroying the foundation of the catapult, and penetrating the main deck. The next two bombs were detonated simultaneously at 1545, a 500kg one in front of the forward 280mm turret jamming a gun at its maximum elevation and peeled open the forecastle. At 1615, the ship began to settle forward, and by 1623 she was listing at 30°, with the bow completely submerged. She sank shortly afterwards, in 113 metres of water. *(Soviet navy)*

the 6th, when she was commissioned as *Novorossiysk*. She then sailed for Sevastopol, where the ship was in dockyard hands from 12 May to 18 June.

That summer, *Novorossiysk* acted as nominal flagship during fleet exercises, but was as yet nowhere near worked up, with many modifications still outstanding, implemented over a series of refits in July 1950, from 29 April to 22 June and October 1951, in June 1952, during 1953, in November 1954, and from 13 February to 29 March 1955. The major refit of 1953 installed new radar, communications gear and main-battery fire control, along with a new light anti-aircraft battery of thirty 37mm/65 guns and new diesel generators.

There was an aspiration to replace her main guns with Soviet 305mm/52 guns, to match the surviving *Sevastopol* class and avoid having to manufacture special ammunition once the 320mm shells delivered with the ship ran out, but before that could be done, *Novorossiysk* detonated a Second World War German mine in Sevastopol harbour on 30 October 1955, and capsized.[25] The wreck was subsequently raised and broken up.

The other ex-enemy capital ship to serve in the Soviet navy was the ex-Finnish *Vyborg*. Handed over on 29 May 1947, she was based for six years at Porkkala, leased by Finland to the Soviet Union by the terms of the Moscow

Armistice of 1944, undertaking a number of training cruises between 1947 and 1949. Following the discovery of major defects during a 1952 refit at Kronstadt, she underwent extensive work at Tallinn from 1953 to 1957, her engines and electronic equipment being replaced. *Vyborg* then returned to training duties, but was then reduced to reserve in 1958. Attempts at interesting the Finns in repurchase having failed, she was stricken in 1966 and broken up.

In addition to these two ships, the USSR was in possession of a number of other capital ships, all of which had been placed in Category C, and were thus due for destruction by 15 August 1946. As already noted (see p 196), this was not achieved, and it was not until October the following year that the destruction of all vessels was certified.[26] In the interim, the Soviet authorities had indeed toyed with the idea of retaining and repairing some vessels, with *Schleswig-Holstein* added to the navy list in March 1946 and *Graf Zeppelin* in September 1945 (as a potential trials ship for future Soviet-built aircraft carriers). However, their poor condition – leaving aside international obligations – made this untenable, and all the ships in question were directed in March 1947 to be destroyed (see p 196, above).

25 S McLaughlin, 'The Loss of the Battleship *Novorossiisk*: Accident or Sabotage?', *Warship* XXIX (2007), pp 139–52.

26 Although no substantive work on breaking up the sunken hulk of *Schlesien* was actually carried out until 1952, when it was formally handed over by the Soviets to the East Germans (although lying in now-Polish waters), before 1950 it had been used as an occasional target.

At the end of the war, *Graf Zeppelin* lay at Stettin, bottomed in shallow water, with her machinery wrecked by demolition charges, but only modest hull damage. She was thus refloated with little difficulty in August, and towed to Swinemünde, where she is shown here on 5 April 1947. *(NHHC NH 78311)*

Left: *Graf Zeppelin* remained at Swinemünde until 14 August 1947 when, now renamed *PB-101*, she was towed to a location off Danzig Bay, arriving the night of 15/16th; like *Lützow*, she carried a number of pre-positioned HE bombs and shells. It had been planned that the carrier should be fully anchored for the trial, but this proved not to be possible. The following detonations were carried out:

– 1,000kg bomb in the funnel; three 100kg bombs and two 180mm shells under the flight deck.
– 1,000kg bomb on the flight deck.
– 250kg bomb on the flight deck; two 180mm shells in the upper hanger.
– 500kg bomb suspended over the flight deck; 250kg bomb on the upper hanger deck; 250kg bomb on the flight deck; 100kg bomb on the main deck.
– 500kg and 100kg bombs on the flight deck.

Next, the ship was attacked by Pe-2 aircraft, scoring six hits out of the eighty-eight bombs dropped, causing minimal damage. It had been intended that further trials should be carried out the next day, but worsening weather, and a concern that the ship might drift into shallow water, led to a decision that she should be sunk by torpedoes on the 17th. The first shot, by the MTB *TK-248*, passed under the carrier; the second, from *TK-503*, hit the bulge; a third, by the destroyer *Slavnyi*, was more successful, the hulk gradually listing to starboard, rolling onto her side and sinking twenty-three minutes after the final torpedo hit. Her wreck was located in 2006, at a depth of 80m. *(Soviet navy)*

To gain maximum value from this, *Lützow, Graf Zeppelin* and *Schleswig-Holstein* (as well as thirteen submarines) were all expended in ordnance trials during the summer of 1947, planning for them having begun in May.[27] The first to be sunk was *Schleswig-Holstein*, which was beached in shallow water on the Nyu Grund bank off the Estonian coast at the mouth of the Gulf of Finland, for long-term use as a target on 26 June. *Lützow* was refloated in the summer of 1947, the ship being sunk in the central Baltic on 22 July 1947 during a trial in which a number of bombs and shells were exploded aboard to assess their effects. Four weeks later, *Graf Zeppelin* (now renamed *PB-101*) was the subject of similar trials in the Baltic, being finally dispatched by MTB and destroyer torpedoes.

Cruisers

Nürnberg sailed from Wilhelmshaven for Liepāja on 2 January 1946, accompanied by the destroyers *Z15 Steinbrinck* and *Z33*, the torpedo boats *T17* and *T33*, and the target ship *Hessen* and her control vessel *Blitz*; they arriving on the 5th. From 15 February 1946 to 2 December 1955, *Admiral Makarov*, as *Nürnberg* had been renamed, was flagship of the 8th (Northern Baltic) fleet, based at Tallinn, undergoing a major refit at Kronstadt during 1949/50. During this, her light AA battery was replaced by twenty 37mm weapons, after which she was generally used for training duties. Although in otherwise good condition, boiler trouble led to her formal reduction to a training cruiser, based at Kronstadt, in February 1957. *Admiral Makarov* was stricken two years later, and handed over to the breakers in Leningrad's Coaling harbour a month later.

The Italian *Z15* (ex-*Emanuele Filiberto Duca d'Aosta*) was delivered to Odessa on 2 March 1949. Initially to be

27 V P Kuzin and D Iu Litinskii, 'Avianosets "Graf Zeppelin"—boevoi trofie Kransnii Armii [Aircraft Carrier *Graf Zeppelin*—Battle Trophy of the Red Army]', *Warship International* XLV/2 (2008), pp 161–5.

Admiral Makarov (ex-*Nürnberg*), little altered from her German form, apart from a reduction in the size of her light AA battery and the fitting of new electronics. (*AD collection*)

Like *Admiral Makarov*, modifications to *Kerch* (ex-*Emanuele Filiberto Duca d'Aosta*) was limited to changes to her light guns, radar and fire-control systems. (*AD collection*)

renamed *Stalingrad*, the names *Admiral Ushakov* and *Odessa* also seem to have been proposed before she definitively became *Kerch*. She served in the Black Sea Fleet until 7 February 1956, when she became a training ship, before being reclassified as an experimental unit, designated *OS32*, on 11 May 1958. Stricken in 20 February, the cruiser was scrapped in 1961.

Although a Category C ship, studies had been undertaken towards completing *Seydlitz*, both as a carrier, and as a cruiser alongside her sister *Tallinn* (ex-*Petropavlovsk*, ex-*Lützow*), with *Seydlitz* given priority (and components from *Tallinn* if necessary) to get her out of her 'to be destroyed' category. Both ships, now to be armed with twelve 152mm and twelve 100mm guns (as in the new Project 68b [*Sverdlov* class] vessels), were due to be completed by the end of 1949. However, *Seydlitz* was stricken on 10 March 1947, in anticipation of the 19 March decree, and broken up.

Destroyers

The four German destroyers allocated to the USSR were due to be handed over by 15 February 1946, work being carried out towards this end. However, the condition of *Z14 Ihn*'s boilers led to a suggestion that she be swapped for the UK's *Z6 Riedel*; this was turned down by the Soviets, and in the event it proved possible to get *Ihn* ready in time, albeit loaded with spares to allow work to be completed after arrival. *Z15 Steinbrinck* and *Z33* having sailed in January with *Nürnberg*, *Z20 Galster* and *Ihn* followed in March.

Like *Nürnberg*, all the destroyers were nominally commissioned on 13 February, taking traditional Russian/Soviet names for such vessels. *Ihn* became *Prytkyi*, and remained in service until stricken in 1952; *Steinbrinck* had a much shorter operational life as *Pylkyi*, becoming an accommodation ship in 1949, although not stricken until 1958. *Galster* became *Prochnyi*, and served until 1954, when she too was

Z33 became *Provornyi* in Soviet service, becoming a training ship in 1954, as more new destroyers came into service. Soon reduced to an accommodation hulk, she was burned out in 1960 and subsequently scrapped. *(AD collection)*

The old *Prozorliviy* (ex-*T158*) survived, latterly as the trials vessel *UTS-67*, until 1961, after over fifty years' service. *(Jerzy Miciński collection)*

relegated to an accommodation role. *Z33* was renamed *Provornyi*, and was refitted at Rostock during 1947–50; she became a training ship in 1954, and in 1958 an accommodation hulk at Leningrad. She sank there following a fire in 1960 and was subsequently scrapped.

The three Soviet ex-German modern torpedo boats, *T12*, *T17* and *T33*, became *Podvizhnyi*, *Porivistiy* and *Primernyi*. *Porivistiy* was reduced to reserve in 1949, but the other two remained active into the mid-50s, when they passed into secondary roles. *Podvizhnyi* had suffered severe machinery damage, and in 1953 became a target ship for nuclear

weapons tests in Lake Ladoga, later being dumped in shallow water there, loaded with radioactive waste, in 1959. The old *T107*, *T158* and *T196*, renamed *Porazaiuskyi*, *Prozorliviy* and *Pronzitelnyi*, all served only briefly in operational roles, although *Prozorliviy* would survive as a trials vessel until 1961.

Of the Japanese destroyers handed over to the USSR, although it had been intended to refit all for operational service, all but the big 'Special Type' ex-*Hibiki* were actually completed as target/trials vessels during 1949. *Hibiki*, renamed successively *Vernyi* and then *Dekabrist*, remained in service, however, only until 1953, although she survived as a target ship until the 1970s. The *Akitsuki* class ex-*Harutsuki* and *Matsu* class ex-*Kiri* survived until 1969, but all the others were gone by 1960.

The first of the two Italian destroyers allocated to the Soviet Union actually handed over (as noted above, p 206, *Riboty* was rejected), *Z12*, ex-*Artigliere*, was commissioned in February 1949. Her sister *Fuciliere* was commissioned on 13 March the following year, having left Italy on 14 November 1949. Her delayed handover (and that of *Ardimentoso*) contributed to the final pair of British

The former *T12*, *Podvizhnyi* was badly damaged by a steam-pipe explosion during the summer of 1949, and was paid off in April 1953, still not fully repaired. That summer, she was moved to Lake Ladoga and anchored off Makarinsaari Island, and in the autumn renamed *Kyt*. Between then and 1955, she was used in a series of nuclear weapons tests, at least three devices being exploded on the ship herself. The hulk was later loaded with radioactive waste and sunk in shallow water off Heinäsenmaa Island in March 1959, as shown here. In the summer of 1991, *Kyt* was salved and towed via the White Sea–Baltic Canal to the Barents Sea, to be scuttled off Novaya Zemlya, alongside other irradiated material, including ships expended in the nuclear tests carried out in the area during the 1950s. *(AD collection)*

Most of the Soviet Union's ex-Japanese ships spent time as target ships, for example *TsL-24* (ex-*Shii*) and *TsL-64* (ex-*Harutzuki*), seen here respectively on 3 September 1958 and in July 1959. *(NHHC NH 87946 NH 87945)*

Legkiy, the former Italian *Fuciliere*, was only on active service for a few years, and like many ex-enemy vessels was reduced to subsidiary service, in her case as a target ship, in 1954. *(AD collection)*

destroyers loaned to the Soviet Union not being returned until August/September 1952.

Both ex-*Artigliere* and ex-*Fuciliere* operated with the Black Sea Fleet after – as with ex-*Aosta* – a number of renamings, as *Lovkyi* (ii) and *Legkyi* (ii), respectively, until the end of 1954, when both became target ships. In October 1955, the ex-*Artigliere* was converted into a telecommunications and air control unit, before, with her sister, becoming a training hulk in March 1958, both being finally stricken at the beginning of 1960. The three ex-Italian torpedo boats, *Ladnyi* (ex-*Animoso*), *Letnyi* (ex-*Fortunale*) and *Lyutyi* (ex-*Ardimentoso*) all entered service in 1949, and were relegated to target status at the same time as the two destroyers, being disposed of in 1958 and 1959. The ex-Romanian *Likhoi* and *Letuchyi* were retained until July 1951, when then were returned to their original owners, renamed *D21* and *D22*, respectively, serving for a further decade before being stricken.

Submarines

As noted above (p 191), the transfer of the USSR's allocated share of German boats from the UK was carried out under Operation 'Cabal'. Half proceeded from the UK to Liepāja under their own power; the others were towed, all arriving on 4 December 1946, except for three being delayed by bad weather and technical difficulties until the 10th (*U3041*), 14th (*U3035*) and 2 February (*U3515*). The Type VIICs (*U1057, U1058, U1064* and *U1305*) commissioned as *N-22–N-25*, the Type IXC/40 (*U1231*) as *N-26*, the Type XXIs (*U2529, U3515, U3041* and *U3035*) as *N-27–N-30*, and the Type XXIII (*U2353*) as *M-31*; all served into the mid-1950s. The two surrendered ex-Italian boats were formally handed over at Valona on 7 February 1949, being commissioning as *N-41* (ex-*Marea*) and *N-42* (ex-*Nichelo*). They were soon, however, renamed *S-41* and *S-42*, serving as such until stricken in 1956 and 1958, respectively.

As already noted (pp 187–188, above), the USSR was also in possession of eleven boats, captured incomplete at

Danzig, and classified as 'unallocated' by the TNC. This of course required that they be sunk by 15 February 1946 but, as with the case of other vessels under Soviet control and due for destruction during that year, nothing was done to meet the deadline. While there is no evidence that the completion of the three Type VIIC boats was contemplated, the eight Type XXIs were all given numbers on the Soviet navy list, suggesting intent to commission, although this never actually occurred.

Nevertheless, the presence of at least some in the Kronstadt/Leningrad area (as well as of sections of such boats) was reported by Western intelligence authorities during 1946/47, fuelling a concern that the USSR was creating a fleet of Type XXIs over and above the four boats actually allocated to it by the TNC. However, directly following the CFM meeting in March 1947 and the subsequent Soviet commitment to have completed destructions by August that year, all the 'potential' sectional boats were stricken on 9 April. *R-1*, *R-2* and *R-3* were all scuttled off the Estonian coast on 8 August, and the rest of the 'whole' boats broken up, all being stricken on 2 February 1948.

Patrol and Escort Vessels

The ex-German *F7* became the Soviet *Buran* in February 1946, becoming a base-ship in May 1951, and stricken in September 1956. Of the seventeen Japanese *Kaibōkan* taken over in the summer of 1947, most were reclassified as target ships in 1948. A number were subsequently modified as oceanographic research, salvage, dispatch or repair vessels, serving into the late 1950s. One, *Kaibōkan No. 142*, was transferred to the People's Republic of China in February 1955, serving into the 1980s.

The fleet tender *Hela*, renamed *Angara*, initially served in the Baltic, but transferred to the Black Sea in 1949, becoming the Black Sea Fleet's command ship/yacht, serving as the USSR state yacht between June 1957 and March 1958,

Six Type C escorts were allocated to the USSR, three of them *Kaibōkan Nos. 79, 105* and *227* later becoming the oceanographic research vessels *Sozh, Khersones* and *Siurkum*. *(NHHC NH 96195)*

The German fleet tender *Hela*, taken over by the Soviet Union as the HQ ship *Angara*, shown here as built. Her stripped hull is shown in the inset on 10 August 2017, allegedly awaiting conversion to a yacht. *(AD collection/ A Brichevsky)*

before reverting to her previous fleet role. On 26 February 1995, she suffered an engine room fire, and was reduced to an accommodation ship in January 1996, being offered for sale in 2000. In 2007, she was sold to Italian interests to be rebuilt as a luxury charter-yacht, work beginning at Sevastopol in 2011. However, after removal of her screws, rudder and all superstructure, the hull was laid up, and remains so at the time of writing.

Mine Warfare Vessels

The Soviet tithe of German minesweepers was divided between the Baltic and Black Sea Fleets, thirteen arriving at Sevastopol during the summer of 1946. The latter were renamed in the *T-900* series, and served down to the late 1950s, ex-*M204* lasting as the salvage vessel *Skalistyi* until 1964 and ex-*M155* as the firefighting training vessel *BRN-31* until March 1980.

Thirty-one vessels were commissioned for service in the Baltic with names in the *T-700* series, most transferring to subsidiary roles in the mid-1950s. Little is known of the service of the R-boats, but six of the *R401* class were transferred to East Germany in 1950, serving into the middle of the decade. One ex-Japanese vessel joined the Pacific Fleet in 1947 but, like most ex-Japanese vessels, became a target ship in 1948. The ex-*W-23* was converted to a repair ship in 1955, serving as *PM-61* until the mid-1980s.

Coastal Forces

Thirty German FPBs were handed over to the USSR, and assigned numbers in the *TK-1000* series. Few lasted long, ex-*S11* being stricken as early as February 1948, most following in the Septembers of 1949 and 1950. Eight were disposed of or reduced to harbour service in June 1952, ex-*S209* being the last to be stricken, in 1957. Ex-Italian boats were likewise only retained briefly, into the mid-1950s.

Auxiliary Vessels

From Italy, the USSR received, alongside tugs and tankers, the sail training ship *Cristoforo Colombo*. She operated in the Black Sea in 1959, but a subsequent refit was never completed, and following a fire she was eventually broken up; her half-sister *Amerigo Vespucci* remains in Italian service at the time of writing.

The depot ship *Otto Wünsche* joined the Northern Fleet as *Pecora* in August 1946, and remained in service until September 1973, when she became an accommodation ship until stricken in 1977. Her half-sister *Waldemar Kophamel*, a Category C wreck at Gdynia, was nevertheless salved in 1950 and rebuilt at the Neptun Werft yard at Rostock from August 1951 to October 1955. Renamed *Kuban*, she also joined the Northern Fleet, being likewise reduced to an accommodation role in September 1973; she was stricken in 1978.

Another vessel salved for further service was the sail training ship *Gorch Fock*, which had been scuttled off Rügen.

The sail training vessel *Cristoforo Colombo* left Taranto on 9 February 1949 for Augusta, where she was decommissioned on the 12th, then proceeding to Odessa, arriving on 2 March and being handed over the following day; renamed *Dunay*, she operated out of Odessa until 1959. Dismantled with a view to a major refit in 1961, she was instead used to transport wood, being badly damaged by a cargo fire in 1963. Stricken as a constructive total loss later that year, her hulk was broken up in 1971. *(AD collection)*

She became the Black Sea-based *Tovarishch*, being transferred to Ukraine after the dissolution of the USSR in 1991. Paid off in 1993, she was subsequently taken to the UK for prospective repairs, and then to Germany, where she became a museum under her original name in 2003.

NORWAY

A significant number of Norwegian warships had been captured by Germany in 1940, including three of the modern *Sleipner*-class destroyers. All three survived as torpedo-recovery vessels at Flensburg, to be returned in May 1945, as were many older vessels kept in Norwegian waters. Most were, however, far too old for further service, and were soon broken up, the Norwegian navy having received numerous modern vessels from the UK during the war.

As already noted (p 192, above), seven largely intact German submarines (*U310*, *U315*, *U995*, *U324*, *U926*, *U1202* and *U4706*) remained in Norwegian waters after the last seaworthy boats had been transferred to the UK in June 1945.[28] All suffered from various defects, with *U926* having major structural issues, and had already been condemned for scrapping in April, before the surrender. There had been proposals that *U4706* be repaired with spares from Germany to allow her to proceed to the UK, but these were rejected. In addition, there were seven derelict boats in Norway (*U92*, *U228*, *U256*, *U437*, *U622* [Bergen], *U985* [Kristiansand-South] and *U995* [Bergen]). All fourteen had been condemned as 'unallocated' or Category C by the TNC and thus to be destroyed by 15 February 1946.

However, unlike vessels in German waters, the TNC had no authority over those in other hands, principally French, Danish and Norwegian. Attempts to apply diplomatic pressure were undermined when the USA made a premature unilateral approach that was not subsequently followed up by the other two major Allies. The UK was in any case ambivalent, being supportive of the French keeping at least one boat (p 192, above) and thus unwilling to put pressure on Norway, while the USSR's position was problematic in view of their own possession of submarines in a not-dissimilar position (p 187–88, above).

In any case, the Norwegian authorities had already begun to take steps towards taking some of the boats into service.[29] *U926* was made seaworthy (although not safe to dive) by September 1945, utilising batteries taken from the old Norwegian submarine *B1*, and sailed from Bergen to Trondheim, being present at the arrival of the ex-British

submarines *Utstein* (ex-*Venturer*), *Utvaer* (ex-*Viking*) and *Uthaug* (ex-*Votary*) from the UK on 1 October. She was then laid up in the ex-German DORA I bunker at Trondheim.

On 12 October, a commission was set up by the Norwegian navy to assess whether any of the ex-German Type VIIC submarines could be made operational at a reasonable cost. This determined that *U228*, *U256*, *U437* and *U993* were write-offs, although two might be cannibalised, as could *U315* and *U324*. On the other hand, *U310*, *U926*, *U995* and *U1202* were judged capable of refitting for service, and the commission's report, issued on 31 October, recommended that they be kept. The Type XXIII *U4706* was also of interest for trials purposes, although she had a major propulsion defect and had lost her *Schnorchel* to a sister that had gone to the UK. All five boats were concentrated at Trondheim, where they were moored unobtrusively, pending a final decision on their future. The remaining nine boats were sold for scrap in 1947, as was *U310*, which was now felt to be in too poor a condition for refitting. She, *U315* and *U324* were first cannibalised for spares for their now-three retained sisters.

Funds were made available for the refitting of *U926*, *U995* and *U1202* in May 1948, but although renamed *Kya*, *Kaura* and *Kinn* in September, it was not until the following month that Norway unilaterally declared ownership. The newly refitted *Kya* (ex-*U926*) made her first dive on 24 April 1949. However, plans to also take *U4706*, renamed *Knerten*, into service were frustrated when she was damaged by a battery explosion and engine room fire before her refit was complete, and was never formally commissioned, being sold as a storage hulk. The three Type VIICs, however, were all commissioned between January 1949 and December 1952, and served into the 1960s. *Kya* was refitted with a streamlined sail and new sonar in the late 1950s, allowing her to remain in commission until the first of the new *Kobben* class boats entered service in 1964. *Kinn* had decommissioned in 1961 and *Kaura* in 1962, but while *Kinn* would be scrapped in 1963, *Kaura* was returned to Germany in October 1965, to become a museum and memorial at the Laboe Naval Memorial near Kiel in 1972. She is now listed as an historic monument within the state of Schleswig-Holstein.

Thirteen M-type minesweepers were given to Norway by the UK in November 1947, but saw no service and were broken up in the early 1950s. Thirteen FPBs also came into Norwegian hands. All came from the USA's share, four (including *S10*, *S21* and *S48*) being intended for cannibalisation. Of the nine given names, *Blink* (ex-*S302*), *Brand* (ex-*S303*), *Kjekk* (ex-*S195*), *Kvikk* (ex-*S98*), *Lyn* (ex-*S64*), *Rapp* (ex-*S174*), *Snaar* (ex-*S210*), *Storm* (ex-*S85*) and *Tross* (ex-*S117*), *Kvikk* and *Snaar* had gone aground during the winter

28 See Waller, *Warships* 179, pp 8–24.

29 D Waller, 'U-boats in Norway, post 08 May 1945 (Part 3)', *Warships* 180 (2015), pp 5–13.

One of a number of German submarines left behind in Norway, and insufficiently seaworthy to be transferred to the UK, *U995* was, together with two sisters and contrary to tripartite Allied policy that required such 'unallocated' vessels be destroyed, refitted for service. As *Kaura*, she entered service in December 1952, operating out of Narvik as a training boat until 1962. In October 1965, she was returned to Germany and, after being loaned to the Deutscher Marinebund, was refitted at Kiel (including a new conning tower), and installed at the foot of the Laboe memorial on 13 March 1972. *(Andrew Wyngaard)*

of 1945/46, and were broken up in 1950, as was *Rapp*. The remainder were transferred to Denmark in 1951 (see below).

DENMARK

Much of the Danish fleet had been scuttled in August 1943 after the Germans imposed direct military occupation, with others seized by Germany. Of the latter, the two incomplete *Najaden*-class torpedo boats would be completed post-war. Six modern torpedo boats had been 'loaned' to Germany in 1941, *Högen* (renamed *TFA1*), *Örnen* (*TFA2*), *Dragen* (*TFA3*), *Glenten* (*TFA4*), *Hvalen* (*TFA5*) and *Laxen* (*TFA6*), and all survived the war. However, ex-*Dragen* was mined in Geltinger Bight on 14 May 1945, and the others became constructive total losses in July while awaiting return, when the depot ship *Donau* blew up alongside at Flensburg.

Denmark was thus keen to rebuild her navy, purchasing two British frigates and a corvette in 1945, as well as ex-German units. Two torpedo boats, *T4* and *T19*, were bought in 1947 from the USA (for $5,000 each) to act as leaders for a planned force of a dozen operational FPBs. The latter force comprised eleven vessels from the USA, together with one from the UK, with another two for cannibalisation. In the event, *T4* and *T19* were not commissioned, and were soon broken up, but the FPBs were put into service with numbers in a *T*-sequence. In 1951, they were joined by six further vessels, transferred from Norway, the whole force then being given names. As support, they had the depot ship *Ægir* (ex-*Tanga*), transferred by the USA in 1948, and rebuilt through to 1951.

All FPBs were given a gun armament of one 40mm and one 20mm, in addition to their two torpedo tubes, and while *Hærfuglen* (ex-*S133*) was stricken as early as 1954, *Viben*

(ex-*S68*) lasted until 1965. The first vessels withdrawn were replaced by an updated version of the *S100* type, built in Denmark to a Lürssen design as the *Flyvefisken* class during 1952–55.

In addition, during 1945 Denmark had operated a number of R-boats alongside the GM/SA in Danish waters, the vessels being formally loaned by the US and UK in September/December 1945 following the TNC's distribution of German warships. Some were formally taken into the Danish navy in 1947, being disposed of between 1948 and the 1960s, the others being returned to the UK/USA.

BELGIUM

As noted above (p 72), Belgium had abolished her navy in the 1920s, with a handful of civilian-owned vessels retained, including two of the ex-German torpedo boats, and the fishery protection vessel (ex-British sloop) *Zinnia*. All, together with the latter's replacement, *Artevelde*, were captured on the slip in 1940, with the extensively modified *Artevelde* and *Zinnia* both retroceded in 1945. However, both were in poor condition (the former with severe engine damage) and were soon replaced by vessels acquired from the UK and USA.

In addition, the ex-German depot ship *Hermann von Wissmann* was also obtained. Laid down at an Antwerp ship-yard to a Polish order (which had resulted in a Polish claim in June 1946 – as well as for her USSR-allocated sister, *Otto Wünsche*),[30] she had served as the British headquarters ship *Royal Harold* at Kiel until paid off in October 1948. Her place of building then led the Belgian Office for Economic

---

30 TNA FO 371/57151 [U5829].

Begun as a Polish merchantman at Antwerp, the German depot ship *Hermann von Wissmann* became the Belgian *Kamina* in 1950. A 670-capacity troop transport, she made her first run, to Korea, on 18 December 1950, being refitted at Ostend on her return. She was then employed between Belgium and the Belgian Congo until the latter's independence in October 1960, then being converted into a logistic support/cadet training ship, before being recommissioned on 6 February 1962. Her last training cruise was to Montreal in April 1967. *(AD collection)*

Reconstruction to make their own request in 1950. Accordingly, her cession to Belgium was requested, the ship being towed to Antwerp for refitting as a troop transport in October 1950, being commissioned as *Kamina* in December.

NETHERLANDS

The principal vessels received from the Axis by the Netherlands were its own units that had been captured in 1940. The most important were the cruisers *De Zeven Provinciën* and *De Ruyter* (German *KH1* and *KH2*), one of which was afloat, and the other still on the stocks; both were finally completed in 1953. There were also the submarine *O27* (*UD5*), the gunboat *Van Speijk* (*K3*) and the minesweeper *Abraham van der Hulst* (*M551*), all completed by the Germans, plus the latter's pre-war sister, *Pieter Florisz* (*M552*). Among other vessels returned were the two former coast defence ships that had served as the German floating AA batteries *Undine* and *Ariadne*. Both would be rebuilt as accommodation ships.

The floating AA batteries *Undine* (ex-*IJmuiden*, ex-*Jacob van Heemskerk*) and *Ariadne* (ex-*Vliereede*, ex-*Hertog Hendrik*), converted from Dutch coast defence ships, laid up at Wilhelmshaven at the end of the war prior to return to the Netherlands. They respectively became the accommodation hulks *Neptunus* and *Hertog Hendrik*, serving until 1968 and 1974. *(AD collection)*

A number of R-boats were Dutch-manned as part of the GM/SA operations in Netherlands waters. All but one were formally transferred from the UK in November 1947, serving into the late 1950s.

YUGOSLAVIA
Torpedo boats
The two surviving ex-Austro-Hungarian boats captured by Italy in 1941 had both been returned in 1943; the damaged hull of the incomplete destroyer *Split* fell back into Yugoslav hands in October 1944 (and was eventually completed in 1958). These were joined by the three major vessels allocated to the Yugoslavs, which were handed over in late April and early May 1949, transfer being delayed pending finalisation of a fishing agreement between the two nations. *Aliseo* and *Indomito* became *Biokovo* and *Triglav*, respectively, serving until stricken in April 1965. The newer *Ariete*, renamed *Durmitor*, lasted two years longer, being stricken at the beginning of 1967.

The torpedo boat *Indomito* was completed shortly before the Italian armistice, and served until she became the Yugoslav *Triglav* in 1949. *(AD collection)*

Her half-sister *Belestra* was still on the stocks at Fiume (Rijeka) at the armistice, and became the German *TA47*; still on the slip, she was damaged by bombs on 2 February 1945. Taken over by Yugoslavia, she was finally launched in 1947, and commissioned as *Učka* in 1950. *(AD collection)*

Found damaged at Pola in 1945, *UIT19* (ex-*Nautilo*) was repaired and recommissioned as the Yugoslav *Sava* in 1949. She was rebuilt during 1958–60 with a streamlined conning tower and no deck gun. *(Yugoslav navy)*

Two of ex-*Ariete*'s sisters, *Balestra* (seized by Germany in 1943 as *TA47*) and *Fionda* (*TA46*) were taken over on the slip at Fiume/Rijeka, and renamed *Učka* and *Velebit*, respectively. Both had been badly damaged by bombing in February 1945 and, in the end, it was only *Ucka* which was completed in 1950. All received US electronics and had their light guns updated.

Submarines
At Pola, *UIT19* (ex-*Nautilo*) was found sunk, having been bombed there by US aircraft on 9 January 1944. In 1947 she was raised and repaired, being commissioned as the Yugoslav *Sava* in 1949. She became a training boat in 1958, having her deck gun removed and conning tower streamlined in 1960; she was stricken in 1971.

Mine Warfare Vessels
Eight minesweepers, of the German M1916 type, had been seized from Yugoslavia by the Italians in 1941. Only one survived to be retroceded in December 1943, and thus seven Italian minesweepers of similar First World War vintage were handed over in August 1948. They remained in service through the 1950s, until replaced by four vessels of the French *Sirius* class from 1957 onwards.

Auxiliary Vessels
Four landing craft, two German (*D203* and *D204*) and two Italian (*D206* [ex-*MZ 713*] and *D219* [ex-*MZ 717*]) were taken over by Yugoslavia, and served through the 1970s. Four tugs – *PR51* (ex-Italian *Porto Conte*, 1936), *PR52* (ex-*San Remo*, 1937), *PR58* (ex-*Molara*, 1937) and *LR11* (ex-*Basiluzzo*) – were also surrendered to Yugoslavia.

GREECE
Greece expressed concerns soon after the signing of the Italian peace treaty that *Eugenio*'s handover might be frus-

To be handed over in part as a reparation for the Italian sinking of the cruiser *Helli* (i) in August 1940, two months before the outbreak of war between Italy and Greece, *Eugenio di Savoia* did not become *Helli* (ii) until July 1951, owing to the need to repair mine-damage dating from 1944. *(AD collection)*

trated by some act of the Italians, and also whether the UK and USA's decision over the fate of ships allocated to them (pp 202–5) might prejudice the Greek position.[31] However, the Italian position was that *Eugenio* was legitimate restitution for the sinking of the Greek cruiser *Helli* (i) in 1940, undertaken in advance of any state of war between the two nations, and thus probably the least problematic of the treaty-required surrenders by Italy.

Negotiations were thus begun, although complicated by the state of the ship, which had been damaged by a mine on 29 February 1944, off Punta Stilo, while repatriating surplus personnel from *Italia* and *Vittorio Veneto*. The need to undertake repairs meant that an early handover, as was the case with ships ceded to France, was not possible. An agreement was finally reached on 29 September 1948, under which repairs (except for her forward gearing) would be completed at Taranto by the end of July 1949; the gearing repair would be carried out on the Greek government's account. In addition, it was agreed that the ship would not be regarded by Greece as war booty, but indeed as restitution for damages inflicted during 1940–44.

As *Helli* (ii), she was commissioned in June 1951, becoming fleet flagship, and was used to carry King Pavlos I to state visits to Istanbul in June 1952, to Yugoslavia in September 1955, to Toulon in June 1956 and to the Lebanon in May 1958. In 1959, she became a command ship of the Ionian Fleet, based at Suda Bay on Crete. Paid off in 1964 as uneconomical to run, she was used as a prison ship for anti-regime navy personnel during the 1967–73 rule of the 'Colonels', and sold for scrap in 1973.

31 TNA ADM 116/5768.

CHINA
Destroyers

After decades of conflict, China needed all the ships she could get to rebuild her navy. However, as ships were delivered without armament, putting them into service was distinctly problematic, given the state of the country and its economy. In addition, the ongoing civil war between the Nationalists and the Communists meant that a number of vessels passed to the new People's Republic of China through defection or capture.

All six destroyers transferred from Japan remained in Nationalist hands, but some never re-entered service, remaining laid up until stricken, this being the case with the old *Shen Yang* (ex-*Namikaze*) and the much newer *Fen Yang* (ex-*Yoizuki*), the largest vessel transferred to China. The latter was used as a training hulk, although a full refurbishment in Japan was contemplated at one point. Others received interim armaments, in particular the big *Tan Yang* (ex-*Yukikaze*) which, initially used as a harbour training ship at Shanghai, was evacuated to Taiwan in May 1949 as the city fell to the Communists. She was then refitted between 1951 and 1953, armed with a twin mount carrying 127mm/40 Type 89 guns forward, with four 100mm/65 Type 98 guns in twin mounts aft (all improvised from shore artillery), plus eight 25mm guns. This temporary armament was replaced in 1956 with US three 5in/38 and two 3in/50 guns in single open mounts, plus ten 40mm. During 1958/59 she undertook anti-mainland activities, before being withdrawn through machinery defects on 16 December 1965. Decommissioned the following November 1966, she was employed as a harbour training ship until running aground during a summer 1969 typhoon; she was subsequently scrapped.

Of the smaller *Matsu/Tachibana*-class vessels, *Xin Yang* (ex-*Hatsuyume*) was given a scratch battery of two 120mm,

Xin Yang (ex-*Hatsuyume*), the one *Matsu/Tachibana* class ship to have substantive service under the Chinese flag, shown here during the late 1950s, as refitted with US guns. *(Republic of China Navy)*

three 57mm, two 40mm and four 20mm guns in March 1948, and operated against Communist forces. She was refitted in 1954, with components taken from her sister *Hui Yang* (ex-*Sugi*, stricken November 1954), and rearmed with two single 5in/38, seven 40mm and six 20mm US guns; she served until the 1960s. However, her sister *Hua Yang* (ex-*Tsuta*), had run aground in the Pescadores Islands en route to Taiwan in 1949 and remained there until stricken in 1954, while *Heng Yang* (ex-*Kaede*) was, like *Hui Yang*, never rearmed or recommissioned after the evacuation from Shanghai, becoming a training hulk until 1960.

Patrol/Escort Vessels

Likewise, of the *Kaibōkan* that remained in Nationalist hands, some were never rearmed. Of these, *Tong An* (ex-*No. 192*) had been stricken as early as 1952, while *Chang An* (ex-*No. 205*) was badly damaged by stranding in the Pescadores on 26 September 1954 while still unarmed. Others, however, were gradually given weapons, *Cheng An* (ex-*Yashiro*), *Chen An* (ex-*No. 40*) and *Tai An* (ex-*No. 104*) being rearmed with

Tan Yang (ex-*Yukikaze*) shown, as provisionally armed with guns taken from coastal batteries, in January 1954, and as definitively rearmed with US weapons in 1956. *(C S Bird/Republic of China Navy)*

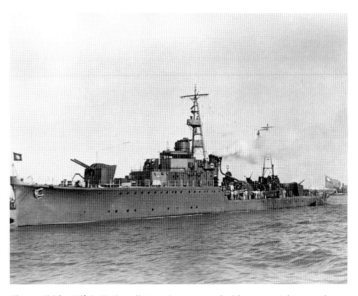

Chang Chi (ex-*Uji*) in Nationalist service, rearmed with ex-coastal guns; she fell into Communist hands and, as *Nan Chang*, was again rearmed, this time with Soviet weapons. *(NHHC NH 96191)*

two US 5in/38s, *Jui An* (ex-*No. 67*) with one 4.7in and one 3in/50, and *Lin An* (ex-*Tsushima*) and *Chao An* (ex-*No. 107*) with two 3in/50 guns, backed up in most cases by 40mm and 20mm weapons.

Also used as an escort was the former minelayer *Yung Ching* (ex-*Saishu*), fitted with a single 3in/50, initially backed up by one 40mm, one 20mm and five 25mm guns, the latter later replaced by two more 40mm and four more 20mm weapons. She retained her minelaying capability, serving until 1964. There was also the ex-Italian minelayer *Sien Hing* (ex-*Okisu*, ex-*Lepanto*), also classified as an escort until broken up in 1956.

The eight vessels that ended up in the People's Republic had various armaments fitted. *Rui Jin* (ex-*Huai An*, ex-*Shisaka*) had two 127cm, her sister *Chang Bai* (ex-*Ku An*, ex-*Oki*) two 100mm, as did *Sheng Yang* (ex-*Huang An*, ex-*No. 81*), together with a light AA battery. *Chang Sha* (ex-*Jie 12*, ex-*No. 118*), *Wu Chang* (ex-*Jie 5*, ex-*No. 14*), *Tsi Nan* (ex-*Wei Hai*, ex-*No. 194*) and *Hsi An* (ex-*Jie 14*, ex-*No. 198*) all had a pair of US 3in/50 guns. *Nan Chang* (ex-*Chang Chi*, ex-*Uji*) was given two Soviet 100mm and two 76mm guns, replacing ex-coastal 127mm guns fitted while in Nationalist hands, and later rearmed once again, with two 130mm and five 37mm weapons, as was also *Shen Yang*. A wide range of other ex-Japanese patrol, escort and gun vessels also served in the Chinese navies, including the retroceded large gunboat *Yi Hsein* (ex-*Atada*, ex-Chinese *Yat Sen*).

TOWARDS NEW GERMAN NAVIES

Although the occupation of Germany by four Allied armies was not intended as a precursor to the dismemberment of what was left of the country (much of the east having already been ceded to Poland). However, in May 1949, the US, UK and French occupation zones together became the Federal Republic of German (Bundesrepublik Deutschland – BRD, or West Germany), and in October the Soviet zone became the communist German Democratic Republic (Deutsches Demokratisches Republik – DDR, or East Germany). They remained separate states until 3 October 1990, when the territory of the former DDR was absorbed into the BRD.

West Germany

In 1951, the US set up a new minesweeping force within its enclave, the nominally civilian US Labor Service Unit B (LSU[B]). Three LSUs had been set up in November 1950 to assist in the manning of US vessels and shore facilities.[32] LSU(B), established on 1 February 1951, beginning with four US-allocated M-boats (*M278*, *M294*, *M388* and *M460*,

The first major ships of the new Federal German navy, *Seehund* (ex-*M388* – see p 220) and *Seelöwe* (ex-*M441*), transferred from the US Labor Service Unit B in July 1956, with which they had served as *M203* and *M205*, respectively. Both were reduced to accommodation ships in 1960. *(AD collection)*

renamed *M202*, *M201*, *M203* and *M204*, respectively), and a few subsidiary vessels, then absorbed the dozen R-boats of the Cuxhaven group in June. Further OMGUS vessels that had been chartered-out were added as they were returned; in particular, *M441* (*M205*) and *M611* (*M206*) were added in October. Eventually, thirty-two minesweepers, three FPBs plus support vessels were formed into three flotillas. Although German-manned, all vessels remained US property and flew the US ensign. As noted above, three trawlers, plus the support vessels *Weser* and *Dievenow*, remained under British control as the Marinedienstgruppe Royal Navy (MDG RN), but were soon demobilised and the vessels disposed of, *Weser* being ultimately sold as a barge, and the trawlers transferred to the new Seegrenzschutz (see below) on 1 July 1951.

In spite of its nominal status, the German 'civilians' contracted to LSU(B) were uniformed and subject to military-style discipline, and it was a fairly open secret that they would form an important part of any new West German naval formation. Thus, training over and above what was needed for the LSU(B) core tasks began to be offered, becoming the priority during 1953–55. Preparations for the transfer of LSU(B) to German control began early in 1955, leading up the establishment of the West German Ministry of Defence in June of that year.[33] Formal transfers began with ex-*R132*, ex-*R134*, ex-*R135* and ex-*R144* on 5 June 1956, and finishing with ex-*R266* and ex-*R407* in January 1957.

The bigger ex-*M388* and ex-*M441* were handed over on 17 July 1956, becoming *Seehund* and *Seelöwe*, with the other three M-boats (ex-*M278* [*Seestern*], ex-*M294* [*Seepferd*] and ex-*M611* [*Seeschlange*]) following in August. In February 1957, five ex-French M-boats (*Ailette* [ex-*M24*], *Laffaux* [ex-*M81*], *Yser* [ex-*M85*], *Belfort* [ex-*M205*] and *Vimy* [ex-*M253*]) were also transferred, becoming respectively *Wespe*, *Hummel*, *Brummer*, *Biene* and *Bremse*.

Also feeding into the new navy was the quasi-coastguard of the Seegrenzschutz, established as part of the Federal Border Guard under the auspices of the Ministry of the Interior in 1951.[34] While the Kiel repair yard was handed over by the British in December 1951, and parts of the Cuxhaven base in October 1952, acquisition of equipment was hindered by a suspicious UK and France, who vetoed an attempt to acquire new-build FPBs in 1953. The vessels in question (the first three of the *Silbermöwe* class, a modified version of the wartime S38b type) were transferred on the stocks to the British, serving with German crews, but under British command, until May 1956 (see p 215, above). Nevertheless, by 1955, some forty patrol vessels were in service. In June 1956 all personnel willing to do so were transferred to the Ministry of Defence, and on 1 July all Seegrenzschutz assets were ceded to the Bundesmarine,

joining the aforementioned first echelons of LSU(B) in what was now well on its way to becoming a fully fledged navy.

New-build frigates (of the *Köln* class) were begun in 1957, and destroyers and frigates acquired from the USA and UK in 1958/39. Two Type XXIII submarines were salved in 1956 and recommissioned in 1957, to serve as training boats for a new series of vessels launched from 1962 onwards, marking the de facto transition of West Germany from a defeated enemy to a trusted naval ally.

East Germany

On the other side of the German divide, a maritime element of the paramilitary and border police forces, established in July 1948, came into existence in December 1949, when purely civilian maritime security entities, in particular Mecklenburg's Maritime Security Police, passed under paramilitary control.[35] From this emerged the maritime sections of the Border Police and Transportation Police, together with a new Sea Police, established in June 1950.

Initial equipment comprised six R-boats and two ex-Kriegsmarine, ex-Danish coastal minelayers, transferred by the USSR in May and June 1950. These were in poor condition, but six new locally built 'Sperber I'-class patrol vessels were added during 1950/51, as was an ex-Danish fishery protection vessel (*Ernst Thälmann*, ex-*Hvidbjörnen*). The first larger ships, 'Habicht'-class mine-warfare vessels were ordered in January 1951.

Following the BRD's accession to NATO in 1955, the Warsaw Pact was created, with the DDR's hitherto-paramilitary forces upgraded in status to participate. The Naval Forces of the National People's Army (Verwaltung Seestreitkräfte der Nationale Volksarmee) was thus created on 1 March 1956, becoming the Volksmarine (People's Navy) in November 1960. By this time, Soviet 'Riga'-class frigates, additional East German-built minesweepers and fast attack craft had been acquired, giving the Volksmarine a useful, if primarily littoral, capability.

---

33 Peifer, *Three German Navies*, pp 170–85.
34 Peifer, *Three German Navies*, pp 161–8.

35 Peifer, *Three German Navies*, pp 116–49.

Ships and fates

1. The German Navy: 8 May 1945

Table 2.1/1. Capital Ships and Cruisers

Class	Disp.	Length	Beam	Machinery	Power/speed	Main gun(s)	TT	Aircraft
Deutschland (i)	13,191t	127.6m	22.2m	8/12 x boilers, 3 x VTE	16–17,000ihp=18.0kt	4 x 28cm/40	–	–
Scharnhorst	35,540t	234.9m	30.0m	12 x boilers, 3 x Tu	160,000shp=31.0kt	[6 x 38cm/47	6 x 53.3cm]	4
Bismarck	42,900t	251.0m	36.0m	12 x boilers, 3 x Tu	138,000shp=29.0kt	8 x 38cm/47	8 x 53.3cm	6
Deutschland (ii)	12,630t	187.9m	20.7m	2 x diesel	54,000bhp=26.0kt	6 x 28cm/55	8 x 53.3cm	2
Admiral Scheer	13,660t	187.9m	21.3m	2 x diesel	54,000bhp=26.0kt	6 x 28cm/55	8 x 53.3cm	2
Admiral Hipper	16,170t	205.0m	21.3m	12 x boilers, 3 x Tu	132,000shp=32.0kt	8 x 20.3cm/60	12 x 53.3cm	3
Prinz Eugen	16,970t	212.0m	21.7m	12 x boilers, 3 x Tu	132,000shp=32.0kt	8 x 20.3cm/60	12 x 53.3cm	3
Seydlitz	17,139t	216.0m	21.8m	12 x boilers, 3 x Tu	132,000shp=32.0kt	[10 x 10.5cm/65	–	20]
Graf Zeppelin	28,090t	262.5m	36.2m	16 x boilers, 4 x Tu	200,000shp=33.8kt	[16 x 15cm/55	–	42]
Emden	6056t	155.1m	14.2m	10 x boilers, 2 x Tu	46,500shp=29.0kt	8 x 15cm/48	2 x 53.3cm	–
Königsberg (ii)	6750t	174.0m	15.2m	6 x boilers, 2 x Tu/diesel	65,000shp/1800bhp=32.0/10.0kt	9 x 15cm/60	9 x 53.3cm	1
Leipzig	6820t	177.0m	16.3m	6 x boilers, 2 x Tu/1 diesel	60,000shp/12,400bhp=32.0/16.5kt	9 x 15cm/60	–	–
Nürnberg	8060t	181.3m	16.3m	6 x boilers, 2 x Tu/1 diesel	60,000shp/12,400bhp=32.0/16.5kt	9 x 15cm/60	–	–
NL De Zeven Provinciën	8350T	185.7m	17.3m	6 x boilers, 2 x Tu	78,000shp = 32.0kt	8 x 15cm/55	–	2

Name	Class	Builder	Launch	Comp / comm	Alloc	Fate
Admiral Hipper	Admiral Hipper	Blohm & Voss (Hamburg)	6 Feb 37	29 Apr 39	Cat C	(scuttled Kiel 3 May 45) Undocked Jul 45; blown up 21 May 46; BU in situ 1948–52
Admiral Scheer	Admiral Scheer	Wilhemshaven DYd	1 Apr 33	12 Nov 34	Cat C	(sunk Kiel 9 Apr 45) BU/buried in situ
Emden	Emden	Wilhelmshaven DYd	7 Jan 25	15 Oct 25	Cat C	(scuttled Kiel 3 May 45) Blown up 21 May 46; BU in situ
Gneisenau	Scharnhorst	Deutsche Werke (Kiel)	8 Dec 36	21 May 38	Cat C	(scuttled Gdynia 27 Mar 45) Salved 12 Sep 51; BU
Graf Zeppelin = PB-101 (3 Feb 47)	Graf Zeppelin	Deutsche Werke (Kiel)	8 Dec 38	–	Cat C	(scuttled Stettin 24 Mar 45) Salved; to Swinemünde; expended target C Baltic (55° 31' 3" N, 18° 17' 9" E) 17 Aug 47
KH1 (ex-De Zeven Provinciën) = De Zeven Provinciën (May 45) = De Ruyter (22 Aug 50) = Almirante Grau (23 May 73) = Proyecto de Modernización 01 (7 Aug 86) = Almirante Grau (15 Feb 88)	NL De Zeven Provinciën	Wilton-Fijenoord (Rotterdam)	24 Dec 44	[18 Nov 53]	–	Retroceded NL May 45; sold PE 7 Mar 73; decommissioned 26 Sep 17
KH2 (ex-Eendracht, ex-Kijkduin) = De Ruyter (May 45) = De Zeven Provinciën (22 Aug 50) = Aguirre (Aug 76) = Almirante Grau (17 Aug 86) = Aguirre (15 Feb 88)	NL De Zeven Provinciën	Rotterdamse Droogd Mij (Rotterdam)	[20 Aug 50]	[17 Dec 53]	–	Retroceded NL May 45; sold PE 17 Aug 76; decommissioned 21 Mar 99; BU 2000
Köln	Königsberg (iii)	Wilhelmshaven DYd	23 May 28	15 Jan 30	Cat C	(sunk Wilhelmshaven 30 Apr 45) BU in situ
Königsberg	Königsberg (iii)	Wilhelmshaven DYd	26 Mar 27	17 Apr 29	Cat C	(being BU Stavanger) BU
Leipzig	Leipzig	Wilhelmshaven DYd	18 Oct 29	8 Oct 31	Cat C	(damaged) Scuttled Skagerrak (57° 53' N, 06° 39' E) 16 Dec 46
Lützow (ex-Deutschland)	Deutschland (ii)	Deutsche Werke (Kiel)	19 May 31	1 Apr 33	Cat C	(sunk Swinemünde 16 Apr 45) Salved Nov 46; expended target C Baltic 22 Jul 47
Nürnberg = Admiral Makarov (Feb 46)	Nürnberg	Deutsche Werke (Kiel)	8 Dec 34	2 Nov 35	SU	SU 13 Feb 46; training ship 21 Feb 57; stricken 20 Feb 59; BU 13 Mar 59–Feb 61

Name	Class	Builder	Launch	Comp / comm	Alloc	Fate
Prinz Eugen	Prinz Eugen	Germania (Kiel)	22 Aug 38	1 Aug 40	US	US 14 Dec 45; US comm 5 Jan 46; expended atomic bomb target Bikini 17 Jun 46; decommissioned 29 Aug 46; foundered Kwajalein (8° 45' 9.85" N, 167° 40' 59.16" E) 22 Dec 46
Schlesien	Deutschland (i)	Schichau (Danzig)	28 May 06	5 May 08	Cat C	(sunk off Swinemünde 4 May 45) BU in situ 1952–57
Schleswig-Holstein	Deutschland (i)	Germania (Kiel)	17 Dec 06	6 Jul 08	Cat C	(sunk Gdynia 18 Dec 44) Salved Aug 45; to Tallinn May 46; grounded as long-term target off Osmussaar 26 Jun 47
Seydlitz	Seydlitz	Deschimag (Bremen)	19 Jan 39	–	Cat C	(scuttled Königsberg 29 Jan 45) Salved; to Leningrad Oct 46; stricken 10 Mar 47; BU
Tirpitz	Bismarck	Wilhelmshaven DYd	1 Apr 39	25 Feb 41	Cat C	(sunk Tromsø 12 Nov 44) BU in situ 1948–57.

Table 2.1/2. Ex-Capital Ships and Cruisers

Class	Disp.	Length	Beam	Machinery	Power/speed	Main gun(s)
NL Hertog Hendrik	4371t	96.6m	15.2m	6 x boilers, 2 x VTE	[6500ihp – inoperable]	8 x 105mm/45
NL Jacob van Heemskerk	4445t	98.0m	15.2m	6 x boilers, 2 x VTE	[6400ihp – inoperable]	8 x 105mm/45
Wittelsbach (mod)	11,800t	125.3m	20.4m	2 x boilers, 2 x VTE	5000ihp=13.0kt	–
Braunschweig (mod)	12,200t	138.1m	21.5m	2 x boilers, 2 x Tu	25,000shp=20.3kt	2 x 105mm/45
NO Tordenskjold	3380t	92.7m	14.8m	3 x boilers, 2 x VTE	4500ihp=14.0kt	6 x 105mm/45
Frauenlob (mod)	2657t	105.0m	12.3m	–	–	4 x 105mm/45
Gazelle (mod)	2650t	105.1m	12.3m	–	–	5 x 105mm/45

Name	Class	Builder	Launch	Comp/comm	Alloc	Fate
Amazone	Gazelle (Table 1.1/2); disarmed)	Germania (Kiel)	6 Oct 00	15 Nov 01	US	Accommodation ship; US 1945; BU Hamburg 1954
Arcona	Frauenlob (mod)	AG Weser (Bremen)	22 Apr 02	13 May 03	Cat C	(scuttled Brunsbüttel May 45) BU 1948–49
Ariadne (ex-Vliereede, ex-Hertog Hendrik) = Hertog Hendrik (Oct 47)	NL Hertog Hendrik	Amsterdam DYd	7 Jun 02	NL: 5 Jan 04 GE: Nov 43	–	Retroceded NL 1945; accommodation hulk 21 Oct 47; decommissioned 27 Sep 68; stricken 28 Aug 69; BU
Berlin	Bremen (Table 1.1/2)	Danzig DYd	22 Sep 03	4 Apr 05	Cat C	(afloat Kiel) Scuttled Skagerrak (58° 08' 09" N, 10° 48' 51" E) 30 May 46
Hessen = Tsel (1946)	Braunschweig (mod)	Germania (Kiel)	18 Sep 03	19 Sep 05	SU	SU 3 Jun 46; stricken & BU 1960
Medusa	Gazelle (mod)	AG Weser (Bremen)	5 Dec 00	26 Jul 01	Cat C	(scuttled Wilhelmshaven May 45) BU 1948–50
Nymphe (ii) (ex-Tordenskjold)	NO Tordenskjold	Armstrong (Elswick)	16 Mar 97	NO: 2 Apr 98 GE: Mar 41	–	Stranded Moldøra (68° 13.3' N, 14° 47' E) 17 May 1945; sold Stavanger shipbreaker 1948; BU
Thetis (ii) (ex-Harald Haarfagre)	NO Tordenskjold (Elswick)	Armstrong	4 Jan 97	NO: 10 Jun 97 GE: Mar 41	–	Retroceded May 45; accommodation hulk; BU 1947
Undine (ex-IJmuiden, ex-Jacob van Heemskerk) = Neptunus (Feb 48)	NL Jacob van Heemskerk	Amsterdam DYd	22 Sep 06	NL: 22 Apr 08 GE: Aug 43	–	Retroceded 1945; accommodation hulk 23 Feb 48; decommissioned 13 Sep 74; stricken 4 Oct 74; sold 11 May 75; BU
Zähringen	Wittelsbach (mod)	Germania (Kiel)	12 Jun 01	25 Oct 02	Cat C	(scuttled Gdynia 27 Mar 45) BU 1949–50.

Table 2.1/3 Destroyers and Torpedo Boats

Class	Disp.	Length	Beam	Machinery	Power/speed	Main gun (s)	TT	Mines
Z1934	2619t	119.3m	11.3m	6 x boilers, 2 x Tu	70,000shp=36.0kt	5 x 12.7cm	8 x 53.3cm	60
Z1934A	2619t	120.0m	11.3m	6 x boilers, 2 x Tu	70,000shp=36.0kt	4/5 x 12.7cm	8 x 53.3cm	60
Z1936	2806t	121.0m	11.8m	6 x boilers, 2 x Tu	70,000shp=36.0kt	5 x 12.7cm	8 x 53.3cm	60
Z1936A	3083t	127.0m	12.0m	6 x boilers, 2 x Tu	70,000shp=36.0kt	3/4/5 x 15cm	8 x 53.3cm	60
Z1936A (Mob)	3083t	127.0m	12.0m	6 x boilers, 2 x Tu	70,000shp=36.0kt	3/4/5 x 15cm	8 x 53.3cm	60
Z1936B (Mob)	2954t	127.0m	12.0m	6 x boilers, 2 x Tu	70,000shp=36.0kt	5 x 12.7cm	8 x 53.3cm	60
Z1942	2330t	114.3m	11.0m	3 x diesel	57,000bhp=36.0kt	4 x 12.7cm	6 x 53.3cm	50
T1935	962t	84.3m	8.6m	2 x boilers, 2 x Tu	31,000shp=34.5kt	1 x 10.5cm	6 x 53.3cm	30
T1937	997t	85.2m	8.9m	2 x boilers, 2 x Tu	31,000shp=34.5kt	1 x 10.5cm	6 x 53.3cm	30
T1939	1512t	102.5m	10.0m	2 x boilers, 2 x Tu	31,000shp=32.5kt	4 x 10.5cm	6 x 53.3cm	50
T1940	2249t	114.5m	11.3m	3 x boilers, 2 x Tu	45,000shp=34.8kt	4 x 12.7cm	8 x 53.3cm	–
T1941	1782t	106.0m	10.7m	2 x boilers, 2 x Tu	40,000shp=34.0kt	4 x 10.5cm	6 x 53.3cm	50
NO Sleipner	590t	74.1m	7.8m	3 x boilers, 2 x Tu	12,500shp=30.0kt	2 x 10cm/40	2/4 x 53.3cm	24
NO Draug	462t	69.0m	7.2m	4 x boilers, 2 x VTE	7500ihp=27.0kt	6 x 76mm/50	3 x 45.6cm	–

Name	Class	Builder	Launch	Comp/comm	Alloc	Fate
Z4 – Richard Beitzen = H97 (Feb 46)	Z1934	Deutsche Werke (Kiel)	30 Nov 35	13 May 37	UK	Target Mar 46; for disposal Jan 47; arrived Gateshead 10 Jan 49 to BU C W Dorkins
Z5 – Paul Jacobi = Desaix (4 Feb 46) = Q2 (Feb 54)	Z1934A	Deschimag (Bremen)	24 Mar 36	29 Jun 37	UK	FR Feb 46; condemned 17 Feb 54; sold Jun 54 to BU Rouen

Name	Class	Builder	Launch	Comp/comm	Alloc	Fate
Z6 – Theodor Riedel = Kléber (4 Feb 46) = Q85 or Q87 (Apr 57)	Z1934A	Deschimag (Bremen)	22 Apr 36	6 Jul 37	UK	FR Feb 46; condemned 10 Apr 57; sold 1958 & BU Rouen
Z10 – Hans Lody = R38 (Jan 46) = H40 (Feb 46)	Z1934A	Germania (Kiel)	14 May 36	17 Sep 38	UK	Training hulk Rosyth Feb 46; accommodation ship Southampton Nov 46; arrived Sunderland to BU by Thomas Young 17 Jul 49
Z14 – Friedrich Ihn = Pritkyi (13 Feb 45)	Z1934A	Blohm & Voss (Hamburg)	5 Nov 35	9 Apr 38	SU	SU 5 Feb 46; stricken 22 Mar 52; BU
Z15 – Erich Steinbrinck = R92 (1945) = Pilkyi (13 Feb 45) = PKZ-2 (1 May 49)	Z1934A	Blohm & Voss (Hamburg)	24 Sep 36	8 Jun 38	SU	SU 2 Jan 46; Accommodation ship 1 May 49; stricken 19 Feb 58; BU
Z20 – Karl Galster = Prochnyi (13 Feb 46) = PKZ-99 (28 Dec 54)	Z1936	Deschimag (Bremen)	15 Jun 38	21 Mar 39	SU	Accommodation ship 30 Nov 54; stricken 25 Jun 56; BU
Z23 = Léopard (1949)	Z1936A	Deschimag (Bremen)	15 Dec 39	15 Sep 40	–	Wreck seized FR; salved 1945; never repaired; condemned 8 Oct 51; BU Brest
Z25 = Hoche (4 Feb 46) = Q102 (Jan 58)	Z1936A	Deschimag (Bremen)	16 May 40	30 Nov 40	UK	FR Feb 46; trials vessel 16 Oct 53; condemned Toulon 2 Jan 58
Z28	Z1936A	Deschimag (Bremen)	4 Aug 40	9 Aug 41	Cat C	(sunk Sassnitz 6 Mar 45) BU
Z29	Z1936A	Deschimag (Bremen)	15 Oct 40	25 Jun 41	Cat C	(damaged Bremerhaven) Scuttled Skagerrak (57° 53' N, 06° 39' E) 10 Mar 46
Z30	Z1936A	Deschimag (Bremen)	8 Dec 40	15 Nov 41	UK	Test hulk Feb 46; arrived Troon Sep 48 to BU
Z31 = Marceau (4 Feb 46) = Q103 (Jan 58)	Z1936A (Mob)	Deschimag (Bremen)	15 Apr 41	11 Apr 42	UK	FR Feb 46; reserve Feb 54; condemned 2 Jan 58; BU
Z33 = Provornyi (13 Feb 46)	Z1936A (Mob)	Deschimag (Bremen)	15 Sep 41	6 Feb 43	SU	SU Feb 46; training ship 1954; accommodation hulk 22 Apr 55; burned and foundered Leningrad 1960; BU 1961.
Z34	Z1936A (Mob)	Deschimag (Bremen)	5 May 42	5 Jun 43	Cat C	(damaged Bremerhaven) Scuttled Skagerrak (~58° 19' N, ~09° 40' E) by US 26 Mar 46
Z37	Z1936A (Mob)	Germania (Kiel)	16 Jul 42	30 Jan 44	-	(scuttled Bordeaux 24 Aug 44) BU 1949
Z38 = R40 (1945) = Nonsuch (Nov 46)	Z1936A (Mob)	Germania (Kiel)	5 Aug 41	20 Mar 43	UK	Trials vessel; target; beached Oct 49; sold Arnott Young 8 Nov 49; stern arrived Dalmuir May 50 to BU
Z39 = DD-939 (14 Sep 45) = Q182 (1947)	Z1936A (Mob)	Germania (Kiel)	2 Dec 41	21 Aug 43	US	FR 10 Nov 47; hulked 1947; condemned 15 Jun 53; floating quay at Brest; BU 1969
Z44	Z1936B (Mob)	Deschimag (Bremen)	20 Jan 44	–	Cat C	(sunk incomplete Bremen) BU in situ Apr 48–Feb 49
Z45	Z1936B (Mob)	Deschimag (Bremen)	15 Apr 44	–	Cat C	(incomplete Bremen) BU Bremen 1946
Z51	Z1942	Deschimag (Bremen)	2 Oct 44	–	Cat C	(sunk incomplete Bremen) BU in situ Deutsches Dampfschiffahrts Hansa Apr 48–Feb 49
T1	T1935	Schichau (Elbing)	19 Feb 38	2 Dec 39	Cat C	(sunk Kiel 10 Apr 45) Blown up 20 May 46
T4	T1935	Schichau (Elbing)	15 Apr 38	3 Feb 40	US	DK 18 Jun 48; stricken 1951; sold H I Hansen (Odensee) Feb 52 to BU
T5	T1935	Deschimag (Bremen)	22 Nov 37	23 Jan 40	Cat C	(sunk off Danzig 14 Mar 45) BU in situ Hela Bay
T7	T1935	Deschimag (Bremen)	18 Jun 38	20 Dec 39	Cat C	(sunk Bremen 29 Jul 44) Salved Bremen; BU Dec 47–Jun 49
T8	T1935	Deschimag (Bremen)	10 Aug 38	8 Oct 39	Cat C	(sunk Kiel 3 May 45) Blown up 10 Dec 45 and 23 Mar 46
T9	T1935	Schichau (Elbing)	3 Nov 38	4 Jul 40	Cat C	(sunk Kiel 3 May 45) Blown up 10 Dec 45 and 23 Mar 46
T10	T1935	Schichau (Elbing)	1939	6 Aug 40	Cat C	(sunk Gdynia 18 Dec 44) BU in situ
T11 = Bir Hacheim (2 Feb 46)	T1935	Deschimag (Bremen)	1 Mar 39	7 May 40	UK	FR 2 Feb 46; stricken 7 Oct 51; condemned 8 Oct 51
T12 = Podvizhnyi (13 Feb 46) = Kyt (30 Dec 53)	T1935	Deschimag (Bremen)	12 Apr 39	3 Jul 40	SU	SU 27 Dec 45; decommissioned 8 Apr 53; scuttled Lake Ladoga 13 Mar 59; salved 1991; scuttled off Novaya Zemlya 1993
T14 = Dompaire (2 Dec 47)	T1937	Schichau (Elbing)	20 Jul 39	14 Jun 41	US	FR Oct 47; condemned 8 Oct 51
T15	T1937	Schichau (Elbing)	16 Sep 39	26 Jun 41	Cat C	(sunk Kiel 13 Dec 43) Blown up 23 Mat 46
T16	T1937	Schichau (Elbing)	23 Nov 39	24 Jul 41	Cat C	(sunk Aarhus 13 Apr 45) BU 1945
T17 = Porivistyi (13 Feb 46) = UTS-6 (7 Sep 49)	T1937	Schichau (Elbing)	13 Mar 40	28 Aug 41	SU	SU 15 Jan 46; reserve 25 Jun 49; trials vessel 7 Sep 49; sunk as target 30 Dec 59
T19	T1937	Schichau (Elbing)	20 Jul 40	18 Dec 41	US	DK 25 Nov 47; BU 1950/51
T20 = Baccarat (2 Feb 46)	T1937	Schichau (Elbing)	12 Sep 40	5 Jun 42	UK	FR Feb 46; condemned 8 Oct 51

Name	Class	Builder	Launch	Comp/comm	Alloc	Fate
T21	T1937	Schichau (Elbing)	21 Nov 40	11 Jul 42	Cat C	(damaged Wesermünde) Scuttled gunfire *T19* Skagerrak (57° 52' N, 16° 15' E by US 10 Jun 46
T23 = *Alsacien* (2 Feb 46) = *Q11* (9 Jun 54)	T1939	Schichau (Elbing)	14 Jun 41	14 Jun 42	UK	FR Feb 46; comm 1 Apr 49; condemned 9 Jun 54; sold 28 Jan 55 to BU
T28 = *Lorrain* (2 Feb 46) = *Q59* (31 Oct 55)	T1939	Schichau (Elbing)	24 Jun 42	19 Jun 43	UK	FR Feb 46; comm 1 Apr 49; reserve May 55; condemned 21 Jul 59
T33 = *Primernyi* (13 Feb 46) = *PKZ-63* (28 Dec 54)	T1939	Schichau (Elbing)	4 Sep 43	15 Jun 44	SU	SU 1945; trials vessel 28 Dec 54; stricken 9 Nov 56; BU 1957–58
T35 = *DD-935*	T1939	Schichau (Elbing)	11 Dec 43	7 Oct 44	US	FR 1947; condemned 3 Oct 52
T37	T1941	Schichau (Elbing)	1944	–	Cat C	(incomplete Bremen) Scuttled Skagerrak (57° 40' N, 06° 30' E) 26 Jul 46
T38	T1941	Schichau (Elbing)	1944	–	Cat C	(incomplete Kiel) Scuttled Skagerrak (58° 07' N, 10° 46' E) 10 May 46
T39	T1941	Schichau (Elbing)	1944	–	Cat C	(incomplete Kiel) Scuttled Skagerrak (58° 08' N, 10° 47' E) 10 May 46
T41	T1941	Schichau (Elbing)	1944	–	Cat C	(incomplete Elbing) BU
T42	T1941	Schichau (Elbing)	1944	–	Cat C	(incomplete Elbing) BU
T43	T1941	Schichau (Elbing)	1944	–	Cat C	(incomplete Elbing) BU
T63	T1940	Rottadamse Droog-dok Mij. (Rotterdam)	28 Oct 44	–	Cat C	(incomplete Kiel) Scuttled Skagerrak 21 Dec 46
T65	T1940	De Schelde (Vlissingen)	8 Jul 44	–	Cat C	(incomplete Wesermünde) Scuttled Skagerrak (58° 17' 09" N, 09° 37' 01" E) 1 Jul 46
T107 (ex-*G7*) = *Porazaiuskyi* (13 Feb 46) = *Kazanka* (22 Dec 50)	G7	Germania (Kiel)	7 Nov 11	30 Apr 12	SU	SU 1945; reserve 28 Nov 50; stricken 12 Mar 57
T108 (ex-*G8*)	G7	Germania (Kiel)	21 Dec 11	6 Aug 12	UK	UK 6 Jan 46; BU
T111 (ex-*G11*)	G7	Germania (Kiel)	23 Apr 12	8 Aug 12	Cat C	(sunk Kiel 3 Apr 45) Blown up 14 Dec 45
T123 Komet (ex-*S23*)	S13	Schichau (Elbing)	29 Mar 13	1 Nov 13	?	?
T151 (ex-*Comet*, ex-*V151*)	V150	Vulcan (Stettin)	19 Sep 07	29 Feb 08	US	GM/SA 20 Nov 45; US 4 Jan 46; BU Bremer Vulkan 1948
T153 Eduard Jungmann (ex-*V153*)	V150	Vulcan (Stettin)	13 Nov 07	9 May 08	US	GM/SA Jul 45; US 22 Dec 45; BU Netherlands 1949
T155 (ex-*V155*)	V150	Vulcan (Stettin)	28 Jan 08	25 Jun 08	Cat C	(sunk Swinemünde 22 Apr 45) BU
T156 Bremse (ex-*V156*)	V150	Vulcan (Stettin)	29 Feb 08	21 Jul 08	Cat C	(damaged Weser) Foundered 10 Jun 46 North Sea en route to be scuttled Skagerrak(?)
T158 (ex-*V158*) = *Prozorliviy* (13 Feb 46) = *Araks* (Dec 50) = *UTS-67* (25 Feb 57)	V150	Vulcan (Stettin)	26 Jun 08	8 Oct 08	SU	SU 13 Feb 46; reserve 28 Nov 50; trials vessel 25 Feb 57; stricken 31 May 61
T190 Claus von Bevern (ex-*V190*)	V186	Vulcan (Stettin)	12 Apr 11	5 Aug 11	Cat C	(damaged Wilhelmshaven) Scuttled Skagerrak (57° 52' N, 16° 15' E) by US 16 Mar 46
T196 (ex-*G196*) = *Pronzitelnyi* (13 Feb 46)	G192	Germania (Kiel)	25 Apr 11	2 Oct 11	SU	SU 27 Dec 45; stricken 30 Apr 49; BU
TA47 (ex-*Balestra*) = *Učka* (1948)	IT *Ariete* (Table 2.2/5)	Cantieri Navale del Quarnaro (Fiume)	[4 Oct 47]	[YU: 1950]	–	Seized YU 1945; stricken 1968; BU 1971
Löwe (ex-*Gyller*) = *Gyller* (May 45)	NO *Sleipner*	Horten DYd	7 Jul 38	NO: 1938 GE: 20 Apr 40	–	Retroceded NO May 1945; stricken 1959; sold 1962; BU
Panther (ex-*Odin*) = *Odin* (May 45)	NO *Sleipner*	Horten DYd	24 Jan 39	NO: 1939 GE: 23 Apr 40	–	Retroceded NO May 1945; stricken 1959; sold 1962; BU
Leopard (ex-*Balder*) = *Balder* (May 45)	NO *Sleipner*	Horten DYd	11 Oct 39	NO: - GE: 26 Jul 40	–	Retroceded NO May 1945; stricken 1959; sold 1962; BU Stavanger
Tiger (ex-*Tor*) = *Tor* (May 45)	NO *Sleipner*	Horten DYd	7 Sep 39	NO: 1940 GE: 13 Jun 40	–	Retroceded NO May 1945; stricken 1959; sold 1962; BU
Troll	NO *Draug*	Horten DYd	7 Jul 10	NO: 1910 GE: 18 May 40	–	Retroceded NO May 1945; stricken 1947; BU 1949

Table 2.1/4. Escorts/Fleet Tenders

Class	Disp.	Length	Beam	Machinery	Power/speed	Main gun (s)	Mines
F1	803t	76.0m	8.8m	2 x boilers, 2 x Tu	14,000shp=28.0kt	2 x 10.5cm/45	–
Grille	2560t	135.0m	13.5m	4 boilers, 2 x Tu	22,000shp=26.0kt	3 x 12.7cm/45	280
Hela	2113t	97.5m	12.3m	2 x diesel	8360bhp=21.0kt	2 x 10.5cm/45	–
Elbe	820t	58.0m	8.5m	2 x diesel	1600bhp=15.0kt	1 x 8.8cm/45	–
K1	1365t	78.0m	10.2m	2 x diesel	2770bhp=14.5kt	4 x 12.0cm/45	200
BE *Artevelde*	1640t	98.5m	10.5m	2 x boilers, 2 x Tu	30,000shp=30.0kt	3 x 10.5cm/45	120
UK *Flower*	1020t	81.2m	10.1m	2 x boilers, 1 x VTE	1400ihp=12.0kt	3 x 10.5cm/45	–
FR *Sans Peur*	1500t	95.0m	11.8m	2 x diesel	4200bhp=18.0kt	3 x 10.5cm/45	–

Name	Class	Builder	Launch	Comp/comm	Alloc	Fate
Barbara (ex-*Zinnia*) = *Breydel* (May 45)	UK *Flower*	Swan Hunter (Low Walker)	12 Aug 15	UK: Sep 15 BE: 19 Apr 20 GE: Jan 42	–	Retroceded BE May 45; BU 1952
Elbe = *Terek* (Dec 45)	*Elbe*	Wilhelmshaven DYd	24 Jan 31	14 Nov 31	SU	GM/SA Jul 45; to SU Dec 45; BU 1962
F1 Jagd (ex-*Libelle*)	*F1*	Germania (Kiel)	1 Mar 35	15 Dec 35	US	GM/SA Jul 45; to FR 1947; BU
F10	*F1*	Wilhelmshaven DYd	11 May 36	12 Mar 38	UK	To UK 21 Dec 45; BU Netherlands 1950
F2	*F1*	Germania (Kiel)	2 Apr 35	27 Feb 36	UK	To UK Jan 46; foundered Scapa Flow 30 Dec 46; wreck sold Metrec Engineering 1967; salvage abandoned
F4	*F1*	Germania (Kiel)	2 Jul 35	5 Apr 36	UK	To UK 16 Jan 46; BU
F7 = *Buran* (Feb 46)	*F1*	Blohm & Voss (Hamburg)	25 May 36	15 Feb 37	SU	To SU 25 Feb 46; base-ship 7 May 51; BU Ventspils 1957/58
F8	*F1*	Blohm & Voss (Hamburg)	27 Jul 36	8 Apr 37	UK	To UK 23 Dec 45; BU Netherlands 1950
Grille	*Grille*	Blohm & Voss (Hamburg)	15 Dec 34	19 May 35	UK	Sold G Adria (Lebanon) 1946; laid up Beirut Nov 47; sold 17 Aug 1950 ($100,000); BU Bordonstown, NJ from 20 Apr 51
Hela = *Angara* (13 May 46) = *PKZ-14* (Jan 96)	*Hela*	Stülcken (Hamburg)	28 Dec 39	16 Oct 40	SU	To SU 25 Dec 45; SU comm 20 Jan 46; accommodation ship Jan 96; sold A Crispino 2007
K2	*K1*	Gusto (Schiedam)	28 Jun 41	14 Nov 42	–	Retroceded NL May 45; foundered Delfzijl; stricken Oct 47; salved 26 Jul 48; BU
K3 = *Van Speyk* (18 Jun 46)	*K1*	Smit (Rotterdam)	23 Mar 41	24 Jan 42	–	Retroceded NL May 45; stricken 1960; BU Amsterdam
K4 Lorelei (ex-*Artevelde*) = *Artevelde* (Jun 45)	BE *Artevelde*	Cockerill (Antwerp)/ Wilton-Fijenoord (Schiedam)	24 Aug 40	25 Apr 43	–	Retroceded BE Jun 45; accommodation ship 1951; stricken 22 Nov 54; BU J Bakker & Zonen (Bruges)
SG3 Uranus (ex-*Sans Souci*) = *Beautemps Beaupré* (1946) = *Q456* (Nov 69)	FR *Sans Peur*	Penhoët (St Nazaire)	2 Oct 40	9 Aug 42	–	Retroceded FR May 45; survey vessel 8 May 47; condemned 20 Nov 69; breakwater; BU Brest 1970
SG4 Merkur (ex-*Sans Peur*) = *Laperouse* (1946) = *Q569* (Jan 77)	FR *Sans Peur*	Penhoët (St Nazaire)	28 Nov 40	2 Sep 43	–	Retroceded FR May 45; survey vessel 1965; condemned 31 Jan 77; breakwater; sold Brest to BU 1984
Weser	*Elbe*	Wilhelmshaven DYd	24 Jan 31	14 Nov 31	UK	GM/SA Jul 45; discarded 1951; sold NL as barge 1953; BU Netherlands 1954.

Table 2.1/5. Submarines

Type	Disp.	Length	Beam	Machinery	Power/speed	TT	Mines
IID	314/364t	44.0m	4.9m	2 x diesel 2 x electric	700bhp=12.7kt 410bhp=7.4kt	3 x 53.3cm	–
VIIC	769/871t	67.1m	6.2m	2 x diesel 2 x electric	2800–3200bhp=17–17.7kt 750bhp=7.6kt	5 x 53.3cm	–
VIID	965/1285t	76.9m	6.4m	2 x diesel 2 x electric	2800–3200bhp=16–16.7kt 750bhp=7.6kt	5 x 53.3cm	15
VIIF	1064/1181t	77.6m	7.3m	2 x diesel 2 x electric	2880–3200bhp=16.9–17.6kt 750bhp=7.9kt	5 x 53.3cm	–
IXB	1051/1178t	76.5m	6.8m	2 x diesel 2 x electric	4400bhp=18.2kt 1000bhp=7.7kt	6 x 53.3cm	–

IXC	1120/1232t	76.8m	6.8m	2 x diesel 2 x electric	4400bhp=18.3kt 1000bhp=7.3kt	6 x 53.3cm	–
IXC/40	1144/1257t	76.8m	6.9m	2 x diesel 2 x electric	4400bhp=18.3kt 1000bhp=7.3kt	6 x 53.3cm	–
IXD^2	1610/1799t	87.6m	7.5m	4 x diesel 2 x electric	2800–3200bhp=15.8–16.5kt 1000bhp=6.9kt	6 x 53.3cm	–
XVIIB^2	312/337t	41.5m	4.5m	1 x diesel 1 x Walter	210–230bhp=8.5kt 77.5bhp=5.0kt	2 x 53.3cm	–
XXI	1621/1819t	76.7m	8.0m	2 x diesel 2 x electric	4000bhp=15.6kt 4200bhp=17.2kt	6 x 53.3cm	–
XXIII	234/258t	34.7m	3.0m	1 x diesel 1 x electric	575–630bhp=9.7kt 580bhp=12.5kt	2 x 53.3cm	–

Name	Type	Builder	Launch	Comp/comm	Surr/cap[4]	Alloc	Fate
U3	IIA	Deutsche Werke (Kiel)	19 Jul 35	6 Aug 35	Neustadt	–	Being broken up Gdynia 1945
U92	VIIC	Flender Werke (Lübeck-Siems)	10 Jan 42	3 Mar 42	Bergen 9 May 45 (sunk)	–	Sold A/S Friis & Tandberg (Drammen) Jan 47 (NOK 400); BU Trondheim
U123 = Blaison (1945) = Q165 (1959)	IXB	Deschimag [Weser] (Bremen)	2 Mar 40	30 May 40	Lorient May 45 (sunk)	–	Salved Oct 45; FR comm 28 Apr 48; condemned 18 Aug 59; target; foundered Gulf of St Tropez 10 Sep 59
U143	IID	Deutsche Werke (Kiel)	10 Aug 40	18 Sep 40	Heligoland 5 May 45	OD (Loch Ryan)	Scuttled gunfire N Atlantic (55° 58' N, 09° 35' W) 22 Dec 45
U145	IID	Deutsche Werke (Kiel)	21 Sep 40	16 Oct 40	Heligoland 5 May 45	OD (Loch Ryan)	Scuttled gunfire N Atlantic (55° 47' N, 09° 35' W) 22 Dec 45
U149	IID	Deutsche Werke (Kiel)	19 Oct 40	13 Nov 40	Heligoland 5 May 45	OD (Loch Ryan)	Scuttled gunfire N Atlantic (55° 40' 05" N, 08° 00' W) 21 Dec 45
U150	IID	Deutsche Werke (Kiel)	19 Oct 40	27 Nov 40	Heligoland 5 May 45	OD (Loch Ryan)	Scuttled gunfire N Atlantic (56° 04' N, 09° 35' W) 21 Dec 45
U155	IXC	Deschimag [Weser] (Bremen)	12 May 41	23 Aug 41	Baring Bay DK 5 May 45	Cat C OD (Loch Ryan)	Scuttled gunfire N Atlantic (55° 35' N, ? W) 21 Dec 45
U170	IXC/40	Deschimag [Seebeck] (Bremen)	6 Jun 42	19 Jan 43	Horten 9 May 45	OD (Loch Ryan)	Scuttled gunfire N Atlantic (55° 44' N, ? W) 30 Nov 45
U181 = I501 (15 Jul 45)	IXD^2	Deschimag [Weser] (Bremen)	30 Dec 41	9 May 42	[Singapore 5 May 45 (captured JP)]	–	See Table 2.3/4
U190	IXC/40	Deschimag [Weser] (Bremen)	8 Jun 42	24 Sep 42	Bay of Bulls 14 May 45 (from sea)	UK	CA trials vessel; paid off 24 Jul 47; aircraft and gunfire target HMCS Nootka and HMCS New Liskeard off Nova Scotia (43° 55N, 63° 00W) 21 Oct 47
U195 = I506 (May 45)	IXD^1	Deschimag [Weser] (Bremen)	8 Apr 42	5 Sep 42	[Surabaya 5 May 45 (captured JP)]	–	See Table 2.3/4
U218	VIID	Germania (Kiel)	5 Dec 41	24 Jan 42	Bergen 12 May 45 (from sea)	OD (Loch Ryan)	Foundered N Atlantic (8.9nm 301° Inistrahull Light) 4 Dec 45
U219 = I505	XB	Germania (Kiel)	6 Oct 42	12 Dec 42	[Jakarta 5 May 45 (captured JP)]	–	See Table 2.3/4
U228	VIIC	Germania (Kiel)	30 Jul 42	12 Sep 42	Bergen 9 May 45 (damaged)	–	Sold 1946 (NOK1,500); BU Bergen
U234	XB	Germania (Kiel)	23 Dec 43	2 Mar 44	Portsmouth, NH 19 May 45 (from sea)	US	Trials vessel 1946; torpedo target USS/M Greenfish 40 miles NE Cape Cod 20 Nov 47
U244	VIIC	Germania (Kiel)	2 Sep 43	9 Oct 43	Loch Eriboll 14 May 45 (from sea)	OD (Lisahally)	Scuttled gunfire ORP Piorun N Atlantic (55° 46' N, ? W) 30 Dec 45
U245	VIIC	Germania (Kiel)	25 Nov 43	18 Dec 43	Bergen 9 May 45 (from sea)	OD (Loch Ryan)	Foundered N Atlantic (55° 25' N, ? W) 7 Dec 45

4 See Waller and A Niestlé, 'The U-boats that Surrendered: "The Definitive List"', *Warship International* XLVIII/4 (2011), pp 356–8.

Name	Type	Builder	Launch	Comp/comm	Surr/cap	Alloc	Fate
U249 = N86	VIIC	Germania (Kiel)	23 Oct 43	20 Nov 43	Portland 10 May 45 (from sea)	UK/ Cat C/ OD (Loch Ryan)	UK comm 29 May 45; expended torpedo target HMS/M *Tantivy* N Atlantic (56° 10' N, 10° 04' W) 13 Dec 45
U255	VIIC	Bremer Vulkan (Vegesack)	8 Oct 41	29 Nov 41	Loch Eriboll 17 May 45 (from sea)	OD (Loch Ryan)	Expended bombing target N Atlantic (55° 50' N, 10° 05' W) 13 Dec 45
U256	VIIC	Bremer Vulkan (Vegesack)	8 Oct 41	18 Dec 41	Bergen 9 May 45 (damaged)	–	Sold 1946 (NOK2,500); BU
U278	VIIC	Bremer Vulkan (Vegesack)	2 Dec 42	16 Jan 43	Loch Eriboll 9 May 45 (from sea)	OD (Lisahally)	Scuttled gunfire N Atlantic (55° 44' N, 08° 21' W) 31 Dec 45
U281	VIIC	Bremer Vulkan (Vegesack)	16 Jan 43	27 Feb 43	9 May 45 Kristiansand- South	OD 30 Dec 45 (Loch Ryan)	Foundered N Atlantic (55° 32' 50" N, 07° 38' 10" W)
U291	VIIC	Bremer Vulkan (Vegesack)	30 Jun 43	4 Aug 43	Cuxhaven 5 May 45	OD (Loch Ryan)	Scuttled gunfire N Atlantic (55° 50' 30" N, 09° 08' W) 21 Dec 45
U293	VIIC	Bremer Vulkan (Vegesack)	30 Jul 43	8 Sep 43	Loch Eriboll 11 May 45 (from sea)	OD	(Loch Ryan) Expended bombing target and Scuttled gunfire N Atlantic (55° 50' N, 10° 05' W) 13 Dec 45
U294	VIIC	Bremer Vulkan (Vegesack)	27 Aug 43	6 Oct 43	Narvik 9 May 45	OD (Lisahally)	Scuttled gunfire N Atlantic (55° 44' N, ? W) 31 Dec 45
U295	VIIC	Bremer Vulkan (Vegesack)	13 May 43	20 Oct 43	Narvik 9 May 45	OD (Loch Ryan)	Scuttled gunfire N Atlantic (56° 14' N, ? W) 17 Dec 45
U298	VIIC	Bremer Vulkan (Vegesack)	25 Oct 43	1 Dec 43	Bergen 9 May 45	OD (Loch Ryan)	Scuttled gunfire N Atlantic (55° 35' N, ? W) 29 Nov 45
U299	VIIC	Bremer Vulkan (Vegesack)	6 Nov 43	15 Dec 43	Kristisansand- South 9 May 45	OD (Loch Ryan)	Foundered N Atlantic (55° 38' 40" N, 07° 54' W) 4 Dec 45.
U310	VIIC	Flender-Werke (Lübeck)	31 Dec 42	24 Feb 43	Trondheim 9 May 45 (damaged)	–	Sold J Taranger A/S Nov 47; BU Trondheim 1948
U312	VIIC	Flender-Werke (Lübeck)	27 Feb 43	21 Apr 43	Narvik 9 May 45	OD (Loch Ryan)	Foundered N Atlantic (55° 35' N, 07° 54' W) 29 Nov 45
U313	VIIC	Flender-Werke (Lübeck)	27 Mar 43	20 May 43	Narvik 9 May 45	OD (Loch Ryan)	Foundered N Atlantic (55° 40' N, ? W) 21 Dec 45
U315	VIIC	Flender-Werke (Lübeck)	29 May 43	10 Jul 43	Trondheim 9 May 45 (damaged)	–	Sold J Taranger A/S Nov 47; BU Trondheim 1948
U318	VIIC	Flender-Werke (Lübeck)	25 Sep 43	13 Nov 43	Narvik 10 May 45 (from sea)	OD (Loch Ryan)	Scuttled gunfire N Atlantic (55° 47' N, 08° 30' W) 21 Dec 45
U324	VIIC	Flender-Werke (Lübeck)	14 Feb 44	5 Apr 44	Bergen 9 May 45 (damaged)	–	Sold J Taranger A/S Nov 47; BU Trondheim 1948
U328	VIIC	Flender-Werke (Lübeck)	15 Jul 44	19 Sep 44	Bergen 9 May 45	OD (Loch Ryan)	Expended bombing target N Atlantic (55° 50' N, ? W) 30 Nov 45
U363	VIIC	Flensburger-Sb (Flensburg)	17 Dec 42	18 Mar 43	Narvik 9 May 45	OD (Lisahally)	Scuttled gunfire N Atlantic (55° 45' N, 08° 18' W) 31 Dec 45
U368	VIIC	Flensburger-Sb (Flensburg)	16 Nov 43	7 Jan 44	Heligoland 5 May 45	OD (Loch Ryan)	Scuttled gunfire N Atlantic (56° 14' N, ? W) 17 Dec 45
U369	VIIC	Flensburger-Sb (Flensburg)	17 Aug 43	15 Oct 43	Kristian- sand-South 9 May 45	OD (Loch Ryan)	Foundered/scuttled by gunfire N Atlantic (55° 31' 40" N, ? W) 30 Nov 45
U427	VIIC	Danziger-Werft (Danzig)	6 Feb 43	2 Jun 43	Narvik 9 May 45	OD (Loch Ryan)	Scuttled gunfire N Atlantic (56° 04' N, 09° 35' W) 21 Dec 45
U437	VIIC	Schichau (Danzig)	15 Jun 41	25 Oct 41	Bergen 9 May 45 (damaged)	–	Sold 1946 (NOK2,300); BU Bergen 1946
U471 = Millé (1947) = Q339 (1963)	VIIC	Deutsche Werke (Kiel)	6 Mar 43	5 May 43	Toulon 1944 (sunk)	–	Salved 1945; FR comm 1947; condemned 9 Jul 63; BU Toulon
U481	VIIC	Deutsche Werke (Kiel)	25 Sep 43	10 Nov 43	Narvik 9 May 45	OD (Loch Ryan)	Scuttled gunfire N Atlantic (56° 11' N, 10° 00' W) 30 Nov 45
U483	VIIC	Deutsche Werke (Kiel)	30 Oct 43	22 Dec 43	Trondheim 9 May 45	OD (Loch Ryan)	Scuttled gunfire N Atlantic (56° 10' N, 10° 05' W) 16 Dec 45
U485	VIIC	Deutsche Werke (Kiel)	15 Jan 44	23 Feb 44	Gibraltar 12 May 45 (from sea)	OD (Loch Ryan)	Expended torpedo target HMS/M *Tantivy* N Atlantic (56° 10' N, 10° 05' W) 8 Dec 45

Name	Type	Builder	Launch	Comp/comm	Surr/cap	Alloc	Fate
U491–U493	XIV	Deutsche Werke (Kiel)	–	–	–	–	Suspended; BU
U510 = *Bouan* (Jun 47) = *Q176* (Nov 59)	IXC	Deutsche Werft (Hamburg)	4 Sep 41	25 Nov 41	St Nazaire 9 May 45	–	FR comm 24 Jun 47; stricken 1 May 59; condemned 23 Nov 59; sold Toulon 1960 to BU
U516	IXC	Deutsche Werft (Hamburg)	16 Dec 41	10 Mar 42	Loch Eriboll 14 May 45 (from sea)	OD (Lisahally)	Foundered N Atlantic (56° 06' 40" N, 09° 00' W) 3 Jan 46
U530	IXC/40	Deutsche Werft (Hamburg)	28 Jul 42	14 Oct 42	Mar del Plata 10 Jul 45 (from sea)	US	Exhibited Texas ports to Dec 45; expended torpedo target USS/M *Toro* NE of Cape Cod 13 Nov 47
U532	IXC	Deutsche Werft (Hamburg)	26 Aug 42	11 Nov 42	Liverpool 13 May 45 (from sea)	OD (Loch Ryan)	Expended torpedo target HMS/M *Tantivy* N Atlantic (56° 08' N, 10° 07' W) 9 Dec 45
U539	IXC/40	Deutsche Werft (Hamburg)	4 Dec 42	24 Feb 43	Bergen 9 May 45	OD (Loch Ryan)	Foundered N Atlantic (55° 38' 30" N, ? W) 4 Dec 45
U541	IXC/40	Deutsche Werft (Hamburg)	5 Jan 43	24 Mar 43	Gibraltar 12 May 45 (from sea)	OD (Lisahally)	Scuttled gunfire HMS *Onslaught* N Atlantic (55° 38' N, 07° 35' 30" W) 5 Jan 46
U555	VIIC	Blohm & Voss (Hamburg)	7 Dec 40	30 Jun 41	Hamburg 3 May 45	–	(decommissioned) BU Hamburg *c.*1946
U622	VIIC	Blohm & Voss (Hamburg)	29 Mar 42	14 Mat 42	Bergen 9 May 45 (damaged)	–	Sold A/S Friis & Tandberg (Drammen) Jan 47 (NOK400); BU Trondheim 1947
U637	VIIC	Blohm & Voss (Hamburg)	7 Jul 42	27 Aug 42	Stavanger 9 May 45	OD (Loch Ryan)	Foundered N Atlantic (55° 35' N, 07° 46' W) 3 Jan 46
U668	VIIC	Hawaldt (Hamburg)	5 Oct 42	14 Nov 42	Narvik 9 May 45	OD (Lisahally)	Scuttled gunfire HMS *Onslaught* N Atlantic (56° 03' N, 09° 24' W) 1 Jan 46
U673	VIIC	Hawaldt (Hamburg)	8 May 43	18 May 43	Stavanger 9 May 45 (damaged)	–	BU 1946
U680	VIIC	Hawaldt (Hamburg)	20 Nov 43	23 Dec 43	Baring Bay DK 5 May 45	OD	(Loch Ryan) Scuttled gunfire N Atlantic (55° 24' N, 06° 29' W) 28 Dec 45
U712	VIIC	Stülcken (Hamburg)	10 Aug 42	5 Nov 42	Kristiansand-South 9 May 45	UK	Arrived Dunston to BU by Clayton & Davie 4 Jun 49.[5]
U716	VIIC	Stülcken (Hamburg)	15 Jan 43	15 Apr 43	Narvik 9 May 45	OD Loch Ryan)	(Expended bombing target N Atlantic (55° 50' N, 10° 05' W) 11 Dec 45
U720	VIIC	Stülcken (Hamburg)	5 Jun 43	17 Sep 43	Heligoland 5 May 45	OD (Loch Ryan)	Scuttled gunfire N Atlantic (56° 04' N, 09° 35' W) 21 Dec 45
U739	VIIC	Schichau (Danzig)	23 Dec 42	6 Mar 43	Emden 13 May 45 (from sea)	Cat C OD (Loch Ryan)	Expended bombing target N Atlantic (55° 50' N, 10° 05' W) 16 Dec 45
U758	VIIC	Wilhelmshaven DYd	1 Mar 42	5 May 42	Kiel 16 Mar 45 (damaged)	–	BU 1946/7
U760	VIIC	Wilhelmshaven DYd	21 Jun 42	15 Oct 42	Loch Ryan 23 Jul 45 (from Ferrol, SP)	Cat C OD (Loch Ryan)	Expended bombing target N Atlantic (55° 50' N, 10° 05' W) 13 Dec 45
U764	VIIC	Wilhelmshaven DYd	13 Mar 43	6 May 43	Loch Eriboll 14 May 45 (from sea)	OD (Lisahally)	Scuttled gunfire ORP *Piorun* N Atlantic (56° 06' N, 09° 00' W) 3 Jan 46
U766 = *Laubie* (1947) = *Q335* (1963)	VIIC	Wilhelmshaven DYd	29 May 43	30 Jul 43	La Pallice May 45 (de-commissioned)	–	FR comm 27 Jun 47; paid off 1961; condemned 11 Mar 63; BU Oct 63
U773	VIIC	Wilhelmshaven DYd	8 Dec 43	20 Jun 44	Trondheim 9 May 45	OD (Loch Ryan)	Expended torpedo target HMS/M *Tantivy* N Atlantic (56° 10' N, 10° 05' W) 8 Dec 45
U775	VIIC	Wilhelmshaven DYd	11 Feb 44	23 Mar 44	Trondheim 9 May 45	OD (Loch Ryan)	Scuttled gunfire Rathlin Sound (55° 04' N, 05° 30' 01" W) 8 Dec 45
U776 = *N65*	VIIC	Wilhelmshaven DYd	4 Mar 44	13 Apr 44	Portland 16 May 45 (from sea)	OD (Loch Ryan)	Exhibited UK east coast ports to Aug 45; trials vessel; foundered N Atlantic (55° 08' 04" N, 05° 30' 01" W) 3 Dec 45
U778	VIIC	Wilhelmshaven DYd	6 May 44	7 Jul 44	Bergen 9 May 45	OD (Loch Ryan)	Foundered N Atlantic (11.2nm, 308° Inistrahull Light) 4 Dec 45
U779	VIIC	Wilhelmshaven DYd	17 Jun 44	24 Aug 44	Cuxhaven 5 May 45	OD (Loch Ryan)	Scuttled gunfire N Atlantic (55° 50' N, 10° 05' W) 17 Dec 45
U802	IXC/40	Deschimag [Seebeck] (Bremen)	31 Oct 42	12 Jun 43	Loch Eriboll 11 May 45 (from sea)	OD (Lisahally)	Foundered N Atlantic (*c.* 55° 30' N, 08° 25' W) 31 Dec 45

[5] See Waller, *Warships* 171, pp 9–10 for the likelihood that *U712* and *U953* were accidentally swapped during delivery to the shipbreakers. *U953* was intended to break up at Dunston, but post-arrival observations and an image of the hulk in question are not consistent with the boat broken up there being her – but are consistent with *U712*.

Name	Type	Builder	Launch	Comp/comm	Surr/cap	Alloc	Fate
U805	IXC/40	Deschimag [Seebeck] (Bremen)	1943	12 Feb 44	Portsmouth NH 15 May 45 (from sea)	–	Torpedo target USS/M *Sirago* off Cape Cod 8 Feb 46
U806	IXC/40	Deschimag [Seebeck] (Bremen)	1943	29 Apr 44	Aarhus 6 May 45 (from sea)	OD (Loch Ryan)	Scuttled gunfire N Atlantic (55° 44' N, 08° 18' W) 21 Dec 45
U825	VIIC	Schichau (Danzig)	27 Feb 44	4 May 44	Portland 13 May 45 (from sea)	OD (Lisahally)	Scuttled gunfire ORP *Blyskawica* N Atlantic (55° 31' N, 07° 30' W) 3 Jan 46
U826	VIIC	Schichau (Danzig)	9 Mar 44	11 May 44	Loch Eriboll 11 May 45 (from sea)	OD (Loch Ryan)	Scuttled gunfire N Atlantic (56° 10' N, 10° 05' W) 1 Dec 45
U858	IXC/40	Deschimag [Weser] (Bremen)	17 Jun 43	30 Sep 43	Lewes, DE 14 May 45 (from sea)	US	Trials vessel early 1946; scuttled USS/M *Sirago* on 21 Nov 47 off New England
U861	IXD²	Deschimag [Weser] (Bremen)	29 Apr 43	2 Sep 43	Trondheim 9 May 45	OD (Lisahally)	Scuttled gunfire ORP *Blyskawica* N Atlantic (55° 25' N, 07° 15' W) 31 Dec 45
U862 = I502 (May 45)	IXD²	Deschimag [Weser] (Bremen)	5 Jun 43	7 Oct 43	[Singapore 5 May 45 (captured JP)]	–	See Table 2.3/4
U868	IXC/40	Deschimag [Weser] (Bremen)	18 Sep 43	23 Dec 43	Bergen 9 May 45	OD (Loch Ryan)	Foundered N Atlantic (55° 48" 30" N, 08° 33' W) 30 Nov 45
U873	IXD²	Deschimag [Weser] (Bremen)	16 Nov 43	1 Mar 44	Portsmouth, NH 16 May 45 (from sea)	US	Trials vessel early 1946; sold at New York to Interstate Metals Corp Mar 48 to BU
U874	IXD²	Deschimag [Weser] (Bremen)	21 Dec 43	8 Apr 44	Horten 9 May 45	OD (Lisahally)	Scuttled gunfire HMS *Offa* N Atlantic (55° 47' N, 09° 27' W) 31 Dec 45
U875	IXD²	Deschimag [Weser] (Bremen)	16 Feb 44	21 Apr 44	Bergen 9 May 45	UK OD (Lisahally)	Trials vessel; scuttled by gunfire HMS *Offa* N Atlantic (55° 41' N, 08° 28' W) 31 Dec 45
U883	IXD/42	Deschimag [Weser] (Bremen)	28 Apr 44	27 Mar 45	Cuxhaven 5 May 45	OD (Lisahally)	Scuttled gunfire N Atlantic (55° 44' N, 08° 40' W) 31 Dec 45
U889	IXC/40	Deschimag [Weser] (Bremen)	5 Apr 44	4 Aug 44	Shelburne, NS 13 May 45 (from sea)	US	To US 12 Jan 1946; torpedo target USS/M *Flying Fish* 20 Nov 47 off Cape Cod
U901	VIIC	Vulkan (Stettin)	9 Oct 43	29 Apr 44	Stavanger 15 May 45 (from sea)	OD (Lisahally)	Scuttled gunfire HMS *Onslaught* N Atlantic (55° 50' N, 08° 30' W) 6 Jan 46
U907	VIIC	Stülcken (Hamburg)	1 Mar 44	18 May 44	Bergen 9 May 45	OD (Loch Ryan)	Foundered Rathlin Sound (55° 17' N, 05° 59' W) 7 Dec 45
U926 = Kya (1949)	VIIC	Neptun (Rostock)	28 Dec 43	29 Feb 44	Bergen 9 May 45 (damaged)	–	NO Oct 48; NO comm 10 Jan 49; decommissioned 4 Apr 64; sold Andreas Stoltenberg (Oslo) May 65; BU W Germany
U928	VIIC	Neptun (Rostock)	15 Apr 44	11 Jul 44	Bergen 9 May 45	OD (Loch Ryan)	Expended bombing target N Atlantic (55° 50' N, 10° 05' W) 16 Dec 45
U930	VIIC	Neptun (Rostock)	Sep 44	6 Dec 44	Bergen 9 May 45	OD (Lisahally)	Scuttled gunfire HMS *Onslow* N Atlantic (55° 22' N, 07° 35' W) 29 Dec 45
U953	VIIC	Blohm & Voss (Hamburg)	28 Oct 42	17 Dec 42	Trondheim 9 May 45	UK	Arrived Hayle to BU by T W Ward 26 Jun 49.[6]
U956	VIIC	Blohm & Voss (Hamburg)	14 Nov 42	6 Jan 43	Loch Eriboll 13 May 45 (from sea)	OD (Loch Ryan)	Scuttled gunfire N Atlantic (55° 50' N, 10° 05' W) 17 Dec 45
U963	VIIC	Blohm & Voss (Hamburg)	30 Dec 42	17 Feb 43	–	–	Scuttled off Nazaré (39° 36' N 09° 05' W) 20 May 45
U968	VIIC	Blohm & Voss (Hamburg)	28 Jan 43	18 Mar 44	Narvik 9 May 45	OD (Loch Ryan)	Foundered N Atlantic (55° 24' N, 06° 22' 45" W) 28 Nov 45
U975	VIIC	Blohm & Voss (Hamburg)	24 Mar 43	29 Apr 43	Horten 9 May 45	OD (Lisahally)	Expended Squid target HMS *Loch Arkaig* N Atlantic (55° 42' N, 09° 01' W) 10 Feb 46
U977	VIIC	Blohm & Voss (Hamburg)	31 Mar 43	6 May 43	Mar del Plata 17 Aug 45 (from sea)	US	Arrived New London CT 12 Oct 45; torpedo target USS/M *Atule* off Cape Cod 13 Nov 46
U978	VIIC	Blohm & Voss (Hamburg)	1 Apr 43	12 May 43	Trondheim 9 May 45	OD (Loch Ryan)	Expended torpedo target HMS/M *Tantivy* N Atlantic (55° 50' N, 10° 05' W) 11 Dec 45
U985	VIIC	Blohm & Voss (Hamburg)	20 May 43	24 Jun 43	Kristiansand-South 9 May 45 (damaged)	–	Sold 1946; BU Kristiansand
U991	VIIC	Blohm & Voss (Hamburg)	24 Jun 43	29 Jul 43	Bergen 9 May 45	OD (Loch Ryan)	Expended torpedo target HMS/M *Tantivy* N Atlantic (56° 10' N, 10° 05' W) 11 Dec 45

[6] See n.5, above.

Name	Type	Builder	Launch	Comp/comm	Surr/cap	Alloc	Fate
U992	VIIC	Blohm & Voss (Hamburg)	23 Jun 43	2 Aug 43	Narvik 9 May 45 (from sea)	OD (Loch Ryan)	Scuttled gunfire N Atlantic (56° 10' N, 10° 05' W) 16 Dec 45
U993	VIIC	Blohm & Voss (Hamburg)	5 Jul 43	19 Aug 43	Bergen 9 May 45 (damaged)	–	Sold 1946 (NOK 1500); BU Bergen 1946
U994	VIIC	Blohm & Voss (Hamburg)	6 Jul 43	2 Sep 43	Trondheim 9 May 45	OD (Loch Ryan)	Foundered N Atlantic (55° 50' N, 08° 30' W) 5 Dec 45
U995 = Kaura (1952) = U995 (1971)	VIIC	Blohm & Voss (Hamburg)	22 Jul 43	16 Sep 43	Trondheim 9 May 45 (damaged)	–	NO Oct 48; NO comm 6 Dec 52; decommissioned 15 Dec 62; sold Deutsches Marinebund 14 Oct 65; museum Laboe 2 Oct 71; inscribed in Schleswig-Holstein register of monuments
U997	VIIC	Blohm & Voss (Hamburg)	18 Aug 43	23 Sep 43	Narvik 9 May 45	OD (Loch Ryan)	Exhibited US East Coast ports to Dec 45; expended bombing target N Atlantic (55° 50' N, 10° 05' W) 11 Dec 45
U1002	VIIC	Blohm & Voss (Hamburg)	27 Oct 43	30 Nov 43	Bergen 9 May 45	OD (Loch Ryan)	Expended torpedo target HMS/M Tantivy N Atlantic (56° 10' N, 10° 05' W) 13 Dec 45
U1004	VIIC	Blohm & Voss (Hamburg)	27 Oct 43	16 Oct 43	Bergen 9 May 45	OD (Loch Ryan)	Scuttled gunfire HMS/M Tantivy N Atlantic (56° 10' N, 10° 05' W) 1 Dec 45
U1005	VIIC	Blohm & Voss (Hamburg)	17 Nov 43	30 Dec 43	Bergen 14 May 45 (from sea)	OD (Loch Ryan)	Foundered N Atlantic (55° 33' N, 08° 27' W) 5 Dec 45
U1009	VIIC	Blohm & Voss (Hamburg)	5 Jan 44	10 Feb 44	Loch Eriboll 10 May 45 (from sea)	OD (Loch Ryan)	Scuttled gunfire HMS/M Tantivy N Atlantic (55° 31' 05" N, 10° 05' W) 16 Dec 45
U1010	VIIC	Blohm & Voss (Hamburg)	5 Jan 44	22 Feb 44	Loch Eriboll 14 May 45 (from sea)	OD (Lisahally)	Scuttled gunfire ORP Garland N Atlantic (55° 37' 09" N, 07° 49' 05" W) 7 Jan 46
U1019	VIIC	Blohm & Voss (Hamburg)	22 Mar 44	4 May 44	Trondheim 9 May 45	OD (Loch Ryan)	Scuttled gunfire N Atlantic (55° 27' N, 07° 56' W) 7 Dec 45
U1022	VIIC	Blohm & Voss (Hamburg)	13 Apr 44	7 Jun 44	Bergen 9 May 45	OD (Loch Ryan)	Scuttled gunfire ORP Piorun N Atlantic (55° 40' N, 08° 15' W) 29 Dec 45
U1023 = N83 (May 45)	VIIC	Blohm & Voss (Hamburg)	3 May 44	15 Jun 44	Portland 10 May 45 (from sea)	OD (Loch Ryan)	Exhibited UK west coast ports to Aug 45; foundered N Atlantic (55° 49' N, 08° 24' W) 8 Jan 46
U1052	VIIC	Germania (Kiel)	16 Dec 43	20 Jan 44	Bergen 9 May 45	OD (Loch Ryan)	Expended rocket projectile target (816 Sqn FAA) N Atlantic (55° 50' N, 10° 05' W) 9 Dec 45
U1054	VIIC	Germania (Kiel)	24 Feb 44	25 Mar 44	Kiel 5 May 45 (damaged)	–	BU
U1057 = N-22 (Feb 46) = S-81 (9 Jun 49)	VIIC	Germania (Kiel)	20 Apr 44	29 Apr 44	Bergen 9 May 45	SU	Delivered Liepāja 4 Dec 45; SU comm 13 Feb 46; atomic bomb target White Sea 1956; badly damaged Novaya Zemlya 24 Sep 57; stricken 16 Oct 57; BU
U1058 = N-23 (Feb 46) = S-82 (9 Jun 49) = PZS-32 (Jan 56)	VIIC	Germania (Kiel)	11 Apr 44	10 Jun 44	Loch Eriboll 10 May 45 (from sea)	SU	Delivered Liepāja 4 Dec 45; SU comm 13 Feb 46; reserve 29 Dec 55; battery charging station 18 Jan 56; stricken 25 Mar 58; BU
U1061	VIIF	Germania (Kiel)	22 Apr 43	25 Aug 43	Bergen 9 May 45	OD (Loch Ryan)	Scuttled gunfire N Atlantic (56° 10' N, 10° 05' W) 1 Dec 45
U1064 = N-24 (Feb 46) = S-83 (9 Jun 49) = PZS-33 (Jan 56) = UTS-49 (Jun 57)	VIIC	Germania (Kiel)	22 Jun 44	29 Jul 44	Trondheim 9 May 45	SU	Delivered Liepāja 4 Dec 45; SU comm 13 Feb 46; reserve 29 Dec 55; battery charging station 18 Jan 56; training hulk 1 Jun 57; stricken 12 Mar 74; BU
U1102	VIIC	Nordseewerke (Emden)	15 Jan 44	22 Feb 44	Hohwacht Bay 13 May 45 (from sea)	Cat C OD (Loch Ryan)	Scuttled gunfire N Atlantic (56° 04' N, 09° 35' W) 21 Dec 45
U1103	VIIC	Nordseewerke (Emden)	12 Oct 43	8 Jan 44	Cuxhaven 5 May 45	OD (Loch Ryan)	Scuttled gunfire N Atlantic (56° 03' N, 10° 05' W) 30 Dec 45
U1104	VIIC	Nordseewerke (Emden)	7 Dec 43	15 Mar 44	Bergen 9 May 45	OD (Loch Ryan)	Scuttled N Atlantic (55° 35' N, 10° 05' W) 15 Dec 45
U1105 = N16 (1945)	VIIC	Nordseewerke (Emden)	20 Apr 44	3 Jun 44	Loch Eriboll 10 May 45 (from sea)	UK	Trials vessel; to US Dec 45; expended target Aug 48; depth charge target off Piney Point (Potomac River MD, 38° 08' 10" N, 76° 33' 10" W) 19 Sep 49; inscribed in US National Register of Historic Places 2001
U1108	VIIC	Nordseewerke (Emden)	5 Sep 44	18 Nov 44	Horten 9 May 45	UK	Arrived Briton Ferry to BU by T W Ward 12 May 49
U1109	VIIC	Nordseewerke (Emden)	19 Jun 44	31 Aug 44	Horten 12 May 45 (from sea)	OD (Lisahally)	Expended torpedo target HMS/M Templar N Atlantic (55° 49' N, 08° 31' W) 6 Jan 46.

Name	Type	Builder	Launch	Comp/comm	Surr/cap	Alloc	Fate
U1110	VIIC/41	Nordseewerke (Emden)	12 Jun 44	24 Sep 44	List, Sylt 14 May 45 (from sea)	OD (Loch Ryan)	Scuttled gunfire N Atlantic (55° 45' N, 08° 19' W) 21 Jan 46
U1163	VIIC	Danziger-Werft (Danzig)	12 Jun 43	6 Oct 44	Kristiansand-South 9 May 45	Cat C OD (Loch Ryan)	Expended bombing target N Atlantic (55° 50' N, 10° 05' W) 11 Dec 45
U1165	VIIC	Danziger-Werft (Danzig)	20 Jul 43	17 Nov 43	Narvik 9 May 45	OD (Lisahally)	Scuttled gunfire N Atlantic (55° 44' N, 08° 40' W) 31 Dec 45.
U1171 = N19 (1945)	VIIC	Danziger-Werft (Danzig)	23 Nov 43	12 Jan 44	Stavanger 9 May 45	UK	Trials vessel; arrived Sunderland to BU by T Young 13 Jun 49
U1174	VIIC	Danziger-Werft (Danzig)	21 Oct 43	–	Danzig 30 Mar 45	–	Transferred Liepāja; BU?
U1176	VIIC	Danziger-Werft (Danzig)	6 Nov 43	–	Danzig 30 Mar 45	–	Transferred Liepāja; BU?
U1177	VIIC	Danziger-Werft (Danzig)	6 Nov 43	–	Danzig 30 Mar 45	–	Transferred Liepāja; BU?
U1194	VIIC	Schichau (Danzig)	2 Sep 43	21 Oct 43	Cuxhaven 9 May 45 (from sea)	OD (Loch Ryan)	Scuttled gunfire N Atlantic (55° 59' N, 09° 55' W) 22 Jan 46.
U1197	VIIC	Schichau (Danzig)	20 Sep 43	2 Dec 43	Wesermünde May 45 (damaged)	–	Scuttled US forces Skagerrak (57° 43' N, 06° 13' E) early 46
U1198	VIIC	Schichau (Danzig)	30 Sep 43	9 Dec 43	Cuxhaven 8 May 45 (from sea)	OD (Loch Ryan)	Scuttled gunfire N Atlantic (56° 14' N, 10° 35' 05" W) 17 Dec 45
U1202 = Kinn (1951)	VIIC	Schichau (Danzig)	11 Nov 43	27 Jan 44	Bergen 9 May 45 (damaged)	–	NO Oct 48; NO comm 1 Jul 51; decommissioned 1 Jun 61; sold 1962; BU Hamburg 1963
U1203	VIIC	Schichau (Danzig)	9 Dec 43	10 Feb 44	Trondheim 9 May 45	OD (Loch Ryan)	Expended bombing target N Atlantic (55° 50' N, 10° 05' W) 8 Dec 45
U1228	IXC/40	Deutsche Werft (Hamburg)	2 Oct 43	22 Dec 43	Portsmouth NH 17 May 45 (from sea)	–	Scuttled torpedoes off Cape Cod 5 Feb 46
U1230	IXC/40	Deutsche Werft (Hamburg)	8 Nov 43	26 Jan 44	Heligoland 5 May 45	OD (Loch Ryan)	Scuttled gunfire N Atlantic (56° 50' N, 10° 05' W) 17 Dec 45
U1231 = N-26 (1945) = B-26 (9 Jun 49) = KBP-33 (15 Sep 53) = UTS-23 (27 Dec 56)	IXC/40	Deutsche Werft (Hamburg)	18 Nov 43	9 Feb 44	Loch Eriboll 13 May 45 (from sea)	SU	Delivered Liepāja 4 Dec 45; SU comm 13 Feb 46; reserve 17 Aug 53; training hulk 15 Sep 53; stricken 13 Jan 68; BU Riga
U1232	IXC/40	Deutsche Werft (Hamburg)	20 Dec 43	8 Mar 44	Wesermünde May 1945 (damaged)	–	Foundered Heligoland Bight (54° 11' N, 07° 24' E) 4 Mar 46
U1233	IXC/40	Deutsche Werft (Hamburg)	23 Dec 43	22 Mar 44	Baring Bay DK 5 May 45	OD (Loch Ryan)	Scuttled gunfire N Atlantic (55° 51' N, 08° 54' W) 29 Dec 45
U1271	VIIC/41	Bremer-Vulkan (Vegesack)	8 Dec 43	12 Jan 44	Bergen 9 May 45	OD (Loch Ryan)	Foundered N Atlantic (55° 28' 50" N, 07° 20' 40" W) 8 Dec 45
U1272	VIIC/41	Bremer-Vulkan (Vegesack)	23 Dec 43	28 Jan 44	Bergen 9 May 45 (from sea)	OD (Loch Ryan)	Expended bombing target N Atlantic (55° 50' N, 10° 05' W) 8 Dec 45
U1277	VIIC/41	Bremer-Vulkan (Vegesack)	18 Mar 44	3 May 44	–	–	Scuttled N Atlantic (41° 09' N, 08° 41' W) 3 Jun 45
U1301	VIIC/41	Flensburger-Werft (Flensburg)	22 Dec 43	11 Feb 44	Bergen 9 May 45	OD (Loch Ryan)	Scuttled gunfire N Atlantic (56° 10' N, 10° 05' W) 16 Dec 45
U1305 = N-25 (Feb 46) = S-84 (9 Jun 49)	VIIC/41	Flensburger-Werft (Flensburg)	11 Jul 44	13 Sep 44	Loch Eriboll 10 May 1945 (from sea)	SU	Delivered Liepāja 4 Dec 45; SU comm 13 Feb 46; reserve 30 Dec 55; expended atomic bomb target off Novaya Zemlya 10 Oct 57
U1307	VIIC/41	Flensburger-Werft (Flensburg)	29 Sep 44	17 Nov 44	Bergen 9 May 45	OD (Loch Ryan)	Expended rocket target (816 Sqn FAA) N Atlantic (55° 50' N, 10° 05' W) 9 Dec 45
U1406	XVIIB	Blohm & Voss (Hamburg)	2 Jan 45	8 Feb 45	Cuxhaven 5 May 45	US	Scuttled GE officer 7 May 45; salved Jun 45 and to Kiel; transported to US but not repaired; for disposal 27 Feb 48; sold Interstate Metals Corp 26 Apr 48; left Portsmouth NYd 18 May 48 to BU
U1407 = N25 (25 Sep 1945) = Meteorite (26 Aug 47)	XVIIB	Blohm & Voss (Hamburg)	Feb 45	29 Mar 45	Cuxhaven 5 May 45	UK	Scuttled GE officer 7 May 45; salved Jun 45 and to Kiel; refitted arrived Barrow; UK comm 26 Aug 47; trials vessel; paid off 8 Jul 49; T W Ward (Barrow) 7 Sep 49 to BU

Name	Type	Builder	Launch	Comp/comm	Surr/cap	Alloc	Fate
U2321	XXIII	Deutsche Werft (Hamburg)	17 Apr 44	12 Jun 44	Kristiansand-South 9 May 45	OD (Loch Ryan)	Scuttled gunfire N Atlantic (56° 10' N, 10° 05' W) 27 Nov 45
U2322	XXIII	Deutsche Werft (Hamburg)	30 Apr 44	1 Jul 44	Stavanger 9 May 45	OD (Loch Ryan)	Scuttled gunfire N Atlantic (56° 10' N, 10° 05' W) 27 Nov 45
U2324	XXIII	Deutsche Werft (Hamburg)	16 Jun 44	18 Jul 44	Stavanger 9 May 45 (from sea)	OD (Loch Ryan)	Scuttled gunfire N Atlantic (56° 10' N, 10° 05' W) 27 Nov 45
U2325	XXIII	Deutsche Werft (Hamburg)	13 Jul 44	3 Aug 44	Kristiansand-South 9 May 45	OD (Loch Ryan)	Scuttled gunfire N Atlantic (56° 10' N, 10° 05' W) 28 Nov 45
U2326 = N35 (1945)	XXIII	Deutsche Werft (Hamburg)	17 Jul 44	10 Aug 44	Dundee 14 May 45 (from sea)	UK	UK trials vessel Jul 45; FR Feb 46; foundered off Toulon 6 Dec46
U2328	XXIII	Deutsche Werft (Hamburg)	17 Aug 44	25 Aug 44	Bergen 9 May 45	OD (Loch Ryan)	Foundered N Atlantic (56° 12' N, 09° 48' W) 27 Nov 45.
U2329	XXIII	Deutsche Werft (Hamburg)	11 Aug 44	1 Sep 44	Stavanger 9 May 45	OD Cat C (Loch Ryan)	Scuttled gunfire N Atlantic (56° 10' N, 10° 05' W) 28 Nov 45
U2334	XXIII	Deutsche Werft (Hamburg)	26 Aug 44	21 Sep 44	Kristiansand-South 9 May 45	OD (Loch Ryan)	Scuttled gunfire N Atlantic (56° 10' N, 10° 05' W) 28 Nov 45
U2335	XXIII	Deutsche Werft (Hamburg)	31 Aug 44	27 Sep 44	Kristiansand-South 9 May 45	OD Cat C (Loch Ryan)	Scuttled gunfire N Atlantic (56° 10' N, 10° 05' W) 28 Nov 45
U2336	XXIII	Deutsche Werft (Hamburg)	10 Sep 44	30 Sep 44	Kiel 15 May 45 (from sea)	OD (Lisahally)	Scuttled gunfire N Atlantic (56° 06' N, 09° 00' W) 3 Jan 46
U2337	XXIII	Deutsche Werft (Hamburg)	15 Sep 44	4 Oct 44	Kristiansand-South 9 May 45	OD (Loch Ryan)	Scuttled gunfire N Atlantic (56° 10' N, 10° 05' W) 28 Nov 45
U2341	XXIII	Deutsche Werft (Hamburg)	3 Oct 44	21 Oct 44	Cuxhaven 5 May 45	OD (Lisahally)	Scuttled gunfire N Atlantic (55° 44' N, 08° 19' W) 31 Dec 45
U2345	XXIII	Deutsche Werft (Hamburg)	28 Oct 44	15 Nov 44	Stavanger 9 May 45	OD (Loch Ryan)	Scuttled N Atlantic (56° 10' N, 10° 05' W) 27 Nov 45
U2348	XXIII	Deutsche Werft (Hamburg)	11 Nov 44	4 Dec 44	Stavanger 9 May 45	UK	Arrived Larne to BU by John Leigh & Co Apr 49
U2350	XXIII	Deutsche Werft (Hamburg)	22 Nov 44	23 Dec 45	Kristiansand-South 9 May 45	OD (Loch Ryan)	Scuttled gunfire N Atlantic (56° 10' N, 10° 05' W) 28 Nov 45.
U2351	XXIII	Deutsche Werft (Hamburg)	25 Nov 44	30 Dec 44	Flensburg 5 May 45	OD (Lisahally)	Scuttled gunfire N Atlantic (56° 06' N, 09° 00' W) 3 Jan 46
U2353 = N-31 (1945) = M-51 (9 Jun 49)	XXIII	Deutsche Werft (Hamburg)	6 Dec 44	9 Jan 45	Kristiansand-South 9 May 45	SU	Delivered Liepāja 4 Dec 45; SU comm 13 Feb 46; training hulk 22 Dec 50; stricken 17 Mar 52; BU 1963
U2354	XXIII	Deutsche Werft (Hamburg)	10 Dec 44	11 Jan 45	Kristiansand-South 9 May 45	OD (Loch Ryan)	Scuttled gunfire N Atlantic (56° 00' N, 10° 05' W) 22 Dec 45
U2356	XXIII	Deutsche Werft (Hamburg)	19 Dec 44	12 Jan 45	Cuxhaven 5 May 45	OD (Lisahally)	Scuttled gunfire HMS Onslaught N Atlantic (55° 50' N, 08° 20' W) 6 Jan 46
U2361	XXIII	Deutsche Werft (Hamburg)	3 Jan 45	3 Feb 45	Kristiansand-South 9 May 45	OD (Loch Ryan)	Scuttled gunfire N Atlantic (56° 10' N, 10° 05' W) 27 Nov 45
U2363	XXIII	Deutsche Werft (Hamburg)	18 Jan 45	5 Feb 45	Kristiansand-South 9 May 45	OD (Loch Ryan)	Scuttled gunfire N Atlantic (56° 10' N, 10° 05' W) 28 Nov 45
U2502	XXI	Blohm & Voss (Hamburg)	15 Jun 44	19 Jul 44	Horten 9 May 45	OD (Lisahally)	Scuttled gunfire ORP Piorun N Atlantic (56° 06' N, 09° 00' W) 3 Jan 46
U2506	XXI	Blohm & Voss (Hamburg)	5 Aug 44	31 Aug 44	Bergen 9 May 45	OD (Lisahally)	Scuttled gunfire HMS Onslaught N Atlantic (55° 37' N, 07° 30' W) 5 Jan 46
U2511	XXI	Blohm & Voss (Hamburg)	2 Sep 44	29 Sep 44	Bergen 9 May 45	OD (Lisahally)	Scuttled gunfire HMS Sole Bay N Atlantic (55° 33' 08" N, 07° 38' 07" W) 7 Jan 46
U2512	XXI	Blohm & Voss (Hamburg)	7 Sep 44	10 Oct 44	Eckernförde 5 May 45 (wreck)	–	BU
U2513	XXI	Blohm & Voss (Hamburg)	14 Sep 44	12 Oct 44	Horten 9 May 45	US	Arrived New London CT 25 Aug 45; trials and training vessel; paid off 1 Jul 49; expended rocket target USS Robert A Owens off Key West FL (24° 53' N, 83° 15' W) 7 Oct 51
U2518 = Roland Morillot (9 Apr 51) = Q426 (1967)	XXI	Blohm & Voss (Hamburg)	4 Oct 44	4 Nov 44	Horten 9 May 45	UK	Transferred FR 14 Feb 46; reserve 15 Apr 67; stricken 17 Oct 67; sold SPA Loti 21 May 69 at Toulon; arrived La Spezia Aug 69 to BU
U2529 = N-27 (1945) = B-27 (9 Jun 49) = BSh-28 (Sep 55) = UTS-3 (Jan 57)	XXI	Blohm & Voss (Hamburg)	18 Nov 44	22 Feb 45	Kristiansand-South 9 May 45	SU	Delivered Liepāja 4 Dec 45; allocated Baltic Fleet on 13 Feb 46. reserve 10 Jun 55; hulked 19 Sep 55; training hulk 1 Jan 57; stricken 1 Sep 72; BU
U3008	XXI	Deschimag [Weser] (Bremen)	15 Sep 44	19 Oct 44	Wilhelmshaven 11 May 45 (from sea)	US	Arrived New London CT 25 Aug 45; trials and training vessel; paid off Jul 48; expended in demolition trials May 54; salved 1955; sold Loudes Iron & Metal Co (Puerto Rico) 15 Sep 55.

Name	Type	Builder	Launch	Comp/comm	Surr/cap	Alloc	Fate
U3017 = N41 (1945)	XXI	Deschimag [Weser] (Bremen)	5 Nov 44	5 Jan 45	Horten 9 May 45	UK	UK trials vessel; arrived Newport to BU by J Cashmore 25 Oct 49
U3035 = N-28 (Feb 46) = B-28 (9 Jun 49) = PZS-34 (Jan 56)	XXI	Deschimag [Weser] (Bremen)	24 Jan 45	1 Mar 45	Stavanger 9 May 45	SU	Delivered Liepāja 4 Dec 45; allocated Baltic Fleet 13 Feb 46; reserve on 29 Dec 55; battery recharging station 18 Jan 56; stricken 25 Mar 58; BU
U3041 = N-29 (Feb 46) = B-29 (Jun 49) = PZS-31 (Jan 56)	XXI	Deschimag [Weser] (Bremen)	23 Feb 45	10 Mar 45	Horten 9 May 45	SU	Delivered Liepāja 4 Dec 45; allocated Baltic Fleet 13 Feb 46; reserve on 29 Dec 55; battery recharging station 18 Jan 56; stricken 25 Sep 58; BU
U3514	XXI	Schichau (Danzig)	21 Oct 44	9 Dec 44	Bergen 9 May 45	OD	(Lisahally) Expended Shark target HMS Loch Arkaig N Atlantic (56° 00' N, 10° 05' W) 11 Feb 46
U3515 = N-30 (1945) = B-30 (9 Jun 49) = PZS-35 (Jan 56) = B-100 (Jul 58)	XXI	Schichau (Danzig)	4 Nov 44	14 Dec 44	Horten 9 May 45	SU	Delivered Liepāja 2 Feb 46; allocated Baltic Fleet 13 Feb 46; reserve on 29 Dec 55; battery recharging station 18 Jan 56; test hulk 2 Jul 58; stricken 25 Sep 59; sold 30 Nov 59 to BU
U3535 = Ts-5 (12 Apr 45) = R-1 (8 Mar 47)	XXI	Schichau (Danzig)	15 Jul 45		Danzig 30 Mar 45	–	Transferred Liepāja; scuttled NW of Cape Riismaa 8 Aug 47
U3536 = Ts-6 (12 Apr 45) = R-2 (8 Mar 47)	XXI	Schichau (Danzig)	15 Jul 45	–	Danzig 30 Mar 45	–	Transferred Liepāja then Tallinn (Oct 45); scuttled NW of Cape Riismaa 8 Aug 47
U3537 = Ts-7 (12 Apr 45) = R-3 (8 Mar 47)	XXI	Schichau (Danzig)	15 Jul 45	–	Danzig 30 Mar 45	–	Transferred Liepāja; scuttled NW of Cape Riismaa 8 Aug 47
U3538 = Ts-8 (12 Apr 45) = R-4 (8 Mar 47)	XXI	Schichau (Danzig)	Jul 45	–	Danzig 30 Mar 45	–	Transferred Liepāja, then Tallinn (Oct 45), then Kronstadt 1945/46; stricken 29 Feb 48; BU 1948
U3539 = Ts-9 (12 Apr 45) = R-5 (8 Mar 47)	XXI	Schichau (Danzig)	Jul 45	–	Danzig 30 Mar 45	–	Transferred Liepāja (Oct 45), then Kronstadt 1945/46; to BU 29 Feb 48
U3540 = Ts-10 (12 Apr 45) = R-6 (8 Mar 47)	XXI	Schichau (Danzig)	Jul 45	–	Danzig 30 Mar 45	–	BU 29 Feb 48
U3541 = Ts-11 (12 Apr 45) = R-7 (8 Mar 47)	XXI	Schichau (Danzig)	Jul 45	–	Danzig 30 Mar 45	–	BU 29 Feb 48
U3542 = Ts-12 (12 Apr 45) = R-8 (8 Mar 47)	XXI	Schichau (Danzig)	Jul 45	–	Danzig 30 Mar 45	–	BU 29 Feb 48
U3543 = Ts-13 (12 Apr 45)	XXI	Schichau (Danzig)	Hull sections only	–	Danzig 30 Mar 45	–	BU 29 Feb 48
U3544 = Ts-15 (12 Apr 45)	XXI	Schichau (Danzig)	Hull sections only	–	Danzig 30 Mar 45	–	BU 29 Feb 48
U3545 = Ts-17 (12 Apr 45)	XXI	Schichau (Danzig)	Hull sections only	–	Danzig 30 Mar 45	–	BU 29 Feb 48
U3546 = Ts-18 (12 Apr 45)	XXI	Schichau (Danzig)	Hull sections only	–	Danzig 30 Mar 45	–	BU 29 Feb 48
U3547 = Ts-19 (12 Apr 45)	XXI	Schichau (Danzig)	Hull sections only	–	Danzig 30 Mar 45	–	BU 9 Apr 47
U3548 = Ts-32 (12 Apr 45)	XXI	Schichau (Danzig)	Hull sections only	–	Danzig 30 Mar 45	–	BU 9 Apr 47
U3549 = Ts-33 (12 Apr 45)	XXI	Schichau (Danzig)	Hull sections only	–	Danzig 30 Mar 45	–	BU 9 Apr 47
U3550 = Ts-34 (12 Apr 45)	XXI	Schichau (Danzig)	Hull sections only	–	Danzig 30 Mar 45	–	BU 9 Apr 47
U3551 = Ts-35 (12 Apr 45)	XXI	Schichau (Danzig)	Hull sections only	–	Danzig 30 Mar 45	–	BU 9 Apr 47
U3552 = Ts-36 (12 Apr 45)	XXI	Schichau (Danzig)	Hull sections only	–	Danzig 30 Mar 45	–	BU 9 Apr 47
U3553 = Ts-37 (12 Apr 45)	XXI	Schichau (Danzig)	Hull sections only	–	Danzig 30 Mar 45	–	BU 9 Apr 47
U3554 = Ts-38 (12 Apr 45)	XXI	Schichau (Danzig)	Hull sections only	–	Danzig 30 Mar 45	–	BU 9 Apr 47
U4706 = Knerter (1948)	XXIII	Germania (Kiel)	19 Jan 45	7 Feb 45	Kristiansand- South 9 May 45 (damaged)	–	NO Oct 48; sold Royal Norwegian Yacht Club 14 Apr 50; hulk; BU 1954.

Name	Type	Builder	Launch	Comp/comm	Surr/cap	Alloc	Fate
UD5 (ex-O 27) = O 27 (1945)	NL O 21	Rotterdam DD	26 Sep 41	30 Jan 42	Bergen 9 May 45	–	Retroceded NL; stricken 14 Nov 59; BU 1961
UF1 (ex-L'Africaine) = L'Africaine (1945) = Q334 (1963)	FR	Ateliers et Chantiers de la Seine-Maritime (Le Trait)	[7 Dec 46]	[1 Jan 50]	–	–	Retroceded FR; trials 8 Nov 48; stricken 28 Feb 63; condemned Toulon 28 Dec 63
UF3 (ex-L'Astrée) = L'Astrée (1945) = Q404 (Nov 65)	FR	Ateliers et Chantiers Dubigeon (Nantes)	[3 May 46]	[1 Jan 50]	–	–	Retroceded FR; stricken 27 Nov 65; condemned 29 Nov 65; sold at Toulon 1966
UIT24 (ex-Commandante Capelli) = I503 (1945)	IT Marcello	Odero-Terni-Orlando (Muggiano)	14 May 39	IT: 23 Sep 39 GE: 10 Sep 43	[Kobe 10 May 45 (captured JP)]	–	See Table 2.3/4
UIT25 (ex-Luigi Torelli) = I504 (1945)	IT Marcello	Odero-Terni-Orlando (Muggiano)	6 Jan 40	IT: 15 May 40 GE: 10 Sep 43	[Kobe 10 May 45 (captured JP)]	–	See Table 2.3/4

Table 2.1/6. Minelayers

Class	Disp.	Length	Beam	Machinery	Power/speed	Main gun(s)	Mines
NO Olav Tryggvason	1596t	97.3m	11.5m	3 x boilers, 2 x Tu 2 x diesel	6000shp=19.0kt 1400bhp	3 x 10.5cm	280
NO Rauma	320t	52.1m	7.1m	1 x boilers, 2 x VTE	900ihp=13.5kt	2 x 7.6cm	?
NO Laugen	335t	43.3m	8.5m	1 x boiler, 1 x VTE	170ihp=9.5kt	2 x 7.6cm	50
NO Gor	270t	31.8m	8.6m	2 x boilers, 2 x VTE	400–450ihp=10.0kt	1 x 12cm	20
NO Nor	255t	29.0m	7.9m	2 x boilers, 2 x VTE	200hp=8.0kt	1 x 4.7cm	20
NO Vale	238t	27.0m	7.9m	2 x boilers, 2 x VTE	200hp=8.0kt	2 x 3.7cm	20

Name	Class	Builder	Launch	Comp/comm	Alloc	Fate
Brummer (ex-Albatross, ex-Olav Tryggvason)	NO Olav Tryggvason	Horten DYd	21 Dec 32	NO: 21 Jun 34 GE: 11 Apr 1940	Cat C	(bombed Kiel 3 Apr 45) BU 1945–48
V5908 Kamerun (ex-Rauma)	NO Rauma	Nylands (Oslo)	1939	NO: 1940 GE: 18 Apr 40	–	Retroceded NO May 45; stricken Apr 63
V6512 Togo (ex-V5908, ex-Otra)	NO Rauma	Nylands (Oslo)	5 Aug 39	NO: 1940 GE: 10 Apr 40	–	Retroceded NO May 45; stricken Apr 63
NN05 Laugen = Rosenberg VI (1950)	NO Laugen	Akers (Oslo)	1916	NO: 1917 GE: 27 Mar 40	–	Retroceded NO May 45; stricken 1950; sold Rosenberg Verft (ferry); sunk as target 1979
Tyr = Bjorn-West (1951)	NO Gor	Horten DYd	16 Mar 1887	NO: 1887 GE: 1 May 40	–	Retroceded NO May 45; stricken; floating crane; mercantile mercantile (cargo) 1951; ferry 1953; still in existence 2019
Gor	NO Gor	Horten DYd	7 May 1884	NO: 1885 GE: May 40	–	Retroceded NO May 45; stricken 1946; sold (oil lighter); BU
NK31 Vidar	NO Nor	Horten DYd	31 Jan 1882	NO: 1882 GE: 1940	–	Retroceded NO May 45; stricken 1947; sold
Brage	NO Nor	Horten DYd	1 Nov 1878	NO: 1879 GE: 1940	–	Retroceded NO May 45; stricken
Nor = Flatholm (1949)	NO Nor	Horten DYd	23 Oct 1878	NO: 1879	–	Retroceded NO May 45; stricken 1949; sold (salvage vessel)
Vale	NO Vale	Horten DYd	14 Apr 1874	NO: 1874	–	Retroceded NO May 45; stricken.

Table 2.1/7. Minesweepers

Class	Disp.	Length	Beam	Machinery	Power/speed	Main gun (s)	Mines
M1914	450t	54.8m	7.3m	2 x boilers, 2 x VTE	1600ihp=16.2kt		
M1915	480t	58.4m	7.3m	2 x boilers, 2 x VTE	1800ihp=16.5kt		
M1916	506t	57.8m	7.3m	2 x boilers, 2 x VTE	1850ihp=16.0kt		
M1935	772t	68.1m	8.7m	2 x boilers, 2 x UE	3500ihp=18.2kt	2 x 10.5cm/45	30
M1938	713t	71.0m	8.8m	2 x boilers, 2 x UE	3200ihp=18.1kt	2 x 10.5cm/45	30
M1939	785t	68.4m	8.7m.	2 x boilers, 2 x UE	3700ihp=18.2kt	2 x 10.5cm/45	30
M1940	637t	62.3m	8.9m.	2 x boilers, 2 x VTE	2400ihp=16.8kt	1 x 10.5cm/45	–
M1943	668t	67.8m	9.0m.	2 x boilers, 2 x VTE	2400ihp=16.5kt	2 x 10.5cm/45	24
Ex-NL	502t	55.8m	8.1m	2 x boilers, 2 x VTE	1600ihp=15.0kt	1 x 75mm/55 or	–
Ex-DK	270t	53.9m	6.3m	1 x boiler, 1 x turbine	2200shp=19.0kt	1/2 x 75mm/50	30

Name	Class	Builder	Launch	Comp/comm	Alloc	Fate
M3 = T-918 (13 May 46) = Issledovatel (1 Apr 47)	M1935	Stülcken (Hamburg)	28 Sep 37	10 Dec 38	SU	SU 5 Nov 45; arrived Sevastopol 2 Aug 46; sonar trials ship 13 Jan 47; target ship 16 Oct 57; stricken 17 Nov 59; target for Caspian Flotilla
M4 = Q108 (1948)	M1935	Oderwerke (Stettin)	16 Oct 37	10 Nov 38	US	GM/SA Jul 45; FR 9 Oct 47; stricken 7 Aug 48; hulked; BU after 1972

Name	Class	Builder	Launch	Comp/comm	Alloc	Fate
M7 = T-912 (13 May 46) = Belbek (17 Oct 55) = ZL-5 (7 May 57)	M1935	Oderwerke (Stettin)	29 Sep 37	21 Oct 38	SU	SU 5 Nov 45; arrived Sevastopol 27 Jul 46; staff ship 1 Sep 55; target ship 8 Apr 57; stricken 26 Oct 57; sunk as target off Theodosia 1958
M9 = Somme (1947) = Q204 (1960)	M1935	Flender (Lübeck)	16 Nov 37	5 May 39	US [SU]	GM/SA Jul 45; FR training ship Oct 47; reserve 18 Jun 54; stricken 8 Mar 60; condemned 8 Mar 61; hulked; BU 1966
M12	M1935	Flender (Lübeck)	6 Aug 38	7 Aug 39	US	GM/SA Jul 45; FR 9 Oct 47; accommodation ship; BU
M16	M1935	Oderwerke (Stettin)	15 Nov 39	1 Jun 40	Cat C	(bombed Kiel 20 Mar 45) Scuttled Kattegat (58° 10' 48" N, 10° 42' 24" E) 18 May 46
M17 = T-921 (13 May 46) = Kacha (17 Oct 55)	M1935	Oderwerke (Stettin)	29 Jul 39	17 Jan 40	SU	SU 5 Nov 45; arrived Sevastopol 27 Jul 46; staff ship 1 Sep 55; target ship 8 Apr 57; stricken 26 Oct 57; stricken 20 Oct 58; target
M21	M1935	Flender (Lübeck)	6 Sep 39	18 Apr 40	US [SU]	GM/SA Jul 45; FR 9 Oct 47; accommodation ship Lorient; BU
M23	M1935	Flender (Lübeck)	11 Jul 40	26 Oct 40	UK	GM/SA Jul 45; BU UK
M24 = Ailette (1947) = Q76 (1956) = Wespe (1957)	M1935	Flender (Lübeck)	12 Oct 40	22 Feb 41	US	GM/SA Jul 45; FR 9 Oct 47; condemned 16 Nov 56; stricken 22 Nov 56; hulk; to GE 28 Feb 57; decommissioned 20 Sep 63; scuttled North Sea (54° 21' 8" N, 6° 42' 2" E) 25 Oct 73 after gunfire target Z4 22 Oct 73
M28 = Meuse (1947) = Q57 (1957)	M1938	Stülcken (Hamburg)	29 Jul 40	22 May 41	UK	GM/SA Jul 45; FR 9 Oct 47; damaged by rock 12 Dec 53; reserve; breakwater Brest Nov 55; condemned 14 Jan 57; BU 1960
M29 = T-913 (13 May 46) = Tuman (11 Nov 47)	M1938	Oderwerke (Stettin)	18 May 40	4 Sep 40	SU	SU 5 Nov 45; arrived Sevastopol 27 Jul 46; survey vessel 3 Oct 47; stricken 8 Sep 56; handed over to BU 30 Sep 56
M30 = T-914 (13 May 46) = Sangesur (12 Jan 55)	M1938	Oderwerke (Stettin)	1 Jun 40	31 Oct 40	SU	SU 5 Nov 45; arrived Sevastopol 27 Jul 46; salvage vessel 18 Dec 54; stricken 22 Oct 58; BU
M32	M1938	Oderwerke (Stettin)	24 Aug 40	8 Mar 41	US	GM/SA Jul 45; OMGUS 1 Nov 47; chartered to Ostdeutsche Dampfschiff & Transport (Hamburg) 18 Jun 48; US 12 Sep 49; BU Ghent 1950
M33	M1938	Lübecker Maschinen-bau (Lübeck)	1 Apr 42	18 Dec 42	UK	GM/SA Jul 45; accommodation ship; BU
M34 = T-920 (13 May 46) = Aragaz (16 Mar 53)	M1938	Lübecker Maschinenbau (Lübeck)	7 Aug 42	26 Jun 43	SU	FR M/S Jun 45–8 Mar 46; to SU 5 Nov 45; arrived Sevastopol 2 Aug 46; Caspian 23 Aug 52; salvage vessel 16 Mar 53; stricken 21 Feb 57; handed over to BU 12 Mar 57.
M35 = Bapaume (1947)	M1938	Schichau (Elbing)	9 Nov 40	6 Sep 41	US	GM/SA Jul 45; FR 9 Oct 47; stricken 1950; condemned Brest 23 Jul 52
M38 = Oise (1947) = Q90 (1958)	M1939	Atlas (Bremen)	12 Oct 40	16 Jun 41	UK	FR M/S May 45–1947; FR 9 Oct 47; reserve Sep 55; condemned 24 Feb 58; BU Brest
M81 = Laffaux (Jul 47) = Q75 (1956) = Hummel (1957)	M1939	Lübecker-Maschinenbau (Lübeck)	20 Dec 40	17 Jul 41	US	GM/SA Jul 45; FR 9 Oct 47; condemned 16 Nov 56; to GE 28 Feb 57; decommissioned 5 Oct 63; target ship; BU Kiel after 19 Mar 76
M82	M1939	Lübecker-Maschinen-bau (Lübeck)	23 Mar 41	17 Nov 41	UK	GM/SA Jul 45; BU UK 1948
M85 = Yser (1947) = Q78 (1956) = Brummer (1957)	M1939	Lübecker-Maschinenbau (Lübeck)	6 Dec 41	18 Sep 42	UK	GM/SA Jul 45; FR 9 Oct 47; condemned 21 Dec 56; to GE 12 Feb 57; decommissioned 5 Oct 63; hulked 9 Jun 66; BU Kiel after 8 Apr 74
M102	M1939	Rickmers (Wesermünde)	1 Aug 41	28 Apr 42	UK	GM/SA Jul 45; BU UK 1948
M104	M1939	Rickmers (Wesermünde)	1 Apr 42	7 Nov 42	UK	GM/SA Jul 45; BU UK 1948
M131	M1939	Lindenau (Memel)	20 Dec 41	31 Aug 42	UK	GM/SA Jul 45; BU UK 1948
M151 = T-915 (13 May 46) = Skalistyi (25 Feb 53)	M1939	Oderwerke (Stettin)	19 Oct 40	5 May 41	SU	SU 5 Nov 45; arrived Sevastopol 27 Jul 46; salvage ship 8 Jan 53; stricken 12 Aug 64; handed over to BU 27 Aug 64
M154 = T-911 (1946)	M1939	Oderwerke (Stettin)	3 May 41	1 Nov 41 [US]	SU	GM/SA Jul 45; to SU 13 Feb 46; BU 1958
M155 = T-924 (13 May 46) = ZL-66 (17 Oct 55) = BRN-31 (4 Dec 56) = PKZ-132 (28 Jan 58)	M1939	Oderwerke (Stettin)	19 Jul 41	27 Jan 42	SU	SU 5 Nov 45; arrived Sevastopol 2 Aug 46; target ship 1 Sep 55; fire-fighting vessel 29 Oct 56; accommodation ship 9 Oct 57; stricken 21 Jun 79; handed over to BU 27 Mar 80
M201	M1939	Neptun (Rostock)	14 May 40	20 Dec 40	UK	GM/SA Jul 45; BU 1948
M202 = Craonne (2 Dec 47)	M1939	Neptun (Rostock)	29 Sep 40	3 Apr 41	US	GM/SA Jul 45; FR 9 Oct 47; condemned 27 Jun 51

Name	Class	Builder	Launch	Comp/comm	Alloc	Fate
M203 = T-919 (13 May 46) = Laila (23 Feb 53)	M1939	Neptun (Rostock)	29 Sep 40	3 Jun 41	SU	SU 5 Nov 45; arrived Sevastopol 2 Aug 46; salvage vessel 8 Jan 53; stricken 1 Jun 61; handed over to BU 1 Dec 61
M204 = T-916 (13 May 46) = Barograf (19 Sep 52)	M1939	Neptun (Rostock)	21 Dec 40	24 Aug 4	SU	SU 5 Nov 45; arrived Sevastopol 2 Aug 46; sonar control vessel 26 Aug 52; stricken 7 Jul 56; BU
M205 = Belfort (2 Dec 47) = Q74 (22 Nov 56) = Biene (1957)	M1939	Neptun (Rostock)	3 May 41	4 Nov 41	US	GM/SA Jul 45; FR 9 Oct 47; stricken 22 Nov 56; GEF 28 Feb 57; decommissioned 20 Sep 63; training hulk 28 May 68; arrived Kiel 8 Jul 74 to BU
M251 = Péronne (Oct 47)	M1939	Deutsche Werft (Hamburg)	12 Jul 40	10 Dec 40	US	GM/SA Jul 45; FR 9 Oct 47; condemned 27 Jun 51
M252 = Ancre (ii) (Oct 47) = Q199 (6 Oct 60)	M1939	Deutsche Werft (Hamburg)	27 Sep 40	15 Feb 41	US	GM/SA Jul 45; FR 9 Oct 47; condemned 6 Oct 60; breakwater Brest; BU 1961
M253 = Vimy (Oct 47) = Q77 (21 Dec 56) = Bremse (1957)	M1939	Deutsche Werft (Hamburg)	23 Nov 40	21 Apr 41	US	GM/SA Jul 45; FR 9 Oct 47; condemned 21 Dec 56; GEF Jan 57; decommissioned 5 Oct 63; target; arrived Wilhelmshaven 24 Aug 74 to BU
M254 = T-917 (13 May 46) = Nerpa (12 Jan 55) = OT-44 (26 Nov 57)	M1939	Deutsche Werft (Hamburg)	17 Feb 41	16 Jun 41	SU	SU 5 Nov 45; arrived Sevastopol 2 Aug 46; trials ship 8 Dec 54; heating vessel 26 Oct 57; stricken 1958; BU Novorossiysk
M255 = T-922 (13 May 46) = Ispytatel (7 Oct 47)	M1939	Deutsche Werft (Hamburg)	1 Apr 41	11 Oct 41	SU	SU 5 Nov 45; arrived Sevastopol 2 Aug 46; trials ship 14 Aug 46; stricken 31 Jan 58; BU
M256 = T-923 (13 May 46) = Beshtau (12 Jan 55) = PKZ-143 (18 Mar 58)	M1939	Deutsche Werft (Hamburg)	31 May 41	19 Jan 42	SU [US]	SU 5 Nov 45; arrived Sevastopol 2 Aug 46; salvage ship 18 Nov 54; accommodation ship 11 Mar 58; stricken 21 Sep 59; handed over to BU 19 Oct 59
M261	M1940	Atlas Werke (Bremen)	10 Apr 42	10 Sep 42	UK	GM/SA Jul 45; NO 19 Nov 47; BU 1950
M265 = T-721 (25 Feb 46) = Kurs (12 Nov 47)	M1940	Atlas Werke (Bremen)	21 Sep 43	15 Aug 44	SU	SU 5 Nov 45; arrived Liepāja 26 Jan 46; survey vessel 12 Nov 47; stricken 31 Jan 64; BU
M266	M1940	Atlas Werke (Bremen)	18 Mar 44	15 Aug 44	Cat C	(bombed Kiel 11 Mar 45) Blown up Kiel 14 Dec 45
M267 = T-701 (27 Dec 45)	M1940	Atlas Werke (Bremen)	16 Jun 44	8 Mar 45	SU	SU 5 Nov 45; arrived Liepāja Dec 45; stricken 20 Oct 60; BU Tallinn 1960
M272	M1940	Rickmers Werft (Wesermünde)	1942	30 Jan 43	UK	GM/SA Jul 45; to NO 19 Nov 47; BU
M275 = Ancre (i) (23 Aug 47) = M275 (2 Dec 47)	M1940	Rickmers Werft (Wesermünde)	25 May 43	4 Sep 43	UK	FR M/S 1945–46; FR 7 Jul 47; training ship; stricken 8 Dec 47; condemned Brest 7 Apr 52; sold 12 May 60
M277 = Q109 (7 Aug 48) = Lucifer (1949)	M1940	Rickmers Werft (Wesermünde)	25 Nov 43	5 Feb 44	UK	FR M/S Jun 45–Feb 46; laid up Lorient Jan 47; condemned 7 Aug 48; damage control hulk Querqueville 1949; sold at Cherbourg to BU 1969
M278 (ex-TS4) = M202 = Seestern (1956) = WBM I (1960)	M1940	Rickmers Werft (Wesermünde)	25 Jan 44	20 Apr 44	US	GM/SA Jul 45; OMGUS 1947; chartered Paulsen & Ivers (Kiel) 1 Apr 48 (to be ferry: M607 substituted); LSU(B) Feb 51; GEF 1956; accommodation ship 1960; BU 1966
M279 = T-702 (27 Dec 45) = Astronom (9 Dec 47)	M1940	Rickmers Werft (Wesermünde)	4 Jul 44	21 Oct 44	SU	SU 5 Nov 45; arrived Liepāja Nov 45; survey vessel 9 Dec 47; stricken 27 Aug 65; BU
M280	M1940	Rickmers Werft (Wesermünde)	1944	–	Cat C	(incomplete Wesermünde) Scuttled off Jutland 26 Jul 46 (57° 40' N, 16° 30' E)
M291 = T-711 (27 Dec 45) = Meridian (24 Oct 51)	M1940	Lindenau (Memel)	27 Mar 43	5 Aug 43	SU	SU 5 Nov 45; arrived Liepāja Nov 45; survey vessel 15 Aug 51; stricken 7 Oct 69; BU
M294 = M201 (1951) = Seepferd (1956) = WBM VI (1960)	M1940	Lindenau (Memel)	4 Mar 44	28 Aug 44	US	GM/SA Jul 45; OMGUS 8 Oct 47; chartered to Paulsen & Ivers (Kiel) 4 Jun 48; LSU(B) Feb 51; GEF 30 Aug 56; accommodation ship 11 Feb 60; BU 1966
M296	M1940	Lindenau (Memel)	–	–	Cat C	(damaged incomplete Rostock 23 Mar 45) BU
M302	M1940	Unterweser (Lehe)	28 Jul 41	18 Apr 42	UK	GM/SA Jul 45; NO 19 Nov 47; BU 1949
M306	M1940	Unterweser (Lehe)	9 Dec 42	4 May 43	UK	GM/SA Jul 45; NO 19 Nov 47; BU 1950
M321	M1940	Oderwerke (Stettin)	29 Mar 41	19 Sep 41	UK	GM/SA Jul 45; NO 19 Nov 47; BU 1953
M322	M1940	Oderwerke (Stettin)	31 May 41	6 Dec 41	UK	Fire damaged; to NO 19 Nov 47; to DK 1953; BU
M323	M1940	Oderwerke (Stettin)	9 Aug 41	11 Jun 42	UK	GM/SA Jul 45; NO 19 Nov 47; BU 1950.

Name	Class	Builder	Launch	Comp/comm	Alloc	Fate
M324 = T-703 (27 Dec 45) = DG-33 (25 May 56) = ZL-16 (19 Feb 59)	M1940	Oderwerke (Stettin)	20 Sep 41	28 Nov 42	SU	SU 5 Nov 45; arrived Liepāja Nov 45; degaussing vessel 7 Apr 56; target ship 19 Jan 59; stricken 21 Jan 60; handed over to BU 27 Mar 60
M326	M1940	Oderwerke (Stettin)	30 Jan 43	23 Oct 43	UK	GM/SA Jul 45; NO 19 Nov 47; BU 1949
M327	M1940	Oderwerke (Stettin)	12 Jun 43	4 Mar 44	US	GM/SA Jul 45; Ostdeutsche Dampfschiff & Transport (Hamburg) 18 Jun 48; fate uncertain
M328 = B1 (Jul 49) = Antilope	M1940	Oderwerke (Stettin)	12 Jun 43	18 Aug 44	US	GM/SA Jul 45; police accommodation ship Bremerhaven Aug 48; IT 20 Jul 49; BU 1959
M330 = T-712 (27 Dec 45) = ZL-35 (10 Feb 59)	M1940	Lübecker Maschinen-baugesellschaft (Lübeck)	7 Feb 44	21 Oct 44	SU	SU 5 Nov 45; target ship 10 Feb 59; stricken 12 Sep 59; handed over to BU 25 Sep 59
M341 = T-722 (25 Feb 46) = Tshugush (6 Oct 51)	M1940	Neptun (Rostock)	10 Jun 41	19 Apr 42	SU	SU 5 Nov 45; arrived Swinemünde 7 Feb 46; salvage vessel 15 Aug 51; stricken 30 Jun 60; BU
M342 = T-704 (27 Dec 45) = OT-91 (12 Feb 60)	M1940	Neptun (Rostock)	11 Jun 41	7 Jun 42	SU	SU 5 Nov 45; heating vessel 20 Jan 60; stricken mid-60s
M348 = T-713 (27 Dec 45) = Vint (17 Oct 55)	M1940	Neptun (Rostock)	7 Nov 42	19 Sep 43	SU	SU 5 Nov 45; survey ship 1 Sep 55; stricken 12 Aug 64; BU
M361	M1940	Schichau (Elbing)	5 Mar 41	25 Jul 42	UK	GM/SA Jul 45; NO 19 Nov 47; BU 1950
M362	M1940	Schichau (Elbing)	1 Apr 41	26 Oct 42	UK	GM/SA Jul 45; NO 19 Nov 47; BU 1953
M364	M1940	Schichau (Elbing)	9 Aug 41	4 Mar 43	UK	GM/SA Jul 45; NO 19 Nov 47; BU 1953
M365	M1940	Schichau (Elbing)	25 Jul 42	20 Apr 43	UK	GM/SA Jul 45; NO 19 Nov 47; BU 1953
M369 = T-723 (25 Feb 46) = Volnomer (6 Oct 51)	M1940	Schichau (Elbing)	18 Jun 43	21 Sep 43	SU	SU 5 Nov 45; arrived Liepāja 7 Jan 46; survey ship 15 Aug 51; stricken 31 Jan 64; BU
M371 (ex-TS1, ex-M371) = Fehmarn (5 May 48)	M1940	Schichau (Elbing)	31 Jul 43	15 Dec 43	US	GM/SA 15 Oct 1945; sold P Zocke 5 May 48 as accommodation ship; sold Walter Riede (Lübeck) 5 May 55; fate uncertain
M373 (ex-TS5, ex-M373)	M1940	Schichau (Elbing)	30 Nov 43	15 May 44	US	GM/SA 4 Oct 45; M Scharpagge (Dusseldorf) as hotel ship 23 Jun 48; US 11 May 49; fate uncertain
M374 (ex-TS6, ex-M374)	M1940	Schichau (Elbing)	18 Dec 43	27 Jun 44	US	GM/SA 17 Oct 45; Eisen & Metall (Hamburg) as accommodation/salvage ship 7 Apr 48; US 29 Aug 49; BU Ghent 1950
M375 (ex-TS8, ex-M375)	M1940	Schichau (Elbing)	10 Mar 44	25 Jul 44	US	GM/SA 15 Oct 1945; H Schammel (Glücksburg) as accommodation ship 22 Jun 48; US 7 Sep 49; fate uncertain
M377 (ex-TS11, ex-M377) = T-705 (27 Dec 45)	M1940	Schichau (Elbing)	27 Jun 44	27 Oct 44	SU	SU 5 Nov 45; stricken 20 Jan 60; BU
M386 = T-714 (17 Mar 46) = Pulkovo (12 Jan 55)	M1940	Elsflether Werft (Elsfleth)	1 Jul 43	9 Oct 43	SU	GM/SA Jul 45; SU 15 Oct 45; added to list 5 Nov 45; arrived Pillau 17 Mar 46; salvage vessel 18 Dec 54; stricken 4 May 63; handed over to BU 27 Jul 63
M388 (ex-TS7, ex-M388) = M203 (Feb 51) = Seehund (1956) = WBM V (1960)	M1940	Elsflether Werft (Elsfleth)	22 Apr 44	22 Jul 44	US	GM/SA Jul 45; Paulsen & Ivers (Kiel) 1 Apr 48; LSU(B) Feb 51; GEF 17 Jul 56; accommodation ship 4 Jan 60; stricken 25 Apr 68; target; sold 7 Sep 73; BU Leer May–Jun 75
M389 (ex-TS12, ex-M389)	M1940	Elsflether Werft (Elsfleth)	22 Jul 44	20 Dec 44	US [SU]	GM/SA Jul 45; Schmidt (Flensburg) 28 Apr 48; US 8 Sep 49; fate uncertain
M401 = T-706 (27 Dec 45)	M1940	Rotterdamsche Droogdok (Rotterdam)	4 Apr 42	30 Nov 42	SU	SU 5 Nov 45; stricken 10 Feb 59; BU from 19 Feb 59 at Tallinn
M404 = Q110 (7 Aug 48)	M1940	Rotterdamsche Droogdok (Rotterdam)	14 Oct 42	26 Mar 43	UK	FR M/S Jun 45–Feb 46; laid up Lorient Jan 47; FR 1948; condemned 7 Aug 48; hulked Lorient; BU 1972
M405 = T-715 (27 Dec 45) = Kengur (12 Jan 55) = SS-7 (6 Nov 57)	M1940	Rotterdamsche Droogdok (Rotterdam)	14 Nov 42	29 Apr 43	SU	SU 5 Nov 45; salvage vessel 18 Dec 54; stricken 28 Jan 58; handed over to BU at Murmansk. 11 Mar 58
M406 = T-707 (27 Dec 45) = DG-34 (25 May 56) = ZL-17 (19 Fen 59)	M1940	Rotterdamsche Droogdok (Rotterdam)	30 Dec 42	2 Jun 43	SU	SU 5 Nov 45; degaussing vessel on 7 Apr 56; target ship 19 Jan 59; stricken 21 Jan 60; handed over to BU 27 Mar 60
M407 = T-724 (25 Feb 46) = Taran 17 Oct 55)	M1940	Rotterdamsche Droogdok (Rotterdam)	15 Feb 43	19 Jun 43	SU	SU 5 Nov 45; survey vessel 1 Sep 55; stricken 31 Jan 64; BU
M408	M1940	Rotterdamsche Droogdok (Rotterdam)	25 Mar 43	3 Jul 43	UK	FR M/S Jun 45–Feb 46; FR 1948; condemned 7 Aug 48

Name	Class	Builder	Launch	Comp/comm	Alloc	Fate
M411 = T-708 (27 Dec 45) = Yurma (12 Jan 55)	M1940	De Schelde (Vlissingen)	22 Aug 42	29 Oct 42	SU	SU 5 Nov 45; salvage vessel 18 Dec 54; stranded off Kildin Island 6 Jan 59; salved and towed to Kola Bay; stricken 2 Jun 59; handed over 21 Aug 59 to BU Murmansk
M415 = T-725 (25 Feb 46) = Reostat (17 Oct 55)	M1940	De Schelde (Vlissingen)	16 Jan 43	15 Mar 43	SU	SU 5 Nov 45; survey vessel 1 Sep 55; stricken 1 Jun 61; handed over to BU 19 Jun 61
M423 = T-709 (27 Dec 45)	M1940	Wilton-Fijenoord (Schiedam)	18 Oct 42	29 Nov 42	SU	SU 5 Nov 45; stricken 10 Feb 59; handed over to BU 19 Feb 59
M424	M1940	Wilton-Fijenoord (Schiedam)	18 Oct 42	22 Dec 42	UK	BU France
M425 = T-716 (27 Dec 45) = DG-35 (25 May 56) = ZL-18 (19 Feb 59)	M1940	Wilton-Fijenoord (Schiedam)	18 Oct 42	31 Jan 43	SU	SU 5 Nov 45; degaussing vessel 7 Apr 56; target ship 19 Jan 59; stricken 12 Sep 59; handed over to BU 25 Sep 59
M431 = T-710 (27 Dec 45)	M1940	Nederlandsche Scheepsbouw (Amsterdam)	7 Mar 42	29 Sep 42	SU	SU 5 Nov 45; stricken 10 Feb 59; handed over to BU at Tallinn 19 Feb 59
M432 = Suippe (23 Aug 47)	M1940	Nederlandsche Scheepsbouw (Amsterdam)	7 Mar 42	27 Oct 42	UK	FR M/S Jun 45–Feb 46; FR 23 Aug 47; special reserve 1 Jul 48; condemned at Brest 15 Jun 53
M434	M1940	Nederlandsche Scheepsbouw (Amsterdam)	11 Apr 42	23 Dec 42	UK	GM/SA Jul 45; laid up Lorient Jan 47; FR Aug 48; condemned 7 Aug 48
M436	M1940	Nederlandsche Scheepsbouw (Amsterdam)	27 Jun 42	6 Mar 43	UK	GM/SA Jul 45; NO 19 Nov 47; BU 1950
M437 = T-726 (25 Feb 46) = Gidrograf (24 Oct 52) = Magnit (17 Oct 55)	M1940	Nederlandsche Scheepsbouw (Amsterdam)	27 Jun 42	28 Apr 43	SU	SU 5 Nov 45; survey vessel Oct 52; stricken 1 Jun 61; BU
M441 = M205 (Feb 51) = Seelöwe (1956) = WBM III (1960)	M1940	P Smit (Rotterdam)	19 Jun 42	26 Nov 42	UK	GM/SA Jul 45; accommodation ship 1947; LSU(B) Oct 51; GEF 17 Jul 56; accommodation ship 4 Jan 60; stricken 8 Jan 69; BU 1970
M442 = Marne (23 Aug 47) = Q93 (19 Jun 57)	M1940	P Smit (Rotterdam)	17 Aug 42	31 Dec 42	UK	GM/SA 15 Dec 45; FR Aug 47; special reserve 1 Jul 48; base ship Nantes; condemned Lorient 19 Jun 57
M443 = T-727 (25 Feb 46) = Dzhinal (25 Feb 53)	M1940	P Smit (Rotterdam)	14 Sep 42	1 Feb 43	SU	SU 5 Nov 45; salvage vessel 8 Jan 53; stricken 20 Apr 64; handed over to BU 28 Jun 64
M446 = T-717 (27 Dec 45) = Bui (24 Oct 51)	M1940	P Smit (Rotterdam)	3 Feb 43	8 Jun 43	SU	SU 5 Nov 45; survey vessel 15 Aug 51; stricken 30 Jun 60; expended as target
M452 = Aisne (23 Aug 47) = Q108 (7 Apr 52)	M1940	Werf Gusto (Schiedam)	19 Dec 42	7 Feb 43	UK	FR M/S Jun 45–Feb 46; FR Aug 47; special reserve 1 Aug 48; condemned at Brest 7 Apr 52; cannibalised
M453	M1940	Werf Gusto (Schiedam)	15 Dec 42	20 Mar 43	US	GM/SA 4 Oct 45; OMGUS 1947; DDG Hansa (Bremen) 24 Feb 48; US Navy Feb 49; BU 1949
M454	M1940	Werf Gusto (Schiedam)	1943	10 May 43	UK	FR M/S Jun 45–Feb 46; laid up Lorient Jan 47; FR Aug 48; condemned 7 Aug 48
M455	M1940	Werf Gusto (Schiedam)	7 Dec 42	11 Jun 43	US	GM/SA Jul 45; fate uncertain
M456 = T-728 (25 Feb 46) = DG-11 (17 Oct 55)	M1940	Werf Gusto (Schiedam)	3 Mar 43	2 Jul 43	SU	SU 5 Nov 45; degaussing vessel 1 Sep 55; stricken 21 Apr 60; BU
M460 = M204 (Feb 51) = Seeigel (1956) = WBM II (1960) = Torpedoklarmach- stelle II (Jun 67)	M1940	Nederlandsche Dok (Amsterdam)	27 Jul 42	6 Feb 43	US	GM/SA (1945); OMGUS 11 Oct 46; Paulsen & Ivers (Kiel) 4 Jun 48; to US Oct 49; LSU(B) Feb 51; GEF 30 Aug 56; accommodation ship 29 Jan 60; torpedo clearance vessel 28 Jun 67; sold Motorenwerke Bremerhaven 4 May 75; foundered 1981; BU 1984
M461 = T-718 (27 Dec 45)	M1940	Nederlandsche Dok (Amsterdam)	24 Oct 42	25 Mar 43	SU	SU 5 Nov 45; arrived Pillau 17 Mar 46; stricken 10 Feb 59; handed over to BU 12 Sep 59
M467 = T-719 (27 Dec 45) = Alagez (6 Oct 51)	M1940	Giessen (Krimpen)	9 Jan 42	31 Oct 42	SU	SU 5 Nov 45; salvage vessel 21 Jun 51; stricken 12 Aug 64; handed over to BU 27 Aug 64
M470 = T-720 (27 Dec 45) = Briz (12 Jan 55)	M1940	Giessen (Krimpen)	29 Oct 42	27 Feb 43	SU	SU 5 Nov 45; arrived Pillau 17 Mar 46; survey vessel 18 Dec 54; stricken 4 Nov 66; BU
M475 = Q111 (21 Aug 48)	M1940	J & K Smit (Kinderdijk)	29 Aug 42	23 Dec 42	UK	FR M/S Jun 45–Feb 46; laid up Lorient Jan 47; FR 1948; condemned 21 Aug 48; hulked Lorient; sold to BU 1978
M476 = Q88 (7 Aug 48)	M1940	J & K Smit (Kinderdijk)	3 Oct 42	20 Mar 43	UK	FR M/S Jun 45–Feb 46; laid up Lorient Jan 47; FR 1948; condemned 7 Aug 48; sold to BU Nantes 1957.

Name	Class	Builder	Launch	Comp/comm	Alloc	Fate
M484 = T-729 (25 Feb 46) = DG-36 (25 May 56) = ZL-19 (19 Feb 59)	M1940	Boele's (Bolnes)	25 Aug 42	20 Jan 43	SU	SU 5 Nov 45; degaussing vessel 7 Apr 56; target ship 19 Jan 59; stricken 21 Jan 60; handed over to BU 7 Mar 60
M495	M1940	Pot (Bolnes)	4 Sep 42	11 Mar 43	US	GM/SA Jul 45; FR Oct 47; cannibalised and BU
M496 = T-730 (25 Feb 46) = DG-12 (17 Oct 55) = Bunar (27 Dec 56) = PKZ-28 (18 Jan 61)	M1940	Pot (Bolnes)	12 Jan 43	7 Jun 43	SU	SU 5 Nov 45; degaussing vessel 1 Sep 55; salvage vessel 7 Dec 56; accommodation ship 1 Dec 60; stricken 5 Jun 70; BU
M502 (ex-M102)	M1916	Atlas-Werke (Bremen)	31 May 18	24 Jul 18	US	GM/SA Jul 45; OMGUS 25 Oct 46; BU Ghent Mar 49
M504 (ex-M104)	M1916	Neptun (Rostock)	27 Apr 18	29 Jun 18	Cat C	(damaged Kiel 9 Apr 45) BU
M508 (ex-Delphin, ex-M108)	M1916	Tecklenborg (Geestemünde)	17 Jul 18	10 Aug 18	SU	GM/SA Jul 45; to SU 17 Nov 45; fate uncertain
M509 (ex-Sundevall, ex-Johan Wittenborg, ex- M109)	M1916	Tecklenborg (Geestemünde)	7 Aug 18	29 Aug 18	US	GM/SA Jul 45; OMGUS 25 Oct 46; D G Neptun as accommodation ship 23 Mar 48; OMGUS 7 Apr 49; US Army Sep 49; BU Aug 50
M510 (ex-M110)	M1916	Tecklenborg (Geestemünde)	27 Aug 18	19 Sep 18	US	GM/SA Jul 45; OMGUS 25 Oct 46; chartered Seebeck Werft (accommodation ship) 19 Sep 47; OMGUS Mar 49; US Army Sep 49; BU Ghent Aug 50
M513 (ex-Acheron, ex-M113)	M1916	Stülcken (Hamburg)	27 May 19	31 Oct 19	US	OMGUS 25 Oct 46; fate uncertain
M517 (ex-M117)	M1916	Atlas-Werke (Bremen)	20 Sep 18	1919	US	GM/SA Jul 45; OMGUS 28 Oct 47; fate uncertain
M522 (ex-M122)	M1916	Neptun (Rostock)	21 Sep 18	27 Feb 19	Cat C	(damaged Kiel 20 Mar 45) Scuttled Skagerrak (58° 10' 12" N, 10° 42' 48" E) 18 May 46
M526 (ex-Alders, ex-M126)	M1916	Flesbeurger Sb (Flensburg)	21 Dec 18	1 Jul 19	US	GM/SA Jul 45; OMGUS 25 Oct 46; fate uncertain
M528 (ex-Pelikan, ex-M28)	M1915	Neptun (Rostock)	6 May 16	24 Jun 16	US	GM/SA Jul 45; OMGUS 28 Oct 46; chartered to Seebeck Werft (accommodation ship) 29 Sep 47; OMGUS 10 Mar 49; US Army Sep 49; BU 1950s
M534 (ex-Jungingen, ex-M534, ex-Frauenlob, ex-M134)	M1916	Frerichs (Eiswerden)	28 Jul 19	31 Oct 19	US	GM/SA Jul 45; fate uncertain
M535 (ex-Gazelle, ex-Hela, ex-M135) = Desna (1946) = Venta (1951)	M1916	Frerichs (Eiswerden)	15 Mar 19	31 Oct 19	SU	GM/SA Jul 45; to SU 8 Feb 46; BU 1960s
M545 (ex-M145)	M1916	Neptun (Rostock)	22 May 19	20 Jun 19	US	GM/SA Jul 45; OMGUS 28 Oct 47; chartered to Reinecke & Brehmer (Hamburg: accommodation ship) 19 Mar 48; stranded Sep 49; BU
M551 (ex-MH1, ex-Willem van Ewijck) = Abraham van der Hulst (May 45)	Ex-NL	P Smit (Rotterdam)	18 Apr 40	26 Aug 40	–	Retroceded NL May 45; netlayer 1952; stricken 1961; sea cadet training hulk; withdrawn 18 Apr 69; BU Hendrik-ibo-Ambacht
M552 (ex- Pieter Florisz) = Pieter Florisz (May 45)	Ex-NL	P Smit (Rotterdam)	11 May 37	NL: 13 Sep 37 GE: 1941	–	Retroceded NL May 45; netlayer 1952; stricken 1961; sea cadet training hulk Feb 62; withdrawn Sep 76; sold to Stolk's Handelsonderneming & BU Hendrik-ibo-Ambacht to 2006
M560 (ex-Hille, ex-Hecht, ex-M60)	M1916	Seebeck (Geestemünde)	28 Nov 17	15 Jan 18	SU	GM/SA Jul 45; to SU 17 Nov 45; fate uncertain
M566 (ex-Störtebeker, ex-M66)	M1916	Tecklenborg (Geestemünde)	2 Jun 17	1 Jul 17	US	GM/SA Jul 45; OMGUS 1 Dec 47; chartered to Ostdeutsche Damfschiff & Transport (Hamburg) 18 Jun 48; OMGUS 12 Sep 49; US Army 13 Sep49; BU 1950s
M572 (ex-M72)	M1916	Bremer Vulcan (Vegesack)	20 Feb 18	28 Apr 18	US	GM/SA Jul 45; OMGUS 25 Oct 46; police accommodation ship Bremen 11 Jun 47; BU Belgium Mar 53
M581 (ex-Nautilus, ex-M81)	M1916	Seebeck (Geestemünde)	8 Sep 19	13 Oct 19	US	GM/SA Jul 45; OMGUS 25 Oct 46; chartered to Schuchman (accommodation ship) 5 Dec 47; OMGUS 10 Mar 49; US Army 13 Sep 49; BU 1950s.
M582 (ex-Jagd, ex-M82)	M1916	Seebeck (Geestemünde)	8 Sep 19	8 Nov 19	US	GM/SA Jul 45; OMGUS 10 Dec 47; chartered to Erfurter Samenversand (Bremerhaven) as accommodation ship 15 Jun 48; sold A Sonnenberg (Bremen) 5 Oct 54 to BU
M598 (ex-M98)	M1916	Tecklenborg (Geestemünde)	16 Apr 18	7 May 18	US	GM/SA Jul 45; OMGUS 26 Oct 46; police accommodation ship Bremen 28 May 47; OMGUS Aug 48; BU Mar 49
M601	M1943	Neptun (Rostock)	31 Aug 44	22 Nov 44	UK	GM/SA Jul 45; BU UK 1948
M602	M1943	Neptun (Rostock)	21 Oct 44	14 Dec 44	UK	GM/SA Jul 45; BU UK 1948
M603	M1943	Neptun (Rostock)	2 Nov 44	31 Dec 44	UK	GM/SA Jul 45; BU UK 1948
M604	M1943	Neptun (Rostock)	10 Nov 44	18 Jan 45	UK	GM/SA Jul 45; BU UK 1948
M605	M1943	Neptun (Rostock)	13 Dec 44	3 Feb 45	UK	GM/SA Jul 45; BU UK 1948
M606	M1943	Neptun (Rostock)	20 Dec 44	16 May 45	US	GM/SA Jul 45; OMGUS 4 Nov 47; chartered to Eisen & Metall (Hamburg) as accommodation ship 9 Jun 48; US Navy 29 Aug 49; BU Ghent 1950.

Name	Class	Builder	Launch	Comp/comm	Alloc	Fate
M607 = Hörnum (Feb 48) = Christian Ivers (1949) = Hanne Scarlett (1954) = Salvatore Lauro (1962)	M1943	Neptun (Rostock)	30 Dec 44	16 Mar 45	US	GM/SA Jul 45; OMGUS 14 Nov 47; sold Hapag Seebärdeinst 19 Feb 48; sold Ivers-Linie (Kiel) 27 Oct 49; sold Kieler Reederei 1954 (chartered to J H J Jensen, [Tuborg]); sold Skandinavisk Linietrafik (Gentofte) 1957; sold Agostino Lauro 1962; sold Libera Navigazione Lauro SAS, Naples 1975; sold Turkey shipbreaker Feb 2006; foundered 10 miles SW of Gerolimena Bay, Peloponnese, 13 Mar 2006
M608 = Amrum (Feb 48) = Harald Ivers (Oct 49) = Lilli Scarlett (1954) = Elena P (1963)	M1943	Neptun (Rostock)	20 Jan 45	20 Mar 45	US	GM/SA Jul 45; OMGUS 14 Nov 47; sold Hapag Seebardeinst 19 Feb 48; sold Ivers-Linie (Kiel) 27 Oct 49; sold Kieler Reederei 1954 (chartered to J H J Jensen [Tuborg], DK); sold Skandinavisk Linietrfik (Gentofte) 1957; sold Ångfartygs Ab (Vaxholm) 1962; sold Christos S Pagouilas (Piraeus) 1963; laid up Perama 1976; BU 1982
M609	M1943	Neptun (Rostock)	29 Jan 45	27 Mar 45	UK	GM/SA Jul 45; OMGUS 14 Nov 47; foundered Finkenwerder 1947; BU Hamburg 1948
M610	M1943	Neptun (Rostock)	27 Feb 45	1945	US	GM/SA Jul 45; OMGUS 14 Nov 47; chartered Norddeutscher Lloyd (Bremen) 10 Feb 48; BU Ghent 1950
M611 = Merc Wangerooge (1948) = M206 (1951) = Seeschlange (1956) = WBM IV (1960)	M1943	Neptun (Rostock)	12 Mar 45	5 Apr 45	US	GM/SA Jul 45; OMGUS 14 Nov 47; chartered Norddeuscher Lloyd Feb 48; LSU(B) 8 Oct 51; GEF 15 Aug 56; accommodation ship Feb 60; stricken 29 May 67; expended air target
M612	M1943	Neptun (Rostock)	23 Mar 45	1 Apr 45	UK	GM/SA Jul 45; BU UK 1948
M613	M1943	Neptun (Rostock)	1945	1945	–	Scuttled off Rostock 1945/46 (?)
M614	M1943	Neptun (Rostock)	1945	1945	–	Scuttled off Rostock 1945/46 (?)
M615	M1943	Neptun (Rostock)	1945	1945	–	Scuttled off Rostock 1945/46 (?)
M616	M1943	Neptun (Rostock)	1945	1945	–	Scuttled off Rostock 1945/46 (?)
M801 = Gazzella (Jul 49)	M1943	Schichau (Königsberg)	9 Sep 44	3 Dec 44	US	GM/SA Jul 45; OMGUS 14 Nov 47; chartered to Deutsch-Amerikanische Petroleum-Gesellschaft (Hamburg) Feb 48; OMGUS 9 Mar 49; IT 20 Jul 49; training ship 1960; stricken 1967; BU 1971
M802	M1943	Schichau (Königsberg)	29 Sep 44	4 Jan 45	Cat C	(sunk Kiel 3 Apr 45) Bombed; blown up Kiel 15 Dec 45
M803 = Daino (Jul 49)	M1943	Schichau (Königsberg)	19 Oct 44	17 Jan 45	US	GM/SA Jul 45; OMGUS 14 Nov 47; chartered to L Nimitz Feb 48; OMGUS 9 Mar 49; IT 20 Jul 49; survey vessel 1960; stricken 1966
M805	M1943	Schichau (Königsberg)	9 Nov 44	25 Jan 45	Cat C	(sunk Kiel 11 Mar 45) Bombed; blown up Kiel 15 Dec 45
M806	M1943	Schichau (Königsberg) [completed Howaldtswerft (Kiel)]	21 Nov 44	31 May 45	UK	GM/SA May 45; BU UK 1948
M807	M1943	Schichau (Königsberg)	21 Nov 44	–	–	To SU at Rostock
M808	M1943	Schichau (Königsberg)	1945	–	–	To SU at Rostock
M809	M1943	Schichau (Königsberg)	1945	–	Cat C	(wreck Kiel) BU
M3800 (ex-M530, ex-Fuchs, ex-M130)	M1916	Reihersteig (Hamburg)	19 Feb 19	29 Jul 29	SU	GM/SA Jul 45; to SU 17 Nov 45; fate uncertain
MA1 (ex-Sölöven) = Sölöven (May 45)	Ex-DK	Copenhagen DYd	3 Dec 38	10 Jul 39 (GE: 29 Aug 43)	–	Retroceded DK May 45; BU 1959
MA4 (ex-Sörridderen) = Sörridderen (May 45)	Ex-DK	Copenhagen DYd	11 Apr 42	25 Sep 42 (GE: 29 Aug 43)	–	Retroceded DK May 45; stricken 1958; BU 1962
MA5 (ex-Söhesten) = Söhesten	Ex-DK	Copenhagen DYd	30 Apr 42	6 Jul 43 (GE: 29 Aug 43)	US	Retroceded DK 22 Nov 45 in damaged condition; repaired; stricken 1958; BU 1959
MA6 (ex-Söhunden) = Söhunden (Nov 45)	Ex-DK	Copenhagen DYd	16 May 42	17 Nov 42 (GE: 29 Aug 43)	–	Retroceded May 45; stricken 1958; BU 1962

Table 2.1/8. Motor Minesweepers

Class	Disp.	Length	Beam	Machinery	Power/speed	Gun(s)	Mines	TT
R17	120t	36.9m	1.4m	2 x diesel	1800bhp=21.0kt	2 x 20mm	12	–
R21	123.6t	37.0m	1.4m	2 x diesel	1800bhp=21.0kt	6 x 20mm	12	–
R25	126t	35.4m	1.4m	2 x diesel	1800bhp=23.5kt	1 x 37mm	12	–
R301	184t	41.0m	6.0m	3 x diesel	3750bhp=25.0kt	1 x 37mm	–	2 x 53.3cm
CH5	114t	37.1m	5.7m	2 x diesel	1836bhp=15.5kt	1 x 37mm	–	–
CH41	126t	37.4m	5.5m	2 x diesel	1836bhp=15.5kt	1 x 37mm	–	–
MZ 1	285t	52.0m	8.3m	1 x diesel	1200bhp=14.0kt	2 x 8.8cm	–	2 x 53.3cm
MGB502	95t	35.7m	5.8m	3 x diesel	3000bhp=25.0kt	2 x 20mm	–	–
RA101	69.9t	28.9m	4.4m	2 x diesel	714bhp=14.5kt	2 x 20mm	–	–
RA106	85t	30.0m	4.6m	2 x diesel	714bhp=14.5kt	2 x 20mm	–	–
RA201	35t	25.0m	4.5m		=14.0kt	2 x 20mm	–	–
MS2	70t	24.6m	4.9m	1 x diesel	200bhp=10.0kt	1 x 20mm	–	–

Name	Class	Builder	Launch	Alloc	Fate
M5401 (ex-RA201)	RA201	Mjellum & Karlsen (Bergen)	1942	US	GM/SA Norway Reserve 1945; BU 1947

Name	Class	Builder	Launch	Alloc	Fate
M5402 (ex-RA202)	RA201	Mjellum & Karlsen (Bergen)	1942	UK	GM/SA Norway Reserve 1945; BU 1947
M5403 (ex-RA203)	RA201	Mjellum & Karlsen (Bergen)	1943	US	GM/SA Jul 45; BU 1947
M5404 (ex-RA204)	RA201	Mjellum & Karlsen (Bergen)	1942	SU	GM/SA Jul 45; to 29 Mar 46
R18	R17	Abeking & Rassmussen (Lemwerder)	29 Aug 35	US	DK 1 Dec 45; returned US 1947; BU UK
R21	R21	Abeking & Rassmussen (Lemwerder)	17 Nov 37	UK	BU UK
R22 = Ostfriesland III (Jun 48) = Twist (18 Mar 52)	R21	Abeking & Rassmussen (Lemwerder)	28 Oct 37	US	Sold J Knecht (Bremen) 17 Jun 48; sold 5 Apr 54 and BU
R23 = KT-101 (1945) = SK-342 (1945)	R21	Abeking & Rassmussen (Lemwerder)	12 Jan 38	SU	SU 26 Oct 45; BU 1954
R24	R21	Schlichting (Travemünde)	22 Dec 37	US	GM/SA Jul 45; OMGUS 1 Dec 47; foundered Bremen 16 May 49; salved and kitchen hulk; to US Navy May 50
R25	R25	Schlichting (Travemünde)	8 Jul 38	SU	GM/SA Jul 45; 20 Jun 46
R26	R25	Schlichting (Travemünde)	3 Aug 38	UK	GM/SA Jul 45; DK 1 Dec 45; BU Odense 1948
R28	R25	Abeking & Rassmussen (Lemwerder)	25 May 38	SU	GM/SA Jul 45; to SU 29 May 46
R31	R25	Abeking & Rassmussen (Lemwerder)	21 Sep 38	UK	GM/SA Jul 45; UK 21 Nov 47; BU
R32	R25	Abeking & Rassmussen (Lemwerder)	27 Oct 38	UK	GM/SA Jul 45; DK 1 Dec 45; UK 1947; BU
R47	R21	Abeking & Rassmussen (Lemwerder)	19 Apr 40	UK	GM/SA Jul 45; UK 5 Dec 47; BU
R48	R21	Abeking & Rassmussen (Lemwerder)	30 Apr 40	UK	GM/SA Jul 45; UK 5 Dec 47; BU
R49	R21	Abeking & Rassmussen (Lemwerder)	5 Jun 40	UK	GM/SA Jul 45; UK 21 Nov 47; BU
R47	R21	Abeking & Rassmussen (Lemwerder)	19 Apr 40	UK	GM/SA Jul 45; UK 5 Dec 47; BU
R53	R21	Abeking & Rassmussen (Lemwerder)	8 Aug 40	SU	GM/SA Jul 45; to SU 20 Dec 45
R55 = Stadt Oldenburg	R21	Abeking & Rassmussen (Lemwerder)	11 Sep 40	US	GM/SA Jul 45; OMGUS 1947; chartered K Kuss (Oldenburg) 24 Jun 48 as restaurant boat; sold Bund Deutscher Pfadfinder 3 Dec 51; accommodation hulk Bremerhaven; (1948) sold 4 Jan 54 to BU
R58	R21	Abeking & Rassmussen (Lemwerder)	25 Oct 40	SU	GM/SA Jul 45; to SU 20 Dec 45
R63_	R21	Abeking & Rassmussen (Lemwerder)	15 Jan 41	SU	GM/SA Jul 45; to SU 20 Dec 45
R65	R21	Abeking & Rassmussen (Lemwerder)	5 Feb 41	SU	GM/SA Jul 45; to SU 26 Oct 45
R67 = Hilligenlei (1948) = Rüstringen (1950) = USN 130 (Sep 53) = Wega (1956) = WBR XII (Mar 62) = Friedrich Lührmann (1967)	R21	Abeking & Rassmussen (Lemwerder)	6 Mar 41	US	GM/SA Jul 45; OMGUS 1 Dec 47; chartered Hapag 27 May 48; ferry; chartered Schiffsgesellschaft Jade (Wilhelmshaven) 23 Nov 50; LSU(B) 15 Sep 53; GEF 30 Oct 56; accommodation vessel 2 Mar 62; Marinejugend Münster 1967; foundered after fire Jul 78
R68 = US 13 Tiger (1948) = Tiger (Jun 48) = USN 143 (1951) = Pegasus (Nov 56) = WBR VI (Apr 61) = Thetis III (May 73)	R21	Abeking & Rassmussen (Lemwerder)	19 Mar 41	US	GM/SA Jul 45; OMGUS 1 Dec 47; chartered Ostdeutsche Dampfschiffe (Hamburg) 8 Jun 48 (tug on Rhein); LSU(B) 30 Jun 51; GEF 16 Nov 56; accommodation vessel 28 Apr 61; stricken 1 Dec 69; sold mercantile 7 May 73; foundered Hamburg-Kohlenschiffhafen 6 Mar 80; salved and BU
R71 = Martha II (Apr 51)	R21	Abeking & Rassmussen (Lemwerder)	25 Apr 41	US	GM/SA Jul 45; OMGUS 5 Dec 47; accommodation vessel 1948; foundered 6 Apr 53 Bremen-Europahafen; salved; BU Jun 53.
R76 = US Leopard (1948) = Leopard (May 48) = USN 145 (Sep 53) = Atair (Oct 56) = WBR V (Apr 60)	R21	Abeking & Rassmussen (Lemwerder)	26 Jun 41	US	GM/SA Jul 45; OMGUS 1 Dec 47; chartered to Ostdeutsche Dampfschiffe (Hamburg) 27 May 48; LSU(B) 15 Sep 53; GEF 30 Oct 56; accommodation vessel 15 Apr 60; stricken 2 Oct 70; sold Seesportclub Büsum 15 Dec 70; BU 1976
R83	R21	Abeking & Rassmussen (Lemwerder)	21 Sep 41	UK	GM/SA Jul 45; UK 21 Nov 47; BU
R85	R21	Abeking & Rassmussen (Lemwerder)	11 Oct 41	–	Mined off Dordrecht 17 Jun 45

Name	Class	Builder	Launch	Alloc	Fate
R87	R21	Abeking & Rassmussen (Lemwerder)	6 Nov 41	SU	GM/SA Jul 45; to SU 4 Nov 45
R90	R21	Abeking & Rassmussen (Lemwerder)	16 Dec 41	SU	GM/SA Jul 45; to SU 19 Jan 46
R91 = USN 131 (Sep 53) = Aldebaran (Nov 56)	R21	Abeking & Rassmussen (Lemwerder)	31 Dec 41	US	GM/SA Jul 45; OMGUS 29 Nov 47; chartered to Norddeutsche Taucherbetrieb (Lübeck) 22 Jun 48; accommodation vessel; H Fleck (Duisburg) 8 Jul 49 (tug on Rhein – not used); LSU(B) 15 Sep 53; GEF 16 Nov 56; stricken 23 Apr 70; yacht 1976; fate uncertain
R96	R21	Abeking & Rassmussen (Lemwerder)	14 Mar 42	US	GM/SA Jul 45; OMGUS 26 Nov 47; sold AG Peglow-Kreutzer Hamburg 1947; fishery research vessel; sold Fish Products Co, Lewes DE 30 Jun 53
R98 = Mars (Jun 48)	R21	Abeking & Rassmussen (Lemwerder)	27 Mar 42	US	GM/SA Jul 45; OMGUS 26 Nov 47; chartered to F Burde (Bremen) 29 Jun 48; accommodation vessel 11 Jul 51; BU 1955
R99 = US 23 Panther (1948) = Panther (May 48) = USN 148 (Sep 53) = Algol (Oct 56) = WBR VIII (Apr 61) = Graf Spee (1970s)	R21	Abeking & Rassmussen (Lemwerder)	11 Apr 42	US	GM/SA Jul 45; OMGUS 26 Nov 47; chartered to Ostdeutsche Dampfschiffe (Hamburg) 28 May 48 (tug on Rhein); LSU(B) 15 Sep 53; GEF 30 Oct 56; accommodation vessel 28 Apr 61; Marinekameradschaft Duisburg 1970s (HQ boat); BU 1977
R100 = Maria-Angela (Jun 48)	R21	Abeking & Rassmussen (Lemwerder)	19 Apr 42	US	GM/SA Jul 45; OMGUS 26 Nov 47; chartered F Gaffling (Kutenhausen) 15 Jun 48; stranded off Blexen (Unterweser) 17 Dec 51
R101 = USN 149 (Jun 51) = UW4 (Dec 56) = Niedersachsen (1971)	R21	Abeking & Rassmussen (Lemwerder)	6 May 42	US	GM/SA Jul 45; OMGUS 26 Nov 47; chartered to H Fleck (Duisburg) 30 Jun49 (tug on Rhein – not used); LSU(B) 30 Jun 51; GEF 11 Dec 56; decommissioned 1 Apr 69; stricken 20 Jul 70; Marinekameradschaft Nienburg 1971 (HQ boat)
R102	R21	Abeking & Rassmussen (Lemwerder)	23 May 42	US	GM/SA Jul 45; OMGUS 26 Nov 47; chartered Norddeutsche Taucherbetrieb (Lübeck) 16 Jun 48 (accommodation vessel); A van Holt (Hamburg) 10 Sep 49 (tug on Rhein); US Navy 15 Sep 53; fate uncertain
R103	R21	Abeking & Rassmussen (Lemwerder)	3 Jun 42	SU	GM/SA Jul 45; to SU 4 Nov 45
R105	R21	Abeking & Rassmussen (Lemwerder)	27 Jun 42	SU	GM/SA Jul 45; to SU 4 Nov 45
R107	R21	Abeking & Rassmussen (Lemwerder)	4 Aug 42	SU	GM/SA Jul 45; to SU 4 Nov 45
R112	R21	Abeking & Rassmussen (Lemwerder)	11 Oct 42	Cat C	(collision off Altenbruch 2 Jun 45); BU.
R113	R21	Abeking & Rassmussen (Lemwerder)	29 Oct 42	SU	GM/SA Jul 45; to SU 20 Dec 45
R115 = ML6115 (Dec 47)	R21	Abeking & Rassmussen (Lemwerder)	19 Nov 42	UK	GM/SA Jul 45; UK 5 Dec 47; trials vessel; BU 1954
R117	R21	Abeking & Rassmussen (Lemwerder)	19 Dec 42	US	GM/SA Jul 45; OMGUS 26 Nov 47; chartered to A Zedler (Lübeck) 28 May 48 (sold Jan 55); accommodation vessel; fate uncertain
R118	R21	Abeking & Rassmussen (Lemwerder)	9 Jan 43	US	GM/SA Jul 45; sunk by ice Kiel Bay 21 Jan 47
R120 = Dorothea (Oct 49) = USN 139 (Sep 53) = Skorpion (Nov 56) = WBR XVI (Aug 62) = Skorpion (Jul 74)	R21	Abeking & Rassmussen (Lemwerder)	17 Feb 43	US	GM/SA Jul 45; OMGUS 1 Dec 47; chartered Wasserstraßenverwaltung Münster 29 Jun 48 (accommodation vessel); W Schnaas (Neuwied) 18 Oct 49 (tug on Rhein); LSU(B) 15 Sep 53; GEF 16 Nov 56; accommodation vessel 3 Aug 62; Marinekameradschaft Borkum 1 Jul 74 (HQ boat); BU 1989
R121	R21	Abeking & Rassmussen (Lemwerder)	11 Mar 43	–	Abandoned Norway
R122	R21	Abeking & Rassmussen (Lemwerder)	19 Mar 43	SU	GM/SA Jul 45; to SU 20 Dec 45
R124	R21	Abeking & Rassmussen (Lemwerder)	8 May 43	SU	GM/SA Jul 45; to SU 20 Dec 45
R127 = USN 141 (Sep 53) = Denib (Nov 56) = WBR VII (Jul 61)	R21	Abeking & Rassmussen (Lemwerder)	2 Jul 43	US	GM/SA Jul 45; OMGUS 1 Dec 47; chartered H Fleck (Duisburg) 29 Jul 49 (tug on Rhein); LSU(B) 15 Sep 53; GEF 30 Nov 56; accommodation vessel 28 Jul 61; Marinekameradschaft Frankfurt/Main 20 Jun 68 (HQ boat); foundered Sep 2006; BU
R128 = Annegret (Oct 49) = USN 151 (Sep 53) = Arkturus (Nov 56) = WBR XVII (May 63) = Moritz (1968)	R21	Abeking & Rassmussen (Lemwerder)	10 Jul 43	US	GM/SA Jul 45; OMGUS 1 Dec 47; chartered Fa Zedler (Lübeck) 28 May 48 (accommodation vessel); W Schnaas (Neuwied) 17 Oct 49 (tug on Rhein); LSU(B) 15 Sep 53; GEF 16 Nov 56; accommodation vessel 31 May 63; target boat 1968; foundered after fire Wilhelmshaven 14 Mar 68; wreck scuttled 1969
R130 = VL.SWO 232 (Jun 48) = Störtebeker (Aug 54)	R21	Abeking & Rassmussen (Lemwerder)	5 Nov 43	US	GM/SA Jul 45; OMGUS 26 Nov 47; Wasserstrassen- und Maschinenamt Minden 18 Jun 48 (accommodation vessel); youth hostel Verden 28 Aug 54; Rolandwerft Bremen 1959 (accommodation vessel); fate uncertain.

Name	Class	Builder	Launch	Alloc	Fate
R132 = USN 132 (Jul 51) = Orion (Jun 56) = WBR IX (Jan 62) = Orion (Dec 68)	R21	Abeking & Rassmussen (Lemwerder)	11 Jan 44	US	GM/SA Jul 45; OMGUS 1 Nov 47; MRVC 1 Jan 48; LSU(B) 1 Jul 51; GEF 5 Jun 56; accommodation vessel 19 Jan 62; Marinekameradschaft Aschaffenburg 18 Dec 68 (HQ boat); BU Oct 2015
R133 = USN 133 (1 Jul 51) = Capella (Jun 56) = Osmagasca (Feb 73)	R21	Abeking & Rassmussen (Lemwerder)	15 Jan 44	US	GM/SA Jul 45; OMGUS 1 Nov 47; MRVC 1 Jan 48; LSU(B) 1 Jul 51; GEF 19 Jun 56; training hulk 20 Feb 59; stricken 1959; sold Fritz Däler Feb 73 (houseboat Bremerhaven); put ashore and burnt 1980
R134 = USN 134 (1 Jul 51) = Merkur (Jun 56) = Cord Widderich (Aug 70)	R21	Abeking & Rassmussen (Lemwerder)	26 Jan 44	US	GM/SA Jul 45; OMGUS 1 Nov 47; MRVC 1 Jan 48; LSU(B) 1 Jul 51; GEF 5 Jun 56; decommissioned 31 Oct 68; Marine-Jugend Büsum 1 Aug 70 (HQ boat); BU 1976
R135 = USN 135 (Jul 51) = Riegel (Jun 56) = WBR X (Dec 51)	R21	Abeking & Rassmussen (Lemwerder)	9 Feb 44	US	GM/SA Jul 45; OMGUS 1 Nov 47; MRVC 1 Jan 48; LSU(B) 1 Jul 51; GEF 5 Jun 56; accommodation vessel 8 Dec 61; stricken 30 Sep 66
R136 = USN 136 (Jul 51) = Mars (Jun 56) = WBR II (Feb 59)	R21	Abeking & Rassmussen (Lemwerder)	24 Feb 44	US	GM/SA Jul 45; OMGUS 1 Nov 47; MRVC 1 Jan 48; LSU(B) 1 Jul 51; GEF 19 Jun 56; accommodation vessel 20 Feb 59; BU Wilhelmshaven 1966
R137 = USN 137 = Regulus (Jul 56) = AT 1 (Aug 61) = Moritz I (Jul 67)	R21	Abeking & Rassmussen (Lemwerder)	23 Mar 44	US	GM/SA Jul 45; OMGUS 1 Nov 47; MRVC 1 Jan 48; LSU(B) 1 Jul 51; GEF (1 Jul 51) 31 Jul 56; training boat 1 Aug 61; stricken 16 Jan 64; target boat Jul 67; foundered after fire Wilhelmshaven 14 Mar 68
R138 = USN 138 (Jul 51) = Castor (Jun 56) = WBR XI (Feb 62) = Schlicktau (19 Sep 69)	R21	Abeking & Rassmussen (Lemwerder)	7 Apr 44	US	GM/SA Jul 45; OMGUS 1 Nov 47; MRVC 1 Jan 48; LSU(B) 1 Jul 51; GEF 9 Jun 56; accommodation vessel 23 Feb 62; BU Wilhelmshaven 1978
R140 = USN 140 (Jul 51) = Pollux (Jun 56) = WBR III (Feb 59)	R21	Abeking & Rassmussen (Lemwerder)	26 May 44	US	GM/SA Jul 45; OMGUS 1 Nov 47; MRVC 1 Jan 48; LSU(B) 1 Jul 51; GEF 19 Jun 56; accommodation vessel 20 Feb 59; stricken 13 Aug 70
R142 = USN 142 (Jul 51) = Spica (Jul 56) = WBR IV (Feb 59)	R21	Abeking & Rassmussen (Lemwerder)	17 Jun 44	US	GM/SA Jul 45; OMGUS 1 Nov 47; MRVC 1 Jan 48; LSU(B) 1 Jul 51; GEF 31 Jul 56; accommodation vessel 20 Feb 59; Schiffswerft Modersitzki (Maasholm) 1970; burnt 1 Feb 79
R143	R21	Abeking & Rassmussen (Lemwerder)	24 Jun 44	UK	GM/SA Jul 45; to DK 1945; to UK; BU?
R144 = USN 144 (Jul 51) = Sirius (Jun 56) = WBR I (Feb 59)	R21	Abeking & Rassmussen (Lemwerder)	1 Jul 44	US	GM/SA Jul 45; OMGUS 1 Nov 47; MRVC 1 Jan 48; LSU(B) 1 Jul 51; GEF 5 Jun 56; accommodation vessel 20 Feb 59; stricken 25 Mar 68; BU 1972
R146 = USN146 (Jul 51) = Jupiter (Jul 56) = OT 1 (Feb 59) = Pulchra Nussia (Oct 70)	R21	Abeking & Rassmussen (Lemwerder)	10 Aug 44	US	GM/SA Jul 45; OMGUS 1 Nov 47; MRVC 1 Jan 48; LSU(B) 1 Jul 51; GEF 31 Jul 56; training boat 20 Feb 59; Marinekameradschaft Neuss 17 Nov 69 (HQ ship); for disposal 2012
R147 = USN147 (Jul 51) = Saturn (Jul 56) = WBR XIII (Nov 61)	R21	Abeking & Rassmussen (Lemwerder)	9 Sep 44	US	GM/SA Jul 45; OMGUS 1 Nov 47; MRVC 1 Jan 48; LSU(B) 1 Jul 51; GEF 31 Jul 56; accommodation vessel 30 Nov 61; fire and damage control training hulk 1960s; Seemannsschule Travemünde 8 Nov 72
R148	R21	Abeking & Rassmussen (Lemwerder)	21 Oct 44	US	GM/SA Jul 45; US 1945; trials vessel; fate uncertain
R149	R21	Abeking & Rassmussen (Lemwerder)	29 Nov 44	SU	SU 4 Nov 45
R150 = USN 150 (Jul 51) = UW 5 (Dec 56) = Schleswig-Holstein (1967)	R21	Abeking & Rassmussen (Lemwerder)	22 Jan 45	US	GM/SA Jul 45; OMGUS 1 Nov 47; chartered Norddeutsche Taucherbetrieb (Lübeck) 16 Jun 48 (diving boat); A van Holt (Hamburg) 5 Sep 49 (tug on Rhein); LSU(B) 1 Jul 51; GEF 11 Dec 56; training boat; decommissioned 28 Apr 67; Marine-Jugend Kiel 1967 (HQ boat); Eberhardtswerft (Arnis) Nov 79.
R152 = MR152 (Dec 45).	R25	Burmester (Burg Lesum)	2 Aug 40	UK	GM/SA Jul 45; DK 1 Dec 45; BU 1951
R153 = MR153 (Dec 45).	R25	Burmester (Burg Lesum)	28 Aug 40	UK	GM/SA Jul 45; DK 1 Dec 45; UK 1947; BU
R154 = MR154 (Dec 45) = Asnaes (1951) = Arion (1961)	R25	Burmester (Burg Lesum)	13 Sep 40	UK	GM/SA Jul 45; DK 1 Dec 45; sold N J Nomikos, (Piraeus) 1961 (ferry)

Name	Class	Builder	Launch	Alloc	Fate
R155 = MR155 (Dec 45) = Bognaes (1951) = Faethon (1961)	R25	Burmester (Burg Lesum)	3 Oct 40	UK	GM/SA Jul 45; DK 1 Dec 45; stricken 1957; sold N J Nomikos, (Piraeus) 1961 (ferry); fate uncertain
R156 = MR156 (Dec 45) = Dyrnaes (1951)	R25	Burmester (Burg Lesum)	23 Oct 40	UK	GM/SA Jul 45; DK 1 Dec 45; stricken 1957; expended as target
R157 = MR157 (Dec 45) = Egenaes (1951)	R25	Burmester (Burg Lesum)	13 Nov 40	UK	GM/SA Jul 45; DK 1 Dec 45; wrecked Jan 61; BU
R159	R25	Burmester (Burg Lesum)	14 Dec 40	–	Abandoned Norway
R160 = MR160 (Dec 45)	R25	Burmester (Burg Lesum)	4 Jan 41	UK	GM/SA Jul 45; DK 1 Dec 45; UK 1948
R167 = MR167 (Jul 49) = Helgenaes (1951)	R25	Burmester (Burg Lesum)	10 May 41	UK	GM/SA Jul 45; UK 19 Nov 47; DK 27 Jul 49; BU 1961
R168 = MR168 (Jul 49) = Lynaes (1951)	R25	Burmester (Burg Lesum)	29 May 41	UK	GM/SA Jul 45; UK 19 Nov 47; DK 27 Jul 49; BU 1962
R170 = MR170 (Nov 47)	R25	Burmester (Burg Lesum)	2 Jul 41	UK	GM/SA Jul 45; DK 19 Nov 47; BU 1948
R172	R25	Burmester (Burg Lesum)	7 Aug 41	US [UK]	GM/SA Jul 45; accommodation vessel; decommissioned 5 Dec 47; BU 1948
R173 = MR173 (Dec 45)	R25	Burmester (Burg Lesum)	23 Aug 41	UK	GM/SA Jul 45; DK 1 Dec 45; BU 1951
R174 = MR174 (Jul 49) = Rinkenaes (1951)	R25	Burmester (Burg Lesum)	11 Sep 41	UK	GM/SA Jul 45; UK 19 Nov 47; DK 27 Jul 49; BU Jun 55
R175 = MR175 (Nov 47)	R25	Burmester (Burg Lesum)	1 Oct 41	UK	GM/SA Jul 45; DK 19 Nov 47; BU 1948
R176 = MR176 (Nov 47)	R25	Burmester (Burg Lesum)	23 Oct 41	US	GM/SA Jul 45; DK 19 Nov 47; BU 1948
R181 = MR181 (Nov 47)	R25	Burmester (Burg Lesum)	21 Jan 42	US	GM/SA Jul 45; DK 26 Nov 47; BU
R183	R25	Burmester (Burg Lesum)	2 Apr 42	–	Abandoned Norway May 1945
R214 = MR214 (Sep 45)	R25	Burmester (Burg Lesum)	28 Jan 43	UK	GM/SA Jul 45; DK 21 Sep 45; BU 1951
R220 = Walcheren (Nov 47)	R25	Burmester (Burg Lesum)	12 Oct 43	UK	GM/SA Jul 45; NL 22 Nov 47; sold Feb 57 to BU
R223	R25	Burmester (Burg Lesum)	13 Oct 43	[UK] Cat C	(abandoned Norway) BU
R225 = MR225 (Sep 45)	R25	Burmester (Burg Lesum)	7 Jan 44	UK	GM/SA Jul 45; DK 3 Sep 45; UK 1947; BU
R226 = MR226 (Sep 45)	R25	Burmester (Burg Lesum)	27 Jan 44	UK	GM/SA Jul 45; DK 29 Sep 45; BU 1950
R229 = MR229 (Sep 45)	R25	Burmester (Burg Lesum)	29 Feb 44	UK	GM/SA Jul 45; DK 3 Sep 45; BU 1951
R230 = MR230 (Sep 45) = Stigsnaes (1951)	R25	Burmester (Burg Lesum)	14 Mar 44	UK	GM/SA Jul 45; DK 3 Sep 45; BU1961
R231	R25	Burmester (Burg Lesum)	30 Mar 44	Cat C	(wreck Bremerhaven) BU
R233 = MR235 (Sep 45)	R25	Burmester (Burg Lesum)	27 Apr 44	UK	GM/SA Jul 45; DK 3 Sep 45; BU 1948
R234	R25	Burmester (Swinemünde)	8 Oct 43	SU	GM/SA; to SU 26 Oct 45
R236 = MR236 (Sep 45) = Trellenaes (1951) = Dedalos (1961)	R25	Burmester (Swinemünde)	1 Feb 44	UK	GM/SA Jul 45; DK 9 Sep 45; sold N J Nomikos (Piraeus) 1961 (ferry); fate uncertain
R238	R25	Burmester (Burg Lesum)	11 May 44	SU	GM/SA Jul 45; to SU 3 Sep 45; fate uncertain
R240 = Goeree (Nov 47)	R25	Burmester (Burg Lesum)	20 Jun 44	UK	GM/SA Jul 45; NL 22 Nov 47; BU 1959
R241	R25	Burmester (Burg Lesum)	20 Jun 44	US	GM/SA Jul 45; OMGUS 22 Nov 47; chartered J A Reinicke (Hamburg) 27 May 48 (workshop hulk); hull sold E Kohse (Heilbronn) 22 May 51; sold H Budde & Co 22 Dec 53 to BU
R242 = MR242 (Sep 45) = Vornaes (1951)	R25	Burmester (Burg Lesum)	8 Jul 44	UK	GM/SA Jul 45; DK 3 Sep 45; BU 1960
R244 = Schouwen (Nov 47)	R25	Burmester (Burg Lesum)	30 Jul 44	UK	GM/SA Jul 45; NL 22 Nov 47; sold to BU 1 Feb 57
R245	R25	Burmester (Burg Lesum)	18 Aug 44	SU	GM/SA Jul 45; to SU 15 Nov 45; fate uncertain

Name	Class	Builder	Launch	Alloc	Fate
R246 = Schiermonnikoog (Nov 47)	R25	Burmester (Burg Lesum)	8 Sep 44	UK	GM/SA Jul 45; NL 29 Nov 47; sold to BU 1 Feb 57
R249 = Gabel-Jürge (1949)	R25	Burmester (Swinemünde)	19 May 44	US	GM/SA Jul 45; OMGUS 24 Nov 47; chartered P Witton (Minden) 1949 (accommodation vessel); sold to BU 1959
R251 = Urk (Nov 47)	R25	Burmester (Swinemünde)	19 Jul 44	UK	GM/SA Jul 45; NL 22 Nov 47; sold to BU 1 Feb 57
R252 = Stortemelk (Nov 47)	R25	Burmester (Swinemünde)	9 Dec 44	UK	GM/SA Jul 45; NL 22 Nov 47; sold to BU 1 Feb 57
R253 = Silesia (Jun 48)	R25	Burmester (Swinemünde)	31 Aug 44	US	GM/SA Jul 45; OMGUS 27 Nov 47; chartered W Kirchner (Minden) 16 Jun 48; sold A Thyselius (Bremenals) 22 Dec 53 to BU
R254	R25	Burmester (Burg Lesum)	22 Sep 44	SU	GM/SA; to SU 26 Oct 45; fate uncertain
R255 = Schulpengat (Nov 47)	R25	Burmester (Burg Lesum)	4 Oct 44	UK	GM/SA Jul 45; NL 22 Nov 47; sold to BU 1 Feb 57
R257	R25	Burmester (Burg Lesum)	21 Oct 44	SU	GM/SA; to SU 4 Nov 45; fate uncertain
R258	R25	Burmester (Burg Lesum)	31 Oct 44	SU	GM/SA; to SU 26 Oct 45; fate uncertain
R259 = MR259 (Sep 45)	R25	Burmester (Burg Lesum)	11 Nov 44	UK	GM/SA Jul 45; DK 3 Sep 45; UK 1947 to BU
R262	R25	Burmester (Burg Lesum)	29 Jan 45	SU	GM/SA; to SU 7 Jan 46; fate uncertain
R263 = MR263 (Sep 45)	R25	Burmester (Burg Lesum)	1 Mar 45	UK	GM/SA Jul 45; DK 24 Sep 45; UK 1947 to BU
R264 = Ilse (Jun 48)	R25	Burmester (Swinemünde)	4 Oct 44	US	GM/SA Jul 45; OMGUS 27 Nov 47; chartered A Zeiske (Bremen) 29 Jun 48; still in service 1955
R265	R25	Burmester (Swinemünde)	31 Oct 44	SU	GM/SA; to SU 20 Dec 45; fate uncertain
R266 = Rewo II (Apr 49) = USN 152 (Sep 53) = AT 1 (Jan 57)	R25	Burmester (Swinemünde)	21 Nov 44	US	GM/SA Jul 45; OMGUS 27 Nov 47; chartered E Wilk (Oldenburg) 10 Apr 49 (tug on Rhine); LSU(B) 15 Sep 53; GEF 21 Jan 57; stricken 15 Feb 61; damage control training hulk; burnt Kiel 31 Jul 68
R267	R25	Burmester (Swinemünde)	24 Jan 45	US	GM/SA Jul 45; OMGUS 27 Nov 47; chartered Wurzel (Minden) 1949 (accommodation vessel); BU 1958
R268 = Malzwin (Nov 47)	R25	Burmester (Swinemünde)	18 Dec 44	UK	GM/SA Jul 45; NL 25 Nov 47; sold to BU 1 Feb 57
R269	R25	Burmester (Swinemünde)	8 Mar 45	SU	GM/SA; to SU 20 Dec 45; fate uncertain
R270	R25	Burmester (Swinemünde)	Feb 45	SU	GM/SA; to SU 20 Nov 45; fate uncertain
R271	R25	Burmester (Swinemünde)	?	Cat C	(incomplete Lübeck) BU
R288	R25	Burmester (Burg Lesum)	Feb 45	SU	GM/SA; to SU 15 Nov 45; fate uncertain
R289	R25	Burmester (Burg Lesum)	Mar 45	SU	GM/SA; to SU 15 Nov 45; fate uncertain
R290 = Vlieter (Nov 47)	R25	Burmester (Burg Lesum)	22 Mar 45	UK	GM/SA Jul 45; NL 22 Nov 47; sold to BU 1 Feb 57
R292	R25	Burmester (Burg Lesum)	–	Cat C	(incomplete Burg Lesum) BU
R302	R301	Abeking & Rassmussen (Lemwerder)	21 Jun 43	SU	GM/SA; to SU 17 Nov 45; fate uncertain
R303	R301	Abeking & Rassmussen (Lemwerder)	26 Aug 43	SU	GM/SA; to SU 17 Nov 45; fate uncertain
R305 = KT-108 (Nov 45)	R301	Abeking & Rassmussen (Lemwerder)	8 Oct 43	SU	GM/SA; to SU 17 Nov 45; fate uncertain
R307 = KT-128 (Nov 45)	R301	Abeking & Rassmussen (Lemwerder)	1 Mar 44	SU	GM/SA; to SU 17 Nov 45; fate uncertain
R308 = KT-109 (Nov 45)	R301	Abeking & Rassmussen (Lemwerder)	31 Mar 44	SU	GM/SA; to SU 17 Nov 45; fate uncertain
R309	R301	Abeking & Rassmussen (Lemwerder)	30 Apr 44	Cat C	(stranded 3 May 45) Cannibalised Bergen
R310 = KT-129 (Nov 45)	R301	Abeking & Rassmussen (Lemwerder)	Jun 44	SU	GM/SA; to SU 17 Nov 45; fate uncertain
R311 = KT-110 (Nov 45)	R301	Abeking & Rassmussen (Lemwerder)	Jul 44	SU	GM/SA; to SU 17 Nov 45; fate uncertain
R312 = KT-111 (Nov 45)	R301	Abeking & Rassmussen (Lemwerder)	Aug 44	SU	GM/SA; to SU 17 Nov 45; fate uncertain
R401 = Koralle (Nov 48)	R25	Abeking & Rassmussen (Lemwerder)	28 Sep 44	US	GM/SA Jul 45; OMGUS 29 Nov 47; chartered Behrendt & Schulte (Bremen), 16 Jun 48; W Schultz (Duisburg) 16 Nov 48
R403 = WS1 (Mar 49) = Atoll (1 Jan 50)	R25	Abeking & Rassmussen (Lemwerder)	22 Oct 44	US	GM/SA Jul 45; OMGUS 27 Nov 47; chartered E Albrecht (Bonn) 26 May 48 (to be . ferry); W Schultz (Duisburg) 17 Mar 49 (tug on Rhine)
R404 = Libelle (May 48)	R25	Abeking & Rassmussen (Lemwerder)	27 Oct 44	US	GM/SA Jul 45; OMGUS 27 Nov 47; chartered E Albrecht (Bonn) 26 May 48 (ferry); Gebr Luwen (Duisburg) 21 Jan 49 (accommodation vessel)
R405 = Hanna (Jun 48)	R25	Abeking & Rassmussen (Lemwerder)	1944	US	GM/SA Jul 45; OMGUS 27 Nov 47; chartered R Wolter (Hamburg) 30 Jun 48; still in service 1954.

Name	Class	Builder	Launch	Alloc	Fate
R406 = Arngast (May 48) = USN 154 (Sep 53) = OT 1 (1956)	R25	Abeking & Rassmussen (Lemwerder)	1944	US	GM/SA Jul 45; OMGUS 27 Nov 47; chartered Schiff Ges Jade (Wilhelmshaven) 27 May 48; LSU(B) 15 Sep 53; GEF 1956; stricken 20 Feb 59 and BU
R407 = Rewo (Jun 48) = Rewo I (12 Aug 49) = USN 153 (Sep 53) = AT 2 (Jan 57)	R25	Abeking & Rassmussen (Lemwerder)	15 Nov 44	US	GM/SA Jul 45; OMGUS 27 Nov 47; chartered E Wilk (Oldenburg) 15 Jun 48 (tug on Rhine); LSU(B) 15 Sep 53; GEF 21 Jan 57; expended as target 18 Jan 63
R408 = Hansa VI (May 48) = USN 155 (Sep 53) = UW 6 (Dec 56) = Stomer (1963)	R25	Abeking & Rassmussen (Lemwerder)	1944	US	GM/SA Jul 45; OMGUS 27 Nov 47; chartered DDG Hansa (Bremen) 19 May 48; LSU(B) 15 Sep 53; GEF 11 Dec 56; stricken 11 Jan 63; generator hulk 1963; BU Kiel 1977
R409	R25	Abeking & Rassmussen (Lemwerder)	1 Dec 44	SU	SU 26 Oct 45; fate uncertain
R410	R25	Abeking & Rassmussen (Lemwerder)	10 Dec 44	SU	SU 4 Nov 45; fate uncertain
R411	R25	Abeking & Rassmussen (Lemwerder)	Dec 44 SU	SU	4 Nov 45; fate uncertain
R412	R25	Abeking & Rassmussen (Lemwerder)	Dec 44 SU	SU	1 Dec 45; fate uncertain
R413	R25	Abeking & Rassmussen (Lemwerder)	Jan 45 SU	SU	1 Dec 45; fate uncertain
R414	R25	Abeking & Rassmussen (Lemwerder)	1945	SU	SU 1 Dec 45; fate uncertain
R415	R25	Abeking & Rassmussen (Lemwerder)	1 Feb 45	SU	SU 1 Dec 45; fate uncertain
R416	R25	Abeking & Rassmussen (Lemwerder)	7 Feb 45	SU	SU 1 Dec 45; fate uncertain
R417	R25	Abeking & Rassmussen (Lemwerder)	14 Feb 45	SU	SU 4 Nov 45; fate uncertain
R418	R25	Abeking & Rassmussen (Lemwerder)	21 Feb 45	SU	SU 15 Nov 45; fate uncertain
R419	R25	Abeking & Rassmussen (Lemwerder)	28 Feb 45	SU	SU 1 Dec 45; fate uncertain
R420	R25	Abeking & Rassmussen (Lemwerder)	Feb 45	SU	SU 24 Nov 45; fate uncertain
R421	R25	Abeking & Rassmussen (Lemwerder)	Mar 45	SU	SU 15 Nov 45; fate uncertain
R422	R25	Abeking & Rassmussen (Lemwerder)	Mar 45	SU	GM/SA Jul 45; to SU 15 Nov 45; fate uncertain
R423	R25	Abeking & Rassmussen (Lemwerder)	Mar 45	SU	SU 15 Nov 45; fate uncertain
R424 = Roompot (Nov 47)	R25	Abeking & Rassmussen (Lemwerder)	Mar 45	UK	GM/SA Jul 45; NL 22 Nov 47; sold 1 Feb 57 to BU
RA1 (ex-CH44) = RN 602 (Jan 46)	FR CH41	Chantiers de la Mediteranée (Le Havre)	10 Jun 40	–	UK Jan 46; to FR 1946; BU
RA3 (ex-CH17) = CH17 (Jan 46) = Tarek ben Said (1952)	FR CH5	Chantiers de la Mediteranée (Le Havre)	1943	–	FR 1945; to SY 1952; stricken 1984
RA5 (ex-CH19) = CH705 (1946) = P705 = Q09 (Jun 54)	FR CH5	Chantiers Navale de Normandie (Fécamp)	1946	–	Retroceded FR 1945; stricken 2 Jun 54.
RA11 (ex-Master Standfast, ex-MG508) = Master Standfast (1945)	UK MGB502	Camper & Nicholson (Gosport)	1942	–	Retroceded UK May 45; BU 1951
RA101 = Codling (1945) = Sparrowhawk (1946)	RA101	Rasmussen (Svendborg)	1 Jun 43	UK	UK May 45; paid off 31 Mar 49
RA102 = RW102 (1945)	RA101	Rasmussen (Svendborg)	8 Jul 43	SU	GM/SA Jul 45; to SU 25 Apr 46; fate uncertain
RA103 = Swallow (1946)	RA101	Rasmussen (Svendborg)	4 Sep 43	UK	UK May 45; GEF Customs Border Guard 1949; stricken 1950

Name	Class	Builder	Launch	Alloc	Fate
RA104 = RN 104 (1945) = Seagull (1946) = Seeadler (1949)	RA101	Rasmussen (Svendborg)	19 Nov 43	UK	UK May 45; GEF Customs Border Guard 1949; fate uncertain
RA105 = Mackerel (1945)	RA101	Rasmussen (Svendborg)	1944	UK	UK May 45; fate uncertain
RA106 = Skate (1945) = Buran (Mar 50)	RA106	Rasmussen (Svendborg)	16 Jul 44	UK	UK May 45; GM/SA Jul 45; sold Waterways & Machinery Office (Minden) 2 Mar 48 (accommodation ship); sold as tug P Müller (Neuwied) 13 Mar 50; still in service Nov 54
RA107 = Herring (1945) = Heimat II (Mar 52)	RA106	Rasmussen (Svendborg)	16 Jul 44	UK	GM/SA Jul 45; sold Waterways & Machinery Office (Minden) 2 Mar 48 (accommodation ship); sold as tug W Bucholz (Lorch) 7 Dec 49; sold J Pawliczek (Münster) 11 Mar 52; sunk 1959; salved? BU 1962
RA108	RA106	Rasmussen (Svendborg)	29 Aug 44	–	UK May 45; GM/SA Jul 45; fate uncertain
RA109 = Shrimp (1945) = USN 28 (1946) = Friesland (1948)	RA106	Rasmussen (Svendborg)	14 Oct 44	–	UK May 45; GM/SA Jul 45; sold C Jansen (Bremen) 25 May 48; sold H Labrecht (Duisburg); still in service Apr 54
RA110 = RW110 (1945)	RA106	Rasmussen (Svendborg)	Nov 44	–	UK May 45; GM/SA Jul 45; fate uncertain
RA111	RA106	Rasmussen (Svendborg)	27 Jan 45	SU	To SU 17 Jan 46; fate uncertain
RA112	RA106	Rasmussen (Svendborg)	4 Mar 45	SU	To SU 1 Dec 45; fate uncertain
Vs820 (ex-Vs119, ex-MS3) = Baagö (1951) = MHV84 (1964)	MS2	Lilleö (Korsør)	21 May 41	–	Retroceded DK 9 Jun 45; stricken 1968
Vs1211 (ex-MS2) == Askö (1951) = MHV81 (1964)	MS2	Holbaek (Korsør)	19 Apr 41	–	Retroceded DK 9 Jun 45; stricken 1971
Vs1212 (ex-MS5) = Enö (1951) = MHV82 (1965)	MS2	Holbaek (Korsør)	19 Apr 41	–	Retroceded DK 9 Jun 45; stricken 1971
Vs1213 (ex-MS6) = Faenö (1951) = DMH69 (1960) = MHV69 (1965) = MHV80 (1965)	MS2	Ring (Svendborg)	19 Apr 41	–	Retroceded DK 9 Jun 45; stricken 1968
MS8 = Lyö (1951) = MHV86 (1965)	MS2	Lilleö (Korsør)	19 Apr 41	–	Retroceded DK 9 Jun 45; stricken 1971
MS10 = Strynö (1951) = Kollund (1956) = Hecht I (1966) = Hecht II (1968) = Orion I (1970)	MS2	Ring (Svendborg)	19 Apr 41	–	Retroceded DK 9 Jun 45; stricken 30 Jun 56 and sold W J Bröndholm; sold Willi Freter (Heiligenhafen) 17 Oct 66; sold Germania Shipping (Laboe) 1970; collision Texaco Ohio 24 Feb 75
MZ1	MZ1	Stülcken (Hamburg)	16 Apr 44	UK	UK 1945.

Table 2.1/9. Fast Patrol Boats

Class	Disp.	Length	Beam	Machinery (diesel)	Power/speed	Gun(s)	TT
S6	80t	32.4m	4.9m	3 x MAN L7	3960bhp=36.6kt	1 x 40mm/37mm + 3–5 x 20mm	2 x 53.3cm
S14	97.5t	34.6m	5.1m	3 x MAN L11	6150bhp=37.5kt	1 x 40mm/37mm + 3–5 x 20mm	2 x 53.3cm
S18	97.5t	34.6m	5.1m	3 x Daimler Benz MB501	6000bhp=39.5kt	1 x 40mm/37mm + 3–5 x 20mm	2 x 53.3cm
S26	92.5t	34.6m	5.1m	3 x Daimler Benz MB501	6000bhp=33.8kt	1 x 40mm/37mm + 3–5 x 20mm	2 x 53.3cm
S30	81t	32.7m	4.9m	3 x Daimler Benz MB502	3960bhp=36.0kt	1 x 40mm/37mm + 3–5 x 20mm	2 x 53.3cm
S38	92.5t	34.9m	5.1m	3 x Daimler Benz MB501	6000bhp=39.0kt	1 x 40mm + 5 x 20mm	2 x 53.3cm
S38b	92.5t	34.9m	5.1m	3 x Daimler Benz MB501	6000bhp=38.6kt	1 x 40mm + 5 x 20mm	2 x 53.3cm
S100	100t	34.9m	5.1m	3 x Daimler Benz MB511	6000bhp=40.0kt	1 x 40mm + 5 x 20mm	2 x 53.3cm
S151	57t	28.3m	4.5m	3 x Daimler Benz MB500	2850bhp=32.3kt	1 x 40mm + 5 x 20mm	2 x 53.3cm
S219	107t	34.9m	5.1m	3 x Daimler Benz MB501	7500bhp=42.0kt	6 x 30mm	2 x 53.3cm

Name	Class	Builder	Launch	Comp/ comm	Surrendered	Alloc	Fate
S7	S6	Lürssen (Vegesack)	14 Aug 33	10 Oct 34	Bergen [UK]	Cat C	(damaged) Scuttled gunfire HMS Cotillion and ramming by tugs Kattegat (58° 08' 50" N, 10° 50' 50") 2 May 46
S8	S6	Lürssen (Vegesack)	22 Jan 34	6 Sep 34	Eckernförde	Cat C	(hulk) Scuttled off Kiel 17 May 1946
S9	S6	Lürssen (Vegesack)	24 Feb 34	12 Jun 35	Bergen [US]	Cat C	(damaged) Scuttled gunfire HMS Cotillion and ramming by tugs Kattegat (58° 09' 00" N, 10° 52' 05") 2 May 46
S10 (ex-V5507, ex-S10)	S6	Lürssen (Vegesack)	26 Aug 34	7 Mar 35	Bergen	US	OMGUS 18 Jan 46; sold Norway for cannibalisation Jul 47; BU 1950

Name	Class	Builder	Launch	Comp/ comm	Surrendered	Alloc	Fate
S11 (ex-*V5508*, ex-*S11*) = *TK-1002* (Jan 46) = *SK-530* (Dec 46)	S6	Lürssen (Vegesack)	24 Oct 34	3 Aug 35	Bergen	SU	To SU Jan 46; stricken Feb 48
S12 (ex-*V5504*, ex-*S12*)	S6	Lürssen (Vegesack)	18 Feb 35	31 Aug 35	Kristiansand	Cat C [US]	(damaged) Scuttled gunfire HMS *Cotillion* Kattegat (58° 09' 12" N, 10° 51' 25") 2 May 46
S13	S6	Lürssen (Vegesack)	29 Mar 35	7 Dec 35	Kristiansand	UK	BU
S15 (ex-*V5511*, ex-*S15*) = *T15* (1947)	S14	Lürssen (Vegesack)	15 Feb 36	27 Feb 37	Bergen	US	To OMGUS 1 Feb 46; DK 1947; cannibalised 1949; sold to Petersen & Albeck 1951; BU 1952
S16 (ex-*V5512*, ex-*S16*) = *TK-1003* (Feb 46)	S14	Lürssen (Vegesack)	7 Apr 37	22 Dec 37	Kristiansand	SU	To SU 13 Feb 46; stricken Sep 50
S19	S18	Lürssen (Vegesack)	13 Jan 38	14 Jul 38	Flensburg	UK	Expended as target 1950
S20	S18	Lürssen (Vegesack)	1 Oct 38	21 Mar 39	Flensburg	UK	Sold 1947/48
S21	S18	Lürssen (Vegesack)	1 Aug 38	19 Dec 39	Flensburg	US	To OMGUS 18 Jan 46; NO 1947; cannibalised 1947; BU 1950
S22	S18	Lürssen (Vegesack)	31 Jan 39	16 May 39	–	Cat C	(wreck Wilhelmshaven) BU
S24 = *TK-1004* (Jan 46)	S18	Lürssen (Vegesack)	4 Jul 39	18 Sep 39	Flensburg	SU	To SU 15 Jan 46; stricken Sep 50
S25	S18	Lürssen (Vegesack)	19 Sep 39	Dec 39	Flensburg	UK	Sold 1947/48
S30	S30	Lürssen (Vegesack)	10 Sep 39	23 Nov 39	Ancona	–	Scuttled off E coast of Malta 11 Aug 47
S36	S30	Lürssen (Vegesack)	20 Apr 40	14 Jun 40	Ancona	–	Scuttled off E coast of Malta Aug 47
S48	S38	Lürssen (Vegesack)	1941	20 Jun 41	Flensburg	US [UK]	To OMGUS Jan 46; to NO 1947; cannibalised 1947; BU 1954
S50 = *TK-1005* (Jan 46)	S38	Lürssen (Vegesack)	1941	25 Jul 41	Flensburg	SU	To SU 15 Jan 46; stricken Sep 50
S61	S30	Lürssen (Vegesack)	Dec 40	1 Feb 41	Ancona	–	Scuttled off E coast of Malta 11 Aug 47
S62	S38	Lürssen (Vegesack)	1941	19 Sep 41	Egersund	UK	Sold 1947/48
S64 = *Lyn* (1947) = *Stormfuglen* (1951)	S38	Lürssen (Vegesack)	1941	2 Nov 41	Flensburg	US	To OMGUS 18 Jan 46; to NO 1947; to DK 1951; stricken 1962; BU 1965
S65	S38	Lürssen (Vegesack)	1942	16 Jun 42	Flensburg	SU	To SU 15 Jan 46; stricken Sep 50
S67 = *TK-1006* (Jan 46) = *Torüs* (1946) = *MV621* (Feb 52) = *MS621* (1 Nov 52) = *MS485* (1 Jan 54) = *MC485* (10 Sep 54)	S38b	Lürssen (Vegesack)	1942	19 Mar 42	Flensburg	UK	Sold merc 1946; to IT 1 Feb 52; IT comm 10 Sep 53; stricken 1 Mar 66; BU
S68 = *T62* (1947) = *Viben* (1951)	S38b	Lürssen (Vegesack)	1942	1 Jul 42	Flensburg	US	To OMGUS 18 Jan 46; to DK 1947; stricken 1965; BU 1966
S69	S38b	Lürssen (Vegesack)	1941	21 Dec 41	Flensburg	UK	Sold 1947/48
S76	S38b	Lürssen (Vegesack)	1942	1 May 42	Flensburg	US	To OMGUS 18 Jan 46; to NO Jul 47; cannibalised 1947; BU Feb 50
S79	S38b	Lürssen (Vegesack)	1942	27 Jun 42	Egersund	US	To OMGUS 18 Jan 46; to DK Jul 47; stricken 1954; BU 1955
S81 = *T58* (Jul 47) = *Musvågen* (1951) = *TK-1001* (Jan 46)	S38b	Lürssen (Vegesack)	1942	28 Jul 42	Flensburg	SU	To SU 4 Jan 46; stricken Sep 50
S82 = *TK-1008* (Jan 46)	S38b	Lürssen (Vegesack)	1942	21 Aug 42	Flensburg	SU	To SU 15 Jan 46; stricken Sep 50
S83	S38b	Lürssen (Vegesack)	1942	7 Sep 42	Flensburg	UK	GM/SA Jul 45; fate uncertain
S85 = *Storm* (1947) = *Tranen* (1951)	S38b	Lürssen (Vegesack)	1942	7 Oct 42	Flensburg	US	To OMGUS 1 Feb 46; to NO Jul 47; to DK 1951; collision off Stavanger 27 Jun 63; salved and BU 1965/66
S86 = *TK-1009* (Jan 46)	S38b	Lürssen (Vegesack)	1942	15 Oct 42	Egersund	SU	To SU 4 Jan 46; stricken Sep 50
S89	S38b	Lürssen (Vegesack)	1942	28 Nov 42	Egersund	UK	Wrecked in tow Tremoutha Haven (50° 46.6' N 04° 38.3' W) Dec 46
S90	S38b	Lürssen (Vegesack)	1942	10 Dec 42	–	Cat C	(wrecked Stavanger 17 Feb 45) BU 1947
S92	S38b	Lürssen (Vegesack)	1942	14 Jan 43	Flensburg	UK	Sold 1947/48
S95	S38b	Lürssen (Vegesack)	1942	28 Feb 43	Flensburg	UK	Sold merc 1949; yacht 1967; fate uncertain
S97 = *T60* (1947) = *Raynen* (1951)	S38b	Lürssen (Vegesack)	1943	25 Mar 43	Flensburg	US	To OMGUS 18 Jan 46; to DK Jul 47; stricken 1962, sold Windway Marine Service (Cardiff) 1963; houseboat; BU 2004
S98 = *Kvikk* (1947)	S38b	Lürssen (Vegesack)	1943	10 Apr 43	Flensburg	US	To OMGUS 8 Mar 46; to NO Jul 47; stricken Feb 50 and BU
S99 = *TK-1010* (Jan 46)	S38b	Lürssen (Vegesack)	1943	17 Apr 43	Flensburg	SU	GM/SA Jul 45; to SU 4 Jan 46; stricken Sep 50

Name	Class	Builder	Launch	Comp/ comm	Surrendered	Alloc	Fate
S101 = TK-1011 (Jan 46)	S38b	Schichting (Travemünde)	25 Sep 40	30 Nov 40	Flensburg	SU	To SU 4 Jan 46; stricken Sep 50
S105	S38b	Schichting (Travemünde)	22 Mar 41	4 May 41	Flensburg	UK	Sold 1947/48
S107 = T52 (1947) = Gribben (1951)	S38b	Schichting (Travemünde)	3 May 41	6 Jul 41	Flensburg	US	To OMGUS 1 Feb 46; to DK Jul 47; stricken 1959; sold 1960 to BU
S108	S38b	Schichting (Travemünde)	28 Jun 41	14 Aug 41	–	Cat C	(wreck Wilhemshaven) Burnt by US Mar 46
S109 = TK-1012 (Jan 46)	S38b	Schichting (Travemünde)	14 Aug 41	14 Sep 41	Flensburg	SU	To SU 4 Jan 46; stricken Sep 50
S110 = TK-1013	S38b	Schichting (Travemünde)	13 Sep 41	19 Oct 41	Flensburg	SU	To SU 15 Jan 46; stricken Sep 49
S112	S38b	Schichting (Travemünde)	2 Dec 41	28 Jan 42	Lorient	–	Sold to BU 27 Jun 51
S113 = TK-1014 (Dec 45)	S38b	Schichting (Travemünde)	7 Feb 42	14 Mar 42	Flensburg	SU	To SU Dec 45; stricken Sep 49
S115	S38b	Schichting (Travemünde)	10 Apr 42	30 May 42	Flensburg	UK	Cannibalised 1946
S116 = US C-105179 (1945)	S38b	Schichting (Travemünde)	7 May 42	4 Jul 42	Cuxhaven	US	Shipped to US; for disposal 19 Mar 48; sold 23 Jul 48; to Bremerhaven for clandestine service; GEF training hulk 1952; damage control hulk 13 Jul 57; burnt out 25 May 65; remains burnt Apr 83.
S117 = Tross (1947) = Hejren (1951)	S38b	Schichting (Travemünde)	13 Jun 42	8 Aug 42	Flensburg	US	To OMGUS 18 Jan 46; to NO Jul 47; to DK 1951; stricken 1956; BU 1965
S118 = TK-1015 (Jan 46)	S38b	Schichting (Travemünde)	30 Jul 42	14 Sep 42	Flensburg	SU	To SU 14 Jan 46; stricken Sep 49
S120	S38b	Schichting (Travemünde)	13 Oct 42	5 Dec 42	Flensburg	UK	Sold 1947/48
S122 = T64 (1947)	S38b	Schichting (Travemünde)	30 Dec 42	21 Feb 43	Flensburg	US	To OMGUS 18 Jan 46; to DK Jul 47; cannibalised 1947; BU 1952
S123 = TK-1016 (Jan 46)	S38b	Schichting (Travemünde)	6 Feb 43	19 Mar 43	Flensburg	SU	To SU 4 Jan 46; stricken Sep 49
S127 = T56 (1947) = Isfuglen (1951)	S38b	Schichting (Travemünde)	5 Jun 43	10 Jul 43	Flensburg	US	To OMGUS 18 Jan 46; to DK Jul 47; stricken 1954; BU Oct 55
S130 = UK MTB5130 (1945) = FPB5130 (1947) = UW10 (7 May 57) = EF3 (15 Aug 63)	S38b	Schichting (Travemünde)	18 Sep 43	21 Oct 43	Rotterdam	UK	UK comm 1945; GEF 1957; sold as houseboat 13 Jan 91; sold British Military Powerboat Trust, Southampton 2003; at Millbrook, Cornwall 2015
S132 = TK-1017 (Jan 46)	S38b	Schichting (Travemünde)	13 Nov 43	10 Dec 43	Flensburg	SU	To SU 16 Jan 46; auxiliary Jun 52
S133 = T54 (1947) = Hærfuglen (1951)	S38b	Schichting (Travemünde)	28 Nov 43	31 Dec 43	Egersund	US	To OMGUS 18 Jan 46; to DK Jul 47; stricken 1954; BU Oct 55
S135 = TK-1018 (Jan 46)	S38b	Schichting (Travemünde)	1943	May 43	Flensburg	SU	To SU 4 Jan 46; Stricken Mar 52
S151 (ex-TM54)	S151	Werf Gusto (Schiedam)	1941	Dec 41	Ancona	–	Scuttled off E coast of Malta 11 Aug 47
S152 (ex-TM55)	S151	Werf Gusto (Schiedam)	1942	1942	Ancona	–	Scuttled off E coast of Malta 11 Aug 47
S155 (ex-TM58)	S151	Werf Gusto (Schiedam)	1942	1942	Ancona	–	Scuttled off E coast of Malta 11 Aug 47
S156 (ex-TM59)	S151	Werf Gusto (Schiedam)	1942	1942	Ancona	–	Scuttled off E coast of Malta 11 Aug 47
S168	S100	Lürssen (Vegesack)	1943	23 Dec 43	Rotterdam	UK	Sold 1947/48
S170 = TK-1007 (Jan 46)	S100	Lürssen (Vegesack)	1943	11 Feb 44		SU	To SU Jan 46; stricken Sep 50
S174 = NO Rapp (1947)	S100	Lürssen (Vegesack)	1943	3 Mar 44	Brunsbüttel	US	To OMGUS 7 Feb 46; to NO Jul 47; BU Feb 50
S175 = TK-1019 (Jan 46)	S100	Lürssen (Vegesack)	1944	11 Mar 44	Rotterdam	SU	To SU 15 Jan 46; stricken Mar 52
S195 = E3 (1947) = Kiekk (1948) = Lommen (1951)	S100	Lürssen (Vegesack)	1944	28 Jun 44	Egersund	US [UK]	To OMGUS 18 Jan 46; to NO Jul 47; to DK 1951; stricken 4 Sep 61; sold Minerva 22 Nov 61; sold Anglo Diesel Co; sold Baron von Waynaghy 1965; laid up; sold E Möller 15 Dec 72 and BU
S196	S100	Lürssen (Vegesack)	1944	3 Jul 44	Flensburg	UK	Cannibalised 1946; BU 1962
S197 = T59 (1947) = Rågen (1951)	S100	Lürssen (Vegesack)	1944	10 Jul 44	Den Helder	US	To OMGUS 7 Feb 46; to DK Jul 47; collision UK MTB5518 North Sea 26 Feb 51; salved; stricken 1957; sold Sundfarten for service as breakwater at Humlebæk/ Øresund; foundered 1959.

Name	Class	Builder	Launch	Comp/ comm	Surrendered	Alloc	Fate
S201 (ii)	S100	Lürssen (Vegesack)	1944	28 Jul 44	–	Cat C	(sunk Kiel 3 May 45) Blown up 20 May 46
S204 = TK-1020 (Feb 46)	S100	Lürssen (Vegesack)	1944	19 Aug 44	Rotterdam	SU	To SU Jan 46; auxiliary Jun 52
S205	S100	Lürssen (Vegesack)	1944	28 Aug 44	Rotterdam	UK	BU
S206 = T55 (1947) = Høgen (1951)	S100	Lürssen (Vegesack)	1944	31 Aug 44	Rotterdam	US	To OMGUS 18 Jan 46; to DK Jul 47; collision Great Belt 11 Sep 57; salved and BU
S207 = T61 (1948) = Skaden (1951)	S100	Lürssen (Vegesack)	1944	19 Sep 44	Rotterdam	US	To OMGUS 18 Jan 46; to DK 30 Jul 48; BU 1960
S208 = FPB5208 (1947) = UW11 (12 Mar 57)	S100	Lürssen (Vegesack)	1944	28 Sep 44	Flensburg	UK	UK comm 1947; GEF 1957; stricken 1964; target; BU 1967
S209 = TK-1021 (Dec 45)	S100	Lürssen (Vegesack)	1944	21 Oct 44	List	SU	To SU Jan 46; stricken 1957
S210 = Snaar (1947)	S100	Lürssen (Vegesack)	1944	27 Sep 44		US	To OMGUS 18 May 46; stranded Østøya 1946; to NO 18 Jul 47; stricken Feb 50
S211 = TK-1022 (Jan 46)	S100	Lürssen (Vegesack)	1944	1 Oct 44	Rotterdam	SU	To SU 15 Jan 46; auxiliary Jun 52
S212 = MTB 5212 (1945) = FPB 5212 (1947)	S100	Lürssen (Vegesack)	1944	11 Oct 44	Rotterdam	UK	UK comm 1945; paid off 1956; BU 1957
S213	S100	Lürssen (Vegesack)	1944	4 Jan 45	Den Helder	Cat C	(wreck Portsmouth) BU Jul 45
S214 = TK-1023 (Jan 46)	S100	Lürssen (Vegesack)	1944	8 Dec 44	Rotterdam	SU	To SU 4 Jan 46; auxiliary Jun 52
S215	S100	Lürssen (Vegesack)	1944	1 Dec 44	Flensburg	UK	Sold 1947/48
S216 = T53 (1947) = Havørnen (1951)	S100	Lürssen (Vegesack)	1944	27 Dec 44	Flensburg	US	To OMGUS 18 Jan 46; to DK Jul 47; stranded off Great Yarmouth Dec 53; salved; sold Sundfarten 1957; BU 1958
S217	S100	Lürssen (Vegesack)	1944	30 Jan 45	Flensburg	UK	Sold 1947/48
S218 = C-105180 (1945)	S100	Lürssen (Vegesack)	1944	18 Jan 45	Flensburg	US	To US 5 Nov 45; for disposal Jan 48; sold Rod Pickard (Miami); handed over 12 Jun 48.
S219 = TK-1024 (Jan 46)	S219	Schichting (Travemünde)	11 Jul 44	9 Aug 44	Rotterdam	SU	To SU 15 Jan 46; stricken 1957
S221	S219	Schichting (Travemünde)	16 Aug 44	10 Sep 44	Den Helder	UK	Sold 1947/48
S222 = TK-1025 (Jan 46)	S219	Schichting (Travemünde)	31 Aug 44	23 Sep 44	Rotterdam	SU	To SU 4 Jan 46; auxiliary Jun 52
S225 = C-105181 (1945)	S219	Schichting (Travemünde)	1944	1 Dec 44	Flensburg	US	To US 5 Nov 45; for disposal 12 Apr 48; sold 1 Sep 48
S227 = TK-1026 (Jan 46)	S219	Schichting (Travemünde)	1944	Dec 44 (?)	Flensburg	SU	To SU 4 Jan 46; stricken Sep 49
S228	S219	Schichting (Travemünde)	1944	19 Apr 45	Flensburg	UK	Cannibalised 1946; BU
S302 = E1 (1947) = Blink (1947) = Falken (1951)	S219	Lürssen (Vegesack)	1944	12 Feb 45	Egersund	US	To OMGUS 7 Feb 46; to NO Jul 47; to DK 1951; stricken 1961; sold 1965; laid up Kiel; BU 1972
S303 = E2 (1947) = Brand (1951) = Tårnfalken (1951)	S219	Lürssen (Vegesack)	1944	24 Feb 45	Egersund	US [UK]	To OMGUS 7 Feb 46; to NO Jul 47; to DK 1951; stricken 1957; sold Sundfarten 1958; BU
S304	S219	Lürssen (Vegesack)	1944	9 Mar 45	Rotterdam	Cat C [UK]	Cannibalised 1945; BU
S305 = T57 (1947) = Jagtfalken (1951)	S219	Lürssen (Vegesack)	1944	29 Mar 45	Flensburg	US	To OMGUS 22 Feb 46; to DK Jul 47; stricken 1962; sold Ing. Büro Minerva 1962; hulk at Hundested 1968
S306 = T51 (1947) = Glenten (1951)	S219	Lürssen (Vegesack)	1945	[Feb 46]	Flensburg	US	To OMGUS 18 Jan 46; to DK 31 Jul 47; stricken 1961; BU
S307	S219	Lürssen (Vegesack)	1945	–	Vegesack	UK	BU
S630 (ex-MS 75)	IT MS, II ser	Cantieri Riuniti dell'Adriatico (Monfalcone)	18 May 43	IT: 30 Jun 43 GE: 10 Dec 44	Venice	–	Retroceded IT (see Table 2.2/9)
S701 = Mijn Vrijbuiter (1951)	S219	Danziger Waggonfabrik (Danzig)	1944 3	Jul 44	Wilhelms- haven	US	To OMGUS Jan 46; sold H Plantega (Amsterdam) 1951; final fate uncertain
S704 = TK-1027 (Jan 46)	S219	Danziger Waggonfabrik (Danzig)	1944	2 Oct 44	Rotterdam	SU	To SU 15 Jan 46; stricken Nov 49
S705	S219	Danziger Waggonfabrik (Danzig)	1944	22 Oct 44	Rotterdam	UK	To UK 4 Jan 46; sold 1947/48

Name	Class	Builder	Launch	Comp/comm	Surrendered	Alloc	Fate
S706	S219	Danziger Waggonfabrik (Danzig)	1944	31 Oct 44	Rotterdam	US	To US 30 Jan 46; for disposal Washington DC Feb 47
S707 = TK-1028 (Jan 46)	S219	Danziger Waggonfabrik (Danzig)	1944	4 Dec 44	Flensburg	SU	To SU 15 Jan 46; stricken Sep 49
S708 = TK-1029 (Mar 46)	S219	Danziger Waggonfabrik (Danzig)	1944	19 Feb 45	Flensburg	SU	To SU 15 Jan 46; stricken Jun 52
S709 = TK-1030 (Mar 46)	S219	Danziger Waggonfabrik (Danzig)	1944	Mar 45	Egersund	SU	To SU 29 Mar 46; stricken Sep 49

Table 2.1/10. Major Auxiliary Ships

FPB Depot Ships

Class	Disp.	Length	Beam	Machinery	Power/speed	Main gun(s)
Tsingtau	1980t	87.5m	13.5m	2 x diesel	4100bhp=17.5kt	2 x 8.8cm/45
Tanga	2190t	96.2m	13.5m	2 x diesel	4100bhp=17.5kt	2 x 10.5cm/45
Adolf Lüderitz	2900t	114.0m	14.5m	2 x diesel	12,000bhp=23.0kt	4 x 10.5cm/45
Gustav Nachtigal	3100t	114.0m	14.7m	1 x diesel	3800bhp=17.0kt	3 x 10.5cm/45

Submarine Depot Ships

Class	Disp.	Length	Beam	Machinery	Power/speed	Main gun(s)
Saar	2710t	100.5m	13.5m	2 x diesel	4800bhp=18.3kt	3 x 10.5cm/45
Wilhelm Bauer	4700t	132.7m	16.0m	2 x diesel	12,400bhp=20.0kt	4 x 10.5cm/45
Otto Wünsche	5000t	139.4m	16.0m	2 x diesel	13,800bhp=21.5kt	2 x 10.5cm/45

Replenishment Ship

Class	Disp.	Length	Beam	Machinery	Power/speed	Main gun(s)
Dithmarschen	8053t	178.0m	22.0m	2 x boilers, 2 x Tu	21,500shp=21.0kt	3 x 15cm

Experimental Vessel

Class	Disp.	Length	Beam	Machinery	Power/speed	Main gun(s)
Walter Holtzapfel	1460t	79.3m	11.6m	2 x diesel	7200bhp=19.5kt	4 x 37mm

Sail Training Vessels

Class	Disp.	Length	Beam	Machinery	Power/speed
Gorch Fock	1354t	74.0m	12.0m	1 x diesel	520bhp=8.0kt
Horst Wessel	1634t	89.0m	12.0m	1 x diesel	750bhp=10.0kt

Name	Class	Builder	Launch	Comp/comm	Alloc	Fate
Adolf Lüderitz = Payserd (1946)	Adolf Lüderitz	Neptun (Rostock)	20 Feb 39	11 Jun 40	SU	To SU 1946; paid off 1964
Albert Leo Schlageter = Guanabara (1948) = Sagres (1961)	Horst Wessel	Blohm & Voss (Hamburg)	30 Oct 37	12 Feb 38	US	To BR 1948; to PT 1961; still in service (2020)
Carl Peters	Adolf Lüderitz	Neptun (Rostock)	13 Apr 39	6 Jan 40	–	Mined Geltinger Bight (54° 47' N, 09° 49' E) 14 May 45; salved 1950; BU Kiel-Wik
Dithmarschen = Southmark (1945) = Conecuh (1 Oct 46)	Dithmarschen	Schichau (Danzig)	12 Jun 37	20 Jul 39	US	To US 15 Jan 46; US comm 2 May 46; decommissioned 3 Apr 56; stricken 1 Jun 60; sold Southeastern Rail & Steel Co ($136,688) 1 Nov 60; BU
Gorch Fock = Tovarishch (1951) = Gorch Fock (29 Nov 2003)	Gorch Fock	Blohm & Voss (Hamburg)	3 May 33	27 Jun 33	–	Scuttled off Rügen 1 May 45; salved 1948; SU comm 1951; UA 1991; GE museum, Stralsund 2003
Hermann von Wissmann (ex-Lewant III) = Royal Harold (1945) = Kamina (Oct 50)	Gustav Nachtigal	Cockerill (Antwerp)	26 Dec 40	16 Dec 43	UK	To UK Aug 45; BE Oct 50; BE comm 8 Dec 50; troop ship; support/training ship 1961; stricken Sep 67; arrived Bruges 26 Sep 68 to BU by Brugse Scheepssloperij
Horst Wessel = Eagle (May 46)	Horst Wessel	Blohm & Voss (Hamburg)	13 Jun 36	17 Sep 36	US	US comm 15 May 46; still in service (2020)
IV [to be Herbert Norkus(?)]	Horst Wessel	Blohm & Voss (Hamburg)	7 Nov 39	–	–	Scuttled Skagerrak 1947
Nordmark = Northmark (1945) = Bulawayo (Jul 47)	Dithmarschen	Schichau (Danzig)	5 Oct 37	16 Jan 39	UK	To UK Jun 45; UK comm 1947; reserve Oct 50; to Arnott Young (Dalmuir) to BU 4 Oct 55
Otto Wünsche = Pecora (Jun 46) = PKZ-14 (Sep 73)	Otto Wünsche	Hawaldt/Kiel DYd	23 May 40	8 Nov 43	SU	To SU 3 Jun 46; accommodation ship 17 Sep 73; stricken 13 Apr 77; BU
Saar = Gustave Zeédé (Oct 47) = Q481 (Jun 71)	Saar	Germania (Kiel)	5 Apr 34	1 Oct 34	US	To US 1 Sep 47; to FR Oct 47; FR comm 17 Jan 48; condemned 29 Jun 71; target 1972; torpedoed Doris S of Marseilles (42° 30' N, 5° 24' E) 26 Feb 76.

Name	Class	Builder	Launch	Comp/ comm	Alloc	Fate
Tanga = Ægir (1948)	Tanga	Neptun	4 Dec 37	21 Jan 39	US	GM/SA Jul 45; to US 3 Dec 47; to DK 29 Jun 48; DK comm 12 Dec 51; training ship 1964; stricken 10 Jan 67; BU Paul Berdsø & Søn (Masendø) 1967
Tsingtau	Tsingtau	Blohm & Voss (Hamburg)	6 Jun 34	24 Sep 34	UK	GM/SA Jul 45; BU Tyne 1950
Waldemar Kophamel = Kuban (1950) = PKZ-12 (Sep 73)	Wilhelm Bauer	Hawaldt/Kiel DYd	15 May 39	21 Oct 40	Cat C	(sunk Gdynia 18 Dec 44) Salved Gdynia 1950; SU list 30 Jul 51; SU comm Oct 55; accommodation ship 10 Sep 73; stricken 9 Feb 78; BU
Walter Holtzapfel = Deepwater (Mar 46)	Walter Holtzapfel	Norderwerft (Hamburg)	1939	7 Aug 40	UK	UK comm Mar 46; sold Northam 13 Sep 60 to BU

2. The Italian Navy: 9 September 1943

Table 2.2/1. Capital Ships

Class	Disp.	Length	Beam	Machinery	Power/speed	Main guns	Aircraft
Guilio Cesare	26,400t	186.4m	28.6m	8 x boilers, 2 x Tu	75,000shp=27.0kt	10 x 320mm/44	–
Caio Duilio	23,887t	186.9m	28.6m	8 x boilers, 2 x Tu	75,000shp=26.0kt	10 x 320mm/44	–
Littorio	41,000t	237.8/240.7m	32.8m	8 x boilers, 4 x Tu	128,200shp=30.0kt	9 x 381mm/50	3

Name	Class	Builder	Launch	Comp/comm	Malta arr & dep	Captured Germany	Alloc	Handed over	Fate
Andrea Doria	Caio Duilio	La Spezia DYd	30 Mar 13	13 Mar 16	10 Sep 43 8 Jun 44	–	–	–	Stricken 1 Nov 56; sold 1957; BU La Spezia 1961
Caio Duilio	Caio Duilio	Castellammare di Stabia DYd	24 Apr 13	10 May 15	10 Sep 43 27 Jul 44	–	–	–	Stricken 15 Sep 56; BU La Spezia 1958
Conte di Cavour	Guilio Cesare	La Sepzia DYd	10 Aug 11	1 Apr 15	–	10 Sep 43 Trieste	–	–	Bombed US aircraft Trieste 17 Feb 45; foundered 23 Feb 45; salved 1951; BU
Guilio Cesare = Z11 (1949) = Novorossiysk (5 Mar 49)	Guilio Cesare	Ansaldo (Genoa)	15 Oct 11	14 May 14	13 Sep 43 17 Jun 44	–	SU	Valona 6 Feb 49	Stricken 15 Dec 1948; to SU 6 Feb 49 at Valona; added to list 24 Feb 49; mined Sevastopol 30 Oct 55; salved 4 May 57; BU
Impero = C320 (Mar 47)	Littorio	Ansaldo (Genoa)	15 Nov 39	–	–	10 Sep 43 Trieste	–	–	Stricken 27 Mar 47; salved 2 Sep 47; stranded Venice 15 Sep 47; BU 1948–50.
Italia (ex-Littorio)	Littorio	Ansaldo (Genoa)	22 Aug 37	6 May 40	11 Sep 43 14 Sep 43	–	US	–	Stricken 1 Jun 48; sold 7 Dec 51; BU La Spezia
Roma	Littorio	Cantieri Riuniti dell'Adriatico (Trieste)	4 Jun 40	14 Jun 42	–	–	–	–	Bombed GE aircraft NW of Sardinia 9 Sep 43
Vittorio Veneto	Littorio	Cantieri Riuniti dell'Adriatico (Trieste)	22 Jul 37	28 Apr 40	11 Sep 43 14 Sep 43	–	UK	–	Stricken 3 Jan 48; sold 23 Jun 51; BU La Spezia

Table 2.2/2. Aircraft Carriers

Ship	Disp.	Length	Beam	Machinery	Power/speed	Main guns	Aircraft
Aquila	23,350t	216.2m	25.3m	8 x boilers, 4 x Tu	140,000shp=30.0kt	8 x 135mm/35	36
Giuseppe Miraglia	4880t	121.2m	15.0m	8 x boilers, 2 x Tu	12,000shp=21.0kt	4 x 102mm/35	20
Sparviero	23.000t	202.4m	30.0m	4 x diesel	28,000bhp=18.0kt	6 x 152mm/45	25

Name	Conversion	Launch	Began conversion	Comp/ comm	Malta arr & dep	Captured Germany	Alloc	Fate
Aquila (ex-Roma) =P227 (1946)	Ansaldo (Genoa)	26 Feb 26	Jul 41	–	–	9 Sep 43 Genoa	–	BU La Spezia 1951–52
Giuseppe Miraglia	La Spezia DYd	20 Dec 23	24 Jan 25	1927	13 Sep 43 21 Oct 43	–	–	Stricken 1950
Sparviero (ex-Falco, ex-Augustus)	Ansaldo (Genoa)	13 Dec 26	Nov 42	–	–	9 Sep 43 Genoa	–	Scuttled Genoa 5 Oct 44; BU 1946

Table 2.2/3. Cruisers

Class	Disp.	Length	Beam	Machinery	Power/speed	Main guns	TT	Mines	Aircraft
Bolzano	11,065t	197.0m	20.6m	10 x boilers, 4 x Tu	150,000shp=36.0kt	8 x 203mm/53	8 x 533mm	–	3
Capitani Romani	3747t	142.2m	14.4m	4 x boilers, 2 x Tu	110,000shp=41.0kt	8 x 135mm/45	8 x 533mm	130	–
Duca d'Aosta	7283t	186.9m	17.5m	6 x boilers, 2 x Tu	110,000shp=36.5kt	8 x 152mm/43	6 x 533mm	100	2
Etna	6000t	153.8m	14.5m	3 x boilers, 2 x Tu	40,000shp=28.0kt	6 x 135mm/45	–	–	–

Class	Disp.	Length	Beam	Machinery	Power/speed	Main guns	TT	Mines	Aircraft
Garibaldi	7874t	187.1m	18.9m	8 x boilers, 2 x Tu	100,000shp=35.0kt	10 x 152mm/43	8 x 533mm	100	2
FR *La Galissonière*	7720t	179.5m	17.5m	4 x boilers, 2 x Tu	97,000shp=32.0kt	9 x 152mm/55	4 x 550mm	–	3
Luigi Cadorna	5316t	169.2m	15.5m	6 x boilers, 2 x Tu	95,000shp=37.0kt	8 x 152mm/43	4 x 533mm	100	2
Montecuccoli	7550t	182.2m	16.5m	6 x boilers, 2 x Tu	106,000shp=37.0kt	8 x 152mm/43	4 x 533mm	100	2
Zara	11,900t	182.8m	20.6m	8 x boilers, 2 x Tu	95,000shp=36.0kt	8 x 203mm/53	8 x 533mm	–	2

Name	Class	Builder	Launch	Comp/ comm	Malta arr & dep	Captured Germany	Alloc	Handed over	Fate
Attilio Regolo = *R4* (Jul 48) = *Châteaurenault* (23 Jul 48) = *Q450* (Jun 69)	Capitani Romani	Odero Terni Orlando (Leghorn)	28 Aug 40	15 May 42	[Interned Port Mahon 10 Sep 43– 21 Jan 45]	–	FR	Toulon 1 Aug 48	Stricken 26 Jul 48; to FR; comm 7 Sep 48; fleet escort 1 May 55; flotilla leader Jul 57; paid off 1962; training ship for marines; condemned 2 Jun 69; BU La Spezia 1969
Bari (ex-*O*, ex-*Pillau*, ex-*Muravev Amurskiy*)	GE *Pillau* (see Table 1.1/3)	Schichau (Danzig)	11 Apr 14	GE: 14 Dec 14 IT: 23 Jan 24	–	Leghorn 9 Sep 43	–	–	Bombed Leghorn 28 Sep 43; BU 1944–48
Bolzano	*Bolzano*	Ansaldo (Genoa)	31 Aug 32	19 Aug 33	–	La Spezia 9 Sep 43	–	–	Sunk human torpedo La Spezia 22 Jun 44; stricken 27 Feb 47; salved Sep 49; BU
Caio Mario	Capitani Romani	Odero Terni Orlando (Leghorn)	17 Aug 41	–	–	La Spezia 9 Sep 43	–	–	Burnt out La Spezia; BU after 1945
Cattaro (ex-*Dalmacija*, ex-*Niobe*) = *Niobe* (Sep 43)	GE *Gazelle* (see Table 1.1/2)	AG Weser (Bremen)	18 Jul 99	GE: 25 Jan 00 YU: 1925 IT: 17 Apr 41	–	Pola 11 Sep 43	–	–	GE comm 8 Nov 43; stranded Silba 19 Dec 43; torpedoed UK *MTB276* and *MTB298* 22 Dec 43; BU 1947–49
Cornelio Silla	Capitani Romani	Ansaldo (Genoa)	28 Jun 41	–	–	Genoa 9 Sep 43	–	–	Bombed Genoa Jul 44; salved; scuttled as blockship; salved 1945; BU 1954
Emanuele Filiberto Duca d'Aosta = *Z15* (Feb 49) = *Stalingrad* (26 Feb 49) = *Kerch* (Mar 49) = *OS-32* (May 58)	*Duca d'Aosta*	Odero Terni Orlando (Leghorn)	22 Apr 34	13 Jul 35	11 Sep 43 14 Sep 43	–	SU	Odessa 2 Mar 49	Stricken 12 Feb 49; to SU; comm 30 Mar 49; training ship 17 Feb 56; experimental vessel 11 May 58; stricken 20 Feb 59; BU 1961.
Etna (ex-*Taksin*)	*Etna*	Cantieri Riuniti dell'Adriatico (Trieste)	28 May 42	–	–	Trieste 10 Sep 43	–	–	RSI Sep 44; scuttled Trieste 1 May 45; BU 1950s
Etna (ex-*Taksin*)	*Etna*	Cantieri Riuniti dell'Adriatico (Trieste)	28 May 42	–	–	Trieste 10 Sep 43	–	–	RSI Sep 44; scuttled Trieste 1 May 45; BU 1950s
Eugenio di Savoia = *G2* (Jun 51) = *Helli* (Jul 51)	*Duca d'Aosta*	Ansaldo (Genoa)	16 Mar 35	16 Jan 36	11 Sep 43 14 Sep 43	–	GR	Piraeus 1 Jul 51	Stricken 26 Jun 51; to GR; stricken 1964; sold 1973; BU Perama 1973–74
FR11 (ex-*Jean de Vienne*)	FR *La Galissonière*	Lorient DYd	31 Jul 35	FR: 1 Sep 36	–	Toulon 9 Sep 43	–	–	Bombed Toulon 24 Nov 43, 4 Feb 44, 11 Mar 44; to FRV 12 May 44; salved 1948; BU
FR12 (ex-*La Galissonière*)	FR *La Galissonière*	Lorient DYd	18 Nov 33	FR: 1 Feb 36	–	Toulon 9 Sep 43	–	–	To FRV 12 May 44; bombed Toulon 18 Aug 44; BU in situ 1955–56.
Giuseppe Garibaldi	*Garibaldi*	Cantieri Riuniti dell'Adriatico (Trieste)	21 Apr 36	20 Dec 37	11 Sep 43 4 Oct 43	–	–	–	Stricken 20 Feb 71; BU La Spezia 1978–79
Gorizia	*Zara*	Odero Terni Orlando (Leghorn)	28 Dec 30	23 Dec 31	–	La Spezia 9 Sep 43	–	–	Stricken 27 Feb 47; BU
Guilio Germanico = *PV2* (1950) = *San Marco* (Mar 51)	Capitani Romani	Navalmeccanica) (Castellammare di Stabia	26 Jul 41	19 Jan 56	–	Castellammare di Stabia 13 Sep 43	– –		Scuttled Castellammare di di Stabia 45; hulked; reinstated Stabia 28 Sep 43; salved Sep Mar 51; stricken 1 Feb 72; BU
Luigi Cadorna	*Luigi Cadorna*	Cantieri Riuniti dell'Adriatico (Trieste)	30 Sep 31	11 Aug 33	10 Sep 43 14 Sep 43	–	–	–	Stricken 1 May 51; BU
Luigi di Savoia Duca Degli Abruzzi	*Garibaldi*	Odero Terni Orlando (Muggiano)	21 Apr 36	1 Dec 37	11 Sep 43 4 Oct 43	–	–	–	Stricken 1 Apr 61; BU 1965
Ottaviano Augusto	Capitani Romani	Cantieri Navali Riuniti (Ancona)	31 May 42	–	–	Ancona 14 Sep 43	–	–	Bombed Ancona 1 Nov 43; BU

Name	Class	Builder	Launch	Comp/ comm	Malta arr & dep	Captured Germany	Alloc	Handed over	Fate
Pompeo Magno = E168 (1949) = PV1 (May 50) = San Giorgio (Mar 51)	Capitani Romani	Cantieri Navali Riuniti (Ancona)	24 Aug 41	24 Jun 43	10 Sep 43 4 Oct 43	–	FR	–	Paid off 1949; stricken 1 May 50; reinstated Mar 51; stricken 1 Jul 82; BU 1987
Raimondo Montecuccoli	Monte-cuccoli	Ansaldo (Genoa)	2 Aug 34	30 Jun 35	11 Sep 43 14 Sep 43	–	–	–	Stricken 1 Jun 64; BU La Spezia 1972
Scipione Africano = S7 (Aug 48) = Guichen (23 Jul 48) = Q554 (Jun 76)	Capitani Romani	Odero Terni Orlando (Leghorn)	12 Jan 41	23 Apr 43	–	–	FR	Toulon 16 Aug 48	Stricken 9 Aug 48; to FR; comm 7 Sep 48; fleet escort 1 Jul 54; flotilla leader Nov 58; paid off 1 Apr 61; hulked 21 Jun 63; condemned 1 Jun 76; sold to BU 1982
Taranto (ex-O, ex-Straßburg)	GE Magdeburg (Table 1.1/2).	Wilhelms-haven DYd	24 Aug 11	GE: 9 Oct 12 IT: 2 Jun 25	–	–	–	–	Scuttled La Spezia 9 Sep 43; salved; bombed 23 Oct 43; salved 13 Apr 44; bombed 23 Sep 44; BU from 1945.

Table 2.2/4. Destroyers

Class	Disp.	Length	Beam	Machinery	Power/speed	Main guns	TT	Mines
Beograd	1210t	98.0m	9.5m	3 x boilers, 2 x Tu	44,000shp=38.0kt	4 x 120mm/50	6 x 533mm	30
FR Bourrasque	1319t	105.8m	9.6m	3 x boilers, 2 x Tu	31,000shp=33.0kt	4 x 130mm/40	3 x 533mm	–
Dardo	1220t	96.0m	9.8m	3 x boilers, 2 x Tu	44,000shp=38.0kt	4 x 120mm/50	6 x 533mm	54
YU Dubrovnik	1880t	113.2m	10.7m	3 x boilers, 2 x Tu	42,000shp=37.0kt	4 x 135mm/45	6 x 533mm	...
FR Guepard	2450t	130.2m	11.8m	4 x boilers, 2 x Tu	64,000shp=35.5kt	5 x 138mm/40	3 x 550mm	–
FR Jaguar	2126t	126.8m	11.3m	5 x boilers, 2 x Tu	55,000shp=35.5kt	5 x 130mm/40	3 x 550mm	–
FR Le Hardi	1772t	117.2m	11.1m	4 x boilers, 2 x Tu	56,000shp=37.0kt	6 x 130mm/45	7 x 550mm	–
Maestrale	1640t	106.7m	10.2m	3 x boilers, 2 x Tu	44,000shp=38.0kt	4 x 120mm/50	6 x 533mm	56
Mirabello	1,811t	103.8m	9.7m	4 x boilers, 2 x Tu	35,000shp=35.0kt	4 x 102mm/45	4 x 450mm	100
Navagatori	1908t	107.2m	10.2m	4 x boilers, 2 x Tu	55,000shp=38.0kt	6 x 120mm/50	4 x 533mm	100
Navagatori (mod)	2125t	110.0m	11.2m	4 x boilers, 2 x Tu	55,000shp=28.0kt	6 x 120mm/50	4 x 533mm	50
Oriani	1685t	106.8m	10.2m	3 x boilers, 2 x Tu	48,000shp=39.0kt	4 x 120mm/50	6 x 533mm	56
Sella	970t	84.9m	8.6m	3 boilers, 2 x Tu	35,000shp=35.0kt	4 x 120mm/45	4 x 533mm	40
Soldati, series 1	1830t	106.8m	10.2m	3 x boilers, 2 x Tu	48,000shp=39.0kt	4/5 x 120mm/50	6 x 533mm	48
Soldati, series 2	1850t	106.8m	10.2m	3 x boilers, 2 x Tu	50,000shp=39.0kt	4/5 x 120mm/50	6 x 533mm	48
YU Split	2040t	121.0m	12.0m	2 x boilers, 2 x Tu	55,000shp=38.0kt	5 x 135mm/45	3 x 533mm	40
Turbine	1090t	93.2m	9.2m	3 boilers, 2 x Tu	40,000shp=36.0kt	4 x 120mm/45	6 x 533mm	52

Name	Class	Builder	Launch	Comp/ comm	Malta arr & dep	Captured Germany	Alloc	Handed over	Fate
Alfredo Oriani = O3 (Jul 47) = D'Estaing (23 Jul 48) = Q15 (Jun 54)	Oriani	Odero Terni Orlando (Leghorn)	30 Jul 36	15 Jul 37	11 Sep 43 14 Sep 43	–	FR	Toulon 23 Jul 48	Stricken 16 Jul 48; to FR; commissioned 6 Aug 48; condemned 12 Jun 54; sold to BU 28 Feb 56
Antonio da Nola	Navagatori (mod)	Canteri del Tirreno (Riva Trigoso)	21 May 29	29 Dec 29	–	–	–	–	Mined Strait of Bonifacio 9 Sep 43
Antonio Pigafetta = TA44 (Sep 43)	Navagatori	Cantieri Navale del Quarnaro (Fiume)	10 Nov 29	1 May 31	–	Fiume 10 Sep 43	–	–	GE comm 14 Oct 44; bombed UK aircraft Trieste 17 Feb 45; salved 1947; BU
Artigliere (ex-Camicia Nera) = Z12 (Dec 48) = Neulovimyi (Feb 49) = Bezposhchadnyi (Feb 49) = Lovkyi (ii) (24 Feb 49) = TsL-58 (Dec 54) = KVN-11 (17 Oct 55)	Soldati, Ser 1	Odero Terni Orlando (Leghorn)	8 Aug 37	30 Jun 38	11 Sep 43 14 Sep 43	–	SU	Odessa 23 Jan 49	Stricken 14 Dec 48; to SU; comm 24 Feb 49; target ship 30 Dec 54; stricken 27 Mar 60; BU
Augusto Riboty = F3 (1950)	Mirabello	Ansaldo (Genoa)	24 Sep 16	5 May 17	13 Sep 43 6 Oct 43	–	SU	–	Stricken 1 May 50; hulked Taranto; BU

Name	Class	Builder	Launch	Comp/ comm	Malta arr & dep	Captured Germany	Alloc	Handed over	Fate
Carabiniere	Soldati, Ser 1	Canteri del Tirreno (Riva Trigoso)	23 Jul 38	20 Dec 38	[Interned Port Mahon Sep 43– 21 Jan 45]	–	–	–	Stricken 18 Jan 65; sold BU Oltona Mar 78; foundered off La Spezia; salved; BU La Spezia 10 1978.
Corazziere	Soldati, Ser 1	Odero Terni Orlando (Leghorn)	22 May 38	4 Mar 39	–	–	–	–	Scuttled Genoa 9 Sep 43; salved and partly dismantled; scuttled Genoa Apr 45; salved 1953; BU
Corsaro (ex-Squadrista) = TA33 (Sep 43)	Soldati, Ser 2	Odero Terni Orlando (Leghorn)	12 Sep 42	–	–	Leghorn 9 Sep 43	–	–	To GE; bombed US aircraft Genoa 4 Sep 44; salved and BU after 1945
Dardo = TA31 (Sep 43)	Dardo	Odero Terni Orlando (Sestri -Ponente)	6 Sep 30	25 Jan 32	–	Genoa 9 Sep 43	–	–	GE comm 17 Jun 44; scuttled Genoa 24 Apr 45; salved 1946; BU
FR21 (ex-Lion)	FR Guepard	Ateliers et Chantiers de France (Dunkirk)	5 Aug 29	FR: Jan 31 IT: 19 Jan 43	–	–	–	–	Scuttled La Spezia 9 Sep 43; salved 1947; BU
FR22 (ex-Panthère)	FR Jaguar	Lorient DYd IT: 1 Feb 43	27 Oct 24	FR: Nov 26	–	–	–	–	Scuttled La Spezia 9 Sep 43; salved; scuttled 1944; salved 1950; BU
FR23 (ex-Tigre)	FR Jaguar	Chantiers de Bretagne (Nantes)	2 Aug 24	FR: Dec 25 IT: 1 Feb 43	–	–	–	–	Retroceded FR Bizerte 28 Oct 43; stricken 4 Jan 54
FR24 (ex-Valmy)	FR Guepard	Penhoët (St Nazaire)	19 May 28	FR: Jan 30 IT: –	–	Savona 9 Sep 43	–	–	Found sunk at Genoa Apr 45; salved; BU
FR31 (ex-Trombe)	FR Bourrasque	Forges et Chantiers de la Gironde (Bordeaux)	29 Dec 25	FR: Feb 28 IT: 1 Feb 43	–	–	–	–	Retroceded FR Bizerte 25 Oct 43; constructive total loss 16 Apr 45; condemned 12 Dec 46; sold Toulon Dec 46 to BU
FR32 (ex-Le Sirocco, ex-Corsaire)	FR Le Hardi	Forges et Chantiers de la Mediterranée (La Seyne)	14 Nov 39	FR: Jun 40 IT: –	–	Genoa 9 Sep 43	–	–	Scuttled as blockship Genoa 28 Oct 44
FR33 (ex-L'Adroit, ex-L'Epée)	FR Le Hardi	Forges et Chantiers de la Gironde (Bordeaux)	26 Oct 38	FR: Jun 40 IT: –	–	Toulon 9 Sep 43	–	–	Bombed Toulon 24 Nov 43, 4 Feb 44; to FRV 12 May 44; salved Sep 45; BU
FR34 (ex-Lansquenet) = TA34 [ii] (Jun 44) = Cyclone (Mar 46)	FR Le Hardi	Chantiers de la Gironde (Bordeaux)	20 May 39	FR: Jun 40 IT: –	–	Genoa 9 Sep 43	–	–	Scuttled Genoa 24 Apr 45; salved and to Toulon 19 Mar 46; stricken 22 Sep 58; BU
FR35 (ex-Bison, ex-Le Filibustier)	FR Le Hardi	Forges et Chantiers de la Mediterranée (La Seyne)	14 Dec 39	FR: – IT: –	–	Toulon 9 Sep 43	–	–	Foundered Toulon after bombing and collision 25 Jun 44; salved 1945; BU
FR36 (ex-Le Foudroyant, ex-Fleuret)	FR Le Hardi	Forges et Chantiers de la Mediterranée (La Seyne)	28 Jul 38	FR: Jun 40 IT: –	–	Toulon 9 Sep 43	–	–	Scuttled Toulon 17 Aug 44; salved 1951; BU 1957
FR37 (ex-Le Hardi)	FR Le Hardi	Ateliers et Chantiers de la Loire (St Nazaire)	4 May 38	FR: Jun 40 IT: –	–	Genoa 9 Sep 43	–	–	Scuttled Genoa 20 Apr 45; BU
Francesco Crispi = TA17 (Oct 43) = TA15 (16 Nov 43)	Sella	Pattison (Naples)	12 Sep 25	1 May 27	–	Piraeus 9 Sep 43	–	–	GE comm 20 Oct 43; bombed UK aircraft Heraklion 8 Mar 44; salved; bombed Piraeus 12 Oct 44
Fuciliere = Z20 (Jan 50) = Nastoitchivyi (Feb 50) = Byedovyi (Feb 50) = Legkyi (ii) (Mar 50) = TsL-57 (Dec 54)	Soldati, Ser 1	Cantieri Navali Riuniti (Ancona)	31 Jul 38	10 Jan 39	[Interned Port Mahon 10 Sep 43– 21 Jan 45]	–	SU	Odessa 31 Jan 50	Stricken 10 Jan 50; to SU comm 13 Mar 50; target ship 30 Nov 54; stricken 21 Jan 60; BU
Granatiere	Soldati, Ser 1	Cantieri Navali Riuniti (Palermo)	24 Apr 38	1 Feb 39	–	–	–	–	Stricken 1 Jul 57; BU
Grecale	Maestrale	Cantieri Navali Riuniti (Ancona)	17 Jun 34	15 Nov 34	11 Sep 43 14 Sep 43	–	–	–	Stricken 1 Jul 65; BU

Name	Class	Builder	Launch	Comp/ comm	Malta arr & dep	Captured Germany	Alloc	Handed over	Fate
Legionario = L6 (Aug 48) = Duchaffault (15 Aug 48) = Q14 (Jun 54)	Soldati, Ser 2	Odero Terni Orlando (Leghorn)	15 Apr 41	1 Mar 42	11 Sep 43 14 Sep 43	–	FR	Toulon 15 Aug 48	Stricken 9 Aug 48; to FR; comm 7 Sep 48; reserve 1 Oct 48; condemned 12 Jun 54; sold to BU 28 Feb 56
Maestrale	Maestrale	Cantieri Navali Riuniti (Ancona)	5 Apr 34	2 Sep 34	–	–	–	–	Scuttled Genoa 9 Sep 43; salved; bombed Apr 44; dismantled; BU after 1945
Mitragliere = M2 (Jul 48) = Jurien de la Gravière (15 Jul 48) = Q12 (Feb 51)	Soldati, Ser 2	Cantieri Navali Riuniti (Ancona)	28 Sep 41	1 Feb 42	[Interned Port Mahon 10 Sep 43– 21 Jan 45]	–	FR	Toulon 15 Jul 48	Stricken 14 Jul 48; to FR; comm for trials 1 Oct 48; hulked 24 Feb 51; sold to BU 28 Feb 56
Nicoló Zeno	Navagatori (mod)	Cantieri Navale del Quarnaro (Fiume)	12 Aug 28	27 May 30	–	–	–	–	Scuttled La Spezia 9 Sep 43; salved 1948; BU
Nicoloso da Recco	Navagatori (mod)	Cantieri Navali Riuniti (Ancona)	5 Jan 30	20 May 30	10 Sep 43 14 Sep 43	–	–	–	Stricken 15 Jul 54; BU
Premuda (ex-Dubrovnik) = TA32 (Sep 43)	YU Dubrovnik	Yarrow (Scotstoun)	11 Oct 31	YU: 1932 IT: Jan 42	–	Genoa 9 Sep 43	–	–	GE comm 18 Aug 44; scuttled Genoa 24 Apr 45; salved 1950; BU
Quintino Sella	Sella	Pattison (Naples)	24 Apr 25	23 Mar 26	–	–	–	–	Torpedoed GE MTB off Venice 11 Sep 43
Sebenico (ex-Beograd) = TA43 (Sep 43)	YU Beograd	Ateliers et Chantiers de la Loire (Nantes)	23 Dec 37	YU: Jan 39 IT: Aug 41	–	Venice 9 Sep 43	–	–	GE comm 22 Feb 45; scuttled Trieste 1 May 45; salved Jun 46; scuttled 19 Jul 46; salved 1948; BU 1949
Spalato (ex-Split) = Split (Oct 44)	YU Split	Yarrow (Split)	18 Jul 43	[YU: 4 Jul 58]	–	Split 24 Sep 43	–	–	Scuttled Split 27 Oct 44; YU Oct 44; stricken 2 Feb 84; BU 1986
Turbine	Turbine	Odero (Sestri- Ponente)	12 Apr 27	27 Aug 27	–	Piraeus 9 Sep 43	–	–	GE comm 28 Oct 43; bombed US aircraft Salamina (37° 57' N, 23° 32' E) 15 Sep 44
Ugolino Vivaldi	Navagatori (mod)	Odero (Sestri- Ponente)	9 Jan 29	6 Mar 30	–	–	–	–	Scuttled NW of Sardinia after gunfire GE shore batteries off Corsica 10 Sep 43
Velite = V3 (Jul 48) = Duperré (30 Jun 47) = Ex-Velite (17 Jun 53) = Q13 (Jun 54)	Soldati, Ser 2	Odero Terni Orlando (Leghorn)	31 Aug 41	31 Aug 42	11 Sep 43 14 Sep 43	–	FR	Toulon 30 Jun 47	Stricken 18 Jul 48; to FR; comm 1 Jul 47; reserve 1 Oct 48; hulked 24 Feb 51; condemned 12 Jun 54; sold to BU 17 Mar 61

Table 2.2/5. Torpedo Boats

Class	Disp.	Length	Beam	Machinery	Power/speed	Main guns	TT	Mines
Ariete	797t	82.3m	8.6m	2 x boilers, 2 x Tu	22,000shp=31.5kt	2 x 100mm/47	6 x 450mm	28
Audace	829t	87.6m	8.4m	3 x boilers, 2 x Tu	22,000shp=30kt	2 x 102mm/35	–	–
Ciclone	1160t	89.5m	9.9m	2 x boilers, 2 x Tu	16,000shp=26kt	3 x 100mm/47	4 x 450mm	20
Curtatone	967t	84.6m	8.4m	4 x boilers, 2 x Tu	22,000shp=30kt	2/4 x 102mm/45	2 x 533mm	16
Generali	635t	73.5m	7.3m	4 x boilers, 2 x Tu	15,000shp=30kt	3 x 102mm/45	4 x 450mm	...
Insidioso	550t	73.0m	7.3m	3 x boilers, 2 x Tu	12,000shp=20kt	1 x 102mm/35	–	–
La Masa	650t	73.5m	7.4m	4 x boilers, 2 x Tu	15,500shp=30kt	2 x 102mm/45	3 x 450mm	10
Orsa	1167t	89.3m	9.5m	2 x boilers, 2 x Tu	16,000shp=28kt	2 x 100mm/47	4 x 450mm	20
Palestro	862t	81.9m	8.0m	4 x boilers, 2 x Tu	22,000shp=32kt	4 x 102mm/45	4 x 450mm	...
Pilo	616t	73.0m	7.4m	4 x boilers, 2 x Tu	15,500shp=30kt	2 x 102mm/35	4 x 450mm	10
Sitori	670t	73.5m	7.4m	4 x boilers, 2 x Tu	15,500shp=30kt	6 x 102mm/45	4 x 450mm	10
Spica	789t	81.0m	8.2m	2 x boilers, 2 x Tu	19,000shp=34kt	3 x 100mm/47	4 x 450mm	20

Name	Class	Builder	Launch	Comp/ comm	Malta arr & dep	Captured Germany	Alloc	Handed over	Fate
Alabarda = TA42 (Oct 43)	Ariete	Cantieri Riuniti dell'Adriatico (Trieste)	7 May 44	GE: 30 Jan 45	–	Trieste 10 Sep 43	–	–	Bombed Venice 21 Mar 45; BU
Aliseo = Y9 (Apr 49) = Biokovo (May 49)	Ciclone	Navalmeccanica (Castellammare di Stabia)	20 Sep 42	28 Feb 43	20 Sep 43 5 Oct 43	–	YU	Split 3 May 49	Stricken 23 Apr 49; to YU May 49; stricken 1963
Animoso = Z16 (Feb 49) = Ladnyi (Mar 49) = TsL-61 (Dec 54)	Ciclone	Ansaldo (Genoa)	15 Apr 42	14 Aug 42	20 Sep 43 5 Oct 43	–	SU	Odessa 16 Mar 49	Stricken 6 Feb 49; to SU; comm 30 Mar 49; target ship 30 Dec 54; stricken 31 Jan 58; expended missile target 28 Aug 59.

Name	Class	Builder	Launch	Comp/ comm	Malta arr & dep	Captured Germany	Alloc	Handed over	Fate
Ardimentoso = Z19 (Oct 49) = Lyutyi (Nov 49) = TsL-60 (Dec 54) = PKZ-150 (Apr 58)	Ciclone	Ansaldo (Genoa)	28 Jun 42	14 Dec 42	20 Sep 43 5 Oct 43	–	SU	Odessa 20 Oct 49	Stricken 6 Oct 49; to SU; comm 23 Nov 49; target ship 30 Dec 54; stricken 4 Dec 59
Ardito = TA25 (Oct 43)	Ciclone	Ansaldo (Genoa)	14 Mar 42	30 Jun 42	–	Portoferraio 18 Sep 43	–	–	GE comm 16 Jan 44; scuttled gunfire TA29 off Viareggio (43° 49' N, 10° 12' E) after torpedo damage US MTBs 21 Jun 44
Aretusa	Spica	Ansaldo (Sestri Ponente)	6 Feb 38	1 Jul 38	–	–	–	–	Stricken 1 Aug 58
Ariete = Y8 (Apr 49) = Durmitor (Apr 49)	Ariete	Ansaldo (Genoa)	6 Mar 43	5 Aug 43	20 Sep 43 6 Oct 43	–	YU	Split	30 Apr 49 Stricken 22 Apr 49; to YU; stricken 1 Jan 67; BU
Arturo = TA24 (Oct 43)	Ariete	Ansaldo (Genoa)	27 Mar 43	GE: 7 Oct 43	–	Genoa 9 Sep 43	–	–	Torpedoed HMS Meteor NE of Corsica (43° 40' N, 09° 40' E) 18 Mar 45
Audace (ex-Intrepido, ex-Kawakaze)	Audace	Yarrow (Scotstoun)	27 Sep 16	1 Mar 17	–	Venice 12 Sep 43	–	–	GE comm 21 Oct 43; gunfire HMS Avon Vale & Wheatland off Pago Island (44° 24' N, 15° 02' E) 1 Nov 44
Auriga = TA27 (Oct 43)	Ariete	Ansaldo (Genoa)	15 Apr 43	GE: 29 Dec 43	–	Genoa 9 Sep 43	–	–	Bombed US aircraft Portoferraio (42°49', 10° 20' E) 9 Jun 44; wreck blown up 14 Jun 44
Balestra = TA47 (Oct 43) = Učka (1948)	Ariete	Cantieri Navale del Quarnaro (Fiume)	[4 Oct 47]	[YU: 1950]	–	Fiume 16 Sep 43	–	–	Seized YU 1945; stricken 1968; BU 1971
Calatafimi = Achilles (Sep 43) = TA15 (28 Oct 43) = TA19 (16 Nov 43)	Curtatone	Odero (Leghorn)	17 Mar 23	24 May 24	–	Piraeus 10 Sep 43	–	–	GE comm 13 Sep 43; torpedoed GR submarine Pipinos Vathi (37° 45' N, 26° 59' E) 9 Aug 44
Calliope	Spica	Ansaldo (Sestri Ponente)	15 Apr 38	28 Oct 38	20 Sep 43 4 Oct 43	–	–	–	Stricken 1 Aug 58
Cassiopea	Spica	Canteri del Tirreno (Riva Trigoso)	22 Nov 36	26 Apr 37	–	–	–	–	Stricken 31 Oct 59
Castelfidardo = TA16 (Oct 43)	Curtatone	Odero (Leghorn)	4 Jun 22	7 Mar 24	–	Suda Bay 9 Sep 43	–	–	GE comm 14 Oct 43; UK aircraft rockets Heraklion 2 Jun 44
Clio	Spica	Ansaldo (Sestri Ponente)	3 Apr 38	2 Oct 38	–	–	–	–	Stricken 31 Oct 59
Daga = TA39 (Oct 43)	Ariete	Cantieri Riuniti dell'Adriatico (Trieste)	14 Aug 43	GE: 27 Mar 44	–	Trieste 10 Sep 43	–	–	Mined S of Cape Dermata 16 Oct 44
Dragone = TA30 (Oct 43)	Ariete	Ansaldo (Genoa)	14 Aug 43	GE: 15 Apr 44	–	Genoa 9 Sep 43	–	–	Torpedoed US PT-552, PT-558 & PT-559 W of La Spezia (43° 58' N, 09° 29' E) 15 Jun 44
Enrico Cosenz (ex-Agostino Bertani)	La Masa	Odero (Sestri Ponente)	6 Jun 16	13 Jun 19	–	–	–	–	Scuttled off Lagosta 27 Sep 43 after damaged GE aircraft
Eridano = TA29 (Oct 43)	Ariete	Ansaldo (Genoa)	12 Jul 43	GE: 6 Mar 44	–	Genoa 9 Sep 43	–	–	Gunfire HMS Lookout NE of Corsica (43° 40' N, 09° 30' E) 18 Mar 45
Fionda = TA46 (Oct 43) = Velebit (1948)	Ariete	Cantieri Navale del Quarnaro (Fiume)	31 Jan 43	GE: 2 Feb 45	–	Fiume 16 Sep 43	–	–	Scuttled Fiume 3 May 45; salved; reconstruction abandoned; BU
Fortunale = Z17 (Feb 42) = Letnyi (Mar 49) = TsL-59 (Dec 54)	Ciclone	Cantieri Riuniti dell'Adriatico (Trieste)	18 Apr 42	16 Aug 42	20 Sep 43 5 Oct 43	–	SU	Odessa 1 Mar 49	Stricken 6 Oct 49; to SU; comm 23 Nov 49; target ship 30 Dec 54; stricken 4 Dec 59; sunk as target Dec 59
Francesco Stocco	Sitori	Odero (Sestri Ponente)	5 Jun 17	19 Jul 17	–	–	–	–	Bombed GE aircraft of Corfu 24 Sep 43
Generale Achille Papa = TA7 (Oct 43) = SG20 (18 Oct 43)	Generale	Odero (Sestri Ponente)	8 Dec 21	9 Feb 22	–	Genoa 9 Sep 43	–	–	GE comm 17 Oct 43; constructive total loss mine 1 Nov 43; foundered Genoa; salved 25 Apr 44 and scuttled as blockship Oneglia
Generale Antonino Cascino	Generale	Odero (Sestri Ponente)	18 Mar 22	8 May 22	–	–	–	–	Scuttled La Spezia 9 Sep 43; salved after 1945; BU
Generale Carlo Montanari	Generale	Odero (Sestri Ponente)	4 Oct 22	9 Nov 22	–	–	–	–	Scuttled La Spezia 9 Sep 43; salved; bombed La Spezia 4 Oct 44; salved 1949; BU
Ghibli	Ciclone	Navalmeccanica (Castellammare di Stabia)	28 Feb 43	24 Jul 43	–	–	–	–	Scuttled La Spezia 9 Sep 43; salved; scuttled Genoa 24 Apr 45

Name	Class	Builder	Launch	Comp/ comm	Malta arr & dep	Captured Germany	Alloc	Handed over	Fate
Giacinto Carini = GM517 (1959)	La Masa	Odero (Sestri Ponente)	7 Nov 17	30 Nov 17	21 Sep 43 5 Oct 43	–	–	–	Minesweeper 1953; stricken 31 Dec 58; training hulk; BU May 63
Giuseppe Cesare Abba	Pilo	Odero (Sestri Ponente)	25 May 15	6 Jul 15	–	–	–	–	Minesweeper 1952; stricken 1 Sep 58
Giuseppe Dezza (ex-Pilade Bronzetti) = TA35 (Oct 43)	Pilo	Odero (Sestri Ponente)	26 Oct 15	1 Jan 16	–	Fiume 16 Sep 43	–	–	GE comm 9 Jun 44; mined Fasana Canal (44° 53' N, 13° 47' E) 17 Aug 44
Giuseppe La Masa	La Masa	Odero (Sestri Ponente)	6 Sep 17	28 Sep 17	–	–	–	–	Scuttled Naples 11 Sep 43
Giuseppe Missori = TA22 (Oct 43)	Pilo	Odero (Sestri Ponente)	20 Dec 15	7 Mar 16	–	Durazzo 10 Sep 43	–	–	GE comm 3 Dec 43; constructive total loss from bombing 11 Aug 44; scuttled Muggia-Trieste 3 May 45; BU 1949
Giuseppe Sitori	Sitori	Odero (Sestri Ponente)	24 Nov 16	22 Dec 16	–	–	–	–	Scuttled Corfu 25 Sep 43
Gladio = TA37 (Oct 43)	Ariete	Cantieri Riuniti dell'Adriatico (Trieste)	15 Jun 43	GE: 8 Jan 44	–	Trieste 10 Sep 43	–	–	Gunfire HMS Termagant & Tuscan off Volos (40° 36' N, 22° 46' E) 19 Oct 44
Impavido = TA1 (Oct 43) = TA23 (Oct 43)	Ciclone	Canteri del Tirreno (Riva Trigoso)	24 Feb 43	30 Apr 43	–	Portoferraio 18 Sep 43	–	–	GE comm 9 Oct 43; scuttled torpedo TA24 NE of Corsica (43° 02' N, 10° 12' E) 25 Apr 44 after mine damage
Impetuoso	Ciclone	Canteri del Tirreno (Riva Trigoso)	20 Apr 43	7 Jun 43	–	–	–	–	Scuttled off Pollensa Bay 11 Sep 43
Indomito = Y10 (Apr 49) = Triglav (Apr 49)	Ciclone	Canteri del Tirreno (Riva Trigoso)	6 Jul 43	4 Aug 43	20 Sep 43 5 Oct 43	–	YU	Split 28 Apr 49	Stricken 20 Apr 49; to YU; stricken 6 Apr 65; BU 1971
Insidioso = TA21 (Oct 43)	Insidioso	Pattison (Naples)	30 Sep 13	6 Jul 14	–	Pola 10 Sep 43	–	–	GE comm 8 Nov 43; US aerial torpedo Fiume 5 Nov 44; BU 1947
Intrepido = TA26 (Oct 43)	Ciclone	Canteri del Tirreno (Riva Trigoso)	8 Sep 43	GE: 16 Jan 44	–	Genoa 9 Sep 43	–	–	Torpedoed US PT552, PT558 & PT559 W of La Spezia (43° 58' N, 09° 29' E) 15 Jun 44
Lancia = TA41 (Oct 43)	Ariete	Cantieri Riuniti dell'Adriatico (Trieste)	7 May 44	GE: 7 Sep 44	–	Trieste 10 Sep 43	–	–	Bombed San Rocco-Trieste 17 Feb 45; scuttled 1 May 48; BU 1949
Libra	Spica	Cantieri Navale del Quarnaro (Fiume)	3 Oct 37	19 Jan 39	12 Sep 43 4 Oct 43	–	–	–	Stricken 1964
Lira = TA49 (Mar 44)	Spica	Cantieri Navale del Quarnaro (Fiume)	12 Sep 37	1 Jan 38	–	–	–	–	Scuttled La Spezia 9 Sep 43; salved after 15 Mar 44; to GE; bombed La Spezia 4 Nov 44; BU
Monzambano	Curtatone	Odero (Leghorn)	6 Aug 23	4 Jun 24	–	–	–	–	Stricken 15 Apr 51; BU
Nicola Fabrizi	La Masa	Odero (Sestri Ponente)	8 Jul 18	12 Jul 18	21 Sep 43 5 Oct 43	–	–	–	Minesweeper 1952; stricken 1 Feb 57; BU La Spezia
Orione	Orsa	Cantieri Navali Riuniti (Palermo)	21 Apr 37	31 Mar 38	12 Sep 43 6 Oct 43	–	–	–	Stricken 1 Jan 65
Orsa	Orsa	Cantieri Navali Riuniti (Palermo)	21 Mar 37	31 Mar 38	–	–	–	–	Stricken 1 Jul 64
Partenope	Spica	Bacini e Scali (Naples)	27 Feb 38	26 Nov 38	–	–	–	–	Scuttled Naples 11 Sep 43; salved; BU Castellammare di Stabia after 1945
Pegaso	Orsa	Bacini e Scali (Naples)	8 Dec 36	30 Mar 38	–	–	–	–	Scuttled off Pollensa Bay 11 Sep 43
Procione	Orsa	Bacini e Scali (Naples)	31 Jan 37	30 Mar 38	–	–	–	–	Scuttled La Spezia 9 Sep 43
Pugnale = TA40 (Oct 43)	Ariete	Cantieri Riuniti Monfalcone dell' Adriatico (Trieste)	1 Aug 43	GE: 17 Oct 44	–	Trieste 10 Sep 43	–	–	Bombed Trieste 20 Feb 45; scuttled 4 May 45
Rigel = TA28 (Oct 43)	Ariete	Ansaldo (Genoa)	22 May 43	GE: 23 Jan 44	–	Genoa 9 Sep 43	–	–	Bombed Genoa 4 Sep 44; salved; scuttled Genoa 24 Apr 45
Rosolino Pilo	Pilo	Odero (Sestri Ponente)	24 Mar 15	25 May 15	–	Defected 9 Sep 43	–	–	Redefected 26 Sep 43; stricken 1 Oct 54
Sagittario	Spica	Cantieri Navale del Quarnaro (Fiume)	21 Jun 36	8 Oct 36	–	–	–	–	Stricken 1 Jul 64
San Martino = TA18 (Oct 43) = TA17 (16 Nov 43)	Palestro	Odero (Leghorn)	8 Sep 20	10 Oct 22	–	Piraeus 9 Sep 43	–	–	GE comm 28 Oct 43; constructive total loss bomb Piraeus 18 Sep 44; scuttled 12 Nov 44.

Name	Class	Builder	Launch	Comp/ comm	Malta arr & dep	Captured Germany	Alloc	Handed over	Fate
Sirio	Spica	Cantieri Navale del Quarnaro (Fiume)	16 Nov 35	1 Mar 36	–	–	–	–	Stricken 31 Oct 59
Solferino = TA18 (16 Nov 43)	Palestro	Odero (Leghorn)	28 Apr 20	31 Oct 21	–	Suda Bay 9 Sep 43	–	–	GE comm 25 Jul 44; gunfire HMS Termagant & Tuscan off Volos (37° 45' N, 26° 59' E) 19 Oct 44
Spada = TA38 (Oct 43)	Ariete	Cantieri Riuniti dell'Adriatico (Trieste)	1 Jul 43	GE: 12 Feb 44	–	Trieste 10 Sep 43	–	–	Stranded Volos (39° 12' N, 22° 56' E) 8 Oct 44; scuttled 19 Oct 44
Spica = TA45 (Oct 43)	Ariete	Cantieri Navale del Quarnaro (Fiume)	30 Jan 44	GE: 6 Sep 44	–	Fiume 16 Sep 43	–	–	Gunfire UK MGBs Morlacca Channel 13 Apr 45
Stella Polare = TA36 (Oct 43)	Ariete	Cantieri Navale del Quarnaro (Fiume)	11 Jul 43	GE: 13 Jan 44	–	Fiume 16 Sep 43	–	–	Mined SW of Fiume (45° 07' N, 14° 21' E) 18 Mar 44
T1 (ex-76T) = Golešnica (1945)	AH 74T	Stab Tecnico Triestino (Trieste)	15 Dec 13	AH: 20 Jul 14 YU: Mar 21 IT: Apr 41	–	–	–	–	Retroceded YU Dec 43; stricken Oct 59
T3 (ex-78T) = TA48 (Oct 43) = T3 (Aug 44) = TA48 (13 Dec 44)	AH 74T	Stab Tecnico Triestino (Trieste)	4 Mar 14	AH: 23 Aug 14 YU: Mar 21 IT: Apr 41	–	Fiume 16 Sep 43	–	–	GE comm 16 Oct 43; to HR 15 Aug 44; to GE 13 Dec 44; bombed Trieste 20 Feb 45; salved 10 May 46; BU Trieste 1948–49
T5 (ex-87F) = Cer (1945)	AH 82F	Danubius (Fiume)	20 Mar 15	AH: 25 Oct 15 YU: Mar 21 IT: Apr 41	–	–	–	–	Retroceded YU at Malta Dec 43; BU 1962
T6 (ex-93F)	AH 82F	Danubius (Fiume)	25 Nov 15	AH: 16 Apr 16 YU: Mar 21 IT: Apr 41	–	–	–	–	Scuttled N of Rimini 11 Sep 43
T7 (ex-96F) = TA34 [i] (Oct 43) = T7 (Jun 44)	AH 82F	Danubius (Fiume)	7 Jul 16	AH: 23 Nov 16 YU: Mar 21 IT: Apr 41	–	Gruz 8 Sep 43	–	–	GE comm Nov 43; to HR 17 Jun 44; beached after gunfire UK MTB659, MTB662 & MTB670 off Kukuljari 24 Jun 44; wreck blown up
T8 (ex-97F)	AH 82F	Danubius (Fiume)	20 Aug 16	AH: 22 Dec 16 YU: Mar 21 IT: Apr 41	–				Bombed GE aircraft NW of Dubrovnik 10/11 Sep 43

Table 2.2/6. Corvettes and Sloop

Class	Disp.	Length	Beam	Machinery	Power/speed	Main guns	Mines
Gabbiano	670t	63.2m	8.7m	2 x diesel	3500bhp=18.0kt	1 x 100mm/47	–
Elan	630t	78.0m	8.5m	2 x diesel	4000bhp=20.0kt	2 x 100mm	–
Eritrea	2200t	96.9m	13.3m	2 x diesel-electric	7800shp=20.0kt	4 x 120mm/45	100
FR Chamois	647t	78.0m	8.5m	2 x diesel	4000bhp=20.0kt	2 x 100mm	–
FR Ardente	266t	60.2m	7.2m	2 x boilers, 1 x VTE	1200ihp=15.0kt	2 x 100mm	–

Name	Class	Builder	Launch	Comp/ comm	Malta arr & dep	Captured Germany	Alloc	Handed over	Fate
Alce = UJ6084 (Sep 43)	Gabbiano	Odero Terni Orlando (Leghorn)	5 Dec 42	GE: Sep 43	–	Leghorn 9 Sep 43	–	–	Scuttled Genoa 24 Apr 45
Antilope = UJ6082 (Sep 43)	Gabbiano	Odero Terni Orlando (Leghorn)	9 May 42	11 Nov 42	–	Leghorn 9 Sep 43	–	–	GE comm Sep 43; gunfire HMS Aphis and Scarab & USS Endicott off Marseilles 17 Aug 44
Ape	Gabbiano	Navalmeccanica (Castellamare di Stabia)	22 Nov 42	15 May 43	20 Sep 43 4 Oct 43	–	–	–	Stricken 31 Jul 81
Ardea = UJ2225 (Oct 43)	Gabbiano	Ansaldo (Genoa)	–	–	–	Genoa 9 Sep 43	–	–	Scuttled Genoa 24 Apr 45
Artemide = UJ2226 (Oct 43)	Gabbiano	Cantieri Riuniti dell'Adriatico (Monfalcone)	10 Aug 42	10 Oct 42	–	Leghorn 9 Sep 43	–	–	GE comm 12 Jul 44; scuttled Genoa 24 Apr 45
Baionetta (ex-Partigiana)	Gabbiano	Breda (Porto Marghera)	5 Oct 42	15 May 43	–	–	–	–	Stricken 1 Oct 71
Berenice	Gabbiano	Cantieri Riuniti dell'Adriatico (Monfalcone)	20 May	43 Sep 43					
Bombarda = UJ206 (Feb 44) = Bombarda (May 45)	Gabbiano	Breda (Porto Marghera)	10 Feb 44	21 Apr 51	–	Porto Marghera 11 Sep 43			Scuttled Venice 26 Apr 45; salved 1945 and completed

Name	Class	Builder	Launch	Comp/ comm	Malta arr & dep	Captured Germany	Alloc	Handed over	Fate
Calabrone	Gabbiano	Navalmeccanica (Castellamare di Stabia)	27 Jun 43	–	–	Castellamare di Stabia 13 Sep 43	–	–	Scuttled Castellamare di Stabia 17 Sep 43; salved; sunk 29 Aug 43
Camoscio = UJ6081 (Sep 43)	Gabbiano	Odero Terni Orlando (Leghorn)	9 May 42	18 Apr 43	–	Leghorn 9 Sep 43	–	–	GE comm Sep 43; gunfire USS Somers S of Toulon 15 Aug 44
Capriolo = UJ2230 (Sep 43) = UJ6083 (Sep 43)	Gabbiano	Odero Terni Orlando (Leghorn)	5 Dec 42	GE: Sep 43	–	Leghorn 9 Sep 43	–	–	Bombed Genoa 5 Sep 44
Carabina = UJ207 (1944)	Gabbiano	Breda (Porto Marghera)	31 Aug 43	–	–	Porto Marghera 11 Sep 43	–	–	Bombed Porto Marghera Feb 44
Cavalletta	Gabbiano	Navalmeccanica (Castellamare di Stabia)	–	–	–	Leghorn 9 Sep 43	–	–	BU on slip
Cervo = UJ6096 (Oct 43)	Gabbiano	Odero Terni Orlando (Leghorn)	?	–	–	Leghorn 9 Sep 43	–	–	Scuttled Genoa 24 Apr 45
Chimera	Gabbiano	Cantieri Riuniti dell'Adriatico (Trieste)	30 Jan 43	26 May 43	–	–	–	–	Stricken 1 May 77
Cicala	Gabbiano	Navalmeccanica (Castellamare di Stabia)	27 Jun 43	–	–	Castellamare di Stabia 13 Sep 43	–	–	Scuttled Castellamare di Stabia 17 Sep 43
Clava	Gabbiano	Breda (Porto Marghera)	–	–	–	Porto Marghera 11 Sep 43	–	–	Broken up on slip
Colubrina =UJ205 (Jan 44)	Gabbiano	Breda (Porto Marghera)	7 Dec 42	GE: 14 Jan 44	–	Venice 11 Sep 43	–	–	Bombed Split 27 Mar 44
Cormorano	Gabbiano	Cerusa (Voltri)	20 Sep 42	6 Mar 43	20 Sep 43 4 Oct 43	–	–	–	Stricken 1 Nov 71
Crisalide	Gabbiano	Navalmeccanica (Castellamare di Stabia)	8 Dec 47	25 Sep 52	–	Castellamare di Stabia 13 Sep 43	–	–	Construction continued 1946; stricken 1 Dec 72
Daino = UJ6087 (Oct 43)	Gabbiano	Odero Terni Orlando (Leghorn)	?	–	–	Leghorn 9 Sep 43	–	–	Scuttled Leghorn 11 Jul 44
Danaide	Gabbiano	Cantieri Riuniti dell'Adriatico (Trieste)	21 Oct 42	27 Feb 43	20 Sep 43 4 Sep 43	–	–	–	Stricken 1 Jan 68
Driade	Gabbiano	Cantieri Riuniti dell'Adriatico (Trieste)	7 Oct 42	14 Jan 43	–	–	–	–	Stricken 1 Jul 66
Egeria = UJ201	Gabbiano	Cantieri Riuniti dell'Adriatico (Monfalcone)	3 Jul 43	GE: 18 Jan 44	–	Monfalcone 10 Sep 43	–	–	Gunfire FR Le Terrible & Le Malin off Dalmatia 29 Feb 44
Eritrea = F1 (27 Jan 48) = Francis Garnier (Jan 50)	Eritrea	Castellammare di Stabia DYd	28 Sep 36	10 Feb 37	–	–	FR Toulon 28 Jan 48		Stricken 27 Jan 48; to FR 12 Feb 48; aircraft and gunfire target La Bourdonnais, Forbin & Jauréguiberry off Papeete 29 Oct 66
Euridice = UJ204 (Oct 43)	Gabbiano	Cantieri Riuniti dell'Adriatico (Monfalcone)	12 Mar 44	–	–	Monfalcone 10 Sep 43	–	–	Bombed Monfalcone 25 May 44
Euterpe = UJ2228 (Oct 43)	Gabbiano	Cantieri Riuniti dell'Adriatico (Monfalcone)	22 Oct 42	20 Jan 43	–	La Spezia 9 Sep 43	–	–	Scuttled La Spezia 9 Sep 43; salved; scuttled Genoa 24 Apr 45
Farfalla	Gabbiano	Navalmeccanica (Castellamare di Stabia)	4 Jan 48	10 Feb 53	–	Castellamare di Stabia 13 Sep 43	–	–	Construction continued 1946; stricken 31 Dec 71
Fenice	Gabbiano	Cantieri Riuniti dell'Adriatico (Trieste)	1 Mar 43	15 Jun 43.	–	–	–	–	Stricken 1 Jul 65
Flora	Gabbiano	Cantieri Riuniti dell'Adriatico (Trieste)	1 Dec 42	26 Apr 43	–	–	–	–	Stricken 1 Jan 70
Folaga	Gabbiano	Ansaldo (Genoa)	14 Nov 42	16 Feb 43	–	–	–	–	Stricken 1 Aug 65
Gabbiano	Gabbiano	Cerusa (Voltri)	23 Jun 42	3 Oct 42	20 Sep 43 4 Oct 43	–	–	–	Stricken 1 Nov 71
Grillo	Gabbiano	Navalmeccanica (Castellamare di Stabia)	21 Mar 43	–	–	Castellamare di Stabia 13 Sep 43	–	–	Scuttled Castellamare di Stabia 17 Sep 43; salved; sunk 3 May 44
Gru	Gabbiano	Ansaldo (Genoa)	23 Dec 42	29 Apr 43	–	–	–	–	Stricken 1 Aug 71.

Name	Class	Builder	Launch	Comp/ comm	Malta arr & dep	Captured Germany	Alloc	Handed over	Fate
Ibis	Gabbiano	Ansaldo (Genoa)	12 Dec 42	3 Apr 43	–	–	–	–	Stricken 1 Jul 71
Libellula	Gabbiano	Navalmeccanica (Castellamare di Stabia)	–	–	–	Leghorn 9 Sep 43	–	–	BU on slip
Lucciola	Gabbiano	Navalmeccanica (Castellamare di Stabia)	21 Mar 43	–	–	Castellamare di Stabia 13 Sep 43	–	–	Scuttled Castellamare di Stabia 13 Sep 43; salved; completed as merchantman
Marangone = UJ2223 (Oct 43)	Gabbiano	Ansaldo (Genoa)	16 Sep 43	GE: 20 Feb 44	–	Genoa 9 Sep 43	–	–	Bombed Genoa 25 May 44
Melpomene = UJ202 (Oct 43)	Gabbiano	Cantieri Riuniti dell'Adriatico (Monfalcone)	29 Aug 43	GE: 24 Apr 44	–	Monfalcone 10 Sep 43	–	–	Gunfire HMS Avon Vale & Wheatland off Pago Island (44° 24' N, 15° 02' E) 1 Nov 44
Minerva	Gabbiano	Cantieri Riuniti dell'Adriatico (Monfalcone)	5 Nov 42	24 Feb 43	20 Sep 43 4 Oct 43	–	–	–	Stricken 1 Jul 69
Pellicano	Gabbiano	Cerusa (Voltri)	12 Feb 43	15 Mar 43	–	–	–	–	Stricken 1 Jul 69
Persefone = UJ2227 (Oct 43)	Gabbiano	Cantieri Riuniti dell'Adriatico (Monfalcone)	21 Sep 42	28 Nov 42	–	La Spezia 9 Sep 43	–	–	Scuttled La Spezia 9 Sep 43; salved; GE comm 15 Oct 43; scuttled Genoa 24 Apr 45
Pomona	Gabbiano	Cantieri Riuniti dell'Adriatico	18 Nov 42	4 Apr 43	–	–	–	–	Stricken 1 Jun 65
Renna = UJ6085 (Sep 43)	Gabbiano	Odero Terni Orlando (Leghorn)	5 Dec 42	GE: Sep 44	–	Leghorn 9 Sep 43	–	–	Bombed Genoa 4 Sep 44
Scimitarra	Gabbiano	Breda (Porto Marghera)	16 Sep 42	15 May 43	–	–	–	–	Stricken 1 Jun 71
Scure = UJ209 (Oct 43)	Gabbiano	Breda (Porto Marghera)	?	–	–	Porto Marghera 11 Sep 43	–	–	Scuttled 24 Apr 43
Sfinge	Gabbiano	Cantieri Riuniti dell'Adriatico (Trieste)	9 Jan 43	12 May 43	–	–	–	–	Stricken 15 Jun 77
Sibilla	Gabbiano	Cantieri Riuniti dell'Adriatico (Trieste)	10 Mar 43	5 Jun 43	–	–	–	–	Stricken 1 Feb 73
Spingarda = UJ208 (Apr 44)	Gabbiano	Breda (Porto Marghera)	22 Mar 43	GE: 22 Apr 44	–	Venice 11 Sep 43	–	–	Gunfire HMS Avon Vale & Wheatland off Pago Island (44° 24' N, 15° 02' E) 1 Nov 44
Stambecco = UJ6088 (Oct 43)	Gabbiano	Odero Terni Orlando (Leghorn)	–	–	–	Leghorn 9 Sep 43	–	–	Bombed on slip, Leghorn
Strolaga = UJ2224 (Oct 43)	Gabbiano	Ansaldo (Genoa)	19 Sep 43	GE: 18 Apr 44	–	Genoa 9 Sep 43	–	–	Bombed Genoa 8 Sep 44
Tersicore = UJ203 (Oct 43)	Gabbiano	Cantieri Riuniti dell'Adriatico (Monfalcone)	16 Oct 43	–	–	Monfalcone 10 Sep 43	–	–	Bombed Monfalcone 20 Apr 44
Tuffetto = UJ2222 (Oct 43)	Gabbiano	Ansaldo (Genoa)	25 Aug 43	GE: 20 Feb 44	–	Genoa 9 Sep 43	–	–	Scuttled 24 Apr 45
Urania	Gabbiano	Cantieri Riuniti dell'Adriatico (Monfalcone)	21 Apr 43	1 Aug 43	–	–	–	–	Stricken 1 Aug 71
Vespa = UJ2221 (Sep 43)	Gabbiano	Navalmeccanica (Castellamare di Stabia)	22 Nov 42	2 Sep 43	–	Pozzuoli 11 Sep 43	–	–	GE comm 29 Sep 43; scuttled Genoa 24 Apr 45
Zagaglia = UJ211 (Oct 43)	Gabbiano	Breda (Porto Marghera)	–	–	–	Porto Marghera 11 Sep 43	–	–	Blown up on slip
FR51 (ex-La Batailleuse) = SG23 (Feb 43) = UJ2231 (Jul 44)	FR Elan	Chantiers de Provence (Port de Bouc)	22 Aug 39	FR: Mar 40 IT: 28 Jan 43	–	La Spezia 9 Sep 43 (scuttled)	–	–	Scuttled La Spezia 9 Sep 43; salved; scuttled Genoa 25 Apr 45
FR54 (ex-Impetueuse) = SG17 (Oct 43)	FR Elan	Ateliers & Chantiers de France (Dunkirk)	17 Aug 39	FR: May 40 IT:	–	–Toulon 9 Sep 43	–	–	Bombed Toulon 24 Nov 43; scuttled Marseilles 7 Aug 44; BU 1945
FR55 (ex-La Curieuse) = SG16 (May 44)	FR Elan	Lorient DYd	11 Nov 39 IT:	FR: 1940	–	–Toulon 9 Sep 43	–	–	GE comm May 44; scuttled Marseilles 7 Aug 44; BU 1945
FR53 (ex-Chamois)	FR Chamois	Lorient DYd	29 Apr 38	1939	–	Toulon 9 Sep 43	–	–	Bombed Toulon 30 Nov 43; salved; BU
FR56 (ex-Dédaigneuse) = M6020 (Oct 43)	FR Ardente	Chantiers de la Gironde (Bordeaux)	1916	1916	–	Toulon 9 Sep 43	–	–	Scuttled Marseilles 21 Aug 44

Table 2.2/7. Submarines

Class	Disp.	Length	Beam	Machinery	Power/speed	Main guns	TT	Mines
Glauco	977/1071t	73.0m	7.2m	2 x diesel 2 x electric	3000bhp=17.1kt 1200shp=8.0kt	2 x 100mm/47	8 x 533mm	–
Calvi	1331/2060t	84.3m	7.2m	2 x diesel 2 x electric	4400bhp=17.1kt 1800shp=8.0kt	2 x 120mm/45	8 x 533mm	–
Foca	1200/1650t	83.9m	7.2m	2 x diesel 2 x electric	2880bhp=16kt 1250shp=8.0kt	1 x 100mm/47	6 x 533mm	36
Marcello	962/1317t	73.0m	7.2m	2 x diesel 2 x electric	3600bhp=17.4kt 1150shp=8.0kt	2 x 100mm/47	8 x 533mm	–
Cappelini	955/1315t	73.0m	7.2m	2 x diesel 2 x electric	3600bhp=17.4kt 1150shp=8.0kt	2 x 100mm/47	8 x 533mm	–
Brin	913/1266t	72.5m	6.7m	2 x diesel 2 x electric	3400bhp=17.3kt 1300shp=8.0kt	1 x 100mm/47	8 x 533mm	–
Liuzzi	1031/1484t	76.1m	7.0m	2 x diesel 2 x electric	3500bhp=18.0kt 1500shp=8.0kt	1 x 100mm/47	8 x 533mm	–
Marconi	1036/1489t	76.5m	6.8m	2 x diesel 2 x electric	3600bhp=18.0kt 1500shp=8.0kt	1 x 100mm/47	8 x 533mm	–
Cagni	1504/2170t	87.9m	7.8m	2 x diesel 2 x electric	4370bhp=16.9kt 1800shp=8.5kt	2 x 100mm/47	14 x 450mm	–
R	1300/2600t	86.5m	7.9m	2 x diesel 2 x electric	2600bhp=14.0kt 900shp=6.5kt	3 x 20mm	0/2 x 450mm	–
Mameli	786/1009t	64.6m	6.5m	2 x diesel 2 x electric	4000bhp=17.2kt 1100shp=7.7kt	1 x 102mm/35	6 x 533mm	–
Pisani	808/1058t	62.8m	6.1m	2 x diesel 2 x electric	3000bhp=15.2kt 1100shp=8.2kt	1 x 102mm/35	6 x 533mm	–
Bandiera	860/1100t	69.8m	7.3m	2 x diesel 2 x electric	3000bhp=15.1kt 1300shp=8.2kt	1 x 102mm/35	8 x 533mm	–
Squalo	857/1143t	69.8m	7.2m	2 x diesel 2 x electric	3000bhp=15.1kt 1300shp=8.0kt	1 x 102mm/35	8 x 533mm	–
Bragadin	833/1086t	71.5m	6.2m	2 x diesel 2 x electric	1500bhp=11.5kt 1000shp=7.0kt	1 x 102mm/35	4 x 533mm	16/24
Argonauta	611/810t	61.5m	5.7m	2 x diesel 2 x electric	1200bhp=14.0kt 800shp=8.0kt	1 x 102mm/35	6 x 533mm	–
Settembrini	872/1153t	69.1m	6.6m	2 x diesel 2 x electric	3000bhp=17.5kt 1400shp=7.7kt	1 x 102mm/35	8 x 533mm	–
Sirena	620/850t	60.2m	6.5m	2 x diesel 2 x electric	1200bhp=14.0kt 800shp=7.7kt	1 x 100mm/47	6 x 533mm	–
Perla	625/850t	60.2m	6.5m	2 x diesel 2 x electric	1400bhp=14.0kt 800shp=7.5kt	1 x 100mm/47	6 x 533mm	–
Adua	625/850t	60.2m	6.5m	2 x diesel 2 x electric	1200bhp=14.0kt 800shp=7.5kt	1 x 100mm/47	6 x 533mm	–
Argo	689/1018t	63.2m	6.9m	2 x diesel 2 x electric	1500bhp=14.0kt 800shp=8.0kt	1 x 100mm/47	6 x 533mm	–
Acciaio	640/865t	60.2m	6.4m	2 x diesel 2 x electric	1400bhp=14.0kt 800shp=7.7kt	1 x 100mm/47	4/6 x 533mm	–
Flutto, I ser	750/1068t	63.2m	7.0m	2 x diesel 2 x electric	2400bhp=16kt 800shp=8.5kt	1 x 100mm/47	6 x 533mm	–

Class	Disp.	Length	Beam	Machinery	Power/speed	Main guns	TT	Mines
Flutto, II ser	766/1131t	64.2m	7.0m	2 x diesel 2 x electric	2400bhp=16.0kt 800shp=8.5kt	1 x 100mm/47	6 x 533mm	–
H	343/441t	44.6m	4.7m	2 x diesel 2 x electric	448bhp=12.0kt 620shp=11.0kt	1 x 76mm/30	4 x 450mm	–
CM	92/114t	33.0m	2.9m	2 x diesel 2 x electric	600bhp=14.0kt 120shp=8.0kt	–	3 x 450mm	–
CC	100/117t	33.0m	2.7m	2 x diesel 2 x electric	700bhp=16.0kt 120shp=9.0kt	–	3 x 450mm	–
YU *Smeli*	665/822t	66.5m	5.4m	2 x diesel 2 x electric	1480bhp=14.5kt 1100shp=9.2kt	1 x 100mm/35	6 x 533mm	–
Requin	974/1441t	78.3m	6.9m	2 x diesel 2 x electric	2900bhp=15.5kt 1800shp=9.0kt	1 x 100mm/35	10 x 550mm	–

Name	Class	Builder	Launch	Comp/ comm	Malta arr & dep	Captured Germany/ Japan	Alloc	Handed over	Fate
Alagi	Adua	Cantieri Riuniti dell'Adriatico (Monfalcone)	15 Nov 36	6 Feb 37	16 Sep 43 13 Oct 43	–	–	–	Stricken 23 Mar 47
Alluminio	Flutto, II ser	Odero Terni Orlando (Muggiano)	–	–	–	Muggiano 9 Sep 43	–	–	BU on slip
Alpino Bagnolini = UIT22 (Sep 43)	Liuzzi	Tosi (Taranto)	28 Oct 39	21 Dec 39	–	Bordeaux 9 Sep 43	–	–	GE comm 10 Sep 43; torpedoed HMS/M *Tally-Ho* Malacca Strait (04° 27' N, 100° 11' E) 11 Mar 44
Ambra	Perla	Odero Terni Orlando (Muggiano)	28 May 36	4 Aug 36	–	–	–	–	Scuttled La Spezia 9 Sep 43
Ametista	Sirena	Odero Terni Orlando (Muggiano)	26 Apr 43	1 Apr 34	–	–	–	–	Scuttled off Ancona 12 Sep 43
Ammiraglio Cagni	Cagni	Cantieri Riuniti dell'Adriatico (Monfalcone)	20 Jul 40	1 Apr 41	–	–	–	–	Stricken 1 Feb 48; BU Taranto DYd
Antimonio	Flutto, II ser	Odero Terni Orlando (Muggiano)	–	–	–	Muggiano 9 Sep 43	–	–	BU on slip.
Antonio Bajamonti (ex-N2, ex-Smeli)	YU Smeli	Atéliers & Chantiers de la Loire (Nantes)	1 Dec 28	YU: 2 Dec 29 IT: 17 Apr 41	–	–	–	–	Scuttled La Spezia 9 Sep 43; salved 1949; BU
Aradam	Adua	Cantieri Riuniti dell'Adriatico (Monfalcone)	18 Oct 36	16 Jan 37	–	–	–	–	Scuttled Genoa 9 Sep 43; RSI Oct 43 (not comm); GE 18 Aug 44; salved; bombed Genoa 4 Sep 44
Argo	Argo	Cantieri Riuniti dell'Adriatico (Monfalcone)	27 Nov 36	31 Aug 37	–	–	–	–	Scuttled Monfalcone 11 Sep 43
Atropo	Foca	Tosi (Taranto)	20 Nov 38	14 Feb 39	13 Sep 43 13 Oct 43	–	UK	–	Stricken 23 Mar 47; BU Taranto
Axum	Adua	Cantieri Riuniti dell'Adriatico (Monfalcone)	27 Sep 36	14 Sep 38	20 Sep 43 9 Oct 43	–	–	–	Stranded on W coast of Morea 28 Dec 43; scuttled
Bario = UIT7 (Sep 43) = Pietro Calvi (Dec 61)	Flutto, II ser	Cantieri Riuniti dell'Adriatico (Monfalcone)	23 Jan 44 [21 Jun 59]	[16 Dec 61] –	–	Monfalcone 10 Sep 43			GE; scuttled Monfalcone 1 May 45; salved 1945; stricken 1 Apr 43
Beilul	Adua	Odero Terni Monfalcone Orlando (Muggiano)	22 May 38	14 Sep 38	–	Monfalcone 9 Sep 43	–	–	RSI Oct 43 (not comm); bombed 25 May 44; salved; scuttled 1 May 45; salved after 1945; BU
Brin	Brin	Tosi (Taranto)	3 Apr 38	30 Jun 38	16 Sep 43 13 Oct 43	–	–	–	Stricken 1 Feb 48; BU Tosi (Taranto)
CC1	CC	Caprioni (Taliedo)	–	–	–	–	–	–	BU
Cernia	Flutto, I ser	Tosi (Taranto)	–	–	–	–	–	–	Stricken 6 Jan 44; BU 1944–48

Name	Class	Builder	Launch	Comp/ comm	Malta arr & dep	Captured Germany/ Japan	Alloc	Handed over	Fate
Ciro Menotti	Bandiera	Odero Terni Orlando (Muggiano)	29 Dec 29	29 Aug 30	12 Sep 43 13 Oct 43	–	–	–	Stricken 1 Feb 48; BU Tosi (Taranto)
CM1 = UIT17 (Sep 43) = CM1 (Apr 45)	CM	Cantieri Riuniti dell'Adriatico (Monfalcone)	5 Sep 43	GE: 4 Jan 45	–	Monfalcone 10 Sep 43	–	–	Seized IT Apr 45; stricken 1 Feb 48; BU Taranto DYd
CM2 = UIT18 (Sep 43)	CM	Cantieri Riuniti dell'Adriatico (Monfalcone)	Feb 44	–	–	Monfalcone 10 Sep 43	–	–	Bombed Monfalcone 25 May 44; scuttled; salved; BU
Commandante Cappellini = UIT24 (Sep 43) = I503 (May 45)	Cappelini	Odero Terni Orlando (Muggiano)	14 May 39	23 Sep 39	–	Sabang 10 Sep 43	–	–	GE comm 10 Sep 43; see Tables 2.1/5 & 2.3/4
Cromo	Flutto, II ser	Cantieri Riuniti dell'Adriatico (Monfalcone)	–	–	–	Monfalcone 10 Sep 43	–	–	BU on slip
Dandolo	Marcello	Cantieri Riuniti dell'Adriatico (Monfalcone)	20 Nov 37	25 Mar 38	–	–	US	–	Stricken 23 Mar 47
Dentice	Flutto, I ser	Tosi (Taranto)	–	–	–	–	–	–	Stricken 6 Jan 44; BU 1944–48
Diaspro	Perla	Cantieri Riuniti dell'Adriatico (Monfalcone)	5 Jul 36	22 Aug 36	–	–	–	–	Stricken 1 Feb 48; BU Tosi (Taranto)
Ferro = UIT12 (Sep 43)	Flutto, II ser	Cantieri Riuniti dell'Adriatico (Monfalcone)	22 Nov 43	–	–	Monfalcone 10 Sep 43	–	–	Scuttled 1 May 45
Filippo Corridoni	Bragadin	Tosi (Taranto)	30 Mar 30	17 Nov 31	20 Sep 43 13 Oct 43	–	–	–	Stricken 1 Feb 48; BU Tosi (Taranto)
Fosforo	Flutto, II ser	Odero Terni Orlando (Muggiano)	–	–	–	Muggiano 9 Sep 43	–	–	BU on slip
FR113 (ex-Requin)	FR Requin	Cherbourg DYd	19 Jul 24	FR: 28 May 26 IT: –	–	–	–	–	Scuttled Genoa 9 Sep 43
FR114 (ex-Espadon)	FR Requin	Toulon DYd	28 May 26	FR: 6 Dec 27 IT: –	–	Castellammare di Stabia 13 Sep 43	–	–	Scuttled Castellammare di Stabia 13 Sep 43
FR115 (ex-Dauphin)	FR Requin	Toulon DYd	2 Apr 25	FR: 22 Nov 27 IT: –	–	Puzzuoli 15 Sep 43	–	–	Scuttled Puzzuoli 15 Sep 43
FR118(?) (ex-Henri Poincaré)	FR Archimede	Lorient DYd	10 Apr 29	FR: 23 Dec 31 IT: –	–	Genoa 9 Sep 43	–	–	BU
Francesco Rismondo (ex-N1, ex-Ostvenik)	YU Smeli	Atéliers & Chantiers de la Loire (Nantes)	14 Feb 29	YU:1929 IT: 17 Apr 41	–	Bonifacio 14 Sep 43	–	–	Scuttled Bonifacio 18 Sep 43
Fratelli Bandiera	Bandiera	Canteri Navali Triestini (Monfalcone)	7 Aug 29	10 Sep 30	–	–	–	–	Stricken 1 Feb 48; BU at Brindisi by Salvagno Pietro (Venice)
Galatea	Sirena	Cantieri Riuniti dell'Adriatico (Monfalcone)	5 Oct 33	25 Jun 34	16 Sep 43 13 Oct 43	–	–	–	Stricken 1 Feb 48; BU Tosi (Taranto)
Giada = PV2 (Feb 48) = Giada (Mar 51)	Acciaio	Cantieri Riuniti dell'Adriatico (Monfalcone)	10 Jul 41	6 Dec 41	16 Sep 43 6 Oct 43	–	FR	–	Stricken 1 Feb 48; battery charging vessel; relisted 1 Mar 51; stricken 1 Jan 66
Giovanni Da Procida	Mameli	Tosi (Taranto)	1 Apr 28	19 Jan 29	–	–	–	–	Stricken 1 Feb 48; BU Tosi (Taranto)
Giuseppe Finzi = UIT21	Calvi	Odero Terni Orlando (Muggiano)	29 Jun 35	8 Jan 36	–	Bordeaux 9 Sep 43	–	–	Scuttled Bordeaux 25 Aug 44
Goffredo Mameli (ex-Masaniello)	Mameli	Tosi (Taranto)	9 Dec 26	19 Jan 29	–	–	–	–	Stricken 1 Feb 48; BU Tosi (Taranto)
Grongo = UIT20 (Mar 44)	Flutto, I ser	Odero Terni Orlando (Muggiano)	6 May 43	–	–	–	–	–	Scuttled La Spezia 9 Sep 43; salved; GE/RSI; bombed Genoa 4 Sep 44; saved Mar 47; BU
H1	'H'	Canadian Vickers (Montreal)	16 Oct 16	23 Dec 16	20 Sep 43 13 Oct 43	–	–	–	Stricken 23 Mar 47; BU Naples
H2	'H'	Canadian Vickers (Montreal)	19 Oct 16	15 Dec 16	20 Sep 43 13 Oct 43	–	–	–	Stricken 23 Mar 47; BU Tosi (Taranto)

Name	Class	Builder	Launch	Comp/ comm	Malta arr & dep	Captured Germany/ Japan	Alloc	Handed over	Fate
H4	'H'	Canadian Vickers (Montreal)	17 Apr 17	15 May 17	20 Sep 43 13 Oct 43	–	–	–	Stricken 23 Mar 47; BU Tosi (Taranto)
H6	'H'	Canadian Vickers (Montreal)	23 Apr 17	23 Jul 17	–	Bonifacio 14 Sep 43	–	–	Scuttled Bonifacio 18 Sep 43
Jalea	Argonauta	Odero Terni Orlando (Muggiano)	15 Jun 32	16 Mar 33	13 Sep 43 13 Oct 43	–	–	–	Stricken 1 Feb 48; BU Taranto DYd
Litio = UIT8 (Sep43)	Flutto, II ser	Cantieri Riuniti dell'Adriatico (Monfalcone)	19 Feb 44	–	–	Monfalcone 10 Sep 43	–	–	Bombed Monfalcone 16 Mar 45; scuttled 1 May 45
Luciano Manara	Bandiera	Canteri Navali Triestini (Monfalcone)	5 Oct 29	6 Jun 30	–	–	–	–	Stricken 1 Feb 48; BU Brindisi by Salvagno Pietro (Venice)
Luigi Settembrini	Settem- brini	Tosi (Taranto)	28 Sep 30	25 Jan 32	17 Sep 43 13 Oct 43	–	–	–	Collision W Atlantic (36° 11' N, 19° 45' W) USS Frament 15 Nov 44
Luigi Torelli = UIT25 (Sep 43) = I504 (May 45)	Marconi	Odero Terni Orlando (Muggiano)	6 Jan 40	15 May 40	–	Singapore 10 Sep 43	–	–	GE comm 10 Sep 43; see Tables 2.1/5 & 2.3/4
Manganese	Flutto, II ser	Odero Terni Orlando (Muggiano)	–	–	–	Muggiano 9 Sep 43	–	–	BU on slip
Marcantonio Bragadin (ex-Marcantonio Bragadino)	Bragadin	Tosi (Taranto)	21 Jul 29	16 Nov 31	17 Sep 43 13 Oct 43	–	–	–	Stricken 1 Feb 48; BU Tosi (Taranto)
Marea = Z13 (Feb 48) = N-41 (Feb 49) = S-41 (16 Jun 49)	Flutto, I ser	Cantieri Riuniti dell'Adriatico (Monfalcone)	10 Dec 42	7 May 43	16 Sep 43 6 Oct 43	–	SU	Valona 7 Feb 49	Stricken 1 Feb 48; SU comm 24 Feb 49; stricken 27 Dec 56; BU Novorossysk
Murena = UIT16 (Sep 43)	Flutto, I ser	Odero Terni Orlando (Muggiano)	11 Aor 43	25 Aug 43	–	–	–	–	Scuttled La Spezia 9 Sep 43; salved; GE/RSI; bombed Genoa 4 Sep 44; saved Mar 47; BU
Nautilo = UIT19 (Sep 43) = Sava (1945)	Flutto, I ser	Cantieri Riuniti dell'Adriatico (Monfalcone)	20 Mar 43	26 Jul 43	–	Venice 10 Sep 43	–	–	Bombed Pola 9 Jan 44; salved 1944; to YU 1945; stricken 1971
Nichelio = Z14 (Feb 48) = N-42 (Feb 49) = S-42 (16 Jun 49)	Acciaio	Odero Terni Orlando (Muggiano)	12 Apr 42	30 Jul 42	20 Sep 43 6 Oct 43	–	SU	Valona	Stricken 1 Feb 48; SU comm 24 Feb 49; 7 Feb 49 stricken 12 Mar 58; BU
Onice (ex-Aguilar Tablada, ex-Onice)	Perla	Odero Terni Orlando (Muggiano)	15 Jun 36	1 Sep 36	17 Sep 43 6 Oct 43	–	–	–	Stricken 23 Mar 47; BU Taranto DYd
Otaria (ex-Espadarte)	Glauco	Cantieri Riuniti dell'Adriatico (Monfalcone)	20 Mar 35	10 Oct 35.	–	–	–	–	Stricken 1 Feb 48; BU Tosi (Taranto)
Piombo = UIT13 (Sep 43)	Flutto, II ser	Cantieri Riuniti dell'Adriatico (Monfalcone)	4 Nov 43	–	–	Monfalcone 10 Sep 43	–	–	Scuttled Monfalcone 1 May 45
Platino	Acciaio	Odero Terni Orlando (Muggiano)	1 Jun 41	2 Oct 41	16 Sep 43 6 Oct 43	–	–	–	Stricken 1 Feb 48; BU Taranto
Potassio = UIT10 (Sep 43)	Flutto, II ser	Cantieri Riuniti dell'Adriatico (Monfalcone)	22 Nov 43	–	–	Monfalcone 10 Sep 43	–	–	Scuttled Monfalcone 1 May 45
R3	R	Tosi (Taranto)	7 Sep 46	–	–	–	–	–	BU 14 Nov 56
R4	R	Tosi (Taranto)	30 Sep 46	–	–	–	–	–	BU 14 Nov 56
R5, R6	R	Tosi (Taranto)	–	–	–	–	–	–	Suspended Sep 43; stricken 8 Jan 44; BU on slip
R7 = UIT4 (Oct 43)	R	Cantieri Riuniti dell'Adriatico (Monfalcone)	21 Oct 43	–	–	Monfalcone 10 Sep 43	–	–	Bombed Monfalcone 25 May 44; salved 3 Jun 46; BU 1948
R8 = UIT5 (Oct 43)	R	Cantieri Riuniti dell'Adriatico (Monfalcone)	28 Dec 43	–	–	Monfalcone 10 Sep 43	–	–	Bombed Monfalcone 20 Apr 44; salved 3 Jun 46; BU 1948
R9 = UIT6 (Oct 43)	R	Cantieri Riuniti dell'Adriatico (Monfalcone)	27 Feb 44	–	–	Monfalcone 10 Sep 43	–	–	Bombed Monfalcone 16 Mar 45; salved 1946; BU 1948

Name	Class	Builder	Launch	Comp/ comm	Malta arr & dep	Captured Germany/ Japan	Alloc	Handed over	Fate
R10 = UIT1 (Oct 43)	R	Cantieri Riuniti dell'Adriatico (Monfalcone)	12 Jul 44	–	–	Monfalcone 10 Sep 43	–	–	Scuttled La Spezia 24 Apr 45; salved 1946; BU
R11 = UIT2 (Oct 43) = GR522 (1946)	R	Cantieri Riuniti dell'Adriatico (Monfalcone)	6 Aug 44	–	–	Monfalcone 10 Sep 43	–	–	Scuttled Genoa 24 Apr 45; salved 1946; floating oil tank
R12 = UIT3 (Oct 43) = GR523 (1946)	R	Cantieri Riuniti dell'Adriatico (Monfalcone)	29 Sep 44	–	–	Monfalcone 10 Sep 43	–	–	Scuttled Genoa 24 Apr 45; salved 1946; floating oil tank; BU Ortona 1980s
Rame = UIT11 (Sep 43)	Flutto, II ser	Cantieri Riuniti dell'Adriatico (Monfalcone)	4 Nov 43	–	–	Monfalcone 10 Sep 43	–	–	Scuttled Monfalcone 1 May 45
Reginaldo Giuliani = UIT23 (Sep 43)	Liuzzi	Tosi (Taranto)	3 Dec 39	3 Feb 40	–	Singapore 10 Sep 43	–	–	GE comm 10 Sep 43; bombed SA aircraft S of Cape of Good Hope (41° 28' N, 17° 40' E) 11 Mar 44
Ruggiero Settimo	Settembrini	Tosi (Taranto)	29 Mar 31	25 Apr 32	–	–	–	–	Stricken 23 Mar 47; BU Tosi (Taranto)
S1 (ex-U426) = U426 (Sep 43)	GE Type VIIC	Danzigerwerft (Danzig)	11 Mar 43	26 Jun 43	–	9 Sep 43	–	–	Recommissioned GE Sep 43; scuttled near Audorf 3 May 45
S2 (ex-U746) = U746 (Sep 43)	GE Type VIIC	Schichau (Danzig)	1943	4 Jul 43	–	9 Sep 43	–	–	Recommissioned GE Sep 43; scuttled Geltinger Bight 5 May 45
S3 (ex-U747) = U747 (Sep 43)	GE Type VIIC	Schichau (Danzig)	1943	18 Jul 43	–	9 Sep 43	–	–	Recommissioned GE Sep 43; bombed Hamburg 1 Apr 45
S4 (ex-U429) = U429 (Sep 43)	GE Type VIIC	Danzigerwerft (Danzig)	30 Mar 43	14 Jul 43	–	9 Sep 43	–	–	Recommissioned GE Sep 43; bombed Wilhelmshaven 30 Mar 45
S5 (ex-U748) = U748 (Sep 43)	GE Type VIIC	Schichau (Danzig)	1943	31 Jul 43	–	9 Sep 43	–	–	Recommissioned GE Sep 43; scuttled Rendsburg 3 May 45
S6 (ex-U430) = U430 (Sep 43)	GE Type VIIC	Danzigerwerft (Danzig)	22 Apr 43	4 Aug 43	–	9 Sep 43	–	–	Recommissioned GE Sep 43; bombed Bremen 30 Mar 45
S7 (ex-U749) = U749 (Sep 43)	GE Type VIIC	Schichau (Danzig)	1943	14 Aug 43	–	9 Sep 43	–	–	Recommissioned GE Sep 43; bombed Kiel 4 Apr 45
S8 (ex-U1161) = U1161 (Sep 43)	GE Type VIIC/42–42	Danzigerwerft (Danzig)	1943	25 Aug 43	–	9 Sep 43	–	–	Recommissioned GE Sep 43; scuttled Flensburg 4 May 45
S9 (ex-U750) = U750 (Sep 43)	GE Type VIIC	Schichau (Danzig)	1943	26 Aug 43	–	9 Sep 43	–	–	Recommissioned GE Sep 43; scuttled Flensburg 4 May 45
Serpente (ex-Nautilus)	Argonauta	Tosi (Taranto)	28 Feb 32	12 Nov 32	–	–	–	–	Scuttled off Ancona 12 Sep 43
Silicio	Flutto, II ser	Odero Terni Orlando (Muggiano)	–	–	–	Muggiano 9 Sep 43	–	–	BU on slip
Sirena	Sirena	Cantieri Riuniti dell'Adriatico (Monfalcone)	26 Jan 33	2 Oct 33	–	–	–	–	Scuttled La Spezia 9 Sep 43
Sodio = UIT9 (Sep 43)	Flutto, II ser	Cantieri Riuniti dell'Adriatico (Monfalcone)	16 Mar 44	–	–	Monfalcone 10 Sep 43	–	–	Bombed Monfalcone 16 Mar 45; scuttled 1 May 45
Sparide = UIT15 (Mar 44)	Flutto, I ser	Odero Terni Orlando (Muggiano)	21 Feb 43	7 Aug 43	–	–	–	–	Scuttled La Spezia 9 Sep 43; salved; GE/RSI; bombed Genoa 4 Sep 44; saved Mar 47; BU
Squalo	Squalo	Cantieri Riuniti dell'Adriatico (Monfalcone)	15 Jan 30	10 Oct 30	17 Sep 43 13 Oct 43	–	–	–	Stricken 1 Feb 48; BU Brindisi by Salvagno Pietro (Venice)
Tito Speri	Mameli	Tosi (Taranto)	25 May 28	10 Aug 29	–	–	–	–	Stricken 1 Feb 48; BU Tosi (Taranto)
Topazio	Sirena	Cantiere Navale del Quarnaro (Fiume)	15 May 33	28 Apr 34	–	–	–	–	Bombed in error UK aircraft SE of Sardinia 12 Sep 43
Turchese	Perla	Cantieri Riuniti dell'Adriatico (Monfalcone)	19 Jul 36	21 Sep 36	–	–	–	–	Stricken 1 Feb 48; BU Tosi (Taranto)
Vettor Pisani	Pisani	Canteri Navali Triestini (Monfalcone)	24 Nov 27	16 Jun 26	–	–	–	–	Stricken 23 Mar 47; BU Tosi (Taranto)
Volframo (ex-Stronzio)	Acciaio	Tosi (Taranto)	9 Nov 41	15 Feb 42	–	–	–	–	Scuttled La Spezia 9 Sep 43; salved; bombed La Spezia 1944
Vortice = PV1 (Feb 48) = Vortice (Nov 52)	Flutto, I ser	Cantieri Riuniti dell'Adriatico (Monfalcone)	23 Feb 43	21 Jun 43	14 Sep 43 6 Oct 43	–	FR	–	Stricken 1 Feb 48; battery charging vessel; relisted 1 Nov 52; stricken 1 Aug 67.

Name	Class	Builder	Launch	Comp/ comm	Malta arr & dep	Captured Germany/ Japan	Alloc	Handed over	Fate
Zinco = *UIT14* (Sep 43)	*Flutto*, II ser	Cantieri Riuniti dell'Adriatico (Monfalcone)	4 Nov 43	–	–	Monfalcone 10 Sep 43	–	–	Scuttled Monfalcone 1 May 45
Zoea	*Foca*	Tosi (Taranto)	5 Dec 37	12 Feb 38	17 Sep 43 13 Oct 43	–	–	–	Stricken 23 Mar 47; BU Naples
Zolfo	*Flutto*, II ser	Odero Terni Orlando (Muggiano)	–	–	–	Muggiano 9 Sep 43	–	–	BU on slip

Table 2.2/8. Minelayers

Class	Disp.	Length	Beam	Machinery	Power/speed	Main guns	Mines
Durazzo	680t	66.0m	9.3m	2 x diesel	700bhp=10.0kt	1 x 76mm/40	54
Ostia	615t	62.2m	8.7m	2 x boilers, 2 x VTE	1500ihp=15.0kt	2 x 102mm/35	80

Name	Class	Builder	Launch	Comp/ comm	Malta arr & dep	Captured Germany	Fate
Buccari	*Durazzo*	Castellammare di Stabia DYd	1926	1927	–	–	Scuttled La Spezia 9 Sep 43
Durazzo	*Durazzo*	Castellammare di Stabia DYd	1 Apr 26	1926	–	–	Torpedoed HMS/M *Safari* 22 Jul 43.
Albona (ex-*RD58*, ex-*MT130*) = *Netztender 57* (Sep 43)	AH *MT130* (Table 1.2/5)	Danubius (Porto Ré)	20 Jul 18	31 Jan 20	–	Syros 10 Sep 43	GE netlayer; scuttled Salonika 31 Oct 44
Laurana (ex-*RD59*, ex-*MT131*)	AH *MT130* (Table 1.2/5)	Danubius (Porto Ré)	24 Aug 18	7 Feb 20	–	Venice 11 Sep 43	Bombed UK aircraft Trieste 20 Feb 45; BU 1949
Rovigno (ex-*RD60*, ex-*MT132*) = *Netztender 56* (Sep 43)	AH *MT130* (Table 1.2/5)	Danubius (Porto Ré)	28 Sep 18	16 Jul 20	–	Syros 10 Sep 43	GE netlayer; scuttled Salonika 31 Oct 44
Fasana	*Durazzo*	Castellammare di Stabia DYd	29 Sep	24 Mar 25	–	Trieste 10 Sep 43	GE comm 20 Apr 44; retroceded Jul 45; stricken 1 Sep 50
Pelagosa	*Durazzo*	Castellammare di Stabia DYd	1926	1927	–	–	Scuttled Genoa 9 Sep 43
Azio	*Ostia*	Cantieri Navali Riuniti (Ancona)	4 May 27	1928	–	–	Stricken Jan 57
Legnano	*Ostia*	Cantieri Navali Riuniti (Ancona)	May 26	1927	–	–	Bombed 5 Oct 43
Lepanto = *Okisu* (Mar 44) = *Sien Hing* (1945)	*Ostia*	Cantieri Navali Riuniti (Ancona)	22 May 27	1928	–	–	Scuttled Shanghai 9 Sep 43; salved; JP 1 Mar 44; see Table 2.4/7
Ugliano (ex-*Marjan*, ex-*MT133*, ex-*MTXXXII*) = *M2* (1945) = *M202* = *M32*	*MT130*	Danubius (Porto Ré)	YU: 1931	YU: 1931	–	–	Retroceded Feb 44; stricken 1978
Pasman (ex-*Mosor*, ex-*MT134*, ex-*MTXXXIII*)	*MT130*	Danubius (Porto Ré)	YU: 1931	YU: 1931	–	Sebenico 20 Dec 43	Stranded Kozja Draga Bay 5 Jan 44; stricken 13 Jan 44; BU 1954
Arbe (ex-*Malinska*, ex-*MT135*, ex-*MTXXXIV*)	*MT130*	Danubius (Porto Ré)	YU: 1931	YU: 1931	–	Sebenico 20 Dec 43	RSI Dec 43; scuttled Genoa 24 Apr 45
Solta (ex-*Meljine*, ex-*MT136*, ex-*MTXXXV*) = *M1* (1945) = *M201* = *M31*	*MT130*	Danubius (Porto Ré)	YU: 1931	YU: 1931	–	–	Retroceded Dec 43; stricken 1968
Meleda (ex-*Mljet*, ex-*MT137*, ex-*MTXXXVI*) = *M3* (1945) = *M203* = *M33*	*MT130*	Danubius (Porto Ré)	YU: 1931	YU: 1931	–	–	Retroceded Dec 43; stricken 1968

Table 2.2/9. Minesweepers

Class	Disp.	Length	Beam	Machinery	Power/speed	Main guns
RD1, RD13	196t	35.3m	5.8m	1 x boiler, 1 x VTE	800ihp=13.5kt	1 x 76mm/40
RD7	215t	35.5m	5.9m	1 x boiler, 1 x VTE	950ihp=14.0kt	1 x 76mm/40
RD15	201t	35.3m	5.8m	1 x boiler, 1 x VTE	800ihp=13.0kt	1 x 76mm/40
RD21	201t	36.5m	5.8m	1 x boiler, 1 x VTE	750ihp=14.0kt	1 x 76mm/40
RD27	200t	36.5m	5.9m	1 x boiler, 1 x VTE	950ihp=14.0kt	1 x 76mm/40
RD31	200t	36.5m	5.8m	1 x boiler, 1 x VTE	750ihp=14.0kt	1 x 76mm/40
RD39	203t	33.2m	5.8m	1 x boiler, 1 x VTE	750ihp=14.0kt	1 x 76mm/40
RD45	212t	38.1m	5.8m	1 x boiler, 1 x VTE	816ihp=13.0kt	1 x 76mm/40
RDV101	101t	34.0m	5.8m	2 x petrol	2300bhp=17kt	1 x 20mm

Name	Class	Builder	Launch	Comp/comm	Captured Germany	Fate
Cotrone (ex-Abastro, ex-M120) = Kehrwieder (Sep 43)	GE M1916 (Table 1.1/6)	AG Neptun (Rostock)	24 Jul 18	GE: 20 Sep 18 IT: Feb 21	–	Scuttled La Spezia 1943; salved and GE; bombed 1944; salved 1947; training hulk 1949; stricken Sep 68; BU
D10 (ex-D2, ex-36, ex-Uhu)	Kibitz	Pola DYd	7 Dec 86	AH: 1886 YU: 1920 IT: Apr 41	Sep 43	To GE Sep 43; sank off Kumbor
Eso (ex-Sokol, ex-M144)	GE M1916 (Table 1.1/6)	AG Neptun (Rostock)	19 Mar 19	GE: 20 Jun 19 YU: Jul 21 IT: Apr 41	–	Aircraft torpedo off Djerba Island 19 Jan 43
Oriole (ex-Zuri, ex-Labud, ex-Gavran, ex-M106)	GE M1916 (Table 1.1/6)	Reiherstieg (Hamburg)	8 Jul 18	GE: 21 Mar 19 YU: Jul 21 IT: Apr 41	–	Scuttled after bombing Augusta 10 Jul 43
RD13	RD13	Poli (Chioggia)	2 Jul 17	1 Apr 18	–	Scuttled Viareggio 9 Sep 43
RD16 = ML302 (Aug 48)	RD15	Castellamare di Stabia DYd	29 Mar 17	11 Apr 17	–	Abandoned Trapani 23 Jul 43; to YU; BU 1960
RD17 = M1227 (Sep 43)	RD15	Castellamare di Stabia DYd	22 Apr 17	2 May 17	Piraeus 9 Sep 43	GE comm Sep 43; scuttled 1945?
RD21 = ML303 (Aug 48)	RD21	Castellamare di Stabia DYd	26 Jan 17	14 Jan 18	–	BU 1960
RD22	RD21	Castellamare di Stabia DYd	31 Feb 17	1 Feb 18	–	Mined(?) off Brindisi 25 Oct 43
RD25 = ML304 (Aug 48)	RD21	Castellamare di Stabia DYd	4 Apr 18	29 May 18	–	Abandoned near Messina 16 Aug 43; to YU; BU 1960
RD26 = M1228 (Sep 43)	RD21	Castellamare di Stabia DYd	15 May 18	7 Jun 18	Piraeus 9 Sep 43	Sunk La Spezia 1944?
RD27 = ML305 (Aug 48)	RD27	Tosi (Taranto)	16 Sep 18	3 Oct 18	–	BU 1960
RD28 = ML306 (Aug 48)	RD27	Tosi (Taranto)	18 Jul 18	20 Dec 18	–	BU 1960
RD29 = ML307 (Aug 48)	RD27	Tosi (Taranto)	28 Aug 18	22 Jan 19	–	BU 1960
RD32 = M5332 (1953)	RD31	Castellamare di Stabia DYd	8 Feb 19	22 Feb 19	–	Stricken 30 Jun 56
RD34 = M5334 (1953)	RD31	Castellamare di Stabia DYd	12 May 19	23 Jul 19	–	Stricken 30 Jun 56
RD35 = M1229 (Nov 43)	RD31	Castellamare di Stabia DYd	17 Jul 19	29 Aug 19	Syra 13 Sep 43	RSI Sep 43; GE 15 Nov 43; lost Aegean 1944?
RD40 = M5340 (1953)	RD39	Tosi (Taranto)	16 Oct 19	2 Mar 20	–	Stricken 15 Apr 55
RD41 = M5341 (1953)	RD39	Tosi (Taranto)	12 Feb 19	31 Mar 20	–	Stricken 1 Jan 53
RD49 = TR106 (Sep 43)	RD45	Pattison (Naples)	24 Jan 21	3 Mar 22	La Spezia 9 Sep 43	RSI Sep 43; scuttled Genoa 23 Apr 45
RD6 = ML301 (Aug 47)	RD1	Castellamare di Stabia DYd	26 Oct 16	22 Feb 17	–	BU 1960
RD9 = M1226 (Sep 43)	RD7	Tosi (Taranto)	2 Feb 17	1 Jul 17	Piraeus 9 Sep 43	GE comm Sep 43; bombed Piraeus 11 Jan 44
RDV101 = RD101 (Sep 43)	RDV101	Baglietto (Varazze)		GE: Nov 44	Varazze 9 Sep 43	GE comm 18 Nov 44; scuttled Genoa 24 Apr 45
RDV102 = RD102 (Sep 43) = DV111 (1949) = DV401 (1953)	RDV101	Baglietto (Varazze)		1949	Varazze 9 Sep 43	Scuttled Varazze 24 Apr 45; salved; stricken Jun 58

Name	Class	Builder	Launch	Comp/comm	Captured Germany	Fate
RDV103 = *RD103* (Sep 43) = *DV112* (1949) = *DV402* (1953)	*RDV101*	Baglietto (Varazze)		1949	Varazze 9 Sep 43	Scuttled Varazze 24 Apr 45; salved; salved; stricken Jun 58
RDV104 = *RD104* (Sep 43) = *DV114* (1949) = *DV404* (1953)	*RDV101*	Baglietto (Varazze)		1949	Varazze 9 Sep 43	Scuttled Varazze 24 Apr 45; salved; salved; sricken Jun 59
RDV105 = *RD105* (Sep 43) = *DV115* (1949) = *DV405* (1953)	*RDV101*	Baglietto (Varazze)		1949	Varazze 9 Sep 43	Scuttled Varazze 24 Apr 45; salved; salved; stricken Sep 54
RDV106 = *RD106* (Sep 43)	*RDV101*	Baglietto (Varazze)		–	Varazze 9 Sep 43	Scuttled Varazze 24 Apr 45
RDV107 = *RD107* (Sep 43)	*RDV101*	Baglietto (Varazze)		–	Varazze 9 Sep 43	Scuttled Varazze 24 Apr 45
RDV108 = *RD108* (Sep 43)	*RDV101*	Baglietto (Varazze)		–	Varazze 9 Sep 43	Scuttled Varazze 24 Apr 45
RDV109 = *RD109* (Sep 43)	*RDV101*	Baglietto (Varazze)		GE: Mar 44	Varazze 9 Sep 43	GE comm 29 Mar 44; scuttled Genoa 24 Apr 45
RDV110 = *RD110* (Sep 43)	*RDV101*	Baglietto (Varazze)		GE: May 44	Varazze 9 Sep 43	GE comm 23 May 44; stranded and burnt out Bay of Cecina (43° 18' N, 10° 29' E) after air attack 3 Jun 44
RDV111 = *RD111* (Sep 43)	*RDV101*	Baglietto (Varazze)		GE: Sep 44	Varazze 9 Sep 43	GE comm 3 Sep 44; scuttled Genoa 24 Apr 45
RDV112 = *RD112* (Sep 43)	*RDV101*	Baglietto (Varazze)		GE: Jan 45	Varazze 9 Sep 43	GE comm 12 Jan 45; scuttled Genoa 24 Apr 45
RDV113 = *DV113* (1949) = *DV408* (1953)	*RDV101*	Baglietto (Varazze)		2 Sep 45	Varazze 9 Sep 43	Survey vessel 1959; stricken Sep 65
RDV114 = *RD114* (Sep 43)	*RDV101*	Baglietto (Varazze)		–	Varazze 9 Sep 43	BU after 1945
RDV115 = *RD115* (Sep 43)	*RDV101*	Cantieri Riuniti dell' Adriatico (Monfalcone)		GE: Mar 45	Monfalcone 9 Sep 43	GE comm 16 Mar 45; bombed Monfalcone 16 Mar 45
RDV116 = *RD116* (Sep 43)	*RDV101*	Cantieri Riuniti dell' Adriatico (Monfalcone)		GE: 1944	Monfalcone 9 Sep 43	GE comm 1944; scuttled Tagliamento estuary (45° 39' N, 13° 06' E) 2 May 45
RDV117 = *RD117* (Sep 43)	*RDV101*	Cantieri Riuniti dell' Adriatico (Monfalcone)		–	Monfalcone 9 Sep 43	BU after 1945
RDV118 = *RD118* (Sep 43)	*RDV101*	Cantieri Riuniti dell' Adriatico (Monfalcone)	–		Monfalcone 9 Sep 43	BU after 1945
RDV119 = *RD119* (Sep 43)	*RDV101*	Cantieri Riuniti dell' Adriatico (Monfalcone)		–	Monfalcone 9 Sep 43	BU after 1945
RDV120 = *RD120* (Sep 43)	*RDV101*	Cantieri Riuniti dell' Adriatico (Monfalcone)		–	Monfalcone 9 Sep 43	BU after 1945
RDV121 = *RD121* (Sep 43)	*RDV101*	Cantieri Riuniti dell' Adriatico (Monfalcone)	–		Monfalcone 9 Sep 43	BU after 1945
RDV122 = *RD122* (Sep 43)	*RDV101*	Cantieri Riuniti dell' Adriatico (Monfalcone)	–		Monfalcone 9 Sep 43	BU after 1945
RDV127 = *RD127* (Sep 43)	*RDV101*	Celli (Venice)		GE: Apr 45	Venice 9 Sep 43	GE comm Apr 45; scuttled Monfalcone 30 Apr 45
RDV128 = *RD128* (Sep 43)	*RDV101*	Celli (Venice)		–	Venice 9 Sep 43	Scuttled Monfalcone 30 Apr 45
RDV129 = *RD129* (Sep 43)	*RDV101*	Celli (Venice)		–	Venice 9 Sep 43	Scuttled Monfalcone 30 Apr 45
RDV130 = *RD130* (Sep 43)	*RDV101*	Celli (Venice)		–	Venice 9 Sep 43	Scuttled Monfalcone 30 Apr 45
RDV131 = *RD131* (Sep 43) = *DV121* (1949) = *DV411* (1953)	*RDV101*	Celli (Venice)		Jun 49	Venice 9 Sep 43	Stricken Jan 59
RDV132 = *RD132* (Sep 43) = *DV122* (1949) = *DV412* (1953)	*RDV101*	Celli (Venice)		Jun 49	Venice 9 Sep 43	Stricken Sep 59
RDV133 = *RD133* (Sep 43) = *DV123* (1949) = *DV413* (1953)	*RDV101*	Celli (Venice)		Jun 49	Venice 9 Sep 43	Stricken 1959

Name	Class	Builder	Launch	Comp/comm	Captured Germany	Fate
RDV134 = *RD134* (Sep 43) = *DV124* (1949) = *DV414* (1953)	*RDV101*	Celli (Venice)		Jun 49	Venice 9 Sep 43	Stricken Sep 59
RDV135 = *RD135* (Sep 43)	*RDV101*	Odero Terni Orlando (Leghorn)	—	-	Leghorn 9 Sep 43	Scuttled Leghorn Apr 45; salved; completion abandoned 1948
RDV136 = *RD136* (Sep 43)	*RDV101*	Picchiotti (Limite sul Arno)		1949?	Limite sul Arno 9 Sep 43	Scuttled Limite sul Arno Apr 45
RDV140 = *RD140* (Sep 43)	*RDV101*	Picchiotti (Limite sul Arno)		1949?	Limite sul Arno 9 Sep 43	Scuttled Limite sul Arno Apr 45
RDV141 = *RD141* (Sep 43)	*RDV101*	Soriente (Salerno)	–	–	Venice 9 Sep 43	Construction abandoned 1943
RDV146 = *RD146* (Sep 43)	*RDV101*	Soriente (Salerno)	–	–	Venice 9 Sep 43	Construction abandoned 1943
RDV147 = *RD147* (Sep 43)	*RDV101*	Costaguta (Voltri)	15 Dec 44	–	Venice 9 Sep 43	Scuttled Genoa 25 Apr 45
RDV148 = *RD148* (Sep 43) = *DV148* (1946) = *DV125* (1949) = *DV415* (1953)	*RDV101*	Costaguta (Voltri)	1946		Voltri 9 Sep 43	Stricken Jul 58
RDV149 = *RD149* (Sep 43) = *DV149* (1945) = *DV116* (1949) = *DV409* (1953)	*RDV101*	Costaguta (Voltri)	1945		Voltri 9 Sep 43	Survey vessel 1954; stricken 1965
Selve (ex-*Galeb*, ex-*M100*)	GE M1916 (Table 1.1/6)	Tecklenborg (Geestemünde)	23 May 18	GE: 16 Jun 18 YU: Jul 21 IT: Apr 41	–	Bombed UK aircraft Benghazi 6 Nov 42; BU 1948
Unie (ex-*Kobac*, ex-*M121*)	GE M1916 (Table 1.1/6)	AG Neptun (Rostock)	10 Sep 18	GE: 25 Oct 18 YU: Jul 21 IT: Apr 41	–	Bombed Bizerte 30 Jan 43
Vergada (ex-*Orao*, ex-*M97*) = *Pionir* (Aug 45) = *Zelenogora*	GE M1916 (Table 1.1/6)	Tecklenborg (Geestemünde)	28 Mar 18	GE: 21 Apr 18 YU: Jul 21 IT: Apr 41	–	Retroceded YU 7 Dec 43; stricken 1962
Vieste (ex-*Meteo*, ex-*M119*)	GE M1916 (Table 1.1/6)	AG Neptun (Rostock)	22 Jun 18	GE: 17 Aug 18 IT: Feb 21	–	Constructive total loss off Naples 11 Sep 43; scuttled Naples 1944; BU after 1945
Zirona (ex-*Jastreb*, ex-*M112*)	GE M1916 (Table 1.1/6)	Tecklenborg (Geestemünde)	12 Jan 18	GE: 31 Oct 19 YU: Jul 21 IT: Apr 41	–	Stranded Benghazi 25 Nov 41; scuttled 18 Nov 42; salved 1948; BU

Table 2.2/9. FPBs

Class	Disp.	Length	Beam	Machinery (diesel)	Power/speed	Gun(s)	TT
MAS423	12.6t	16.0m	3.0m	2 x petrol	1500bhp=40.0kt	2 x 6.5mm	2 x 450mm
MAS424	19.0t	16.0m	3.0m	2 x petrol	200bhp=45.0kt	2 x 6.5mm	2 x 450mm
MAS430	13.8t	16.0m	3.3m	2 x petrol	1500bhp=40.0kt	2 x 6.5mm	2 x 450mm
MAS431	12.3t	16.0m	3.9m	2 x petrol	1500bhp=40.0kt	2 x 8mm	2 x 450mm
MAS432	14.1t	16.0m	3.3m	2 x petrol	1500bhp=40.0kt	2 x 6.5mm	2 x 450mm
MAS437	13.7t	16.0m	3.3m	2 x petrol	1500bhp=40.0kt	2 x 6.5mm	2 x 450mm
MAS502	21t	17.0m	4.7m	2 x petrol	2000bhp=41.0kt	1 x 13.2mm	2 x 450mm
MAS510	24t	17.0m	4.4m	2 x petrol	2000bhp=41.0kt	1 x 13.2mm	2 x 450mm
MAS513	24t	17.0m	4.4m	2 x petrol	2000bhp=42.0kt	1 x 13.2mm	2 x 450mm
MAS526	26t	18.7m	4.7m	2 x petrol	2000bhp=41.8kt	1 x 13.2mm	2 x 450mm
MAS536	26t	18.7m	4.7m	2 x petrol	2000bhp=42.0kt	1 x 13.2mm	2 x 450mm
MAS552	23t	18.7m	4.7m	2 x petrol	2000bhp=41.0kt	1 x 13.2mm	2 x 450mm
MAS555	28t	18.7m	4.7m	2 x petrol	2000bhp=41.0kt	1 x 13.2mm	2 x 450mm
MS, I ser	63t	28.0m	4.3m	3 x petrol	3450bhp=33.0kt	2/4 x 20mm/65	2 x 533mm
YU MS	63t	28.0m	4.3m	3 x petrol	3300bhp=32.0kt	2 x 20mm/65	2 x 533mm
MS, II ser	66t	28.0m	4.3m	3 x petrol	3450bhp=33.0kt	2/4 x 20mm/65	2 x 533mm

Name	Class	Builder	Launch	Comp/comm	Malta arr & dep	Captured Germany	Alloc	Handed over	Fate
MAS423	*MAS423*	SVAN (Venice)	Mar 29 9	Mar 29	–	–	–	–	Scuttled Pola 11 Sep 43.; salved; fate uncertain
MAS424 (ii) = *SA17* (1943)	*MAS424*	Baglietto (Varazze)	24 Oct 37	18 Dec 37	–	–	–	–	Scuttled Toulon 9 Sep 43; salved; GE; sunk May 45.

Name	Class	Builder	Launch	Comp/comm	Malta arr & dep	Captured Germany	Alloc	Handed over	Fate
MAS430	MAS430	SVAN (Venice)	1929 11	Sep 29	–	Sebenico Sep 43	–	–	RSI Sep 43; bombed Sebenico 6 Dec 43
MAS431	MAS431	Baglietto (Varazze)	1931	16 Jun 32	–	Sebenico Sep 43	–	–	RSI Sep 43; disappeared in passage Zara–Sebenico Nov 43
MAS432	MAS432	SVAN (Venice)	1930	2 Jul 30	–	–	–	–	Stricken 12 Dec 43; BU Brindisi
MAS433	MAS432	SVAN (Venice)	1930	1930	–	Sebenico Sep 43	–	–	RSI Sep 43; IT 19 Nov 43; stricken 1 Aug 49
MAS434	MAS432	SVAN (Venice)	1930	1930	–	–	–	–	Stricken 1 Aug 49
MAS437 = SA18 (1943)	MAS437	SVAN (Venice)	1934	1 Nov 34	–	–	–	–	Scuttled Toulon 9 Sep 43; salved; GE; sunk May 45
MAS502	MAS502	Baglietto (Varazze)	24 Apr 36	6 Apr 37	–	Voltri 8 Sep 43	–	–	RSI Feb 44; erroneous gunfire GE artillery off Anzio 5 Mar 44; scuttled Follonica Apr 44
MAS504	MAS502	Baglietto (Varazze)	24 Aug 36	20 Jul 37	–	Voltri 8 Sep 43	–	–	RSI Mar 44; rammed HMS Grenville off Anzio 25 Mar 44
MAS505	MAS502	Baglietto (Varazze)	19 Feb 37	9 Jun 37	–	Defected 10 Apr 44	–	–	RSI 10 Apr 44; scuttled Porto Maurizio 24 Apr 45
MAS509	MAS509	Baglietto (Varazze)	15 Feb 36	16 Jun 37	–	–	–	–	Fire Bastia 12 Aug 44
MAS510 = ME B1 = MAS1	MAS510	Cantieri Riuniti dell'Adriatico (Monfalcone)	1936	30 Jan 37	–	–	–	–	Stricken 28 Jun 50
MAS514 = ME B2 = MAS2	MAS513	Cantieri Riuniti dell'Adriatico (Monfalcone)	2 Feb 37	28 Apr 37	–	–	–	–	Stricken 1 Jul 50
MAS515	MAS513	Picchiotti (Limite sull'Arno)	15 Apr 37	21 Jun 37	–	–	–	–	Stricken 1 Oct 45
MAS516 = TK-975 (Jul 49)	MAS513	Picchiotti (Limite sull'Arno),	1937	21 Jan 37	–	–	SU	Odessa Jul 49	To SU; stricken 1950s
MAS517	MAS513	Picchiotti (Limite sull'Arno)	21 Jan 37	27 Apr 37	–	–	–	–	Stricken 16 Dec 44
MAS518	MAS513	Picchiotti (Limite sull'Arno)	19 May 37	21 Jun 37	–	–	–	–	Scuttled Venice 12 Sep 43; salved; BU
MAS519 = TK-976 (Jul 49)	MAS513	Celli (Venice)	1937	9 Aug 37	–	–	SU	Odessa Jul 49	Stricken 18 May 49; to SU; stricken 1950s
MAS520 = ME B3 = MAS3	MAS513	Celli (Venice)	1937	3 Oct 37	–	–	–	–	Stricken 1 Jul 50
MAS521 = ME B4 = MAS4	MAS513	Celli (Venice)	1937	4 Sep 37	–	–	–	–	Stricken 1 Jul 50
MAS522 = S511 (Sep 43)	MAS513	Celli (Venice)	1937	21 Aug 37	–	Defected 18 Sep 43	–	–	To GE 15 Nov 43; bombed off Makronisos 4 Dec 43
MAS523 =MASMT 523 (1944)	MAS513	SACIN	1937	3 Jul 37	–	–	–	–	Stricken 1949
MAS525 = S508 (1943) = ME B9 (1946) = MAS9	MAS513	Cantieri Riuniti dell'Adriatico (Monfalcone)	1937	15 Oct 37	–	–	–	–	Scuttled La Spezia 9 Sep 43; salved; scuttled Genoa 24 Apr 45; salved 1946; stricken 1 Jul 50
MAS531	MAS526	Baglietto (Varazze)	24 May 39	4 Sep 39	–	Bocche de Magra 9 Sep 43	–	–	RSI comm Feb 44; gunfire FR Sabre 11 Dec 44
MAS538 = ME B5 = MAS5	MAS536	Picchiotti (Limite sull'Arno)	1939	29 Dec 39	–	–	–	–	Stricken 1 Jul 50
MAS540 = MASMT 540 (1944)	MAS536	Celli (Venice)	1939	20 May 39	–	–	–	–	Stricken 1 Nov 49
MAS542 = S601 (Aug 44)	MAS536	Celli (Venice)	5 Jul 39	7 Sep 39	–	Piraeus 9 Sep 39	–	–	GE comm 1 Aug 44; bombed Aegean 1944
MAS543 = V782 (Sep 49) = Y782	MAS536	Celli (Venice)	1939	14 Sep 39	–	–	FR 26 Sep 49		To FR; BU 1955
MAS544	MAS536	Celli (Venice)	9 Oct 39	26 Oct 39	–	Portoferraio 16 Sep 43	–	–	RSI comm Mar 44; bombed US aircraft Genoa 1 Sep 44.

Name	Class	Builder	Launch	Comp/comm	Malta arr & dep	Captured Germany	Alloc	Handed over	Fate
MAS545 = MASMT 545 (1944) = ME B6 = MAS6	MAS536	Picchiotti (Limite sull'Arno)	1939	11 Oct 39	–	–	–	–	Stricken 1 Jul 50
MAS546	MAS536	Cantieri Riuniti dell'Adriatico (Monfalcone)	1939	31 Aug 39	–	–	–	–	Mined off Capraia 21 Feb 44
MAS547 = ME B7 = MAS7 = GLV 1 (1950)	MAS536	Cantieri Riuniti dell'Adriatico (Monfalcone)	1939	31 Aug 39	–	–	–	–	Stricken 1 Jul 50; to Coast Guard; stricken 1967; BU
MAS549 = S509 (Sep 43) = MAS549 (Oct 43)	MAS536	Cantieri Riuniti dell'Adriatico (Monfalcone)	1939	1 Sep 39	–	Bocche di Magra 9 Sep 43	–	–	RSI 26 Oct 43; bombed La Spezia 22 May 44
MAS550 = TC1 (1945)	MAS536	Cantieri Riuniti dell'Adriatico (Monfalcone)	23 Sep 39	6 Nov 39	–	Monfalcone 9 Sep 39	–	–	RSI (not comm); to YU 1945; fate uncertain
MAS551 = S510 (Sep 43) = MAS551 (Jan 44)	MAS536	Cantieri Riuniti dell'Adriatico (Monfalcone)	1941	1941	–	Portoferraio 16 Sep 43	–	–	RSI 22 Jan 44; scuttled Imperia 24 Apr 45
MAS553 = S512 (Sep 43) = MAS553 (Jan 45)	MAS552	Cantieri Riuniti dell'Adriatico (Monfalcone)	10 May 41	31 May 41	–	–	–	–	Scuttled Lerici 9 Sep 43; salved; GE; RSI comm Jan 45; scuttled Porto Maurizio 24 Apr 45
MAS554 = S513 (Oct 43) = SA20 (30 Sep 44?)	MAS552	Cantieri Riuniti dell'Adriatico (Monfalcone)	20 May 41	31 May 41	–	Venice 12 Sep 43	–	–	GE comm 12 Oct 43; sunk near Trieste May 45; salved Jul 45; BU
MAS555	MAS555	Picchiotti (Limite sull'Arno)	1940	16 Mar 41	–	–	–	–	Scuttled Leros 12 Nov 43
MAS556	MAS555	Picchiotti (Limite sull'Arno)	7 Mar 41	18 Apr 41	–	La Spezia 9 Sep 43	–	–	RSI comm Feb 44; scuttled Porto Maurizio 24 Apr 45
MAS557	MAS555	Picchiotti (Limite sull'Arno)	7 Mar 41	12 Jun 41	–	Bocche di Magra 9 Sep 43	–	–	RSI comm Mar 44; scuttled Ostia after damage off Anzio 30 Ap 44
MAS558	MAS555	Celli (Venice)	1940	27 Sep 41	–	Varazze 9 Sep 43	–	–	RSI 8 Nov 43; scuttled Trieste 2 May 45
MAS559	MAS555	Celli (Venice)	1941	22 Apr 41	–	Leros 13 Nov 43	–	–	Scuttled Leros 13 Nov 43
MAS561	MAS555	Baglietto (Varazze)	4 Feb 41	24 Feb 41	–	Verazze 9 Sep 43	–	–	RSI 8 Nov 44; sunk US MTBs 23 Apr 45
MAS562 = ME B8 (1 Jul 50) = MAS8 (1954)	MAS555	Baglietto (Varazze)	1941	22 Apr 41	–	Voltri 8 Sep 43	–	–	RSI comm 8 Nov 43; captured US MTBs off Portoferaio 30 Jun 44; IT recommission Sep 44; stricken 1 Jul 50; Guardia Finanza 1954
MS11 = MV 611 (1 Jan 49) = MS611 (1 Nov 52) = MS471 (1 Jan 54)	MS, I ser	Cantieri Riuniti dell'Adriatico (Monfalcone)	31 Jan 42	29 Apr 42	–	–	–	–	Stricken 1 May 65
MS12 (ex-MS13)	MS, I ser	Cantieri Riuniti dell'Adriatico (Monfalcone)	5 Feb 42	1 Jun 42	–	–	–	–	Bombed GE aircraft Stampalia 19 Sep 43
MS15 (ex-MS19)	MS, I ser	Cantieri Riuniti dell'Adriatico (Monfalcone)	2 Feb 42	2 Jun 42	–	–	–	–	Bombed GE aircraft Leros 26 Oct 43
MS16 (ex-MS21)	MS, I ser	Cantieri Riuniti dell'Adriatico (Monfalcone)	3 Feb 42	13 Jun 42	–	–	–	–	Scuttled Voltri 9 Sep 43; to RSI 11 Oct 43 (not comm); bombed Genoa Jan 44
MS21 (ex-MS23)	MS, I ser	Cantieri Riuniti dell'Adriatico (Monfalcone)	27 May 42	13 Jun 42	–	–	–	–	Scuttled after mining off Gaeta 25 Sep 43
MS23 (ex-MS27)	MS, I ser	Cantieri Riuniti dell'Adriatico (Monfalcone)	6 Feb 42	24 Jun 42	–	–	–	–	Bombed GE aircraft Aegean 18 Sep 43
MS24 (ex-MS10) = MV 612 (1 Jan 49) = MS612 (1 Nov 52) = MS472 (1 Jan 54)	MS, I ser	Cantieri Riuniti dell'Adriatico (Monfalcone)	3 Jun 42	24 Jun 42	–	–	–	–	Stricken 1975; preserved Ravenna

Name	Class	Builder	Launch	Comp/comm	Malta arr & dep	Captured Germany	Alloc	Handed over	Fate
MS26 (ex-MS14)	MS, I ser	Cantieri Riuniti dell'Adriatico (Monfalcone)	16 Jun 42	9 Jul 42	–	–	–	–	Stranded off Leros 9 Oct 43
MS31 (ex-MS16) = MV 613 (1 Jan 49) = MS613 (1 Nov 52) = MS473 (1 Jan 54)	MS, I ser	Cantieri Riuniti dell'Adriatico (Monfalcone)	9 Jun 42	16 Jul 42	–	–	–	–	Stricken 1975; preserved Venice
MS32 (ex-MS18)	MS, I ser	Cantieri Riuniti dell'Adriatico (Monfalcone)	18 Jun 42	20 Jul 42	–	–	–	–	Scuttled Viareggio 9 Sep 43
MS33 (ex-MS20)	MS, I ser	Cantieri Riuniti dell'Adriatico (Monfalcone)	23 Jun 42	4 Aug 42	–	–	–	–	GE shore gunfire off Ortona-Pescara 3 Nov 43
MS34 (ex-MS22)	MS, I ser	Cantieri Riuniti dell'Adriatico (Monfalcone)	3 Jul 42	5 Aug 42	–	–	–	–	Scuttled Bocche di Magra; salved; to RSI 25 Nov 43 (not comm); scuttled La Spezia May 45
MS35 (ex-MS24) = V780 (Dec 48)	MS, I ser	Cantieri Riuniti dell'Adriatico (Monfalcone)	4 Jul 42	5 Aug 42	20 Sep 43 4 Oct 43	–	FR	Toulon Dec 48	Stricken 15 Dec 48; to FR; condemned 8 Sep 50
MS36 (ex-MS26)	MS, I ser	Cantieri Riuniti dell'Adriatico (Monfalcone)	10 Jul 42	5 Aug 42	–	–	–	–	Scuttled La Spezia 9 Sep 43
MS41 (ex-MAS3D, ex-Orjen) = S605 (Sep 43?) = MS41 (Feb 44)	YU MS	Lürssen (Vegesack)		1936	–	–	–	–	Scuttled Monfalone 9 Sep 43; salved; RSI Dec 43; mined off Montone estuary 27 Sep 44
MS42 (ex-MAS4D, ex-Velebit) = S601 (Sep 43)	YU MS	Lürssen (Vegesack)		1938	–	Piraeus 9 Sep 43	–	–	GE comm 6 Dec 43; bombed Salonika Oct 44
MS43 (ex-MAS5D, ex-Dinara) = S602 (Sep 43)	YU MS	Lürssen (Vegesack)		1939	–	Crete 9 Sep 43	–	–	GE comm 24 Jan 44; sunk Salonika Oct 44
MS44 (ex-MAS6D, ex-Triglav) = S603 (Sep 43)	YU MS	Lürssen (Vegesack)		1939	–	Crete 9 Sep 43	–	–	GE comm 24 Jan 44; scuttled Salonika Oct 44
MS45 (ex-MAS7D, ex-Suvobor)	YU MS	Lürssen (Vegesack)		1937	–	–	–	–	Scuttled Cattolica 18 Sep 43
MS46 (ex-MAS8D, ex-Rudnik) = S604 (Sep 43)	YU MS	Lürssen (Vegesack)		1939	–	Crete 9 Sep 43	–	–	GE trials 14 Nov 43; scuttled Salonika Oct 44
MS51	MS, II ser	Cantieri Riuniti dell'Adriatico (Monfalcone)	14 Oct 42	15 Feb 43	–	–	–	–	Scuttled Bocche di Magra 9 Sep 43; salved; GE; sunk La Spezia May 45
MS52 = TK-970 (Jul 49)	MS, II ser	Cantieri Riuniti dell'Adriatico (Monfalcone)	17 Oct 42	15 Feb 43	–	–	SU	Odessa 11 May 49	Stricken 11 May 49; to SU; stricken 1950s
MS53 = TK-971 (Jul 49)	MS, II ser	Cantieri Riuniti dell'Adriatico (Monfalcone)	22 Oct 42	9 Mar 43	–	–	SU	Odessa 18 May 49	Stricken 18 May 49; to SU; stricken 1950s
MS54 = MV 614 (1 Jan 49) = MS614 (1 Nov 52) = MS474 (1 Jan 54)	MS, II ser	Cantieri Riuniti dell'Adriatico (Monfalcone)	28 Oct 42	24 Mar 43	23 Sep 43 4 Oct 43	–	–	–	Stricken 1979
MS55 = MV 615 (1 Jan 49) = MS615 (1 Nov 52) = MS481 (1 Jan 54)	MS, II ser	Cantieri Riuniti dell'Adriatico (Monfalcone)	4 Nov 42	23 Mar 43	20 Sep 43 4 Oct 43	–	–	–	Stricken 1979
MS56 = MV 616 (1 Jan 49) = MS616 (1 Nov 52) = MS482 (1 Jan 54)	MS, II ser	Cantieri Riuniti dell'Adriatico (Monfalcone)	11 Nov 42	23 Mar 43	23 Sep 43 4 Oct 43	–	–	–	Stricken 1 Mar 63
MS61 = TK-972 (Jul 49)	MS, II ser	Cantieri Riuniti dell'Adriatico (Monfalcone)	7 Dec 42	12 Apr 43	23 Sep 43 4 Oct 43	–	SU	Odessa Jul 49	Stricken Jul 49; to SU; stricken 1950s
MS63	MS, II ser	Cantieri Riuniti dell'Adriatico (Monfalcone)	22 Dec 42	20 Apr 43	–	Varazze (damaged)	–	–	Scuttled Alto Tirreno Apr 45

Name	Class	Builder	Launch	Comp/comm	Malta arr & dep	Captured Germany	Alloc	Handed over	Fate
MS64	MS, II ser	Cantieri Riuniti dell'Adriatico (Monfalcone)	30 Dec 42	29 Apr 43	20 Sep 43 4 Oct 43	–	–	–	Stricken 21 Jan 47
MS65 = *TK-973* (Jul 49)	MS, II ser	Cantieri Riuniti dell'Adriatico (Monfalcone)	9 Jan 43	14 May 43	–	–	SU	6 Jul 49 Odessa	Stricken 18 May 49; to SU; stricken 1950s
MS71	MS, II ser	Cantieri Riuniti dell'Adriatico (Monfalcone)	5 Mar 43	22 May 43	–	Gaeta 10 Sep 43	–	–	BU
MS72 = *MV 617* (1 Jan 49) = *MS617* (1 Nov 52) = *MS483* (1 Jan 54)	MS, II ser	Cantieri Riuniti dell'Adriatico (Monfalcone)	21 Mar 43	24 May 43	–	–	–	–	Stricken 1 Mar 63
MS73 = *MV 618* (1 Jan 49) = *MS618* (1 Nov 52) = *MS484* (1 Jan 54)	MS, II ser	Cantieri Riuniti dell'Adriatico (Monfalcone)	18 Mar 43	20 Jun 43	–	–	–	–	Stricken 1 Mar 63
MS74 = *MV 619* (1 Jan 49) = *MS619* (1 Nov 52) = *MS485* (1 Jan 54)	MS, II ser	Cantieri Riuniti dell'Adriatico (Monfalcone)	15 May 43	30 Jun 43	–	Venice 12 Sep 43	–	–	To RSI; IT May 45; stricken 1965
MS75 = *S630* (Dec 44) = *MS75* (Feb 44) = *TK-974* (Jul 49)	MS, II ser	Cantieri Riuniti dell'Adriatico (Monfalcone)	18 May 43	30 Jun 43	–	Venice 10 Sep 43	SU	Odessa 6 Jul 49	RSI comm 12 Oct 43; GE 10 Dec 44; surrendered Venice 29 Apr 45; stricken 18 May 49; to SU 6 Jul 49; stricken 1950s
MS76 = *S629* (Feb 44)	MS, II ser	Cantieri Riuniti dell'Adriatico (Monfalcone)	7 Apr 43	GE: 12 Nov 43	–	Monfalcone 10 Sep 43	–	–	RSI comm 25 Nov 43; GE 1 Feb 44; sunk Adriatic Apr 45

Table 2.2/10. Vedette Boats

Class	Disp.	Length	Beam	Machinery	Power/speed	Gun(s)	TT
I ser	63t	28.0m	4.3m	3 x petrol	1920bhp=19.0kt	2 x 20mm	2 x 450mm
II ser	68.5t	28.0m	4.7m	3 x petrol	1750bhp=19.0kt	2 x 20mm	2 x 450mm
III ser	75t	30.0m	4.5m	3 x diesel (*VAS 301–4*) 3 x petrol (*VAS 305–12*)	1500bhp=18.0kt 2300bhp=19.0kt	2 x 20mm	2 x 450mm

Name	Class	Builder	Launch	Comp/ comm	Malta arr & dep	Captured Germany	Alloc	Handed over	Fate
VAS 201 = *VAS 711* (1949)	I ser	Baglietto (Varazze)	1942	1942	20 Sep 43 4 Oct 43	–	–	–	Stricken 1953
VAS 203	I ser	Baglietto (Varazze)	1942	1942	–	–	–	–	Scuttled Varazze 9 Sep 43.
VAS 204 = *VAS 711* (1949) = *VAS 491* (1954)	I ser	Baglietto (Varazze)	1942	1942	20 Sep 43 4 Oct 43	–	–	–	Stricken 1957
VAS 205 = *VAS 716* (1949)	I ser	Baglietto (Varazze)	1942	1942	–	–	–	–	Scuttled Mergellina Sep 43; salved; stricken 1953
VAS 206	I ser	Baglietto (Varazze)	1942	1942	–	–	–	–	Stranded off Capri 13 Feb 44
VAS 207	I ser	Baglietto (Varazze)	1942	1942	–	–	–	–	Scuttled Bocche di Magra 9 Sep 43; salved; sunk La Spezia 1945
VAS 208	I ser	Baglietto (Varazze)	1942	1942	–	–	–	–	Gunfire GE shore artillery Piombino 11 Sep 43; salved 1947; BU
VAS 209	I ser	Picchiotti (Limite sull'Arno)	1942	1942	–	Portoferraio 17 Sep 43	–	–	Sunk Leghorn 1944; salved 1947; BU
VAS 210	I ser	Picchiotti (Limite sull'Arno)	1942	1942	–	Cannes 9 Sep 43	–	–	Fate uncertain
VAS 211 = *VAS 713* (1949) = *VAS 492* (1954)	I ser	Picchiotti (Limite sull'Arno)	1942	1942	–	–	–	–	Stricken 1957
VAS 214	I ser	Picchiotti (Limite sull'Arno)	1942	1942	–	–	–	–	Gunfire GE shore artillery Piombino 11 Sep 43; salved 1946; BU
VAS 215	I ser	Navalmeccanica (Castellammare di Stabia)	26 Mar 42	9 Apr 42	–	Cannes 9 Sep 43	–	–	Fate uncertain
VAS 217	I ser	Navalmeccanica (Castellammare di Stabia)	12 Jun 42	27 Jun 42	–	Portoferraio 17 Sep 43	–	–	Sunk Portoferraio 1944/45
VAS 218 = *VAS 714* (1949) = *VAS 493* (1954)	I ser	Navalmeccanica (Castellammare di Stabia)	7 Jul 42	28 Jul 42	–	Naples 11 Sep 43	–	–	GE; retroceded; stricken 1957

Name	Class	Builder	Launch	Comp/ comm	Malta arr & dep	Captured Germany	Alloc	Handed over	Fate
VAS 219	I ser	Navalmeccanica (Castellammare di Stabia)	22 Sep 42	9 Oct 42	–	–	–	–	Gunfire GE shore artillery Piombino 11 Sep 43; salved 1947; BU
VAS 220	I ser	Navalmeccanica (Castellammare di Stabia)	28 Oct 42	16 Nov 42	–	–	–	–	Gunfire GE shore artillery Piombino 11 Sep 43; salved 1947; BU
VAS 221	I ser	Celli (Venice)	1942	1942	–	Cannes 9 Sep 43	–	–	Fate uncertain
VAS 222 = VAS 715 (1949)	I ser	Celli (Venice)	1942	1942					Stricken 1953
VAS 224 = VAS 721 (1949) = VAS 494 (1954)	I ser	Celli (Venice)	1942	1942	20 Sep 43 4 Oct 43	–	–	–	Stricken 1957.
VAS 225	I ser	Celli (Venice)	1942	1942	–	–	–	–	Scuttled Bocche di Magra 9 Sep 43; salved; fate uncertain
VAS 226	I ser	Celli (Venice)	1942	1942	–	–	–	–	Scuttled Naples 11 Sep 43; salved; sunk Ischia
VAS 227	I ser	Celli (Venice)	1942	1942	–	Cannes 9 Sep 43	–	–	Fate uncertain
VAS 228	I ser	Celli (Venice)	1942	1942	–	–	–	–	Scuttled Portoferraio Sep 43
VAS 232	II ser	Baglietto (Varazze)	1942	1942	–	Portoferraio 17 Sep 43	–	–	Cannibalised; scuttled Portoferraio Sep 43
VAS 233 = VAS 722 (1949) = VAS 495 (1954)	II ser	Baglietto (Varazze)	1942	1942	20 Sep 43 4 Oct 43	–	–	–	Stricken 1957
VAS 234	II ser	Baglietto (Varazze)	1942	1943	–	–	–	–	Gunfire GE MTBs off Gorgona Island 9 Sep 43
VAS 235 = VAS 723 (1949)	II ser	Baglietto (Varazze)	1943	1943	–	–	–	–	Stricken 1953
VAS 236 = RA261 (Sep 43)	II ser	Baglietto (Varazze)	1943	1943	–	–	–	–	Scuttled Portovnere 9 Sep 43; salved; GE; bombed Genoa 5 Sep 44
VAS 237 = VAS 722 (1949) = VAS 495 (1954)	II ser	Picchiotti (Limite sull'Arno)	1942	1942	20 Sep 43 4 Oct 43	–	–	–	Stricken 1957
VAS 238	II ser	Picchiotti (Limite sull'Arno)	1942	1942	–	Leghorn 9 Sep 43	–	–	Scuttled Genoa 25 Apr 45
VAS 239 = RA262 (Sep 43)	II ser	Navalmeccanica (Castellammare di Stabia)	1942	1943	–	Legnana 9 Sep 43	–	–	Bombed off Genoa 5 Sep 44; salved; sunk Genoa 25 Apr 45
VAS 240 = VAS 725 (1949)	II ser	Navalmeccanica (Castellammare di Stabia)	1943	1943	20 Sep 43 4 Oct 43	–	–	–	Stricken 1953
VAS 241 = VAS 726 (1949) = VAS 497 (1954)	II ser	Navalmeccanica (Castellammare di Stabia)	1943	1943	20 Sep 43 4 Oct 43	–	–	–	Stricken 1957
VAS 242	II ser	Navalmeccanica (Castellammare di Stabia)	1943	–	–	–	–	–	Scuttled Castellammare di Stabia Sep 43
VAS 243	II ser	Navalmeccanica (Castellammare di Stabia)	1943	–	–	–	–	–	Scuttled Castellammare di Stabia Sep 43
VAS 244	II ser	Navalmeccanica (Castellammare di Stabia)	1943	1943	–	–	–	–	Sunk Allied MTBs off Salerno 9 Sep 43
VAS 245 = SK-748 (1949)	II ser	Navalmeccanica (Castellammare di Stabia)	1943	1943	20 Sep 43 4 Oct 43	–	SU	Odessa 30 Jun 49	To SU; stricken 1950s
VAS 247	II ser	Celli (Venice)	1943	1943	–	–	–	–	Gunfire GE warships 10 Sep 43
VAS 248 = SK-750 (1949)	II ser	Celli (Venice)	1943	1943	20 Sep 43 4 Oct 43	–	SU	Odessa 30 Jun 49	To SU; stricken 1950s
VAS 301 = RA254 (Sep 43) I	II ser	Ceruasa (Voltri)	17 Jul 42	22 Sep 42	–	Genoa 9 Sep 43	–	–	GE comm 1943; sunk Genoa 25 Apr 45
VAS 302 = RA257 (Sep 43) I	II ser	Ceruasa (Voltri)	16 Sep 42	2 Nov 42	–	Cittaveccia 9 Sep 43	–	–	GE comm 1943; stranded after bomb damage Genoa 2 Aug 44
VAS 303 = RA256 (Sep 43) I	II ser	Ceruasa (Voltri)	16 Sep 42	2 Nov 42	–	Cittaveccia 9 Sep 43	–	–	GE comm 18 Oct 43; constructive total loss bombing off Leghorn 30 Mar 44; stricken 21 Jun 44
VAS 304 = RA255 (Sep 43) I	II ser	Ceruasa (Voltri)	17 Oct 42	27 Jan 43	–	Genoa 9 Sep 43	–	–	GE comm 1943; gunfire UK warships Gulf of Genoa (44° 20' N, 08° 30' E) 21 Aug 44
VAS 305 = RA252 (Sep 43) I	II ser	Ceruasa (Voltri)	24 Dec 42	25 Jun 43	–	Leghorn 9 Sep 43	–	–	GE comm Oct 43; RSI comm May 44; scuttled Genoa 25 Apr 45
VAS 306 = RA251 (Sep 43) I	II ser	Ceruasa (Voltri)	28 Jan 43	14 Aug 43	–	Genoa 9 Sep 43	–	–	GE comm 13 Oct 43; sunk UK warships San Juan Bay (43° 34' N, 07° 04' E) 22 Aug 44.

Name	Class	Builder	Launch	Comp/ comm	Malta arr & dep	Captured Germany	Alloc	Handed over	Fate
VAS 307 = RA253 (Sep 43) I	II ser	Ceruasa (Voltri)	26 Jan 43	GE: 9 Nov 43	–	Voltri 9 Sep 43	–	–	RSI comm Sep 44; scuttled Genoa 24 Apr 45
VAS 308 = RA263 (Sep 43) I	II ser	Ceruasa (Voltri)	9 Feb 43	GE: 9 Dec 43	–	Voltri 9 Sep 43	–	–	RSI comm 16 May 44; sunk Genoa 25 Apr 45
VAS 309 = RA258 (Sep 43) I	II ser	Ceruasa (Voltri)	9 Feb 43	GE: 15 Mar 44	–	Voltri 9 Sep 43	–	–	GE comm 21 Mar 44; sunk Genoa 25 Apr 45
VAS 310 = RA264 (Sep 43) I	II ser	Ceruasa (Voltri)	20 May 43	GE: 1944	–	Voltri 9 Sep 43	–	–	GE comm 1944; sunk Genoa 25 Apr 45
VAS 311 = RA259 (Sep 43) I	II ser	Ceruasa (Voltri)	21 May 43	GE: 1 Jun 44	–	Voltri 9 Sep 43	–	–	GE comm 1943; gunfire UK warships Gulf of Genoa (44° 20' N, 08° 30' E) 21 Aug 44
VAS 312 = RA260 (Sep 43) I	II ser	Ceruasa (Voltri)	13 Apr 43	GE: 16 Jun 44	–	Voltri 9 Sep 43	–	–	GE comm 3 Aug 44; stranded off Cape Mortula 10 Aug 44; scuttled 2 Sep 44.

Table 2.2/11. Major Auxiliary Vessels

Depot/Support Vessels

Class	Disp.	Length	Beam	Machinery	Power/speed	Main guns
Quarnaro	7386t	114.8m	14.8m	3 x boilers, 1 x VTE	2300ihp=12.0kt	3 x 102mm
Anteo	1253t	50.0m	24.0m	2 x boilers, 2 x VYE	800ihp=8.2kt	–

Sail Training Vessels

Class	Disp.	Length	Beam	Machinery	Power/speed	Main guns
Amerigo Vespucci	4083t	82.4m	15.6m	1 x diesel	1900bhp=10.5kt	4 x 76mm/40
Cristiforo Colombo	3513t	78.3m	14.8m	1 x diesel	1600bhp=11.0kt	4 x 76mm/40
YU Jadran	720t	58.2m	8.9m	1 x diesel	...... bhp=8.0kt	–

Name	Builder	Launch	Comp/comm	Captured Germany	Alloc	Handed over	Fate
Quarnaro	Scoglio Ulivi (Pola)	30 Jul 24	8 Jan 27	Genoa 9 Sep 43	–	–	Scuttled Genoa 20 Sep 43; salved 1949; BU
Anteo	Smulders (Schiedam)	20 Dec 12	6 Nov 14	La Spezia 9 Sep 43	UK	–	Sunk La Spezia 1944/45; salved 1946; stricken 30 Apr 54
Amerigo Vespucci	Castellammare di Staba DYd	22 Feb 31	26 May 31	–	–	–	Still in service (2018)
Cristiforo Colombo (ex-Patria) = Dunay (Mar 49)	Castellammare di Staba DYd	4 Apr 28	1 Jul 28	–	SU	Odessa 3 Mar 49	Stricken 12 Feb 19; to SU Mar 49; BU 1963
Marco Polo (ex-Jadran) = Jadran (1946)	Stülcken (Hamburg)	25 Jun 31	YU: 19 Aug 33 IT: Apr 41	Venice Sep 43	–	–	YU 1945; ME 2006; still in service (2018)

✳ 3. The Japanese Navy: 15 August 1945

Table 2.3/1. Capital Ships and Carriers

Class	Disp.	Length	Beam	Machinery	Power/speed	Main guns	Aircraft
Nagato	39,120t	224.9m	33.0m	10 x boilers, 4 x Tu	82,000shp=25.0kt	8 x 16in/45	3
Hosho	7470t	168.1m	22.7m	8 x boilers, 2 xTu	30,000shp=25.0kt	2 x 76mm/40	8
Ryuho	13,360t	215.6m	23.0m	4 x boilers, 2 x Tu	52,000shp=26.5kt	8 x 127mm/40	18
Hiyo	24,140t	219.3m	27.3m	6 x boilers, 2 x Tu	56,250shp=25.5kt	12 x 127mm/40	54
Unryu	17,460t	227.4m	27.0m	8 x boilers, 2 x Tu	152,000shp=34.0kt	12 x 127mm/40	65
Katsuragi	17,260t	227.4m	27.0m	8 x boilers, 2 x Tu	104,000shp=32.0kt	12 x 127mm/40	65
Ibuki	12,500t	205.0m	23.0m	4 x boilers, 2 x Tu	72,000shp=29.0kt	4 x 76mm/60	27

Name	Class	Builder	Launch	Comp/Comm	Surrendered	Fate
Nagato	Nagato	Kure DYd	9 Nov 19	25 Nov 20	Yokosuka	Stricken 15 Sep 45; expended US atom bomb target Bikini Atoll 1 Jul 46; sank 29 Jul 46
Hosho	Hosho	Asano (Yokohama)/ Yokosuka DYd	13 Nov 21	27 Dec 22	Moji	Stricken 5 Oct 45; repatriation 10 Oct 45; decommissioned Jun 46; to Home Ministry 31 Aug 46; BU Hitachi Zosen, Sakurajima to 1 May 47
Ryuho (ex-Tagei)	Ryuho	Yokosuka DYd	16 Nov 33	31 Mar 35	Kure 28 Nov 45	Stricken 30 Nov 45; BU Harima Apr–Sep 46
Junyo (ex-Kashiwara Maru)	Hiyo	Mitsubishi (Nagasaki)	26 Jun 41	3 May 42	Sasebo	Stricken 30 Nov 45; BU Sasebo 1 Jun 46–1 Aug 47
Katsuragi	Katsuragi	Kure DYd	19 Jan 44	15 Aug 44	Sasebo	Repatriation 13 Oct 45; decommissioned Jun 46; stricken 15 Nov 46; to Home Ministry 20 Nov 46; BU Hitachi Zosen, Osaka 22 Dec 46–30 Nov 47.

Name	Class	Builder	Launch	Comp/Comm	Surrendered	Fate
Aso	Katsuragi	Kure DYd	1 Nov 44	–	Kure	BU Sasebo 21 Dec 46–26 Apr 47
Kasagi	Unryu	Mitsubishi (Nagasaki)	19 Oct 44	–	Sasebo	BU Sasebo 1 Sep 46–31 Dec 47
Ikoma	Unryu	Kawasaki (Kobe)	17 Nov 44	–	–	BU Tamano 4 Jul 46–10 Mar 47
Ibuki	Ibuki	Kure DYd/ Sasebo DYd	21 May 43	–	Sasebo	BU Sasebo 22 Oct 46–1 Aug 47

Table 2.3/2. Cruisers

Class	Disp.	Length	Beam	Machinery	Power/speed	Main guns	TT
Yakumo	9646t	132.3m	19.6m	6 x boilers, 2 x VTE	7000ihp/16.0kt	4 x 127mm/40	–
Myoko	13,000t	203.8m	17.3m	12 x boilers, 4 x Tu	130,250shp=33.8kt	10 x 203mm/50	8 x 610mm
Takao	13,400t	203.8m	19.0m	12 x boilers, 4 x Tu	133,100shp=34.2kt	10 x 203mm/50	16 x 610mm
Agano	6652t	174.5m	15.2m	6 x boilers, 4 x Tu	100,000shp=35.0kt	6 x 152mm/50	4 x 610mm
Kuma (mod)	5780t	163.0m	17.5m	12 x boilers, 2 x Tu	35,110shp=23.0kt	4 x 127mm/40	–
Katori	5890t	133.5m	16.6m	3 x boilers, 2 xTu +2 x diesel	4400shp+3600bhp=18.0kt	4 x 140mm/50	–

Name	Class	Builder	Launch	Comp/Comm	Surrendered	Fate
Kashima	Katori	Mitsubish (Yokohama)	25 Sep 39	31 May 40	Kure	Stricken 5 Oct 45; Repatriation Service 1 Dec 45; BU Kawanami Heavy Industries (Koyagishima) 15 Nov 46–15 Jun 47
Kitakami	Kuma (mod)	Sasebo DYd	3 Jul 20	15 Apr 21	Kurahashi-jima	Stricken 30 Nov 45; Sasebo Repatriation Assistance Office 10 Feb 46 (repair ship); BU Nagasaki Oct 46–31 Mar 47
Myoko	Myoko	Yokosuka DYd	16 Apr 27	31 Jul 29	Singapore 21 Sep 45	Scuttled Malacca Strait (03° 05' 06" N, 100° 40' 06" E) 8 Jul 46
Sakawa	Agano	Sasebo DYd	9 Apr 44	30 Nov 44	Maizuru	Stricken 5 Oct 45; Repatriation Service 1 Dec 45; to US 25 Feb 46; expended US atom bomb target Bikini Atoll 1 Jul 46; sank 2 Jul 46
Takao	Takao	Yokosuka DYd	12 May 30	31 May 32	Singapore 21 Sep 45	Scuttled and gunfire HMS Newfoundland Malacca Strait (03° 05' 05" N, 100° 41' 00" E) 27 Oct 46
Yakumo	Yakumo	Vulcan (Stettin)	8 Jul 99	Jun 00	Kure	Stricken 1 Oct 45; Repatriation Service 1 Dec 45; arrived Maizuru 20 Jul 46 to BU by Hitachi to 1 Apr 47

Table 2.3/3 Destroyers

Class	Disp.	Length	Beam	Machinery	Power/speed	Main guns	TT
Akatsuki	1780t	118.4m	10.4m	3 x boilers, 2 x Tu	50,000shp=38.0kt	6 x 127mm/50	9 x 610mm
Akizuki	2743t	134.2m	11.6m	3 x boilers, 2 x Tu	52,000shp=35.5kt	8 x 100mm/65	4 x 610mm
Ayanami	1780t	118.4m	10.4m	4 x boilers, 2 x Tu	50,000shp=38.0kt	6 x 127mm/50	9 x 610mm
Chidori	610t	82.0m	7.4m	2 x boilers, 2 x Tu	11,000shp=28.0kt	2 x 127mm/40	2 x 533mm
Kagero	2032t	118.5m	10.8m	3 x boilers, 2 x Tu	52,000shp=35.5kt	4 x 127mm/50	8 x 610mm
Kamikaze	1400t	102.6m	9.1m	4 x boilers, 2 x Tu	38,500shp=37.0kt	4 x 120mm/45	6 x 533mm
Matsu	1260t	100.0m	9.35m	2 x boilers, 2 x Tu	19,000shp=27.8kt	3 x 127mm/40	2 x 610mm
Minekaze	1367t	102.6m	9.0m	4 x boilers, 2 x Tu	38,500shp=39.0kt	4 x 120mm/45	4 x 533mm
Momi	864t	83.8m	7.9m	3 x boilers, 2 x Tu	21,500shp=36.0kt	3 x 120mm/45	4 x 533mm
Otori	840t	88.5m	8.2m	2 x boilers, 2 x Tu	19,000shp=30.5kt	2 x 120mm/45	3 x 533mm
Tachibana	1350t	100.0m	9.35m	2 x boilers, 2 x Tu	19,000shp=27.3kt	3 x 127mm/40	2 x 610mm
Wakatake	910t	85.5m	7.9m	3 x boilers, 2 x Tu	21,500shp=36.0kt	2 x 120mm/45	2 x 533mm

Name	Class	Builder	Launch	Comp/Comm	Surrendered	Alloc	Fate
Asagao	Wakatake	Ishikawajima	4 Nov 22	10 May 23	–	–	Mined Kanmon Straits 22 Aug 45; salved, BU Jun 48
Hatsukari	Chidori	Fujinagata	19 Dec 33	15 Jul 34	Hong Kong	UK	Stricken; to UK 3 May 47 at Hong Kong; BU
Fuyutsuki	Akizuki	Maizuru DYd	20 Jan 44	25 May 44	Moji		Stricken 20 Nov 45; scuttled as breakwater Kitakyūshū Jul 48
Hagi	Tachibana	Yokosuka DYd	27 Nov 44	1 Mar 45	Kure	UK	Stricken 5 Oct 45; to UK 16 Jul 47; BU Singapore
Hanazuki = DD-934	Akizuki	Maizuru DYd	10 Oct 44	28 Dec 44		US	Stricken 5 Oct 45; to US 29 Aug 47; expended as target off Goto-retto (35° 30' 0" N, 122° 49' 0" E) 3 Feb 48
Harukaze	Kamikaze	Maizuru DYd	18 Dec 22	31 May 23	Sasebo	US	Stricken 10 Nov 45; scuttled as breakwater Takeno Port
Harutsuki = Vnimatelnyi (Aug 47) = Vnezapny (25 Sep 47) = Oskoli (Apr 49) = PKZ-65 (Mar 55) = TsL-64 (Jun 55) = PKZ-37 (Aug 65)	Akizuki	Sasebo DYd	3 Aug 44	28 Dec 44		SU	Stricken 5 Oct 45; to SU 28 Aug 47; SU comm 25 Sep 47; reserve 15 Apr 48; training ship 28 Apr 49; accommodation ship 12 Mar 55; target vessel 2 Jun 55; accommodation ship 27 Aug 65; stricken 4 Jun 69
Hasu	Momi	Uraga Dock	8 Dec 21	31 Jul 22	Tsingtau 16 Sep 45	–	Stricken 12 Oct 45; scuttled as breakwater in Fukui 1946
Hatsuyume = Xin Yang (Jul 47)	Tachibana	Maizuru DYd	25 Apr 45	18 Jun 45	Maizuru	CN	Stricken 5 Oct 45; to CN 6 Jul 47; stricken Dec 61

Name	Class	Builder	Launch	Comp/Comm	Surrendered	Alloc	Fate
Hatsuzakura = *Vetrenny* (Jul 47) = *Vyrazitelny* (2 Oct 47) = *TsL-26* (Jun 49)	*Tachibana*	Yokosuka DYd	10 Feb 45	28 May 45	Yokusuka	SU	Stricken 5 Oct 45; to SU 29 Jul 47 at Nakhodka; target vessel 17 Jun 49; stricken 19 Feb 59
Hibiki = *Vernyi* (Apr 47) = *Dekabrist* (5 Jul 48)	*Akatsuki*	Maizuru DYd	16 Jun 32	31 Mar 33	Maizuru	SU	Stricken 5 Oct 45; Repatriation Service 1 Dec 45; to SU 5 Apr 47; comm 22 Jul 47; stricken 20 Feb 53; expended target off Karamzina Island 1970s
Kaba	*Tachibana*	Fujinagata	27 Feb 45	29 May 45	Kure	US	Stricken 5 Oct 45; to US 4 Aug 47; BU 1 Mar 48
Kaede = *Heng Yang* (Jul 47)	*Matsu*	Yokosuka DYd	25 Jun 44	30 Oct 44	Kure	CN	Stricken 5 Oct 45; to CN 6 Jul 47; training hulk 1 Oct 49; stricken 1960; BU 1962
Kaki	*Tachibana*	Yokosuka DYd	11 Dec 44	5 Mar 45	Maizuru	US	Stricken 5 Oct 45; to US 4 Jul 47; expended as target Yellow Sea (35° 29' N 123° 35' E) 19 Aug 47
Kamikaze	*Kamikaze*	Mitsubishi (Nagasaki)	25 Sep 22	19 Dec 22	Singapore	–	Stricken 5 Oct 45; Repatriation Service 1 Dec 45; stranded off Cape Omaezaki (34° 38' N 138° 8' E.) 7 Jun 46
Kashi	*Matsu*	Fujinagata	13 Aug 44	30 Sep 44	Kure	US	Stricken 5 Oct 45; to US 7 Aug 47; BU 20 Mar 48
Katsura	*Tachibana*	Fujinagata	23 Jun 45	–	–	–	Expended as breakwater
Kaya = *Volevoy* (1947) = *TsL-23* (Jun 49) = *OT-61* (Jun 58)	*Matsu*	Maizuru DYd	30 Jul 44	30 Sep 44	Kure	SU	Stricken 5 Oct 45; to SU 5 Jul 47; comm 22 Jul 47; target vessel 17 Jun 49; heating hulk 10 Jun 58; stricken 1 Aug 59
Keyaki	*Matsu*	Yokosuka DYd	30 Sep 44	15 Dec 44	Yokusuka	US	Stricken 5 Oct 45; to US 5 Jul 47; expended as target off Bōsō Peninsula (34° 44' N, 140° 01' E) 29 Oct 47
Kiji = *Vnimatelnyi* (Oct 47)	*Otori*	Mitsui (Tamano)	26 Jan 37	31 Jul 37	Surabaya	SU	Stricken 5 Oct 45; to SU 3 Oct 47; comm 21 Oct 47; trials vessel 17 Jun 49; stricken 31 Oct 57
Kiri = *Vozrozhdionny* (Jul 47) = *TsL-25* (Jun 49) = *PM-65* (3 Oct 57)	*Matsu*	Yokosuka DYd	27 May 44	14 Aug 44	Kure	SU	Stricken 5 Oct 45; to SU 29 Jul 47 at Nakhodka; target ship 17 Jun 49; stricken 20 Dec 69
Kuri	*Momi*	Kure DYd	19 Mar 20	30 Apr 20	Tsingtau	–	Mined off Pusan 8 Oct 45
Kusunoki	*Tachibana*	Yokosuka DYd	8 Jan 45	28 Apr 45	Maizuru	UK	Stricken 5 Oct 45; to UK; BU
Kuzu	*Matsu*	Yokosuka DYd	–	–	–	–	BU
Maki	*Matsu*	Maizuru DYd	10 Jun	44 10 Aug 44	Kure	UK	Stricken 5 Oct 45; to UK 14 Aug 47; BU Singapore 1947
Mitaka (ex-*Sumire*)	*Momi*	Ishikawajima	14 Dec 21	31 Mar 23	–	–	BU Mar 48
Namikaze = *Shen Yang* (Oct 47)	*Minekaze*	Maizuru DYd	24 Jun 22	11 Nov 22	Maizuru	CN	Stricken 5 Oct 45; Repatriation Service 1 Dec 45; to CN 3 Oct 47; BU 1960
Nara	*Matsu*	Fujinagata (Osaka)	12 Oct 44	26 Nov 44	Moji	–	Stricken 5 Oct 45; BU 1 Jul 48
Natsuzuki	*Akizuki*	Sasebo DYd	2 Dec 44	8 Apr 45	Moji	UK	Stricken 5 Oct 45; to UK 25 Aug 47; BU Uraga 1948
Nire	*Tachibana*	Maizuru DYd	25 Nov 44	31 Jan 45	Kure	–	Stricken 5 Oct 45; BU 1948
Odake	*Tachibana*	Maizuru DYd	10 Mar 45	15 May 45	Maizuru	US	To US 14 Jul 47; target Yellow Sea (35° 29' N 122° 52' E), 17 Sep 47
Sawakaze	*Minekaze*	Mitsubishi (Nagasaki)	7 Jan 19	6 Mar 20	Yokusuka	–	Stricken 15 Sep 45; BU 1948
Shii = *Volny* (Jul 47) = *TsL-24* (Jun 49) = *OT-5* (11 Nov 59)	*Tachibana*	Maizuru DYd	13 Jan 45	13 Mar 45	Kure	SU	Stricken 5 Oct 45; to SU 5 Jul 47; comm 22 Jul 47; target ship 17 Jun 49; stricken 8 Aug 60
Sugi = *Hui Yang* (Jul 47)	*Matsu*	Fujinagata	3 Jul 44	25 Aug 44	Kure	CN	Stricken 5 Oct 45; to CN 6 Jul 47; stricken 11 Nov 54; BU
Sumire	*Tachibana*	Yokosuka DYd	27 Dec 44	28 Mar 48	Maizuru	UK	To UK 23 Aug 47; expended target off Hong Kong 1947
Suzutsuki	*Akizuki*	Mitsubishi (Nagasaki)	3 Mar 42	29 Dec 42	Sasebo		Stricken 20 Nov 45; scuttled as breakwater Kitakyūshū Jul 48
Take	*Matsu*	Yokosuka DYd	28 Mar 44	16 Jun 44	Maizuru	UK	Stricken 5 Oct 45; to UK 16 Jul 47; BU Singapore 1948
Tochi	*Tachibana*	Maizuru DYd	28 May 45	–	–	–	Expended breakwater
Tomariura Kaibōkan No. 2 (ex-*Ashi*)	*Momi*	Kawasaki (Kobe)	3 Sep 21	29 Oct 21		–	BU 1947
Tsubaki	*Matsu*	Maizuru DYd	30 Sep 44	30 Nov 44	Kure	–	Stricken 5 Oct 45; BU 28 Jul 48
Tsuta = *Hua Yang* (Jul 47)	*Tachibana*	Yokosuka DYd	2 Nov 44	8 Feb 45	Kure	CN	Stricken 5 Oct 45; to CN 31 Jul 47; stricken 11 Nov 54
Ushio	*Ayanami*	Uraga Dock	17 Nov 30	14 Nov 31	Yokosuka	–	Stricken 15 Sep 45; BU Aug 48
Yadake	*Matsu*	Yokusuka DYd	1 May 45	–	–	–	Expended breakwater 1948
Yoizuki = *Fen Yang* (Aug 47)	*Akizuki*	Uraga Dock	25 Sep 44	31 Jan 45	Kure	CN	Stricken 5 Oct 45; Repatriation Service 1 Dec 45; to CN 29 Aug 47; training hulk 1 Oct 49; BU 1963
Yukaze	*Minekaze*	Mitsubishi (Nagasaki)	28 Apr 21	24 Aug 21	Inland Sea	UK	Stricken 5 Oct 45; Repatriation Service 1 Dec 45; to UK 14 Aug 47; BU Singapore
Yukikaze = *Tan Yang* (Jul 47)	*Kagero*	Sasebo DYd	24 Mar 39	20 Jan 40	Kure	CN	Stricken 5 Oct 45; Repatriation Service 1 Dec 45; to CN 6 Jul 47; decommissioned 16 Nov 66; BU 1970–71.

Table 2.3/4. Submarines

Class	Disp.	Length	Beam	Machinery	Power/speed	Main gun(s)	TT	Mines	Aircraft
Ha101	429/493t	44.5m	6.1m	1 x diesel 1 x electric	400bhp=10.0kt 150shp=5.0kt	–	–	–	–
Ha201	377/440t	53.0m	4.0m	1 x diesel 1 x electric	400bhp=10.5kt 1250shp=13.0kt	1 x 77mm/80	2 x 533mm	–	–
I13 [Type AM]	3603/4762t	113.7m	11.7m	2 x diesel 2 x electric	4400bhp=16.7kt 600shp=5.5kt	1 x 140mm/40	6 x 533mm	–	2
I15 [Type B1]	2589/3654t	108.7m	9.3m	2 x diesel 2 x electric	12,400bhp=23.6kt 2000shp=8.0kt	1 x 140mm/40	6 x 533mm	–	1
I46 [Type C2]	2557/3564t	109.3m	9.1m	2 x diesel 2 x electric	11,000bhp=25.6kt 2000shp=8.0kt	1 x 140mm/40	8 x 533mm	–	–
I52 [C3]	2564/3644t	108.7m	9.3m	2 x diesel 2 x electric	4700bhp=17.7kt 1200shp=6.5kt	1 x 140mm/40	6 x 533mm	–	–
I54 [Type B3]	2607/3688t	108.7m	9.3m	2 x diesel 2 x electric	4700bhp=17.7kt 1200shp=6.5kt	1 x 140mm/40	6 x 533mm	–	1
I21 [Type KRS]	1383/1768t	85.2m	7.5m	2 x diesel 2 x electric	2400bhp=14.5kt 1100shp=7.0kt	1 x 140mm/40	4 x 533mm	–	–
I53 [Type KD3A]	1800/2300t	100.6m	8.0m	2 x diesel 2 x electric	6800bhp=20.0kt 1800shp=8.0kt	1 x 120mm/45	8 x 533mm	–	–
I61 [Type KD4]	1720/2300t	97.7m	7.8m	2 x diesel 2 x electric	6000bhp=20.0kt 1800shp=8.5kt	1 x 120mm/45	6 x 533mm	–	–
I201 [Type ST]	1291/1450t	79.0m	5.8m	2 x diesel 2 x electric	2750bhp=15.8kt 5000shp=19.0kt	2 x 25mm/60	4 x 533mm	–	–
I361 [Type D1]	1779/2215t	73.5m	8.9m	2 x diesel 2 x electric	1750bhp=13kt 1200shp=6.5kt	1 x 140mm/40	–	–	–
I400 [Type STo]	5223/6560t	122.0m	12.0m	2 x diesel 2 x electric	7700bhp=18.7kt 2400shp=6.5kt	1 x 140mm/40	8 x 533mm	–	3
Ro35 [Type K6]	1115/1447t	80.5m	7.1m	2 x diesel 2 x electric	4200bhp=19.7kt 1200shp=8.0kt	1 x 76mm/40	4 x 533mm	–	–
Ro60 [Type L4]	996/1322t	76.2m	7.4m	2 x diesel 2 x electric	2400bhp=16.5kt 1600shp=9.0kt	1 x 76mm/40	6 x 533mm	–	–

Name	Class	Builder	Launch	Comp/Comm	Surrendered	Fate
I1	I13 [Type AM]	Kawasaki (Kobe)	10 Jun 44	–	–	Foundered Kobe 18 Sep 45; salved and BU 1947
I14	I13 [Type AM]	Kawasaki (Kobe)	14 May 44	14 Mar 45	At sea 27 Aug 45	Stricken 15 Sep 45; torpedo target USS/M Bugara off Pearl Harbor (21° 13' N, 158° 08' W) 28 May 1946
I15	I13 [Type AM]	Kawasaki (Kobe)	12 Apr 44	–	–	BU 1945
I36	I15 [Type B1]	Yokosuka DYd	1 Nov 41	30 Sep 42	Kure 2 Sep 45	Stricken 30 Nov 45; scuttled off Goto-retto (32° 37' N, 129° 17' E) 1 Apr 46
I47	I46 [Type C2]	Sasebo DYd	29 Sep 43	10 Jul 44	Kure 2 Sep 45	Stricken 30 Nov 45; scuttled off Goto-retto (32° 37' N, 129° 17' E) 1 Apr 46
I53	I52 [Type C3]	Kure DYd	24 Dec 42	15 Feb 44	Otsushima	Stricken 30 Nov 45; gunfire USS Nereus off Goto-retto (32° 37' N, 129° 17' E) 1 Apr 46
I58	I54 [Type B3]	Yokosuka DYd	9 Oct 43	7 Sep 44	At sea	Stricken 30 Nov 45; scuttled off Goto-retto (32° 37' N, 129° 17' E) 1 Apr 46
I121 (ex-I21, ex-48)	I21 [i] [Type KRS]	Kawasaki (Kobe)	30 Mar 26	31 Mar 27	Maizuru	Stricken 30 Nov 45; scuttled off Maizuru Bay 30 Apr 46
I153 (ex-I53, ex-64)	I53 [Type KD3A]	Kure NY	5 Aug 25	30 Mar 27	Hirao	Stricken 20 Nov 45; BU 1948
I154 (ex-I54, ex-77)	I53 [Type KD3A]	Sasebo NY	15 Mar 26	15 Dec 27	Kure	Stricken 20 Nov 45; scuttled Inland Sea May 46
I155 (ex-I55, ex-78)	I53 [Type KD3A]	Kure NY	2 Sep 25	5 Sep 27	Kure	Stricken 20 Nov 45; gunfire HMAS Quiberon and HMIS Sutlej Inland Sea 9 May 46
I156 (ex-I56)	I56 [Type KD3B]	Kure NY	23 Mar 28	31 Mar 29	Kure 2 Sep 45	Stricken 30 Nov 45; scuttled off Goto-retto (32° 37' N, 129° 17' E) 1 Apr 46.

Name	Class	Builder	Launch	Comp/Comm	Surrendered	Fate
I157 (ex-I157)	I56 [Type KD3B]	Kure NY	1 Oct 28	24 Dec 29	Kure 2 Sep 45	Stricken 30 Nov 45; scuttled off Goto-retto (32° 37' N, 129° 17' E) 1 Apr 46
I158 (ex-I158)	I56 [Type KD3B]	Yokusuka NY	3 Oct 25	15 May 28	Kure 2 Sep 45	Stricken 30 Nov 45; scuttled off Goto-retto (32° 37' N, 129° 17' E) 1 Apr 46
I159 (ex-I159)	I56 [Type KD3B]	Yokusuka NY	25 Mar 29	31 Mar 30	Kure 2 Sep 45	Stricken 30 Nov 45; scuttled off Goto-retto (32° 37' N, 129° 17' E) 1 Apr 46
I162 (ex-I62)	I61 [Type KD4]	Mitsubishi (Kobe)	29 Nov 28	24 Apr 30	Kure	Stricken 30 Nov 45; scuttled off Goto-retto (32° 37' N, 129° 17' E) 1 Apr 46
I201	I201 [Type ST]	Kure DYd	22 Jul 44	2 Feb 45	Maizuru	Stricken 30 Nov 45; torpedo target USS/M Queenfish off Pearl Harbor (21° 13' N, 158° 08' W) 23 May 46
I202	I201 [Type ST]	Kure DYd	2 Sep 44	12 Feb 45	Maizuru	Stricken 30 Nov 45; scuttled off Kongo (Kougo) Point 5 Apr 46
I203	I201 [Type ST]	Kure DYd	20 Oct 44	29 May 45		Stricken 30 Nov 45; torpedo target USS/M Caiman off Hawaii (21° 13' N, 158° 08' W) 21 May 46
I205	I201 [Type ST]	Kure DYd	15 Feb 45	–	Kure	BU Jul 48
I206	I201 [Type ST]	Kure DYd	26 Mar 45	–	Kure	Foundered Kobe 25 Aug 45; salved and BU Nov 46
I207	I201 [Type ST]	Harima (Harima)	–	–	–	BU Apr 46
I208	I201 [Type ST]	Harima (Harima)	–	–	–	BU Apr 46
I363	I361 [Type D1]	Kure DYd	12 Dec 43	8 Jul 44	Kure 2 Sep 45	Mined off Miyazaki 29 Oct 45; stricken 10 Nov 45; salved 26 Jan 66; BU Etajima
I366	I361 [Type D1]	Mitsubishi (Kobe)	9 Mar 44	3 Aug 44	Kure 2 Sep 45	Stricken 30 Nov 45; scuttled off Goto-retto (32° 37' N, 129° 17' E) 1 Apr 46
I367	I361 [Type D1]	Mitsubishi (Kobe)	28 Apr 44	15 Aug 44	Kure 2 Sep 45	Stricken 30 Nov 45; scuttled off Goto-retto (32° 37' N, 129° 17' E) 1 Apr 46
I369	I361 [Type D1]	Yokosuka DYd	9 Mar 44	9 Oct 44	Yokosuka 30 Aug 45	Stricken 15 Sep 45; BU Yokusuka 1946
I400	I400 (STo)	Kure DYd	18 Jan 44	30 Dec 44	At sea 27 Aug 45	Stricken 15 Sep 45; torpedo target USS/M Trumpetfish off Pearl Harbor (21° 13' N, 158° 07' W) 4 Jun 46
I401	I400 (STo)	Sasebo DYd	11 Mar 44	8 Jan 45	At sea 29 Aug 45	Stricken 15 Sep 45; torpedo target USS/M Cabezon off Pearl Harbor (21° 12' N, 158° 07' W) 31 May 46
I402	I400 (STo)	Sasebo DYd	5 Sep 44	24 Jul 45	Kure 2 Sep 45	Stricken 30 Nov 45; gunfire target USS Everett F Larson and Goodrich off Goto-retto (32° 37' N, 129° 17' E) 1 Apr 46
I501 (ex-U181)	GE IXD2 (Table 2.1/5)	Deschimag [Weser] (Bremen)	30 Dec 41	GE: 9 May 42 JP: 15 Jul 45	Singapore 16 Aug 45	Stricken 30 Nov 45; scuttled gunfire HMS Loch Lomond and Loch Glendhu Malacca Strait (03° 05' 30" N, 100° 41' 30" E) 15 Feb 46
I502 (ex-U862)	GE IXD2 (Table 2.1/5)	Deschimag [Weser] (Bremen)	5 Jun 43	GE: 7 Oct 43 JP: 15 Jul 45	Singapore 16 Aug 45	Stricken 30 Nov 45; scuttled gunfire HMS Loch Lomond and Loch Glendhu Malacca Strait (03° 05' N, 100° 38' 45" E) 15 Feb 46
I503 (ex-UIT24 ex-Commandante Capelli)	IT Cappelini (Table 2.2/7)	Odero-Terni-Orlando (Muggiano)	14 May 39	IT: 23 Sep 39 GE: 10 Sep 43 JP: 10 May 45	Kobe 30 Aug 45	Stricken 30 Nov 45; scuttled Kii Suido 16 Apr 46
I504 (ex-UIT25 ex-Luigi Torelli)	IT Marcello (Table 2.2/7)	Odero-Terni-Orlando (Muggiano)	6 Jan 40	IT:15 May 40 JP: 10 Sep 43	Kobe 30 Aug 45	Stricken 30 Nov 45; scuttled Kii Suido 16 Apr 46
I505 (ex-U219)	GE XB (Table 2.1/5)	Germania (Kiel)	6 Oct 42	GE: 12 Dec 42 JP: 15 Jul 45	Tanjong Priok 12 Sep 45	Stricken 30 Nov 45; scuttled gunfire HrMS Kortenaer S of Sunda Strait (006° 31' S, 104° 54.5' E) 3 Feb 46
I506 (ex-U195)	GE IXD1 (Table 2.1/5)	Deschimag [Weser] (Bremen)	8 Apr 42	GE: 5 Sep 42 JP: 15 Jul 45	Surabaya Oct 45	Stricken 30 Nov 45; scuttled gunfire HMS Sussex, E of Kangean Island (006° 50' S, 114° 42' E) 15 Feb 46
Ro50	Ro35 [Type K6]	Tamano (Tamano)	27 Nov 43	31 Jul 44	Maizuru Sep 45	Stricken 30 Nov 45; scuttled off Goto-retto (32° 37' N, 129° 17' E) 1 Apr 46
Ro62 (ex-73)	Ro60 [Type L4]	Mitsubishi (Kobe)	19 Sep 23	24 Jul 24	Maizuru Sep 45	Stricken 20 Nov 45: gunfire HMAS Quiberon and HMIS Sutlej Inland Sea May 45
Ro63 (ex-48)	Ro60 [Type L4]	Mitsubishi (Kobe)	24 Jan 24	20 Dec 24	Maizuru Sep 45	Stricken 20 Nov 45: gunfire HMAS Quiberon and HMIS Sutlej Inland Sea May 45
Ro67	Ro60 [Type L4]	Mitsubishi (Kobe)	18 Mar 26	15 Dec 26	Sasebo	(hulk) BU 1946
Ro68	Ro60 [Type L4]	Mitsubishi (Kobe)	23 Feb 25	29 Oct 25	Maizuru Sep 45	Stricken 30 Nov 45: scuttled off Maizuru Bay 30 Apr 46
Ro500 (ex-U511)	GE IXC (Table 2.1/5)	Deutsche Werft (Hamburg)	22 Sep 41	16 Sep 43 (GE: 8 Dec 41)	Maizuru Sep 45	Stricken 10 Oct 45; scuttled Wasaka Bay (nr Maizuru) 30 Apr 46
Ha101	Ha101	Kawasaki (Tanagawa)	22 Aug 44	22 Nov 44	Yokosuka	Stricken 15 Sep 45; BU Uraga Dockyard (Tokyo) Oct 45
Ha102	Ha101	Mitsubishi (Kobe)	22 Aug 44	6 Dec 44	Yokosuka	Stricken 15 Sep 45; BU Uraga Dockyard (Tokyo) Oct 45
Ha103	Ha101	Mitsubishi (Kobe)	21 Oct 44	3 Feb 45	Kure	Stricken 30 Nov 45; scuttled off Goto-retto (32° 30' N, 128° 40' E) 1 Apr 46
Ha104	Ha101	Kawasaki (Tanagawa)	30 Sep 44	1 Dec 44	Yokusaka	Stricken 15 Sep 45; scuttled off Shimizi Oct 45
Ha105	Ha101	Mitsubishi (Kobe)	31 Oct 44	19 Feb 45	Kure	Stricken 30 Nov 45; scuttled off Goto-retto (32° 37' N, 129° 17' E) 1 Apr 46

Name	Class	Builder	Launch	Comp/Comm	Surrendered	Fate
Ha106	Ha101	Kawasaki (Tanagawa)	30 Oct 44	15 Dec 44	Kure	Stricken 30 Nov 45; scuttled off Goto-retto (32° 37' N, 129° 17' E) 1 Apr 46
Ha107	Ha101	Kawasaki (Tanagawa)	20 Dec 44	7 Feb 45	Maizuru	Stricken 30 Nov 45; scuttled off Goto-retto (32° 37' N, 129°17' E) 1 Apr 46
Ha108	Ha101	Kawasaki (Tanagawa)	28 Dec 44	6 May 45	Maizuru	Stricken 30 Nov 45; scuttled off Goto-retto (32° 37' N, 129° 17' E) 1 Apr 46
Ha109	Ha101	Mitsubishi (Kobe)	10 Jan 45	10 Mar 45	Matsuura	Stricken 30 Nov 45; scuttled off Goto-retto (32° 37' N, 129° 17' E) 1 Apr 46
Ha110	Ha101	Kawasaki (Tanagawa)/ Kawasaki (Kobe)	12 Jan 45	–	Kobe	Scuttled off Kii Suido 15 Apr 46
Ha111	Ha101	Mitsubishi (Kobe)	2 Mar 45	13 Jul 45	Saeki	Stricken 30 Nov 45; scuttled off Goto-retto (32° 37' N, 129° 17' E) 1 Apr 46
Ha112	Ha101	Mitsubishi (Kobe)	15 Apr 45	–	Kobe	Scuttled off Kii Suido 15 Apr 46
Ha201	Ha201	Sasebo DYd	23 Apr 45	30 May 45	Sasebo	Stricken 30 Nov 45; gunfire target USS *Everett F Larson* & *Goodrich* off Goto-retto (32° 37' N, 129° 17' E) 1 Apr 46
Ha202	Ha201	Sasebo DYd	23 Apr 45	31 May 45	Sasebo	Stricken 30 Nov 45; scuttled off Goto-retto (32° 37' N, 129° 17' E) 1 Apr 46
Ha203	Ha201	Sasebo DYd	25 May 45	20 Jun 45	Sasebo	Stricken 30 Nov 45; scuttled off Goto-retto (32° 37' N, 129° 17' E) 1 Apr 46
Ha204	Ha201	Sasebo DYd	1 Jun 45	25 Jun 45	Sasebo	Stranded Aburatsu Bay Oct 45; stricken 30 Nov 45; BU Nishimura Tekkosho Ironworks Aug–Oct 48
Ha205	Ha201	Sasebo DYd	14 May 45	3 Jul 45	Sasebo	Stricken 30 Nov 45; gunfire HMAS *Quiberon* and HMIS *Sutlej* Inland Sea 9 May 46
Ha206	Ha201	Kawasaki (Tanagawa)	10 Jul 45	–	Senshu	Foundered Senshu 25 Aug 45; salved Apr 46; scuttled off Kii Suido Channel 6 May 46; salved 1952; BU Kawasaki (Kobe)
Ha207	Ha201	Sasebo DYd	26 May 45	14 Aug 45	Sasebo	Stricken 30 Nov 45; scuttled Sasebo Bay 5 Apr 46
Ha208	Ha201	Sasebo DYd	26 May 45	4 Aug 45	Sasebo	Stricken 30 Nov 45; scuttled off Goto-retto (32° 37' N, 129° 17' E) 1 Apr 46
Ha209	Ha201	Sasebo DYd	31 May 45	4 Aug 45	Hikoshima	Purposely stranded Ganryu Jima Island 18 Aug 45; blown up 11 Nov 45; stricken 30 Nov 45; salved and BU Mitsubishi (Hikoshima) Aug–Nov 47
Ha210	Ha201	Sasebo DYd	10 Jun 45	11 Aug 45	Sasebo	Stricken 30 Nov 45; scuttled Sasebo Bay 5 Apr 46
Ha211	Ha201	Kawasaki (Tanagawa)	24 Apr 46	–	Tanagawa	BU 1946
Ha212	Ha201	Kawasaki (Tanagawa)	25 Jun 45	–	Tanagawa	BU 1946
Ha213	Ha201	Kawasaki (Tanagawa)	29 Jul 45	–	Tanagawa	BU 1946
Ha214	Ha201	Kawasaki (Tanagawa)	15 Aug 45	–	Tanagawa	BU 1946
Ha215	Ha201	Sasebo DYd	15 Jun 45	–	Sasebo	Stricken 30 Nov 45; scuttled Sasebo Bay 5 Apr 46
Ha216	Ha201	Sasebo DYd	19 Jun 45	16 Aug 45	Sasebo	Stricken 30 Nov 45; scuttled Sasebo Bay 5 Apr 46
Ha217	Ha201	Sasebo DYd	26 Jun 45	–	Sasebo	Stricken 30 Nov 45; scuttled Sasebo Bay 5 Apr 46
Ha218	Ha201	Sasebo DYd	2 Jul 45	–	Sasebo	Stricken 30 Nov 45; scuttled Sasebo Bay 5 Apr 46
Ha219	Ha201	Sasebo DYd	12 Jul 45	–	Sasebo	Stricken 30 Nov 45; scuttled Sasebo Bay 5 Apr 46
Ha220	Ha201	Kawasaki (Tanagawa)	–	–	–	BU 1946
Ha221	Ha201	Kawasaki (Kobe)	4 Aug 45	–	Kobe	BU 1946
Ha222 –Ha227	Ha201	Kawasaki (Tanagawa)	–	–	–	BU 1946
Ha228	Ha201	Sasebo DYd	18 Jul 45	–	Sasebo	Stricken 30 Nov 45; scuttled Sasebo Bay 5 Apr 46
Ha229	Ha201	Sasebo DYd	27 Jul 45	–	Sasebo	BU 1946
Ha230	Ha201	Sasebo DYd	1946	–	Sasebo	BU 1946
Ha231, Ha232	Ha201	Sasebo DYd	–	–		BU 1946
Ha233	Ha201	Kawasaki (Tanagawa)	–	–		BU 1946
Ha234	Ha201	Kawasaki (Kobe)	–	–		BU 1946
Ha235	Ha201	Kawasaki (Tanagawa)	–	–		BU 1946
Ha236	Ha201	Kawasaki (Kobe)	–	–		BU 1946
Ha237–Ha240	Ha201	Mitsubishi (Kobe)	–	–		BU 1946
Ha246–Ha247	Ha201	Kawasaki (Tanagawa)	–	–		BU 1946.

Table 2.3/5. Minelayers

Class	Disp.	Length	Beam	Machinery	Power/speed	Main guns	Mines
Sokuten/Harashima	750t	73.3m	7.9m	2 x Diesels	3600bhp=20.0kt	1 x 76mm	120
Hatsutaka	1890t	90.9m	11.3m	3 x boilers, 2 x Tu	6000shp=20.0kt	2 x 76mm	360
Kamishima	800t	73.3m	7.9m	2 x Diesels	1900bhp=16.5kt	2 x 40mm	120

Name	Class	Builder	Launch	Comp/Comm	Surrendered	Alloc	Fate
Awashima	*Kamishima*	Sasebo DYd	1945	18 Apr 46	Sasebo	US	Stricken 15 Sep 45; Repatriation Service 3 Apr 46; to US 1 Oct 47; BU
Ishizaki	*Harashima*	Mitsubishi (Hiroshima)	13 Aug 41	28 Feb 42	Yokosuka	US	Stricken 30 Nov 45; Minesweeping Service 1 Dec 45; hulked Sasebo Jul 46; to US 1 Oct 47; BU Tsingtau
Kamishima = *Katun* (Oct 47)	*Kamishima*	Sasebo DYd	12 Jun 45	30 Jul 45	Yokosuka	SU	Stricken 15 Sep 45; Repatriation Service 1 Dec 45; to SU at Nakhodka 3 Oct 47; stricken 9 Nov 56; BU
Kyosai	*Sokuten*	Ishikawajima	29 Jun 39	27 Dec 39	Uraga	UK	Stricken 5 Sep 45; Repatriation Service 1 Dec 45; to UK 20 Nov 47; BU by Tohoku Shiogama to 31 March 1948
Niizaki	*Harashima*	Mitsui (Tamano)	2 Mar 42	31 Aug 42	Hong Kong	–	Damaged by mine off Muroran 4 Oct 45; stricken 5 Oct 45; BU 1947
Saishu = *Yung Ching* (Oct 47)	*Harashima*	Osaka Iron Works (Sakurajima)	5 Aug 41	25 Apr 42	Hong Kong	CN	Stricken 22 Oct 45; Repatriation Service 1 Dec 45; to CN at Tsingtau 3 Oct 47; stricken 1964; BU
Wakataka = *Laburnum* (Sep 49) = *Singapura* (5 May 67)	*Hatsutaka*	Harima	12 Jul 41	30 Nov 41	Surabaya	UK	Stricken 1 Mar 46; repatriation; to UK 17 Oct 47; Malayan Navy Volunteer Force Sep 49; Royal Malayan Navy Aug 52; paid off 1956; Singapore Naval Volunteer Force 1 Jan 66; sold 1968; BU

Table 2.3/6. Minesweepers

Class	Disp.	Length	Beam	Machinery	Power/speed	Main guns
W-1	610t	76.2m	8.0m	3 x boilers, 2 x VTE	4000ihp=20.0kt	2 x 120mm/45
W-7	640t	72.5m	7.9m	2 x boilers, 2 x VTE	3850ihp=20.0kt	3 x 120mm/45
W-17	578t	72.5m	7.9m	2 x boilers, 2 x Tu	3200shp=19.0kt	2 x 120mm/45
W-19	648t	72.5m	7.9m	2 x boilers, 2 x Tu	3250shp=20.0kt	3 x 120mm/45
UK *Bangor*	643t	52.3m	8.7m	2 x boilers, 2 x VTE	2400ihp=16.0kt	1 x 120mm/45

Name	Class	Builder	Launch	Comp/Comm	Alloc	Fate
W-4	*W-1*	Sasebo DYd	24 Apr 24	29 Apr 25	–	Scuttled off Singapore 11 Jul 46.
W-8	*W-7*	Uraga Dock	28 May 38	15 Feb 39	–	Scuttled off Singapore 10 Jul 46.
W-17	*W-17*	Hitachi (Sakurajima)	3 Aug 35	15 Jan 36	–	Stricken 20 Nov 45; BU Sasebo 1 Apr 48
W-21	*W-19*	Harima	28 Feb 41	30 Jun 42	US	Stricken 25 Oct 45; Repatriation Service 1 Dec 45; to US 1 Oct 47 at Tsingtao; expended gunnery target Yellow Sea (35° 19' N, 123° 31' E) 7 Oct 47
W-23 = *T-28* (Oct 47) = *TsL-28* (Jul 48) = *PM-61* (Mar 55)	*W-19*	Ishikawajima	13 Jan 43	31 Mar 43	SU	Stricken 30 Nov 45; to SU 3 Oct 47; target ship 5 Jul 48; repair ship 12 Mar 55; stricken 7 Mar 86; BU
W-102 (ex-*Waglan*, ex-*Seaford*)	UK *Bangor*	Taikoo (Hong Kong)	20 Mar 43	28 Sep 44	–	Stricken 30 Nov 45; Allied Minesweeping Service 1 Dec 45; retro-ceded UK 20 Nov 47; BU Uraga Dockyard (Tokyo) from 31 Mar 48.

Table 2.3/7. Patrol, Escort and Gun Vessels

Class	Disp.	Length	Beam	Machinery	Power/speed	Main guns	TT
Type A	874t	77.7m	9.1m	2 x diesel	4200bhp=19.5kt	3 x 120mm/45	–
Type A (Mod)	884t	77.7m	9.1m	2 x diesel	4200bhp=19.7kt	3 x 120mm/45	–
Type B, Type B (Mod)	955t	77.7m	9.1m	2 x diesel	4400bhp=19.5kt	3 x 120mm/45	–
Type C	757t	67.5m	8.4m	2 x diesel	1900bhp=16.5kt	2 x 120mm/45	–
Type D	752t	67.5m	8.6m	2 x boilers, 1 x Tu	1900bhp=17.5kt	2 x 120mm/45	–
NL *Fazant*	623t	48.0m	6.9m	2 x boilers, 1 x VTE	525ihp=12.0kt	1 x 76mm/40	–
NL *Valk*	775t	70.1m	8.8m	2 x boilers, 2 x VTE	3350ihp=15.0kt	1 x 76mm/40	–
NL *Van Galen*	1316t	81.8m	9.5m	4 x boilers, 2 x Tu	31,000shp=36.0kt	2 x 76mm/40	–
UK 'S'	1168t	84.1m	8.2m	2 x boilers, 2 x Tu	10,000shp=25.0kt	2 x 13mm/40	4 x 610mm + 2 x 533mm
US *Clemson*	1707t	98.7m	9.1m	3 x boilers, 2 x Tu	38,500shp=26.0kt	2 x 76mm/40	4 x 450mm
CN *Yat Sen*	1520t	83.8m	10.3m	3 x boilers, 2 x VTE	2800ihp = 16.0kt	1 x 76mm/40	–
Ataka	725t	68.0m	9.7m	2 x boilers, 1 x VTE	1700ihp = 16.0kt	1 x 120mm/45	–

Name	Class	Builder	Launch	Comp/Comm	Alloc	Fate
Aguni	Type B (Mod)	Nihon Kōkan (Tsurumi)	12 Sep 44	2 Dec 1944	–	Stricken 30 Nov 45; BU Maizuru from 20 May 48
Amami	Type B (Mod)	Nihon Kōkan (Tsurumi)	30 Nov 44	8 Apr 45	UK	Stricken 5 Oct 45; Repatriation Service 1 Dec 45; to UK 10 Dep 47; BU Mitsubishi (Hiroshima) from 20 Dec 47; hull pontoon to 1982
Atada (ex-Yat Sen) = Yi Hsein (Aug 46)	CN Yat Sen	Kaingnan (Shanghai)	12 Nov 30	CN: Dec 30 JP: 1938	–	Retroceded CN 25 Aug 46; stricken 1960s
Ataka (ex-Nakoso) = CN An Tung (1945)	Ataka	Yokohama	11 Apr 22	Aug 23	CN	To CN Aug 45; stricken 1970s
Chikubu = Chikubu Maru (Dec 47) = Atsumi (Jan 49)	Type B (Mod)	Uraga Dock (Tokyo)	24 Nov 44	31 Dec 44	–	Stricken 30 Nov 45; minesweeper; MTB weather ship 26 Dec 47; MSA 1 Jan 49; sold to BU 4 Oct 62
Daito	Type B (Mod)	Hitachi (Sakurajima)	24 Jun 44	7 Aug 44	–	Stricken 20 Nov 45; minesweeper; mined Tsushima Strait (33° 59' N, 129° 35' E) 16 Nov 45
Etorofu	Type A (Mod)	Hitachi (Sakurajima)	29 Jan 43	25 Mar 43	US	Stricken 5 Oct 45; Repatriation Service 1 Dec 45; to US 5 Aug 47; BU Kure from 13 Oct 47
Fukue	Type A (Mod)	Uraga Dock (Tokyo)	2 Apr 43	15 Jul 43	UK	Stricken 5 Oct 45; Repatriation Service 1 Dec 45; to UK 16 Jul 47; BU
Habushi	Type B (Mod)	Mitsui (Tamano)	20 Nov 44	10 Jan 45	US	Stricken 5 Oct 45; Repatriation Service 1 Dec 45; to US 4 Sep 47; BU from 17 Oct 47
Habuto	Type B (Mod)	Hitachi (Sakurajima)	28 Feb 45	7 Apr 45	UK	Stricken 23 Oct 45; Repatriation Service 1 Dec 45; to UK 16 Jul 47 at Singapore; BU
Hachijo	Type A	Sasebo DYd	10 Apr 40	31 Mar 41	–	Stricken 30 Nov 45; BU Maizuru to 30 Apr 48
Hodaka	Type B (Mod)	Uraga dock	28 Jan 45	30 Mar 45	US	Stricken 5 Oct 45; Repatriation Service 1 Dec 45; to US 19 Jul 47; BU Uraga from 1 Mar 48
Ikuna = Okija (Dec 45)	Type B (Mod)	Hitachi (Sakurajima)	4 Sep 44	15 Oct 44	–	Stricken 30 Nov 45; minesweeper 1 Dec 45; minesweeper tender 10 Jul 46; MTB weather ship 26 Dec 47; MSA 1 Jan 49; sold to BU 25 May 63
Ikuno = EK-41 (Aug 47) = TsL-41 (1948) = Val (1949)	Type B (Mod)	Uraga Dock (Tokyo)	11 Mar 45	17 Jul 45	SU	Stricken 15 Sep 45; Repatriation Service 1 Dec 45; to SU 29 Jul 47 at at Nakhodka; comm 26 Aug 47; target ship 1948; oceanographic research ship 1949; stricken 1 Jun 61; BU
Iwo	Type B (Mod)	Maizuru DYd	12 Feb 45	24 Mar 45	–	Stricken 5 Oct 45; Repatriation Service 1 Dec 45; accommodation ship Senzaki Apr 46; BU Sasebo from 2 Jul 48
Kaibōkan No. 8	Type D	Mitsubishi Nagasaki	11 Jan 44	29 Feb 44	UK	Stricken 5 Oct 45; Repatriation Service 1 Dec 45; to UK 16 Jul 47; BU
Kaibōkan No. 12	Type D	Yokosuka DYd	22 Mar 44	14 Apr 44	US	Stricken 30 Nov 45; minesweeper; to US 5 Sep 47; BU 10 Sep–30 Nov 47
Kaibōkan No. 14 = Jie-6 = Tsin An (Jul 47) = Wu Chang (1949)	Type D	Yokosuka DYd	27 Mar 44	5 May 44	CN	Stricken 30 Nov 45; to CN 6 Jul 47; CNP 1949; stricken 1986; BU
Kaibōkan No. 16	Type D	Yokosuka DYd	31 Mar 44	25 Apr 44	UK	Stricken 30 Nov 45; Repatriation Service 1 Dec 45; to UK 14 Aug 47 Singapore; BU
Kaibōkan No. 22	Type D	Mitsubishi (Nagasaki)	27 Jan 44	24 Apr 44	US	Stricken 30 Nov 45; minesweeper 1 Dec 45; to US 5 Sep 47; BU Sasebo 20 Oct–31 Dec 47
Kaibōkan No. 26	Type D	Mitsubishi (Nagasaki)	11 Apr 44	31 May 44	US	Stricken 30 Nov 45; minesweeper 1 Dec 45; to US 6 Sep 47; BU 7 Sep–13 Oct 47
Kaibōkan No. 27	Type C	Nihon Kōkan (Tsurumi)	3 Jun 44	20 Jul 44	UK	Stricken 15 Sep 45; Repatriation Service 1 Dec 45; to UK 14 Aug 47; BU Singapore
Kaibōkan No. 29	Type C	Nihon Kōkan (Tsurumi)	26 Jun 44	8 Aug 44	–	Stricken 20 Nov 45; BU Sasebo from 1 Mar 48
Kaibōkan No. 32	Type D	Mitsubishi (Nagasaki)	10 May 44	30 Jun 44	UK	Stricken 5 Oct 45; repatriation; to UK 16 Jul 47; BU
Kaibōkan No. 34 = EK-32 (1947) = TsL-63 (1954) = PM-75 (1957)	Type D	Tōkyō (Ishikawajima)	25 Aug 44	4 Nov 44	SU	Stricken 5 Oct 45; Repatriation Service 1 Dec 45; to SU 5 Jul 47; comm 22 Jul 47; target ship 30 Dec 54; repair ship 1957; stricken 23 Jul 58; BU.
Kaibōkan No. 36	Type D	Fujinagata	21 Oct 44	28 Dec 44	US	Stricken 5 Oct 45; Repatriation Service 1 Dec 45; to US 19 Jul 47; BU Tsurumi 1 Feb–1 Mar 48
Kaibōkan No. 37	Type C	Nihonkai Dock	5 Aug 44	3 Nov 44	US	Stricken 15 Sep 45; Repatriation Service; to US 4 Sep 47; BU Osaka from 30 Oct 47
Kaibōkan No. 40 = Cheng An (Aug 47)	Type D	Fujinagata	22 Dec 44	1 Feb 45	CN	Stricken 30 Nov 45; minesweeper 1 Dec 45; to CN 29 Aug 47; stricken 1963
Kaibōkan No. 44	Type D	Mitsubishi (Nagasaki)	7 Jul 44	31 Aug 44	US	Stricken 5 Oct 45; Repatriation Service 1 Dec 45; to US 5 Jul 47; expended target off Oshima (34° 48' N, 139° 42' E) 25 Aug 47
Kaibōkan No. 48 = EK-42 (Aug 47) = TsL-42 (1948) = Abakan (1949)	Type D	Fujinagata	30 Jul 44	13 Mar 45	SU	Stricken 30 Nov 45; minesweeper 1 Dec 45; to SU 28 Aug 47 at Nakhodka; target ship 1948; dispatch vessel 1949; stricken 2 Jun 59; BU

Name	Class	Builder	Launch	Comp/Comm	Alloc	Fate
Kaibōkan No. 49	Type C	Nihon Kōkan (Tsurumi)	15 Oct 44	16 Nov 44	US	Stricken 30 Nov 45; minesweeper; to US 1 Sep 47; BU Shimizu from 1 Feb–2 Aug 48
Kaibōkan No. 50	Type D	Tōkyō (Ishikawajima)	13 Oct 44	5 Dec 44	–	Stricken 20 Nov 45; BU Osaka by 5 May 48
Kaibōkan No. 52 = EK-36 (1947) = Naryn (1954)	Type D	Mitsubishi (Nagasaki)	7 Aug 44	25 Sep 44	SU	Stricken 5 Oct 45; Repatriation Service 1 Dec 45; to SU 29 Jul 47 at Nakhodka; comm 26 Aug 47; dispatch vessel 1954; stricken 11 Mar 58; BU
Kaibōkan No. 55	Type C	Nihon Kōkan (Tsurumi)	4 Nov 44	20 Dec 44	UK	Stricken 5 Oct 45; Repatriation Service 1 Dec 45; to UK 16 Jul 47; BU
Kaibōkan No. 57	Type C	Nihon Kōkan (Tsurumi)	15 Nov 44	13 Jan 45	–	Stricken 5 Oct 45; Repatriation Service 1 Dec 45; expended breakwater at Ube May 48
Kaibōkan No. 58	Type D	Fujinagata	15 Ap 45	8 Apr 46	US	Repatriation 8 Apr 46; to US 31 Jul 47; BU Sasebo to 30 Nov 47
Kaibōkan No. 59	Type C	Nihon Kōkan (Tsurumi)	2 Feb 45	5 Apr 45	–	Stricken 5 Oct 45; Repatriation Service 1 Dec 45; foundered after collision with wreck of Hyūga, Kure, 30 Jul 46; salved 9 Nov 47; BU
Kaibōkan No. 60	Type D	Kawasaki (Kobe)	9 Nov 44	16 Dec 44	UK	Stricken 5 Oct 45; Repatriation Service 1 Dec 45; to UK 14 Aug 47; BU
Kaibōkan No. 61	Type C	Maizuru Naval Arsenal	15 Sep 44	20 Nov 45	–	Stricken 5 Mar 47; BU Saigon
Kaibōkan No. 62	Type D	Hitachi Zōsen (Mukōjima)	1945	–	–	Foundered Kure 14 Jan 46; salved 27 Mar 46; BU from 31 May 48 by Amakusa Kaiji
Kaibōkan No. 67 = Ying Kou (Jul 47) = Rui An (1955)	Type C	Maizuru Naval Arsenal	12 Nov 44	28 Dec 44	CN	Stricken 25 Oct 45; Repatriation Service 1 Dec 45; to CN 6 Jul 47; stricken 1963
Kaibōkan No. 71 = EK-43 (Sep 47) = West (1948) = Ostrovnoy (1953)	Type C	Nihon Kōkan (Tsurumi)	12 Mar 45	20 May 45	SU	Stricken 5 Oct 45; Repatriation Service 1 Dec 45; to SU 28 Aug 47; comm 25 Sep 47; oceanographic research ship 1948; stricken 31 Jan 64; BU
Kaibōkan No. 76 = EK-44 (1947) = TsL-44 (1948), = SKR-49 (1954)	Type D	Mitsubishi (Nagasaki)	23 Dec 44	20 Feb 45	CN	Stricken 30 Nov 45; minesweeper 1 Dec 45; to SU 28 Aug 47 at Nakhodka; comm 25 Sep 47; target ship 1948; patrol ship 1954; to CNP 25 Jun 55
Kaibōkan No. 77 = EK-45 (Sep 47) = TsL-45 (1948) = PM-63 (1955).	Type C	Nihon Kōkan (Tsurumi)	31 Mar 45	Aug 45	SU	Stricken 30 Nov 45; minesweeper 1 Dec 45; to SU 28 Aug 47; comm 25 Sep 47; target ship 1948; repair ship 1955; stricken 25 Jan 69; BU
Kaibōkan No. 78 = EK-37 (1947) = Murgab (1954)	Type D	Kawasaki (Senshū)	1945	4 Apr 46	SU	Repatriation Service 4 Apr 46; to SU 29 Jul 47 at Nakhodka; comm 16 Aug 47; dispatch vessel 1954; stricken 11 Mar 58; BU
Kaibōkan No. 79 = EK-39 (Sep 47) = TsL-39 (1948) = Sozh (1949).	Type C	Nihon Kōkan (Tsurumi)	6 May 45	16 Jul 45	SU	Stricken 5 Oct 45; Repatriation Service 1 Dec 45; to SU 29 Jul 47 at Nakhodka; comm 26 Sep 47; target ship 1948; oceanographic research ship 1949; stricken 30 Aug 60; BU
Kaibōkan No. 81 = Huang An (Aug 47) = Sheng Yang (1949)	Type C	Maizuru Naval Arsenal	15 Dec 44	25 Jan 45	CN	Stricken 5 Oct 45; Repatriation Service 1 Dec 45; to CN 29 Aug 47, CNP 13 Feb 49; stricken 1980
Kaibōkan No. 83	Type C	Kyōwa Zōsen/ Naniwa Dock	16 Jan 45	–	–	BU from 17 Mar 48
Kaibōkan No. 85 = Ji An (Jul 47)	Type C	Nihon Kōkan (Tsurumi)	27 Jan 45	31 May 45	CN	Stricken 25 Oct 45; Repatriation Service 1 Dec 45; to CN 6 Jul 47, CNP 23 Apr 49; bombed Yanziji, 28 Apr 49
Kaibōkan No. 87	Type C	Nihon Kōkan (Tsurumi)	20 May 45	20 May 45	US	Stricken 5 Oct 45; Repatriation Service 1 Dec 45; to US 29 Jul 47 at Tsingtau; BU from 1 Mar 48
Kaibōkan No. 89	Type C	Nihonkai Dock	3 May 45	–		BU Toyama Nov 47
Kaibōkan No. 95	Type C	Nihon Kōkan (Tsurumi)	14 Apr 45	4 Jul 45	–	Stricken 15 Sep 45. BU Tsurumi from 20 Jul 48
Kaibōkan No. 97	Type C	Nihon Kōkan (Tsurumi)	25 May 45	16 Dec 45	–	Stricken 1 Apr 46. BU Kure from 27 Oct 47
Kaibōkan No. 102 = EK-46 (1947) = TsL-46 (1948)	Type D	Mitsubishi (Nagasaki)	4 Dec 44	20 Jan 45	SU	Stricken 30 Nov 45; minesweeper; to SU 28 Aug 47; comm 25 Sep 47; target ship 1948; stricken 21 Jan 60; BU
Kaibōkan No. 104 = Tai An (Aug 47)	Type D	Mitsubishi (Nagasaki)	16 Dec 44	31 Jan 45	CN	Stricken 30 Nov 45; minesweeper; to CN 29 Aug 47; stricken 1963
Kaibōkan No. 105 = EK-34 (Jul 47) = TsL-34 (1948) = Khersones (1949)	Type C	Nihon Kōkan (Tsurumi)	Jan 46	15 Apr 46	SU	Repatriation 1946; to SU 5 Jul 47; comm 22 Jul 47; target ship 1948; oceanographic research ship 1949; stricken 3 Dec 60; BU
Kaibōkan No. 106	Type D	Tōkyō (Ishikawajima)	14 Jan 45	5 Mar 44	US	Stricken 5 Oct 45; Repatriation Service 1 Dec 45; to US 5 Jul 47; expended target off Oshima (34° 45' N, 139° 44' E) 21 Jul 47
Kaibōkan No. 107 = Chao An (Aug 47)	Type C	Nihon Kōkan (Tsurumi)	16 Mar 46	30 May 46	CN	Repatriation 1946; to CN 29 Aug 47; stricken 1963

Name	Class	Builder	Launch	Comp/Comm	Alloc	Fate
Kaibōkan No. 116	Type D	Ishikawajima Heavy Industries	3 Mar 45	28 Nov 45	–	Repatriation Service 28 Nov 45; stranded off Makurazaki (31° 16' N, 130° 18' E) 25 Mar 46; BU
Kaibōkan No. 118 = *Jie-12* (Jul 47) = *Chang Sha* (1949)	Type D	Kawasaki (Kobe)	20 Nov 44	27 Dec 44	CN	Stricken 5 Oct 45; Repatriation Service 1 Dec 45; to CN 31 Jul 47; to CNP May 49; stricken 1986
Kaibōkan No. 124	Type D	Kawasaki (Senshū)	5 Sep 44	9 Feb 45	–	Stricken 30 Nov 45; BU Kawanami from 1 Feb 48
Kaibōkan No. 126	Type D	Kawasaki (Senshū)	25 Feb 45	26 Mar 45	UK	Stricken 5 Nov 45; Repatriation Service 1 Dec 45; to UK 14 Aug 47 at Singapore; BU
Kaibōkan No. 132	Type D	Harima Zōsen	25 Jun 44	7 Sep 44		Stricken 5 Oct 45; Repatriation Service 1 Dec 45; BU Sasebo from 2 Jul 48
Kaibōkan No. 142 = *EK-38* (1947) = *TsL-38* (1948) = *Arkhara* (1949) = *SKR-48* (1954) = *Chih-17* (Feb 55)	Type D	Kawasaki (Senshū)	8 May 45	7 Apr 46	SU	Repatriation Service 7 Apr 46; to SU 29 Jul 47 at Nakhodka; target ship 1948; dispatch vessel 1949; patrol ship 1954; CNP 11 Feb 55; stricken 1987
Kaibōkan No. 150	Type D	Harima Zōsen	15 Nov 44	24 Dec 44	US	Stricken 5 Oct 45; Repatriation Service 1 Dec 45; to US 4 Jul 47; expended target Yellow Sea (35° 28' N, 123° 25' E) 18 Aug 47
Kaibōkan No. 154	Type D	Harima Zōsen	26 Dec 44	7 Feb 45	UK	Stricken 30 Nov 45; minesweeper 1 Dec 45; to UK 4 Sep 47 at Innoshima; BU from 1 Mar 48
Kaibōkan No. 156	Type D	Harima Zōsen	25 Jan 45	8 Mar 45	UK	Stricken 30 Nov 45; minesweeper 1 Dec 45; to UK 4 Sep 47 at Maizuru; BU from 11 Dec 47 by Iino Shoji
Kaibōkan No. 158	Type D	Harima Zōsen	25 Feb 45	23 Apr 45	US	Stricken 5 Oct 45; Repatriation Service 1 Dec 45; to US 25 Jul 47; BU at Maizuru by Iino Iino Shoji to 31 Dec 47
Kaibōkan No. 160	Type D	Harima Zōsen	10 Apr 45	16 Aug 45	UK	Stricken 5 Oct 45; Repatriation Service 1 Dec 45; to UK 8 Sep 47; BU by Nanao from 21 Feb 48
Kaibōkan No. 190	Type D	Mitsubishi (Nagasaki)	16 Jan 45	21 Feb 45	–	Stricken 30 Nov 45; BU by Moji 31 Mar 48
Kaibōkan No. 192 = *Ton An* (Jul 47)	Type D	Mitsubishi (Nagasaki)	30 Jan 45	28 Feb 45	CN	Stricken 25 Oct 45; Repatriation Service 1 Dec 45; to CN 31 Jul 47 at Shanghai; stricken 1952
Kaibōkan No. 194 = *Wei Hai* (Jul 47) = *Tsi Nan* (Apr 49)	Type D	Mitsubishi (Nagasaki)	15 Feb 45	15 Mar 45	CN	Stricken 5 Oct 45; Repatriation Service 1 Dec 45; to CN 6 Jul 47; CNP 23 Apr 49; stricken 1986
Kaibōkan No. 196 = *EK-33* (1947) = *Turgai* (1954)	Type D	Mitsubishi (Nagasaki)	26 Feb 45	31 Mar 45	SU	Stricken 30 Nov 45; Repatriation Service 1 Dec 45; to SU 5 Jul 47 at Nakhodka; comm 22 Jul 47; dispatch vessel 1954; stricken 11 Mar 58; BU
Kaibōkan No. 198 = *Jie-14* (Jul 47) = *Hsi An* (May 49)	Type D	Mitsubishi (Nagasaki)	26 Feb 45	11 Mar 45	CN	Stricken 5 Oct 45; Repatriation Service 1 Dec 45; to CN 31 Jul 47; to CNP May 49; stricken 1986
Kaibōkan No. 200	Type D	Mitsubishi (Nagasaki)	19 Mar 45	20 Apr 45	–	Stricken 30 Nov 45; BU at Maizuru by Iino Shoji from 1 Jul 48
Kaibōkan No. 202	Type D	Mitsubishi (Nagasaki)	2 Apr 45	7 Jul 45	–	Stricken 30 Nov 45; BU Sasebo from 1 Jan 48
Kaibōkan No. 204	Type D	Mitsubishi (Nagasaki)	14 Apr 45	11 Jul 45	–	Stricken 20 Nov 45; BU Nagasaki from 31 Jan 48
Kaibōkan No. 205 = *Chang An* (Jul 47)	Type C	Nihonkai Dock	30 Oct 44	16 Dec 44	CN	Stricken 5 Oct 45; Repatriation Service 1 Dec 45; to CN 31 Jul 47; stricken 1960
Kaibōkan No. 207	Type C	Naniwa Dock	15 Oct 44	21 Nov 44	US	Stricken 5 Oct 45; Repatriation Service 1 Dec 45; to US 4 Jul 47; expended target 13 Aug 47
Kaibōkan No. 213	Type C	Mitsubishi (Kobe	12 Feb 45	23 Mar 45	–	Mined off Pusan (35° 10' N, 129° E) 18 Aug 45
Kaibōkan No. 215 = *Liao Hai* (Jul 47) = *Jie-8*	Type C	Niigata Iron Works	1945	30 Dec 45	CN	Stricken 5 Oct 45; Repatriation Service 1 Dec 45; to CN 6 Jul 47; stricken 1960
Kaibōkan No. 217	Type C	Mitsubishi (Kobe)	26 Feb 45	17 Jul 45	UK	Stricken 30 Nov 45; minesweeper 1 Dec 45; to UK 5 Sep 47; BU Nagasaki by Koyakishima 10 Feb 48
Kaibōkan No. 221 = *EK-40* (Aug 47) = *TsL-40* (1948) = *Zhiguli* (1949)	Type C	Niigata Iron Works	26 Dec 44	2 Apr 45	SU	Stricken 30 Nov 45; Repatriation Service 1 Dec 45; to SU 29 Jul 47 at Nakhodka; comm 26 Aug 47; target ship 1948; salvage vessel 1949; stricken 11 Mar 58; BU
Kaibōkan No. 223	Type C	Mitsubishi (Kobe)	4 Jul 45	–	–	BU Kobe from 23 Oct 47
Kaibōkan No. 225	Type C	Niigata Iron Works	26 Mar 45	28 May 45	–	Stricken 5 Oct 45; BU from 30 Apr 48 by Amakisa Kaiji
Kaibōkan No. 227 = *EK-35* (1947) = *TsL-35* (1948) = *Siurkum* (1949)	Type C	Naniwa Dock	10 Feb 45	15 Jun 45	SU	Stricken 5 Oct 45; Repatriation Service 1 Dec 45; to SU 5 Jul 47 Nakhodka; comm 22 Aug 47; target ship 1948; oceanographic research ship 1949; stricken 11 Mar 58; BU
Kanawa	Type B (Mod)	Mitsui, Tamano	15 Nov 44	25 Mar 45	UK	Stricken 5 Oct 45; Repatriation Service 1 Dec 45; to UK 14 Aug 47; BU
Kasado	Type A (Mod)	Uraga Dock (Tokyo)	9 Dec 43	30 Mar 44	–	Stricken 5 Oct 45; BU by Amaksusa Kaiji from 31 May 48

Name	Class	Builder	Launch	Comp/Comm	Alloc	Fate
Kozu = *EK-47* (Sep 47) = *Nord* (1948) = *Glubomer* (1953) = *PM-62* (1955)	Type B (Mod)	Uraga dock	31 Dec 44	7 Feb 45	SU	Stricken 30 Nov 45; minesweeper; SU 28 Aug 47; comm 25 Sep 47; oceanographic research ship 1948; repair ship 1955; stricken 25 Jan 69; BU
Kuga	Type B (Mod)	Sasebo Navy Yard	19 Nov 44	25 Jan 45	–	Stricken 30 Nov 45; BU Maizuru from 30 May 47
Kunashiri	Type A	Nihon Kōkan (Tsurumi)	6 May 40	3 Oct 40	–	Stricken 5 Oct 45; Repatriation Service 1 Dec 45; stranded off Omaezaki (34° 35' N, 138° 15' E) 4 Jun 46; abandoned 25 Jun 46; BU Aug 46–Jul 47
Kurahashi	Type B	Nihon Kōkan (Tsurumi)	15 Oct 43	10 Mar 44	UK	Stricken 30 Nov 45; minesweeper 1 Dec 45; to UK 14 Sep 47; BU Nagoya to 15 Jan 48
Manju	Type A (Mod)	Mitsui (Tamano)	31 Jul 43	30 Nov 43	–	BU 1946; stricken 5 Mar 47
Miyake	Type B	Nihon Kōkan (Tsurumi)	30 Aug 43	30 Nov 43	–	Stricken 30 Nov 45; Repatriation Service 1 Dec 45; BU Sasebo 2 Jul 48
Oki = *Ku An* (Aug 47) = *Chang Bai* (1949)	Type A (Mod)	Uraga Dock (Tokyo)	20 Dec 42	31 Mar 43	CN	Stricken 20 Nov 45; Repatriation Service 1 Dec 45; to CN 29 Aug 47 at Tsingtau; to CNP 1949; stricken 1982; BU
Okisu (ex-*Lepanto*) = *Sien Hing* (1945)	IT *Ostia* (Table 2.2/8)	Cantieri Navali Riuniti (Ancona)	22 May 27	1928	CN	To CN 1945; BU 1956
Renshu-Tei No. 1 (ex-*Shōkaitei No. 101*, ex-UK *Thracian*) = *Thracian* (Sep 45)	UK 'S'	Hawthorn Leslie (Hebburn)/ Sheerness DYd	5 Mar 20	UK: 1 Apr 22 JP: 25 Nov 42	–	Retroceded UK 4 Sep 45; sold at Hong Kong Feb 46; BU
Sakito	Type B (Mod)	Hitachi (Sakurajima)	29 Nov 44	10 Jan 45	–	Stricken 20 Nov 45; BU Sasebo to 1 Dec 47
Shiga = *Kojima* (1949) = *Shiga Maru* (Dec 50) = *Kojima* (1954)	Type B (Mod)	Sasebo Navy Yard	9 Feb 45	20 Mar 45	–	Stricken 30 Nov 45; minesweeper 1 Dec 45; ferry 1 Feb 46; MTB 26 Dec 47; MSA 1 Jan 49; weather ship 31 Dec 50; MSA 1 Jan 54; discarded 6 May 64; hulked as pavilion Maritime Amusement Park, Chiba City 31 Aug 65; BU 1998
Shimushu = *EK-31* (Jul 47)	Type A	Mitsui (Tamano)	13 Dec 39	30 Jun 40	SU	Stricken 5 Oct 45; Repatriation Service 1 Dec 45; to SU 22 Jul 47 at Nakhodka; base-ship 16 Sep 57; stricken 16 May 59; BU
Shinnan = *Tsugaru* (Jan 49)	Type B (Mod)	Uraga Dock (Tokyo)	4 Sep 44	21 Oct 44	–	Stricken 30 Nov 45; minesweeper 1 Dec 45; minesweeping tender; MTB weather ship 26 Dec 47; MSA 1 Jan 49; Petrol Development Agency accommodation hulk Oct 67; BU 1975
Shisaka = *Huai An* (Jul 47) = *Rui Jin* (1949)	Type B (Mod)	Hitachi (Sakurajima)	31 Oct 44	15 Dec 44	CN	Stricken 15 Sep 45; Repatriation Service 1 Dec 45; to CN 6 Jul 47; to CNP 1949; training ship 1955; stricken 1986
Shōkaitei No. 36 (ex-*Fuji*)	*Momi*	Fujinagata (Osaka)	27 Nov 20	31 May 21	–	BU Surabaya 1947
Shōkaitei No. 102 (ex-*Stewart*) = *DD-224* (Aug 45)	US *Clemson*	Cramp (Philadelphia)	4 Mar 20	US: 15 Sep 20 JP: 20 Sep 43	–	Retroceded US 25 Oct 45; US recommission 29 Oct 45; stricken 17 April 46; expended target off San Francisco (37° 44' 56.4" N, 122° 43' 44.4" W) 24 May 46
Shōkaitei No. 104 (ex-*Valk*)	NL *Valk*	Wilton-Fijenoord (Schieldam)	19 Oct 29	NL: 1930 JP: 31 Jan 44	–	Mined 24 Aug 45
Shōkaitei No. 106 (ex-*Banckert*)	NL *Van Galen*	Burgerhout (Rotterdam)	14 Nov 29	NL: 14 Nov 30 JP: –	–	Retroceded NL 23 Oct 45; stricken 5 Mar 47; expended target Madura Strait Sep 49
Shōkaitei No. 109 (ex-*Fazant*) = *Kartika* (1951)	NL *Fazant*	Marine-Etablissement (Surabaya)	1930	1931	–	Retroceded NL 21 Apr 46; stricken 5 Mar 47; to ID 1949; BU 1954
Takane	Type B (Mod)	Mitsui (Tamano)	13 Feb 45	26 Apr 45	–	Stricken 5 Oct 45; BU Kure 27 Nov 47
Tsushima = *Lin An* (Jul 47)	Type A (Mod)	Nihon Kōkan (Tsurumi)	20 Mar 43	15 Aug 43	CN	Stricken 5 Oct 45; Repatriation Service 1 Dec 45; to CN 31 Jul 47; stricken 1963
Uji = *Chang Chi* (1947) = *Nan Chang* (1949)	*Hasahadate*	Sakurajima (Osaka)	25 Sep 40	30 Apr 41	CN	Stricken 25 Oct 45; to CN 1947; CNP 1949; stricken 1986
Uku	Type B (Mod)	Sasebo DYd	12 Nov 44	30 Dec 44	US	Stricken 5 Oct 45; Repatriation Service 1 Dec 45; to US 4 Jul 47 at Tsingtau; BU
Ukuru = *Ukuru Maru* (Dec 47) = *Satsuma* (Jan 54)	Type B (Mod)	Nihon Kōkan (Tsurumi)	15 May 44	31 Jul 44	–	Stricken 30 Nov 45; minesweeper 1 Dec 45; minesweeping tender 10 Jul 46; MTB weather ship 26 Dec 47; MSA 1 Jan 54; sold to BU 24 Nov 65
Yashiro = *Wei Tai* (Aug 47) = *Cheng An* (1951)	Type B	Hitachi, Sakurajima	16 Feb 44	6 Jun 44	CN	Stricken 30 Nov 45; minesweeper 1 Dec 45; to CN 29 Aug 47 at Tsingtau; discarded 1954; stricken 1963; BU

Table 2.3/8. Depot Ship

	Disp.	Length	Beam	Machinery	Power/speed	Main guns
Chogai	6,600t	124m	17m	6 x boilers, 2 x Tu	7500shp=18kt	4 x 140mm/50

Name	Builder	Launch	Comp/Comm	Fate
Chogai	Mitsubishi (Nagaski)	24 Mar 24	2 Aug 24	Stricken 5 Oct 45; Repatriation Service 1 Dec 45; BU Hitachi (Mukaishima) 20 Sep 46–1947.

4. The Romanian Navy: 24 August 1944

Table 2.4/1. Destroyers

Class	Disp.	Length	Beam	Machinery	Power/speed	Main gun(s)	TT	Mines
Regele Ferdinand	1400t	102.0m	9.6m	4 x boilers 2 x Tu	52,000shp=37.0kt	5 x 120mm/50	6 x 533mm	50
Mărăşti	1410t	94.7m	9.5m	5 x boilers 2 x Tu	45,000shp=34.0kt	4 x 120mm/50	4 x 457mm	50

Name	Class	Builder	Launch	Comp / comm	Seized	SU	Fate
Regele Ferdinand = *Likhoi* (Sep 44) = *D21* (1952) = *D1* (1956) = *D9* (1959)	*Regele Ferdinand*	Pattison (Naples)	2 Dec 28	7 Sep 30	5 Sep 44	Constanţa	SU comm 20 Oct 44; retroceded 3 Jul 51; stricken Apr 61
Regina Maria = *Letuchyi* (Sep 44) = *D22* (1952) = *D2* (1956) = *D10* (1959)	*Regele Ferdinand*	Pattison (Naples)	2 Mar 29	7 Sep 30	5 Sep 44	Constanţa	SU comm 20 Oct 44; retroceded 3 Jul 51; stricken Apr 61
Mărăşti (ex-*Sparviero*, ex-*Vijelie*) = *Lovkyi* (i) (Sep 44) = *D1* (1948) = *D11* (1952) = *D3* (1956)	*Mărăşti*	Pattison (Naples)	26 Mar 17	IT: 15 Jul 17 RO: 1 Jul 20	5 Sep 44	Constanţa	SU comm 20 Oct 44; retroceded 12 Oct 45; stricken Apr 61
Mărăşeşti (ex-*Nibbio*, ex-*Vartez*) = *Legkyi* (i) (Sep 44) = *D2* (1948) = *D12* (1952) = *D4* (1956)	*Mărăşti*	Pattison (Naples)	30 Jan 18	IT: 15 May 18 RO: 1 Jul 20	5 Sep 44	Constanţa	SU comm 20 Oct 44; retroceded 12 Oct 45; stricken Apr 61

Table 2.4/2. Submarines

Class	Disp.	Length	Beam	Machinery	Power/speed	Main gun(s)	TT	Mines
Delfinul	600/650t	68.6m	5.9m	2 x diesel 2 x electric	1600bhp=14.0kt 800shp=9.0kt	1 x 102mm/35	6 x 533mm	–
Requinul	585/789t	58.0m	5.6m	2 x diesel 2 x electric	1840bhp=17.0kt 860shp=8.0kt	1 x 88mm/42	6 x 533mm	–
Marsouinul	637/680t	68.7m	6.4m	2 x diesel 2 x electric	1840bhp=16.6kt 860shp=8.0kt	1 x 88mm/42	6 x 533mm	20

Name	Builder	Launch	Comp / comm	Seized SU	Fate
Delfinul = *TS-3* (14 Sep 44) = *S1* (1948) = *S51* (1956)	Cantieri Navale del Quarnaro (Fiume)	22 Jun 30	May 36	Galaţi 12 Sep 44	SU comm 20 Oct 44; retroceded 12 Oct 45; comm 1954; stricken Jan 58
Requinul = *TS-1* (14 Sep 44) = *N-39* (4 Aug 47) = *S-39* (16 Jun 49) = *S2* (1951) = *S11* (1952) = *S52* (1956)	Santieri Galaţi (Galaţi)	4 May 41	May 43	Constanţa 5 Sep 44	SU comm 20 Oct 44; retroceded 3 Jul 51; stricken 1959
Marsouinul = *TS-2* (14 Sep 44) = *N-40* (4 Aug 47) = *S-40* (16 Jun 49)	Santieri Galaţi (Galaţi)	22 May 41	Jul 43	Constanţa 5 Sep 44	SU comm 20 Oct 44; constructive total loss torpedo explosion Poti 20 Feb 45; stricken 28 Nov 50; BU

Table 2.4/3. Torpedo Boats

Class	Disp.	Length	Beam	Machinery	Power/speed	Main gun(s)	TT	Mines
Viforul	32t	21.9m	5.0m	3 x petrol	3450bhp=42.0kt	8 x 7.7mm/66	2 x 533mm	4
Vedenia	30.8t	21.4m	6.1m	3 x petrol	2850bhp=35.0kt	2 x 20mm/80	2 x 533mm	–

Name	Class	Builder	Launch	Comp / comm	Seized SU	Fate
Smeul (ex-83F) = Toros (Oct 44) = E1 (Oct 45)	AH 82F (see Table 1.2/3)	Danubius (Fiume)	7 Nov 14	7 Aug 15	Constanţa 5 Sep 44	SU comm 20 Oct 44; retroceded 12 Oct 45; BU 1960
Sborul (ex-81T) = Musson (Oct 44) = E2 (Oct 45)	AH 74T (see Table 1.2/3)	Stab Tecnico Triestino (Trieste)	6 Aug 14	1 Dec 14	Constanţa 5 Sep 44	SU comm 20 Oct 44; retroceded 12 Oct 45; BU 1958
Viscolul (ex-MTB23) = TK-955 (5 Sep 43)	Viforul	Vosper (Portsmouth)	16 Feb 40		Constanţa 5 Sep 44	SU comm 20 Oct 44; retroceded Sep 45; BU
Vedenia = TK-951 (5 Sep 43) (ex-S203, ex-TM63)	Vedenia	Werf Gusto (Schiedam)/ Santieri Galati (Galatz)	1943		Constanţa 5 Sep 44	SU comm 20 Oct 44; retroceded 12 Oct 45; BU
Vantul = TK-952 (5 Sep 43) (ex-S204, ex-TM64)	Vedenia	Werf Gusto (Schiedam)/ Santieri Galati (Galatz)	1943		Constanţa 5 Sep 44	SU comm 20 Oct 44; retroceded 12 Oct 45; BU
Vijelia = TK-953 (5 Sep 43) (ex-S205, ex-TM65)	Vedenia	Werf Gusto (Schiedam)/ Santieri Galati (Galatz)	1943		Constanţa 5 Sep 44	SU comm 20 Oct 44; retroceded 12 Oct 45; BU
Viforul = TK-954 (5 Sep 43) (ex-S206, ex-TM66)	Vedenia	Werf Gusto (Schiedam)/ Santieri Galati (Galatz)	Apr/May 44		Constanţa 5 Sep 44	SU comm 20 Oct 44; retroceded 12 Oct 45; BU
Vartejul = TK-956 (5 Sep 43) (ex-S207, ex-TM67)	Vedenia	Werf Gusto (Schiedam)/ Santieri Galati (Galatz)	Apr/May 44		Constanţa 5 Sep 44	SU comm 20 Oct 44; retroceded 12 Oct 45; BU
Vulcanul = TK-957 (5 Sep 43) (ex-S208, ex-TM68)	Vedenia	Werf Gusto (Schiedam)/ Santieri Galati (Galatz)	Apr/May 44		Constanţa 5 Sep 44	SU comm 20 Oct 44; retroceded 12 Oct 45; BU

Table 2.4/4. Minelayer

Class	Disp.	Length	Beam	Machinery	Power/speed	Main gun(s)	Mines
Amiral Murgescu	812t	76.9m	9.1m	2 x diesel	2100bhp=16kt	2 x 105mm/32	135

Name	Builder	Launch	Comp / comm	Seized SU	Fate
Amiral Murgescu = Don (Sep 44) = PKZ-107 (May 56) = PM-76 (Jan 58) = PMR-76 (8 Jun 66)	Santieri Galaţi (Galaţi)	14 Jun 39	2 Mar 41	Constanţa 5 Sep 44	SU comm 20 Oct 44; depot ship 18 Jan 47; command ship 9 Feb 48; accommodation ship 7 May 56; repair ship 4 Jan 58; stricken 27 May 88; sold 4 Jul 88; BU Sevastopol

Table 2.4/5. Minesweepers

Class	Disp.	Length	Beam	Machinery	Power/speed	Main gun(s)
FR Friponne	375t	60.2m	7.0m	2 x diesel	900bhp=14.5kt	1 x 37mm/80

Name	Class	Builder	Launch	Comp / comm	Seized SU	Fate
Căpitan Dumitrescu Constantin (ex-Impatiente) = Araks (Sep 44)	FR Friponne	Brest DYd	1916	FR: 1917 RO: Jan 20	Constanţa 5 Sep 44	SU comm 20 Oct 44; mined Odessa 10 Jan 45; salved 19 Jan 45; BU
DB13 =Democraţia (1949) = Vice-Amiral Mihai Gavrilescu (1993) = Descătuşarea (1949) = Vice-Amiral Ioan Balanescu (1993)	GE M1940 (see Table 2.1/7)	Santieri Galaţi (Galaţi)	1944	19 Oct 54	–	Stricken 2001.
DB14 = Desrobiriea (1949) = Vice-Amiral Emil Grescescu (1993)	GE M1940 (see Table 2.1/7)	Santieri Galaţi (Galaţi)	1944	19 Oct 54	–	Stricken 2001.
DB15 = Dreptatia (1949) = Vice-Amiral Ioan Georgescu (1993)	GE M1940 (see Table 2.1/7)	Santieri Galaţi (Galaţi)	1944	19 Oct 54	–	Stricken 2001.
DB16	GE M1940 (see Table 2.1/7)	Santieri Galaţi (Galaţi)	1944	19 Oct 54	–	Stricken 2000

Locotenent-Comandor Stihi Eugen (ex-*Friponne*) = *Akhtuba* (Sep 44) = *D61* (1947) = *Eugen Stihi* (1960)	FR *Friponne*	Lorient DYd	1916	FR: 1917 RO: Jan 20	Constanţa 5 Sep 44	SU comm 20 Oct 44; retroceded Oct 45; survey vessel 1960; stricken 2002; potential museum ship Mangalia 2011
Sublocotenent Ghiculescu Ion (ex-*Mignonne*) = *Angara* (Sep 44) = *D62* (1947) = *Ghiculescu Ion* (1960)	FR *Friponne*	Brest DYd	1917	FR: 1918 RO: Jan 20	Constanţa 5 Sep 44	SU comm 20 Oct 44; retroceded Oct 45; survey vessel 1960; stricken 2002

Table 2.4/6. River Monitors

Class	Disp.	Length	Beam	Machinery	Power/speed	Main gun(s)
Ion C. Brătianu	680t	63.5m	10.5m	2 x boilers 2 x VTE	1800ihp=13.0kt	3 x 120mm/33

Name	Class	Builder	Launch	Comp / comm	Seized SU	Fate
Ardeal (ex-*Drina*, ex-*Temes*) = *Berdyansk* (Sep 44) = *M207* (Jul 51)	AH *Temes* (see Table 1.2/6)	H Schönischen (Budapest)	26 Apr 04	AH: 10 Nov 04 RO: 15 Apr 20	Izmail 5 Sep 44	SU comm 30 Oct 44; retroceded 3 Jul 51; stricken 1960
Ion C. Brătianu = *Azov* (Sep 44) = *M202* (Jul 51)	*Ion C. Brătianu*	Stab Tecnico Triestino (San Marco)/ Santieri Galaţi (Galaţi)	Jul 07	Sep 07	Izmail 5 Sep 44	SU comm 30 Oct 44; retroceded 3 Jul 51; stricken 1960
Alexandru Lachovari = *Mariupol* (Sep 44) = *M201* (Jul 51)	*Ion C. Brătianu*	Stab Tecnico Triestino (San Marco)/ Santieri Galaţi (Galaţi)	Oct 07	Jan 08	Izmail 5 Sep 44	SU comm 30 Oct 44; retroceded 3 Jul 51; stricken 1960
Bucovina (ex-*Soca*, ex-*Sava*) = *Izmail* (Sep 44) = *M205* (Jul 51)	AH *Sava* (see Table 1.2/6)	Stab Tecnico Triestino (Linz)	31 May 15	AH: 15 Sep 15 RO: 15 Apr 20	Izmail 5 Sep 44	SU comm 30 Oct 44; retroceded 3 Jul 51; stricken 1959
Basarabia (ex-*Marx*, ex-*Ujvidek*, ex-*Inn*) = *Kerch* (Sep 44) = *M206* (Jul 51)	AH *Enns* (see Table 1.2/6)	Danubius, (Budapest)	25 Feb 15	AH: 11 Apr 15 RO: 15 Apr 20	Izmail 5 Sep 44	SU comm 30 Oct 44; retroceded 3 Jul 51; stricken 1960

Table 2.4/7. Submarine Depot Ship

Class	Disp.	Length	Beam	Machinery	Power/speed	Main gun(s)
Constanţa	2300t	77.3m	11.3m	2 x diesel	2000bhp=13.0kt	2 x 76mm

Name	Builder	Launch	Comp / comm	Seized SU	Fate
Constanţa = *Bug* (Sep 44) = *PZK-87*	Cantieri Navale del Quarnaro (Fiume)	8 Nov 28	1931	Constanţa 5 Sep 44	To SU; BU 1977

Table 2.4/8. Sail Training Ship

Name	Class	Builder	Launch	Comp / comm	Seized SU	Fate
Mircea	GE *Gorch Fock* (Table 2.1/10)	Blohm & Voss (Hamburg)	1938	17 May 38	Constanţa 5 Sep 44	Retroceded 27 May 46; still in service (2019)

5. The Bulgarian Navy: 9 September 1944

Table 2.5/1. Torpedo Boats

Class	Disp.	Length	Beam	Machinery	Power/speed	Main gun(S)	TT
Druzki	97.5t	38.0m	4.4m	2 x boilers; 1 x VTE	1950ihp=26.0kt	2 x 37mm/80	–

Name	Class	Builder	Launch	Comp / comm	Seized SU	Fate
Druzki = *Ingul* (Sep 44) = *Druzki* (Jul 45)	*Druzki*	Schneider (Chalons-sur-Saône)	10 Aug 07	Jan 08	Varna 9 Sep 44	To SU Sep 44; BG Jul 45; stricken 1954; components to preserved '*Druzki*' at Varna 21 Nov 57
Khrabri = *Vychegda* (Sep 44) = *Khrabri* (Jul 45)	*Druzki*	Schneider (Chalons-sur-Saône)	10 Aug 07	Jan 08	Varna 9 Sep 44	To SU Sep 44; BG Jul 45; stricken 1954; BU 1962
Strogi	*Druzki*	Schneider (Chalons-sur-Saône)	6 Apr 08	Aug 09	Varna 9 Sep 44	To SU Sep 44; BG Jul 45; stricken 1954; hull to preserved '*Druzki*' at Varna 21 Nov 57.

+ 6. The Finnish Navy: 19 September 1944

Table 2.6/1. Coast Defence Ship

Class	Disp.	Length	Beam	Machinery	Power/speed	Main gun(S)
Väinämöinen	3900t	93.0m	16.9m	2 x Diesel-electric	6000bhp=15.0kt	4 x 254mm/45

Name	Builder	Launch	Comp / comm	Fate
Väinämöinen = Vyborg (May 47)	Crichton-Vulcan (Turku)	28 Dec 30	28 Dec 32	Stricken May 47; to SU 29 May 47; stricken 25 Sep 66; BU Leningrad

Table 2.6/2. Submarines

Class	Disp.	Length	Beam	Machinery	Power/speed	Main gun(S)	TT	Mines
Vetehinen	600/716t	63.5m	6.1m	2 x Diesel 2 x electric	1160bhp=13.5kt 700shp=8.5kt	1 x 76mm/48	4 x 533mm	20
Saukko	130/140t	32.4m	4.1m	1 x Diesel 1 x electric	170bhp=7kt 120shp=5.7kt	1 x 12.7mm/62	2 x 450mm	9
Vesikko	254/303t	40.9m	4.1m	2 x Diesel 2 x electric	700bhp=13.1kt 360shp=8.1kt	1 x 20mm/60	5 x 450mm	9

Name	Builder	Launch	Comp / comm	Fate
Iku-Turso	Crichton-Vulcan (Turku)	5 May 31	13 Oct 31	Stricken 1947; BU Belgium 1953
Saukko	Hietalahti (Laatokka)	2 Jul 30	16 Dec 30	Stricken 1947; BU Belgium 1953
Vesihiisi	Crichton-Vulcan (Turku)	1 Aug 30	2 Dec 31	Stricken 1947; BU Belgium 1953
Vesikko	Hietalahti (Laatokka)	10 May 33	30 Apr 34	Stricken 1947; preserved 1962; museum at Sveaborg 9 Jul 73
Vetehinen	Crichton-Vulcan (Turku)	1 Jun 30	13 Oct 30	Stricken 1947; BU Belgium 1953

Table 2.6/3. Escort Vessels

Class	Disp.	Length	Beam	Machinery	Power/speed	Main gun(S)	Mines
RU Vodorez	342t	50.1m	6.8m	2 x boilers 2 x VTE	1150ihp=15.0kt	2 x 75mm/48	30
RU Gulob	406t	52.0m	7.5m	3 x boilers 2 x VTE	1400ihp=15.0kt	2 x 105mm/45	40

Name	Builder	Launch	Comp / comm	Fate
Hämeenmaa (ex-Wulf, ex-Pingvin)	Kone-ja-Silta (Helsinki)	1917	GE: Apr 18 Fl: 1919	Stricken 1953
Karjala (ex-Filin)	Crichton-Vulcan (Turku)	1918	1918	Stricken 1953
Turunmaa (ex-Orlan)	Crichton-Vulcan (Turku)	1918	1918	Stricken 1953
Uusimaa (ex-Bär, ex-Golub)	Kone-ja-Silta (Helsinki)	1917	GE: Apr 18 Fl: 1919	Stricken 1953

Table 2.6/4. Fast Patrol Boats

Class	Disp.	Length	Beam	Machinery	Power/speed	Main gun(s)	TT	mines
MTV4	12t	16.8m	3.4m	2 x petrol	750bhp=40.0kt	1 x 7.6mm	–	–
SU D-3	31t	22.4m	4.0m	3 x petrol	2550bhp=32.0kt	1 x 20mm/60	2 x 533mm	–
SU G-5	15–20t	19.1m	3.4m	2 x petrol	1700–2000bhp=45.0–52.0kt	1 x 76mm/94	2 x 533mm or	3–4
H1	20t	16.5m	4.3m	2 x petrol	1600bhp=36.0kt	1 x 20mm/60	2 x 450mm	–
T1	22t	17.8m	4.6m	2 x petrol	2300bhp=48.0kt	1 x 20mm/60	2 x 450mm	–

Name	Class	Builder	Launch	Comp / comm	Fate
H1 Hyöky	H1	Baglietto (Varazze)	1943	1943	Stricken 1963; sold
H2 Hirmu	H1	Baglietto (Varazze)	1943	1943	Stricken 1963; sold
H3 Hurja	H1	Baglietto (Varazze)	1943	1943	Stricken 1963; sold
H4 Hyrsky = Odysses (1963)	H1	Baglietto (Varazze)	1943	1943	Stricken 1963; sold; mercantile
H5 Häijy	H1	Baglietto (Varazze)	1943	1943	Stricken 1963; sold
J1 Jylhä (ex-MAS526)	IT MAS526 (Table 2.2/9)	Baglietto (Varazze)	22 Aug 38 Fl: 5 Jun 43	IT: 2 Mar 39	Stricken 1961
J2 Jyry (ex-MAS527)	IT MAS526 (Table 2.2/9)	Baglietto (Varazze)	30 Jan 39 Fl: 5 Jun 43	IT: 30 Mar 39	Stricken 1961
J3 Jyske (ex-MAS528)	IT MAS526 (Table 2.2/9)	Baglietto (Varazze)	28 Feb 39 Fl: 5 Jun 43	IT: 29 Aug 39	Stricken 1961

Name	Class	Builder	Launch	Comp / comm	Fate
J4 Jymy (ex-MAS529)	IT MAS526 (Table 2.2/9)	Baglietto (Varazze)	3 Apr 39	IT: 30 Jun 39 FI: 5 Jun 43	Stricken 1961
T2 Taisto	T1	Turun Veneveistämö (Turku)	1943	1943	Stricken 1964
T3 Tyrsky	T1	Turun Veneveistämö (Turku)	1943	1943	Stricken 1977; preserved Turku,
T4 Tuima	T1	Turun Veneveistämö (Turku)	1943	1943	Stricken 1964
T5 Tuisku	T1	Turun Veneveistämö (Turku)	1943	1943	Stricken 1964
T6 Tuuli	T1	Turun Veneveistämö (Turku)	1943	1943	Stricken 1964
V3 (ii) (ex-TK-51, ex-No51, ex-No54, ex-No51, ex-No71) = TK-90 (Sep 44)	SU G-5	194 (Marti) Yard (Leningrad)	1934	SU: 1934 FI: Jun 44	Retroceded SU Sep 44
Vasama (ex-V1, ex-No52) = SK-37 (Oct 44)	SU D-3	5 Yard (Leningrad)	1941	SU: 1941 FI: Oct 41	Retroceded SU Oct 44
Vihuri (ex-V2, ex- No141, ex-No144, ex-No141) = TK-80 (Sep 44)	SU G-5	194 (Marti) Yard (Leningrad)	1938	SU: 1938 FI: Nov 41	Retroceded SU Sep 44
Viima (ex-V1, ex-V3, ex-No64, ex-No121, ex-No184) = TK-70 (Sep 44)	SU G-5	194 (Marti) Yard (Leningrad)	1939	SU: 1939 FI: Nov 41	Retroceded SU Sep 44
Vinha (ex-MTV6)	MTV4	Thornycroft (Woolston)	1929	1929	Stricken 1945

Table 2.6/5. Minelayers

Class	Disp.	Length	Beam	Machinery	Power/speed	Main gun(s)	mines
Louhi	640t	50.0m	8.0m	3 x boilers 1 x VTE	800ihp=12.0kt	2 x 40mm/39	150
Ruotsinsalmi	310t	50.0m	7.9m	2 x diesel	1120bhp=15.0kt	1 x 75mm/48	100

Name	Builder	Launch	Comp / comm	Fate
Louhi (ex-M1, ex-Voin)	Kolomna (Moscow)	1916	RU: 1916 FI: Apr 18	Torpedoed U370 off Hanko 12 Jan 45
Ruotsinsalmi	Crichton-Vulcan (Turku)	May 40	Feb 41	Diving support vessel 1973; stricken 1975; BU early 1990s

Table 2.6/6. Minesweepers

Class	Disp.	Length	Beam	Machinery	Power/speed	Main gun(s)	mines
RU Udarnik	190t	43.6m	6.1m	2 x boilers 2 x VTE	400ihp = 11.0kt	1 x 47mm/40	30
Pukkio	162t	27.0m	6.7m	1 x diesel	300ihp = 10.0kt	1 x 45mm/43	20
Viipuri	335t	31.6m	7.5m	1 x ...	368...hp = 10.0kt	2 x 45mm/43	–
Narvi	400t	39.3m	8.5m	2 x boilers 2 x VTE	400ihp = 10.0kt	1 x 45mm/43	40
Ajonpää	52t	20.0m	5.3m	1 x diesel	200bhp = 10.0kt	1 x 20mm/60	–

Name	Class	Builder	Launch	Comp / comm	Fate
Ajonpää	Ajonpää	[Denmark]	1941/42	1943	Stricken 1960
Jurmo	Narvi		1944	1944	To SU late 1944
Kallanpää	Ajonpää	[Denmark]	1941/42	1943	Stricken 1962
Luppi	Narvi		1944	1944	To SU late 1944
Narvi	Narvi		1944	1944	To SU late 1944
No 761 Viipuri = EMTShch-70 (Nov 44)	Viipuri	Crichton-Vulcan (Turku)	1941	Jun 41	To SU Nov 44
No 762 = EMTShch-71 (Nov 44)	Viipuri	Crichton-Vulcan (Turku)	1941	Jun 41	To SU Nov 44
No 763 = EMTShch-72 (Nov 44)	Viipuri	Crichton-Vulcan (Turku)	1941	Jun 41	To SU Nov 44
No 764 = EMTShch-73 (Nov 44)	Viipuri	Crichton-Vulcan (Turku)	1941	Jun 41	To SU Nov 44
Pansio	Pukkio	Valmet (Helsinki)	1940	May 47	Stricken 1979, LCU 1984, sold 1990
Porkkala	Pukkio	Valmet (Helsinki)	1940	1940	Stricken 1974, LCU 1979, sold 1990
Pukkio	Pukkio	Valmet (Helsinki)	1939	1940	Stricken 1974, LCU 1979, sold 1982
Rautu (ex-T1, ex-Fortral)	RU Udarnik	Russo-Baltic Works (Reval)	1916	RU: Jan 18 FI: Apr 18	Stricken 1952

9

Retrospect

Comparing the events after each of the two World Wars, one sees a number of similarities and differences. Among the latter was the fact that after the Second World War both Germany and Japan were under full Allied occupation, with no national government. Accordingly, the matter of distributing or otherwise disposing of vessels was wholly within the control of the principal victorious powers. In contrast, after the First World War, Germany retained its own government, and thus had an active (if unwilling) role in the transfers, in many ways mirrored by Italy's position in 1947. The situation regarding the former Austro-Hungarian navy in 1918 was similarly akin to that of Germany and Japan in 1945, in that its ships were almost entirely under Allied control, and subject entirely to their decisions as to its fate – in spite of the aspirations of the new Yugoslavia.

Similarities are particularly visible when one looks at the squabbling between the victors over who would get what – and what they could do with it when it was formally in their hands. In this, we see a consistency in the underlying positions of the UK and USA at the end of both wars, that ideally everything should be destroyed, contrasting with the 1918/19 French and 1945 Soviet positions, that victorious nations should have largely untrammelled discretion as to what could be done with surrendered tonnage. The inter-Allied negotiations were thus in both cases a matter of squaring these circles, with restrictions on submarine and submarine-technology proliferation an important motif, especially for the British, brought close to defeat by submarine warfare during both wars.

Nevertheless, the acquisition of ex-enemy ships would never be a true substitute for new-build vessels, most such tonnage being war-weary and, most importantly, labouring under the logistic burdens of non-standardisation and the provision of spares. Thus, ships taken over by the USSR and France after the Second World War had generally been withdrawn by the mid-1950s, by which time, in any case, post-war naval programmes were delivering replacements.

Likewise, most post-First World War surrenders had passed out of service within a decade or so.

On the other hand, some of the vessels thus acquired had much longer careers in the hands of their new owners, in particular two of the three ex-German light cruisers taken over by Italy after the First World War, which remained in service into the Second World War, and a few ships ceded after the latter conflict, with some of the ex-German sail training ships still active at the time of writing and much valued not only as the last gasp of the sailing ship era, but also in an eminently modern role as goodwill ambassadors. But these were very much exceptions to the rule. Most were soon broken up for the benefit of whichever victorious nation they had been allocated, or sunk or otherwise destroyed to meet some joint agreement between the winning powers.

The Austro-Hungarian torpedo boats *81T* and *83F* present interesting case-studies of not only long service – launched in 1915, but not broken up until 1958/60 – but also successive geopolitical realities over that period. Having served the dual monarchy, they were assigned in 1920 to Romania, a state that also acquired some former Austro-Hungarian territory, seized by the Soviets in 1944, and, returned once more to Romania, now serving behind the Iron Curtain as part of the Communist eastern bloc.

Treaties and commercial realities in the wake of the wars also led to some unusual fates for 'surplus' vessels. Perhaps most extraordinary were the conversions of the unfinished German destroyers *S178* and *S179*, on the stocks at the end of the First World War, which, with new bows and sterns, became sailing schooners, *S179* undergoing further conversion into a refrigerated trawler, still under sail.

Over and above the practical sides of the acquisitions of ex-enemy tonnage by the victorious nations were the political aspects, especially regarding a nation's position in the shifting absolute or relative hierarchies of world powers. This can be seen in particular with Italy's position after the First World War, when its overarching requirement was to have the same as France – whether the latter got something or nothing. The Potsdam Agreement's refusal in 1945 to allocate any tonnage to France was a pointed act of humiliation (by the USSR), undermining France's perception of itself as again one of the victorious powers – in spite of the events of 1940 and the acts of the Vichy regime.

The consequent handover of UK-allocated ex-German tonnage to France by the British was an opportunity for the latter to show generosity towards the French, while also implicitly underlining the two powers' relative standings in the contemporary world. It also relieved the British of the costs of maintaining – or even preparing for the scrapping of – vessels in which it had little interest. Similar motives probably stalked the UK's implicit support for France and Norway's ignoring of the TNC 'guidance' to these two powers over the destruction of submarines within their jurisdiction.

The question of the status of the defeated powers was also, of course, part of the process. At one level, the removal of weapons from such a defeated nation could be presented as making it more difficult for an 'aggressor' to threaten peace in future, but the desire to inflict humiliation was very much another. The downgrading of the German fleet from the world's second-strongest to something with capabilities little better than that of Sweden was an unmistakable statement about Germany's future status as seen in 1919. Even the new names assigned to vessels after both World Wars had a punitive element to them, alluding particularly to redrawn boundaries following cession of territory or asserting a new nationhood. Following both wars France was particularly pointed in rechristening former German vessels taken into its fleet.

The debates and negotiations surrounding the future of the Italian fleet between 1943 and 1947 reflected the tensions between 'punishing' Italy as a former Axis power; recognising her contributions to Allied victory as a co-belligerent; and fixing her position in the post-war world (both as an ally of the Western powers, and a potential enemy of the Soviet Union). The two-sided implications of 'generosity' can also be seen in the way that France's waiving of the transfer of *some* of her Italian allocation allowed her to *both* indicate a positive attitude to the 'new' Italy, *and* to humiliate her old rival by insisting on the public handover of the tonnage actually ceded.

Thus, the story of the fates of the various enemy fleets after the two World Wars picks up an array of threads. These range from the relatively simple age-old tradition of 'to the victor the spoils', through to international wrangling surrounding the unpicking of wartime alliances. The fates of the various vessels involved are now in most cases well known and understood, but others have long been subject to error, misunderstanding and, in a few cases, apparent omission from surviving records. Material now available means that only a few loose ends remain, with the wrecks of a few – and a tiny handful of still-active vessels and museum ships – surviving as memorials to their era, with an increasing appreciation of their heritage values.

Maps

Map 1. The English Channel, showing the known sinking-locations of ships covered in this book. *(AD graphic)*

Map 2. The eastern Atlantic, North Sea and Baltic. *(AD graphic)*

A Y

Kristiana
(Oslo)

GULF OF BOTHNIA

FINLAND

ÅLAND ISLANDS

Kotka

Helsinki

Kronsdadt

Petrograd/
Leningrad
St Petersburg

Mariehamm

Hanko

Louhi+

RUSSIA

S W E D E N

Stockholm

Schleswig-Holstein+

Tallinn

E S T O N I A

Berlin
T38
Z34+ T39
T65   M16+
      M522+
S7 S9 S12

GULF OF
RIGA

L A T V I A

R A K

KATTEGAT

GOTLAND

Riga

B A L T I C

Libau/
Liepāja

Karlskrona

S E A

Memel/
Klaipėda

L I T H U A N I A

D E N M A R K

Copenhagen

Graf Zeppelin+
~Lützow

sbjerg

Nyborg

THE
SOUND   BORNHOLM

Vilna/
Vilnius

Flensberg

HEIKEN
DORFER
BAY

Königsberg/
Kaliningrad

Kiel

KIEL CANAL

Stralsund

Rostock

Gdynia/
Gotenhafen

Danzig/
Gdansk

EAST PRUSSIA

Lübeck

Swinemünde
(Świnoujście)

B E L A R U S

Hamburg

Bremerhaven
Geestemünde

Stettin
(Szczecin)

Bremen

Warsaw

P O L A N D

G E R M A N Y

U K R A I N E

Prague

Krakow

C Z E C H O - S L O V A K I A

0   100nm

0   200km

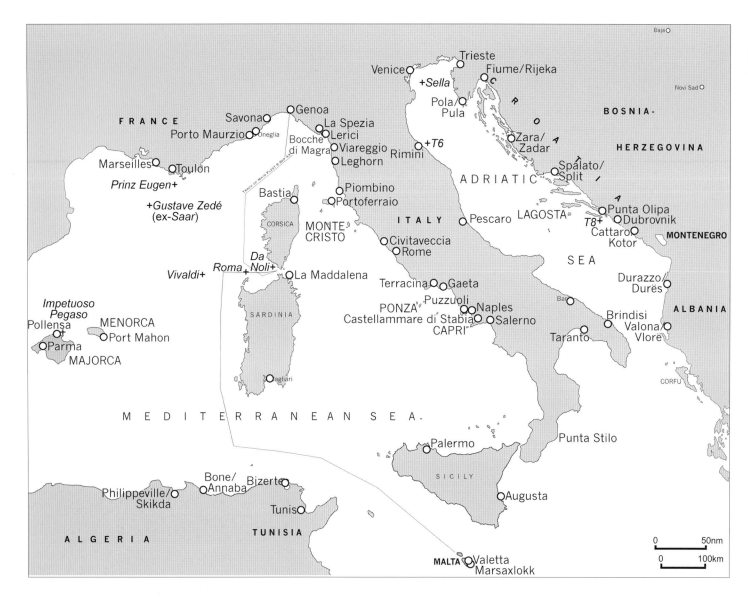

Map 3. The Mediterranean and Adriatic. *(AD graphic)*

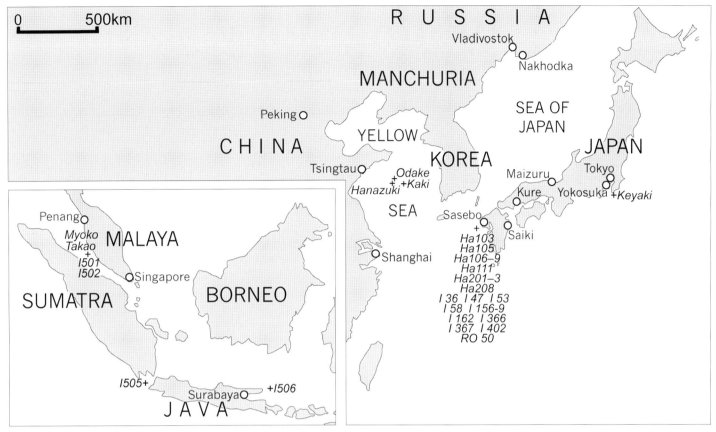

Map 4. The Far East. *(AD graphic)*

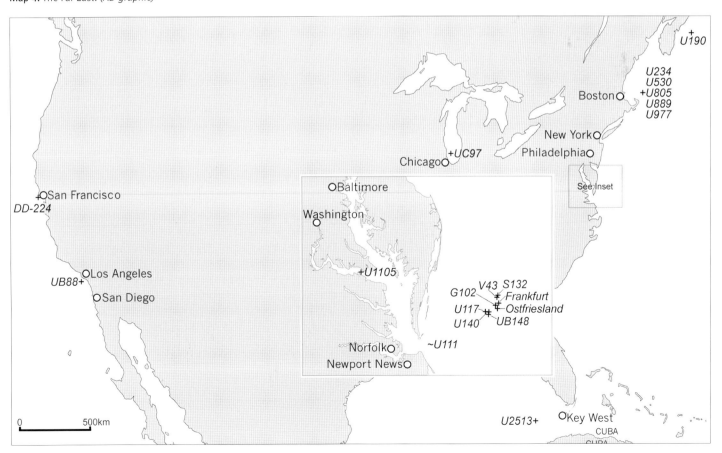

Map 5. North America. *(AD graphic)*

Bibliography

PUBLISHED WORKS

Auf dem Garten, K, *Boote, Yachten und Kleinschiffe aus Bremen: ein (fast) vergessenes Industriegeschichte 1847–1997* (Bremen: Hauschild, 2012).

Bagnasco, E and E Cernuschi, 'La Regia Marina e l'incrociatore antiaerei', *Storia Militare* 40 (1997), pp 24–34.

Bevans, C (ed.), *Treaties and Other International Agreements of the United States of America, 1776–1949*, 13 vols (Washington, DC: US Government Printing Office, 1968–76).

Booth, T, *Cox's Navy: Salvaging the German High Seas Fleet at Scapa Flow, 1924–1931* (Barnsley: Pen & Sword, 2005).

Boury, M, 'Le froid appliqué à la conservation du poisson', *Révue générale du froid*, 20/4 (April 1939), pp 103–19.

Bowen, F, 'The Shipbreaking Industry', *Shipping Wonders of the World* 38 (10 November 36), pp 1265–74.

Branfill-Cook, R, *X.1: The Royal Navy's Mystery Submarine* (Barnsley: Seaforth Publishing, 2013).

Brown, D K, 'Post War Trials: Test Against Destroyers', *Warship* XI (1987), pp 28–34.

Burrows, C W, *Scapa with a Camera: Pictorial Impressions of Five Years Spent at the Grand Fleet Base* (London: Country Life, 1921).

Buxton, I, *Big Gun Monitors: Design, Construction and Operations 1914–1945*, 2nd edition (Barnsley: Seaforth Publishing, 2008).

_____, *Metal Industries: Shipbreaking at Rosyth and Charlestown* (Kendal: World Ship Society, 1992).

_____, 'Admiralty Floating Docks', *Warship* XXXII (2010), pp 27–42.

_____, 'Shipbreaking on the East Coast of Scotland – Some Corrections', *Warships* 184 (2016), pp 42–3.

Caruana, J, *Destination Malta: The Surrender of the Italian Fleet, September 1943* (Rabat: Wise Owl Publications, [2010]).

Cernuschim E and V P O'Hara, 'The Naval War in the Adriatic', *Warship* XXXVII (2015), pp 161–73; [XXXVIII] (2016), pp 62–75.

Cosentino, M, 'The Colonial Sloop *Eritrea*', *Warship* [XXXVIII] (2016), pp 30–41.

Crăciunoiu, C, and M Axworthy, 'Romanian Minelaying Operations in the Second World War', *Warship* XI (1991), pp 146–59.

_____, 'Romanian Submarine Operations in the Second World War', *Warship* XVI (1992), pp 142–59.

Davidonis, A C, *American Naval Mission in the Adriatic, 1918–1921* (Washington, DC: Navy Department, 1943) <www.history.navy.mil/research/library/online-reading-room/title-list-alphabetically/a/american-naval-mission-adriatic-1918-1921.html>.

Dent, S, and I Johnston 'Japan's U-boats, Sasebo, 1921', *Warship* [XL] (2018), pp 220–4.

Dodson, A, *The Kaiser's Battlefleet: German Capital Ships* (Barnsley: Seaforth Publishing, 2016).

_____, '*Derfflinger*: An Inverted Life', *Warship* [XXXVIII] (2016), pp 175–8.

_____, 'After the Kaiser: The Imperial German Navy's Light Cruisers after 1918', *Warship* [XXXIX] (2017), pp 143–4.

_____, 'Beyond the Kaiser: The Imperial German Navy's Destroyers and Torpedo Boats after 1918', *Warship* [XLI] (2019), pp 129–44.

Dodson, A, and D Nottelmann, *The Kaiser's Cruisers, 1871–1918* (Barnsley: Seaforth Publishing, in preparation).

Dubbs, C, *America's U-Boats: Terror Trophies of World War I* (Lincoln and London: University of Nebraska Press, 2014).

Finamore, D, and G Wood, *Ocean Liners: Speed and Style* (London: V&A Publishing, 2018).

Fisher, S and J Whitewright, 'Hidden Heritage: The German Torpedo Boats in Portsmouth Harbour', *Warship* [XXXIX] (2017), pp 166–70.

Frampton, V, V Toyka, D Waller and H Visser, 'U-boats Surrendered in Argentina', *Warship International* LI/2 (2014), pp 120–2.

Freivogel, Z, *Beute-Zerstörer und Torpedoboote der Kriegsmarine*, Marine-Arsenal 48 (Wölfersheim-Brstadt: Podzun-Pallas-Verlag, 2000).

Freivogel, Z and A Rastelli, *Adriatic Naval War 1940–1945* (Zagreb: Despot Infinitus, 2015).

Fukui, S (ed.), *[Japanese Naval Vessels Survived: Their Post-War Activities and Final Disposition]* (Tokyo: Shuppan Kyodo, 1961).

George, S C, *Jutland to Junkyard: The Raising of the Scuttled German High Seas Fleet from Scapa Flow – The Greatest Salvage Operation of All Time* (Cambridge: Patrick Stevens Ltd, 1973).

Gibson, R H and M Prendergast, *The German Submarine War 1914–1918* (London: Constable, 1931).

Gothling, W, O Lorscher and S Schnetzke, *Ausgeliefert: Die deutschen U-Boote 1918-1920 und ihr Verbleib – Eine Dokumentation* (Berlin: Digital Business and Printing GmbH, 2012).

Greger, R, 'The Bulgarian Nadezda', *Warship International* X/2 (1973), pp 183–5.

_____, 'Yugoslav Naval Guns and the Birth of the Yugoslav Navy 1918–1941', *Warship International* XXIV/4 (1987), pp 344–5.

Gröner, E, *Die deutschen Kriegsschiffe 1815–1945*, 9 vols (Munich: Bernard & Graefe, 1982–94).

_____, *German Warships 1815–1945*, 2 vols (London: Conway Maritime Press, 1990–91).

Grossman, M, 'The Allied Assault on *Aquila* – Operation Toast', *Warship International* XXVII/2 (1990), pp 166–73.

Hamilton, A S, *German Submarine U1105 'Black Panther': The*

Naval Archaeology of a U-boat (Oxford: Osprey, 2019).

Harding, S, *Great Liners at War* (Cirencester: Tempus Publishing, 2008)

Hazlett, E E, 'The Austro-American Navy', *US Naval Institute Proceedings* 66 (1940), pp 1757–68.

Hervieux, P, 'German TA Torpedo Boats at War', *Warship XXI* (1997–98), pp 133–48.

————, 'The Royal Romanian Navy at War, 1941–1944', *Warship XXIV* (2001–2), pp 70–88.

Hird, D M, *The Grey Wolves of Eriboll* (Caithness: Whittles Publishing, 2010).

Jones, G P, *Under Three Flags: The Story of* Nordmark *and the Armed Supply Ships of the German Navy* (London: William Kimber, 1973).

Jones, J W, *U.S. Battleship Operations in World War I* (Annapolis, MD: Naval Institute Press, 1998).

Klar, J W, 'USS *DD-224* (ex-*Stewart*) – The Voyage Home', *Warship International XXVII* (1990), pp 74–82.

Kunimoto, Y, 'The Maruyu Submarines', *Warship International XXXVI/3* (1999), pp 267–73.

Kuzin, V P, and D Iu Litinskii, 'Avianosets "Graf Zeppelin"— boevoi trofie Kransnii Armii [Aircraft Carrier *Graf Zeppelin*— Battle Trophy of the Red Army]', *Warship International XLV/2* (2008), pp 161–5.

Lehmann, E, 'Die Entwicklung der Schwimmdocks', *Deutsches Schiffahrtsarchiv* 25 (2002), pp 253–68.

MacMillan, M, *Peacemakers: The Paris Peace Conference of 1919 and its Attempt to End War* (London: John Murray, 2001).

Madsen, C, *The Royal Navy and German Naval Disarmament 1942–1947* (London: Routledge, 1998).

Maritime Archaeology Trust, *Forgotten Wrecks of the First World War: SM U-90 Site Report* (April 2018) <https://forgotten-wrecks.maritimearchaeologytrust.org/uploads/images/Articles/Site%20Reports/FW_Site%20report_U-90_FINAL.pdf>.

Marshall, C, 'Easy Boats: Schnellboote in the US Navy' <www.prinzeugen.com/USNSchnell.htm>, with *S144* identified at <http://s-boot.net/sboats-kriegsmarine-Losses.html>.

McCallum, I, 'The Riddle of the Shells', *Warship XXV* (2002–3), pp 3–25; XXVI (2004), pp 9–20; XXVII (2005), pp 9–24.

McCartney, I, *Lost Patrols: Submarine Wrecks of the English Channel* (Penzance: Periscope Publishing, 2003).

————, *Scapa 1919: The Archaeology of a Scuttled Fleet* (Oxford: Osprey, 2019).

————, 'Scuttled in the Morning: The Discoveries and Surveys of HMS *Warrior* and HMS *Sparrowhawk*, the Battle of Jutland's Last Missing Shipwrecks', *International Journal of Nautical Archaeology* 47/2 (2018), pp 256–66.

McLaughlin, S, 'The Loss of the Battleship *Novorossiisk*: Accident or Sabotage?', *Warship XXIX* (2007), pp 139–52.

Messimer, D R, *The Baltimore Sabotage Cell: German Agents, American Traitors, and the U-boat* Deutschland *during World War I* (Annapolis, MD: Naval Institute Press, 2015).

Milburn, M, 'The U-boat Coast', *Diver* 63/7 (2018), pp 20–3 .

Miller, D. 'Operation "Deadlight"', *Warship XXI* (1997–98), pp 115–32.

Monakov, M, and J Rohwer, *Stalin's Ocean-Going Fleet: Soviet Naval Strategy and Shipbuilding Programmes, 1935–53* (London: Routledge, 2001).

O'Driscoll, P, 'WW1 Medway U-boats', *After the Battle* 36 (1982), pp 39–42.

O'Hara, V P and E Cernuschi, *Black Phoenix: History and Operations of the Marina Repubblicana 1943–1945* (Chula Vista, CA: Propeller Press, 2014).

————, *Dark Navy: The Italian Regia Marina and the Armistice of 8 September 1943* (Ann Arbor, MI: Nimble Books, 2009).

Office of the Historian, Joint Task Force One, *Operation Crossroads: The Official Pictorial Record* (New York: Wm H Wise & Co, n.d.).

Peifer, D C, 'Forerunners to the West German Bundesmarine: The Klose Fast Patrol Group, the Naval Historical Team Bremerhaven, and the U.S. Navy's Labor Service Unit (B)', *International Journal of Naval History* 1/1 (2002).

————, *The Three German Navies: Dissolution, Transition, and New Beginnings* (Gainesville, FL: University Press of Florida, 2002).

Philips, F, *14–18 op zee. Belgische Schepen en zeelui tijdens de Grote oorlog* (Tielt: Lannoo, 2013).

Prasky, F, *Donaumonitoren Österreich-Ungarns – von 1872 bis zur Gegenwart* (Vienna: Neuer Wissenschaftlicher Verlag, 2004).

Rastelli, A and E Bagnasco, 'The Sinking of the Italian Aircraft Carrier Aquila – A Controversial Question', *Warship International XXVII/1* (1990), pp 55–70

Rössler, E, *The U-boat: The Evolution and Technical History of German Submarines* (London: Arms & Armour Press, 1981).

Schenk, P, 'German Aircraft Carrier Developments', *Warship International XLV/2* (2008), pp 128–60.

Schiffbautechnischen Gesellschaft, *Jahrbuch der Schiffbautechnischen Gesellschaft*, 27th edition (Berlin: Verlag Julius Springer, 1926)

Schleihauf, W, 'The *Baden* Trials', *Warship XXIX* (2007), pp 81–90.

Sieche, E F, 'The German Heavy Cruiser *Prinz Eugen*: A Career Under Two Flags', *Warship* 49 (1989), pp 44–8; *Warship International XXVII/3* (1990), pp 278–306.

————, 'Guns of the the Austro-Hungarian Battleship *Prinz Eugen*', *Warship International XLVIII/2* (2011), pp 153–4.

Smith, K F, 'The Ex-German Battleship *Ostfriesland*', *Journal of the American Society of Naval Engineers* 32 (1920), pp 652–87.

Sondhaus, L, *The Naval Policy of Austria-Hungary 1867–1918: Navalism, Industrial Development and the Politics of Dualism* (West Lafyette, IN: Purdue University Press, 1994).

Tamura, T, 'The Career of the Imperial Japanese Patrol Boat No. 102 (ex-USS *Stewart*, DD-224), *Warship International LII/3* (2015), pp 227–54.

Todorov, I, 'Fifty Years of the Bulgarian Navy', *Warship International XXXIII/1* (1996), 16–44.

US State Department, *US Treaties and Other International Agreements*, 35 vols (Washington, DC: US Department of State, 1950–84).

Vego, M, 'The Yugoslav Navy 1918–41', *Warship International XIX/4* (1982), pp 342–61.

Walker, K E and S J Webster, *Strategic Assessment of Submarines in English* Waters (Cirencester: Cotswold Archaeology, 2014).

Waller, D, 'U-boats that Survived', *Warship International* VII/2 (1970), pp 110–21.

_____, 'The U-Boats that Surrendered: U-1407 (HMS Meteorite) in the Royal Navy – 1945 to 1949', <https://uboat.net/articles/97.html>.

_____, 'Fact or Fiction – Did U-1197 Surrender in 1945?', <https://uboat.net/articles/86.html>.

_____, 'The U-boats that Surrendered: U-boats in the Royal Navy Post-May 1945', *Warships* 168 (2012), pp 2–15; 169 (2012), pp 2–10; 170 (2012), pp 2–12; 171 (2012), pp 2–13.

_____, 'Japanese Submarines that Surrendered (Including Ex U-Boats)', *Warships* 174 (2013), pp 21–6.

_____, 'The U-boats Captured by the Red Army in Danzig – March 1945', *Warships* 175 (2014), pp 4–25.

_____, 'U-boats Surrendered in Argentina', *Warship International* LII/2 (2015), pp 126–7.

_____, 'U-boats in Norway, Post 08 May 1945', *Warships* 178 (2015), pp 18–30; 179 (2015), pp 8–24; 180 (2015), pp 5–13.

_____, 'The Secret US Navy Submarine Mission in Europe in 1945', *Warships* 181 (2015), pp 9–23; 182 (2016), pp 5–18.

_____, 'The French Connection', *Warships* 183 (2016), pp 6–19; 184 (2016), pp 4–22.

_____, 'USCG Cutter ARGO: The Surrender of U-boats in North East USA in May 1945 (Part 1)', *Warships* 185 (2016), pp 7–21.

_____, 'Operation Cabal', *Warships* 186 (2017), pp 4–24.

_____, 'U-boats in Loch Ryan – May to December 1945', *Warships* 190 (2018), pp 24–35.

_____, 'The Potsdam Conference and Agreement: The Kriegsmarine's U-boats', *Warships* 192 (2018), pp 7–18.

Waller, D and A Niestlé, 'The U-boats that Surrendered: "The Definitive List"', *Warship International* XLVIII/4 (2011), pp 356–8.

Wessex Archaeology, *U-boat off Castle Beach, Falmouth: Photographic Survey* (Salisbury: unpublished report for Historic England, 2013).

Wildenberg, T, *Billy Mitchell's War with the Navy: The Interwar Rivalry Over Naval Air Power*, (Annapolis, MD: Naval Institute Press, 2013).

Wise, J, 'The Royal Navy and the Evolution of the "True Submarine", 1945–1963', *Warship* XXXI (2009), pp 22–38.

Witt, J, *Das Marine-Ehrenmal* (Laboe: Deutscher Marinebund, nd).

_____, *Technisches Museum U995: Geschichte und Fakten* (Laboe: Deutscher Marinebund, nd).

Woodward, D, *The Collapse of Power: Mutiny in the High Seas Fleet* (London: Arthur Barker, 1973).

Woodward, E L and R Butler (eds), *Documents of British Foreign Policy 1919–1939*, First Series, Volume II: 1919 (London: His Majesty's Stationery Office, 1948).

_____, *Documents of British Foreign Policy 1919–1939*, First Series, Volumes I, II: 1919 (London: His Majesty's Stationery Office, 1947–48).

Wright, C C, 'The U.S. Navy's Operation of the Former Imperial Japanese Navy Submarines *I-14*, *I-400* and *I-401* 1945–1946', *Warship International* XXXVII/4 (2000), pp 348–401.

_____, 'Re: Mystery Photo No. 176 (*W.I.* 46, no. 3:240)', *Warship International* XLVII/1 (2010), pp 68–76.

UK NATIONAL ARCHIVES FILES

ADM 1/8576/337 Disposal of Surrendered enemy Ships.

ADM 1/8558/132 Submarines. Disposal of German Vessels.

ADM 1/8565/231 Hungarian claims re proposed Naval clauses of Treaty of Peace.

ADM 1/8641/119 Scrapping of ex-Austrian Warship TEGETHOFF. Demolition of "ADMIRAL SPAUN".

ADM 1/13650 FOREIGN COUNTRIES (52): Allocation of ships of Italian Fleet for air training duties.

ADM 1/14983 Disposal of Italian Fleet: question of use of Littorio battleships by RN in war against Japan.

ADM 1/18449 Disposal of captured German war material in Norway: modification of instructions.

ADM 116/2113. Naval Inter-Allied Commission of Control – Progress Reports.

ADM 116/5768 Italian Fleet: disposal in accordance with peace treaty: papers and correspondence with Four Power Naval Commission, Foreign Office and Italian Government concerning allocation of ships; progress report.

ADM 116/5655 German auxiliary vessels allocated to UK by Tripartite Naval Commission: disposal as gifts to allied navies.

ADM 116/2945. Germany's breach of the Versailles Treaty.

ADM 116/1992 Berlin Office German war vessels to be surrendered Pack 12A.

ADM 116/1974 Particulars of floating and submarine pressure docks.

ADM 116/1975 Submarines, pressure docks and German salvage vessels Vulkan and Cyclops; Docks, tugs and dredgers. Correspondence and telegrams.

ADM 116/1976 German Submarines Disposal, storage and delivery of engines; Allocation of submarines; Correspondence, etc. – Salvage vessels and pressure docks; Submarines to be broken up – Hulls for commerce; Submarines building in Denmark and alleged construction in Germany.

ADM 116/1826 Handing over of German Submarines.

ADM 116/1994 Pack 13A – 4. Vessels to be broken up – Definition of the term "breaking up" and conversion of war vessels for mercantile purposes.

ADM 137/2483 Surrender of German ships.

ADM 186/360 Report on Explosive Trials carried out against ex-German submarines, 1920 and 1921.

ADM 228/22 Transfer of German minesweepers to the Russians.

FO 371/57146 German fleet: report of the Tripartite Naval Commission: disposal and destruction of submarines and warships.

FO 371/57151 German fleet: report of the Tripartite Naval Commission: disposal and destruction of submarines and warships.

FO 371/79492 Arrangements regarding transfer of ships before the wind up of the Four Power Naval Commission.

FO 608/248/29 Peace terms and treaty: Naval: Disposal of enemy ships.

FO 893/20 Minutes of meeting No 202 held 29 January 1923.

Index of Ships